Franklin Benjamin

Constitution of the State of New York Adopted in 1846

With a comparative arrangement of the constitutional provisions of other states

Franklin Benjamin Hough

Constitution of the State of New York Adopted in 1846
With a comparative arrangement of the constitutional provisions of other states

ISBN/EAN: 9783337723200

Printed in Europe, USA, Canada, Australia, Japan

Cover: Foto ©Suzi / pixelio.de

More available books at **www.hansebooks.com**

CONSTITUTION

OF THE

STATE OF NEW YORK,

ADOPTED IN 1846.

WITH A

COMPARATIVE ARRANGEMENT OF THE CONSTITUTIONAL
PROVISIONS OF OTHER STATES, CLASSIFIED
BY THEIR SUBJECTS.

PREPARED UNDER THE DIRECTION OF A COMMITTEE OF THE NEW YORK CONSTITUTIONAL
CONVENTION OF 1867,

BY FRANKLIN B. HOUGH.

ALBANY:

WEED, PARSONS & COMPANY, PRINTERS.

PREFACE.

Previous to the meeting of the present Constitutional Convention, a summary of the various provisions found in the existing Constitutions of the several States had been prepared by Dr. Franklin B. Hough, with the design of affording facilities for comparison and reference in the revision of the Constitution of the State of New York. This summary was examined by several delegates to the Convention, and soon after organization the undersigned were appointed a committee to take into consideration the expediency of printing in bill form the present Constitution of New York, with such comparative references as might be proper. This committee after a careful examination of the plan proposed by Dr. Hough, approved of its general arrangement, but recommended a more extended list of references, a specification of the *page*, in the volume of Constitutions forming the first volume of the "Manual," where the subject referred to would be found in its proper connection, and the adoption of the exact phraseology used in the several Constitutions whenever practicable. A concise statement was thought proper in cases where it might be desirable to present the various provisions upon particular subjects at a single glance.

It would have been desirable to include in this connection references to legal decisions upon constitutional points, but the brief time allowed for the preparation, upon the plan as modified, rendered this altogether impracticable.

From the blending of several subjects into one section, which in other cases are stated separately, a strict classification could not in all cases be secured, but to render this inconvenience less sensible, an extended index has been prepared, which will obviate much of the difficulty of reference.

As a general rule, provisions of a strictly local character, and such as refer to circumstances and conditions that have passed away, are omitted. Whenever these have been retained, the analogies which they suggest, were thought worthy of notice, as in some cases having relation to a similar application in the revision now before the Convention. Whenever reference is made to sections "nearly similar," it will be understood that they differ somewhat in the phraseology, but that they agree in their general statement. In some instances, lengthy sections, embracing minute details, are referred to without insertion, or with but a brief analysis of their subject.

> JOHN STANTON GOULD, *Chairman,*
> G. M. BECKWITH,
> JAMES A. BELL,
> G. J. TUCKER,
> MARIUS SCHOONMAKER.

CONSTITUTION OF NEW YORK,

ADOPTED IN 1846.

We, the people of the State of New York, grateful to Almighty God for our freedom, in order to secure its blessings, do establish this Constitution.(¹)

ARTICLE I.

1   SECTION 1. No member of this State shall be disfranchised, or deprived of

2 any of the rights or privileges secured to any citizens thereof, unless by the law

3 of the land, or the judgment of his peers.(²)

(1) *N. Y.*, (1821), 41; *Minn.*, 319.
(2) *N. Y.*, (1777), 28; (1821), 41.

PREAMBLE.

—In order to form a more perfect Union, establish justice, insure domestic tranquility, provide for the common defense, promote the general welfare, and secure the blessings of liberty to ourselves and our posterity, do ordain and establish this Constitution. *U. S.*, 9. [Same except "government." in place of "Union,"] *Ill.* 151.

—And secure to ourselves and to our posterity the rights of life, liberty and property; invoking the favor and guidance of Almighty God, do ordain and establish the following Constitution and form of government. *Ala.* 72.

—Having the right to establish for ourselves a Constitution in conformity with the Constitution of the United States of America, to secure to ourselves and our posterity the protection and blessings of the Federal Constitution, and the enjoyment of all the rights of liberty and the free pursuit of happiness, do agree to continue ourselves as a free and independent State, by the name and style of ——, and do ordain and establish the following Constitution for the government thereof. *Ark.* 83.

—In order more effectually to define, secure and perpetuate the liberties, rights and privileges which they have derived from their ancestors, hereby, after a careful consideration and revision, ordain and establish the following Constitution and form of civil government. *Ct.* 107.

—In order to secure to ourselves and our posterity the enjoyment of all the rights of life, liberty and property, and the pursuit of happiness, do mutually agree, each with the other, to form the following Constitution and form of government in and for the said State. *Fla.* 128.

—In order to form a permanent government, establish justice, insure domestic tranquility and secure the blessing of liberty to ourselves and our posterity—acknowledging and invoking the guidance of Almighty God, the author of all good government, do ordain and establish this Constitution. *Ga.* 142.

—To the end that justice be established, public order maintained, and liberty perpetuated, we, the people of. *Ind.* 109; *Or.* 447.

—Grateful to the Supreme Being for the blessings hitherto enjoyed, and feeling our dependence on Him for a continuation of those blessings, do ordain and establish a free and independent government by the name of. *Iowa*, 182.

—Grateful to Almighty God for our civil and religious privileges, in order to insure the full enjoyment of our rights as American citizens, do ordain and establish this Constitution. *Kan.* 198.

—We, the representatives of the people of ——,

in Convention assembled, to secure to all the citizens thereof the enjoyment of the rights of life, liberty and property, and of pursuing happiness, do ordain and establish this Constitution for its government. *Ky.* 209.

—We, the people of the State of ——, grateful to Almighty God for our civil and religious liberty, and taking into our serious consideration the best means for establishing a good Constitution in this State, for the sure foundation and more permanent security thereof, declare: *Md.* 253.

—Acknowledging, with grateful hearts, the goodness of the Sovereign Ruler of the Universe in affording us an opportunity so favorable to the design; and imploring his aid and direction in its accomplishment, do agree to form ourselves into a free and independent State, by the style and title of ——, *Me.*, 239.

—The end of the institution, maintenance and administration of Government, is to secure the existence of the body politic, to protect it, and to furnish the individuals who compose it with the power of enjoying in safety and tranquility, their natural rights, and the blessings of life; and whenever these great objects are not obtained, the people have a right to alter the government, and to take measures necessary for their safety, prosperity and happiness.

—The body politic is formed by a voluntary association of individuals; it is a social compact, by which the whole people covenants with each citizen, and each citizen with the whole people, that all shall be governed by certain laws for the common good. It is the duty of the people, therefore, in framing a Constitution of government, to provide for an equitable mode of making laws, as well as for an impartial interpretation and a faithful execution of them; that every man may, at all times, find his security in them, We, therefore, the people of ——, acknowledging, with grateful hearts, the goodness of the great Legislator of the Universe, in affording us, in the course of His providence, an opportunity, deliberately and peaceably, without fraud, violence or surprise, of entering into an original, explicit and solemn compact with each other; and of forming a new Constitution of civil government for ourselves and posterity; and devoutly imploring His direction in so interesting a design, do agree upon, ordain and establish the following *Declaration of Rights and Frame of Government*, as the CONSTITUTION of the COMMONWEALTH of ——. *Mass.*, 279.

—Grateful to God for our civil and religious liberty, and desiring to perpetuate its blessings, and secure the same to ourselves and our posterity, do ordain and establish this Constitution. *Min.*, 319.

—Grateful to Almighty God, the Sovereign Ruler of Nations, for our State government, our liberties, and our connection with the American Union, and acknowledging our dependence upon Him for the

2

continuance of those blessings to us and our posterity, do, for the more certain security thereof, and for the better government of this State, ordain and establish this revised and amended Constitution. *Mo.*, 346.

—That the general, great, and essential principles of liberty and free government may be recognized and established, and that the relations of this State to the Union and government of the United States, and those of the people of this State to the rest of the American people, may be defined and affirmed, we do declare: *Mo.* 346.

—Grateful to Almighty God for our freedom, in order to secure its blessings, form a more perfect government, insure domestic tranquility and promote the general welfare, do establish this Constitution. *Neb.* 370; (nearly identical), *Nev.* 379; *Ohio*, 432; *Wis.* 559.

—Grateful to Almighty God for the civil and religious liberty which He hath so long permitted us to enjoy, and looking to Him for a blessing upon our endeavors to secure and transmit the same unimpaired to succeeding generations, do ordain and establish this Constitution. *N. J.*, 411.

—That the general, great and essential principles of liberty and free government may be recognized and established, we declare. *Miss.*, 334.

—Acknowledging, with gratitude the grace and beneficence of God in permitting us to make a choice of our form of government, do ordain and establish this Constitution. *Tex.*, 505.

—That the general, great and essential principles of liberty and free government may be recognized and established, we declare. *Ala.*, 72; *Ct.*, 107; *Fl.*, 129; *Ill.* 165; *Pa.*, 467; *Tex.*, 505; *Tenn.*, 490.

[A simple declaration of establishment.] *Del.*, 116; *Pa.* 461; *S. C.*, 482.

[Authority of U. S., recited.] *Tenn.*, 490.

[No preamble.] *Cal.*, *La.*, *Md.*, *Mich.*, *N. H.*, *N. C.*, *R. I.*, *Vt.*, *Va.*, *W. Va.*

INHERENT RIGHTS.

—The free inhabitants of each of these States, paupers, vagabonds and fugitives from justice excepted, shall be entitled to all the privileges of free citizens. *Art. Confed.*, 3.

—All men are born free and equal, and have certain natural, essential and unalienable rights; among which may be reckoned the right of enjoying and defending their lives and liberties; that of acquiring, possessing and protecting property; in fine, that of seeking and obtaining their safety and happiness. *Mass.*, 280; (nearly similar), *Neb.*, 370; *Nev.*, 379; *N. H.*, 398; *N. J.*, 412; *Ohio*, 432; *Pa.*, 467; *Vt.*, 521; *Va.*, 531; *Wis.*, 559.

—Therefore, no male person, born in this country, or brought from over sea, ought to be holden, by law, to serve any person, as a servant, slave or apprentice, after he arrives to the age of twenty-one years, nor female, in like manner, after she arrives to the age of eighteen years, unless they are bound by their own consent after they arrive to such age, or bound by law for the payment of debts, damages, fines, costs or the like. *Vt.*, 521.

—No attainder shall work corruption of blood, nor, except during the life of the offender, forfeiture of estate. The estates of those who destroy their own lives shall descend or vest as in case of natural death, and if any person be killed by accident, no forfeiture shall be thereby incurred. *Del.*, 117.

—The estate of such persons as may destroy their own lives shall not for that offense be forfeited, but descend or ascend in the same manner as if such person had died in a natural way. Nor shall any article which shall accidentally occasion the death of any person be henceforth deemed a deodand, or in any wise forfeited on account of such misfortune. *N. H.*, 409; *Vt.* 526.

—That the estates of suicides shall descend, or vest, as in cases of natural death; and that, if any person shall be killed by casualty, there shall be no forfeiture by reason thereof. *Ala.*, 73; *Ky.*, 224.

—Emigration from the State shall not be prohibited. *Ala.*, 74; *Ind.*, 171; *Ky.*, 224; *Or.*, 448; *Pa.*, 463.

—Nor shall any free white citizen of this State ever be exiled under any pretence whatever. *Miss.*, 335.

—That all the people have a natural and inherent right to emigrate from one State to another that will receive them. *Vt.*, 522.

—No capitation or other direct tax shall be laid unless in proportion to the census or enumeration herein before directed to be taken. *U. S.*, 13.

—The General Assembly shall have power to authorize the levying of a capitation tax. *Fl.*, 137.

—Capitation tax shall be equal throughout the State, upon all individuals subject to the same. *N. C.*, 430.

—No poll-tax shall be assessed for other than county purposes. *Ark.*, 93.

—The General Assembly may, whenever they shall deem it necessary, cause to be collected from all able-bodied, free white male inhabitants of this State, over the age of twenty-one years and under the age of sixty years, who are entitled to the right of suffrage, a capitation tax of not less than fifty cents, nor more than one dollar each. *Ill.*, 163.

—That the levying of taxes by the poll is grievous and oppressive, and ought to be prohibited; that paupers ought not to be assessed for the support of the Government, but every other person in the State, or persons holding property therein, ought to contribute his proportion of public taxes for the support of Government, according to his actual worth in real or personal property; yet fines, duties or taxes may properly and justly be imposed or laid with a political view, for the good government and benefit of the community. *Md.*, 254.

—No special privileges or immunities shall ever be granted by the Legislature, which may not be altered, revoked or repealed by the same body; and this power shall be exercised by no other tribunal or agency. *Kan.*, 197.

—That a long continuance in the Executive Departments, of power or trust, is dangerous to liberty; a rotation, therefore, in those departments, is one of the best securities of permanent freedom. *Md.* 255.

—Government is instituted for the common good; for the protection, safety prosperity and happiness of the people: and not for the profit, honor or private interest of any one man, family or class of men; therefore, the people alone have an incontestable, unalienable and indefeasible right to institute government, and to reform, alter or totally change the same, when their protection, safety, prosperity and happiness require it. *Mass.*, 280; (nearly similar), *Min.*, 319; *New.*, 379; *Vt.*, 520; *Va.*, 531; *N. H.*, 399.

—No man, nor corporation or association of men, have any other title to obtain advantages, or particular and exclusive privileges, distinct from those of the community, than what rises from the consideration of services rendered to the public; and this title being in nature neither hereditary, nor transmissible to children or descendants, or relations by blood, the idea of a man born a magistrate, law-giver or judge, is absurd and unnatural. *Mass.*, 280.

—No title of nobility or hereditary distinction, privilege, honor or emolument, shall ever be granted or confirmed; nor shall any office be created, the appointment to which shall be for a longer time than during good behavior. *Me.*, 240.

—No office or place whatsoever in government shall be hereditary—the abilities and integrity requisite in all not being transmissible to posterity or relations. *N. H.*, 399.

—That the Legislature shall not grant any title of nobility or hereditary distinction, nor create any office, the appointment of which shall be for a longer term than during good behavior. *Pa.*, 468; *S. C.*, 488.

—No title of nobility shall be granted; and no person holding any office of profit or trust under them, shall, without the consent of the Congress, accept of any present, emolument, office or title, of any kind whatever, from any king, prince, or foreign State. *U. S.*, 13.

—That no person ought to hold at the same time more than one office of profit created by the Constitution or Laws of this State; nor ought any person in public trust to receive any present from any foreign prince, or State, or from the United States, or any of them, without the approbation of this State. *Md.*, 255.

—No hereditary emoluments, privileges or honors shall ever be granted or conferred in this State. *Ct.*, 108; (nearly similar), *Fl.*, 130; *Kan.*, 197; *Ky.*, 224; *N. C.*, 422; *Or.*, 448.

—No hereditary distinction shall be granted, nor any office created or exercised, the appointment to which shall be for a longer term than during good behavior; and no person holding any office under this State, shall accept of any office or title of any kind whatever, from any king, prince, or foreign State. *Del.*, 117.

—That no title of nobility, or hereditary distinction, privilege, honor, or emolument, shall ever be granted or conferred in this State; and that no office shall be created, the appointment of which shall be for a longer term than during good behavior. *Ala.*, 74.

—That no title of nobility or hereditary honors ought to be granted in this State. *Md.*, 256; *Ind.*, 171.

—All freemen, when they form a social compact, have equal rights; and no man, or set of men, is entitled to exclusive, separate public emoluments or privileges, but in consideration of public services. *Ky.*, 223; *Tex.*, 505.

—Economy being a most essential virtue in all States, especially in a young one; no pension should be granted but in consideration of actual services; and such pension ought to be granted with great caution by the Legislature, and never for more than one year at a time. *N. H.*, 401.

—The powers of government reside in all the citizens of the State, and can be rightfully exercised only in accordance with their will and appointment. *W. Va.*, 546.

—None but citizens of the United States shall be appointed to any office of trust or profit in this State. *La.*, 233.

—That absolute, arbitrary power over the lives, liberty, and property of freemen, exists nowhere in a republic—not even in the largest majority. *Ky.*, 253.

—No authority shall, on any pretense whatever, be exercised over the people or members of this State, but such as shall be derived from and granted by them. *N. Y.* (1777). 26.

—The people of this State have the sole and exclusive right of governing themselves as a free, sovereign and independent State, and do, and forever hereafter shall exercise and enjoy every power, jurisdiction and right pertaining thereto, which is not or may not hereafter be by them expressly delegated to the United States of America, in Congress assembled. *N. H.*, 399.

—Nor are the people bound by any law but such as they have in like manner assented to, for their common good. *Vt.*, 522.

—That every citizen of this State owes paramount allegiance to the Constitution and government of the United States, and that no law or ordinance of this State in contravention or subversion thereof can have any binding force. *Mo.*, 346.

—That this State shall ever remain a member of the American Union; that the people thereof are a part of the American nation; and that all attempts, from whatever source and upon whatever pretext, to dissolve said Union, or to sever said nation, ought to be resisted with the whole power of the State. *Mo.*, 346.

—The Constitution of the United States and the laws made in pursuance thereof being the supreme law of the land, every citizen of this State owes paramount allegiance to the Constitution and Government of the United States, and is not bound by any law or ordinance of this State in contravention or subversion thereof. *Md.*, 254.

—But the paramount allegiance of every citizen is due to the Federal government, in the exercise of all its Constitutional powers as the same have been or may be defined by the Superior Court of the United States; and no power exists in the people of this or any other State of the Federal Union to dissolve their connection therewith, or perform any act tending to impair, subvert or resist the supreme authority of the United States. The Constitution of the United States confers full powers on the Federal government to maintain and perpetuate its existence, and whensoever any portion of the States, or the people thereof, attempt to secede from the Federal Union, or forcibly resist the execution of its laws, the Federal government may by warrant of the Constitution employ armed force in compelling obedience to its authority. *Nev.*, 379.

—Every member of the community has a right to be protected by it in the enjoyment of his life, liberty, and property. He is therefore bound to contribute his share in the expense of such protection, and to yield his personal service, when necessary, or an equivalent. *N. H.*399; (nearly similar), *Vt.*, 520.

—Protection to person and property is the duty of government. *Ga.* 142.

—All political power is inherent in the people, and all free governments are founded on their authority, and instituted for their benefit; and they have, at all times, the unalienable right to alter, reform, or abolish their form of government, in such manner as they may think expedient. *Tex.* 505; (nearly similar) *Ohio* 473; *Pa.* 467; *S. C.* 487; *N. C.* 421; *Mo.* 340; *N. H.* 399.

—That we hold it to be self-evident that all men are created equally free; that they are endowed by their Creator with certain unalienable rights, among which are life, liberty, the enjoyment of the proceeds of their own labor, and the pursuit of happiness. *Md.*, 253.

—That the people of this State, by their legal Representatives, have the sole, inherent and exclusive right of governing and regulating the internal police of the same. *Vt.*, 521.

—That all government of right originates from the people, is founded in compact only, and instituted solely for the good of the whole; and they have at all times the unalienable right to alter, reform or abolish their form of government in such manner as they may deem expedient. *Md.*, 253.

—That all men, when they form a social compact, are equal in rights; and that no man or set of men, are entitled to exclusive public emoluments, or privileges, from the community. *Ct.*, 107; *Or.*, 447; *Miss.*, 334.

—That all men when they form a social compact, are equal, and have certain inherent and indefeasible rights, amongst which are those of enjoying and defending life and liberty; of acquiring, possessing and protecting property and reputation, and of pursuing their own happiness. *Ark.*, 84; *Fl.*, 129.

—That the people of this State ought to have the sole and exclusive right of regulating the internal government and police thereof. *Md.*, 253.

—All power residing originally in the people, and being derived from them, the several magistrates and officers of government, vested with authority, whether legislative, executive or judicial, are the substitutes and agents, and are at all times accountable to them. *Mass.*, 280.

—All men are by nature free and independent, and have certain unalienable rights, among which are those of enjoying and defending life and liberty, acquiring, possessing, and protecting property, and pursuing and obtaining safety and happiness. *Cal.*, 96; (substantially similar), *Ill.*, 165; *Iowa*, 183; *Kan.*, 196; *Me.*, 239; *Mo.*, 396.

—When men enter into a state of society they surrender up some of their natural rights to that society, in order to procure the protection of others, and without such equivalent the surrender is void. *N. H.*, 398.

—Through Divine goodness all men, have, by nature, the rights of worshipping and serving their Creator according to the dictates of their consciences, of enjoying and defending life and liberty, of acquiring

4

1 § 2. The trial by jury in all cases in which it has been heretofore used, shall

2 remain inviolate forever (¹); but a jury trial may be waived by the parties in

3 all civil cases in the manner prescribed by law.(²)

and protecting reputation and property, and, in general of attaining objects suitable to their condition, without injury by one to another; and as these rights are essential to their welfare, for the due exercise thereof, power is inherent in them; and therefore all just authority in the institutions of political society is derived from the people, and established with their consent, to advance their happiness: And they may for this end, as circumstances require, from time to time, alter their Constitution of government. *Del.*, 116.
—The General Assembly shall not grant to any citizen, or class of citizens, privileges, or immunities, which, upon the same terms, shall not equally belong to all citizens. *Ind.*, 171.
—That no man, and no set of men, are entitled to exclusive, separate public emoluments or privileges, but in consideration of public services. *Ala.*, 72; *Tex.*, 508; *Va.*, 531; *N. C.*, 421.
—The Legislature shall pass no law requiring a property qualification for office. *Ga.*, 235.
—We declare that all men are created equal; that they are endowed by their Creator with certain unalienable rights; that among these are life, liberty, and the pursuit of happiness; that all power is inherent in the people; and that all free governments are, and of right ought to be, founded on their authority, and instituted for their peace, safety and well being. For the advancement of these ends, the people have, at all times, an indefeasible right to alter and reform their government. *Ind.*, 170.
—All political power is inherent in the people. Government is instituted for the protection, security and benefit of the people; and they have the right to alter or reform the same whenever the public good may require it. *Cal.*, 96; (nearly similar) *Iowa*, 183; *Kan.*, 197; *Ky.*, 223; *Miss.*, 334; *N. J.*, 412; *Or.*, 447; *R. I.*, 473; *Tenn.*, 490; *Va.*, 531; *Vt.*, 521.
—That all power is inherent in the people, and all free governments are founded on their authority, and instituted for their peace, safety and happiness. *Ill.*, 165; *Me.*, 239.
—They have, therefore, an unalienable and indefeasible right to institute government, and to alter, reform, or totally change the same, when their safety and happiness require it. *Me.*, 239.
—That all persons invested with the Legislative or Executive powers of Government are the trustees of the public, and as such accountable for their conduct; *wherefore*, whenever the ends of Government are perverted, and public liberty manifestly endangered, and all other means of redress are ineffectual, the people may and of right ought to reform the old or establish a new government. The doctrine of nonresistance against arbitrary power and oppression is absurd, slavish and destructive of the good and happiness of mankind. *Md.*, 254.
—That the people of this State have the inherent, sole, and exclusive right of regulating the internal government and police thereof, and of altering and abolishing their Constitution and form of government, whenever it may be necessary to their safety and happiness; but every such right should be exercised in pursuance of law, and consistently with the Constitution of the United States. *Mo.*, 346.
—That every foreigner who comes to settle in this State, having first taken an oath of allegiance to the same, may purchase, or, by other just means, acquire, hold, and transfer land, or other real estate, and after one year's residence be deemed a free citizen. *N. C.*, 426.
Naturalization of foreigners allowed. *N. Y.*, (1777), 33.
—That all political power is inherent in the people, and all free governments are founded on their authority, and instituted for their benefit; and that,

therefore, they have at all times an inalienable and indefeasible right to alter, reform or abolish their form of government in such manner as they may deem expedient. *Ala.* 72; (substantially similar), *Ark.* 84; *Ct.* 107; *Fl.* 129.

RIGHT OF TRIAL; TRIAL BY JURY.

(1) [Thus far in Constitution of 1821, with the following addition :] " And no new court shall be instituted, but such as shall proceed according to the course of the common law; except such courts of equity, as the Legislature is herein authorized to establish." *P.* 41.
(2) [Similar provision], *N. Y.*, (1777), and *Minn.*, 319; *Mich.*, 307; *Nev.* 370.
—The Legislative Assembly shall so provide that the most competent of the permanent citizens of the county shall be chosen for jurors; and out of the whole number in attendance at the court, seven shall be drawn by lot as grand jurors, five of whom must concur to find an indictment; but the Legislative Assembly may modify or abolish grand juries. *Or.*, 454.
—The right of trial by jury shall remain inviolate; and shall extend to all cases at law, without regard to the amount in controversy; but a jury trial may be waived by the parties in all cases, in the manner prescribed by law. *Wis.* 560.
—That the inhabitants of —— are entitled to the common law of England, and the trial by jury according to the course of that law, and to the benefit of such of the English statutes as existed on the fourth day of July, seventeen hundred and seventy-six, and which, by experience, have been found applicable to their local and other circumstances, and have been introduced, used and practiced by the courts of law or equity, and also of all acts of Assembly in force on the first day of June, eighteen hundred and sixty-four, except such as may have since expired or may be inconsistent with the provisions of this Constitution, subject, nevertheless, to the revision and amendment or repeal by the Legislature of this State; and the inhabitants are also entitled to all property derived to them from or under the charter granted by His Majesty Charles the First. *Md.*, 253.
—That no person shall be accused, arrested, or detained, except in cases ascertained by law, and according to the forms which the same has prescribed; and that no person shall be punished, but by virtue of a law established and promulgated prior to the offense, and legally applied. *Ala.*, 73.
—That the right of trial by jury shall remain inviolate; and shall extend to all cases at law, without regard to the amount in controversy. *Ill.*, 165.
—That the trial of facts where they arise is one of the greatest securities of the lives, liberties and estate of the people. *Md.*, 254.
—No person shall be held to answer for treason, felony or other crime not cognizable by a justice, unless on presentment or indictment of a grand jury. *W. Va.*, 547.
—The Legislature may authorize a trial by a jury of a less number than twelve men. *Mich.*, 304.
—No person shall be deprived of life, liberty, or property, except by due process of law. *Ga.*, 142.
—In criminal prosecutions, the verification of facts, in the vicinity where they happen, is one of the greatest securities of the life, liberty and property of the citizens. *Mass.*, 251.
—That the ancient mode of trial by jury shall be held sacred, and the right thereof remain inviolate, subject to such modifications as may be authorized by this Constitution. *Ky.*, 223.
—The Jurors of this State shall be white men, pos-

sessed of such qualifications as may be prescribed by law. *Fl.*, 140.

—Trials of issues proper for the cognizance of a jury, in the Supreme and County Courts, shall be by jury, except where the parties otherwise agree; and great care ought to be taken to prevent corruption, or partiality, in the choice and return, or appointment of juries. *Vt.*, 526.

—That no person shall be debarred from prosecuting or defending, before any tribunal in this State, by himself or counsel, any civil cause to which he is a party. *Ala.*, 73.

—Every court in which any person shall be summoned to serve as a grand or petit juror, shall require him, before he is sworn as a juror, to take such oath, in open court; and no person refusing to take the same shall serve as a juror. *Mo.*, 350.

—No fine shall be laid on any citizen of this State, that shall exceed fifty dollars; unless it shall be assessed by a jury of his peers, who shall assess the fine at the time they find the fact, if they think the fine should be more than fifty dollars. *Tenn.*, 497.

—In all cases of law or equity, where the matter in controversy shall be valued at or exceed twenty dollars, the right of trial by jury shall be preserved. *Tex.*, 512.

—That no freeman shall be imprisoned, or disseized of his freehold, liberties, or privileges, or outlawed or exiled, or in any manner deprived of his life, liberty, or property, but by the judgment of his peers or the law of the land. *Ill.*, 166; *Md.*, 255; (nearly similar), *N. C.* 422; *Tex.* 506.

—That when any issue in fact, proper for the cognizance of a jury, is joined in a court of law, the parties have a right to trial by jury, which ought to be held sacred. *Vt.*, 522.

—No person shall be held to answer for an offense unless on the presentment or indictment of a grand jury, except in cases of impeachment, or in cases cognizable by justices of the peace, or arising in the army or navy, or in the militia when in actual service in time of war or public danger. *Me.*, 240; *N. J.*, 412; *R. I.*, 473; *Provided,* That Justices of the Peace shall try no person, except as a court of inquiry, for any offense punishable with imprisonment or death, or fine above one hundred dollars. *Ill.* 166.

—That no freeman shall be put to answer any criminal charge but by presentment, indictment, or impeachment. *Tenn.*, 491; *N. C.*, 422.

—The trial of crimes and misdemeanors, unless herein otherwise provided, shall be by jury, and shall be held publicly and without unreasonable delay, in the county where the alleged offense was committed, unless upon petition of the accused and for good cause shown, or in consequence of the existence of war or insurrection in such county, it is removed to, or instituted in, some other county. In all such trials the accused shall be informed of the character and cause of the accusation, and be confronted with the witnesses against him, and shall have the assistance of counsel for his defense, and compulsory process for obtaining witnesses in his favor. *W. Va.*, 547.

—In all criminal cases whatever the jury shall have the right to determine the law and the facts. *Ind.*, 170. Under the direction of the court as to the law, and the right of new trial, as in civil cases. *Or.*, 443.

—In all controversies concerning property, and in all suits between two or more persons, except in cases in which it has heretofore been otherways used and practiced, the parties have a right to a trial by jury; and this method of procedure shall be held sacred, unless, in causes arising on the high seas, and such as relate to mariners' wages, the Legislature shall hereafter find it necessary to alter it. *Mass.* 281.

—Every man being presumed innocent, until he is pronounced guilty by the law, no act of severity which is not necessary to secure an accused person shall be permitted. *R. I.*, 473.

—The right of trial by jury shall remain inviolate; *Ala.*, 73; *Ct.*, 108; but the General Assembly may

authorize trial by a jury of a less number than twelve men in inferior courts; *Neb.*, 370; but no person shall be deprived of life, liberty, or property, without due process of law. *Iowa*, 183.

—That every freeman restrained of his liberty is entitled to a remedy, to inquire into the lawfulness thereof, and to remove the same, if unlawful; and that such remedy ought not to be denied or delayed. *N. C.*, 422.

—Every person is entitled to a certain remedy in the laws, for all injuries or wrongs which he may receive in his person, property, or character; he ought to obtain justice freely and without being obliged to purchase it; completely and without denial; promptly and without delay, conformably to the laws. *Mln.* 319; *N. H.*, 399; *R. I.*, 473; *Vt.*, 521; *Wis.*, 560.

—The Legislature shall provide by law a suitable and impartial mode of selecting juries; and their usual number and unanimity, in indictments and convictions, shall be held indispensable. *Me.*, 240.

—That no freedman shall be convicted of any crime, but by the unanimous verdict of a jury of good and lawful men, in open court, as heretofore used. *N. C.*, 422.

—In all civil suits, and in all controversies concerning property, the parties shall have a right to a trial by jury, except in cases where it has heretofore been otherwise practiced; the party claiming the right may be heard by himself and his counsel, or either, at his election. *Me.*, 240.

—It is essential to the preservation of the rights of every individual, his life, liberty, property and character, that there be an impartial interpretation of the laws and administration of justice. It is the right of every citizen to be tried by judges as free, impartial and independent as the lot of humanity will admit. It is, therefore, not only the best policy, but for the security of the rights of the people, and of every citizen, that the Judges of the Supreme Judicial Court should hold their offices as long as they behave themselves well, and that they should have honorable salaries ascertained and established by standing laws. *Mass.*, 282.

—That no person shall be put to answer any criminal charge, but by presentment, indictment or impeachment, except in such cases as the Legislature shall otherwise provide; but the Legislature shall pass no law whereby any person shall be required to answer any criminal charge involving the life of the accused, except upon indictment or presentment by a Grand Jury. *Fl.*, 129.

—In every criminal prosecution, the accused shall have the right to a speedy and public trial by an impartial jury, which may consist of less than twelve men in all courts not of record; to be informed of the nature of the accusation; to be confronted with the witnesses against him; to have compulsory process for obtaining witnesses in his favor, and have the assistance of counsel for his defense. *Mich.*, 307.

—That, in all criminal prosecutions, the accused has a right to be heard by himself and counsel, to demand the nature and cause of the accusation, to have a copy thereof, to be confronted by the witnesses against him, to have compulsory process for obtaining witnesses in his favor, and, in all prosecutions by indictment or information, a speedy public trial by an impartial jury of the county or district in which the offense was committed; and that he shall not be compelled to give evidence against himself, nor be deprived of his life, liberty or property, but by due course of law. *Ala.*, 73; (nearly similar), *Ky.*, 223.

--That all courts shall be open; and that every person, for any injury done him, in his lands, goods, person or reputation, shall have a remedy by due course of law, and right and justice administered, without sale, denial or delay. *Ala.*, 73; *Ky.*, 223.

—The statutes of limitations shall not be pleaded upon any claim in the hands of any person whomsoever, not sued upon when such claim was not barred by the statutes of limitation on the 10th day of January, 1861. *Fl.*, 141.

—No law of this State providing that claims or demands against the estates of decedents shall be barred if not presented within two years, shall be considered as being in force within this State between the 10th day of January, 1861, and the 25th day of October, 1865. *Fl.*, 141.

—In all criminal prosecutions and in cases involving the life or liberty of an individual, the accused shall have a right to a speedy and public trial by an impartial jury; to be informed of the accusation against him; to have a copy of the same when demanded; to be confronted with the witnesses against him; to have compulsory process for his witnesses; and to have the assistance of counsel. *Neb.*, 370.

—That in all prosecutions for criminal offenses, a person hath a right to be heard, by himself and his counsel; to demand the cause and nature of his accusation; to be confronted with the witnesses; to call for evidence in his favor, and a speedy public trial by an impartial jury of the country, without the unanimous consent of which jury, he cannot be found guilty; nor can he be compelled to give evidence against himself; nor can any person be justly deprived of his liberty except by the laws of the land, or the judgment of his peers. *Ti.*, 522.

—That, in controversies respecting property, and in suits between man and man, the ancient trial by jury of twelve men is preferable to any other, and ought to be held sacred. *Va.*, 532.

—In suits at common law, where the value in controversy exceeds twenty dollars, the right of trial by jury, if required by either party, shall be preserved. No fact tried by a jury shall be otherwise re-examined in any case than according to the rules of the common law. *W. Va.*, 547.

—The trial by jury, as heretofore used in this State, and the liberty of the press, shall be forever inviolably preserved. But the General Assembly shall have power to determine the number of persons who shall constitute the jury in the inferior and District Courts. *S. C.*, 488.

—No person shall be taken, or imprisoned, or disseized of his freehold, liberties or privileges, or outlawed or exiled, or in any manner deprived of his life, liberty or property, but by due process of law; nor shall any bill of attainder, *ex post facto* law, or law impairing the obligation of contracts, ever be passed by the General Assembly. *S. C.*, 487.

—That no freeman shall be taken or imprisoned, or disseized of his freehold, liberties or privileges, or outlawed or exiled, or in any manner destroyed or deprived of his life, liberty or property, but by the judgment of his peers, or the law of the land. *Tenn.*, 491.

—No person, in time of peace, shall be deprived of life, liberty or property without due process of law. *W. Va.*, 547.

—In order to reap the fullest advantage of the inestimable privilege of the trial by jury, great care ought to be taken that none but qualified persons should be appointed to serve; and such ought to [be] fully compensated for their travel, time and attendance. *N. H.*, 400.

—That no person can, for an indictable offense, be proceeded against criminally by information, except in cases arising in the land or naval forces, or in the militia when in actual service in the time of war or public danger, or by leave of court, for oppression or misdemeanor in office. *Mo.*, 347.

—That in all controversies at law, respecting property, the ancient mode of trial by jury is one of the best securities of the rights of the people, and ought to remain sacred and inviolable. *N. C.*, 422.

—The right of trial by jury shall be secured to all, and remain inviolate forever; but a jury trial may be waived by the parties in all civil cases, in the manner to be described by law; and in civil cases if three-fourths of the jury agree upon a verdict, it shall stand and have the same force and effect as a verdict by the whole jury: *Provided*, The Legislature, by a law passed by a two-thirds vote of all the members elected to each branch thereof, may require a unanimous verdict notwithstanding this provision. *Nev.*, 379.

—The right of trial by jury shall remain inviolate; but the Legislature may authorize the trial of civil suits, when the matter in dispute does not exceed fifty dollars, by a jury of six men. *N. J.*, 412.

—In all controversies concerning property, and in all suits between two or more persons, except in cases in which it has been heretofore otherwise used and practiced, the parties have a right to trial by jury; and this method of procedure shall be held sacred, unless, in cases arising on the high seas, and such as relate to mariners' wages, the Legislature shall think it necessary hereafter to alter it. *N. H.*, 400.

—In criminal prosecutions, the trial of the facts in the vicinity where they happen is so essential to the security of the life, liberty and estate of the citizen, that no crime or offense ought to be tried in any other county than that in which it is committed; except in cases of general insurrection in any particular county, when it shall appear to the Judges of the Superior Court that an impartial trial cannot be had in the county where the offense may be committed, and upon their report, the Legislature shall think proper to direct the trial in the nearest county in which an impartial trial can be obtained. *N. H.*, 400.

—That no person shall, for any indictable offense, be proceeded against criminally by information; except in cases arising in the land or naval forces, or in the militia when in actual service, or by leave of the court, for misdemeanor in office. *Provided*, That the Legislature in case of petit larceny, assault, assault and battery, affray, riot, unlawful assembly, drunkenness, vagrancy, and other misdemeanors of like character, may dispense with an inquest of a grand jury, and may authorize prosecutions before Justices of the Peace, or such other inferior court or courts as may be established by the Legislature; and the proceedings in such cases shall be regulated by law. *Miss.*, 335; (nearly similar), *Ala.*, 73.

—No person shall be held to answer for a criminal offense unless on the presentment or indictment of a grand jury except in cases of impeachment, or in cases cognizable by Justices of the Peace, or arising in the army or navy, or in the militia, when in actual service in time of war, or public danger; and no person for the same offense shall be put twice in jeopardy of punishment, nor shall be compelled in any criminal case to be a witness against himself. All persons shall, before conviction, be bailable by sufficient sureties, except for capital offenses, when the proof is evident or the presumption great; and the privilege of the writ of *habeas corpus* shall not be suspended, unless when, in cases of rebellion or invasion, the public safety may require. *Neb.*, 370.

—The House of Delegates may inquire, on the oath of witnesses, into all complaints, grievances and offenses, as the Grand Inquest of the State, and may commit any person, for any crime, to the public jail, there to remain until discharged by due course of law; they may examine and pass all accounts of the State, relating either to the collection or expenditure of the revenue, and appoint auditors to state and adjust the same; they may call for all public or official papers and records, and send for persons whom they may judge necessary in the course of their inquiries concerning affairs relating to the public interest, and may direct all office bonds, which shall be made payable to the State, to be sued for any breach thereof. *Md.*, 262.

1   § 3. The free exercise and enjoyment of religious profession and worship,

2 without discrimination or preference, shall forever be allowed in this State to

3 all mankind ; (¹) and no person shall be rendered incompetent to be a witness

4 on account of his opinions on matters of religious belief ; (²) but the liberty of

5 conscience hereby secured shall not be so construed as to excuse acts of licentious-

6 ness, or to justify practices inconsistent with the peace or safety of this State.(³)

(1). [The clause relating to incompetency of witnesses on account of religious belief, is not included in N. Y. Constitution of 1821.]

(2). *Ind.*, 170; *Ohio*, 432; *S. C.*, 488.

(3). *Cal.*, 96; *Ct.*, 107; *Miss.*, 334; *Nev.*, 379.

[A preamble giving reasons]. *N. Y.*, (1777), 32.

RELIGIOUS FREEDOM.

—Congress shall make no law respecting an establishment of religion, or prohibiting the free exercise thereof. *U. S.*, 18.

—That religion, or the duty which we owe to our Creator, and the manner of discharging it, can be directed only by reason and conviction, not by force or violence ; and, therefore, all men are equally entitled to the free exercise of religion, according to the dictates of conscience ; and that it is the mutual duty of all to practice Christian forbearance, love and charity towards each other. *Va.*, 532.

—That no person within this State shall, upon any pretense whatever, be deprived of the inestimable privilege of worshipping God in the manner most agreeable to his own conscience; nor be hurt, molested or restrained in his religious profession, sentiments or persuasions, provided he does not disturb others in their religious worship. *Ala.*, 72.

—That all men have a natural and indefeasible right to worship Almighty God according to the dictates of their own consciences; and no man can, of right, be compelled to attend, erect or support any place of worship, or to maintain any ministry against his consent; that no human authority can, in any case whatever, interfere with the rights of conscience; and that no preference shall ever be given to any religious establishment or mode of worship. *Ark.*, 84; *Ill.*, 165; *Tenn.*, 400; *Pa.*, 467; *Tex.*, 506; *Mo.*, 346.

—But nothing herein shall be construed to dispense with oaths and affirmations. Religion, morality and knowledge, however, being essential to good government, it shall be the duty of the General Assembly to pass suitable laws to protect every religious denomination in the peaceable enjoyment of its own mode of public worship, and to encourage schools and the means of instruction. *Ohio*, 432; *Neb.*, 371.

—That no religion shall be established by law ; that no preference shall be given by law to any religious sect, society, denomination, or mode of worship, that no one shall be compelled by law to attend any place of worship, nor to pay any tithes, taxes, or other rate, for building or repairing any place of worship, or for maintaining any minister or ministry; that no religious test shall be required as a qualification to any office or public trust under this State; and that the civil rights, privileges and capacities of any citizen shall not be in any manner affected by his religious principles. *Ala.*, 72.

—That no other test or qualification ought to be required on admission to any office of trust or profit than such oath of allegiance and fidelity to this State and the United States as may be prescribed by this Constitution, and such oath of office and qualification as may be prescribed by this Constitution, or by the laws of the State, and a declaration of belief in the Christian religion, or in the existence of God, and in a future state of rewards and punishments. *Md.*, 25.

—That the civil rights, privileges or capacities of any citizen shall in no wise be diminished or enlarged on account of his religion. *Ark.*, 84; *Ky.*, 223.

—The right to worship God according to the dictates of conscience shall never be infringed; nor shall any person be compelled to attend or support any form of worship; nor shall any control of, or interference with, the rights of conscience be permitted; nor any preference be given by law to any religious establishment or mode of worship. No religious test or property qualification shall be required for any office of public trust, nor for any vote at any election; nor shall any person be incompetent to testify on account of religious belief. *Kan.*, 187.

—And whereas, the ministers of the gospel are, by their profession, dedicated to the service of God, and the cure of souls, and ought not to be diverted from the great duties of their functions; therefore, no minister of the gospel, or priest of any denomination whatsoever, shall at any time hereafter under any pretense or description whatever, be eligible to, or capable of holding, any civil or military office or place within this State. *N. Y.*, (1777), 33, (1821,) 41.

—Therefore no minister of the gospel, or priest of any denomination whatever, shall be eligible to a seat in either House of the Legislature. *Tenn.*, 498; (similar provision), *La.*, 229; *N. C.*, 425; *Va.*, 536.

—No licensed minister of the Gospel shall be required to perform military duty, work on roads, or serve on juries in this State. *Tex.*, 514.

—No sectarian instruction shall be imparted or tolerated in any school or university that may be established under this Constitution. *Nev.*, 391.

—Therefore no minister of the gospel, or public preacher of any religious persuasion, whilst he continues in the exercise of his pastoral functions, shall be eligible to the office of Governor, Lieutenant-Governor, or to a seat in the Senate or House of Representatives. *S. C.*, 484; *Tex.*, 509.

—The Legislature shall not diminish or enlarge the civil or political rights, privileges and capacities of any person on account of his opinion or belief concerning matters of religion. *Mich.*, 304.

—No man shall be compelled to frequent or support any religious worship, place or ministry whatsoever; nor shall any man be enforced, restrained, molested or burdened in his body or goods, or otherwise suffer, on account of his religious belief; but all men shall be free to profess, and by argument to maintain, their opinions in matters of religion, and the same shall in no wise affect, diminish or enlarge their civil capacities. And the Legislature shall not prescribe any religious test whatever; or confer any peculiar privileges or advantages on any sect or denomination; or pass any law requiring or authorizing any religious society, or the people of any district within this State, to levy on themselves or others, any tax for the erection or repair of any house for public worship, or for the support of any church or ministry; but it shall be left free to every person to select his religious instructor, and to make for his

8

support, such private contract as he shall please. *Va.*, 537 ; *W. Va.*, 547.

—The militia of this State shall, at all times hereafter, be armed and disciplined, and in readiness for service; but all such inhabitants of this State, of any religious denomination whatever, as from scruples of conscience, may be adverse to bearing arms, shall be excused therefrom by paying to the State an equivalent in money; and the Legislature shall provide by law for the collection of such equivalent, to be estimated according to the expense, in time and money, of an ordinary, able-bodied militia-man. *N. Y.*, (1821), 41.

—Among the natural rights, some are in their very nature unalienable, because no equivalent can be given or received for them. One of this kind are rights of conscience. *N. H.*, 398.

—No person shall be rendered incompetent to be a witness on account of his opinions on matters of religious belief. *Mich.*, 307.

—As the public worship of God, and instructions in piety, religion and morality, promote the happiness and prosperity of a people, and the security of a republican government, therefore the several religious societies of this Commonwealth, whether corporate or unincorporate, at any meeting legally warned and holden for that purpose, shall ever have the right to elect their pastors or religious teachers, to contract with them for their support, to raise money for erecting and repairing houses for public worship, for the maintenance of religious instruction, and for the payment of necessary expenses; and all persons belonging to any religious society shall be taken and held to be members, until they shall file with the clerk of such society a written notice declaring the dissolution of their membership, and thenceforth shall not be liable for any grant or contract which may be thereafter made or entered into by such society ; and all religious sects and denominations, demeaning themselves peaceably, and as good citizens of the Commonwealth, shall be equally under the protection of the law ; and no subordination of any one sect or denomination to another shall ever be established by law. *Mass.*, 296.

—That there shall be no establishment of any one religious church or denomination in this State in preference to any other; neither shall any person, on any pretense whatsoever, be compelled to attend any place of worship contrary to his own faith or judgment, nor be obliged to pay for the purchase of any glebe, or the building of any house of worship, or for the maintenance of any minister or ministry, contrary to what he believes right and has voluntarily and personally engaged to perform; but all persons shall be at liberty to exercise their own mode of worship : *Provided*, That nothing herein contained shall be construed to exempt preachers of treasonable or seditious discourses from legal trial and punishment. *N. C.*, 425.

—That all men have a natural and indefeasible right to worship Almighty God according to the dictates of their own consciences; that no man shall be compelled to attend, erect or support any place of worship, or to maintain any ministry against his consent; that no human authority ought, in any case whatever, to control or interfere with the rights of conscience; and that no preference shall ever be given by law to any religious societies or modes of worship. *Ky.*, 223.

—Perfect freedom of religious sentiment, be and the same is hereby secured, and no inhabitant of this State, shall ever be molested in person or property; nor prohibited from holding any public office or trust on account of his religious opinion. *Ga.*, 142.

—That no person shall be molested for his opinions on any subject whatever, nor suffer any civil or political incapacity, or acquire any civil or political advantages, in consequence of such opinions, except in cases provided for in this Constitution. *Miss.*, 334.

—All men shall be secured in the natural right to worship Almighty God according to the dictates of their own consciences. *Ind.*, 170 ; *Me.*, 239 ; *Or.*, 447.

—And no one shall be hurt, molested or restrained in his person, liberty or estate, for worshipping God in the manner and season most agreeable to the dictates of his own conscience, nor for his religious professions or sentiments, provided he does not disturb the public peace, nor obstruct others in their religious worship ;—and all persons demeaning themselves peaceably, as good members of the State, shall be equally under the protection of the laws, and no subordination nor preference, of any one sect or denomination to another, shall ever be established by law, nor shall any religious test be required as a qualification for any office or trust under this State ; and all religious societies in this State, whether incorporate or unincorporate, shall at all times have the exclusive right of electing their public teachers, and contracting with them for their support and maintenance. *Me.*, 239.

—No law shall, in any case whatever, control the free exercise and enjoyment of religious opinions, or interfere with the rights of conscience. *Ind.*, 170 ; *Or.*, 447.

—Nor can any man, who is conscientiously scrupulous of bearing arms, be justly compelled thereto, if he will pay such equivalent. *N. H.*, 399; (nearly similar), *Ala.*, 74; *Tex.*, 514; *Ill.*, 163; *Ind.*, 180; *Vt.*, 522.

—The Legislature shall pass laws, exempting citizens belonging to any sect or denomination of religion the tenets of which are known to be opposed to the bearing of arms, from attending private and general musters. *Tenn.*, 498.

—That no person who acknowledges the being of God and a future state of rewards and punishments, shall, on account of his religious sentiments, be disqualified to hold any office or place of trust or profit under this Commonwealth. *Pa.*, 467.

—No person who shall deny the being of God, or the truth of the Christian religion, or the divine authority of the old or new Testament, or who shall hold religious principles incompatible with the freedom or safety of the State, shall be capable of holding any office or place of trust or profit in the civil department within this State. *N. C.*, 430.

—No person who denies the being of a God shall hold any office in the civil department of this State, nor be allowed his oath in any court. *Ark.*, 93; [*Tenn.*, 498].

—No person who denies the being of a God, or a future state of rewards and punishments, shall hold any office in the civil department of this State. *Miss.*, 342.

—No contract of marriage, if otherwise duly made, shall be invalidated for want of conformity to the requirements of any religious sect. *Cal.*, 104.

—It being the duty of all men to worship the Supreme Being, the Great Creator and Preserver of the universe, and their right to render that worship in the mode most consistent with the dictates of their conscience, no person shall by law be compelled to join or support, or be classed with or associated to any congregation, church, or religious association. But every person now belonging to such congregation, church, or religious association, shall remain a member thereof until he shall have separated himself therefrom in the manner hereinafter provided. And each and every society or denomination of Christians in this State shall have and enjoy the same and equal powers, rights and privileges, and shall have power and authority to support and maintain the ministers or teachers of their respective denominations, and to build and repair houses for public worship by a tax on the members of any such society only, to be laid by a major vote of the legal voters assembled at any society meeting, warned and held according to law, or in any other manner. *Ct.*, 112.

—If any person shall choose to separate himself from the society or denomination of Christians to which he may belong, and shall leave a written notice thereof with the clerk of such society, he shall thereupon be no longer liable for any future expenses which may be incurred by said society. *Ct.*, 112.

—That all men have a natural and inalienable right

to worship Almighty God according to the dictates of their own conscience, [*N. C.*, 722,] and that no preference shall ever be given by law to any religious establishment or mode of worship in this State. *Fl.,* 124.

—The Legislature shall pass no law to prevent any person from worshipping Almighty God according to the dictates of his own conscience, or to compel any person to attend, erect or support any place of religious worship, or to pay tithes, taxes or other rates for the support of any minister of the Gospel or teacher of religion. *Mich.,* 307.

—Although it is the duty of all men frequently to assemble together for the public worship of the Author of the Universe, and piety and morality, on which the prosperity of communities depends, are thereby promoted; yet no man shall, or ought to be compelled to attend any religious worship, to contribute to the erection or support of any place of worship, or to the maintenance of any ministry, against his own free will and consent, and no power shall or ought to be vested in or assumed by any magistrate, that shall in any case interfere with, or in any manner control the rights of conscience, in the free exercise of religious worship: nor shall a preference be given by law to any religious societies, denomination or modes of worship. *Del,* 116.

—The General Assembly shall make no law respecting an establishment of religion, or prohibiting the free exercise thereof; nor shall any person be compelled to attend any place of worship, pay tithes, taxes, or other rates for building or repairing places of worship, or the maintenance of any minister or ministry. *Iowa,* 183.

—No religious test shall be required as a qualification to any office, or public trust, under this State. *Del.,* 116; *Ill.,* 165; *Ind.,* 170; *Iowa,* 183; *Or.,* 447; *Ohio,* 432; *N. J.,* 912; *Neb.,* 371; *Tex.,* 505; *Tenn.,* 490; *Wis.,* 560.

—That every gift, sale or devise of land, to any minister, public teacher or preacher of the Gospel, as such, or to any religious sect, order or denomination, or to or for the support, use or benefit of, or in trust for any minister, public teacher, or preacher of the Gospel, as such, or any religious sect, order or denomination, and every gift or sale of goods or chattels to go in succession, or to take place after the death of the seller or donor, to or for such support, use or benefit; and also, every devise of goods or chattels, to or for the support, use or benefit of any minister, public teacher or preacher of the Gospel, as such; or any religious sect, order or denomination, without the prior or subsequent sanction of the Legislature, shall be void; except always any sale, gift, lease or devise of any quantity of land not exceeding five acres, for a church, meeting-house or other house of worship, or parsonage, or for a burying-ground, which shall be improved, enjoyed or used only for such purpose, or such sale, gift, lease or devise shall be void. *Md.,* 255.

—That every gift, sale, or devise of any land to any minister, public teacher, or preacher of the Gospel, as such, or to any religious sect, order or denomination; or to, or for the support, use or benefit of, or in trust for, any minister, public teacher or preacher of the Gospel, as such, or any religious sect, order or denomination; and every gift or sale of goods or chattels to go in succession, or to take place after the death of the seller or donor, to or for the support, use or benefit; and also every devise of goods or chattels, to or for the support, use or benefit of any minister, public teacher or preacher of the Gospel, as such, or any religious sect, order or denomination, shall be void; except any gift, sale or devise of land to a church, religious society or congregation, or to any person or persons in trust, for the use of a church, religious society or congregation, whether incorporated or not, for the uses and purposes, and within the limitations of the next preceding clause of this article. *Mo.,* 347.

—No money shall be appropriated or drawn from the treasury for the benefit of any religious sect or

society, theological or religious seminary, nor shall property belonging to the State be appropriated for any such purpose. *Mich.,* 304.

—No preference shall be given by law to any christian sect or mode of worship. *Ct.,* 107.

—No preference shall ever be given by law to any religious sect, or mode of worship. *Miss.,* 334.

—No preference shall be given by law to any creed, religious society, or mode of worship; no man shall be compelled to attend, erect or support any place of worship, or to maintain any ministry, against his consent. *Ind.,* 170.

—The rights, privileges, immunities and estates of religious societies and corporate bodies shall remain as if the Constitution of this State had not been altered or amended. *Pa.,* 466; *Del,* 125.

—No ordained clergyman or ordained preacher of the gospel, of any denomination, shall be capable of holding any civil office in the State, or of being a member of either branch of the Legislature while he continues in the exercise of the pastoral or clerical functions. *Del.,* 125.

—That no person shall be compelled to erect, support or attend any place of worship, or maintain any minister of the Gospel or teacher of religion; but whatever contracts any person may enter into for any such object ought, in law, to be binding and capable of enforcement, as other contracts. *Mo.,* 347.

—No money shall be drawn from the treasury for the benefit of any religious or theological institution. *Ind.,* 170; *Or.,* 447.

—The Legislature may authorize the employment of a chaplain for the State prison; [*Mich.,* 303,] but no money shall be appropriated for the payment of any religious service, in either House of the Legislative Assembly. *Or.,* 447.

—If any person shall declare that he has conscientious scruples against taking an oath, or swearing in any form, the said oath may be changed into a solemn affirmation, and be made by him in that form. *Mo.,* 350.

—The mode of administering any oath or affirmation shall be such as may be most consistent with, and binding upon the conscience of the person to whom such oath or affirmation may be administered. *Ind.* 170; *Or.,* 447.

—That the manner of administering an oath or affirmation to any person ought to be such as those of the religious persuasion, profession or denomination of which he is a member, generally esteem the most effectual confirmation by the attestation of the Divine Being. *Md.,* 256.

—The manner of administering an oath or affirmation shall be such as is most consistent with the conscience of the deponent, and shall be esteemed by the General Assembly the most solemn appeal to God. *Ky.,* 220.

—No person, while he continues to exercise the functions of a clergyman, priest, or teacher of any religious persuasion, society or sect, nor while he holds or exercises any office of profit under this Commonwealth, or under the government of the United States, shall be eligible to the General Assembly, except attorneys-at-law, justices of the peace, and militia officers: *Provided,* That attorneys for the Commonwealth, who receive a fixed annual salary, shall be ineligible. *Ky.,* 212.

—No person shall be deprived of any of his rights, privileges, or capacities, or disqualified from the performance of any of his public or private duties, or rendered incompetent to give evidence in any court of law or equity, in consequence of his opinions on the subject of religion; and any party to any judicial proceeding shall have the right to use as a witness, or take testimony of, any other person not disqualified on account of interest, who may be cognizant of any fact material to the case; and parties to suits may be witnesses, as provided by law. *Iowa,* 183.

—That, as it is the duty of every man to worship God in such manner as he thinks most acceptable to him, all persons are equally entitled to protection in their religious liberty; wherefore, no person ought, by any law, to be molested in his person or estate, on account of his religious persuasion or profession, or for his religious practice, unless under the color of religion any man shall disturb the good order, peace, or safety of the State, or shall infringe the laws of morality, or injure others in their natural, civil or religious rights; nor ought any person to be compelled to frequent or maintain, or contribute, unless on contract to maintain, any place of worship or any ministry; nor shall any person be deemed incompetent as a witness or juror who believes in the existence of a God, and that under his dispensation such person will be held morally accountable for his acts, and be rewarded or punished therefor, either in this world or the world to come. *Md.*, 255.

—It is the right as well as the duty of all men in society, publicly, and at stated seasons, to worship the Supreme Being, the great Creator and Preserver of the universe. And no subject shall be hurt, molested or restrained, in his person, liberty, or estate, for worshipping God in the manner and season most agreeable to the dictates of his own conscience; or for his religious profession or sentiments; provided he doth not disturb the public peace, or obstruct others in their religious worship. *Mass.*, 280.

—As the happiness of a people, and the good order and preservation of civil Government, essentially depend upon piety, religion and morality; and as these cannot be generally diffused through a community, but by the institution of the public worship of God, and of public instructions in piety, religion and morality; *Therefore*, To promote their happiness, and to secure the good order and preservation of their Government, the people of this Commonwealth have a right to invest their Legislature with power to authorize and require, and the Legislature shall, from time to time, authorize and require the several towns, parishes, precincts, and other bodies politic, or religious societies, to make suitable provision, at their own expense, for the institution of the public worship of God, and for the support and maintenance of public protestant teachers of piety, religion and morality, in all cases where such provision shall not be made voluntarily. *Mass.*, 280.

—The right of every man to worship Almighty God according to the dictates of his own conscience, shall never be infringed; nor shall any man be compelled to attend, erect, or support any place of worship, or to maintain any ministry, against his consent. Nor shall any control of, or interference with the rights of conscience be permitted, or any preference be given by law to any religious establishments, or modes of worship. Nor shall any money be drawn from the treasury for the benefit of religious societies or religious or theological seminaries. *Wis.*, 500; (nearly similar), *Min.*, 320.

—And the people of this Commonwealth have also a right to, and do, invest their Legislature with authority to enjoin upon all the subjects an attendance upon the instructions of the public teachers aforesaid, at stated times and seasons, if there be any on whose instructions they can conscientiously and conveniently attend. *Mass.*, 280.

Provided, notwithstanding, That the several towns, parishes, precincts, and other bodies politic, or religious societies, shall at all times have the exclusive right of electing their public teachers, and of contracting with them for their support and maintenance. *Mass.*, 280.

—And all moneys, paid by the subject, to the support of public worship, and of the public teachers aforesaid shall, if he require it, be uniformly applied to the support of the public teacher or teachers of his own religious sect or denomination, provided there be any on whose instructions he attends; otherwise it may be paid toward the support of the teacher or teachers of the parish or precinct in which the said moneys are raised. *Mass.*, 280.

—And every denomination of Christians, demeaning themselves peaceably, and as good subjects of the Commonwealth, shall be equally under the protection of the law; and no subordination of any one sect or denomination to another shall ever be established by law. *Mass.*, 280.

—That no religious corporation can be established in this State; except that by a general law, uniform throughout the State, any church, or religious society, or congregation, may become a body corporate, for the sole purpose of acquiring, holding, using, and disposing of so much land as may be required for a house of public worship, a chapel, a parsonage, and a burial ground, and managing the same, and contracting in relation to such land, and the buildings thereon, through a board of trustees, selected by themselves; but the quantity of land to be held by any such body corporate, in connection with a house of worship or a parsonage, shall not exceed five acres in the country, or one acre in a town or city. *Mo.*, 347.

—There shall be no establishment of one religious sect in preference to another; no religious test shall be required as a qualification for any office or public trust; and no person shall be denied the enjoyment of any civil right merely on account of his religious principles. *N. J.*, 412.

—As morality and piety, rightly grounded on evangelical principles, will give the best and greatest security to government, and will lay in the hearts of men the strongest obligations to due subjection; and as a knowledge of these is most likely to be propagated through a society by the institution of the public worship of the Deity, and of public instruction in morality and religion; therefore, to promote those important purposes, the people of this State have a right to empower, and do hereby fully empower the Legislature to authorize, from time to time, the several towns, parishes, bodies corporate, or religious societies within this State, to make adequate provisions, at their own expense, for the support and maintenance of public Protestant teachers of piety, religion, and morality. *N. H.*, 399.

—The rights, privileges, immunities and estates of both civil and religious societies and of corporate bodies, shall remain as if the Constitution of this State had not been altered or amended. *S. C.*, 488.

—No religious test or amount of property shall ever be required as a qualification for any office of public trust under the State. No religious test or amount of property shall ever be required as a qualification of any voter at any election in this State; nor shall any person be rendered incompetent to give evidence in any court of law or equity in consequence of his opinion upon the subject of religion. *Minn.*, 320.

—That all men have a natural and inalienable right to worship Almighty God according to the dictates of their own consciences and understandings, as in their opinion shall be regulated by the word of God; and that no man ought to, or of right can be compelled to attend any religious worship, or erect or support any place of worship, or maintain any ministry, contrary to the dictates of his conscience; nor can any man be justly deprived or abridged of any civil right as a citizen on account of his religious sentiments or peculiar mode of religious worship; and that no authority can, or ought to be vested in or assumed by any power whatever, that shall in any case interfere with or in any manner control the rights of conscience in the free exercise of religious worship; nevertheless, every sect or denomination of Christians ought to observe the Sabbath or Lord's day, and keep up some sort of religious worship which to them shall seem most agreeable to the revealed will of God. *Vt.* 521.

—But the liberty of conscience hereby secured shall not be so construed as to excuse acts of licentiousness, nor to justify practices inconsistent with the good order, peace, or safety of the State, or with the rights of others. *Mo.* 346; *S. C.*, 488.

—Every individual has a natural and unalienable right to worship God according to the dictates of his own conscience and reason; and no subject shall be hurt, molested or restrained in his person, liberty or estate, for worshipping God in the manner and season most agreeable to the dictates of his own conscience, or of his religious profession, sentiments, or persuasion:

1   § 4. The privileges of the writ of *habeas corpus* shall not be suspended, unless

2 when, in cases of rebellion or invasion, the public safety may require its suspension(¹).

Provided, He doth not disturb the public peace, or disturb others in their religious worship. *N. H.*, 398.

Provided notwithstanding, That the several towns, parishes, bodies corporate, or religious societies, shall at all times have the exclusive right of electing their own public teachers, and of contracting with them for their support and maintenance. And no person, or any one particular religious sect or denomination shall ever be compelled to pay toward the support of the teacher or teachers of another persuasion, sect or denomination. *N. H.*, 399.

—And every denomination of Christians demeaning themselves quietly, and as good subjects of the State, shall be equally under the protection of the law; and no subordination of any one sect or denomination to another shall ever be established by law.

—And nothing herein shall be understood to affect any former contracts made for the support of the ministry; but all such contracts shall remain and be in the same state as if this Constitution had not been made. *N. H.*, 399.

—No person shall be deprived of the inestimable privilege of worshipping Almighty God in a manner agreeable to the dictates of his own conscience; nor under any pretense whatever be compelled to attend any place of worship contrary to his faith and judgment; nor shall any person be obliged to pay tithes, taxes, or other rates for building or repairing any church or churches, place or places of worship, or for the maintenance of any minister or ministry, contrary to what he believes to be right, or has deliberately and voluntarily engaged to perform. *N. J.*, 412.

—Whereas, Almighty God hath created the mind free, and all attempts to influence it by temporal punishment; or burdens, or by civil incapacitations, tend to beget habits of hypocrisy and meanness; and, whereas, a principal object of our venerated ancestors in their migration to this country and their settlement of this State, was, as they expressed it, to hold forth a lively experiment that a flourishing civil State may stand and be best maintained with full liberty in religious concernments; we, therefore declare that no man shall be compelled to frequent or to support any religious worship, place or ministry whatever, except in fulfillment of his own voluntary contract; nor enforced, restrained, molested or burdened in his body or goods; nor disqualified from holding any office; nor otherwise suffer on account of his religious belief; and that every man shall be free to worship God according to the dictates of his own conscience, and to profess, and by argument to maintain, his opinion in matters of religion; and that the same shall in no wise diminish, enlarge, or affect his civil capacity. *R. I.*, 473.

—In order effectually to secure the religious and political freedom established by our venerated ancestors, and to preserve the same for our posterity, we do declare that the essential and unquestionable rights and principles hereinafter mentioned shall be established, maintained, and preserved, and shall be of paramount obligation in all legislative, judicial, and executive proceedings. *R. I.*, 472.

—No charter of incorporation shall be granted to any church or religious denomination. Provision may be made by general laws for securing the title to church property, so that it shall be held and used for the purpose intended. *W. Va.*, 557.

—The General Assembly shall not grant a charter of incorporation to any church or religious denomination, but may secure the title to church property to an extent to be limited by law. *Va.*, 518.

—No person shall be rendered incompetent as a witness or juror in consequence of his opinions on matters of religion, nor be questioned in any court of justice touching his religious belief to affect the weight of his testimony. *Or.*, 447.

—No person shall be rendered incompetent to give evidence in any court of law or equity in consequence of his opinions on the subject of religion. *Wis.*, 560.

(1). *U. S.*, 13; *N. Y.*, (1821) 42; *Ala.* 73; *Ark.*, 84; *Cal.*, 96; *Del.*, 117; *Ga.*, 142; *Ill.*, 166; *Ind.*, 171; *Kan.*, 197; *La.*, 233; *Mich.*, 304; *Pa.*, 468; *Mo.*, 347; *Nev.*, 379; *N. J.*, 412; *Ohio*, 432; *Or.*, 448; *S. C.*, 487; *Tenn.*, 491; *Tex.*, 508; *W. Va.*, 546; *Miss.*, 335.

WRIT OF HABEAS CORPUS—EX POST FACTO LAWS—EXEMPTION FROM SEIZURES AND SEARCHES.

—The writ of *habeas corpus* shall in no case be suspended. It shall be a writ, issuable of right; and the General Assembly shall make provision to render it a speedy and effectual remedy in all cases proper therefor. *Vt.*, 529,

—Retrospective laws are highly injurious, oppressive and unjust. No such laws, therefore, should be made, either for the decision of civil causes or the punishment of offences. *N. H.*, 400.

The writ of *habeas corpus* shall not be suspended or refused when application is made as required by law, unless in case of rebellion or invasion, the public safety may require it. *Iowa*, 184.

—The privilege and benefit of the writ of *habeas corpus* shall be enjoyed in this Commonwealth, in the most free, easy, cheap, expeditious and ample manner; and shall not be suspended by the Legislature, except upon the most urgent and pressing occasions, and for a limited time, not exceeding twelve months. *Mass.*, 293; *N. H.*, 410.

—No bill of attainder or *ex post facto* law shall be passed. *U. S.*, 13; *Ark.*, 84; *Cal.*, 97; *Iowa*, 184; *Me.*, 240; *Min.*, 320; *Neb.*, 371; *Nev.*, 380; *Miss.*, *Vt.*, 537, nor vested rights be divested, unless for purposes of public utility, and for adequate compensation previously made. *La.*, 234.

That no *ex post facto* law, or law impairing the obligations of contracts shall ever be made. *Ala.*, 73; *Ark.*, 84; *Cal.*, 97; *Fl.*, 120; *Ill.*, 166; *Ind.*, 171; *Iowa*, 184; *Ky.*, 224; *La.*, 233; *Me.*, 240; *Va.*, 537; *R. I.*, 473; *Tenn.*, 491; *Mich.*, 304; *Pa.*, 468; *Miss.*, 335; *Mo.*, 348; *Nev.*, 380; *Tex.*, 506; *Or.*, 448; *W. Va.*, 547; *Wis.*, 560.

—That retrospective laws punishing acts committed before the existence of such laws, and by them only declared penal or criminal, are oppressive, unjust and incompatible with liberty; wherefore no *ex post facto* law shall ever be made. *Fl.*, 120; *N. C.*, 422; *Md.*, 254; *Tenn.*, 497.

—*Ex post facto* laws, laws impairing the obligation of contracts, and retroactive laws injuriously affecting any right of the citizen, are prohibited. *Ga.*, 142.

—Laws made to punish for actions done before the existence of such laws, and which have not been declared crimes by preceding laws, are unjust, oppressive and inconsistent with the fundamental principles of a free government. *Mass.*, 282.

—Writs of error shall never be prohibited by law. *Wis.*, 561.

—The writ of error shall be a writ of right in all capital cases, and shall operate as a supersedeas to stay the execution of the sentence of death until the further order of the Supreme Court in the premises. *Neb.*, 371.

—The right of the people to be secure in their persons, houses, papers and effects, against unreasonable seizures and searches, shall not be violated; and no warrant shall issue but on probable cause, supported by oath or affirmation, particularly describing the place to be searched, and the persons and things to

13

be seized. *Cal.*, 97; *Ga.*, 143; *Ind.*, 170; *Iowa*, 183; *Kan.*, 197; *La.*, 233; *Miss.*, 319; *Neb.*, 371; *Nev.*, 380; *N. J.*, 412; *Ohio*, 433; *Or.*, 447; *R. I.*, 473; *W. Va.*, 547; *Wis.*, 560.

Every subject has a right to be secure from all unreasonable searches and seizures of his person, his houses, his papers, and all his possessions. All warrants, therefore, are contrary to this right, if the cause or foundation of them be not previously supported by oath or affirmation, and if the order in the warrant to a civil officer, to make search in suspected places, or to arrest one or more suspected persons, or to seize their property, be not accompanied with a special designation of the persons or objects of search, arrest or seizure; and no warrant ought to be issued but in cases, and with the formalities prescribed by the laws. *Mass.*, 281.

—No person shall be accused, arrested or detained, except in cases ascertained by law, and according to the form which the same has prescribed; and no person shall be punished but in virtue of a law established and promulgated prior to the offense, and legally applied. *Miss.*, 335.

—That the people shall be secure in their persons, houses, papers and possessions, from unreasonable seizures or searches; and that no warrant shall issue to search any place, or to seize any person or thing, without describing them as nearly as may be, nor without probable cause, supported by oath or affirmation. *Ala.*, 72; *Ark.*, 84; *Ct.*, 107; *Del.*, 116; *Fl.*, 129; *Id.*, 165; *Me.*, 239; *Min.*, 335; *Mo.*, 347; *Pa.*, 467; *Tex.*, 506.

— That all warrants, without oath or affirmation, to search suspected places, or to seize any person or property, are grievous and oppressive; and all general warrants to search suspected places, or to apprehend suspected persons, without naming or describing the place, or the person in special, are illegal, and ought not to be granted. *Md.*, 255; and that general warrants, whereby any officer may be commanded to search suspected places without evidence of the fact committed, or to seize any person or persons not named, whose offenses are not particularly described and supported by evidence, are dangerous to liberty, and shall not be granted. *Ark.*, 84; *Ill.*, 165; (nearly similar), *N. C.*, 422; *Va.*, 532; *Vt.*, 522; *Tenn.*, 490.

Every subject has a right to be secure from all unreasonable searches and seizures of his person, his houses, his papers, and all his possessions; *Therefore*, All warrants to search suspected places, or arrest a person for examination or trial, in prosecutions for criminal matters, are contrary to this right, if the cause or foundation of them be not previously supported by oath or affirmation; and if the order in a warrant to a civil officer, to make search in suspected places, or to arrest one or more suspected persons, or to seize their property, be not accompanied with a special designation of the persons or object of search, arrest or seizure, and no warrant ought to be issued but in cases and with the formalities prescribed by law. *N. H.*, 400.

MILITARY RIGHTS AND RESTRICTIONS.

—The military shall in all cases and at all times be kept in strict subordination to the civil power. *Ark.*, 85; *Cal.*, 96; *Ct.*, 108; *Del.*, 117; *Fl.*, 120; *Ill.*, 166; *Ind.*, 171; *Iowa*, 184; *Ky.*, 224; *Md.*, 255; *Neb.*, 371; *N. C.*, 422; *Miss.*, 335; *Or.*, 448; *Pa.*, 468; *W. Va.*, 547; *Mich.*, 314; *Min.*, 320; *N. J.*, 412; *R. I.*, 474; *Nev.*, 380; *N. H.*, 400; *S. C.*, 487; *Tex.*, 506; *Wis.*, 561; *Vt.*, 522.

—The law martial shall be used and exercised in such cases only as occasion shall necessarily require. *R. I.*, 474.

—That every citizen has a right to bear arms in defense of himself and the State. *Ala.*, 74.

—Every citizen has a right to keep and bear arms for the common defense; and this right shall never be questioned. *Me.*, 240; *Pa.*, 468.

—That no standing army shall be kept up, without the consent of the General Assembly; and in that case no appropriation for its support shall be for a longer term than one year; and that the military shall, in all cases and at all times, be in strict subordination to the civil power. *Ala.*, 74.

—That the rights of the citizens to bear arms in defense of themselves and the State shall not be questioned; but the General Assembly may pass laws to prevent persons from carrying concealed arms. *Ky.*, 224.

—The people have a right to keep and to bear arms for the common defense. And as, in time of peace, armies are dangerous to liberty, they ought not to be maintained without the consent of the Legislature; and the military power shall always be held in an exact subordination to the civil authority, and be governed by it. *Mass.*, 281.

—The right of the people to keep and bear arms shall not be infringed. *R. I.*, 474.

—That the free white men of this State shall have a right to keep and to bear arms for their common defense. *Ark.*, 85; *Mo.*, 346; *Tenn.*, 492.

—The people shall have a right to bear arms for the defense of themselves and the State. *Ct.*, 108; *Ind.*, 171; (of lawful authority of the State), *Mo.*, 346; *Miss.*, 335; *Mich.*, 314; *N. C.*, 422; *Tex.*, 506; *Vt.*, 522.

—The people have the right to bear arms for their defense and security; but standing armies, in time of peace, are dangerous to liberty, and shall not be tolerated, and the military shall be in strict subordination to the civil power. *Kan.*, 197; *N. C.*, 422; *Or.*, 448; *Ohio*, 432.

That no soldier shall, in time of peace, be quartered in any house without the consent of the owner, nor in time of war, but in a manner prescribed by law. *U. S.*, 18; *Ala.*, 74; *Ark.*, 85; *Cal.*, 96; *Ct.*, 108; *Del.*, 117; *Fl.*, 130; *Ill.*, 166; *Ind.*, 171; *Iowa*, 184; *Kan.* 197; *Ky.*, 224; *Me.*, 240; *Md.*, 255; *Mass.*, 282; *Mich.*, 314; *Miss.*, 335; *Nev.*, 380; *N. H.*, 400; *N. J.*, 412; *Ohio*, 433; *Or.*, 448; *Pa.*, 465; *R. I.*, 474; *Tenn.*, 492; *Tex.*, 517. [By a civil magistrate]. *Del.* 117; *N. H.*, 399.

—That no citizen of this State shall be compelled to bear arms, provided he will pay an equivalent, to be ascertained by law. *Tenn.*, 492.

—That the military is, and in all cases and at all times, ought to be, in strict subordination to the civil power; that no soldier can, in time of peace, be quartered in any house without the consent of the owner; nor in time of war, but in such manner as may be prescribed by law; nor can any appropriation for the support of an army be made for a longer period than two years. *Mo.*, 348.

—No standing army shall be kept up by this State in time of peace. *Cal.*, 96; *Del.*, 111; *Fl.*, 130; *Iowa*, 184; *Ky.*, 224; *Me.*, 240.

—That standing armies are dangerous to liberty, and ought not to be raised or kept up without the consent of the Legislature. *Md.*, 255; *N. H.*, 400; *Pa.*, 468; *Miss.*, 335; *Va.*, 533; *Nev.*, 380; *Vt.*, 522.

—A well-regulated militia, being necessary to the security of a free State, the right of the people to keep and bear arms, shall not be infringed. *Ga.*, 142; *Va.*, 532.

—That a well-regulated militia is the proper and natural defense of a free government. *Md.*, 255; *N. H.*, 400.

—That the sure and certain defense of a free people is a well-regulated militia; and, as standing armies in time of peace are dangerous to freedom, they ought to be avoided, and as the circumstances and safety of the community will admit; and that in all cases the military shall be kept in strict subordination to the civil authority. *Tenn.*, 491.

SLAVERY—RIGHTS OF COLORED PERSONS.

—Neither slavery nor involuntary servitude, unless for the punishment of crime, whereof the party shall have been duly convicted, shall exist within the

13

United States, or any place subject to their jurisdiction. *U. S.*, 20; [similar provision, with preambles and provisos, in some]. *Ala.*, 74; *Ill.*; *Cal.* 97; *Fl.*, 140; *Ga.*, 143; *Ill.*, 166; *Ind.*, 171; *Iowa*, 184; *Kan.*, 197; *La.*, 225; *Mich.*, 314; *Md.*, 255; *Miss.*, 343; *Mo.*, 364; *N. C.*, 431; *Ohio*, 413; *Mo.*, 346; *Wis.*, 559; *Neb.*, 376; *Nev.*, 380; *Tex.*, 518; *Va.*, 357; *R. I.*, 473; *Tenn.*, 503; *Min.*, 319; *Or.*, 459.

—The Legislature shall make no law recognizing the right of property in man. *La.*, 225.

—No indenture of any negro or mulatto, made and executed out of the bounds of the State, shall be valid within the State. *Ind.*, 171.

[A Constitutional guaranty of right of property in the slave and its increase, and prohibition against their emancipation.] *Ky.*, 221.

—That no person can, on account of color, be disqualified as a witness; or be disabled to contract, otherwise than as others are disabled; or be prevented from acquiring, holding and transmitting property; or be liable to any other punishment for any offense, than that imposed upon others for a like offense; or be restricted in the exercise of religious worship; or be hindered in acquiring education; or be subjected, in law, to any other restraints or disqualifications, in regard to any personal rights, than such as are laid upon others under like circumstances. *Mo.*, 346.

—All contracts made with any negro or mulatto coming into the State, contrary to the provision of the foregoing section, shall be void; and any person who shall employ such negro or mulatto, or otherwise encourage him to remain in the State, shall be fined in any sum not less than ten dollars nor more than five hundred dollars. *Ind.*, 180.

—Nor shall any male person arrived at the age of twenty-one years, nor female arrived at the age of eighteen years, be held to serve any person as a servant, under any indenture or contract hereafter made, unless such person shall enter into such indenture or contract while in a state of perfect freedom, and on condition of a *bona fide* consideration received or to be received for their services. *Ark.*, 88.

—Nor shall any indenture of any negro or mulatto hereafter made and executed out of this State, or if made in this State, where the term of service exceeds one year, be of the least validity, except those given in the case of apprenticeship, which shall not be for a longer term than until the apprentice shall arrive at the age of twenty-one years, if a male, or the age of eighteen years, if a female. *Ark.*, 88.

—The marriage relation between white persons and persons of African descent is forever prohibited, and such marriage shall be null and void; and it shall be the duty of the General Assembly to enact laws for the punishment of any officer who shall knowingly issue a license for the celebration of such marriage, or any officer or minister of the gospel who shall marry such persons together. *Ga.*, 150.

—It shall be the duty of the General Assembly, at its next session, and from time to time thereafter, to enact such laws as will protect the freedmen of this State in the full enjoyment of all their rights of person and property, and guard them against any evils that may arise from their sudden emancipation. *Ala.*, 78.

—Be it ordained, that on and after the ratification of the Constitution, no person, save under the military arm of the Federal government, shall be permitted to bring within the limits of this State any indentured or freed negro or mulatto; nor shall any negro or mulatto not now in the State be ever permitted to reside within its limits, save by authority of the government of the United States, or under some proclamation of the President. *Ark.*, 95.

—Africans and their descendants shall be protected in their rights of person and property by appropriate legislation; they shall have the right to contract and be contracted with; to sue and be sued; to acquire, hold and transmit property; and all criminal prosecutions against them shall be conducted in the same manner as prosecutions for like offenses against the

white race, and they shall be subject to like penalties. *Tex.*, 518.

—Africans and their descendants shall not be prohibited, on account of their color or race, from testifying orally, as witnesses, in any case, civil or criminal, involving the right of injury to, or crime against any of them, in person or property, under the same rules of evidence that may be applicable to the white race; the credibility of their testimony to be determined by the court or jury hearing the same; and the Legislature shall have power to authorize them to testify as witnesses in all other cases, under such regulations as may be prescribed, as to facts hereafter occurring. *Tex.*, 518.

—Any person who shall, after this Constitution shall have gone into effect, detain in slavery any person emancipated by the provisions of this Constitution, shall, on conviction, be fined not less than five hundred dollars nor more than five thousand dollars, or be imprisoned not more than five years; and any of the judges of this State shall discharge, on *habeas corpus*, any person so detained in slavery. *Md.*, 266.

—The General Assembly shall pass no law, nor make any appropriation to compensate the masters or claimants of slaves emancipated from servitude by the adoption of this Constitution. *Md.*, 264.

—The General Assembly shall have no power to make compensation for emancipated slaves. *Mo.*, 354.

—The General Assembly shall, at the first session under the amended Constitution, pass such laws as will effectually prohibit free persons of color from immigrating to and settling in this State; and effectually prevent the owners of slaves from bringing them into this State for the purpose of setting them free. *Ill.*, 169.

—No negro or mulatto shall come into or settle in the State after the adoption of this Constitution. *Ind.*, 180.

—All fines which may be collected for a violation of the provisions of this article, or any law which may hereafter be passed for the purpose of carrying the same into execution, shall be set apart and appropriated for the colonization of such negroes and mulattoes and their descendants, as may be in the State at the adoption of this Constitution, and may be willing to emigrate. *Ind.*, 180.

—All the inhabitants of the State, without distinction of color, are free, and shall enjoy the rights of person and property, without distinction of color. *Fl.*, 140.

—Persons emancipated by ordinance can not be apprenticed except in pursuance of laws. *Mo.*, 302.

—Courts of competent jurisdiction may apprentice minors of African descent on like conditions provided by law for apprenticing white children. *Va.*, 537.

—Nothing in this Constitution shall prevent the General Assembly from passing such laws in relation to the apprenticeship of minors, during their minority, as may be necessary and proper. *Ill.*, 169.

TREASON.—ATTAINDER.—BANISHMENT.—CONFISCATION OF ESTATES.

—Treason against the State shall consist only in levying war against it, adhering to its enemies, or giving them aid and comfort. [*Mo.*, 348.] No person shall be convicted of treason unless on the evidence of two witnesses to the same overt act, or confession in open court. *U. S.*, 16; *Ala.*, 73; *Ark.*, 93; *Cal.*, 97; *Ct.*, 113; *Del.*, 121; *Fl.*, 140; *Ind.*, 171; *Iowa*, 184; *Kan.*, 197; *Ky.*, 219; *La.*, 239; *Me.*, 240; *Mich.*, 307; *Miss.*, 342; *Minn.*, 319; *Neb.*, 374; *Nev.*, 380; *N. J.*, 412; *Or.*, 449; *Tex.*, 515; *W. Va.*, 547; *Wis.*, 560.

—Treason shall be punished, according to the character of the acts committed, by the infliction of one or more of the penalties of death, imprisonment, fine, or confiscation of the real and personal property of the offender, as may be prescribed by law. *W. Va.*, 547.

—No person shall be attainted of treason or felony by the Legislature. *Ct.*, 108; *Ky.*, 224; *Mass.*, 232; *Mo.*, 348; *Pa.*, 465; *Vt.*, 525.

4

1 § 5. Excessive bail shall not be required nor excessive fines imposed(¹), nor
2 shall cruel and unusual punishments be inflicted (²), nor shall witnesses be
3 unreasonably detained(³).

—No conviction can work corruption of blood; that there can be no forfeiture of estate for any crime, except treason; and that the estates of such persons as may destroy their own lives shall descend or vest, as in cases of natural death. *Mo.*, 348; *Tenn.*, 491.

—That no attainder shall work corruption of blood; nor, except during the life of the offender, forfeiture of estate to the Commonwealth; that the estates of such persons as shall destroy their own lives, shall descend or vest as in case of natural death; and if any person shall be killed by casualty, there shall be no forfeiture by reason thereof. *Pa.*, 468.

—That the estates of suicides shall descend or vest as in cases of natural death; and if any person shall be killed by casualty, there shall be no forfeiture by reason thereof. *Miss.*, 335; *Tenn.*, 491.

—No person shall be attainted of treason or felony by the Legislature. *Ct.*, 108; *Mass.*, 282.

—That no person shall be liable to be transported out of this State for any offense committed within the same. *Ill.*, 166; *Kan.*, 197; *Vt.*, 522; *Ohio*, 433.

—No person shall be transported out of the State for any offense committed within the same; and no conviction shall work corruption of blood, or forfeiture of estate. *Ohio*, 433.

—That no conviction shall work corruption of blood, nor shall there be any forfeiture of the estate of any person for any crime, except treason, and then only on conviction. *Md.*, 255.

—That no conviction shall work corruption of blood or forfeiture of estate, under any law of this State. *Ala.*, 73; *Ark.*, 84; *Fl.*, 129; *Ga.*, 142; *Ill.*, 166; *Ind.*, 171; *Kan.*, 197; *Ky.*, 224; *Me.*, 270; *Mo.*, 348; *Or.*, 448; *Tenn.*, 419.

—That no law to attaint particular persons of treason or felony ought to be made in any case, or at any time hereafter. *Md.*, 254.

—The Legislature shall have power to declare the punishment of treason; but no attainder of treason shall work corruption of blood or forfeiture, except during the life of the person attainted. *La.*, 233.

(1). *Ala.*, 73; *Ark.*, 84; *Ct.*, 108; *Fl.*, 129; *Ind.*, 255; *Mass.*, 282.

(2). *Cal.*, 96; *Del.*, 217; *Ga.*, 142; *Iowa*, 184; *Kan.*, 197; *Me.*, 240; *Nev.*, 379; *Neb.*, 370.

(3). *Fl.*, 129; *Ind.*, 170; *La.*, 233; *Miss.*, 337; *Min.*, 317; *Mo.*, 347; *N. C.*, 422; *N. J.*, 412; *Wis.*, 660; *Va.*, 532; *S. C.*, 488; *N. H.*, 400; *Pa.*, 468; *R. I.*, 473; *Tenn.*, 491; *Or.*, 448; *Ohio*, 432; *Tex.*, 506; *W. Va.*, 547.

EXCESSIVE BAIL.—PUNISHMENT FOR CRIMES.

—That all prisoners shall be bailable by sufficient securities, unless in capital offenses, where the proof is evident or the presumption great. *Ala.*, 73; *Ark.*, 84; *Cal.*, 96; *Ill.*, 166; *Iowa*, 184; *Kan.*, 197; *Ky.*, 224; *Mich.*, 307; *Ohio*, 432; *Pa.*, 468.

—That all penalties shall be reasonable, and proportioned to the nature of the offense. *Ark.*, 84; *Ind.*, 170; *Ill.*, 166; *La.*, 233; *Me.*, 240; *W. Va.*, 547.

—The true design of all punishment being to reform, not to exterminate mankind. *Ill.*, 166.

—The penal code shall be founded on the principles of Reformation, and not of vindictive justice. *Ind.*, 170; *Or.*, 448.

—And all prisoners, unless in execution, or committed for capital offenses, when the proof is evident or presumption great, shall be bailable, by sufficient sureties; nor shall excessive bail be exacted for bailable offenses.

—Sanguinary laws shall not be passed. *Me.*, 240.

—That sanguinary laws ought to be avoided as far as it is consistent with the safety of the State; and no law to inflict cruel and unusual pains and penalties ought to be made in any case, or at any time hereafter. *Md.*, 254.

—All courts shall be open, and every man for an injury done him in his reputation, person, movable or immovable possessions, shall have remedy by the due course of law [*Tenn.*, 506], and justice administered according to the very right of the cause and the law of the land, without sale, denial, or unreasonable delay or expense; and every action shall be tried in the county in which it shall be commenced, unless when the judges of the court in which the cause is to be tried, shall determine that an impartial trial therefor cannot be had in that county. *Del.*, 116.

—No person shall be subject to corporal punishment under military law, except such as are employed in the army or navy, or in the militia when in actual service, in time of war, or public danger. *Me.*, 240; *Tenn.*, 491.

—All punishments ought to be proportioned to the offense. *Or.*, 448; *R. I.*, 473.

—No wise Legislature will affix the same punishment to the crimes of theft, forgery, and the like, which they do to those of murder and treason. Where the same undistinguishing severity is exerted against all offenses, the people are led to forget the real distinction in the crimes themselves, and to commit the most flagrant with as little compunction as they do the lightest offenses. For the same reason a multitude of sanguinary laws is both impolitic and unjust; the true design of all punishments being to reform, not to exterminate mankind. *N. H.*, 400.

—All prisoners shall be bailable by sufficient sureties, unless for capital offenses, when the proof is evident, but this provision shall not be so construed as to prohibit bail after indictment found, upon an examination of the evidence by a Judge of the Supreme or District Court, upon the return of a writ of *habeas corpus*, returnable in the county where the offense is committed; [or to such other counties as the same may by consent of parties be made returnable]. *Tex.*, 506.

—All prisoners shall be bailable by sufficient sureties, unless for capital offenses, when the proof is positive or the presumption great; [*Mo.*, 347; *Miss.*, 335; *Nev.*, 379; *N. C.*, 426; *Or.*, 447]; and when persons are confined on accusation for such offenses, their friends and counsel may at proper seasons have access to them. *Del.*, 117.

—All prisoners shall, before conviction, be bailable, by sufficient sureties, except for capital offenses, where the proof is evident, or the presumption great; and the privileges of the writ of *habeas corpus* shall not be suspended, unless when in case of rebellion or invasion, the public safety may require it, nor in any case but by the Legislature. *Ct.*, 108; substantially similar, *Fl.*, 129; *Me.*, 240; *R. I.* 473.

—All persons shall be bailable by sufficient sureties, unless for capital offenses, where the proof is evident or presumption great; or, unless after conviction for any offense or crime punishable with death or imprisonment at hard labor. *La.*, 233.

—No person, before conviction, shall be bailable for any of the crimes which now are or have been denominated capital offenses since the adoption of the Constitution, when the proof is evident or the presumption great, whatever the punishment of the crime may be. *Me.*,252.

—No person can in any case be subjected to law-martial, or to any penalties or pains, by virtue of that law, except those employed in the army or navy, [*Vt.*, 522; *N. H.*, 401], and except the militia in actual service, but by authority of the Legislature. *Mass.*, 282.

—In the construction of jails, a proper regard shall be had to the health of prisoners. *Del.*, 117; *Pa.*, 468.

1 § 6. No person shall be held to answer for a capital or otherwise infamous

2 crime (except in cases of impeachment, and in cases of militia when in active (¹)

3 service; and the land and naval forces in time of war, or which this State may

4 keep, with the consent of Congress, in time of peace, and in cases of petit larceny,

5 under the regulation of the Legislature), unless on presentment or indictment

6 of a grand jury; and in any trial in any court whatever, the party accused

7 shall be allowed to appear and defend in person and with counsel as in civil

8 actions.(²) No person shall be subject to be twice put in jeopardy(²) for the same

9 offense; nor shall he be compelled in any criminal case to be a witness against

10 himself,(³) nor be deprived of life, liberty or property without due process of law;

11 nor shall private property be taken for public use, without just compensation.(⁴)

—No person arrested or confined in jail shall be treated with unnecessary rigor. *Tenn.,* 491.
—No commission of oyer and terminer or jail delivery shall be issued. *Del.,* 117.
—That no person, except regular soldiers, mariners, and marines in the service of this State, or militia when in actual service, ought in any case to be subject to, or punishable by, martial law. *Md.,* 255.

IMPRISONMENT FOR DEBT.

No person shall be imprisoned for debt [*Tex.,* 506] in any civil action on mesne or final process, unless in cases of fraud [*Neb.,* 371; *Ohio,* 433; *Kan.,* 197;] and no person shall be imprisoned for a militia fine in time of peace. *Cal.,* 97; *Iowa,* 184.
—That imprisonment for debt cannot exist in this State, except for fines or penalties imposed for violation of law. *Mo.,* 348.
—No person shall be imprisoned for debt. *Md.,* 246.
—§ 11. Imprisonment for debt shall not be allowed in this State, except when an allegation of fraud on the part of the debtor shall be clearly proved. *Ark.,* 93.
—In any action, or in any judgment founded upon contract, unless in cases of fraud; nor shall any person be imprisoned for a militia fine in time of peace. *N. J.,* 412.
—Except in cases of fraud or absconding debtors. *Or.,* 448.
—That the person of a debtor, when there is not strong presumption of fraud shall not be detained in prison, after delivering up his estate for the benefit of his creditors, in such manner as shall be prescribed by law. *Miss.* 335; *Ky.,* 224.
—That the person of a debtor, where there is not strong presumption of fraud, shall not be continued in prison after delivering up his estate for the benefit of his creditor or creditors in such manner as shall be prescribed by law. *Ala.,* 73; *Tenn.,* 491.
That the person of a debtor, where there is not strong presumption of fraud, shall not be continued in prison after delivering up his estate for the benefit of his creditors in such manner as shall be prescribed by law. *Pa.,* 468; *R. I.,* 473; *Vt.,* 526.
—Shall not be continued in prison after delivering up *bona fide* all his estate, real and personal, for the use of his creditors, in such manner as shall hereafter be regulated by law.
—No person shall be imprisoned for debt arising out of or founded on a contract expressed or implied. *Mich.,* 307; *Wis.,* 560.
—Except in cases of fraud or breach of trust, or of moneys collected by public officers, or in any profes-

sional employment. No person shall be imprisoned for a militia fine in time of peace. *Mich.,* 307.
—The privilege of the debtor to enjoy the necessary comforts of life shall be recognized by wholesome laws, exempting a reasonable amount of property from seizure or sale, for the payment of any debt or liability hereafter contracted. *Wis.,* 560.
—The privilege of the debtor to enjoy the necessary comforts of life shall be recognized by wholesome laws, exempting a reasonable amount of property from seizure or sale for payment of any debts or liabilities hereafter contracted; and there shall be no imprisonment for debts except in cases of fraud, libel, or slander, and no person shall be imprisoned for a militia fine in time of peace. *Nev.,* 380.
—No person shall be imprisoned for debt in this State, but this State shall not prevent the Legislature from providing for imprisonment, or holding to bail persons charged with fraud in contracting said debt. A reasonable amount of property shall be exempt from seizure or sale, for the payment of any debt or liability; the amount of such exemption shall be determined by law. *Min.,* 320.
—The person of a debtor shall not be detained in prison, after delivery, for the benefit of his creditors of all his estate, not expressly exempted by law from levy and sale. *Ga.,* 143.
—No person shall be imprisoned for debt, unless upon refusal to deliver up his estate for the benefit of his creditors, in such manner as shall be prescribed by law, or in cases where there is strong presumption of fraud. *Ill.,* 166.
—The privilege of the debtor to enjoy the necessary comforts of life, shall be recognized by wholesome laws, exempting a reasonable amount of property from seizure or sale for the payment of any debt or liability hereafter contracted; and there shall be no imprisonment for debt, except in case of fraud. *Ind.,* 170.

(1) [Actual.] *N. Y.,* (1821) 42.
(2) In every trial on impeachment or indictment, the party accused shall be allowed counsel as in civil actions. *N. Y.,* (1821) 42.
(3) *Ind.,* 170; *Kan.,* 197. Of life or limb. *N. Y.,* (1821), 42; *Ala.,* 73; *Ark.,* 84; *Fl.* 120; *Ill.,* 166; *Me.,* 240; *Tenn.,* 491; *Miss.,* 335; *Tex.,* 506; *U. S.,* 16; *Ky.,* 223.
(4) This section was embraced in 1821, except as above noted. Also, *Cal.,* 96; *Nev.,* 360.
(5) *Ind.,* 170; *Kan.,* 197; *Md.,* 255; *Mich.,* 307; *W. Va.,* 547; *Or.,* 447; *U. S.,* 16.

SECOND TRIAL—RIGHT OF SPEEDY TRIAL.

—That no person, after having been once acquitted by a jury, can, for the same offense, be again put in jeopardy of life or liberty : but if, in any criminal prosecution, the jury be divided in opinion, the court before which the trial shall be had may, in its discretion, discharge the jury, and commit or bail the accused for trial at the next term of said court. *Mo.*, 347.

—No person, for the same offense, shall be twice put in jeopardy of life or limb; nor shall a person be again put upon trial for the same offense, after a verdict of not guilty ; and the right of trial by jury shall remain inviolate. *Tex.*, 506.

—No subject shall be liable to be tried, after an acquittal, for the same crime or offense. Nor shall the Legislature make any law that shall subject any person to a capital punishment (except for the government of the army and navy, and militia in actual service) without trial by jury. *N. H.*, 399.

—That no person shall for any indictable offense, be proceeded against criminally by information ; except in cases arising in the land or naval forces or in the militia when in actual service in time of war or public danger ; or by leave of the court for oppression and misdemeanor in office. No person shall for the same offense be twice put in jeopardy of life or limb; nor shall any man's property be taken, or applied to public use, without the consent of his representatives, and without just compensation being made. *Pa.*, 467.

—No person shall be held to answer for a criminal offense, unless on the presentment or indictment of a grand jury, except in cases of impeachment, or in cases cognizable by Justices of the Peace, or arising in the army or navy, or in the militia when in actual service in time of war or public danger ; and no person for the same*offense shall be put twice in jeopardy of punishment, nor shall be compelled in any criminal case to be a witness against himself. All persons shall, before conviction, be bailable by sufficient sureties, except for capital offenses, when the proof is evident or the presumption great ; and the privilege of the writ of *habeas corpus* shall not be suspended unless when, in case of rebellion or invasion, the public safety may require. *Wis.*, 560.

—No person shall, after acquittal, be tried for the same offense. All persons shall, before conviction, be bailable by sufficient sureties, except for capital offenses, when the proof is evident or presumption great. *N. J.*, 412.

—No person shall be put in jeopardy of life or liberty more than once for the same offense, save on his or her own motion for a new trial after conviction, or in case of a mis-trial. *Ga.*, 142.

—Prosecutions shall be by indictment or information. The accused shall have a speedy public trial, by an impartial jury of the parish in which the offense shall have been committed. He shall not be compelled to give evidence against himself; he shall have the right of being heard, by himself or counsel ; he shall have the right of meeting the witnesses face to face, and shall have compulsory process for obtaining witnesses in his favor. He shall not be twice put in jeopardy for the same offense. *La.*, 233.

—No person shall for any indictable offense be proceeded against criminally by information, except in cases arising in the land and naval forces, or in the militia when in actual service in time of war or public danger, and no person shall be for the same offense twice put in jeopardy of life or limb; nor shall any man's property be taken or applied to public use without the consent of his representatives, and without compensation being made. *Del.*, 116.

—In all criminal prosecutions the accused shall have the right to a public trial by an impartial jury, in the county in which the offense shall have been committed ; to be heard by himself and counsel; to demand the nature and cause of the accusation against him, and to have a copy thereof; to meet the witnesses face to face, and to have compulsory process

for obtaining witnesses in his favor. *Ind.*, 170 *Kan.*, 197.

—All offenses less than felony, and in which the punishment does not exceed a fine of one hundred dollars, or imprisonment for thirty days, shall be tried summarily before a Justice of the Peace, or other officer authorized by law, on information under oath, without indictment or the intervention of a grand jury, saving to the defendant the right of appeal ; and no person shall be held to answer for any higher criminal offense, unless on presentment or indictment by a grand jury, except in cases arising in the army or navy, or in the militia when in actual service, in time. of war or public danger. *Iowa*, 184.

—All persons, for injuries suffered in person, reputation, or property, shall have remedy by due course of law, and justice- administered without delay. *Kan.*, 197 ; substantially the same, *Me.*, 240.

—That every man, for any injury done to him in his person or property, ought to have remedy by the course of the law of the land, and ought to have justice and right freely without sale, fully without any denial, and speedily without delay, according to the law of the land. *Md.*, 254.

—Every subject of the Commonwealth ought to find a certain remedy, by having recourse to the laws, for all injuries or wrongs which he may receive in his person, property or character. He ought to obtain right and justice freely, and without being obliged to purchase it; completely, and without any denial ; promptly, and without delay, conformably to the laws. *Mass.*, 281.

—No person shall be debarred from prosecuting or defending any civil cause for or against him or herself before any tribunal in this State, by him or herself, or counsel or both. *Miss.*, 335.

—No subject shall be held to answer for any crime or offense until the same is fully and plainly, substantially and formally described to him; or be compelled to accuse or furnish evidence against himself. And every subject shall have a right to produce all proofs that may be favorable to himself; to meet the witnesses against him face to face, and to be fully heard in his defense by himself and counsel. And no subject shall be arrested, imprisoned, despoiled or deprived of his property, immunities or privileges, put out of the protection of the law, exiled, or deprived of his life, liberty, or estate, but by the judgment of his peers, or the law of the land. *N. H.*, 399.

—No man in a court of common law, shall be compelled to give evidence criminating himself. *R. I.*, 473.

—That no freeman shall be taken, imprisoned, or disseized of his freehold, liberties or privileges, or outlawed or exiled, or in any manner destroyed or deprived of his life, liberty or property, but by the law of the land. *Fl.*, 129.

--That no man shall be put to answer any criminal charge, but by presentment, indictment or impeachment, except as hereinafter provided. *Ark.*, 84.

—No person shall be arrested, detained or punished, except in cases clearly warranted by law. *Ct.*, 107.

—In all criminal prosecutions the accused shall have a right to be heard by himself and by counsel [or both. *Fl.*]; to demand the nature and cause of the accusation ; to be confronted by the witnesses against him; to have compulsory process to obtain witnesses in his favor; and in all prosecutions by indictment or information [or presentment. *Fl.*], a speedy public trial by an impartial jury [of the county or district where the offense was committed. *Fl.*] He shall not be compelled to give evidence against himself nor be deprived of life, liberty or property but by due course of law. And no person shall be holden to answer for any crime the punishment of which may be death or imprisonment for life, unless on a presentment or an indictment of a grand jury, except in the land or naval forces, or in the militia, when in actual service, in time of war, or public danger. *Ct.*, 107 ; (substantially similar), *U. S.*, 19 ; *Me.*, 239 ; *Ohio*, 432 ; *Ark.*, 84 ; *Del.*, 116 ; *Ill.*, 166 ; *Kan.*, 197 ; *Iowa*,

1 § 7. When private property shall be taken for any public use, the compen-

2 sation to be made therefor,(¹) when such compensation is not made by the State,

3 shall be ascertained by a jury, or by not less than three commissioners appointed

4 by a court of record, as shall be prescribed by law. Private roads may be

5 opened in the manner to be prescribed by law; but in every case the necessity of

6 the road, and the amount of all damage to be sustained by the opening thereof

7 shall be first determined by a jury of freeholders, and such amount, together

8 with the expenses of the proceeding, shall be paid by the person to be benefited.

185; *Me.*, 230; *Min.*, 319; *Mo.*, 347; *Miss.*, 335; *N. J.*, 412; *N. C.*, 422; *Or.*, 447; *Pa.*, 467; *R. I.*, 473; *Tenn.*, 491; *Tex.*, 506; *Va.*, 532.

—All courts shall be open, and every person, for an injury done him in his person, property or reputation, shall have remedy by due course of law, and right and justice administered without sale, denial or delay. *Ct.*, 108; *Fl.*, 129; *Ind.*, 170; *La.*, 234; *Miss.*, 315; *Mo.*, 347; *Neb.*, 370; *Ohio*, 433; *Or.*, 447; *Pa.*, 467; *Tenn.*, 491.

—Justice shall be administered freely and without purchase; completely, and without denial; speedily, and without delay. *Ind.*, 170.

—That in all criminal prosecutions every man hath a right to be informed of the accusation against him; to have a copy of the indictment or charge in due time (if required) to prepare for his defense; to be allowed counsel; to be confronted with the witnesses against him; to have process for his witnesses; to examine the witnesses for and against him on oath; and to a speedy trial by an impartial jury, without whose unanimous consent he ought not to be found guilty. *Md.*, 254.

—Every person charged with an offense against the State, shall have the privilege and benefit of counsel, shall be furnished on demand with a copy of the accusation, and list of the witnesses on whose testimony the charge against him is founded; shall have compulsory process to obtain the attendance of his own witnesses; shall be confronted with the witnesses testifying against him, and shall have a public and speedy trial by an impartial jury, as heretofore practiced. *Ga.*, 142.

—The powers of the courts to punish for contempt shall be limited by legislative acts. *Ga.*, 142,

—Every person within this State ought to find a certain remedy in the laws for all injuries or wrongs which he may receive in his person, property, or character; he ought to obtain right and justice freely, and without being obliged to purchase it; completely and without denial, promptly and without delay, conformably to the laws. *Ill.*, 166.

—No subject shall be held to answer for any crimes or no offense until the same is fully and plainly, substantially and formally, described to him; or be compelled to accuse, or furnish evidence against himself; and every subject shall have a right to produce all proofs that may be favorable to him; to meet the witnesses against him face to face, and to be fully heard in his defense by himself or his counsel, at his election. And no subject shall be arrested, imprisoned, despoiled or deprived of his property, immunities or privileges, put out of the protection of the law, exiled or deprived of his life, liberty or estate, but by the judgment of his peers, or the law of the land. *Mass.*, 281.

—And the Legislature shall not make any law that shall subject any person to a capital or infamous punishment, excepting for the government of the army and navy, without trial by jury. *Miss.*, 281.

—In the trial of all criminal cases the jury shall be the judges of law as well as fact. *Md.*, 277.

—That no person shall, for any indictable offense, be proceeded against criminally, by information, except in cases arising in the land or naval forces, or in the militia when in actual service, in time of war or public danger, or by leave of the court for oppression or misdemeanor in office. *Ky.*, 223.

—In the trial of all causes in equity in the District Courts, the plaintiff or defendant shall, upon application made in open court, have the right of trial by jury, to be governed by the rules and regulations prescribed in trials at law. *Tex.*, 510.

—The General Assembly shall provide for the compensation of jurors, but appropriations for that purpose shall not be made from the State treasury, except in prosecutions for felony and misdemeanor. *Va.*, 543.

—The General Assembly may modify or abolish the grand jury system. *Ind.*, 177.

DUELING.

—Any person who shall, after the adoption of this Constitution, fight a duel, or send or accept a challenge for that purpose, or be aider or abettor in fighting a duel, shall be deprived of the right of holding any office of honor or profit in this State, and shall be punished otherwise, in such manner as is or may be prescribed by law. *Ill.*, 166.

—[A stringent oath, relating to dueling, required.] *Ill.*, 166; *Miss.*, 343.

[Disqualification from holding office and other penalties.] *Cal.*, 104; *Fl.*, 136; *Ky.*, 220; *Md.*, 264; *Mo.*, 362; *Ohio*, 443; *La.*, 466; *Tenn.*, 498; *Tex.*, 515; *Va.*, 537; *W. Va.*, 548; *Wis.*, 570.

(1). *Ct.*, 107; *Fl.*, 129; *Miss.*, 335.

COMPENSATION FOR PRIVATE PROPERTY OR SERVICES FOR PUBLIC USE.

—Each individual of the society has a right to be protected by it in the enjoyment of his life, liberty and property, according to standing laws. He is obliged, consequently, to contribute his share to the expense of this protection; to give his personal service, or an equivalent, when necessary; but no part of the property of any individual can, with justice, be taken from him, or applied to public uses, without his own consent, or that of the representative body of the people. In fine, the people of this Commonwealth are not controllable by any other laws than those to which their Constitutional representative body have given their consent. And whenever the public exigencies require that the property of any individual should be appropriated to public uses, he shall receive a reasonable compensation therefor. *Mass.*, 281.

—No person's property shall be taken, or applied to public use, without adequate compensation being made, unless by the consent of such person. *Tex.*, 506.

5

18

—The assent of two-thirds of the members elected to each House of the General Assembly shall be required to every bill appropriating the public money or public property for local or private purpose. *Pa.*, 476.

—Lands may be taken for public way, for the purpose of granting to any corporation the franchise of way for public use. In all cases, however, a fair and equitable compensation shall be paid for such land and the damages arising from the taking of the same; but all corporations being common carriers, enjoying the right of way in pursuance to the provisions of this section, shall be bound to carry the mineral, agricultural and other productions or manufactures on equal and reasonable terms. *Min.*, 328.

—The Legislature shall not authorize by private or special law, the sale or conveyance of any real estate belonging to any person; nor vacate, nor alter any road laid out by commissioners of highways, or any street in any city or village, or in any recorded town plat. *Mich.*, 303.

—The General Assembly shall have no power to authorize, by private or special law, the sale of any lands or other real estate belonging in whole or in part to any individual or individuals. *Ill.*, 154.

—Private property shall not be taken for public improvements in cities and villages without the consent of the owner, unless the compensation therefor shall first be determined by a jury of freeholders, and actually paid or secured in the manner provided by law. *Mich.*, 313.

—No person's property shall be taken by any corporation under authority of law, without compensation being first made or secured in such manner as may be prescribed by law. *Or.*, 457.

—No right of way shall be appropriated to the use of any corporation, until full compensation therefor shall be first made in money, or first secured by a deposit of money, to the owner, irrespective of any benefit from any improvement proposed by such corporation; which compensation shall be ascertained by a jury of twelve men, in a Court of Record, as shall be prescribed by law. *Ohio*, 443.

—The General Assembly shall enact no law authorizing private property to be taken for public use, without just compensation, as agreed upon between the parties, or awarded by a jury, being first paid or tendered to the party entitled to such compensation. *Md.*, 264.

—That private property shall not be taken or applied for public use, unless just compensation be made therefor; nor shall private property be taken for private use, or for the use of corporations other than municipal, without the consent of the owner; *Provided*, however, that laws may be made securing to persons or corporations the right of way over the lands of other persons or corporations, and, for works of internal improvement, the right to establish depots, stations, and turn-outs; but just compensation shall, in such cases, be first made to the owner. *Ala.*, 73.

—No man's property shall be taken by law without just compensation; nor except in case of the State, without such compensation first assessed and tendered. *Ind.*, 170.

—When private property is taken for the use or benefit of the public, the necessity for using such property and the just compensation to be made therefor, except when to be made by the State, shall be ascertained by a jury of twelve freeholders, residing in the vicinity of such property, or by not less than three commissioners, appointed by a Court of Record, as shall be prescribed by law. *Mich.*, 314.

—In cases of necessity, private ways may be granted upon just compensation being first paid; and with this exception private property shall not be taken, save for public use, and then only on just compensation to be first provided and paid, unless there be a pressing, unforeseen necessity; in which event the General Assembly shall make early provision for such compensation. *Ga.*, 143.

—The property of no person shall be taken for public use without just compensation therefor. Private

roads may be opened in the manner to be prescribed by law; but in every case the necessity of the road and the amount of all damages to be sustained by the opening thereof, shall be first determined by a jury of freeholders; and such amount, together with the expenses of proceedings, shall be paid by the person or persons to be benefited. *Mich.*, 314.

—Nor shall any man's property be taken or applied to public use without the consent of his Representatives in the General Assembly, nor without just compensation being made to him. *Ill.*, 166; *Va.*, 537.

—Private property shall not be taken for public use without just compensation first being made or secured, to be paid to the owner thereof, as soon as the damages shall be assessed by a jury, who shall not take into consideration any advantages that may result to said owner on account of the improvement for which it is taken. *Iowa*, 186.

—Private property shall not be taken for public uses without just compensation: [*Mo.*, 344; *Neb.*, 371; *N. J.*, 412; *R. I.*, 453; *W. Va.*, 547; *Wis.*, 560;] nor unless the public exigencies require it. [*Me.*, 240; to be previously paid. *Min.*, 320]; except in cases of war, riot, fire or great public peril, in which cases compensation shall be afterwards made. *Nev.*, 380.

—Private property shall not be taken for public use, nor the particular services of any man be demanded, without just compensation; nor except in the case of the State, without such compensation first assessed and tendered. *Or.*, 448.

—That private property ought to be subservient to public uses, when necessity requires it; nevertheless, whenever any person's property is taken for the use of the public, the owner ought to receive an equivalent in money. *Vt.*, 521. But land may be taken for public highways, as heretofore, until the Legislature shall direct compensation to be made. *N. J.*, 412.

—Private property shall ever be held inviolate, but subservient to the public welfare. When taken in time of war or other public exigency, imperatively requiring its immediate seizure, or for the purpose of making or repairing roads, which shall be open to the public, without charge, a compensation shall be made to the owner, in money, and in all other cases where private property shall be taken for public use, a compensation therefor shall be first made in money, or first secured by a deposit of money; and such compensation shall be assessed by a jury, without deduction for the benefits to any property of the owner. *Ohio*, 433.

—No part of a man's property shall be taken from him or applied to public uses, without his own consent, or that of the Representative body of the people. Nor are the inhabitants of this State controllable by any other laws than those to which they, or their representative body have given their consent. *N. H.*, 399; *Vt.*, 522.

—Laws should have a general operation, and no general law affecting private rights shall be varied in any particular case by special legislation, except with the free consent, in writing, of all persons to be affected thereby; and no person being under a legal disability to contract, is capable of such free consent. *Ga.*, 142.

—No man's particular service shall be demanded without just compensation. *Or.*, 448; *Ind.*, 170.

—That no man's particular services shall be demanded, or property taken, or applied to public use, without the consent of his Representatives, or without just compensation being made therefor. *Tenn.*, 491.

SUITS AGAINST THE STATE.

—Suits may be brought against the State, according to such regulations as shall be made by law. *Ala.*, 73; *Cal.*, 104; *Del.*, 117.

—The General Assembly may direct, by law, in what manner, and in what courts, suits may be brought against the State. *Ark.*, 87; *Ill.*, 154; *Ind.*, 174; *Ky.*, 220; *Mis.*, 343; *Nev.*, 383; *Wis.*, 563.

1   § 8. Every citizen may freely speak, write and publish his sentiments on

2   all subjects, being responsible for the abuse of that right; and no law shall be

3   passed to restrain or abridge the liberty of speech or the press. In all criminal

4   prosecutions or indictments for libels, the truth may be given in evidence to the

5   jury; and if it shall appear to the jury that the matter charged as libelous is

6   true, and was published with good motives and for justifiable ends, the party shall

7   be acquitted; and the jury shall have the right to determine the law and the fact(¹)

—But no special act authorizing such suit to be brought, or making compensation to any person claiming damages against the State, shall ever be passed. *Ind.*, 174; *Or.*, 451.

—It shall be the duty of the Clerk of the Court of Appeals and the Commissioner of the Land Office respectively, whenever a case shall be brought into said court or office, in which the State is a party or has an interest, immediately to notify the Attorney-General thereof. *Md.*, 271.

—No State officer or member of the Legislative Assembly shall, directly or indirectly, receive a fee, or be engaged as counsel, agent, or attorney in the prosecution of any claim against this State. *Or.*, 458.

(1). *N. Y.* (1821), 42; *Cal.*, 96; (nearly similar), *Ct.*, 107; *Fl.*, 129; *Neb.*, 370; *Miss.*, 334; *Tex.*, 506; *Wis.*, 559.

FREEDOM OF SPEECH AND OF THE PRESS.

—That the free communication of thought and opinions is one of the invaluable rights of man, and that every person may freely speak, write, and print, on any subject, being responsible for the abuse of that liberty; and in all prosecutions for libel, the truth thereof may be given in evidence, and the jury may determine the law and the facts, under the direction of the court. *Mo.*, 348.

—That every citizen may freely speak, write and publish his sentiments on all subjects, being responsible for the abuse of that liberty. *Ala.*, 72; *Fl.*, 129.

—The press shall be free; every citizen may freely speak, write and publish his sentiments on all subjects, being responsible for an abuse of this liberty. *La.*, 234.

—That printing presses shall be free to every person; and no law shall ever be made to restrain the rights thereof. The free communication of thoughts and opinions is one of the invaluable rights of man; and every citizen may freely speak, write and print, on any subject, being responsible for the abuse of that liberty. *Ark.*, 84; *Pa.*, 467.

—That the liberty of the press ought to be inviolably preserved; that every citizen of the State ought to be allowed to speak, write and publish his sentiments on all subjects, being responsible for the abuse of that liberty. *Md.*, 256.

—In prosecutions for the publication of papers investigating the official conduct of officers or men in public capacity, or where the matter published is proper for public information, the truth thereof may be given in evidence, and in all indictments for libels the jury shall have the right to determine the law and the facts. *Ala.*, 73; *Ark.*, 84; *Fl.*, 166; *Ky.*, 223; *Pa.*, 467; *Tex.*, 506.

—In all indictments for libels, the jury, after having received the direction of the court, shall have a right to determine, at their discretion, the law and the fact. *Me.*, 239.

—The liberty of the press is essential to the security of freedom in a State; it ought, therefore, to be inviolably preserved. *N. H.*, 400.

—The press shall be free to every citizen who undertakes to examine the official conduct of men acting in a public capacity; and any citizen may print on any such subject, being responsible, for the abuse of that liberty. In prosecutions for publications investigating the proceedings of officers, or where the matter published is proper for public information, the truth thereof may be given in evidence; and in all indictments for libels, the jury may determine the facts and the law, as in other cases. *Ill.*, 116.

—No law abridging freedom of speech or of the press shall be passed; but the Legislature may provide for the restraint and punishment of the publishing and vending of obscene books, papers and pictures, and of libel and defamation of character, and for the recovery, in civil actions, by the aggrieved party, of suitable damages for such libel or defamation. Attempts to justify and uphold an armed invasion of the State, or an organized insurrection therein, during the continuance of such invasion or insurrection, by publicly speaking, writing, or printing, or by publishing or circulating such writing or printing, may be, by law, declared a misdemeanor, and punished accordingly. *W. Va.*, 547.

—The liberty of the press is essential to the security of freedom in a State; it ought not, therefore, to be restrained in this Commonwealth. *Mass.*, 281.

—That the freedom of the press is one of the great bulwarks of liberty, and can never be restrained but by despotic governments. *N. C.*, 422; *Va.*, 532.

—No law shall ever be passed to curtail or restrain the liberty of speech of the press. *Miss.*, 334; *Mich.*, 304.

—The liberty of the press shall be inviolate; and all persons may freely speak, write, or publish their sentiments on all subjects, being responsible for the abuse of such right; and in all civil or criminal actions for libel, the truth may be given in evidence to the jury, and if it shall appear that the alleged libellous matter was published for justifiable ends, the accused party shall be acquitted. *Kan.*, 197.

—Freedom of speech, and freedom of the press, are inherent elements of political liberty. But while every citizen may freely speak or write, or print on any subject, he shall be responsible for the abuse of the liberty. *Min.*, 319.

—That the people have a right to freedom of speech, and of writing and publishing their sentiments concerning the transactions of government, therefore the freedom of the press ought not to be restrained. *Vt.*, 522.

—The liberty of the press being essential to the security of freedom in a State, any person may publish his sentiments on any subject, being responsible for the abuse of that liberty; and in all trials for libel, both civil and criminal, the truth, unless published from malicious motives, shall be sufficient defense to the person charged. *R. I.*, 474.

—The printing presses shall be free to every person who undertakes to examine the proceedings of the General Assembly, or of any branch of government; and no law shall ever be made to restrain the right thereof. The free communication of thoughts and

1 · § 9. The assent of two-thirds of the members elected to each branch of the

2 Legislature, shall be requisite to every bill appropriating the public moneys

3 or property for local or private purposes(¹).

opinions is one of the invaluable rights of man; and every citizen may freely speak, write and print on any subject, being responsible for the abuse of that liberty. *Ill.*, 166; *Ky.*, 222; *Tenn.*, 491.

—But in prosecutions for the publication of papers investigating the official conduct of officers or men in public capacity, the truth thereof may be given in evidence; and in all indictments for libels, the jury shall have a right to determine the law and the facts, under the direction of the court, as in other criminal cases. *Tenn.*, 491.

—No law shall be passed restraining the free interchange of thought and opinion, or restricting the right to speak, write or print freely on any subject whatever; but for the abuse of that right every person shall be responsible. *Ind.*, 170; *Or.*, 447.

—In prosecutions and civil suits for libel, the truth may be given in evidence; and if it shall appear to the jury that the matter charged as libelous is true, and was published with good motives and for justifiable ends, the verdict shall be for the defendant. *W. Va.*, 547.

—In all prosecutions for libel, the truth of the matters alleged to be libelous may be given in justification. *Ind.*, 170.

—In all prosecutions for libels, the truth may be given in evidence to the jury; and if it shall appear to the jury that the matter charged as libelous is true, and was published with good motives and for justifiable ends, the party shall be acquitted. The jury shall have the right to determine the law and the fact. *Mich.*, 307.

—Every person may speak, write and publish his sentiments on all subjects, being responsible for the abuse of that right. No law shall be passed to restrain or abridge the liberty of speech, or of the press. In all prosecutions or indictments for libel, the truth may be given in evidence to the jury, and if it appear to the jury that the matter charged as libelous was true, and was published with good motives and justifiable ends, the party shall be acquitted. *Iowa*, 183; substantially the same, *Me.*, 239; *Ohio*, 413; *Nev*, 380; *N. J.*, 412.

(1). *Mich.*, 304; [or creating, continuing, altering or renewing any body politic or corporate]. *N. Y.*, (1821), 42.

LAWS FOR APPROPRIATION OF MONEY.

—The assent of two-thirds of the members elected to each branch of the Legislature shall be requisite to every bill appropriating the public moneys or property for local or private purposes, or creating, continuing, altering or renewing any body politic or corporate. *N. Y.*, (1821), 42.

—No money shall be drawn from the treasury of the State except in accordance with an appropriation by law, and every such law shall distinctly specify the sum appropriated, and the object to which it shall be applied; *Provided*, That nothing herein contained shall prevent the General Assembly from placing a contingent fund at the disposal of the Executive, who shall report to the General Assembly at each session the amount expended and the purposes to which it was applied; an accurate statement of the receipts and expenditures of the public money shall be attached to and published with the laws after each regular session of the General Assembly. *Md.*, 263.

—No moneys shall be issued out of the Treasury of this Commonwealth and disposed of (except such sums as may be appropriated for the redemption of bills of credit or Treasurer's notes, or for the payment of interest arising thereon) but by warrant under the hand of the Governor for the time being, with the advice and consent of the council for the necessary defense and support of the Commonwealth, and for the protection and preservation of the inhabitants thereof, agreeably to the acts and resolves of the General Court. *Mass.*, 288.

—No money shall be drawn from the Treasury except in pursuance of a specific appropriation made by law; and no appropriation shall be made for a longer period than two years. *Neb.*, 373; *Ohio*, 434.

—No money shall be drawn from the treasury but in consequence of an appropriation made by law, nor shall any appropriation. of money for the support of an army be made for a longer time than one year. *Miss.*, 342.

—No money shall be drawn from the treasury except in pursuance of a specific appropriation made by law, and no appropriation shall be for a longer term than one year. *Kan.*, 200.

—No vote, resolution, law or order shall pass granting a donation or gratuity in favor of any person, except by the concurrence of two-thirds of the General Assembly. *Ga.*, 146.

—No money shall be drawn from the treasury but in consequence of appropriations made by law; and a regular statement and account of the receipts and expenditures of all public money shall be published at least once in every two years. *Del.*, 119.

—No money shall be appropriated except by bill. *Miss.* 322.

—No moneys shall be issued out of the treasury of this State, and disposed of (except such sums as may be appropriated for the redemption of bills of credit or treasurer's notes, or for the payment of interest arising thereon) but by warrant under the hand of the Governor for the time being, by and with the advice and consent of Council, for the necessary support and defense of this State, and for the necessary protection and preservation of the inhabitants thereof, agreeably to the acts and resolves of the General Court. *N. H.*, 406.

—No money shall be drawn from the treasury, but in pursuance of specific appropriations made by law; nor shall any appropriation of money be made for a longer term than two years, except for purposes of education; and no appropriation for private or individual purposes, or for purposes of internal improvement, shall be made, without the concurrence of two-thirds of both houses of the Legislature. A regular statement and account of the receipts and expenditures of all public money shall be published annually in such manner as shall be prescribed by law. And in no case shall the Legislature have the power to issue "treasury warrants." "treasury notes," or paper of any description, intended to circulate as money. *Tex.*, 515.

—Laws making appropriations for the salaries of public officers, and other current expenses of the State, shall contain provisions upon no other subject. *Or.*, 456.

—In all cases where sums of money are mentioned in this Constitution, the value thereof shall be computed in silver, at six shillings and eight pence per ounce; and it shall be in the power of the Legislature, from time to time, to increase such qualifications, as to property, of the persons to be elected to offices, as the circumstances of the Commonwealth shall require. *Mass.*, 293.

—In all cases where sums of money are mentioned in this Constitution, the value thereof shall be computed in silver at six shillings and eight pence per ounce. *N. H.*, 410.

[Two-thirds vote requisite for a tax]. *Vt.*, 523.

—No money shall be drawn from the treasury but in pursuance of [specific, *La.*,] appropriations made by law, nor shall any appropriations of money for the support of an army be made for a longer time than two years, and a regular statement and account of the receipts and expenditures of all public money shall be published annually. [*Ky.*, 220; *La.*, 233; *Tenn.*, 494; *W. Va.*, 556], in such manner as shall be prescribed by law. *La.*, 233; *S. C.*, 484.

—No money shall be drawn from the treasury, but in consequence of appropriations made by law, [*Ala.*, 78; *Ark.*, 93; *Cal.*, 99; *Fl.*, 137; *Ga.*, 146; *Ind.*, 179; *Iowa*, 186; *Mich.*, 312; *Miss.*, 342; *Mo.*, 362; *Neb.*, 376; *Nev.*, 382; *N. J.*, 414; *Ohio*, 440; *Or.*, 456; *Pa.*, 462; *Vt.*, 525; *Wis.*, 567], and a regular statement and account of the receipts and expenditures of all public money shall be published from time to time. *U. S.*, 13; (similar provision), *Va.*, 539.

—No subsidy, charge, tax, impost or duties, ought to be established, fixed, laid or levied, under any pretext whatsoever, without the consent of the people, or their Representatives in the Legislature. *Mass.*, 282; *N. H.*, 400; *Md.*, 251; *Or.*, 448.

—That the people of this State ought not to be taxed or made subject to the payment of any impost or duty, without the consent of themselves, or their Representatives in General Assembly freely given. *N. C.*, 422.

—An accurate statement of the receipts and expenditures of the public moneys shall be attached to and published with the laws, at every regular session of the Legislature. *Mich.*, 314; (nearly similar), *Ala.*, 78; *Ark.*, 93; *Cal.*, 99; *Ct.*, 111; *Fl.*, 137; *Ga.*, 146; *Ind.*, 179; *Iowa*, 186; *Kan.*, 201; *Me.*, 246; *Mo.*, 362; *Nev.*, 382; *Ohio*, 443; *Or.*, 456.

—And previous to any law being made to raise a tax, the purpose for which it is to be raised ought to appear evident to the Legislature to be of more service to the community than the money would be if not collected. *Vt.*, 522.

EXTRA COMPENSATION FOR SERVICES AND CONTRACTS.

—No extra compensation shall be made to any officer, public agent, or contractor, after the service shall have been rendered, or the contract entered into; nor shall any money be paid on any claim, the subject-matter of which shall not have been provided for by pre-existing laws, and no public money or property shall be appropriated for local or private purposes, unless such appropriation, compensation, or claim be allowed by two-thirds of the members elected to each branch of the General Assembly. *Iowa*, 187.

—No extra compensation shall be granted or allowed by the General Assembly to any public officer, agent, servant, or contractor, after the services shall have been rendered or the contract entered into; nor shall the salary or compensation of any public officer be increased or diminished during his term of office. *Md.*, 263.

—The Legislature shall not grant nor authorize extra compensation to any public officer, agent, or contractor, after the service has been rendered or the contract entered into. *Mich.*, 303; *Ill.*, 154.

—The Legislature shall never grant any extra compensation to any public officer, agent, servant, or contractor, after the services shall have been rendered or the contract entered into. Nor shall the compensation of any public officer be increased or diminished during his term of office. *Neb.*, 371; *Wis.*, 503.

—No extra compensation shall be made to any officer, public agent, or contractor, after the service shall have been rendered, or the contract entered into; nor shall any money be paid, on any claim, the subject-matter of which shall not have been provided for by the pre-existing law, unless such compensation, or claim, be allowed by two-thirds of the members elected to each branch of the General Assembly. *Ohio*, 435.

—The Legislature shall provide by law for the compensation of all officers, servants, agents, and public contractors, not provided for by this Constitution, and shall not grant extra compensation to any officer, agent, servant, or public contractor, after such public service shall have been performed, or contract entered into for the performance of the same; nor grant, by appropriation, or otherwise, any amount of money out of the treasury of the State, to any individual on a claim, real or pretended, where the same shall not have been provided for by pre-existing law; *Provided*, That nothing in this section shall be so construed as to affect the claims of persons against the Republic of Texas, heretofore existing. *Tex.*, 515.

—No money shall be drawn from the State treasury as salary or compensation for any officer or employee of the Legislature, or either branch thereof, except in such cases where such salary or compensation has been fixed by a law in force prior to the election or appointment of such officer or employee of the Legislature, or either branch thereof, at such session of the Legislature. *Nev.*, 383.

—No extra compensation shall be granted or allowed to any public officer, agent, or contractor, after the services shall have been rendered, or the contract entered into. Nor shall the salary or compensation of any public officer be increased or diminished during his term of office. *W. Va.*, 548.

—No money shall be drawn from the treasury but in consequence of appropriations made by law; and an accurate statement of the receipts and expenditures of the public money shall be attached to, an l published with the laws at the rising of each session of the General Assembly. And no person who has been or may be a collector of public moneys shall be eligible to a seat in either House of the General Assembly, nor be eligible to any office of profit or trust in this state, until such person shall have accounted for and paid into the treasury all sums for which he may be accountable. *Ill.*, 153.

—The officers mentioned in this article shall, at stated times, receive for their services a compensation to be established by law, which shall neither be increased nor diminished during the period for which they shall have been elected. *Ohio*, 436.

—As every freeman, to preserve his independence (if without a sufficient estate), ought to have some profession, calling, trade or farm whereby he may honestly subsist, there can be no necessity for nor use in establishing offices of profit, the usual effects of which are dependence and servility, unbecoming freemen, in the possessors or expectants, and faction, contention and discord among the people. But if any man is called into public service to the prejudice of his private affairs, he has a right to a reasonable compensation; and whenever an office, through increase of fees, or otherwise, becomes so profitable as to occasion many to apply for it, the profits ought to be lessened by the Legislature. And if any officer shall wittingly and wilfully take greater fees than the law allows him, it shall ever after disqualify him from holding any office in this State, until he shall be restored by act of legislation. *Vt.*, 525.

DEDUCTION FROM SALARIES.

—All salaries and fees annexed to offices shall be moderate; and no officer shall receive any fees whatever without giving to the person who pays a receipt for them, if required, therein specifying every particular and the charge for it. *Del.*, 125.

—It shall be the duty of the General Assembly to regulate by law in what cases and what deductions from the salaries of public officers shall be made, for any neglect of duty in their official capacity. *Fl.*, 136; *Ky.*, 220.

6

1 § 10. No law shall be passed abridging the right of the people peaceably

2 to assemble and petition the government, or any department thereof, nor shall

3 any divorce be granted, otherwise than by due judicial proceedings; nor shall

4 any lottery hereafter be authorized or any sale of lottery tickets allowed

5 within this State.

—The Legislature shall reduce the salaries of officers who shall neglect the performance of any legal duty. *Kan.*, 206.

—The officers mentioned in this article shall, at stated times, receive for their services a compensation to be established by law, which shall neither be increased nor diminished during the period for which they shall have been elected. *Kan.*, 198.

—It shall be the duty of the Legislature to regulate, by law, the cases in which deductions shall be made from salaries of public officers for neglect of duty in their official capacity, and the amount of such deduction. *Ala.*, 71; *Miss.*, 343.

—The Legislature may, at any time, provide by law for increasing or diminishing the salaries or compensation of any of the officers whose salary or compensation is fixed in this Constitution; *Provided*, No such change of salary or compensation shall apply to any officer during the term for which he may have been elected. *Nev.*, 392.

—The Legislature shall have power to provide for deduction from the salaries of public officers who may neglect the performance of any duty that may be assigned them by law. *Tex.*, 515.

RIGHT OF PETITION — RIGHT OF ASSEMBLING.

—That every man hath a right to petition the Legislature for the redress of grievances, in a peaceable and orderly manner. *Md.*, 254.

—That the people shall have a right [at all times— *Me.*], in a peaceable manner, to assemble together to consult for the common good; and to apply to those invested with the powers of government for redress of grievances, or other proper purposes, by petition, address or remonstrance. *Ala.*, 74; *Fl.*, 130; *Me.*, 240.

—The citizens have a right, in a peaceable manner, to assemble together for their common good, to instruct their representatives, and to apply to those invested with the power of the government for redress of grievances, or other proper purposes, by [petition] address or remonstrance. *Ark.*, 85; *Ct.*, 108.

The people have a right, in an orderly and peaceable manner, to assemble to consult upon the common good; give instructions to their representatives, and to request, of the legislative body, by the way of addresses, petitions or remonstrances, redress of the wrongs done them, and of the grievances they suffer. *Mass.*, 282.

—The people shall have the right freely to assemble together to consult for the common good, to instruct their representatives, and to petition the Legislature for redress of grievances. *Cal.*, 961; *Ill.*, 166; *Iowa*, 184; *Kan.*, 197; *Mich.*, 314; *Neb.*, 370; *N. J.*, 413; *N. C.*, 422; *Nev.*, 380; *Or.*, 448; or other purpose by petition, address or remonstrance. *Miss.*, 335; *Pa.*, 463; *N. H.*, 400; *R. I.*, 474; *Tenn.*, 491; *Tex.*, 506; *Vt.*, 522.

—No law shall restrain any of the inhabitants of the State from assembling together in a peaceable manner to consult for their common good, nor from instructing their representatives, nor from applying to the General Assembly for redress of grievances. *Ind.*, 171.

—The people have a right to assemble together in a peaceable manner, to consult for their common good, to instruct their representatives, and to petition the General Assembly for the redress of grievances. *Ohio*, 432.

—Although disobedience to laws by a part of the people upon suggestions of impolicy or injustice in them, tends by immediate effect and the influence of example, not only to endanger the public welfare and safety, but also in governments of a republican form, contravenes the social principles of such governments founded on common consent for common good; yet the citizens have a right in an orderly manner to meet together, and to apply to persons intrusted with the powers of government, for redress of grievances or other proper purposes, by petition, remonstrance or address. *Del.*, 117.

—The right of the people to appeal to the courts, to petition government on all matters of legitimate cognizance and peaceably to assemble for the consideration of any matter of public concern shall never be impaired. *Ga.*, 142.

DIVORCES.

—Divorces from the bonds of matrimony shall not be granted, but in the cases by law provided for, and by suit in chancery, but decrees in chancery for divorce shall be final, unless appealed from, in the manner prescribed by law, within three months from the date of the enrollment thereof. *Ala.*, 77.

—The General Assembly shall not have power to pass any bill of divorce, but may prescribe by law the manner in which such cases may be investigated in the courts of justice, and divorces granted. *Ark.*, 87.

—No divorce shall be granted by the Legislature. *Cal.*, 99; *Iowa*, 186; *Mich.*, 303; *Min.*, 323; *N. J.*, 415; *Tex.*, 516.

—Divorces from the bonds of matrimony shall not be allowed but by the judgment of a court, as shall be prescribed by law. *Fl.*, 140.

—The Superior Court shall have exclusive jurisdiction in all cases of divorce, both total and partial; but no total divorce shall be granted except on the concurrent verdicts of two special juries. In each divorce case, the court shall regulate the rights and disabilities of the parties. *Ga.*, 148.

—The General Assembly shall have no power to grant divorces, but may authorize the courts of justice to grant them for such causes as may be specified by law; *Provided*, That such laws shall be general and uniform in their operation. *Ill.*, 154.

—All power to grant divorces is vested in the District Courts, subject to regulation by law. *Kan.*, 200.

—The General Assembly have no power to grant divorces, to change the names of individuals, or direct the sales of estates belonging to infants, or other persons laboring under legal disabilities, by special legislation; but by general laws shall confer such powers on the courts of justice. *Ky.*, 212.

—The Legislature may enact general laws regulating the adoption of children, emancipation of minors, changing of names, and the granting of divorces; but no special laws shall be enacted relating to particular or individual cases. *La.*, 234.

—All causes of marriage, divorce and alimony, and all appeals from the Judges of Probate, shall be heard and determined by the Governor and Council until the Legislature shall, by law, make other provision. *Mass.*, 200.

1   § 11. The people of this State, in their right of sovereignty, are deemed to
2 possess the original and ultimate property in and to all lands within the juris-
3 diction of the State; and all lands the title to which shall fail, from a defect
4 of heirs, shall revert or escheat to the people.

1   § 12. All feudal tenures of every description, with all their incidents, are
2 declared to be abolished, saving, however, all rents and services certain which
3 at any time heretofore have been lawfully created or reserved.

1   § 13. All lands within this State are declared to be allodial, so that, subject
2 only to the liability to escheat, the entire and absolute property is vested in
3 the owners, according to the nature of their respective estates.

1   § 14. No lease or grant of agricultural land, for a longer period than twelve
2 years, hereafter made, in which shall be reserved any rent or service of any
3 kind, shall be valid.

—Divorces from the bonds of matrimony shall not be granted, but in cases provided for by law, by suit in chancery. *Miss.*, 343.
—The Legislature shall never authorize any lottery, or grant any divorce. *Neb.*, 373; *Wis.*, 563.
--All causes of marriage, divorce and alimony, and all appeals from the respective Judges of Probate, shall be heard and tried by the Superior Court, until the Legislature shall by law make other provision. *N. II.*, 408.
—The General Assembly shall have power to pass general laws regulating divorce and alimony, but shall not have power to grant a divorce or secure alimony in any individual case. *N. C.*, 428.
—The General Assembly shall grant no divorce, nor exercise any judicial power, not herein expressly conferred. *Ohio*, 435.
—The Legislature shall not have power to enact laws annulling the contract of marriage in any case where by law, the courts of this Commonwealth are, or hereafter may be, empowered to decree a divorce. *Pa.*, 462.
—The Legislature shall have no power to grant divorces, but may authorize the courts of justice to grant them for such causes as may be specified by law; *Provided*, That such laws be general and uniform throughout the State. *Tenn.*, 499.
—The General Assembly shall confer on the courts the power to grant divorces, change the names of persons, and direct the sale of estates belonging to infants and other persons under legal disabilities, but shall not, by special legislation, grant relief in such cases, or in any other case of which the courts or other tribunals may have jurisdiction. *Va.*, 539.

LOTTERIES.

[Lotteries forbidden in Constitution of 1821, and sale of tickets forbidden except of lotteries provided by laws then existing]. *p.* 43; *R. I.*, 476; (forbidden) *Ill.*, 154; *Va.*, 538; *W. Va.*, 557; *Ark.*, 73; *Cal.*, 99; *Ind.*, 181; *Iowa*, 186; *Kan.*, 206; *Md.*, 263; *Mich.*, 303; *Min.*, 323; *Mo.*, 354; *Nev.*, 343; *N. J.*, 415; *Ohio*, 443; *Tenn.*, 499; *Tex.*, 576.

—Lotteries and the sale of lottery tickets for any purpose whatever are prohibited, and the Legislative Assembly shall prevent the same by penal laws. *Or.*, 458.
—The Legislature shall have the power to license the selling of lottery tickets and the keeping of gambling houses; said houses in all cases shall be on the first floor, and kept with open doors; but in all cases not less than ten thousand dollars per annum shall be levied as a license or tax on each vendor of lottery tickets, and on each gambling house, and five hundred dollars on each tombola. *La.*, 234.

PUBLIC LANDS—TENURE OF LANDS— LEASES—EMINENT DOMAIN.

[Limitation of leases of agricultural lands in Michigan to twelve years]. *p.* 314.
[The Constitution of 1821 pledged the public lands as a perpetual fund, the interest of which was to be inviolably devoted to schools]. *p.* 42.
—All the lands within this State are declared to be allodial, and feudal tenures of every description, with all their incidents, are prohibited. Leases and grants of agricultural land for a longer period than twenty-one years, hereafter made, in which shall be reserved any rent or service of any kind, shall be void. *Min.* 320.
—All lands within the State are declared to be allodial, and feudal tenures are prohibited. Leases and grants of agricultural land, for a longer term than fifteen years in which rent or service of any kind shall be reserved, and all fines and like restraints upon alienation, reserved in any grant of land, hereafter made, are declared to be void. *Wis.*, 560.
—That no purchase of lands shall be made of the Indian natives, but on behalf of the public, by authority of the General Assembly. *N. C.*, 426.
—The people of the State in their right of sovereignty, are declared to possess the ultimate property in and to all lands within the jurisdiction of the State; and all lands the title to which shall fail from defect of heirs, shall revert or escheat to the people. *Neb.*, 376; *Wis.*, 568.

1 § 15. All fines, quarter sales, or other like restraints upon alienation, reserved

2 in any grant of land hereafter to be made, shall be void.

—No entry by warrant on land in this State shall be hereafter made; and in all cases where an entry has been heretofore made and has been or shall be so perfected as to entitle the locator to a grant, the Legislature shall make provision by law for issuing the same. *W. Va.*, 556.

—The State shall have concurrent jurisdiction on all rivers and lakes bordering on this State, so far as such rivers or lakes shall form a common boundary to the State and any other State or Territory, now or hereafter to be formed and bounded by the same. And the river and the navigable waters leading into the same, shall be common highways, and forever free as well to the inhabitants of the State as to the citizens of the United States, without any tax, impost or duty therefor. *Wis.*, 568; (nearly similar), *Neb.*, 376.

—No navigable stream in this State shall be either bridged or dammed without authority from the Board of Supervisors of the proper county, under the provisions of law. No such law shall prejudice the right of individuals to the free navigation of such streams, or preclude the State from the further improvement of the navigation of such stream. *Miss.*, 314.

[Pre-emption and other rights secured to certain classes]. *Tenn.*, 492, 500.

—In the event of the annexation of any foreign territory to this State, the General Assembly shall enact laws, extending to the inhabitants of the acquired territory all the rights and privileges which may be required by the terms of the acquisition; anything in this Constitution to the contrary notwithstanding. *Ala.*, 78; *Ark.*, 93.

—That the General Assembly may at any time cede to the United States government a sufficient parcel or fraction of land for the purpose of coast defense and other national purposes. *Fl.*, 133.

—It shall be the duty of the General Assembly to provide for the prevention of waste and damage to the public lands, that may be hereafter ceded to the State, and it may pass laws for the sale of any part or portion thereof; and, in such cases, provide for the safety, security, and appropriation of the proceeds, but in no wise to affect the purposes for which said lands have been heretofore appropriated. *Fl.*, 138.

—The following grounds, owned by the State, in Indianapolis, namely: the State House Square, the Governor's Circle, and so much of out lot numbered one hundred and forty-seven as lies north of the arm of the central canal, shall not be sold or leased. *Ind.*, 181.

—It shall be the duty of the General Assembly to provide for the permanent inclosure and preservation of the Tippecanoe battle-ground. *Ind.*, 181.

—Persons residing on Indian lands within the State, shall enjoy all the rights and privileges of citizens, as though they lived in any other portion of the State, and shall be subject to taxation. *Min.*, 329.

—The title to all lands and other property, which have accrued to the Territory of Nebraska, by grant, gift, purchase, forfeiture, escheat, or otherwise, shall vest in the State of Nebraska. *Neb.*, 376.

—There shall be one general land office in the State, which shall be at the seat of government, where all titles which have heretofore emanated, or may hereafter emanate from government, shall be registered; and the Legislature may establish, from time to time, such subordinate officers as they may deem requisite. *Tex.*, 520.

—That the State of Texas hereby releases to the owner of the soil all mines and mineral substances that may be on the same, subject to such uniform rate of taxation as the Legislature may impose. All islands along the gulf coast of the State, not now patented or appropriated by locations under valid land certificates, are reserved from location or appro-

priated (appropriations) in any other manner by private individuals than as the Legislature may direct. *Tex.*, 518.

—All certificates for head-right claims to land, issued to fictitious persons, or which were forged, and all locations and surveys thereon, are, and the same were null and void from the beginning.

—There shall be a Commissioner of the Land Office, elected by the qualified voters of the State, on the Tuesday after the first Monday in the month of November, in the year eighteen hundred and seventy, and on the same day in every sixth year thereafter, who shall hold his office for the term of six years from the first Monday in January ensuing his election. The returns of said election shall be made to the Governor, and in the event of a tie between two or more candidates, the Governor shall direct a new election to be held, by writs to the Sheriffs of the several counties, and of the city of Baltimore, who shall hold said election after at least twenty days' notice, exclusive of the day of election. He shall perform such duties as are now required of the Commissioner of the Land Office, or such as may hereafter be prescribed by law, and shall also be the keeper of the chancery records. He shall receive a salary of two thousand dollars per annum, to be paid out of the treasury, and shall charge such fees as are now or may be hereafter fixed by law. He shall make a semi-annual report of all the fees of his office, both as Commissioner of the Land Office and as Keeper of the Chancery Records, to the Comptroller of the Treasury, and shall pay the same semi-annually into the treasury. In case of vacancy in such office by death, resignation or other cause, the Governor shall fill such vacancy until the next general election for members of the General Assembly thereafter, when a Commissioner of the Land Office shall be elected for the full term of six years ensuing. *Md.*, 273.

—No lease or grant of agricultural lands, reserving any rent, or service of any kind, shall be valid for a longer period than twenty years. *Iowa*, 184.

—None of the lands granted by Congress to the State of Louisiana for aiding in constructing the necessary levees and drains, to reclaim the swamp and overflowed lands of the State, shall be diverted from the purposes for which they were granted. *La.*, 235.

—All lands in this State heretofore vested in the State by forfeiture, or by purchase at the sheriff's sales for delinquent taxes, and not released or exonerated by the laws thereof, or by the operation of the preceding section, may be redeemed by the former owners by payment to this State of the amount of taxes and damages due thereon at the time of such redemption, within five years from the day this Constitution goes into operation; and all such lands not so released, exonerated or redeemed, shall be treated as forfeited, and proceeded against and sold as provided. *W. Va.*, 557.

—The former owner of any tract of land in this State sold under the provisions of this article shall be entitled to receive the excess of the sum for which such tract may be sold over the taxes and damages charged and chargeable thereon, and the costs, if his claim be filed in the Circuit Court which decreed the sale, within two years thereafter. *W. Va.*, 557.

—The Legislature shall have power to extend this Constitution and the jurisdiction of this State over any territory acquired by compact with any State, or with the United States, the same being done by consent of the United States. *La.*, 235.

PERPETUITIES—MONOPOLIES.

—That perpetuities and monopolies are contrary to the genius of a republic, and shall not be allowed; [*N. C.*, 422; *Tenn.*, 491], nor shall any hereditary

1 § 16. No purchase or contract for the sale of lands in this State, made since
2 the fourteenth day of October, one thousand seven hundred and seventy-five,
3 or which may hereafter be made, of, or with the Indians, shall be valid, unless
4 made under the authority and with the consent of the Legislature.

1 § 17. Such parts of the common law, and of the acts of the Legislature of
2 the colony of New York, as together did form the law of the said colony, on
3 the nineteenth day of April, one thousand seven hundred and seventy-five,
4 and the resolutions of the Congress of the said colony, and of the Convention
5 of the State of New York, in force on the twentieth day of April, one thou-
6 sand seven hundred and seventy-seven,(') which have not since expired, or been
7 repealed or altered, and such acts of the Legislature of this State as are now
8 in force, shall be and continue the law of this State, subject to such alterations
9 as the Legislature shall make concerning the same. But all such parts of the
10 common law, and such of the said acts or parts thereof as are repugnant to
11 this Constitution are hereby abrogated,(²) and the Legislature, at its first session

emoluments, privileges or honors, ever be granted or conferred in this State. *Ark.*, 84; *Fl.*, 130.
—Nor shall the law of primogeniture or entailments ever be in force in this State. *Tex.*, 506.
—That monopolies are odious, contrary to the spirit of a free government and the principles of commerce, and ought not to be suffered. *Md.*, 256.
—That no hereditary emoluments, privileges or honors, shall ever be granted or conferred in this State. *Miss.*, 335; *Ohio*, 433; *Tenn.*, 492.
—That no title of nobility, or hereditary emolument, privilege, or distinction, can be granted. *Mo.*, 348.
—No law shall be passed granting to any citizen, or class of citizens, privileges or immunities which, upon the same terms, shall not equally belong to all citizens. *Or.*, 448.
—The rights of primogeniture shall not be re-established, and there shall not fail to be some legislative provision for the equitable distribution of the estates of intestates. *S. C.*, 488.
—No perpetuities shall be allowed, except for eleemosynary purpose. *Cal.*, 104; *Ner.*, 392.
—That the future Legislature of this State shall regulate entails, in such a manner as to prevent perpetuities, *N. C.*, 426; *Vt.*, 526.

RIGHTS OF ALIENS.

(1). *N. Y.*, (1821) 43.
—No distinction shall ever be made between citizens and aliens in reference to the purchase, enjoyment, or descent of property. *Kan.*, 197; *Neb.*, 371; *Wis.*, 560.
—Foreigners who are, or who may hereafter become *bona fide* residents of this State, shall enjoy the same rights in respect to the possession, enjoyment, and inheritance of property, as native born citizens. *Cal.*, 37; *Iowa*, 184; *Nev.*, 380; *Mich.*, 314.
—White foreigners, who are or may hereafter become residents of this State, shall enjoy the same rights in respect to the possession, enjoyment and descent of property as native-born citizens. And the Legislative Assembly shall have power to restrain and regulate the immigration to this State of persons not qualified to become citizens of the United States. *Or.*, 448.

7

CONTINUANCE OF LAWS AND GRANTS.

(1). On this day the first Constitution went into operation.
(2). Thus far in the Constitution of 1821, *p.* 43; substantially embraced in Constitution of 1777, 31.
—All laws which, on the first day of June, one thousand seven hundred and ninety-two, were in force in the State of *Virginia*, and which are of a general nature, and not local to that State, and not repugnant to this Constitution, nor to the laws which have been enacted by the General Assembly of this Commonwealth, shall be in force within this State, until they shall be altered or repealed by the General Assembly.
—All laws and parts of laws in force in the Territory at the time of the acceptance of this Constitution by Congress, not inconsistent with this Constitution, shall continue and remain in full force until they expire or shall be repealed. *Kan.*, 201; *Wis.*, 571.
—All laws now in force in this State, and not repugnant to this Constitution, shall remain and be in force, until altered or repealed by the Legislature or shall expire by their own limitation. *Me.*, 249; *Tenn.*, 419.
—All statute laws of this State now in force, not inconsistent with this Constitution, shall continue in force until they shall expire by their own limitation, or be amended or repealed by the General Assembly; and all writs, prosecutions, actions, and causes of action, except as herein or otherwise provided, shall continue; and all indictments which shall have been found, or may hereafter be found, for any crime or offense committed before this Consti ution takes effect, may be proceeded upon as if no change had taken place, except as hereinafter specified. *Mo.*, 362.
—All laws in force in the Territory of Oregon when the Constitution takes effect, and consistent therewith shall continue in force until altered or repealed. *Or.*, 460.
—All the laws of this State existing at the time of making this Con-titution, and not inconsistent with it, shall remain in force, unless they shall be altered by future laws; and all actions and prosecutions now pending shall proceed as if this Constitution had not been made. *Del.*, 125.

12 after the adoption of this Constitution, shall appoint three Commissioners,

13 whose duty it shall be to reduce into a written and systematic code the whole

14 body of the law of this State, or so much and such parts thereof as to the said

15 Commissioners shall seem practicable and expedient. And the said Commis-

16 sioners shall specify such alterations and amendments therein as they shall deem

17 proper, and they shall at all times make reports of their proceedings to the

18 Legislature, when called upon to do so; and the Legislature shall pass laws

19 regulating the tenure of office, the filling of vacancies therein, and the com-

20 pensation of the said Commissioners, and shall also provide for the publication

21 of the said code, prior to its being presented to the Legislature for adoption.

—All fines, penalties, forfeitures, obligations and escheats, heretofore accruing to the State of ——, and not made unlawful by the Constitution or laws of the United States, shall continue to accrue to the use of the State. *Fl.,* 140.

—The General Assembly may grant aid to said districts out of the funds arising from the swamp and overflowed lands, granted to the State by the United States for that purpose or otherwise. *La.,* 236.

—No person shall be prosecuted in any civil action or criminal proceeding, for or on account of any act by him done, performed, or executed, after the first day of January, one thousand eight hundred and sixty-one, by virtue of military authority vested in him by the government of the United States, or that of this State, to do such act, or in pursuance of orders received by him from any person vested with such authority ; and if any action or proceeding shall have heretofore been, or shall hereafter be, instituted against any person for the doing of any such act, the defendant may plead this section in bar thereof. *Me.,* 360.

—All the laws, which have heretofore been adopted, used and approved, in the Province, Colony or State of ——, and usually practiced on in the courts of law, shall still remain and be in full force, until altered or repealed by the Legislature ; such parts only excepted as are repugnant to the rights and liberties contained in this Constitution. *Mass.,* 293.

—All laws which have heretofore been adopted, used and approved in the province, colony or State, and usually practiced on in the courts of law, shall remain and be in full force until altered and repealed by the Legislature, such parts thereof only excepted, as are repugnant to the rights and liberties contained in this Constitution ; *Provided,* That nothing herein contained, when compared with the twenty-third article in the bill of rights, shall be construed to affect the laws already made respecting the persons or estates of absentees. *N. H.,* 410.

—All laws of this State, in force on the first day of September, one thousand eight hundred and fifty-one, and not inconsistent with this Constitution, shall continue in force until amended or repealed. *Ohio,* 444.

—Nothing contained in this Constitution shall impair the validity of any debts or contracts, or affect any rights of property, or any suits, actions, rights of action, or other proceedings in courts of justice. *Tenn.,* 499.

—The common laws and statute laws now in force not repugnant to this Constitution, shall remain in force until they expire of their own limitation, or be altered or repealed by the Legislature ; and all writs, actions, causes of action, prosecution, contracts, claims, and rights of individuals and of bodies corporate, and of the State, and all charters of incorpora-

tion, shall continue, and all indictments which shall have been found, or which may hereafter be found, for any crime or offense committed before the adoption of this Constitution, may be proceeded upon as if no change had taken place. The several courts of law and equity, except as herein otherwise provided, shall continue with the like powers and jurisdiction as if this Constitution had not been adopted. *N. J.,* 420.

—Such parts of the common law as are now in force in the Territory of Wisconsin, not inconsistent with this Constitution, shall be and continue part of the law of this State until altered or suspended by the Legislature. *Wis.,* 575.

—The compact with the State of Virginia, subject to such alterations as may be made therein agreeably to the mode prescribed by the said compact, shall be considered as part of this Constitution. *Ky.,* 220. [Corresponding provisions in many States, with reference to territorial grants, rights and privileges.]

—All laws of force in this State at the adoption of this Constitution, and not repugnant hereto, shall so continue until altered or repealed, except where they are temporary, in which case they shall expire at the times respectively limited for their duration, if not continued by act of the General Assembly. *S. C.,* 487.

—The laws, public records and the judicial and legislative written proceedings of the State shall be promulgated, preserved, and conducted in the language in which the Constitution of the United States is written. *La.,* 233.

REVISION OF THE LAWS.

—At its first session, after the adoption of this Constitution, the General Assembly shall appoint not more than three persons, learned in the law, whose duty it shall be to revise and arrange the statute laws of this Commonwealth, both civil and criminal, so as to have but one law on any one subject; and, also, three other persons, learned in the law, whose duty it shall be to prepare a code of practice for the courts, both civil and criminal, in this Commonwealth, by abridging and simplifying the rules of practice and laws in relation thereto; all of whom shall, at as early a day as practicable, report the result of their labors to the General Assembly, for their adoption or modification. *Ky.,* 221.

—No general revision of the laws shall hereafter be made. When a reprint thereof becomes necessary! the Legislature, in joint convention, shall appoint a suitable person to collect together such acts and parts of acts as are in force, and without alteration, arrange them under appropriate heads and titles. The laws so arranged shall be submitted to two commissioners

1 § 18. All grants of land within this State, made by the king of Great

2 Britain, or persons acting under his authority, after the fourteenth day of

3 October, one thousand seven hundred and seventy-five, shall be null and void;

4 but nothing contained in this Constitution shall affect any grants of land

5 within this State, made by the authority of the said king or his predecessors,

6 or shall annul any charters to bodies politic or corporate, by him or them made

7 before that day; or shall affect any such grants or charters, since made by

8 this State, or by persons acting under its authority; or shall impair the obli-

9 gation of any debts contracted by this State, or individuals, or bodies cor-

10 porate, or any other rights of property, or any suits, actions, rights of action,

11 or other proceedings in courts of justice.(¹)

appointed by the Governor, for examination, and if certified by them to be a correct compilation of all general laws in force, shall be printed in such manner as shall be prescribed by law. *Mich.*, 314.

—The Legislature, at its first session after the adoption of this Constitution, shall provide for the appointment of three commissioners, whose duty it shall be to inquire into, revise and simplify the rules of practice, pleadings, forms and proceedings, and arrange a system adapted to the courts of record of this State, and report the same to the Legislature, subject to their modification and adoption; and such commission shall terminate upon the rendering of the report, unless otherwise provided by law. *Wis.*, 567.

—The Legislature shall never adopt any system or code of laws by general reference to such system or code of laws; but in all cases shall specify the several provisions of the laws it may enact. *La.*, 234.

—It shall also be the duty of the General Assembly, within five years after the adoption of this Constitution, and within every subsequent period of ten years, to make provision by law for the revision, digesting and promulgation of all the public statutes of this State, both civil and criminal. *Ala.*, 77.

—Within five years after the adoption of this Constitution, the laws, civil and criminal, shall be revised, digested and arranged, and promulgated in such manner as the General Assembly may direct, and a like revision, digest and promulgation shall be made within every subsequent period of ten years. *Ark.*, 93; nearly similar, *Tex.*, 516.

—The Legislature shall, as soon as conveniently may be, provide by law for ascertaining what statutes and parts of statutes shall continue to be in force within this State; for reducing them and all acts of the General Assembly into such order, and publishing them in such manner, that thereby the knowledge of them may be generally diffused; for choosing Inspectors and Judges of elections, and regulating the same in such manner as shall most effectually guard the rights of the citizens entitled to vote; for better securing personal liberty, and easily and speedily redressing all wrongful restraints thereof; for more certainly obtaining returns of impartial juries; for dividing lands and tenements in sales by Sheriffs, where they will bear a division, into as many parcels as may be without spoiling the whole, and for advertising and making the sales in such manner, and at such times and places as may render them most beneficial to all persons concerned; and for establishing schools, and promoting arts and sciences. *Del.*, 125.

—The General Assembly, at its first session after the adoption of this Constitution, shall provide for the appointment of three Commissioners, whose duty it

shall be to revise, simplify and abridge the rules, practice, pleadings and forms of the courts of justice. And they shall provide for abolishing the distinct forms of action at law, now in use, and that justice shall be administered in a uniform mode of pleading, without distinction between law and equity. And the General Assembly may also make it the duty of said Commissioners to reduce into a systematic code the general statute law of the State; and said Commissioners shall report the result of their labors to the General Assembly, with such recommendations and suggestions as to abridgment and amendment as to said Commissioners may seem necessary or proper. Provision shall be made by law for filling vacancies, regulating the tenure of office and the compensation of said Commissioners. *Ind.*, 177.

—The Legislature shall provide for the speedy publication of all statute laws of a general nature, and such decisions of the Supreme Court as it may deem expedient; and all laws and judicial decisions shall be free for publication by any person; *Provided*, That no judgment of the Supreme Court shall take effect and be operative until the opinion of the court in such case shall be filed with the clerk of said court. *Nev.*, 392.

—The Legislature, in cases not provided for in this Constitution, shall prescribe by general laws the terms of office, powers, duties, and compensation of all public officers and agents, and the manner in which they shall be elected, appointed, and removed. *W. Va.*, 548.

(1) Substantially embraced in Constitution of 1777. 32. Identical with § 15, Article VII, Constitution of 1821. *p.* 43.

DUELING.

—Any citizen of this State who may hereafter be engaged either directly or indirectly in a duel, either as principal or accessory before the fact, shall forever be disqualified from holding any office under the Constitution and laws of this State. *Iowa*, 183.

—[Oaths concerning dueling required of public officers]. *Ky.*, 219.

—[Prohibitions against the practice.] *Ala.*, 77; *Ct.*, 112; *Ind.*, 171; *Kan.*, 202; *Ky.*, 220; *Or.*, 449; *Va.*, 537; *W. Va.*, 548; *Wis.*, 570.

FUNDAMENTAL PRINCIPLES — RESERVATION OF RIGHTS.

—A frequent recurrence to the fundamental principles of the Constitution, and a constant adherence to those of piety, justice, moderation, temperance, industry and frugality, are absolutely necessary to preserve the advantages of liberty, and to maintain a free government. The people ought, consequently, to have a particular attention to all those principles, in the choice of their officers and representatives; and they have a right to require of their lawgivers and magistrates an exact and constant observance of them, in the formation and execution of the laws necessary for the good administration of the Commonwealth. *Mass.*, 282; *N H.*, 401; *Vt*, 523.

—This enumeration of certain rights shall not be construed to deny or disparage others retained by the people, [*U. S.*, 19], and to guard against any encroachment on the rights hereby retained, or any transgression of any of the high powers by this Constitution delegated, we declare, that everything in this article is excepted out of the general powers of government, and shall forever remain inviolate, and that all laws contrary thereto, or to the following provisions, shall be void. *Ala*, 74; *Tenn.*, 500.

—The declaration of rights hereto prefixed, is declared to be a part of the Constitution of this State, and shall never be violated on any pretense whatever. *Tenn*, 500.

—To guard against transgressions of the high powers which we have delegated, we declare, that everything in this article is excepted out of the general powers of government, and shall forever remain inviolate; and that all laws contrary thereto, or contrary to this Constitution, shall be void. *Ky.*, 224; *Miss.*, 336; *Tenn.*, 500.

—That a frequent recurrence to fundamental principles is absolutely necessary to preserve the blessings of liberty. *Fl.*, 130; *Ill.*, 166; *N. C.*, 422.

—The powers not delegated to the United States by the Constitution, nor prohibited by it to the States, are reserved to the States respectively, or to the people. *U. S.*, 19.

—No law shall be passed, the taking effect of which shall be made to depend upon any authority, except as provided in this Constitution, *Ind.*, 171; *Or.*, 448.

—Provided, that laws locating the capital of the State, locating county seats, and submitting town and city corporate acts and other local and special laws, may take effect or not, upon a vote of the electors interested. *Or.*, 448.

—That no free government, or the blessings of liberty, can be preserved to any people, but by a firm adherence to justice, moderation, temperance, frugality, and virtue, and by a frequent recurrence to fundamental principles. *Va.*, 532; *Wis.*, 561; *N b.*, 371.

—Legislative acts in violation of the Constitution are void, and the judiciary shall so declare them. *Ga.*, 142.

—That no power of suspending laws or the execution of laws, unless by or derived from the Legislature, ought to be exercised or allowed. *Md.*, 254; *Miss.*, 335.

—The power of suspending the laws, or the execution of the laws, ought never to be exercised but by the Legislature, or by authority derived from it to be exercised in such particular cases only as the Legislature shall expressly provide for. *Mass.*, 282; *N. C.*, 422; *N., H.*, 400; *Vt.*, 522; *Va.*, 532.

—No power of suspending laws shall be exercised but by the authority of the Legislature. *Del.*, 117; (Similar provisions) *Ind.*, 171; *La.*, 233; *Mr.*, 240; *Ohio*, 433; *Or.*, 448; *Pa.*, 468; *Tex.*, 506.

—We declare, that everything in this article is reserved out of the general powers of government hereinafter mentioned. *Del.*, 117.

—The enumeration in the Constitution of certain rights shall not be construed to deny or disparage others retained by the people. *U. S.*, 19.

—This enumeration of rights shall not be construed to deny or disparage others retained by the people

[*Iowa*, 184; *Kan.*, 197; *Md.*, 256; *Min.*, 320; *Neb.*, 371; *Nev.*, 380; *N. J.*, 413; *Ohio*, 433; *Or.*, 445; *R. I.*, 474], and to guard against any encroachments on the rights herein retained, or any transgression of any of the higher powers herein delegated, we declare that everything in this article is excepted out of the general powers of the government, and shall forever remain inviolate; and that all laws contrary thereto, or to the other provisions herein contained, shall be void. *Ark.*, 85; *Ga.*, 143.

—The Legislature shall assemble for the redress of public grievances, and for making such laws as the public good may require. *N. H.*, 400.

—The declaration of the political rights and privileges of the inhabitants of this State, is hereby declared to be a part of the Constitution of this Commonwealth, and ought not to be violated on any pretense whatsoever. *Vt.*, 527.

—That to guard against transgressions upon the rights of the people, we declare that everything in this article is excepted out of the general powers of government, and shall forever remain inviolate [*Tex.*, 507]; and all laws to the contrary thereto, or to the following provisions, shall be void. *Fl.*, 130; (analogous provisions) *Pa.*, 468.

HOMESTEAD EXEMPTIONS.

—The Legislature shall protect by law from forced sale a certain portion of the homestead and other property of all heads of families. *Cal.*, 104.

—A homestead to the extent of one hundred and sixty acres of farming land, or of one acre within the limits of an incorporated town or city, occupied as a residence by the family of the owner, together with all the improvements on the same shall be exempted from forced sale under any process of law, and shall not be alienated without the joint consent of both husband and wife, when that relation exists; but no property shall be exempt from sale for taxes, or for the payment of obligations contracted for the purchase of said premises, or for the erection of improvements thereon; *Provided*, The provisions of this section shall not apply to any process of law obtained by virtue of a lien given by the consent of both husband and wife. *Kan*, 206.

—Laws shall be passed by the General Assembly to protect from execution a reasonable amount of property of a debtor, not exceeding in value the sum of five hundred dollars. *Md.*, 204.

—The personal property of every resident of this State, to consist of such property only as shall be designated by law, shall be exempted to the amount of not less than five hundred dollars from sale on execution, or other final process of any court, issued for the collection of any debt contracted after the adoption of this Constitution. *Mich.*, 313.

—Every homestead of not exceeding forty acres of land, and the dwelling house thereon, and the appurtenances to be selected by the owner thereof, and not included in any town plat, city, or village; or instead thereof, at the option of the owner, any lot in any city, village, or recorded town plat, or such parts of lots as shall be equal thereto, and the dwelling-house thereon and its appurtenances, owned and occupied by any resident of the State, not exceeding in value fifteen hundred dollars, shall be exempt from forced sale on execution, or any other final process from a court for any debt contracted after the adoption of this Constitution. Such exemption shall not extend to any mortgage thereon lawfully obtained; but such mortgage or other alienation of such land, by the owner thereof, if a married man, shall not be valid without the signature of the wife to the same. *Mich.*, 313.

—The homestead of a family, after the death of the owner thereof, shall be exempt from the payment of his debts, contracted after the adoption of this Constitution, in all cases, during the minority of his children. *Mich.*, 313.

—If the owner of a homestead die, leaving a widow, but no children, the same shall be exempt, and the rents and profits thereof shall accrue to her benefit during the time of her widowhood, unless she be the owner of a homestead in her own right. *Mich.*, 313.

—A homestead as provided by law, shall be exempt from forced sale under any process of law, and shall not be alienated without the joint consent of husband and wife where that relation exists; but no property shall be exempt from sale for taxes, or for the payment of obligations contracted for the purchase of said premises, or for the erection of improvements thereon; *Provided*, The provisions of this section shall not apply to any process of law obtained by virtue of a lien given by the consent of both husband and wife; and laws shall be enacted providing for the recording of such homestead within the county in which the same shall be situated. *Nev.*, 383.

—The homestead of a family not to exceed two hundred acres of land, (not included in a town or city) or any town or city lot or lots, in value not to exceed two thousand dollars, shall not be subject to forced sale for any debts hereafter contracted, nor shall the owner, if a married man, be at liberty to alienate the same, unless by the consent of the wife in such manner as the Legislature may hereafter point out. *Tex.*, 516.

—The Legislature shall have power to protect by law, from forced sale, a certain portion of the property of all heads of families. *Tex.*, 516.

—The Legislature shall have power to provide by law for [exemption] from taxation, two hundred and fifty-dollars' worth of household furniture, or other property belonging to each family in this State. *Tex.*, 516.

—All property used exclusively for State, county, municipal, scientific, religious, benevolent, and charitable purposes, and personal property to the amount of at least two hundred dollars for each family, shall be exempted from taxation. *Kan.*, 214.

PROPERTY OF MARRIED WOMEN.

—All property, both real and personal, of the wife, owned or claimed by marriage, and that acquired afterward by gift, devise, or descent, shall be her separate property; and laws shall be passed more clearly defining the rights of the wife, in relation as well to her separate property as to that held in common with her husband. Laws shall also be passed providing for the registration of the wife's separate property. *Cal.*, 104; *Nev.*, 383; *Tex.*, 516.

—The Legislature shall provide for the protection of the rights of women in acquiring and possessing property, real, personal and mixed, separate and apart from the husband; and shall also provide for their equal rights in the possession of their children. *Kan.*, 206.

—The General Assembly shall pass laws necessary to protect the property of the wife from the debts of the husband during her life, and for securing the same to her issue after her death. *Md.*, 266.

—The real and personal estate of every female, acquired before marriage, and all property to which she may afterward become entitled, by gift, grant, inheritance or devise, shall be and remain the estate and property of such female, and shall not be liable for the debts, obligations, or engagements of her husband; and may be devised or bequeathed by her as if she were unmarried. *Mich.*, 313.

—The property and pecuniary rights of every married woman, at the time of marriage, or afterward, acquired by gift devise, or inheritance, shall not be subject to the debts or contracts of the husband, and laws shall be passed providing for the registration of the wife's separate property. *Or.*, 458.

MISCELLANEOUS PROVISIONS.

—The State shall be and remain one of the United States of America. The Constitution of the United States, and the laws and treaties made in pursuance thereof, shall be the supreme law of the land. *W. Va.*, 546.

—The people of this Commonwealth have the sole and exclusive right of governing themselves as a free, sovereign and independent State; and do, and forever hereafter shall, exercise and enjoy every power, jurisdiction and right, which is not, or may not hereafter be by them expressly delegated to the United States of America, in Congress assembled. *Mass.*, 280.

—That the Legislature shall pass no law providing for an alteration, change or abolishment of this Constitution, except in the manner therein prescribed and directed. *Md.*, 256.

—Suits may be brought against the Commonwealth in such manner, in such courts, and in such cases, as the Legislature may, by law, direct. *Pa.*, 467.

—All civil officers, whose authority is limited to a single judicial district, a single election district, or part of either, shall be appointed, hold their office, be removed from office, and, in addition to liability to impeachment, may be punished for official misconduct, in such manner as the General Assembly, previous to their appointment, may provide. *S. C.*, 487.

—No person shall hold or exercise, at the same time, more than one civil office of trust or profit, except that of Justice of the Peace. *La.*, 234.

—The Legislature shall pass no law excluding citizens of this State from office for not being conversant with any language except that in which the Constitution of the United States is written. *La.*, 235.

—All officers elected or appointed under this Constitution may be removed from office for misconduct, incompetence, neglect of duty, or other causes, in such manner as may be prescribed by general laws; and unless so removed, shall continue to discharge the duties of their respective offices, until their successors are elected or appointed and qualified. *W. Va.*, 548.

—The Legislature may determine the mode of filling vacancies in all offices for which provision is not made in this Constitution. *La.*, 235.

—No mechanical trade shall hereafter be taught to convicts in the State prison of this State, except the manufacture of those articles, of which the chief supply for home consumption is imported from other States or countries. *Mich.*, 314.

—To deter more effectually from the commission of crimes, by continued visible punishments of long duration, and to make sanguinary punishments less necessary, means ought to be provided for punishing by hard labor, those who shall be convicted of crimes not capital, whereby the criminal shall be employed for the benefit of the public, or for the reparation of injuries done to private persons; and all persons, at proper times, ought to be permitted to see them at their labor. *Vt.*, 526.

—The Legislature shall not pass any act authorizing the grant of license for the sale of ardent spirits or other intoxicating liquors. *Mich.*, 304.

—Laws may be passed regulating or prohibiting the sale of intoxicating liquor within the limits of this State. *W. Va.*, 558.

—The Legislature shall provide by law that the furnishing of fuel and stationery for the use of the State. *Mich.*, 303.

—It shall be the duty of the General Assembly at its next session, and from time to time thereafter as it may deem proper to enact laws prohibiting the intermarriage of white persons with negroes, or with persons of mixed blood, declaring such marriages null and void *ab initio*, and making the parties to any such marriage subject to criminal prosecutions, with such penalties as may be by law prescribed. *Ala.*, 77.

—The inhabitants of this State shall have liberty, in seasonable times, to hunt and fowl on the lands they hold, and on other lands not inclosed, and in like

ARTICLE II.

1   SECTION 1. Every male citizen of the age of twenty-one years who shall
2 have been a citizen for ten days and an inhabitant of this State one year
3 next preceding an election, and for the last four months a resident of the
4 county where he may offer his vote, shall be entitled to vote at such election
5 in the election district of which he shall at the time be a resident, and not
6 elsewhere, for all officers that now are or hereafter may be elective by the
7 people; but such citizen shall have been for thirty days next preceding the
8 election, a resident of the district from which the officer is to be chosen for
9 whom he offers his vote. But no man of color, unless he shall have been for
10 three years a citizen of this State, and for one year next preceding any elec-
11 tion, shall have been seized and possessed of a freehold estate of the value of

manner to fish in all boatable and other waters (not private property), under proper regulations to be hereafter made and provided by the General Assembly. *Va.*, 527.

—The people shall continue to enjoy and freely exercise all the rights of fishery, and privileges of the shore, to which they have been heretofore entitled, under the charter and usages of this State. But no new right is intended to be granted, nor any existing right impaired by this declaration. *R. I.*, 473.

—The Legislature is forbidden to pass any laws imposing disabilities, or impairing civil rights, on account of acts done in late rebellion. *S. C.*, 489.

—That, for redress of grievances, and for amending and strengthening the laws, elections ought to be often held. *N. C.*, 422.

—The rate of interest in this State shall not exceed six per centum per annum, and no higher rate shall be taken or demanded; and the General Assembly shall provide by law all necessary forfeitures and penalties against usury. *Md.*, 265.

—The Legislature shall fix the rate of interest; and the rate so established shall be equal and uniform throughout the State. *Tenn.*, 499.

QUALIFICATIONS OF ELECTORS FORMERLY REQUIRED IN NEW YORK ASSEMBLY.

—1777. That every male inhabitant, of full age, who shall have personally resided within one of the counties of this State for six months immediately preceding the day of election, shall at such election be entitled to vote for representatives of the said county in Assembly; if, during the time aforesaid he shall have been a freeholder, possessing a freehold of the value of twenty pounds, within the said county, or have rented a tenement therein of the yearly value of forty shillings, and been rated and actually paid taxes to this State: *provided, always,* that every person who now is a freeman of the city of Albany, or who was made a freeman of the city of New York, on or before the fourteenth day of October, in the year of our Lord one thousand seven hundred and seventy-five, and shall be actually and usually resident in the said cities respectively, shall be entitled to vote for representatives in Assembly, within his said place of residence. *P.* 27.

—[Senate and Governor.] Freeholders possessed of freeholds of the value of one hundred pounds charged thereon. *P.* 28.

—1821. Every male citizen of the age of twenty-one years who shall have been an inhabitant of this State one year next preceding any election, and for the last six months a resident of the town or county where he may offer his vote, and shall have, within the year next preceding the election paid a tax to the State or county assessed upon his real or personal property, or shall by law be exempted from taxation, or, being armed and equipped according to law shall have performed within that year military duty in the militia of this State, or who shall be exempted from performing militia duty in consequence of being a fireman in any city, town or village in this State, and also, every male citizen of the age of twenty-one years, who shall have been for three years next preceding such election, an inhabitant of this State, and for the last year a resident in the town or county where he may offer his vote, and shall have been, within the last year assessed to labor upon the public highways, and shall have performed the labor, or paid an equivalent therefor, according to law, shall be entitled to vote in the town or ward where he actually resides, and not elsewhere, for all officers that now are or hereafter may be elective by the people; but no man of color, unless he shall have been for three years a citizen of this State, and for one year next preceding any election shall be seized and possessed of a freehold estate of the value of two hundred and fifty dollars, over and above all debts and incumbrances charged thereon; and shall have been actually rated, and paid a tax thereon, shall be entitled to vote at any such election. And no person of color shall be subject to direct taxation unless he shall be seized and possessed of such real estate as aforesaid. *p.* 37.

[Property qualification abrogated in 1826], *p.* 45.

QUALIFICATIONS OF AGE, CITIZENSHIP AND RESIDENCE.

[Age 21, in every State except Delaware, where it is 22 years.]

Citizen of United States. *Ala.*, 82; *Ark.*, 82., *Ct.*, 111; *Fl.*, 135; *Ga.*, 149; *Ind.*, 171; *Iowa*, 184; *Ky.*, 218; *La.*, 227; *Me.*, 240; *Md.*, 256; *Miss.*, 336; *Mo.*,

12 two hundred and fifty dollars over and above all debts and incumbrances

13 charged thereon, and shall have been actually rated and paid a tax thereon,

14 shall be entitled to vote at such election. And no person of color shall be

15 subject to direct taxation unless he shall be seized and possessed of such real

16 estate as aforesaid : Provided, that in time of war no elector in the actual

17 military service of the United States, in the army or navy thereof, shall

18 be deprived of his vote by reason of his absence from the State, and the Leg-

19 islature shall have power to provide the manner in which, and the time and

20 place at which such absent electors may vote, and for the canvass and returns

21 of their votes in the election districts in which they respectively reside or

22 otherwise.

350; *Neb.*, 373; *Nev.*, 380; *N. J.*, 413; *N. C.*, 428; *Ohio*, 438; *Or.*, 448; *R. I.*, 474; *Tenn.*, 495; *Tex.*, 507; *Wis.*, 561.

Citizen of U. S. 2 years after naturalization, if of foreign birth. *Mass.*, 300.

Citizen of State. *Ct.*, 111; *Ga.*, 149; *Ill.*, 162; *Mich.*, 307; *W. Va.*, 547.

Citizen of State 2 years. *S. C.*, 486.

Residence in U. S. 1 year. 325.

Residence in State 3 months. *Me.*, 240; *Mich.*, 308.
do do 4 months. *Minn.*, 325.
do do 6 months. *Cal.*, 97; *Ind.*, 171; *Iowa*, 184; *Kan.*, 202; *Nev.*, 380; *Or.*, 448.

Residence in State 1 year. *Ala.*, 82; *Ct.*, 115; *Del.*, 120; *Fl.*, 135; *Ill.*, 162; *La.*, 227; *Md.*, 256; *Mass.*, 294; *Miss.*, 336; *Mo.*, 350; *N. J.*, 413; *Ohio*, 438; *Pa.*, 464; *R. I.*, 474; *Tex.*, 507; *Vt.*, 525; *Va.*, 533; *W. Va.*, 567; *Wis.*, 561. If formerly a resident of State 6 months, after return entitles to vote. *Pa.*, 464.

Residence in State 2 years. *Ga.*, 149; *Ky.*, 218.
do do time to be provided by law. *Neb.*, 371.

Residence in State 1 year (if alien) after declaring intentions to become a citizen. *Ind.*, 171; *Mo.*, 350; *Or.*, 448.

Residence in State 2 years (if alien). *S. C.*, 486.
do do no time mentioned after declaration. *Minn.*, 325; *Neb.*, 371; *Wis.*, 561.

Resident in county 1 month. *Del.*, 120; *Neb.*, 380; *W. Va.*, 547.

Residence in the county 2 months. *Iowa*, 184; *Mo.*, 350.

Residence in county 3 months. *Ala.*, 82; *La.*, 227.
do do 4 months. *Miss.*, 336.
do do 5 months. *N. J.*, 413.
do do 6 months. *Fl.*, 135; *Ga.*, 149; *Md.*, 256; *Tenn.*, 495; *Tex.*, 507; *Va.*, 533.

Residence in county 1 year. *Ky.*, 212.
do do time to be fixed by law. *Neb.*, 371; *Ohio*, 438.

Residence in town 4 months. *Miss.*, 336.
do do 6 months. *Ct.*, 111, 115; *R. I.*, 474; *Tex.*, 507; *Va.*, 533.

Residence in town — time to be fixed by law. *Ohio*, 438.

Residence in district 10 days. *Mich.*, 308; *Minn.*, 325; *Pa.*, 464.

Residence in district 30 days. *Cal.*, 97; *Kan.*, 202; *Nev.*, 380.

Residence in district 6 months. *Fl.*, 135; *Ga.*, 149; *Mass.*, 294; *S. C.*, 484; *Tex.*, 507.

Residence in district 1 year. *Ky.*, 218; *N. C.*, 428.
do do time to be fixed by law. *Ohio*, 438.

QUALIFICATIONS OF ELECTORS.

—Every free white male citizen, of the age of twenty-one years, who has resided in the State two years, or in the county, town or city, in which he offers to vote, one year next preceding the election, shall be a voter ; but such voter shall have been, for sixty days next preceding the election, a resident of the precinct in which he offers to vote, and he shall vote in said precinct, and not elsewhere. *Ky.*, 210.

—Shall have paid, by himself, master or guardian, any State or county tax, which shall, within two years next preceding such election, have been assessed upon him, in any town or district of this Commonwealth ; and also, every citizen who shall be by law exempted from taxation, and who shall be in all other respects qualified as above mentioned, shall have a right to vote in such election of Governor, Lieutenant-Governor, Senators and Representatives ; and no other person shall be entitled to vote in such elections. *Mass.*, 294.

—And every white male of foreign birth of the age of twenty-one years and upwards, who shall have resided in the United States one year, and shall have resided in this State during the six months immediately preceding such election, and shall have declared his intention to become a citizen of the United States, conformably to the laws of the United States on the subject of naturalization, shall be entitled to vote in the township or precinct where he may reside. *Ind.*, 171.

—Every white male inhabitant residing in the State on the twenty-fourth day of June, one thousand eight hundred and thirty-five ; every white male inhabitant residing in this State on the first day of January, one thousand eight hundred and fifty, who has declared his intention to become a citizen of the United States, pursuant to the laws thereof, six months preceding an election, or who has resided in this State two years and six months, and declared his intention as aforesaid. *Mich.*, 307.

—And who has paid all taxes assessed to him, after the adoption of this Constitution, under the laws of the Commonwealth after the re-organization of the county, city or town where he offers to vote. *Va.*, 533.

—And having within two years next before the election paid a county tax, which shall have been assessed at least six months before the election, shall enjoy the right of an elector ; and every free white male citizen of the age of twenty-one years, and under the age of twenty-two years, having resided as aforesaid, shall be entitled to vote without payment of any tax. *Del.*, 120.

—And the qualifications of electors of the Governor shall be the same as those for Senators; and if no person shall have a majority of votes, the Senate and House of Representatives shall, by joint ballot, elect one of the two persons having the highest number of votes, who shall be declared Governor. *N. H.*, 405.
—And every white male of foreign birth, of the age of twenty-one years and upwards, who shall have resided in the United States one year, and shall have resided in this State during the six months immediately preceding such election, and shall have declared his intention to become a citizen of the United States one year preceding such election, conformably to the laws of the United States on the subject of naturalization, shall be entitled to vote at all elections authorized by law. *Or.*, 448.
—A plurality of the votes given at an election shall constitute a choice, where not otherwise directed in this Constitution. *Cal.*, 105; *Neb.*, 373; *Nev.*, 392.
—All elections ought to be free; and all the inhabitants of this Commonwealth, having such qualifications as they shall establish by their frame of government, have an equal right to elect officers, and to be elected for public employments. *Mass.*, 281; *N. H.*, 399.
—All elections shall be free and equal. *Ark.*, 84; *Del.*, 116; *Ill.*, 165; *Ind.*, 171; *Ky.*, 223; *Miss.*, 347, *N. H.*, 399; *Or.*, 448; *Pa.*, 467; *Tenn.*, 490; *Va.*, 532.
—All elections should be free and open. *Mo.*, 347.
—No property qualification for eligibility to office, or for the right of suffrage shall ever be required in this State. *Fl.*, 129.
—That elections of members to serve as Representatives in General Assembly ought to be free. *N. C.*, 422.
—Every person of good character, who comes to settle in this State, having first taken an oath or affirmation of allegiance to the same, may purchase, or by other means acquire, hold, and transfer land, or other real estate, and after one year's residence shall be deemed a free denizen thereof, and entitled to all rights of a natural born subject of this State; except that he shall not be capable of being elected Governor, Lieutenant-Governor. Treasurer, Councillor, or Representative in Assembly, until after two years' residence. *Vt.*, 527.
—Every citizen shall be entitled to equal representation in the government, and in all apportionments of representation, equality of numbers of those entitled thereto shall, as far as practicable, be preserved. *W. Va.*, 546.
—And who is really and truly possessed in his own right of real estate in such town or city of the value of one hundred and thirty-four dollars, over and above all incumbrances, or which shall rent for seven dollars per annum, over and above any rent reserved, or the interest of any incumbrances thereon, being an estate in fee simple, fee tail, for the life of any person, or an estate in reversion of remainder, which qualifies no other person to vote, the conveyance of which estate, if by deed, shall have been recorded at least ninety days, shall hereafter have a right to vote at the election of all civil officers, and on all questions in all legal town or ward meetings, so long as he continues so qualified. And if any person hereinbefore described shall own any such estate within this State, out of the town or city in which he resides, he shall have a right to vote in the election of all general officers and members of the General Assembly, in the town or city in which he shall have had his residence and home for the term of six months next preceding the election, upon producing a certificate from the clerk of the town or city in which his estate lies, bearing date within ten days of the time of his voting, setting forth that such person has a sufficient estate therein to qualify him as a voter, and that the deed, if any, has been recorded ninety days. *R. I.*, 474.
—Every male citizen of the United States, of the age of twenty-one years, who has had his residence and home in this State two years, and in the town or city in which he may offer to vote six months next pre-

ceding the time of voting, whose name is registered pursuant to the act calling the Convention to frame this Constitution, or shall be registered in the office of the clerk of such town or city, at least seven days before the time he shall offer to vote, and before the last day of December in the present year; and who has paid or shall pay a tax or taxes, assessed upon his estate within this State, and within a year of the time of voting, to the amount of one dollar, or who shall voluntarily pay, at least seven days before the time he shall offer to vote, and before the said last day of December, to the Clerk or Treasurer of the town or city where he resides, the sum of one dollar, or such sums as, with his other taxes, shall amount to one dollar, for the support of public schools therein, and shall make proof of the same, by the certificate of the Clerk, Treasurer, or Collector of any town or city where such payment is made; or who, being so registered, has been enrolled in any military company in this State, and done military service or duty therein, within the present year, pursuant to law, and shall (until other proof is required by law), prove by the certificate of the officer legally commanding the regiment, or chartered, or legally authorized, or volunteer company, in which he may have served or done duty, that he has been equipped and done duty according to law, or by the certificate of the commissioners upon military claims, that he has performed military service, shall have a right to vote in the election of all civil officers, and on all questions in legally organized town or ward meetings, until the end of the first year after the adoption of this Constitution, or until the end of the year eighteen hundred and forty-three. *R. I.*, 474.
—But no compulsory process shall issue for the collection of any registry tax; *Provided*, That the registry tax of every person who has performed military duty according to the provisions of the preceding section, shall be remitted for the year he shall perform such duty; and the registry tax assessed upon any mariner, for any year while he is at sea, shall, upon his application, be remitted; and no person shall be allowed to vote whose registry tax for either of the two years next preceding the time of voting is not paid or remitted, as herein provided. *R. I.*, 475.
—And have paid all taxes which may have been required of them, and which they have had an opportunity of paying agreeable to law, for the year preceding the election. *Ga.*, 140.
—No property qualification shall be necessary to the holding of any office in this State, except the office of Senator in the General Assembly, and the office of Assessor, Inquisitor on lands, and levy Court Commissioner, and except such offices as the General Assembly shall by law designate. *Del.*, 125.
—No property qualification for eligibility to office, or for the right of suffrage, shall ever be required by law in this State. *Miss.*, 335.
—No possession of a freehold, or of any other estate, shall be required as a qualification for holding a seat in either branch of the General Court, or in the Executive Council. *Mass.*, 297.
[*Freehold qualifications.*] *N. Y.*, (1777), 27, 28; (1821), 37; (abolished in 1826, *p.* 45). Formerly in *Ct.*, $7, annually 111; *N. H.*, 402; *N. C.*, 50 acres, 424.
—[Property qualification without regard to color.] *N. Y.* (1777), 27.
—[Residence in State at time of adoption of Constitution, gives right to vote.] *Mich.*, 307.
—And within two years paid a State or county tax, which shall have been assessed at least ten days before the election, shall enjoy the rights of an elector. But a citizen of the United States, who had previously been a qualified voter of this State, and removed therefrom and returned, and who shall have resided in the election district, and paid taxes as aforesaid, shall be entitled to vote, after residing in the State six months; *Provided*, That white freemen, citizens of the United States, between the ages of twenty-one and twenty-two years, and having resided in the State one year, and in the election district ten days

as aforesaid, shall be entitled to vote, although they shall not have paid taxes. *Pa.*, 446.

—White male citizens of Mexico at time of treaty of 1848, who have elected to become citizens of the United States, declared electors. *Cal.*, 97.

—That all elections ought to be free, and without corruption, and that all freemen, having a sufficient evident common interest with and attachment to the community, have a right to elect and be elected to office, agreeably to the regulations made in this Constitution. *Vt.* 521.

—Must be taxpayer two years. *Del.*, 120; within two years, *Pa.*, 454; not specific, *Ga.*, 149; *Mass.*, 294; *N. C.*, 424.

—No property qualification for eligibility to office, or for the right of suffrage, shall ever be required in this State. *Fl.*, 129.

—That the right of the people to participate in the Legislature is the best security of liberty and the foundation of all free government; for this purpose elections ought to be free and frequent, and every free white male citizen having the qualifications prescribed by the Constitution, ought to have the right of suffrage. *Md.*, 254.

—No person shall be eligible to any civil office, (except the office of school committee), unless he be a qualified elector for such office. *R. I.*, 479.

—From and after that time, every such citizen, who has had the residence herein required, and whose name shall be registered in the town where he resides, on or before the last day of December in the year next preceding the time of his voting, and who shall show by legal proof that he has for and within the year next preceding the time he shall offer to vote, paid a tax or taxes assessed against him in any town or city in this State, to the amount of one dollar; or that he has been enrolled in a military company in this State, been equipped and done duty therein, according to law, and at least for one day during such year, shall have a right to vote in the election of all civil officers, and on all questions in all legally organized town or ward meetings. *R. I.*, 475.

—All persons who have been or shall hereafter, previous to the ratification of this Constitution, be admitted freemen, according to the existing laws of this State, shall be electors. *Ct.*, 111.

—Every white male citizen of the United States, and every white male person of foreign birth who may have declared his intention to become a citizen of the United States, according to law, not less than one year nor more than five years before he offers to vote, who is over the age of twenty-one years, who is not disqualified by or under any of the provisions of this Constitution, and who shall have complied with its requirements, and have resided in this State one year next preceding any election, or next preceding his registration as voter, and during the last sixty days of that period shall have resided in the county, city, or town where he offers to vote, or seeks registration as a voter, shall be entitled to vote at such election, for all officers, State, county, or municipal, made elective by the people; but he shall not vote elsewhere than in the *Mo.*, 350.

—And the inhabitants of plantations unincorporated, qualified as this Constitution provides, who are or shall be empowered and required to assess taxes upon themselves toward the support of government, shall have the same privilege of voting for Councillors and Senators, in the plantations where they reside, as town inhabitants have in their respective towns; and the plantation meetings for that purpose shall be held annually, [on the same first Monday in April], at such place in the plantations respectively, as the Assessors thereof shall direct: which Assessors shall have like authority for notifying the electors, collecting and returning the votes, as the Selectmen and Town Clerks have in their several towns, by this Constitution. And all other persons living in places unincorporated (qualified as aforesaid), who shall be assessed to the support of government by the Assessors of an adjacent town, shall have the privilege of giving in their votes for Councillors and Senators in the town

where they shall be assessed, and be notified of the place of meeting by the selectmen of the town where they shall be assessed, for that purpose, accordingly. *Mass.*, 284.

—The qualifications of voters and the limitation of the elective franchise, may be determined by the General Assembly, which shall first assemble under the amended Constitution. *Tenn.*, 504.

—The General Assembly shall have power to regulate by law, not inconsistent with this Constitution, all matters which relate to the Judges of Election, time, place and manner of holding elections in this State, and of making returns thereof. *Md.*, 256.

—The Selectmen and Town Clerk of the several towns shall decide on the qualifications of electors, at such times and in such manner as may be prescribed by law. *Ct.*, 112.

—[Militia service formerly a qualification of electors for Assembly.] *N. Y.* (1821), 37; *Ct.*, 112.

—[Electors required to take an oath of allegiance.] *N. Y.* (1777), 27; *Ct.*, 112, 115; *Md.*, 256; *Mo.*, 340, 350; *Va.*, 534.

—Every man of the full age of twenty-one years, having resided in the State for the space of one whole year next before the election of Representative, and is of a quiet and peaceful behavior, and will take the following oath or affirmation, shall be entitled to all the privileges of a freeman of this State: "You solemnly swear (or affirm) that whenever you give your vote or suffrage, touching any matter that concerns the State of Vermont, you will do it so as in your conscience you shall judge will most conduce to the best good of the same, as established by the Constitution, without fear or favor of any man." *Vt.*, 525.

PROVISIONS CONCERNING COLORED PERSONS AND INDIANS.

—No free negro, free mulatto, or free person of mixed blood, descended from negro ancestors to the fourth generation inclusive (though one ancestor of each generation may have been a white person), shall vote for members of the Senate or House of Commons. *N. C.*, 428.

—*Provided*, That nothing herein contained shall be construed to prevent the Legislature, by a two-thirds concurrent vote, from admitting to the right of suffrage Indians or the descendants of Indians, in such special cases as such a proportion of the legislative body may deem just and proper. *Cal.*, 97.

—[Indians not taxed, excluded from voting.] *Mo.*, 240; *Tenn.*, 507.

—[Narraganset Indians excluded from voting.] *R. I.*, 475.

—Civilized persons of Indian descent and not belonging to any tribe, may vote. *Mich.*, 307; *Wis.*, 562.

—Persons of mixed white and Indian blood who have adopted the customs and habits of civilization, may vote. *Min.*, 325.

—Persons of Indian blood residing in this State, who have adopted the language, customs and habits of civilization, after an examination before any District Court of the State, in such manner as may be provided by law, and shall have been pronounced by said court capable of enjoying the rights of citizenship within the State. *Min.*, 325.

—Persons of Indian blood who have once been declared by law of Congress to be citizens of the United States, any subsequent law of Congress to the contrary notwithstanding. *Wis.*, 562.

—Colored persons expressly excluded from voting. *Ind.*, 171; *Or.*, 449; *Tex.*, 507.

—Excluded from elections by the word "white." *Ala.*, 82; *Ark.*, 85; *Cal.*, 97; *Ct.*, 111, 115; *Del.*, 120; *Fl.*, 135; *Ga.*, 149; *Ill.*, 162; *Ind.*, 171; *Iowa*, 184; *Kan.*, 201; *Ky.*, 215; *La.*, 227; *N. J.*, 413; *Me.*, 240; *Md.*, 256; *Mich.*, 307; *Min.*, 325; *Mo.*, 350; *Neb.*, 371; *Nev.*, 390; *Ohio*, 438; *Or.*, 448; *Pa.*, 464; *S. C.*, 436; *Tenn.*, 495; *Va.*, 533; *W. Va.*, 347.

—The word "white," not used. *Mass.*, 281; *N. H.*, 403; *R. I.*, 474; *Vt.*, 525.

—Freemen are voters, and the word "white" not used. *N. C.*, 424.

—Legislature may provide for election of such other persons, citizens of United States, as by military service, by taxation to support the Government, or by intellectual fitness, may be deemed entitled thereto. *La.*, 227.

—[Freemen of color excused from military duty, and from poll tax.] *Tenn.*, 495.

—That no person shall be disqualified from voting in any election on account of color, who is now, by the laws of this State, a competent witness in a court of justice against a white man. All free men of color shall be exempt from military duty in time of peace, and also from paying a free poll tax. *Tenn.*, 495.

—[The word "white," stricken out.] *Wis.* 561.

—[Proposition pending to strike out "white."] *Kan.*

LITERARY QUALIFICATIONS OF VOTERS.

—Every person shall be able to read any article of the Constitution, or any section of the statutes of this State, before being admitted as an elector. *Ct.*, 115.

—No person shall have the right to vote, or be eligible to office under the Constitution of this Commonwealth, who shall not be able to read the Constitution in the English language and write his name: *Provided, however,* That the provisions of this amendment shall not apply to any person prevented by a physical disability from complying with its requisitions, nor to any person who now has the right to vote, nor to any person who shall be sixty years of age or upwards at the time this amendment shall take effect. *Mass.*, 222.

—After the first day of January, one thousand eight hundred and seventy-six, every person who was not a qualified voter prior to that time shall, in addition to the other qualifications required, be able to read and write in order to become a qualified voter; unless his inability to read or write shall be the result of a physical disability. *Mo.*, 351.

SOLDIERS' VOTE.

—The right of suffrage shall be enjoyed by all persons otherwise entitled to the same, who may be in the military or naval service of the United States; *Provided,* The votes so cast shall be made to apply to the county and township of which said voters were *bona fide* residents at the time of their enlistment; *Provided, further,* That the payment of a poll tax, or a registration of such voters shall not be required as a condition to the right of voting. Provision shall be made by law regulating the manner of voting, holding elections, and making returns of such elections, wherein other provisions are not contained in this Constitution. *Nev.*, 380.

—Any qualified voter who may be absent from the place of his residence, by reason of being in the volunteer army of the United States, or in the militia force of this State, in the service thereof, or of the United States, whether within or without the State, shall, without registration, be entitled to vote in any election occurring during such absence. The votes of all such persons, wherever they may be, may be taken on the day fixed by law for such election, or on any day or days within twenty days next prior thereto; and the General Assembly shall provide by law for the taking, return and counting of such votes. Every such person shall take the same oath that all other voters may be required to take in order to vote. *Mo.*, 351.

Whenever any of the qualified electors of this Commonwealth, shall be in any actual military service, under a requisition from the President of the United States, or by the authority of this Commonwealth, such electors may exercise the right of suffrage in all elections by the citizens, under such

regulations as are, or shall be prescribed by law, as fully as if they were present at their usual place of election. *Pa.*, 472.

[Entitled to vote in district where he resides.] Or in case of volunteer soldiers, within their several military departments or districts. *Ark.*, 85.

[Regulation for soldiers' vote similar to that of New York.] *Ct.*, 115; *Mich.*, 308.

[Special and minute provision for soldiers' vote.] *Md.*, 278.

—Officers and privates in army, and marines of the navy of United States, and seamen, excluded from voting. *S. C.*, 486.

—The provisions of this ordinance in regard to the soldiers' vote shall apply to future elections under this Constitution, and be in full force until the Legislature shall provide by law for taking the votes of citizens of said Territory in the army of the United States. *Nev.*, 398.

—The General Assembly shall also provide by law for taking the votes of soldiers in the army of the United States serving in the field. *Md.*, 256.

—Every elector of this State who shall be in the military service of the United States, either as a drafted person or volunteer, during the present rebellion, shall, when absent from this State, because of such service, have the same right to vote in any election of State officers, Representatives in Congress, and electors of President and Vice-President of the United States, as he would have if present at the time appointed for such election, in the town in which he resided at the time of his enlistment into such service. This provision shall in no case extend to persons in the regular army of the United States, and shall cease, and become inoperative and void, upon the termination of the present war. The General Assembly shall prescribe by law, in what manner and in what time the votes of electors absent from this State in the military service of the United States, shall be received, counted, returned and canvassed. *Ct.*, 115.

—For the purpose of taking the vote of the electors of said Territory who may be in the army of the United States, the Adjutant-General of said Territory shall, on or before the fifth day of August next following, make out a list in alphabetical order, and deliver the same to the Governor, of the names of all the electors, residents of said Territory, who shall be in the army of the United States, stating the number of the regiment, battalion, squadron or battery to which he belongs, and also the county or township of his residence in the said Territory. *Nev.* 397.

—No soldier, seaman, or marine, in the army or navy of the United States, or of their allies, shall be deemed to have acquired a residence in the State in consequence of being stationed within the same; nor shall any soldier, seaman, or marine have the right to vote. *Kan.* 202.

—No soldier, seaman or marine, in the army or navy of the United States, shall be deemed a resident of this State, in consequence of being stationed at any military or naval place within the State. *Ala.*, 82; *Ark.*, 85; *Ill.*, 162; (nearly similar), *Del.*, 120; *Fl.*, 135; *Ill.*, 162; *Ind.*, 174; *Iowa*, 194; *Me.*, 240; *Mich.*, 308; *Min.*, 326; *N. J.*, 413; *Ohio*, 438; *Or.*, 449; *Va.*, 534; *W. Va.*, 546; *Wis.*, 462.

—No officer, soldier, or marine, in the regular army or navy of the United States, shall be entitled to vote at any election in this State [*Miss.*, 350], and no soldier, sailor, or marine in the army or navy of the United States shall be entitled to vote at any election created by this Constitution. *Tex.*, 507.

—Any other person in the employ or pay of the United States, unless he be a qualified elector of the State previous to his appointment or enlistment as such officer, soldier, seaman or marine, in the regular army or navy of the United States, or of the revenue service, shall be considered a resident in the State in consequence of being stationed within the same. *Fl.*, 135.

—Electors of this State, who, in time of war, are absent from the State, in the actual military service

1 § 2. Laws may be passed excluding from the right of suffrage all persons
2 who have been or may be convicted of (¹) bribery, (²) larceny, or of any
3 infamous crime; and for depriving every person who shall make, or become
4 directly or indirectly interested in any bet or wager, depending upon the
5 result of any election, from the right to vote at such election.(³)

of the United States, being otherwise qualified, shall have a right to vote in all elections in the State for electors of President and Vice President of the United States, Representatives in Congress, and general officers of the State. The General Assembly shall have full power to provide by law for carrying this article into effect; and until such provision shall be made by law, every such absent elector on the day of such elections, may deliver a written or printed ballot, with the names of the persons voted for thereon, and his christian and surname, and his voting residence in the State, written at length on the back thereof, to the officer commanding the regiment or company to which he belongs; and all such ballots, certified by such commanding officer to have been given by the elector whose name is written thereon, and returned by such commanding officer to the Secretary of State within the time prescribed by law for counting the votes in such elections, shall be received and counted with the same effect as if given by such elector in open town, ward or district meeting; and the clerk of each town or city, until otherwise provided by law, shall, within five days after any such election, transmit to the Secretary of State a certified list of the names of all such electors on their respective voting lists. *R. I.*, 491.

-But persons in the military, naval, or marine service of the United States, or this State, shall not be considered as having obtained such established residence by being stationed in any garrison, barrack, or military place, in any town or plantation. *Me.*, 240.

—No person in the military, naval or marine service of the United States shall be deemed a resident of this State by reason of being stationed therein; but citizens of this State, when in the military service of the United States, shall be permitted to vote under such regulations as may be prescribed by the General Assembly, wherever they may be stationed, the same as if they were within their respective cities, counties or districts. No person shall have the right to vote who is of unsound mind or a pauper, or who has been convicted of a bribery in an election, or of any infamous offense. *Va.*, 534.

EXCLUSION FROM THE RIGHT OF SUFFRAGE.

[Idiots excluded]. *Del.*, 120; *Iowa*, 184; *Kan.*, 202; *Md.*, 256; *Min.*, 326; *Nev.*, 380; *N. J.*, 413; *Ohio*, 438; *Or.*, 449; *R. I.*, 475; *Wis.*, 562.

[Lunatics excluded]. *Del.*, 120; *Iowa*, 180; *Kan.*, 202; *Md.*, 256; *Min.*, 326; *Nev.*, 381; *N. J.*, 413; *Ohio*, 438; *Or.*, 449; *R. I.*, 475; *W. Va.*, 547; *Wis.*, 562.

[Paupers excluded]. *N. Y.*, (1821), 37; *Cal.*, 97; *La.*, 227; *Me.*, 240; *Mass.*, 294; *N. H.*, 403; *N. J.*, 413; *R. I.*, 475; *S. C.*, 486; *W. Va.*, 547.

[Persons under guardianship excluded]. *Kan.*, 202; *Me.*, 240; *Mass.*, 294; *Min.*, 326; *Wis.*, 562.

[Persons under interdiction excluded]. *La.*, 227.

[Persons excused from paying taxes at their own request]. *N. H.*, 403.

[Prisoners excluded]. *Cal.*, 97.

[Chinamen excluded]. *Or.*, 449.

—Persons residing on lands ceded by this State to the United States, shall not be entitled to exercise the privileges of electors. *R. I.*, 475.

—If any person shall give, or offer to give, directly or indirectly, or hath given or offered to give, since the fourth day of July, eighteen hundred and fifty-one, any bribe, present, or reward, or any promise, or any security for the payment or delivery of money or any other thing, to induce any voter to refrain from casting his vote, or forcibly to prevent him in any way from voting, or to procure a vote for any candidate or person, proposed or voted for as elector of President and Vice-President of the United States, or Representative in Congress, or for any office of profit or trust created by the Constitution or laws of this State, or by the ordinances or authority of the Mayor and City Council of Baltimore, the person giving or offering to give, and the persons receiving the same, and any person who gives or causes to be given an illegal vote, knowing it to be such, at any election to be hereafter held in this State, or who shall be guilty of or accessory to any fraud, force, surprise, or bribery to procure himself or any other person to be nominated to any office, national, State, or municipal, shall, on conviction in a court of law, in addition to the penalties now or hereafter to be imposed by law, be forever disqualified to hold any office of profit or trust, or to vote at any election thereafter. *Md.*, 257.

—But the foregoing provisions in relation to acts done against the United States shall not apply to any person not a citizen thereof, who shall have committed such acts while in the service of some foreign country at war with the United States, and who has, since such acts, been naturalized, or may hereafter be naturalized, under the laws of the United States, and the oath of loyalty hereinafter prescribed, when taken by any such person, shall be considered as taken in such sense. *Mo.*, 349.

—Whoever shall be convicted of having directly or indirectly, given or offered any bribe, to procure his election or appointment to any office, shall be disqualified for any office of honor, trust or profit under this State; and whoever shall give or offer any bribe to procure the election or appointment of any other person to any office, shall, on conviction thereof, be disqualified for a voter, or any office of honor, trust or profit under this State, for ten years after such conviction. *Mo.*, 350.

—The Legislature may pass laws to deprive persons of the right of suffrage who shall be convicted of bribery at elections. *N. J.*, 413; *W. Va.*, 547.

—Every person shall be disqualified from holding office, during the term for which he may have been elected, who shall have given or offered a bribe, threat, or reward, to procure his election. [*Or.*, 449; *Cal.*, 104; *Kan.*, 202; *Tex.*, 515.] Or procured any other person to offer a bribe. *Ark.*, 86; *R. I.*, 479.

—Every person shall be disqualified from serving as Governor, Senator, Representative, or from holding any other office of honor or profit in this State, for the term for which he shall have been elected, who shall have been convicted of having given or offered any bribe to procure his election. *Ala.*, 81; *Fl.*, 136.

—Or has ever, with a view to avoid enrollment in the militia of this State, or to escape the performance of duty therein. *Mo.*, 348.

—Or, having ever voted at any election by the people in this State, or in any other of the United States, or in any of their Territories, or held office in this State, or in any other of the United States, or in any of their Territories, or under the United States, shall thereafter have sought or received, under claim of alienage, the protection of any foreign government, through any consul or other officer thereof, in order to secure exemption from military duty in the militia of this State, or in the army of the United States. *Mo.*, 349.

—And no person shall ever be admitted to hold a seat in the Legislature, or any office of trust or importance under the government of this Commonwealth, who shall, in the due course of law, have been convicted of bribery or corruption, in obtaining an election or appointment. *Mass.*, 242.

—No person shall ever be admitted to hold a seat in the Legislature, or any office of trust or importance under this government, who, in the due course of law, has been convicted of bribery or corruption in obtaining an election or appointment. *N. H.*, 410.

—All elections, whether by the people, or the Legislature, shall be free and voluntary; and any elector, who shall receive any gift or reward, for his vote, in meat, drink, moneys, or otherwise, shall forfeit his right to elect at that time, and suffer such other penalty as the law shall direct; and any person who shall directly or indirectly give, promise, or bestow, any such reward to be elected, shall thereby be rendered incapable to serve for the ensuing year, and be subject to such further punishment as a future Legislature may direct. *Il.*, 526.

—Any person who shall be convicted of the embezzlement or defalcation of the public funds of this State, or who may be convicted of having given or offered a bribe to secure his election or appointment to office, or received a bribe to aid in the procurement of office for any other person, shall be disqualified from holding any office of profit or trust in this State; and the Legislature shall, as soon as practicable, provide by law for the punishment of such defalcation, bribery, or embezzlement, as a felony. *Nev.*, 582.

—No person who may hereafter be a collector or holder of public money shall be eligible to any office of trust or profit until he shall have accounted for and paid over according to law, all sums for which he may be liable. *Ga.*, 143; *Ind.*, 172; *Mich.*, 303; *Or.*, 449.

—No person who may have collected, or been intrusted with public money, whether State, county, township, or municipal, shall be eligible to the Legislature, or to any office of honor, trust or profit, until he shall have duly accounted for and paid over such money according to law. *Fl.*, 136; *Iowa*, 186; *Mo.*, 353; *N. C.*, 425; *Ohio*, 433; *Tenn.*, 494; *Tex.*, 509; *W. Va.*, 550.

—Any elector who shall receive any gift or reward for his vote, in meat, drink, money, or otherwise, shall suffer such punishment as the laws shall direct. And any person who shall directly or indirectly give, promise, or bestow any such reward to be elected, shall thereby be rendered incapable, for six years, to serve in the office for which he was elected, and be subject to such further punishment as the Legislature shall direct. *Tenn.*, 498.

—Or person convicted of a crime which now excludes him from being a witness, unless pardoned or restored by law to the right of suffrage, shall enjoy the right of an elector. *N. J.*, 413.

—No person who, since the first day of June, 1861, has given or shall give voluntary aid or assistance to the rebellion against the United States, shall be a citizen of this State, or be allowed to vote at any election held therein, unless he has volunteered into the military or naval services of the United States, and has been or shall be honorably discharged therefrom. *W. Va.*, 548.

—Every person who shall give or accept a challenge to fight a duel, or shall knowingly carry to another person such challenge, or who shall agree to go out of the State to fight a duel, shall be ineligible to any office of trust or profit. *Ark.*, 93; *Ind.*, 171; *Nev.*, 392; *Or.*, 449; *Ct.*, 112; *Kan.*, 202; *Or.*, 449; *Va.*, 537; *W. Va.*, 548; *Wis.*, 570.

—Any inhabitant who may hereafter be engaged in a duel, either as principal or accessory before the fact, shall be disqualified from holding any office under the Constitution and laws of this State, and shall not be permitted to vote at any election. *Mich.*, 308.

[Rigid exclusion of those who have participated in the rebellion.] *Md.*, 256; *Mo.*, 348; *Nev.*, 380.

[Amnesty of President required in case a person has served in rebel army.] *Nev.*, 380.

[Service in the United States army restores those who had lost their franchise by rebellion.] *Mo.*, 350.

[Bribery specified as cause of disqualification.] *Ala.*, 82; *Ct.*, 112; *Fl.*, 135; *La.*, 233; *Miss.*, 342; *Mo.*, 352; *Ohio*, 438; *R. I.*, 475; *Wis.*, 562, and some others.

[Forgery, specified.] *Ala.*, 82; *Cal.*, 104; *Ct.*, 112; *Fl.*, 136.

[Fraudulent bankruptcy.] *Ct.*, 112.

[Felony.] *Del.*, 121; *Miss.*, 325; *W. Va.*, 547, &c. [Larceny.] *Wis.*, 561. [Theft.] *Ct.* 112. [Perjury.] *Ala.*, 82; *Ct.*, 112; *Fl.*, 135; *Il.*, 154; *La.*, 233; *Mo.*, 352; *Ohio*, 438, &c.

[Treason.] *La.*, 233; *Min.*, 326; *Nev.*, 380; *W. Va.*, 547; *Wis.*, 627.

Treason or felony committed in any State.] *Nev.*, 380.

[Crimes punished by imprisonment in penitentiary.] *Or.*, 447.

[Crimes punishable by hard labor.] *La.*, 227.

["Other high crimes," and "infamous crimes."] *Ala.*, 82; *Cal.*, 97, 104; *Ct.*, 112; *Fl.*, 135; *Il.*, 162; *Iowa*, 184; *Kan.*, 202; *Min.*, 322; *Mo.*, 352; *Ohio*, 438; *R. I.*, 475; *Tenn.*, 495; *Wis.*, 562.

[Right lost as above may be restored.] *Ga.* 143; *Kan.*, 202; *Md.*, 256; *Miss.*, 326; *R. I.*, 475; *Wis.*, 526, &c.

[Exclusion on account of crimes, applied to those over 21 years of age.] *Md.*, 256.

—The Legislature may impose the forfeiture of the right of suffrage as a punishment for crime. *Del.*, 120; *Il.*, 162.

PRIVILEGES OF ELECTORS.

—No elector shall be obliged to do militia duty on the day of election, except in time of war or public danger, or attend court as a suitor or witness, [*Mich.*, 308], nor work on the public roads, [*Va.*, 545; *W. Va.*, 548; *Cal.*, 97; *Il.*, 162; *Iowa*, 184; *Me.*, 241; *Miss.*, 336; *Or.*, 449;] nor serve as a juror. *Va.*, 534.

—Every elector, in all cases, except treason, felony, or breach of the peace, shall be privileged from arrest during his attendance at election, and in going to and returning from the same. *Ala.*, 82; *Cal.*, 97; *Del.*, 121; *Il.*, 162; *Iowa*, 184; *Ind.*, 172; *Kan.*, 202; *Ky.*, 210; *La.*, 227; *Me.*, 241; *Mich.*, 308; *Mo.*, 251; *Ohio*, 438; *Or.*, 449; *Pa.*, 464; *Tenn.*, 495; *Tex.*, 507; *Va.*, 545.

—Privilege from summons. *Tenn.*, 495.

—Privilege from service of civil process. *Ct.*, 112; *Nev.*, 381; *Va.*, 534; *W. Va.*, 548; *Min.*, 326.

1 § 3. For the purpose of voting, no person shall be deemed to have gained
2 or lost a residence, by reason of his presence or absence, while employed in
3 the service of the United States; (¹) nor while engaged in the navigation of
4 the waters of this State, or of the United States, or of the high seas; (²) nor
5 while a student of any seminary of learning; nor while kept at any alms
6 house, or other asylum, at public expense; nor while confined in any public
7 prison.(³)

(1). *Ill.*, 162; *Md.*, 171; *R. I.*, 415; *Wis.*, 562.
(2). *Cal.*, 97.
(3). *Cal.*, 97; *Mich.*, 308 *Min.*, 326; *Mo.*, 351; *Nev.*, 381; *Or.*, 449; &c.

RESIDENCE OF ELECTORS.

—All civil officers for the State at large shall be voters of and reside within the State; and all district or parish officers shall be voters of and reside within their respective districts or parishes, and shall keep their offices at such places therein as may be required by law. *La.*, 233.
—No person shall be entitled to vote at any election held in this State except in the parish of his residence, and in cities and towns divided into election precincts, in the election precinct in which he resides. *La.*, 227; *Md.*, 256.
—No voter, on removing from one parish to another within the State, shall lose the right of voting in the former until he shall have acquired it in the latter. *La.*, 227.
—But a person who shall have acquired a residence in such county or city entitling him to vote at any such election, shall be entitled to vote in the election district from which he removed, until he shall have acquired a residence in the part of the county or city to which he has removed. *Md.*, 256.
—All persons residing upon Indian lands within any county of the State, and qualified to exercise the right of suffrage under this Constitution, shall be entitled to vote at the polls which may be held nearest their residence, for State, United States, or county officers: *Provided*, That no person shall vote for county officers out of the county in which he resides. *Wis.*, 571.
—All qualified electors shall vote in the election precinct in the county where they may reside, for county officers, and in any county in the State for State officers, or in any county of a congressional district in which such electors may reside, for members of Congress. *Or.*, 449.
[Electors allowed to vote for State officers, anywhere in the State.] *Tex.* 507.
—That any one entitled to vote in this State in the county where he resides, may vote for the adoption or rejection of this constitution in any county in this State. *Ark.*, 85.
—And every person, qualified as the constitution provides, shall be considered as an inhabitant for the purpose of electing and being elected into any office or place within this State, in the town, parish or plantation where he dwelleth and hath his home. *N. H.*, 403.

—All persons qualified to vote in the election of Senators shall be entitled to vote within the district where they dwell, in the choice of Representatives. *N. H.*, 402.
—Nor shall the residence of a student at any Seminary of learning, entitle him to the right of suffrage in the town or plantation where such seminary is established. *Me.*, 240.
—And any such qualified elector, who may happen to be in any county, city or town other than that of his residence at the time of an election, or who shall have moved to any county, city, or town within four months preceding the election, from any county, city, or town in which he would have been a qualified elector had he not so removed, may vote for any State or district officer, or member of Congress, for whom he could have voted in the county of his residence, or the county, city or town from which he may have so removed. *Miss.*, 336.
—And to remove all doubts concerning the meaning of the word "inhabitant," in this Constitution, every person shall be considered as an inhabitant, for the purpose of electing and being elected into any office or place within this State, in that town, district or plantation where he dwelleth or hath his home. *Mass.*, 284.
—It shall be the duty of the General Assembly to pass laws to punish with fine and imprisonment any person who shall remove into any election district or precinct of any ward of the city of Baltimore, not for the purpose of acquiring a *bona fide* residence therein, but for the purpose of voting at an approaching election, or who shall vote in any election district or ward in which he does not reside (except in the case provided for in this article), or shall at the same election vote in more than one election district, or precinct, or shall vote or offer to vote in any name not his own, or in place of any other person of the same name, or shall vote in any county in which he does not reside. *Md.*, 258.
[Provision relating to students similar to N. Y.] *Me.*, 240.
[Absence on business of State not a disqualification.] *Cal.*, 105; *Ind.*, 171; *Wis.*, 562.
—Temporary absence from the State shall not cause a forfeiture of residence once obtained. *Ala.*, 94.
—Absence on business of this State, or of the United States, or on a visit, or necessary private business, shall not cause a forfeiture of a residence once obtained. *Ark.*, 93; *Miss.*, 343.
—Absence on the business of this State, or of the United States, shall not forfeit a residence once obtained, so as to deprive any one of the right of suffrage, or of being elected or appointed to any office, under the exceptions contained in this Constitution. *Ky.*, 220; *Tex.*, 515.

1 § 4. Laws shall be made for ascertaining by proper proofs the citizens who

2 shall be entitled to the right of suffrage hereby established.(¹)

(1). *N. Y.*, (1777), 37; *Kan.*, 202.

REGISTRY OF VOTERS—REGISTRATION OF BIRTHS, MARRIAGES AND DEATHS.

—The Legislature may provide for a registry of voters. They shall prescribe the manner of conducting and making returns of elections, and of determining contested elections; and shall pass such laws as may be necessary and proper to prevent intimidation, disorder or violence at the polls, and corruption or fraud in voting. *W. Va.*, 548.

—The General Assembly shall immediately provide by law for a complete and uniform registration, by election districts, of the names of qualified voters in this State; which registration shall be evidence of the qualification of all registered voters to vote at any election thereafter held; but no person shall be excluded from voting at any election, on account of not being registered, until the General Assembly shall have passed an act of registration, and the same shall have been carried into effect; after which, no person shall vote, unless his name shall have been registered at least ten days before the day of the election; and the fact of such registration shall be no otherwise shown, than by the register, or an authentic copy thereof, certified to the judges of election by the registering officer, or other constituted authority. A new registration shall be made within sixty days next preceding the tenth day prior to every biennial general election; and after it shall have been made, no person shall establish his right to vote, by the fact of his name appearing on any previous register. *Mo.*, 356.

—The General Assembly shall provide for the periodical registration in the several counties, cities and towns of the voters therein; and for the annual registration of births, marriages and deaths in the white population, and of the births and deaths in the colored population. *Va.*, 539.

—The General Assembly shall provide by law for the registration of births, marriages and deaths, and shall pass laws providing for the celebration of marriage between any persons legally competent to contract marriage, and shall provide that any persons prevented by conscientious scruples from being married by any of the existing provisions of law, may be married by any Judge or Clerk of any Court of Record, or any Mayor of any incorporated city in this State. *Md.*, 264.

[The Recorder, in addition to the duties incident to the recording of inventories, and other papers relating to estates, and to deeds and other writings, attends to the registering of births, marriages and deaths, and issuing of marriage licenses]. *W. Va.*, 554.

—The General Assembly shall pass laws for the preservation of the purity of elections by the registration of voters, and by such other means as may be deemed expedient; and to make effective the provisions of the Constitution disfranchising certain persons, or disqualifying them from holding office. *Md.*, 264.

—Until such a system of registration shall have been established, every person shall, at the time of offering to vote, and before his vote shall be received, take an oath in the terms prescribed in the next succeeding section. After such a system shall have been established, the said oath shall be taken and subscribed by the voter at each time of his registration. Any person declining to take said oath shall not be allowed to vote, or to be registered as a qualified voter. The taking thereof shall not be deemed conclusive evidence of the right of the person to vote, or to be registered as a voter; but such right may, notwithstanding, be disproved. And, after a system of registration shall have been established, all evidence for and against the right of any person as a qualified

voter, shall be heard and passed upon by the registering officer or officers, and not by the judges of election. The registering officer or officers shall keep a register of the names of persons rejected as voters, and the same shall be certified to the judges of election; and they shall receive the ballot of any such rejected voter offering to vote, marking the same and certifying the vote thereby given, as rejected; but no such vote shall be received, unless the party offering it take, at the time, the oath of loyalty hereinafter prescribed. *Mo.*, 349.

—The Legislature shall provide by law that the names and residence of all qualified electors shall be registered, in order to entitle them to vote; but the registry shall be free of cost to the elector. *La.*, 227; *Md.*, 256.

—But no person shall be excluded from voting at any election on account of not being registered until the General Assembly shall have passed an act of registration, and the same shall have been carried into effect, after which no person shall vote unless his name appears on the register. *Md.*, 256.

—Provision shall be made by law for the registration of the names of the electors within the counties of which they may be residents, and for the ascertainment by proper proofs of the persons who shall be entitled to the right of suffrage, as hereby established; to preserve the purity of election, and to regulate the manner of holding and making returns of the same; and the Legislature shall have power to prescribe by law any other or further oaths as may be deemed necessary as a test or electoral qualification. *Nev.*, 381.

—The General Assembly shall have full power to provide for a registry of voters; to prescribe the manner of conducting the elections; the form of certificates; the nature of the evidence to be required in case of a dispute as to the right of any person to vote, and generally to enact all laws necessary to carry this article into effect, and to prevent abuse, corruption and fraud in voting. [*R. I.*, 475.] *Provided, however,* That the General Assembly may, by requiring a registry of voters, or other suitable legislation, guard against frauds in elections and usurpations of the right of suffrage; may impose disqualification to vote as a punishment for crime, and may prescribe additional qualifications for voters in municipal elections. *S. C.*, 486.

MANNER OF HOLDING AND REPORTING ELECTIONS.

—The General Assembly shall have power to regulate by law, not inconsistent with this Constitution, all matters which relate to the judges of election, time, place, and manner of holding elections in this State, and of making returns thereof. *Md.*, 265.

—Each of the boards of judges shall safely keep one poll-book and tally-list, and the ballots cast at each election; and shall, within ten days after such election, cause the other poll-book and tally-list to be transmitted, by the hands of a sworn officer, to the clerk of the board transacting county business in their respective counties, or to which the county may be attached for municipal purposes. *Kan.*, 207.

—Laws shall be made to support the privilege of free suffrage, prescribing the manner of regulating and conducting meetings of the electors, and prohibiting, under adequate penalties, all undue influence therein, from power, bribery, tumult and other improper conduct. *Ala.*, 74; *Cal.*, 104; *Ct.*, 112; *Fl.*, 136; *La.*, 233; *Miss.*, 342; *Nev.*, 383; *Or.*, 449; *Tex.*, 515.

—Laws may be passed to preserve the purity of elections, and guard against abuses of the elective franchise. *Mich.*, 308.

—Elections for Senators and Representatives shall be general throughout the State, and shall be regulated by law. *Tex.*, 509.

—The manner of calling and conducting the meetings for the choice of Representatives, and of ascertaining their election, shall be prescribed by law. *Mass.*, 299.

—Elections to be held in one day. *La.*, 225; *Miss.*, 344; *Mo.*, 348.

—All elections by the people shall be held between the hours of six o'clock in the morning and seven o'clock in the evening. *Ky.*, 220.

—At each of the elections provided for in this schedule the polls shall be opened between the hours of nine and ten o'clock A. M., and closed at sunset. *Kan.*, 207.

—No special election, State, county or municipal, shall be held on a Monday. *Mo.*, 348.

—It shall be proper and legal for the voters of any county, when it shall be unsafe by reason of the presence of insurgent troops to open a poll or polls at the usual places of holding elections, to open the same in any other part of said county. *Va.*, 545.

—The election for Senators, next after the first apportionment under this Constitution, shall be general throughout the State, and at the same time that the election for Representatives is held, and thereafter, there shall be a biennial election for Senators to fill the places of those whose term of service may have expired. *Ky.*, 211.

—The Legislature shall, by standing laws, direct the time and manner of convening the electors, and of collecting votes, and of certifying to the Governor the officers elected. *Mass.*, 288.

—Elections for the members of the General Assembly shall be held at the several election precincts established by law. *Ia.*, 226.

—The existing laws relative to the manner of notifying, holding and conducting elections, making returns, and canvassing votes, shall be in force, and observed in respect to the elections hereby directed to commence on the first Monday of November, in the year one thousand eight hundred and twenty-two, so far as the same are applicable. And the present Legislature shall pass such other and further laws as may be requisite for the execution of the provisions of this Constitution in respect to elections. *N. Y.*, (1821), 44.

[The General Assembly may change the day of election]. *Ga.*, 143.

—The General Assembly, as occasion may require, shall cause every city or town, the white population of which exceeds five thousand, to be laid off into convenient wards, and a separate place of voting to be established in each; and thereafter no inhabitant of such city or town shall be allowed to vote except in the ward in which he resides. *Va.*, 534, 541.

—All elections by the people shall be held at such times and places in the several counties, cities, or towns, as are now, or may hereafter be designated by law. *Tex.*, 507.

—The names of the persons voted for as Governor, Lieutenant-Governor, Secretary of State, Attorney-General, and General Treasurer, shall be placed upon one ticket, and all votes for these officers shall in open town or ward meeting, be sealed up by the moderators and town clerks, and by the wardens and ward clerks, who shall certify the same, and deliver or send the same to the Secretary of State, whose duty it shall be securely to keep and deliver the same to the grand committee after the organization of the two Houses, at the annual May session; and it shall be the duty of the two Houses at said session, after their organization, upon the request of either House, to join in grand committee for the purpose of counting and declaring such votes, and of electing other officers. *R. I.*, 478.

—At said election the polls shall be opened, the election held, returns made, and certificates issued in all respects as provided by law for opening, closing and conducting elections and making returns of the same, except as hereinbefore specified, and excepting also that polls may be opened and elections held at any point or points, in any of the counties where precincts may be established as provided by law, ten days previous to the day of election, and not less than ten miles from the place of voting in any established precinct. *Min.*, 332.

—In all elections held by the people, under this Constitution, a majority of all the electors voting shall be necessary to the election of the person voted for. *R. I.*, 479; *Or.*, 449; *Vt.*, 528.

—In all elections of civil officers by the people of this Commonwealth, whose election is provided for by the Constitution, the person having the highest number of votes shall be deemed and declared to be elected. *Mass.*, 297.

—The return of every election for Governor and Lieutenant-Governor shall be sealed up and transmitted to the seat of government of the State, directed to the Speaker of the House of Representatives, who shall open and publish them in the presence of both Houses of the General Assembly. *Iowa*, 187.

—The said judges of election, before entering upon the duties of their office, shall take and subscribe an oath faithfully to discharge their duties as such. They shall appoint two clerks of election, who shall be sworn by one of said judges faithfully to discharge their duties as such. In the event of a vacancy in the board of judges, the same shall be filled by the electors present. *Kan.*, 207.

—No vote in any election by the people shall be cast up for, nor shall any certificate of election be granted to any person, who shall not, within fifteen days next preceding such election, have taken, subscribed and filed said oath [of allegiance]. *Mo.*, 350.

—It shall be the duty of the judges and clerks of election, in addition to the returns required by law for each precinct, to forward to the Secretary of the Territory by mail, immediately after the close of the election, a certified copy of the poll-book, containing the name of each person who has voted in the precinct, and the number of votes polled for and against the adoption of this Constitution. *Min.*, 332.

—The returns of election for Senators and members of Assembly shall be transmitted to the Clerk of the Board of Supervisors, or County Commissioners, as the case may be, and the votes shall be canvassed, and certificates of election issued, as now provided by law. *Wis.*, 572.

—The returns of every election for the officers named in the foregoing section, shall be made to the Secretary of State, and by him transmitted to the Speaker of the House of Representatives, who shall cause the same to be opened and canvassed before both Houses of the Legislature, and the result declared within three days after each House shall be organized. *Min.*, 323.

—The Treasurer, Secretary and Comptroller, for the time being, shall canvass the votes publicly. The twelve persons having the greatest number of votes for Senators shall be declared to be elected. But in cases where no choice is made by the electors in consequence of an equality of votes, the House of Representatives shall designate, by ballot, which of the candidates having such equal number of votes shall be declared to be elected. The return of votes and the result of the canvass shall be submitted to the House of Representatives, and also to the Senate, on the first day of the session of the General Assembly; and each House shall be the final judge of the election returns and qualifications of its own members. *Ct.*, 100.

—Until otherwise provided by law, elections for judges and clerks shall be held, and the poll-books returned, as is provided for Governor, and the abstract therefrom certified to the Secretary of State, shall be by him opened, in the presence of the Governor, who shall declare the result, and issue commissions to the persons elected. *Ohio*, 445.

—The returns of all elections of Governor, Lieutenant-Governor, and other State officers shall be made to the Secretary of State in such manner as may be prescribed by law. *Miss.*, 343; *Mo.* 356.

--Returns of elections for all civil officers elected by the people who are to be commissioned by the Governor, and also for members of the General Assembly, shall be made to the Secretary of State. *Ala.*, 82.

—Contested elections for Governor shall be determined by the Legislative Assembly in such manner as may be prescribed by law. *Or.*, 452.

—Contested elections for Governor and Lieutenant-Governor shall be determined by both Houses of the General Assembly, according to such regulations as may be established by law. *Ky.*, 214.

—The returns of the votes for Governor at the said next ensuing election, shall be transmitted to the Secretary of State, the votes counted, and the election declared, in the manner now provided by law in the case of the election of Electors of President and Vice-President. *N. J.*, 421.

--The Speaker of the House of Delegates shall then open the said returns in the presence of both Houses, and the person having the highest number of votes and being constitutionally eligible, shall be the Governor, and shall qualify in the manner herein prescribed, on the second Wednesday of January next ensuing his election, or as soon thereafter as may be practicable. *Md.*, 258.

—The returns of every election for the officers named in the foregoing section, shall be sealed up and transmitted to the seat of Government by the returning officers, directed to the President of the Senate, who during the first week of the session, shall open and publish them, and declare the result in the presence of a majority of the members of each House of the Legislature. *Neb.*, 373.

—If no person shall have a majority of votes for Governor, it shall be the duty of the grand committee to elect one by ballot from the two persons having the highest number of votes for the office, except when such a result is produced by rejecting the entire vote of any town, city or ward, for informality or illegality, in which case a new election of the electors throughout the State shall be ordered; and in case no person shall have a majority of votes for Lieutenant-Governor, it shall be the duty of the grand committee to elect one by ballot from the two persons having the highest number of votes for the office. *R. I.*, 478.

—The General Assembly shall, at its first session after the adoption of this Constitution, provide by law for the mode of voting by ballot, and also for the manner of returning, canvassing and certifying the number of votes cast at any election; and until said law shall be passed all elections shall be *viva voce*, and the laws now in force regulating elections shall continue in force until the General Assembly shall provide otherwise, as herein directed. *Ill.*, 168.

—And the Governor shall exclude from the count the votes of any county or city the return judges of which shall fail to certify in the returns, as prescribed by this schedule, that all persons who have taken the oath prescribed to be taken, unless the Governor shall be satisfied that such oath was actually administered, and that the failure to make the certificate has been from inadvertence or mistake. *Md.*, 278.

—The returns of every election for Governor shall be sealed up and transmitted to the Speaker of the House of Representatives, who shall, during the first week of the session, open and publish them in the presence of both houses of the General Assembly. The person having the highest number of votes shall be Governor; but if two or more shall be equal and highest in votes, one of them shall be chosen Governor by the joint vote of both houses of the General Assembly, in such manner as shall be prescribed by law. *Ark.*, 88; (nearly similar) *Cal.*, 100; *S. C.*, 485.

—The ballots for Senators and Representatives in the several towns, shall, in each case after the polls are declared to be closed, be counted by the moderator, who shall announce the result, and the clerk shall give certificates to the persons elected. If, in any case there be no election, the polls may be re-opened, and the like proceedings shall be had until an election shall take place; *Provided, however,* that an adjournment or adjournments of the election may be made at a time not exceeding seven days from the first meeting. *R. I.*, 478.

—The vote for Governor, Lieutenant-Governor and Treasurer of the State shall be sorted and counted, and the result declared by a committee appointed by the Senate and House of Representatives. If at any time there shall be no election by the freemen, of Governor, Lieutenant-Governor and Treasurer of the State, the Senate and House of Representatives shall by a joint ballot, elect to fill the office not filled by the freemen, as aforesaid, one of the three candidates for such office (if there be so many), for whom the greatest number of votes shall have been returned. *Vt.*, 529.

—The General Assembly shall make provision for all cases of contested elections, of any of the officers not herein provided for. *Md.*, 264; (nearly similar), *Ohio*, 434.

—Contested elections of Judges of the Supreme Court shall be tried by the Senate, and of Judges of the Circuit Court, by the Supreme Court, and the General Assembly shall prescribe the manner of proceeding therein. *Ill.*, 169.

—The General Assembly shall provide by law for the trial of any contested election of Auditor, Register, Treasurer, Attorney-General, Judges of Circuit Courts, and all other officers not otherwise herein specified, *Ky.*, 221.

—Returns of all elections by the people shall be made to the Secretary of State, for the time being, except in those cases otherwise provided for in this Constitution, or which shall be otherwise directed by law. *Ky.*, 220; (nearly similar), *Ark.*, 93.

—Returns of elections for members of Congress and the General Assembly shall be made to the Secretary of State, in manner to be prescribed by law. *Fl.*, 136; *La.*, 229; *Mo.*, 357.

—Until otherwise provided by law, an abstract of the returns of every election, for the officers named in the foregoing section, shall be sealed up and transmitted by the clerks of the boards of canvassers of the several counties to the Secretary of State, who, with the Lieutenant-Governor and Attorney-General, shall constitute a board of State Canvassers, whose duty it shall be to meet at the State Capital on the second Tuesday of December succeeding each election for State officers and canvass the vote for such officers and proclaim the result; but in case any two or more have an equal and the highest number of votes, the Legislature shall, by joint ballot, choose one of said persons so having an equal and the highest number of votes for said office. *Kan.*, 198.

—The town and ward clerks shall also keep a correct list or register of all persons voting for general officers, and shall transmit a copy thereof to the General Assembly, on or before the first day of said May session. *R. I.*, 478.

—That returns of the election of Justices of the Supreme and Judges of the Circuit Courts, Secretary of State, Auditor, and Treasurer, shall be made and canvassed, as is now provided by law for Representatives in Congress; and returns for members of the General Assembly and county officers shall be made and canvassed as is now provided by law. *Ill.*, 168.

—In case two or more persons have an equal and the highest number of votes for any office, as canvassed by the Board of State Canvassers, the Legislature, in joint convention, shall choose one of said persons to fill such office. When the determination of the Board of State Canvassers is contested, the Legislature, in joint convention, shall decide which person is elected. *Mich.*, 308.

—The Legislature shall prescribe by law the manner in which evidence in cases of contested seats in either House shall be taken. *Min.*, 322.

—In case of a contested election, the person only shall receive from the State per diem compensation and mileage, who is declared to be entitled to a seat by the House in which the contest takes place. *Mich.*, 303.

—The Legislature shall, by law, direct the manner of notifying the electors, conducting the elections, and making the returns to the Governor of the officers elected; and if the electors shall neglect or refuse to make such elections, after being duly notified according to law, the Governor shall appoint suitable persons to fill such offices. *Me.*, 240.

—It shall not be necessary for the town or ward clerks to keep and transmit to the General Assembly a list or register of all persons voting for general officers; but the General Assembly shall have power to pass such laws on the subject as they may deem expedient. *R. I.*, 481.

—The General Assembly shall direct, by law, the mode and manner of conducting and making due returns to the Secretary of State, of all elections of the Judges and Clerk or Clerks of the Court of Appeals, and of determining contested elections of any of these officers. *Ky.*, 210.

—If two or more persons shall have the highest and an equal number of votes, one of them shall be chosen Governor by the Senate and House of Delegates; and all questions in relation to the eligibility of Governor, and to the returns of said election, and to the number and legality of votes therein given, shall be determined by the House of Delegates; and if the person or persons having the highest number of votes be ineligible, the Governor shall be chosen by the Senate and House of Delegates. Every election of Governor by the General Assembly shall be determined by a joint majority of the Senate and House of Delegates, and the vote shall be taken *viva voce*. But if two or more persons shall have the highest and an equal number of votes, then a second vote shall be taken, which shall be confined to the persons having an equal number; and if the votes should be again equal, then the election of Governor shall be determined by lot between those who shall have the highest and an equal number on the first vote. *Md.*, 259.

—The manner of conducting and making returns of elections, of determining contested elections, and of filling vacancies in office, in cases not specially provided for by this Constitution, shall be prescribed by law; but special elections to fill vacancies in the office of judge of any court shall be for a full term. And the General Assembly may declare the cases in which any office shall be deemed vacant, where no provision is made for that purpose in this Constitution. *Va.*, 539.

—The person having the highest number of votes for Governor shall be elected; but in case two or more persons shall have an equal and the highest number of votes for Governor, the two Houses of the Legislative Assembly, at the next regular session thereof, shall forthwith, by joint vote, proceed to elect one of the said persons Governor. *Or.*, 452.

—Should there be no session of the General Assembly in January next after an election for any of the officers aforesaid, the returns of such election shall be made to the Secretary of State, and opened, and the result declared by the Governor, in such manner as may be provided by law. *Ohio*, 435; *Neb.*, 371.

—The General Assembly shall provide by law for the making of the returns by the proper officers, of the election of all officers to be elected under this Constitution. *Ky.*, 221.

[Detailed provisions made for returning and canvassing elections.] *Ct*, 108, 114, 115; *Mass.*, 284, 286; *Me.*, 242, 244, 252; *N. II.*, 404; *R. I.*, 474; *Vt.*, 528, 530.

RESTRICTIONS UPON THE HOLDING OF OFFICE.

—That no person in the State shall hold more than one lucrative office at any one time; *Provided*, That no appointment in the militia, or of the office of a Justice of the Peace, shall be considered as a lucrative office. *N. C.*, 426.

—No member of Congress, or person holding any office under the United States, or minister of any religious society, shall be eligible to the office of Governor. *Ky.*, 213.

—No member of Congress, nor person holding or exercising any office of profit or trust under the United States, or either of them, or under any foreign power, shall be eligible as a member of the Legislature, or hold or exercise any office of profit or trust under this State. *Tex.*, 516.

—No member of Congress, nor any person holding any office of profit or trust under the United States (postmasters excepted) or under any foreign power; no person convicted of any infamous crime in any court within the United States, and no person being a defaulter to the United States, or to this State, or to any county or town therein, or to any State or Territory within the United States, shall be eligible to any office of trust, profit or honor in this State. *Wis.*, 570.

—No member of Congress, nor person holding any office under the United States (post officers excepted), nor office of profit under this State, Justices of the Peace, Notaries Public, Coroners, and officers of the militia, excepted, shall have a seat in either House during his being such member of Congress, or his continuing in such office. *Me.*, 214.

—No member of Congress or officer of the United States shall be eligible to a seat in the Legislature. If any person, after his election to the Legislature, be elected to Congress, or elected or appointed to any office under the United States, his acceptance thereof shall vacate his seat. *Kan.*, 199.

—No member of Congress, nor any person holding any office of profit or trust under the United States (the office of Postmaster excepted), or any other State of the Union, or under any foreign power, shall hold or exercise any office of trust or profit under this State. *Miss.*, 343.

—No member of Congress or person holding any civil or military office under the United States shall be eligible as a Senator or Delegate; and if any person shall, after his election as a Senator or Delegate, be elected to Congress, or be appointed to any office, civil or military, under the government of the United States, his acceptance thereof shall vacate his seat. *Md.*, 261.

—No member of Congress or person holding an office under the United States, or this State, shall exercise the office of Governor; and in case the Governor, or person administering the government, shall accept of any office under the United States or this State, his office of Governor shall thereupon be vacant. *N. Y.*, 416.

—No member of Congress, or person holding any lucrative office under the United States or this State (militia officers, Justices of the Peace, and Notaries Public excepted), shall be eligible to either House of the General Assembly, or shall remain a member thereof after having accepted any such office, or a seat in either House of Congress. *Mo.*, 353.

—No member of Congress, or of the Legislature of this State, nor any person holding any office under the United States (post offices excepted), nor any civil officers under this State (Justices of the Peace and Notaries Public excepted), shall be Counsellors. And no Counsellor shall be appointed to any office during the time for which he shall have been elected. *Me.*, 245.

—No member of Congress or person holding or exercising any office of profit under the United States, or under any foreign power, shall be eligible as a member of the General Assembly of this State, or hold or exercise any office of profit under the State; and no person in this State shall ever hold two offices of profit at the same time, except the office of Justice of the Peace, Notary Public, Constable, and Militia offices, except by special act of the Legislature; but the Legislature shall never unite in the same person two offices, the duties of which are incompatible. *Fla.*, 136.

—No person holding any office or place under the United States, this State, or any other power, shall exercise the office of Governor. *Me.*, 244.

—No person holding any military commission, or other appointment, having any emolument or compensation annexed thereto, under this State or the United States, or either of them (except Justices of the Inferior Court, Justices of the Peace, and officers of the militia), nor any defaulter for public money, or for any legal taxes required of him, shall have a seat in either branch of the General Assembly, nor shall any Senator or Representative, after his qualification as such, be elected by the General Assembly, be appointed by the Governor, with the advice and consent of two-thirds of the Senate, to any office having any emolument or compensation annexed thereto, during the time for which he shall have been elected. *Ga.*, 143.

—No person holding a lucrative office or appointment under the United States, or under this State, shall be eligible to a seat in the General Assembly; nor shall any person hold more than one lucrative office at the same time, except as in this Constitution expressly permitted. *Provided,* That officers in the militia, to which there is attached no annual salary, and the office of deputy postmaster, where the compensation does not exceed ninety dollars per annum shall not be deemed lucrative; *And provided, also,* That counties containing less than one thousand polls may confer the office of Clerk, Recorder and Auditor, or any two of said offices, upon the same person. *Ind.*, 171.

—No person holding any office under the government of the United States, or of any other State or country, shall act as a general officer or as a member of the General Assembly, unless at the time of taking his engagement he shall have resigned his office under such government; and if any general officer, Senator, Representative, or Judge, shall, after his election and engagement, accept any appointment under any other government, his office under this shall be immediately vacated; but this restriction shall not apply to any person appointed to take depositions or acknowledgments of deeds, or other legal instruments, by the authority of any other State or country. *R. I.*, 479.

—That no officer in the regular army or navy, in the service and pay of the United States, of this State, or any other State, nor any contractor or agent for supplying such army or navy with clothing or provisions, shall have a seat either in the Senate, House of Commons, or Council of State, or be eligible thereto; and any member of the Senate, House of Commons, or Council of State, being appointed to, and accepting of such office, shall thereby vacate his seat. *N. C.*, 425.

—No Governor or Judge of the Supreme Judicial Court shall hold any office or place under the authority of this State, except such as by this Constitution they are admitted to hold, saving that the judges of said court may hold the offices of Justices of the Peace throughout the State; nor shall they hold any place or office, or receive any pension or salary from any other State, government or power whatever. *N. H.*, 410.

—No person holding any lucrative office under the United States, or any other power, shall be eligible to any civil office of profit under this State; provided, that officers in the militia, to which there is attached no annual salary, or local officers and postmasters whose compensation does not exceed five hundred dollars per annum, shall not be deemed lucrative. *Cal.*, 99.

—No person in this State shall be capable of holding or exercising more than one of the following offices at the same time, viz.: Governor, Lieutenant-Governor, Judge of the Supreme Court, Treasurer of the State, member of the Council, member of the General Assembly, Surveyor-General or Sheriff. Nor shall any person, holding any office of profit or trust under the authority of Congress, be eligible to any appointment in the Legislature, or of holding an executive or judiciary office under this State. *Vt.*, 525.

—No person shall be capable of exercising at the same time more than one of the following offices in this State, viz.: Judge of Probate, Sheriff, Register of Deeds, and never more than two offices of profit, which may be held by appointment of the Governor, or Governor and Council, or Senate and House of Representatives, or superior or inferior courts: military offices and offices of Justices of the Peace excepted. *N. H.*, 410.

—No Judge of any court of law or equity, Secretary of State, Attorney-General, Attorney for the State, Recorder, Clerk of any Court of Record, Sheriff or Collector, member of either House of Congress, or person holding any lucrative office under the United States or of this State; *Provided,* That appointments in the militia, or Justices of the Peace, shall not be considered lucrative offices; shall have a seat in the General Assembly; nor shall any person, holding any office of honor or profit under the government of the United States, hold any office of honor or profit under the authority of this State. *Ill.*, 153.

—No person holding any lucrative office under the government of the United States, or any other power, shall be eligible to any civil office of profit under this State; *Provided,* That Postmasters, whose compensation does not exceed five hundred dollars per annum, or Commissioners of Deeds, shall not be deemed as holding a lucrative office. *Nev.*, 382.

—No person being a member of Congress, or holding any military or civil office under the United States, shall be eligible to a seat in the Legislature; and if any person shall, after his election as a member of the Legislature, be elected to Congress, or be appointed to any office, civil or military, under the government of the United States, his acceptance thereof shall vacate his seat. *Neb.*, 372.

—No person holding any lucrative office under the United States or this State, or any other power, shall be eligible to hold a seat in the General Assembly; but offices in the militia, to which there is no annual salary, or the office of Justice of the Peace, or Postmaster, whose compensation does not exceed one hundred dollars per annum, or Notary Public, shall not be deemed lucrative. *Iowa*, 186.

—No person convicted of embezzlement or misuse of the public funds shall have a seat in the Legislature. *Kan.*, 109.

—No person who may hereafter be a collector or holder of public moneys shall have a seat in either House of the General Assembly, or be eligible to any office of trust or profit under this State, until he shall have accounted for and paid into the Treasury all sums for which he may be accountable. *Fl.*, 136; *Iowa*, 186; *Mo.*, 359; *N. C.*, 425; *Ohio*, 433; *Tenn.*, 494; *Tex.*, 509; *W. Va.*, 550.

—No member of Congress, nor any person holding or exercising any office under the United States, shall at the same time hold or exercise the office of Judge, Treasurer, Attorney-General, Secretary, Prothonotary, Register for the probate of wills and granting letters of administration, Recorder, Sheriff, or any office under this State, with a salary by law annexed to it, or any other office which the Legislature shall declare incompatible with offices or appointments under the United States. No person shall hold more than one of the following offices at the same time, to wit: Treasurer, Attorney-General, Prothonotary, Register or Sheriff. *Del.*, 119.

—No person shall hold or exercise at the same time more than one civil office of emolument, except that of Justice of the Peace. *Tex.*, 516.

—No person shall be elected or appointed to any office in this State, unless he possess the qualifications of an elector. *Ohio*, 443.

—No person except a citizen of the United States and a qualified elector of the State shall be eligible to any office provided for by this Constitution. *Neb.*, 373.

—No person holding the office of judge of any court except special Judges, Secretary, Treasurer of the State, Attorney-General, Commissary-General, military officers receiving pay from the continent or this State, excepting officers of the militia, occasionally

1 § 5. All elections by the citizens shall be by ballot, except for such town

2 officers as may by law be directed to be otherwise chosen.(¹)

called forth on an emergency, Register of Deeds, Sheriff, or officers of the customs, including naval officers, collectors of excise and State and continental taxes, hereafter appointed, and not having settled their accounts with the respective officers with whom it is their duty to settle such accounts, members of Congress, or any person holding any office under the United States, shall at the same time hold the office of Governor, or have a seat in the Senate, or House of Representatives, or Council; but his being chosen and appointed to and accepting the same, shall operate as a resignation of their seat in the chair, Senate or House of Representatives, or Council, and the place so vacated shall be filled up. No member of the Council shall have a seat in the Senate or House of Representatives. *N. H.*, 410.

—But no person shall be appointed to an office within a county, who shall not have a right to vote for Representatives, and have been an inhabitant therein one year next before his appointment, nor hold the office longer than he continues to reside in the county. *Del.*, 119.

—No person who shall be convicted of the embezzlement or defalcation of the public funds of this State, shall ever be eligible to any office of honor, trust, or profit under this State; and the Legislature shall, as soon as practicable, pass a law providing for the punishment of such embezzlement or defalcation as a felony. *Cal.*, 90.

—No person shall be appointed to any office within any county who shall not have been a citizen and an inhabitant therein one year next before his appointment, if the county shall have been so long erected; but if it shall not have been so long erected, then within the limits of the county or counties out of which it shall have been taken. No member of Congress from this State, or any person holding or exercising any office or appointment of trust or profit under the United States, shall at the same time hold or exercise any office in this State, to which a salary is, or fees or perquisites are, by law, annexed; and the Legislature may by law declare what State offices are incompatible. No member of the Senate or of the House of Representatives shall be appointed by the Governor to any office during the term for which he shall have been elected. *Pa.*, 466.

—Every elector shall be eligible to any office in this State, except in cases provided for in this Constitution. *Ct.*, 112; (nearly similar), *Ga.*, 149; *Neb.*, 371; *Min.*, 326; [none but voters eligible to office]; *Del.*, 119; *W. Va.*, 548; *Min.*, 326.

(1). *N. Y.*, (1821) 37; *Ala.*, 82; *Mich.*, 308; *Min.*, 326; (unless otherwise ordered) *Ga.*, 150; *Tex.* 515.

ELECTIONS BY BALLOT AND VIVA VOCE.

[All elections by the people to be by ballot]. *Cal.*, 97; *Ct.*, 112; *Del.*, 120; *Fla.*, 136; *Ill.*, 102; *Iowa*, 184; *Kan.*, 201; *La.*, 233; *Md.*, 258; *Mo.*, 348; *Miss.*, 336; *Nev.*, 380; *Pa.*, 464; *Tenn.*, 495; *Va.*, 534; *Vt.*, 527; *W. Va.*, 548.

[Elections to be by written ballot]. *Me.*, 240.

[The experiment of voting by ballot to be tried]. *N. Y.*, (1777) 27.

[Elections to office in Legislature to be viva voce]. *Ala.*, 76; *Cal.*, 100; *Fla.*, 136; *Iowa*, 187; *Kan.*, 201; *La.*, 233; *Me.*, 240; *Md.*, 258; *Mich.*, 302; *Min.*, 323; *Mo.*, 348; *Neb.*, 373; *Nev.*, 380; *N. C.*, 428; *Ohio*, 435; *Or.*, 449; *Pa.*, 464; *S. C.*, 484; *Tenn.*, 495; *Tex.*, 515; *Wis.*, 563. (In most of these States the vote is required to be entered on the journals.)

—In all elections, votes shall be given openly or

viva voce, and not by ballot; but dumb persons, entitled to suffrage, may vote by ballot. *Va.*, 595; (amendment).

—All general elections shall be *viva voce* until otherwise directed by law, and commence and be holden every two years, on the first Monday in August, until altered by law, (except that) the first election under this Constitution shall be held on the second Monday in March, 1864, and the electors in all cases except in cases of treason, felony and breach of the peace, shall be privileged from arrest during their attendance on elections and in going to and returning therefrom. *Ark.*, 86.

—In all elections by the people, and by the Senate and House of Representatives, jointly or separately, the votes shall be personally and publicly given, *viva voce; Provided*, That dumb persons, entitled to suffrage, may vote by ballot. *Ky.*, 220.

—Whenever an officer, civil or military, shall be appointed by the joint or concurrent vote of both Houses, or by the separate vote of either House of the General Assembly, the vote shall be taken *viva voce*, and entered upon the journal. *Ark.*, 86; (nearly similar), *Ala.*, 76; *Cal.*, 100; *Iowa*, 187; *Min.*, 323; *Mo.*, 354; *Neb.*, 373; *S. C.*, 484; *Wis.*, 563.

—The voting for Governor, Lieutenant-Governor, Secretary of State, Attorney-General, General Treasurer, and Representatives to Congress, shall be by ballot; Senators and Representatives to the General Assembly, and town or city officers, shall be chosen by ballot, on demand of any seven persons entitled to vote for the same; and in all cases where an election is made by ballot or paper vote, the manner of balloting shall be the same as is now required in voting for general officers until otherwise prescribed by law. *R. I.*, 478.

—All elections by the General Assembly shall be *viva voce* and the vote shall always appear on the journal of the House of Representatives, and where the Senate and the House of Representatives unite for the purpose of electing, they shall meet in the Representative Chamber, and the President of the Senate shall in such cases preside and declare the person or persons elected. *Ga.*, 179.

ELECTION OF GOVERNOR — CONTESTED ELECTIONS.

—Statedly, once in every three years, and as often as the seat of government shall become vacant, a wise and discreet freeholder of this State, shall be, by ballot, elected governor, by the freeholders of this State, qualified, as before described, to elect Senators; which elections shall be always held at the times and places of choosing representatives in Assembly for each respective county; and that the person who hath the greatest number of votes within the said State shall be governor thereof. *N. Y.* (1777), 28.

—The Governor and Lieutenant-Governor shall be elected at the times and places of choosing members of the Legislature. The persons respectively having the highest number of votes for Governor and Lieutenant-Governor, shall be elected; but in case two or more shall have an equal and the highest number of votes for Governor, or for Lieutenant-Governor, the two houses of the Legislature shall, by joint ballot, choose one of the said persons so having an equal and the highest number of votes, for Governor, or Lieutenant-Governor. *N. Y.* (1821), 38.

—Every person qualified to vote for delegates shall be qualified and entitled to vote for Governor; the election to be held in the same manner as the election of delegates, and the returns thereof, under seal, to be addressed to the Speaker of the House of Delegates, and inclosed and transmitted to the Secretary of State, and delivered to the said Speaker at the commencement of the session of the General Assembly next ensuing said election. *Md.*, 258.

—The returns for every election for Governor shall be sealed up, and transmitted to the seat of government, directed to the Speaker of the House of Representatives, who shall, during the first week of the session, open and publish them in the presence of both Houses of the General Assembly. The person having the highest number of votes, shall be Governor; but if two or more shall be equal and highest in votes, one of them shall be chosen Governor by the joint vote of both Houses. Contested elections for Governor shall be determined by both Houses of the General Assembly, in such manner as shall be prescribed by law. *Ala.*, 78; (nearly similar) *Fl.*, 130; *Ill.*, 157; *Ind.*, 174; *Or.*, 452; *Tex.*, 512.

[Returns to be made to presiding officer of the Senate, and published as above.] *N. C.*, 424; *Ohio*, 435; *Pa.*, 463; *Tenn.*, 494.

—Returns of the election of Governor shall be made, in the manner and by the persons designated by the Legislature, to the Secretary of the State, who shall deliver them to the Speaker of the House of Delegates on the first day of the next session of the Legislature The Speaker shall, within ten days thereafter, in the presence of a majority of each branch of the Legislature, open the said returns, when the votes shall be counted. The person having the highest number of votes, if duly qualified, shall be declared elected; but if two or more have the highest and an equal number of votes, one of them shall thereupon be chosen Governor by the joint vote of the two branches. Contested elections for Governor shall be decided by a like vote, and the mode of proceeding in such cases shall be prescribed by law. *W. Va.*, 552.

—The qualified electors for Representatives shall vote for Governor and Lieutenant-Governor at the time and place of voting for Representatives; the returns of every election shall be sealed up and transmitted by the proper returning officer to the Secretary of State, who shall deliver them to the Speaker of the House of Representatives on the second day of the session of the General Assembly then to be holden. The Members of the General Assembly shall meet in the House of Representatives to examine and count the votes. The person having the greatest number of votes for Governor shall be declared duly elected; but if two or more persons shall be equal and the highest in the number of votes polled for Governor, one of them shall be immediately chosen Governor by joint vote of the members of the General Assembly. The person having the greatest number of votes polled for Lieutenant-Governor shall be Lieutenant-Governor; but if two or more persons shall be equal and highest in the number of votes polled for Lieutenant-Governor, one of them shall be immediately chosen Lieutenant-Governor by joint vote of the members of the General Assembly. *La.*, 229.

[Returns to be directed to the President of the Senate and Speaker of the House, and transmitted to the Governor, who shall lay the same, without opening, before the Senate on the next day after the organization. The Senate to transmit them to the House, and they are to be published at a joint meeting. Contested elections to be decided as above.] *Ga.*, 146.

—Votes shall deliver, or cause them to be delivered, to the Secretary, within fifteen days after next said election. The votes so returned shall be counted by the Treasurer, Secretary and Comptroller, within the month of April. A fair list of the persons, and number of votes given for each, together with the returns of the presiding officers, shall be, by the Treasurer, Secretary and Comptroller, made and laid before the General Assembly, then next to be holden, on the first day of the session thereof; and said Assembly shall, after examination of the same, declare the person whom they shall find to be legally chosen, and give him notice accordingly. If no person shall have a majority of the whole number of said votes, or if two or more shall have an equal and the greatest number of said votes, then said Assembly, on the

second day of their session, by joint ballot of both Houses, shall proceed, without debate, to choose a Governor from a list of the names of the two persons having the greatest number of votes, or of the names of the persons having an equal and highest number of votes so returned as aforesaid. The General Assembly shall by law prescribe the manner in which all questions concerning the election of a Governor or Lieutenant-Governor shall be determined. *Ct.*, 109.

—The Governor shall be chosen annually in the month of March; the votes for Governor shall be received, sorted, counted, certified and returned, in the same manner as the votes for Senators; and the Secretary shall lay the same before the Senate and House of Representatives, on the first Wednesday of June, to be by them examined; and in case of an election by a majority of votes through the State, the choice shall be by them declared and published. *N. H.*, 405.

—The Governor and Lieutenant-Governor shall be elected by the qualified electors of the State, at the times and places of choosing members of the Legislature. The persons respectively having the highest number of votes for Governor and Lieutenant-Governor shall be elected. But in case two or more shall have an equal and the highest number of votes for Governor or Lieutenant-Governor, the two Houses of the Legislature, at its next annual session, shall forthwith, by joint ballot, choose one of the persons so having an equal and the highest number of votes for Governor and Lieutenant-Governor. The returns of election for Governor and Lieutenant-Governor shall be made in such manner as shall be provided by law. *Wis.*, 564.

—The returns of every election for Governor and other State officers voted for at the general election, shall be sealed up and transmitted to the seat of government, directed to the Secretary of State, and on the third Monday of December succeeding such election, the Chief Justice of the Supreme Court and the Associate Justices, or a majority thereof, shall meet at the office of the Secretary of State, and open and canvass the election returns for Governor and all other State officers, and forthwith declare the result and publish the names of the persons elected. The persons having the highest number of votes for the respective offices, shall be declared elected; but in case any two or more have an equal, and the highest number of votes for the same office, the Legislature shall, by joint vote of both Houses, elect one of said persons to fill said office. *Nev.*, 384.

—In case two or more persons shall have an equal and the highest number of votes for Governor or Lieutenant-Governor, the Legislature shall, by joint vote, choose one of such persons. *Mich.*, 304; (nearly similar), *Mo.*, 355; *Iowa*, 188; *N. J.*, 416; *Ind.*, 174; *Mo.*, 356.

—Contested elections for Governor shall be determined by both Houses of the General Assembly, in such manner as shall be prescribed by law. *N. C.*, 429; *Iowa*, 188; *Ind.*, 174.

—The person having the highest number of votes shall be Governor; but if two or more shall be equal and highest in votes, the election shall be determined by lot, in such manner as the General Assembly may direct. *Ky.*, 213.

—Contested elections of a Governor shall be determined by a joint committee, consisting of one-third of all the members of each branch of the Legislature, to be selected by ballot of the House, respectively; every person of the committee shall take an oath or affirmation that, in determining the said election, he will faithfully discharge the trust reposed in him; and the committee shall always sit with open doors. *Del.*, 119.

—The Governor shall be chosen by the qualified voters for the members of the House of Commons, at such time and place as members of the General Assembly are elected. *N. C.*, 429; *Cal.*, 100; *Ark.*, 88; *Ala.*, 781; *Ind.*, 174; *Tex.*, 512.

—And that there may be no delay in the organization of the government on the first Wednesday of

ARTICLE III.

1   SECTION 1. The legislative power of this State shall be vested in a Senate

2 and Assembly.

January, the Governor, with at least five Councillors for the time being, shall, as soon as may be, examine the returned copies of the records for the election of Governor, Lieutenant-Governor and Councillors; and ten days before the said first Wednesday in January he shall issue his summons to such persons as appear to be chosen, to attend on that day to be qualified accordingly; and the Secretary shall lay the returns before the Senate and the House of Representatives on the said first Wednesday in January, to be by them examined; and in case of the election of either of said officers, the choice shall be by them declared and published: but in case there shall be no election of either of said officers, the Legislature shall proceed to fill such vacancies in the manner provided in the Constitution for the choice of such officers. *Mass.*, 297.

—And the Senate and House of Representatives may try and determine all cases where their rights and privileges are concerned, and which, by the Constitution, they have authority to try and determine, by committees of their own members, or in such other way as they may, respectively, think best. *Mass.*, 286.

—A contested election shall be determined in such manner as shall be directed by law. *Fla.*, 132; *Iowa*, 185; *Miss.*, 337.

DISTRIBUTION OF THE POWERS OF GOVERNMENT.

—The powers of the government shall be divided into three distinct departments — the Legislative, Executive and Judicial; and no person or persons belonging to, or constituting one of these departments, shall exercise any of the powers properly belonging to either of the others, except as herein expressly provided. *N. J.*, 413; (nearly similar), *Ala.*, 74; *Ark.*, 85; *Cal.*, 97; *Ct.*, 108; *Fl.*, 130; *Ga.*, 143; *Ill.*, 151; *Ind.*, 172; *Iowa*, 184; *Ky.*, 209; *La.*, 225; *Me.*, 241; *Mich.*, 304; *Min.*, 321; *Miss.*, 336; *Neb.*, 381; *Or.*, 449; *Tenn.*, 492; *Tex.*, 507.

—In the government of this Commonwealth, the legislative department shall never exercise the executive and judicial powers, or either of them; the executive shall never exercise the legislative and judicial powers, or either of them; the judicial shall never exercise the legislative and executive powers, or either of them; to the end it may be a government of laws, and not of men. *Mass.*, 282.

—That the Legislative, Executive and Judicial powers of government ought to be forever separate and distinct from each other, and no person exercising the functions of one of said departments shall assume or discharge the duties of any other. *Md.*, 254.

—That the Legislative, Executive and Supreme Judicial powers of government, ought to be forever separate and distinct from each other. *N. C.*, 421.

—In the government of this State, the three essential powers thereof, to wit, the legislative, executive and judicial, ought to be kept as separate from, and independent of each other, as the nature of a free government will admit, or as is consistent with that chain of connection that binds the whole fabric of the Constitution in one indissoluble bond of union and amity. *N. H.*, 401.

—The powers of the government shall be distributed into three departments: the Legislative, Executive and Judicial. *R. I.*, 475; *Tenn.*, 492.

—The Legislative, Executive and Judiciary departments shall be separate and distinct, so that neither exercise the powers properly belonging to either of the others; nor shall any person exercise the powers of more than one of them at the same time, except

that Justices of the Peace shall be eligible to either House of Assembly. *Va.*, 533.

—The Legislative, Executive and Judiciary department shall be separate and distinct, so that neither exercise the powers properly belonging to the other. *Vt.*, 523.

—That the Legislative, Executive and Judicial powers should be separate and distinct, and that the members thereof may be restrained from oppression, by feeling and participating the burdens of the people, they should, at fixed periods, be reduced to a private station, return into that body from which they were originally taken, and the vacancies be supplied by frequent, certain and regular elections, in which all, or any part of the former members, to be again eligible, or ineligible, as the laws shall direct. *Va.*, 531.

—The Legislative, Executive and Judicial departments of the government shall be separate and distinct. Neither shall exercise the powers properly belonging to either of the others. No person shall be invested with or exercise the powers of more than one of them at the same time. *W. Va.*, 546.

LEGISLATIVE POWER — HOW VESTED.

—The supreme legislative power within this State shall be vested in two separate and distinct bodies of men, the one to be called the Assembly of the State of New York, the other to be called the Senate of the State of New York, who together shall form the Legislature, and meet once at least in every year, for the despatch of business. *N. Y.* (1777), 26.

—The Legislative power of this State shall be vested in a Senate and Assembly. *N. Y.* (1821), 35; *Wis.*, 562.

—The legislative power of this State shall be vested in two distinct branches, the one to be styled the "*Senate*," and the other the "*House of Representatives*," and both together the "*General Assembly.*" *Ala.*, 75; (nearly similar) *Ct.*, 108; *Fl.*, 132; *Ky.*, 209; *La.*, 225; *Miss.*, 336; *Me.*, 241; *R. I.*, 475; *Vt.*, 523, 528.

—The legislative power of this State shall be invested in a General Assembly, which shall consist of a Senate and House of Representatives. *Ark.*, 87; (nearly similar) *Del.*, 117; *Ga.*, 143; *Ill.*, 151; *Ind.*, 172; *Iowa*, 185; *Kan.*, 198; *Mich.*, 301; *Min.*, 321; *Mo.*, 352; *Neb.*, 371; *Or.*, 449; *S. C.*, 482.

—The Legislature shall consist of two distinct branches, a Senate and a House of Delegates, which shall be styled "The General Assembly of Maryland." *Md.*, 200.

—The department of legislation shall be formed by two branches, a Senate and House of Representatives, each of which shall have a negative on the other. *Mass.*, 282; *N. H.*, 401.

—The Legislative power shall be vested in a Senate and General Assembly. *N. J.*, 413.

—That the Legislative authority shall be vested in two distinct branches, both dependent on the people, to wit, a Senate and House of Commons. *N. C.*, 423.

—That the Senate and House of Commons, assembled for the purpose of legislation, shall be denominated the General Assembly. *N. C.*, 423.

—The Legislative power of this State shall be vested in a General Assembly, which shall consist of a Senate and House of Representatives. *Ohio*, 433; (nearly similar), *Pa.*, 461.

—The Legislative authority of this State shall be vested in a General Assembly, which shall consist of a Senate and House of Representatives, both dependent on the people. *Tenn.*, 492.

—The Legislative powers of this State shall be vested in two distinct branches; the one to be styled the

1 § 2. The Senate shall consist of thirty-two members, and the senators shall

2 be chosen for two years. The assembly shall consist of one hundred and

3 twenty-eight members, who shall be annually elected.

Senate and the other the House of Representatives, and both together, the Legislature of the State. *Tex.*, 507.
—The Legislative power of this Commonwealth shall be vested in a General Assembly, which shall consist of a Senate and House of Delegates. *Va.*, 534.
—The Legislative power shall be vested in a Senate and House of Delegates. *W. Va.*, 549.
—The concurrence of the two Houses shall be necessary to the enactment of laws. *R. I.*, 475.
—The Legislative authority of this State shall be vested in a Senate and Assembly, which shall be designated "The Legislature of the State of ———," and the sessions of such Legislature shall be held at the seat of government of the State. *Neb.*, 381; (nearly similar), *Cal.*, 97.

SENATORS—THEIR CLASSIFICATION AND TERMS.

[Under the N. Y. Constitution, of 1777, Senators were elected in four great districts, for a term of four years, and were classed so that one-fourth of the number were elected annually. In 1821, the number of districts was increased to eight, the term and classes being as before]. *p.* 28, 34, 35.
—Senators shall be chosen for the term of four years; yet, at the first general election after each new apportionment, elections shall be held anew in all the senatorial districts; and the Senators elected, when convened at the next ensuing session of the General Assembly, shall be divided by lot into two classes, as nearly equal to each other as may be; the seats of the Senators of the first class shall be vacated at the expiration of two years, and those of the second class at the expiration of four years from the day of election, so that (except as above provided) one-half of the Senators may be chosen biennially. *Ala.*, 75.
—Senators shall be chosen for the term of two years, at the same time and places as members of Assembly; and no person shall be a member of the Senate or Assembly who has not been a citizen and inhabitant of the State one year, and of the county or district for which he shall be chosen six months next before his election. *Cal.*, 98.
—The Senators shall be chosen for [four] years by the citizens residing in the several counties. *Del.*, 117.
—The Senators at their first session herein provided for shall be divided by lot, as near as can be, into two classes. The seats of the first class shall be vacated at the expiration of the second year, and those of the second class at the expiration of the fourth year; so that one-half thereof, as near as possible, may be biennially chosen forever thereafter. *Ill.*, 152.
—Senators shall be elected for the term of four years, and Representatives for the term of two years, from the day next after their general election; *provided, however,* That the Senators elect, at the second meeting of the General Assembly under this Constitution, shall be divided by lot into two equal classes, as nearly as may be; and the seats of Senators of the first class shall be vacated at the expiration of two years, and of those of the second class at the expiration of four years; so that one-half, as nearly as possible, shall be chosen biennially forever thereafter. And in case of increase in the number of Senators, they shall be so annexed by lot to one or the other of the two classes, as to keep them as nearly equal as practicable. *Ind.*, 172; (nearly similar) *Or.*, 450.
—Senators shall be chosen for the term of four years, at the same time and place as Representatives; they shall be twenty-five years of age and possess the qualifications of Representatives as to residence and citizenship. *Iowa*, 185.

—Senators shall be chosen for the term of four years, and the Senate shall have power to choose its officers biennially. *Ky.*, 210.
—At the session of the General Assembly next after the first apportionment under this Constitution, the Senators shall be divided by lot, as equally as may be, into two classes; the seats of the first class shall be vacated at the end of two years from the day of the election, and those of the second class at the end of four years, so that one-half shall be chosen every two years. *Ky.*, 211.
—The members of the Senate shall be chosen for the term of four years. The Senate, when assembled, shall have the power to choose its own officers. *La.*, 227.
—At the first session of the General Assembly, after this Constitution takes effect, the Senators shall be equally divided by lot into two classes; the seats of the Senators of the first class shall be vacated at the expiration of the term of the first House of Representatives; of the second class, at the expiration of the term of the second House of Representatives; so that one-half shall be chosen every two years, and a rotation thereby kept up perpetually. In case any district shall have elected two or more Senators, said Senators shall vacate their seats respectively at the end of the term aforesaid, and lots shall be drawn between them. *La.*, 228.
—The period for which the Governors, Senators and Representatives, Counsellors, Secretary and Treasurer, first elected or appointed, are to serve in their respective offices and places, shall commence on the last Wednesday of May, in the year of our Lord one thousand eight hundred and twenty, and continue until the first Wednesday of January, in the year of our Lord one thousand eight hundred and twenty-two. *Me.*, 249.
—Immediately after the Senate shall have convened, after the first election under this Constitution, the Senators shall be divided by lot into two classes, as nearly equal in number as may be; Senators of the first class shall go out of office at the expiration of two years, and Senators shall be elected on the Tuesday next after the first Monday in the month of November, eighteen hundred and sixty-six, for the term of four years, to supply their places; so that after the first election, one-half of the Senators may be chosen every second year. In case the number of Senators be hereafter increased, such classification of the additional Senators shall be made as to preserve as nearly as may be, an equal number in each class. *Md.*, 201.
—The whole number of Senators shall, at the several periods of making the enumeration before mentioned, be fixed by the Legislature, and apportioned among the several Districts to be established by law, according to the number of free white inhabitants in each, and shall never be less than one-fourth, nor more than one-third of the whole number of Representatives. *Miss.*, 337.
—Such mode of classifying new additional Senators shall be observed as will, as nearly as possible, preserve an equality of members in each class. *Miss.*, 337.
—At the regular session of the General Assembly chosen at said election, the Senators shall be divided into two equal classes. Those elected from districts bearing odd numbers shall compose the first class, and those elected from districts bearing even numbers shall compose the second class. The seats of the first class shall be vacated at the end of the second year after the day of said election, and those of the second class at the end of the fourth year after that day; so that one-half of the Senators shall be chosen every second year. In districting any county for the

election of Senators, the districts shall be numbered, so as to effectuate the division of Senators into classes, as required in this section. *Mo.*, 353.

—The Senators to be elected at the first election under this Constitution shall draw lots, so that the term of one-half of the number, as nearly as m iy be, shall expire on the day succeeding the general election in A. D. eighteen hundred and sixty-six, and the term of the other half shall expire on the day succeeding the election in A. D. eighteen hundred and sixty-eight; *Provided*, That in drawing lots for all Senatorial terms, the Senatorial representation shall be allotted by the Legislature in long and short terms as hereinbefore provided, so that one-half the number, as nearly as may be, shall be elected every two years. *Nev.*, 304.

—The terms of the members of the Assembly elected at the second general election under this Constitution, shall expire on the day succeeding the general election in A. D. eighteen hundred and sixty-five; and the terms of those elected at the general election in A. D., eighteen hundred and sixty-five shall expire on the day succeeding the election in A. D. eighteen hundred and sixty-six. *Nev.*, 304.

—Senators and Representatives shall be elected biennially, by the electors in the respective counties or districts, on the second Tuesday of October; their term of office shall commence on the first day of January next thereafter, and continue two years. *Ohio*, 433.

—And that there may be a due meeting of Senators on the first Wednesday of June, annually, the Governor, and a majority of the Council, for the time being, shall, as soon as may be, examine the return copies of such records, and fourteen days before the first Wednesday of June, he shall issue his summons to such persons as appear to be chosen Senators by a majority of votes, to attend and take their seats on that day; *Provided, nevertheless*, That, for the first year, the said returned copies shall be examined by the President and the majority of the Council then in office; and the said President shall, in like manner, notify the persons elected to attend and take their seats accordingly. *N. H.*, 402.

—The freeholders and other inhabitants of each district, qualified as in this Constitution is provided, shall annually give in their votes for a Senator, at some meeting holden in the month of March. *N. H.*, 403.

—As soon as the Senate shall meet after the first election to be held in pursuance of this Constitution, they shall be divided as equally as may be into three classes. The seats of the Senators of the first class shall be vacated at the expiration of the first year; of the second class, at the expiration of the second year, and of the third class, at the expiration of the third year; so that one class may be elected every year, and if vacancies happen, by resignation or otherwise, the persons elected to supply such vacancies shall be elected for the unexpired terms only. *N. Y.*, 413; (nearly similar), *Pa.*, 461.

—Members of the Senate and General Assembly shall be elected yearly and every year, on the second Tuesday of October; and the two Houses shall meet separately on the second Tuesday in January next, after the said day of election; at which time of meeting the legislative year shall commence; but the time of holding such election may be altered by the Legislature. *N. Y.*, 413.

—The Senators shall be chosen for three years by the citizens [of Philadelphia and of the several counties], at the same time, in the same manner, and at the same places where they shall vote for Representatives. *Pa.*, 461.

—Upon the meeting of the first General Assembly which shall be chosen under the provisions of this Constitution, the Senators shall be divided, by lot, into two classes; the seats of the Senators of the one class to be vacated at the expiration of two years after the Monday following the general election, and of those of the other class at the expiration of four years; and the number of these classes shall be so proportioned that one-half of the whole number of Senators may, as nearly as possible, continue to be chosen thereafter every second year. *S. C.*, 483.

—The terms of office of the Senators and Representatives chosen at the general election shall begin on the Monday following such election. *S. C.*, 483.

—Such mode of classifying new additional Senators, shall be observed as will as nearly as possible preserve an equality of number in each class. *Tex.*, 507.

—The Senators shall be chosen by the qualified electors, for the term of four years, and shall be divided, by lot, into two classes, as nearly equal as can be. The seats of the Senators of the first class shall be vacated at the expiration of the first two years; and of the second class at the expiration of four years; so that one-half thereof shall be chosen biennially thereafter. *Tex.*, 507.

—The term of office of Senators shall be two years, and that of Delegates one year. The Senators first elected shall divide themselves into two classes, one Senator from every district being assigned to each class; and of these classes, the first, to be designated by lot in such manner as the Senate may determine, shall hold their offices for one year, and the second for two years; so that after the first election one-half of the Senators shall be elected annually. *W. Va.*, 549.

—The Senators shall be elected for the term of four years, for the election of whom the counties, cities and towns shall be divided into thirty-four districts. *Va.*, 535.

NUMBER OF MEMBERS IN THE TWO HOUSES.

—That the Assembly shall consist of at least seventy members, to be annually chosen in the several counties, in the proportions following, viz.: *N. Y.*, (1777), 26.

[Limited in 1801 to 100, and never to exceed 150. *p.* 34. Fixed in 1821 at 128. The original number of Senators was 24, with a conditional increase, based upon a census of electors. The number was fixed in 1801 at 32, and has since thus remained. *p.* 34].

[The whole number of members in House not to exceed one hundred]. *Ala.*, 75.

—The whole number of Senators shall be not less than one-fourth, nor more than one-third, of the whole number of Representatives. *Ala.*, 75.

[Number in House, 24 to 100, on ratio of 1 to 500 free white males in each county, till the number reaches 75, and then no increase till the population amounts to 500,000; but each county has at least one. In Senate, on ratio of 1 to 1,500 free white males, till the number reaches 25, and then no increase till the population amounts to 500,000]. *Ark.*, 85, 86.

—The House of Representatives shall consist of electors residing in towns from which they are elected. The number of Representatives from each town shall be the same as at present practiced and allowed. In case a new town shall hereafter be incorporated, such new town shall be entitled to one Representative only; and if such new town shall be made from one or more towns, the town or towns from which the same shall be made shall be entitled to the same number of Representatives as at present allowed, unless the number shall be reduced by the consent of such town or towns. *Ct.*, 108.

—The number of Senators shall not be less than one-third, nor more than one-half of that of the members of Assembly; and at the first session of the Legislature after this Constitution takes effect, the Senators shall be divided by lot as equally as may be, into two classes; the seats of the Senators of the first class shall be vacated at the expiration of the first year, so that one-half shall be chosen annually. *Cal.*, 98.

—When the number of Senators is increased, they shall be apportioned by lot, so as to keep the two classes as nearly equal in number as possible. *Cal.*, 98.

48

—From and after the first Wednesday of May in the year of our Lord one thousand eight hundred and thirty, the Senate of this State shall consist of not less than eighteen nor more than twenty-four members, and be chosen by districts. *Ct.*, 114.

[Provision relating to House stated in Art. III, § 3.] *Ct.*, 108.

—There shall be seven Representatives chosen in each county, until a greater number of Representatives shall by the General Assembly be judged necessary; and then, two-thirds of each branch of the Legislature concurring, they may by law make provision for increasing their number. *Del.*, 117.

—There shall be three Senators chosen in each county. When a greater number of Senators shall by the General Assembly be judged necessary, two-thirds of each branch concurring, they may by law make provision for increasing their number; but the number of Senators shall never be greater than one-half, nor less than one-third of the number of Representatives. *Del.*, 118.

—The General Assembly shall also, after every such enumeration, proceed to fix by law the number of Senators which shall constitute the Senate of the State of Florida, and which shall never be less than one-fourth nor more than one-half of the whole same number of the House of Representatives; and they shall lay off the State into the same number of Senatorial Districts, as nearly equal in the number of inhabitants as may be, according to the ratio of representation established in the preceding section, each of which districts shall be entitled to one Senator. *Fl.*, 137.

[Number in House, specified by counties]. *Fl.*, 137.

—The House of Representatives shall be composed as follows: The thirty-seven counties having the largest Representative population, shall have two Representatives each. Every other county shall have one Representative. The designation of the counties having two Representatives shall be made by the General Assembly immediately after the taking of each census. *Ga.*, 145.

[Number of Senators 44. Specified by counties]. *Ga.*, 144.

—The Senate shall consist of twenty-five members, and the House of Representatives shall consist of seventy-five members, until the population of the State shall amount to one million of souls, when five members may be added to the House, and five additional members for every five hundred thousand inhabitants thereafter, until the whole number of Representatives shall amount to one hundred; after which the number shall be neither increased nor diminished; to be apportioned among the several counties according to the number of white inhabitants. In all future apportionments, where more than one county shall be thrown into a representative district, all the Representatives to which said counties may be entitled shall be elected by the entire district. *Ill.*, 152.

—The Senate shall not exceed fifty, nor the House of Representatives one hundred members; and they shall be chosen by the electors of the respective counties or districts into which the State may from time to time be divided. *Ind.*, 172.

—The number of Senators and Representatives shall, at the session next following each period of making such enumeration, be fixed by law, and apportioned among the several counties, according to the number of white male inhabitants above twenty-one years of age in each; *Provided*, That the first and second elections of members of the General Assembly under this Constitution shall be according to the apportionment last made by the General Assembly, before the adoption of this Constitution. *Ind.*, 172.

—The number of Senators shall not be less than one-third, nor more than one-half of the Representative body; and shall be so classified by lot that one class, being as nearly one-half as possible, shall be elected every two years. When the number of Senators is increased, they shall be annexed by lot to one or the other of the two classes, so as to keep them as nearly equal in numbers as practicable. *Iowa*, 185.

— The Senate shall not consist of more than fifty members, nor the House of Representatives of more than one hundred; and they shall be apportioned among the several counties and Representative districts of the State according to the number of white inhabitants in each, upon ratios to be fixed by law. But no Representative district shall contain more than four organized counties, and shall be entitled to one Representative. Every county and district which shall have a number of inhabitants equal to one-half of the ratio fixed by law, shall be entitled to one Representative; and any one county containing, in addition to the ratio fixed by law, one-half of that number, or more, shall be entitled to one additional Representative. No floating district shall hereafter be formed. *Iowa*, 187.

—The first House of Representatives under this Constitution shall consist of seventy-five members, who shall be chosen for one year. The first Senate shall consist of twenty-five members, who shall be chosen for two years. After the first election, the number of Senators and members of the House of Representatives shall be regulated by law; but shall never exceed one hundred Representatives and thirty-three Senators. *Kan.*, 199.

—The number of Representatives shall be one hundred, and the number of Senators thirty-eight. *Ky.*, 211.

—One Senator for each district shall be elected by the qualified voters therein, who shall vote in the precincts where they reside, at the places where elections are by law directed to be held. *Ky.*, 211.

—The House of Representatives shall consist of one hundred and fifty-one members, to be elected by the qualified electors for one year from the next day preceding the annual meeting of the Legislature—which shall first be convened under this Constitution, shall, on or before the fifteenth day of August, in the year of our Lord one thousand eight hundred and twenty-one, and the Legislature within every subsequent period of at most ten years, and at least five, cause the number of the inhabitants of the State to be ascertained, exclusive of foreigners not naturalized, and Indians not taxed. The number of Representatives shall, at the several periods of making such enumeration, be fixed and apportioned among the several counties, as near as may be, according to the number of inhabitants, having regard to the relative increase of population. The number of Representatives shall, on said first apportionment, be not less than one hundred nor more than one hundred and fifty. *Me.*, 241, 252.

—The Senate shall consist of not less than twenty, nor more than thirty-one members; elected at the same time, and for the same term as the Representatives, by the qualified electors of the district into which the State shall, from time to time, be divided. *Me.*, 242.

[Representation in House based upon white population, and in Senate one from each county except Baltimore, which has three.] *Md.*, 260.

—The House of Representatives shall consist of two hundred and forty members. *Mass.*, 299.

—The Senate shall consist of forty members. *Mass.*, 299.

—The House of Representatives shall consist of not less than sixty-four, nor more than one hundred members. Representatives shall be chosen for two years, and by single districts. Each representative district shall contain, as nearly as may be, an equal number of white inhabitants, and civilized persons of Indian descent, not members of any tribe, and shall consist of convenient and contiguous territory. But no township or city shall be divided in the formation of a representative district. When any township or city shall contain a population which entitles it to more than one representative, then such township or city shall elect by general ticket the number of Representatives to which it is entitled. Each county hereafter organized, with such territory as may be attached thereto, shall be entitled to a separate Representative when it has attained a population equal to a moiety of the ratio of representation. In every county entitled to more than one representative, the Board of Supervisors shall assemble at such time and place as the Legislature shall prescribe, and divide the same into representative districts, equal to the number of Representatives to which such county is entitled by law, and shall cause to be filed in the office of the Secretary of State and Clerk of such county a description of such representative districts, specifying the number of each district, and the population thereof, according to the last preceding enumeration. *Mich.*, 301.

—The Senate shall consist of thirty-two members. Senators shall be elected for two years and by single districts. Such districts shall be numbered from one to thirty-two, inclusive, each of which shall choose one Senator.. No county shall be divided in the formation of senate districts, except such county shall be equitably entitled to two or more Senators. *Mich.*, 301.

[Number of Representatives fixed at one hundred, and of Senators thirty-five. With specific rules for apportionment]. *Ohio*, 440, 441.

—The Senate shall consist of sixteen and the House of Representatives of thirty-four members, which number shall not be increased until the year eighteen hundred and sixty; after which time the Legislative Assembly may increase the number of Senators and Representatives, always keeping as near as may be the same ratio as to the number of Senators and Representatives. *Provided*, That the Senate shall never exceed thirty and the House of Representatives sixty members. *Or.*, 450.

[Number of House to be 60 to 100. The Senate to be not less than one-fourth nor more than one-third the number in the House of Representatives. *Pa.*, 461.

—The House of Representatives shall never exceed seventy-two members. *R. I.*, 476.

—The Senate shall consist of the Lieutenant-Governor and of one Senator from each town or city in the State. *R. I.*, 477.

—The Senate shall be composed of one member from each election district, except the election district of Charleston, to which will be allowed two Senators. *S. C.*, 483.

[The House to consist of one hundred and twenty-four members]. *S. C.*, 482.

[Number of Representatives not to exceed seventy-five, until the population amounts to 1,500,000. The Senate not to exceed one-third that of the House]. *Tenn.*, 492, 493.

—The members of the House of Representatives shall be chosen by the qualified electors, and their term of office shall be two years from the day of the general election; and the sessions of the Legislature shall be biennial, at such times as shall be prescribed by law. *Tex.*, 507.

[Representation to be fixed by law. House from 75 to 90; Senate, 19 to 33. *Tex.*, 509.

—The Senate shall be composed of thirty Senators, to be of the freemen of the county for which they are elected, respectively, who shall have attained the age of thirty years, and they shall be elected annually by the freemen of each county, respectively. *Vt.*, 530.

[Representation in House by towns]. *Vt.*, 528.

—The House of Delegates shall consist of not less than eighty and of not more than one hundred and four members. The Senate shall never be less than one-fourth, nor more than one-third the number of the House of Delegates. *Va.*, 534.

—The number of the House of Delegates shall, instead of forty-seven, be in the first case fifty-seven, and in the last, fifty-two. *W. Va.*, 550.

—The Senate shall be composed of eighteen, and the House of Delegates of forty-seven members, subject to be increased according to the provisions hereinafter contained. *W. Va.*, 549.

—The number of the members of the Assembly shall never be less than fifty-four, nor more than one hundred. The Senate shall consist of a number not

more than one-third, nor less than one-fourth of the number of the members of the Assembly. *Wis.*, 562.

—The number of members who compose the Senate and House of Representatives, shall be prescribed by law, but the Representatives in the Senate shall never exceed one member for every five thousand inhabitants, and in the House of Representatives, one member to every ten thousand inhabitants. The representation in both houses shall be apportioned equally throughout the different sections of the State, in proportion to the population thereof, exclusive of Indians not taxable under the provisions of law. *Min.*, 321.

[Number in house to be from 36 to 100.] *Miss.*, 337.

—The Senators shall be chosen by the qualified electors, for four years, and on their being convened in consequence of the first election, they shall be divided by lot from their respective districts into two classes, as nearly equal as can be. And the seats of the Senators of the first class shall be vacated at the expiration of the second year. *Miss.*, 337.

—The Senate shall consist of thirty-four members, to be chosen by the qualified voters, for four years; for the election of whom the State shall be divided into convenient districts. *Mo.*, 352; (number in house, fixed at 200). *Mo.*, 352.

—Senators and members of Assembly shall be duly qualified electors in the respective counties and districts which they represent, and the number of Senators shall not be less than one-third nor more than one-half of that of the Assembly. *Neb.*, 381.

—The Senate shall consist of thirteen members, and the House of Representatives shall consist of thirty-nine members, and shall not be increased for the term of ten years after the adoption of this Constitution; *Provided*, That after the expiration of said ten years, the Legislature shall have power to increase the number of Senators and Representatives, so as to correspond with the increase of the population of the State: *Provided*, Such number shall at no time be more than twenty-five in the Senate and seventy-five in the House of Representatives. *Neb.*, 372.

—The aggregate number of members of both branches of the Legislature shall never exceed seventy-five. *Nev.*, 392.

—The Senate shall consist of twelve members, who shall hold their office for one year, from the first Wednesday in June, next ensuing their election. *N. H.*, 403.

[Representation in House, by towns and parishes.] *N. H.*, 402.

—The Senate shall be composed of one Senator from each county in the State, elected by the legal voters of the counties, respectively for three years. *N. Y.*, 413.

[Number in House not to exceed 60.] *N. J.*, 413.

—The House of Commons shall be composed of one hundred and twenty Representatives, biennially chosen by ballot, to be elected by counties according to their federal population, that is, according to their respective numbers, which shall be determined by adding to the whole number of free persons, including those bound to service for a term of years, and excluding Indians not taxed, three-fifths of all other persons; and each county shall have at least one member in the House of Commons, although it may not contain the requisite ratio of population. *N. C.*, 427.

—The Senate of this State shall consist of fifty Representatives, biennially chosen by ballot, and to be elected by districts; which districts shall be laid off by the General Assembly, at its first session after the year one thousand eight hundred and fifty-one; and then, every twenty years thereafter, in proportion to the public taxes paid into the treasury of the State, by the citizens thereof; and the average of the public taxes paid by each county into the treasury of the State, for the five years preceding the laying off of the districts, shall be considered as its proportion of the public taxes, and constitute the basis of apportionment; *Provided,* That no county shall be divided in the formation of a senatorial district. And when there are one or more counties having an excess of taxation above the ratio to form a senatorial district, adjoining a county or counties deficient in such ratio, the excess or excesses aforesaid shall be added to the taxation of the county or counties deficient; and if, with such addition, the county or counties receiving it shall have the requisite ratio, such county and counties each shall constitute a senatorial district. *N. C.,* 427.

ELECTIONS TO THE LEGISLATURE—TERM OF OFFICE.

—The Governor and Council shall, as soon as may be, examine returned copies of such list, and twenty days before the said first Wednesday of January, issue a summons to such persons as shall appear to be elected by a majority of the votes in each district, to attend that day and take their seats. *Me.,* 243.
—Members of both Houses of the General Assembly shall be chosen by the qualified electors, and the regulations for holding such elections shall, as to time, place and manner, be the same for each House, and shall be prescribed by law. After the special election to be held on the first Monday in November, 1865, such elections shall, until otherwise directed by law, take place on the first Monday in August. *Ala.,* 75.
—The members of the Assembly shall be chosen annually, by the qualified voters of their respective districts, on the Tuesday next after the first Monday in November, unless otherwise ordered by the Legislature, and their term of office shall be one year. *Cal.,* 98.
—The Representatives shall be chosen for two years, by the citizens residing in the several counties. *Del.,* 117; *Fl.,* 132; *Ala.,* 75.
—The members of the House of Representatives shall be chosen by the qualified voters, and shall serve for the term of two years from the day of the general election, and no longer, and the sessions of the General Assembly shall be annual, and commence on the second Wednesday in November in each year. *Fl.,* 132.
—The Representatives shall be chosen every two years on the first Monday in the month of October, until otherwise directed by law. *Fl.,* 132.
[Members elected biennially, 1st Wednesday in Oct.] *Ga.,* 143.
—The members of the House of Representatives shall be chosen every second year, by the qualified electors of their respective districts, on the second Tuesday in October, except the years of the Presidential election, when the election shall be on the Tuesday next after the first Monday in November; and their term of office shall commence on the first day of January next after their election, and continue two years, and until their successors are elected and qualified. *Iowa,* 185.
—Representatives shall be chosen on the first Monday of November every two years. *La.,* 225.

—The members of the House of Representatives shall continue in service for the term of two years from the day of the closing of the general elections. *La.,* 225.
—The members of the House of Delegates shall be elected by the qualified voters of the counties and the legislative districts of Baltimore city respectively, to serve for two years from the day of their election. *Md.,* 261.
[The members of the House of Representatives shall be chosen annually in the month of May, ten days at least before the last Wednesday of that month.] *Mass.,* 286.
—The members of the House of Representatives shall be chosen by the qualified electors, and shall serve for the term of two years, from the day of the commencement of the general election, and no longer. *Miss.,* 336.
—The Representatives shall be chosen every two years, on the first Monday and day following in November. *Miss.,* 336.
—The members of the Assembly shall be chosen biennially, by the qualified electors of their respective districts, on the Tuesday next after the first Monday in November, and their term of office shall be two years from the day next after their election. *Neb.,* 381.
—Senators and Representatives shall be elected biennially, by the electors in the respective counties or districts, on the second Tuesday of October. Their term of office shall commence on the first day of January next thereafter, and continue two years, except the Senators and Representatives to the first Legislature under this Constitution, whose election and term of office shall be as hereinafter provided. *Neb.,* 371.
—That the Senate shall be composed of Representatives, [annually] chosen by ballot, one for each county in the State. *N. C.,* 423.
—The members of the House of Representatives shall be chosen annually, in the month of March, and shall be the second branch of the Legislature. *N. H.,* 402.
—The Representatives shall be chosen annually, by the citizens, on the second Tuesday of October. *Pa.,* 461.
—The House of Representatives shall be composed of members chosen by ballot, every second year, by the citizens of this State, qualified as in this Constitution is provided. *S. C.,* 482.
—Senators and members of the House of Representatives shall be chosen at a general election on the third Wednesday in October in the present year, and on the same day in every second year thereafter, in such manner and for such terms of office as are herein directed. They shall meet on the fourth Monday in November, annually, at Columbia (which shall remain the seat of Government, until otherwise determined by the concurrence of two-thirds of both branches of the whole representation), unless the casualties of war or contagious disorders shall render it unsafe to meet there; in either of which cases, the Governor, or Commander-in-Chief, for the time being, may, by proclamation, appoint a more secure and convenient place of meeting. *S. C.,* 483.
—The House of Delegates shall be elected biennially by the voters of the cities of Norfolk and Richmond, and the several counties, on the fourth Tuesday in May. *Va.,* 534.

1 § 3. The State shall be divided into thirty-two districts, to be called senate
2 districts, each of which shall choose one senator. The districts shall be
3 numbered from one to thirty-two inclusive.

4 District number one (1) shall consist of the counties of Suffolk, Richmond
5 and Queens.

6 District number two (2) shall consist of the county of Kings.

7 District number three (3), number four (4), number five (5) and number
8 six (6) shall consist of the city and county of New York. And the board of
9 supervisors of said city and county shall, on or before the first day of May,
10 one thousand eight hundred and forty-seven, divide the said city and county
11 into the number of Senate districts to which it is entitled, as near as may be,
12 of an equal number of inhabitants excluding aliens and persons of color not
13 taxed, and consisting of convenient and contiguous territory ; and no Assembly
14 district shall be divided in the formation of a Senate district. The board of
15 supervisors when they shall have completed such division, shall cause certifi-
16 cates thereof, stating the number and boundaries of each district, and the
17 population thereof, to be filed in the office of the Secretary of State, and of
18 the clerk of the said city and county.

19 District number seven (7) shall consist of the counties of Westchester,
20 Putnam and Rockland.

21 District number eight (8) shall consist of the counties of Dutchess and
22 Columbia.

23 District number nine (9) shall consist of the counties of Orange and
24 Sullivan.

25 District number ten (10) shall consist of the counties of Ulster and Greene.

26 District number eleven (11) shall consist of the counties of Albany and
27 Schenectady.

28 District number twelve (12) shall consist of the county of Rensselaer.

29 District number thirteen (13) shall consist of the counties of Washington
30 and Saratoga.

31 District number fourteen (14) shall consist of the counties of Warren,
32 Essex and Clinton.

33 District number fifteen (15) shall consist of the counties of St. Lawrence
34 and Franklin.

35 District number sixteen (16) shall consist of the counties of Herkimer,
36 Hamilton, Fulton and Montgomery.

37 District number seventeen (17) shall consist of the counties of Schoharie
38 and Delaware.

39 District number eighteen (18) shall consist of the counties of Otsego and
40 Chenango.

41 District number nineteen (19) shall consist of the county of Oneida.

42 District number twenty (20) shall consist of the counties of Madison and
43 Oswego.

44 District number (21) shall consist of the counties of Jefferson and Lewis.

45 District number twenty-two (22) shall consist of the county of Onondaga.

46 District number twenty-three (23) shall consist of the counties of Cortland,
47 Broome and Tioga.

48 District number twenty-four (24) shall consist of the counties of Cayuga
49 and Wayne.

50 District number twenty-five (25) shall consist of the counties of Tompkins,
51 Seneca and Yates.

52 District number twenty-six shall consist of the counties of Steuben and
53 Chemung.

54 District number twenty-seven (27) shall consist of the county of Monroe.

55 District number twenty-eight (28) shall consist of the counties of Orleans,
56 Genesee and Niagara.

57 District number twenty-nine (29) shall consist of the counties of Ontario
58 and Livingston.

59 District number thirty (30) shall consist of the counties of Allegany and
60 Wyoming.

61 District number thirty-one (31) shall consist of the county of Erie.

62 District number thirty-two shall consist of the counties of Chautauque and
63 Cattaraugus.

1   § 4. An enumeration of the inhabitants of the State shall be taken under

2 the direction of the Legislature, in the year one thousand eight hundred and

3 fifty-five, and at the end of every ten years thereafter; and the said districts

4 shall be so altered by the Legislature at the first session after the return of

5 every enumeration, that each Senate district shall contain, as nearly as may

6 be, an equal number of inhabitants, excluding aliens and persons of color not

7 taxed; and shall remain unaltered until the return of another enumeration,

8 and shall at all times consist of contiguous territory; and no county shall be

9 divided in the formation of a Senate district except such county shall be equit-

10 ably entitled to two or more Senators.

1   § 5. The members of Assembly shall be apportioned among the several

2 counties of this State by the Legislature, as nearly as may be, according to

3 the number of their respective inhabitants, excluding aliens and persons of

4 color not taxed, and shall be chosen by single districts.

APPORTIONMENT.--REPRESENTATION.

—That the Legislature at their next session shall apportion the said one hundred members of the Assembly among the several counties of this State, as nearly as may be, according to the number of electors which shall be found to be in each county by the census directed to be taken in the present year. *N. Y.*, (1777,) 34.

[The classification of Senators, and future arrangement of districts, detailed in constitution.] *N. Y.*, (1777,) 28, 34; (founded on a septennial census.)

—The members of the Assembly shall be chosen by counties, and shall be apportioned among the several counties of the State, as nearly as may be, according to the numbers of their respective inhabitants, excluding aliens, paupers, and persons of color not taxed. An apportionment of members of Assembly shall be made by the Legislature, at its first session after the return of every enumeration; and when made, shall remain unaltered until another enumeration shall have been taken. But an apportionment of members of the Assembly shall be made by the present Legislature, according to the last enumeration taken under the authority of the United States, as nearly as may be. Every county heretofore established, and separately organized, shall always be entitled to one member of the Assembly; and no new county shall hereafter be erected, unless its population shall entitle it to a member. *N. Y.*, (1821,) 36.

[A census to be taken in 1825, and every ten years after, as a basis of representation.] *N. Y.* (1821,) 36.

—A census of whites ordered in 1866, 1875, and every ten years after, as a basis of representation. *Ala.*, 75.

—A census of inhabitants ordered in 1865, and every ten years after. *Ark.*, 87; *Ill.*, 152; *Kan.*, 200; *Mass.*, 298, 299; *Min.*, 322; *Wis.*, 562.

—A census of inhabitants to be taken in 1852, 1855, and every ten years after. *Cal.*, 99.

—The census of United States taken as a basis. *Ct.*, 114; *N. C.*, 427; *Or.*, 450.

—A census of all the inhabitants to be taken in 1867 and 1875, and every tenth year after. The representation founded on whites, and three-fifths of the colored people. *Fl.*, 137.

—The General Assembly shall at its second session after the adoption of this Constitution, and every sixth year thereafter, cause an enumeration to be made of all the white male inhabitants over the age of twenty-one years. *Ind.* 172.

—The General Assembly shall, in the years 1859, 1863, 1865, 1867, 1869 and 1875, and every ten years thereafter, cause an enumeration to be made of all the white inhabitants of the State. *Iowa*, 187.

—Representation shall be equal and uniform in this Commonwealth, and shall be forever regulated and ascertained by the number of qualified voters therein. In the year 1850, again in the year 1857, and every eighth year thereafter, an enumeration of all the qualified voters of the State shall be made; and to secure uniformity and equality of representation, the State is hereby laid off into ten districts. *Ky.*, 210; (nearly similar), *La.*, 226.

—A census to be taken in 1866, 1870, 1876, and at such times after (at least every ten years), as may be ordered by law, for ascertaining the number of population and of electors. *La.*, 226.

—A census of 1854, and every tenth year thereafter, as a basis of representation, which is founded on the number of whites and civilized Indians. *Mich.*, 301.

—Representative districts formed by the Supervisors. *Mich.*, 301.

—The Legislative Assembly shall, in the year eighteen hundred and sixty-five, and every ten years after, cause an enumeration to be made of all the white population of the State. *Or.*, 450.

—An enumeration of the qualified voters and an apportionment of the Representatives in the General Assembly, shall be made in the year one thousand eight hundred and forty-one, and within every subsequent term of ten years. *Tenn.*, 492.

—The Legislature shall cause an enumeration to be made every ten years, commencing on the 6th day of February, A. D., 1875, of all the inhabitants (including Indians taxed) of the State, designating particularly the number of qualified electors and the age, sex and color of all others, herein following the classification of the United States census, and the whole number of Representatives shall, at the several periods of making such enumeration, be fixed by the Legislature, and apportioned among the several counties, cities or towns, according to the number of

14

5   The several Boards of Supervisors in such counties of this State as are now

6   entitled to more than one member of Assembly, shall assemble on the first

7   Tuesday of January next, and divide their respective counties into Assembly

8   districts equal to the number of members of Assembly to which such counties

9   are now severally entitled by law, and shall cause to be filed in the office of the

10 Secretary of State, and the clerks of their respective counties, a description of

11 such Assembly districts, specifying the number of each district and the popu-

12 lation thereof, according to the last preceding State enumeration, as near as

white population in each; and shall not be less than forty-five, nor more than ninety. *Provided,* That there shall be an enumeration and an apportionment made in the year 1870, in the manner here indicated. *Tex.,* 500.

—Each county shall be entitled to at least one representative. *Ala.,* 75; *Ark.,* 88; *Kan.,* 204.

—Where two or more adjoining counties shall each have a residuum or fraction over and above the ratio then fixed by law, which fractions, when added together, equal or exceed that ratio, in that case, the county having the largest fraction shall be entitled to one additional Representative. *Ala.,* 75.

—When a Congressional, Senatorial or Assembly District shall be composed of two or more counties, it shall not be separated by any county belonging to another district; and no county shall be divided, in forming a Congressional, Senatorial or Assembly District. *Cal.,* 90.

—And it shall be the duty of the General Assembly, at its first session after the making of each enumeration, as provided by the last preceding section, to fix by law the number of Senators, and to divide the State into as many senatorial districts as there are Senators; which districts shall be as nearly equal to each other as may be in the number of white inhabitants, and each shall be entitled to one Senator, and no more; *Provided,* That in the formation of said districts, no county shall be divided, and no two or more counties, which are separated entirely by a county belonging to another district, shall be joined into one district; *And provided further,* That the senatorial district when formed, shall not be changed until after the next census shall have been taken. *Ala.,* 75.

—Senatorial and representative districts shall be composed of contiguous territory bounded by county lines; and only one Senator allowed to each senatorial, and not more than three Representatives to any representative district; *Provided,* That cities and towns, containing the requisite population, may be erected into separate districts. *Ill.,* 152.

—In forming senatorial and representative districts, counties containing a population of not more than one-fourth over the existing ratio, shall form separate districts, and the excess shall be given to the nearest county or counties not having a Senator or Representative, as the case may be, which has the largest white population. *Ill.,* 152.

—A Senatorial or Representative district, where more than one county shall constitute a district, shall be composed of contiguous counties; and no county for senatorial apportionment shall ever be divided. *Ind.,* 172.

—The number of Senators shall, at the next session following each period of making such enumeration, and the next session following each United States census, be fixed by law, and apportioned among the several counties according to the number of white inhabitants in each. *Iowa,* 187.

—At the first session under this Constitution, and at every subsequent regular session, the General Assembly shall fix the ratio of representation, and also form into Representative districts those counties which will not be entitled singly to a Representative. *Iowa,* 187.

—When a Congressional, Senatorial, or Representative district shall be composed of two or more counties, it shall not be entirely separated by any county belonging to another district; and no county shall be divided in forming a Congressional, Senatorial, or Representative district. *Iowa,* 187.

—In the future apportionment of the State, each organized county shall have at least one Representative; and each county shall be divided into as many districts as it has Representatives. *Kan.,* 204.

—It shall be the duty of the first Legislature to make an apportionment, based upon the census ordered by the last Legislative Assembly of the Territory; and a new apportionment shall be made in the year 1866, and every five years thereafter, based upon the census of the preceding year. *Kan.,* 204.

—When any city or town shall have a separate representation, such city or town, and the county in which it is located, may have such separate municipal courts, and executive and ministerial officers as the General Assembly may, from time to time, provide. *Ky.,* 217.

—The General Assembly shall divide each county of this Commonwealth into convenient election precincts, or may delegate power to do so to such county authorities as may be designated by law, and elections for Representatives for the several counties shall be held at the places of holding their respective courts, and in the several election precincts into which the counties may be divided; *Provided,* That when it shall appear to the General Assembly that any city or town hath a number of qualified voters equal to the ratio then fixed, such city or town shall be invested with the privilege of a separate representative in either or both Houses of the General Assembly which shall be retained so long as such city or town shall contain a number of qualified voters equal to the ratio which may, from time to time be fixed by law; and thereafter, elections for the county in which such city or town is situated shall not be held therein, but such city or town shall not be entitled to a separate representation, unless such county, after the separation, shall also be entitled to one or more representatives. That whenever a city or town shall be entitled to a separate representation in either House of the General Assembly, and by its numbers shall be entitled to more than one representative, such city or town shall be divided, by squares which are contiguous, so as to make the most compact form, into representative districts, as nearly equal as may be, equal to the number of Representatives to which such city or town may be entitled; and one Representative shall be elected from each district. In like manner shall said city or town be divided into Senatorial districts, when, by the apportionment, more than one Senator shall be allotted to such city or town; and a Senator shall be elected from each Senatorial district, but no ward or municipal division shall be divided by such divis-

13 can be ascertained. Each Assembly district shall contain, as nearly as may

14 be, an equal number of inhabitants, excluding aliens and persons of color not

15 taxed, and shall consist of convenient and contiguous territory; but no town

16 shall be divided in the formation of Assembly districts.

17   The Legislature, at its first session after the return of every enumeration,

18 shall re-apportion the members of Assembly among the several counties of this

19 State, in manner aforesaid, and the Boards of Supervisors in such counties as

20 may be entitled, under such re-apportionment, to more than one member, shall

21 assemble at such time as the Legislature making such re-apportionment shall

22 prescribe, and divide such counties into Assembly districts, in the manner

ion of Senatorial or Representative districts, unless it be necessary to equalize the elective, Senatorial, or Representative districts. *Ky.*, 209.

—Representation based upon the number of free white males. *Ark.*, 88.

— Representation based upon population. *Nev.*, 380; *Va.*, 537.

—Representation based upon number of white inhabitants. *Cal.*, 99; *Ill.*, 152; *Md.*, 260; *Miss.*, 336; *Or.*, 450; *Va.*, 549; *W. Va.*, 599.

—No county now organized shall be divided into new counties, so as to reduce the inhabitants of either below the ratio of representation. *Fla.*, 137.

—When any Senatorial District shall be composed of two or more counties, the counties of which such district consists shall not be entirely separated by any county belonging to another district, and no county shall be divided in forming a district. *Fla.*, 137.

—Apportionment ordered after every State and Federal census. *Ill.*, 152; *Me.*, 242; *Vt.*, 523; *Wis.*, 562.

—The number of Representatives shall, at the several sessions of the General Assembly, next after the making of the enumerations, be apportioned among the ten several districts, according to the number of qualified voters in each; and the Representatives shall be apportioned, as near as may be, among the counties, towns, and cities in each district; and in making such apportionment the following rules shall govern, to wit: Every county, town, or city having the ratio shall have one Representative; if double the ratio, two Representatives, and so on. Next, the counties, towns, or cities having one or more Representatives, and the largest number of qualified voters above the ratio, and counties having the largest number under the ratio shall have a Representative. regard being always had to the greatest number of qualified voters; *Provided*, That when a county may not have a sufficient number of qualified voters to entitle it to one Representative, then such county may be joined to some adjacent county or counties, which counties shall send one Representative. When a new county shall be formed of territory belonging to more than one district, it shall form a part of that district having the least number of qualified voters. *Ky.*, 210.

—It shall be the duty of the General Assembly which shall convene in the year 1850, to make an apportionment of the representation of this State, upon the principle set forth in this Constitution; and until the first apportionment shall be made as herein directed, the apportionment of Senators and Representatives among the several districts and counties in this State, shall remain as at present fixed by law; *Provided*, That on the first Monday in August, 1850, all Senators shall go out of office, and on that day an election for Senators and Representatives shall be

held throughout the State, and those then elected shall hold their offices for one year, and no longer; *Provided further*, That at the elections to be held in the year 1850, that provision in this Constitution which requires voters to vote in the precinct within which they reside, shall not apply. *Ky.*, 224.

—At the first session of the Legislature after the making of each enumeration, the Legislature shall apportion the representation amongst the several parishes and election districts on the basis of qualified electors as aforesaid. A representative number shall be fixed, and each parish and election district shall have as many Representatives as the aggregate number of its electors will entitle it to, and an additional Representative for any fraction exceeding one-half the representative number. The number of Representatives shall not be more than one hundred and twenty, nor less than ninety. *La.*, 226.

—The Legislature in every year in which they apportion representation in the House of Representatives, shall divide the State into Senatorial districts. *La.*, 228.

—No parish shall be divided in the formation of a Senatorial district, the parish of Orleans excepted. And whenever a new parish shall be created, it shall be attached to the Senatorial district from which most of its territory was taken, or to another contiguous district, at the discretion of the Legislature, but shall not be attached to more than one district. The number of Senators shall be thirty-six; and they shall be apportioned among the Senatorial districts according to the electoral population contained in the several districts; *Provided*, That no parish be entitled to more than nine Senators. *La.*, 228.

—At every apportionment of representation, the State shall be laid off into thirty-eight Senatorial districts, which shall be so formed as to contain, as near as may be, an equal number of qualified voters, and so that no county shall be divided in the formation of a Senatorial district, except such county shall be entitled, under the enumeration, to two or more senators; and where two or more counties compose a district, they shall be adjoining. *Ky.*, 211.

—No new parish shall be created with a territory less than six hundred and twenty-five square miles, nor with a number of electors less than the full number entitling it to a Representative; nor when the creation of such new parish would leave any other parish without the said extent of territory and number of electors. *La.*, 228.

—In all apportionments of the Senate, the electoral population of the whole State shall be divided by the number thirty-six, and the result produced by this division shall be the Senatorial ratio entitling a Senatorial district to a Senator. Single or contiguous parishes shall be formed into districts, having a population the nearest possible to the number entitling

23 herein directed; and the apportionment and districts so to be made shall
24 remain unaltered until another enumeration shall be taken under the provi-
25 sions of the preceding section.

26   Every county heretofore established and separately organized, except the
27 county of Hamilton, shall always be entitled to one Member of the Assembly,
28 and no new county shall be hereafter erected unless its population shall
29 entitle it to a member.

30   The county of Hamilton shall elect with the county of Fulton, until the
31 population of the county of Hamilton shall, according to the ratio, be entitled
32 to a member.

a district to a Senator; and if in the apportionment to make a parish or district fall short of or exceed the ratio, then a district may be formed having not more than two Senators, but not otherwise. No new apportionment shall have the effect of abridging the term of service of any Senator already elected at the time of making the apportionment. After an enumeration has been made, as directed in the tenth article, the Legislature shall not pass any law until an apportionment of representation in both Houses of the General Assembly be made. *La.*, 228.

[Towns are entitled to representation as follows, according to population, viz.: 1,500 to one; 3,750 to two; 6,750 to three; 10,500 to four; 15,000 to five; 20,250 to six, and 26,250 to seven; but no town to have more than seven. This apportionment may be changed by the Legislature.] *Me.*, 241.

—Every county in the State and each legislative district of Baltimore city, as hereinbefore provided for, shall be entitled to one Senator, who shall be elected by the qualified voters of the counties and of the legislative districts of Baltimore city respectively, and shall serve for four years from the date of his election, subject to the classification of Senators hereinafter provided for. *Md.*, 260.

—There shall be in the Legislature of this Commonwealth, a representation of the people, annually elected, and founded upon the principle of equality. *Mass.*, 285.

—In the census aforesaid, a special enumeration shall be made of the legal voters; and in each city said enumeration shall specify the number of such legal voters aforesaid, residing in each ward of such city. The enumeration aforesaid shall determine the apportionment of Representatives for the periods between the taking off the census. 298.

[Mode of representation by towns specified in detail.] *Mass.*, 296, 297, 298, 299; *N. H.*, 402, 403; *R. I.*, 476; *Vt.*, 523, 528.

—The several senatorial districts now existing shall be permanent. The Senate shall consist of forty members, and in the year one thousand eight hundred and forty, and every tenth year thereafter, the Governor and Council shall assign the number of Senators to be chosen in each district, according to the number of inhabitants in the same. But, in all cases, at least one Senator shall be assigned to each district. *Mass.*, 297.

—At their first session after each enumeration so made, and also at their first session after each enumeration made by the authority of the United States, the Legislature shall have the power to prescribe the bounds of congressional, senatorial and representative districts, and to apportion anew the Senators and Representatives among the several districts, according to the provisions of section second of this article. *Min.*, 322.

—The Senators shall also be chosen by single districts of convenient contiguous territory, at the same time that the members of the House of Representatives are required to be chosen, and in the same manner, and no representative district shall be divided in the formation of a senate district. The senate districts shall be numbered in regular series, and the Senators chosen by the districts designated by odd numbers shall go out of office at the expiration of the first year, and the Senators chosen by the districts designated by even numbers shall go out of office at the expiration of the second year; and thereafter the Senators shall be chosen for the term of two years, except there shall be an entire new election of all the Senators at the election next succeeding each new apportionment provided for in this article. *Min.*, 322.

—The number of members who compose the Senate and House of Representatives shall be prescribed by law, but the representation in the Senate shall never exceed one member for every five thousand inhabitants, and in the House of Representatives one member for every two thousand inhabitants. The representation in both houses shall be apportioned equally throughout the different sections of the State, in proportion to the population thereof, exclusive of Indians not taxable under the provisions of law. *Min.*, 321.

—When a senatorial district shall be composed of two or more counties, it shall not be entirely separated by any county belonging to another district; and no county shall be divided in forming a district. *Miss.*, 337.

—Until the first enumeration shall *be made, as directed by this Constitution, the apportionment of Senators and Representatives among the several districts and counties in this State shall remain as at present fixed by law. *Miss.*, 344.

—Elections for representatives for the several counties shall be held at the places of holding their respective courts, or in the several election districts into which the county may be divided; *Provided,* That when it shall appear to the Legislature that any city or town hath a number of free white inhabitants equal to the ratio then fixed, such city or town shall have a separate representation, according to the number of free white inhabitants therein, which shall be retained so long as such city or town shall contain a number of free white inhabitants equal to the existing ratio, and thereafter and during the existence of the right of separate representation in such city or town, elections for the county in which such city or town entitled to a separate representation is situated, shall not be held in such city or town; *And provided,* That if the residuum or fraction of any city or town entitled to separate representation shall, when added to the residuum in the county in which it may lie, be equal to the ratio fixed by law for one representative, then the aforesaid county, city or town, having the largest residuum, shall be entitled to such representation; *And provided also,* That when there are two or more counties adjoining, which have residuums over and above the ratio then fixed by law, if said residuums, when added together, will amount to such ratio, in that case one Representative shall be added to that county having the largest residuum. *Miss.,* 336.

—The Legislature shall at their first session, and at periods of not less than every four, nor more than every six years, until the year 1815, and thereafter at periods of not less than every four, nor more than every eight years, cause an enumeration to be made of all the free white inhabitants of this State, and the whole number of Representatives shall, at the several periods of making such enumeration, be fixed by the Legislature, and apportioned among the several counties, cities or towns entitled to separate representation, according to the number of free white inhabitants in each, and shall not be less than thirty-six nor more than one hundred; *Provided, however,* That each county shall always be entitled to at least one Representative. *Miss.,* 337.

—When any county shall be entitled to more than one Senator, the County Court shall cause such county to be subdivided into as many compact and convenient districts as such county may be entitled to Senators; which districts shall be, as near as may be, of equal population; and the qualified voters of each of such districts shall elect one Senator, who shall be a resident of such district. *Mo.,* 352.

—Senators shall be apportioned among their respective districts, as nearly as may be, according to the number of permanent inhabitants in each. *Mo.,* 352.

—Senators and Representatives shall be chosen according to the rule of apportionment established in this Constitution, until the next decennial census taken by the United States shall have been made, and the result thereof as to this State ascertained, when the apportionment shall be revised and adjusted on the basis of that census. In the year one thousand eight hundred and seventy-six, and every tenth year thereafter, there shall be taken, under the authority of this State, a census of the inhabitants thereof, and after every such census the apportionment of Senators and Representatives may be based thereon until the next succeeding national census, after which it may be based upon the national census until the next succeeding decennial State census; and so on from time to time; the enumerations made by the United States and this State shall be used, as they respectively occur, as the basis of apportionment. *Mo.,* 353.

—Senatorial and representative districts may be altered, from time to time, as public convenience may require. When any senatorial district shall be composed of two or more counties, they shall be contiguous. *Mo.,* 353.

—The House of Representatives shall consist of members to be chosen every second year, by the qualified voters of the several counties. and apportioned in the following manner. *Mo.,* 352.

—The ratio of representation shall be ascertained at each apportioning session of the General Assembly, by dividing the whole number of permanent inhabitants of the State by the number two hundred. Each county having one ratio, or less, shall be entitled to one Representative; each county having three times said ratio shall be entitled to two Representatives; each county having six times said ratio shall be entitled to three Representatives; and so on above that number, giving one additional member for every three additional ratios. When any county shall be entitled to more than one Representative, the County Court shall cause such county to be subdivided into as many compact and convenient districts as such county may be entitled to Representatives; which districts shall be, as near as may be, of equal population; and the qualified voters of each

of such districts shall elect one representative, who shall be a resident of such district.

—No person shall be a member of the House of Representatives who shall not have attained the age of twenty-four years; who shall not be a white male citizen of the United States; who shall not have been a qualified voter of this State two years, and an inhabitant of the county which he may be chosen to represent one year next before the day of his election, if such county shall have been so long established; but if not, then of the county from which the same shall have been taken; and who shall not have paid a State and county tax. *Mo.,* 352.

—The Senators and Representatives shall be chosen by districts of convenient contiguous territory, as compact as may be, to be defined by law, except as to the first election which is hereinafter provided for. *Neb.,* 171.

—The Legislature shall provide by law for an enumeration of the inhabitants of the State in the year one thousand eight hundred and seventy-five, and at the end of every ten years thereafter; and at their first session after such enumeration, and also after each enumeration made by the authority of the United States, the Legislature shall apportion and district anew the members of the Senate and House of Representatives, according to the number of inhabitants, excluding Indians not taxed, and soldiers and officers of the United States army and navy. *Neb.,* 371.

—The enumeration of the inhabitants of this State shall be taken under the direction of the Legislature, if deemed necessary, in A. D. eighteen hundred and sixty-seven; A. D., eighteen hundred and seventy-five, and every ten years thereafter; and these enumerations, together with the census that may be taken under the direction of the Congress of the United States, in A. D., eighteen hundred and seventy, and every subsequent ten years, shall serve as the basis of representation in both Houses of the Legislature. *Nev.,* 392.

—The General Assembly shall be composed of members annually elected by the legal voters of the counties, respectively. who shall be apportioned among the said counties as nearly as may be, according to the number of their inhabitants. The present apportionment shall continue until the next census of the United States shall have been taken, and an apportionment of members of the General Assembly shall be made by the Legislature at its first session after the next and every subsequent enumeration or census, and when made shall remain unaltered until another enumeration shall have been taken; *Provided,* That each county shall at all times be entitled to one member; and the whole number of members shall never exceed sixty. *N. J.,* 413.

—For the first ten years, after the year one thousand eight hundred and fifty-one, the apportionment of Representatives shall be, as provided in the schedule, and no change shall ever be made in the principles of representation, as herein established, or in the senatorial districts, except as above provided. All territory, belonging to a county at the time of any apportionment, shall, as to the right of representation and suffrage, remain an integral part thereof, during the decennial period. *Ohio,* 441.

—The Governor, Auditor, and Secretary of State, or any two of them, shall, at least six months prior to the October election, in the year one thousand eight hundred and sixty-one, and at each decennial period thereafter, ascertain and determine the ratio of representation, according to the decennial census, the number of Representatives and Senators each county or district shall be entitled to elect, and for what years, within the next ensuing ten years, and the Governor shall cause the same to be published, in such manner as shall be directed by law. *Ohio,* 442.

—Where two or more counties are joined in a senatorial, representative, or judicial district, the returns of elections shall be sent to the county having the largest population. *Ohio,* 445.

—The Senators and Representatives shall be chosen

by the electors of the respective counties or districts into which the State may, from time to time, be divided by law. *Or.*, 450.

—And in case any county shall not have the requisite population to entitle such county to a member, then such county shall be attached to some adjoining county for senatorial or representative purposes. *Or.*, 450.

—A senatorial district, when more than one county shall constitute the same, shall be composed of contiguous counties; and no county shall be divided in creating senatorial districts. *Or.*, 450.

—In the year one thousand eight hundred and sixty-four, and in every seventh year thereafter, Representatives to the number of one hundred shall be apportioned and distributed equally throughout the State by districts, in proportion to the number of taxable inhabitants in the several parts thereof, except that any county containing at least three thousand five hundred taxables, may be allowed a separate representation, but no more than three counties shall be joined, and no county shall be divided in the formation of a district. Any city containing a sufficient number of taxables to entitle it to at least two Representatives, shall have a separate representation assigned it, and shall be divided into convenient districts of contiguous territory, of equal taxable population as near as may be, each of which districts shall elect one Representative. *Pa.*, 471.

[Senators apportioned according to taxable inhabitants.] *Pa.*, 461, 471.

—The House of Representatives shall consist of one hundred and twenty-four members, to be apportioned among the several election districts of the State, according to the number of white inhabitants contained in each, and the amount of all taxes raised by the General Assembly, whether direct or indirect, or of whatever species, paid in each, deducting therefrom all taxes paid on account of property held in any other district, and adding thereto all taxes elsewhere paid on account of property held in such district. An enumeration of the white inhabitants for this purpose was made in the year one thousand eight hundred and fifty-nine, and shall be made in the course of every tenth year thereafter, in such manner as shall be by law directed; and Representatives shall be assigned to the different districts in the above-mentioned proportion, by act of the General Assembly at the session immediately succeeding every enumeration; *Provided*, That until the apportionment, which shall be made upon the next enumeration, shall take effect, the representation of the several election districts, as herein constituted, shall continue as assigned at the last apportionment, each district which has been heretofore divided into smaller districts, known as parishes, having the aggregate number of Representatives which the parishes heretofore embraced within its limits have had since that apportionment, the Representative to which the parish of All Saints has been heretofore entitled, being, during this interval, assigned to Horry election district. *S. C.*, 482.

—In assigning Representatives to the several districts, the General assembly shall allow one Representative for every sixty-second part of the whole number of white inhabitants in the State, and one Representative, also, for every sixty-second part of the whole taxes raised by the General Assembly. There shall be further allowed one Representative for such fractions of the sixty-second part of the white inhabitants, and of the sixty-second part of the taxes as, when added together, form a unit. *S. C.*, 483.

—If, in the apportionment of Representatives, any election district shall appear not to be entitled, from its population and its taxes, to a Representative, such election district shall nevertheless send one Representative; and if there be still a deficiency of the number of Representatives required by section fifth, such deficiency shall be supplied by assigning Representatives to those election districts having the largest surplus fractions, whether those fractions consist of a combination of population and taxes, or of population

or taxes separately, until the number of one hundred and twenty-four members are made up; *Provided, however*, That not more than twelve Representatives shall, in any apportionment, be assigned to any one election district. *S. C.*, 483.

—No apportionment of Representatives shall be construed to take effect, in any manner, until the general election which shall succeed such apportionment. *S. C.*, 483.

—The number of Representatives shall, at the several periods of making the enumeration, be apportioned among the several counties or districts according to the number of qualified voters in each; and shall not exceed seventy-five until the population of the State shall be one million and a half; and shall never thereafter exceed ninety-nine; *Provided*, That any county having two-thirds of the ratio, shall be entitled to one member. *Tenn.*, 492.

—The number of Senators shall, at the several periods of making the enumeration, be proportioned among the several counties or districts, according to the number of qualified electors in each, and shall not exceed one-third the number of Representatives. In apportioning the Senators among the different counties, the fraction that may be lost by any county or counties, in the apportionment of members to the House of Representatives, shall be made up to such county or counties in the Senate as near as may be practicable. When a district is composed of two or more counties, they shall be adjoining; and no county shall be divided in forming a district. *Tenn.*, 492.

—When a senatorial district shall be composed of two or more counties it shall not be separated by any county belonging to another district. *Tex.*, 507.

—The Senators shall be apportioned to the several counties, according to the population as ascertained by the census taken under the authority of Congress in the year 1840, regard being always had, in such apportionment, to the counties having the largest fraction, and giving to each county at least one Senator. *Vt.*, 530.

—The Legislature shall make a new apportionment of the Senators to the several counties, after the taking of each census of the United States, or after a census taken for the purpose of such apportionment, under the authority of this State, always regarding the above provisions of this article. *Vt.*, 530.

—Each county, city and town of the respective districts at the time of the first election of its Delegates under this Constitution, shall vote for one Senator, and the Sheriffs or other officers holding the election for each county, city or town within ten days at the farthest after the last election in the district, and from the polls so taken in their respective counties, cities and towns, return as Senator the person who has received the greatest number of votes in the whole district. *Va.*, 535.

—The whole number of members to which the State may at any time be entitled in the House of Representatives of the United States, shall be apportioned as nearly as may be, amongst the several counties, cities and towns of the State according to their population. *Va.*, 537.

—In the apportionment, the State shall be divided into districts corresponding in number with the Representatives to which it may be entitled in the House of Representatives of the Congress of the United States, which shall be formed respectively of contiguous counties, cities and towns, be compact, and include, as nearly as may be, an equal number of population. *Va.*, 537.

—For the election of Senators, the State shall be divided into nine senatorial districts; which number shall not be diminished, but may be increased as hereinafter provided. Every district shall choose two Senators, but after the first election both shall not be chosen from the same county. The districts shall be equal, as nearly as practicable, in white population, according to the returns of the United States census. They shall be compact, formed of contiguous territory, and bounded by county lines. After every such census the Legislature shall alter the senatorial districts, so far as may be necessary to make them conform to the foregoing provisions. *W. Va.,* 549.

—Any senatorial district may at any time be divided, by county lines or otherwise, into two sections, which shall be equal, as nearly as practicable, in white population. If such division be made, each section shall elect one of the Senators for the district; and the Senators so elected shall be classified in such manner as the Senate may determine. *W. Va.,* 549.

—For the election of Delegates, every county containing a white population of less than half the ratio of representation for the House of Delegates, shall, at each apportionment, be attached to some contiguous county or counties, to form a delegate district. *W. Va.,* 549.

—When two or more counties are formed into a delegate district, the Legislature shall provide by law that the Delegates to be chosen by the voters of the district shall be in rotation, residents of each county, for a greater or less number of terms, proportioned, as nearly as can be conveniently done to the white population of the several counties in the district. *W. Va.,* 549.

—After every census the Delegates shall be apportioned as follows:

The ratio of representation for the House of Delegates shall be ascertained by dividing the whole white population of the State by the number of which the House is to consist, and rejecting the fraction of a unit, if any, resulting from such division.

Dividing the white population of every delegate district, and of every county not included in a delegate district, by the ratio thus ascertained, there shall be assigned to each a number of Delegates equal to the quotient obtained by this division, excluding the fractional remainder.

The additional Delegates necessary to make up the number of which the House is to consist, shall then be assigned to those delegate districts, and counties not included in a delegate district, which would otherwise have the largest fractions unrepresented. But every delegate district and county not included in a delegate district, shall be entitled to at least one Delegate. *W. Va.,* 549.

—The arrangement of senatorial and delegate districts, and appointment of Delegates, shall hereafter be declared by law, as soon as possible after each succeeding census taken by authority of the United States. When so declared, they shall apply to the first general election for members of the Legislature to be thereafter held, and shall continue in force, unchanged until such districts are altered and Delegates apportioned under the succeeding census. *W. Va.,* 550.

—For the election of Representatives to Congress, the State shall be divided into districts, corresponding in number with the Representatives to which it may be entitled; which district shall be formed of contiguous counties and be compact. Each district shall contain, as nearly as may be, an equal federal number, to be determined according to the rule prescribed in the second section of the first article of the Constitution of the United States. *W. Va.,* 558.

—Additional territory may be admitted into and become part of this State with the consent of the Legislature. And in such case provision shall be made by law for the representation of the white population thereof in the Senate and House of Delegates, in conformity with the principles set forth in this Constitution. And the number of members of which each branch of the Legislature is to consist, shall thereafter be increased by the representation assigned to such additional territory. *W. Va.,* 550.

—The Legislature shall provide by law for an enumeration of the inhabitants of the State, in the year one thousand eight hundred and fifty-five, and at the end of every ten years thereafter; and at their first session after such enumeration, and also after each enumeration made by the authority of the United States, the Legislature shall apportion and district anew the members of the Senate and Assembly, according to the number of inhabitants, excluding Indians not taxed, and soldiers and officers of the United States army and navy. *Wis.,* 562.

—The members of the Assembly shall be chosen annually by single districts on the Tuesday succeeding the first Monday of November, by the qualified electors of the several districts, such districts to be bounded by county, precinct, town or ward lines, to consist of contiguous territory, and be in as compact form as practicable. *Wis.,* 562.

—The Senators shall be chosen by single districts of convenient contiguous territory, at the same time and in the same manner as members of the Assembly are required to be chosen, and no assembly district shall be divided in the formation of a senate district. The senate districts shall be numbered in regular series, and the Senators chosen by the odd numbered districts shall go out of office at the expiration of the first year, and the Senators chosen by the even numbered districts shall go out of office at the expiration of the second year, and thereafter the Senators shall be chosen for the term of two years. *Wis.,* 562.

—Until there shall be a new apportionment, the Senators and members of the Assembly shall be apportioned among the several districts, as hereinafter mentioned, and each district shall be entitled to elect one Senator or member of the Assembly, as the case may be. *Wis.,* 573.

—The foregoing districts are subject, however, so far to be altered that when any new town shall be organized, it may be added to either of the adjoining assembly districts. *Wis.,* 575.

—The population of the townships in the several counties of the State, and of the several wards, shall be ascertained by the last preceding census of the United States, until the Legislature shall provide, by law, some other mode of ascertaining it. *N. J.,* 418.

—This apportionment shall be made by the General Assembly, at the respective times and periods when the districts for the Senate are hereinbefore directed to be laid off, and the said apportionment shall be made according to an enumeration to be ordered by the General Assembly, or according to the census which may be taken by order of Congress, next preceding the making such apportionment. *N. C.,* 427.

—In making the apportionment in the House of Commons, the ratio of representation shall be ascertained by dividing the amount of federal population in the State, after deducting that comprehended within those counties which do not severally contain the one hundred and twentieth part of the entire federal population aforesaid by the number of Representatives less than the number assigned to the said counties. To each county containing the said ratio, and not twice the said ratio, there shall be assigned one Representative; to each county containing twice, but not three times the said ratio, there shall be assigned two Representatives, and so on progressively; and then the remaining Representatives shall be assigned severally to the counties having the largest fractions. *N. C.,* 427.

—The apportionment of this State for members of the General Assembly, shall be made every ten years after the year one thousand eight hundred and fifty-one, in the following manner: The whole population of the State, as ascertained by the federal census, or in such other mode as the General Assembly may direct, shall be divided by the number "one hundred," and the quotient shall be the ratio of representation in the House of Representatives for ten years next succeeding each apportionment. *Ohio* 440.

—Every county, having a population equal to one-half of said ratio, shall be entitled to one Representative; every county containing said ratio and three-fourths over, shall be entitled to two Representatives; every county containing three times said ratio, shall be entitled to three Representatives; and so on, requiring, after the first two, an entire ratio for each additional Representative. *Ohio,* 441.

—When any county shall have a fraction above the ratio, so large, that being multiplied by five, the

1 § 6. The Members of the Legislature shall receive for their services a sum
2 not exceeding three dollars a day, from the commencement of the session;
3 but such pay shall not exceed in the aggregate three hundred dollars for per
4 diem allowance, except in proceedings for impeachment. The limitation as to
5 the aggregate compensation shall not take effect until the year one thousand
6 eight hundred and forty-eight. When convened in extra session by the Gov-
7 ernor, they shall receive three dollars per day. They shall also receive the
8 sum of one dollar f.r every ten miles they shall travel, in going to and return-
9 ing from their place of meeting, on the most usual route. The speaker of the
10 Assembly shall, in virtue of his office, receive an additional compensation
11 equal to one-third of his per diem allowance as a member.

result will be equal to one or more ratios, additional Representatives shall be apportioned for such ratios, among the several sessions of the decennial period, in the following manner: If there be only one ratio, a Representative shall be allotted to the fifth session of the decennial period; if there are two ratios, a Representative shall be allotted to the fourth and third sessions, respectively; if three, to the third, second, and first sessions respectively; if four, to the fourth, third, second and first sessions respectively. *Ohio,* 441.

—Any county, forming with another county or counties a representative district, during one decennial period, if it have acquired sufficient population at the next decennial period, shall be entitled to a separate representation, if there shall be left, in the district from which it shall have been separated, a population sufficient for a Representative; but no such change shall be made, except at the regular decennial period for the apportionment of Representatives. *Ohio,* 441.

—If, in fixing any subsequent ratio, a county, previously entitled to separate representation, shall have less than the number required by the new ratio for a Representative, such county shall be attached to the county adjoining it, having the least number of inhabitants; and the representation of the district, so formed, shall be determined as herein provided. *Ohio,* 441.

—The ratio for a Senator shall, forever hereafter, be ascertained, by dividing the whole population of the State, by the number thirty-five. *Ohio,* 441.

—The same rules shall be applied, in apportioning the fractions of senatorial districts, and in annexing districts, which may hereafter have less than three-fourths of a senatorial ratio, as are applied to representative districts. *Ohio,* 441.

—Any county forming part of a senatorial district, having acquired a population equal to a full senatorial ratio, shall be made a separate senatorial district, at any regular decennial apportionment, if a full senatorial ratio shall be left in the district from which it shall be taken. *Ohio,* 441.

QUALIFICATIONS OF LEGISLATORS.

Age (for House), 21 years. *Ala.,* 75; *Fl.,* 132; *Ind.,* 172; *Iowa,* 185; *Me.,* 241; *Md.,* 261; *Miss.,* 336; *N. J.,* 413; *Or.,* 450; *Pa.,* 461; *S. C.,* 483; *Tenn.,* 493; *Va.,* 536. 24 years, *Del.,* 117. 25 years, *U. S.,* 9; *Ark.,* 85; *Ill.,* 151.

Age (for Senate), 21 years. *Or.,* 450. 25 years. *Ark.* 85; *Fl.,* 132; *Ga.,* 144; *Ind.,* 172; *Me.,* 243;

Md., 261; *Pa.,* 461; *Va.* 536. 27 years. *Ala.,* 75; *Del.,* 117. 30 years. *U. S.,* 10; *Ill.,* 151; *Ky.,* 211; *Miss.,* 337; *Mo.,* 352; *N. II.,* 403; *N. J.,* 413; *S. C.,* 483; *Tenn.,* 493; *Tex.,* 508; *Vt.,* 528.

Sex and color: White male. *Ala.,* 75; *Ark.,* 85; *Fl.,* 132; *Ill.,* 185; *Mo.,* 352; *Neb.,* 371; *S. C.,* 485; *Tex.,* 508.

Citizenship: Must be a citizen of the United States. *Ala.,* 75; *Ark.,* 85; *Fl.,* 132; *Ga.,* 145; *Ill.,* 151; *Ind.,* 172; *Me.,* 241, (53); *Md.,* 261; *Mich.,* 301; *Miss.,* 336; *Or.,* 450; *Tenn.,* 493; *Tex.,* 508.

Must have been a citizen of State 3 years. *Del.,* 117.

Residence: In State, 1 year. *Ark.,* 85; *Del.,* 117; (for House); *Min.,* 323; *N. J.,* 413; *Wis.,* 562. 2 years. *Ala.,* 75; *Fl.,* 132; *Ind.,* 173; *Miss.,* 336; *N. II.,* 402; *S. C.,* 483 (for House); *Vt.,* 525. 3 years. *Del.,* 117 (Senate); *Ga.,* 144; *Ill.,* 151; *Ind.,* 261; *Mo.,* 352; *Pa.,* 461; *Tenn.,* 493. 4 years. *Miss.,* 337; *N. J.* 413; *Pa.,* 461. 5 years. *S. C.,* 484 (Senate); *Tex.,* 507. 6 years. *Ky.,* 211.

In county. 60 days. *Iowa,* 185. 6 months. *Min.,* 323; *S. C.,* 483, 484. 1 year. *Ala.,* 75 (Senate); *Ga.,* 145; *Kan.,* 199; *Ky.,* 211; *Mass.,* 299; *Mo.,* 352; *N. C.,* 428; *Ohio,* 433; *Pa.,* 461; *Tenn.,* 493; *Tex.,* 507; *W. Va.,* 550. 5 years. *Mass.,* 299 (Senate.)

In town, 1 year. *N. II.* 402; *Vt.,* 522.

Absence from the State on business of the State or of United States, during the above periods, not a disqualification. *Ohio,* 433; *Pa.,* 461, &c.

Qualifications of an elector. *Kan.,* 199; *La.,* 226; *Min.,* 323; *N. J.,* 403; *Wis.,* 562.

An elector of district, 3 months. *Me.,* 241. 1 year. *Cal.,* 98; *Ky.,* 211; *La.,* 226; *Mich.,* 301; *Neb.,* 371; *Nev.,* 381; *Va.,* 536.

Freehold qualifications. *N. C.* (300 acres in fee in district; 100 acres in fee or term of his life, in district for 1 year) 423, 428.

Taxpayer. *Ill.,* 151; *Mo.,* 352.

Religion. Protestant. *N. II.,* 402, 403.

Representatives must be persons most noted for wisdom and virtue. *Vt.,* 523.

Removal from district, vacates office. *Mass.,* 299; *Mich.,* 301; *Mo.,* 353; *N. II.,* 402; *S. C.,* 483; *W. Va.,* 550.

PAY OF LEGISLATORS.

—The members of the Legislature shall receive for their services a compensation to be ascertained by law, and paid out of the public treasury; but no increase of the compensation shall take effect during the year in which it shall have been made. And no law shall be passed increasing the compensation of the members of the Legislature beyond the sum of three dollars a day. *N. Y.* (1821), 36.

—Each member of the General Assembly shall receive from the public treasury such compensation for his services as may be fixed by law; but no increase of compensation shall take effect during the session at which such increase shall have been made. *Ala.*, 76; (nearly similar), *Ark.*, 87; *Cal.*, 79; *Del.*, 118; *Fl.*, 133; *Ind.*, 174; *Miss.*, 338; *Mo.*, 353; *Nev.*, 383; *Tex.*, 508; *Va.*, 536.

—The pay of the members of the Legislature, until some general system of salaries shall be fixed by law, shall be for each member, five dollars per diem, and twenty cents per mile in going to, and the same in returning from the capital. *Ark.*, 95.

—But no law varying the compensation shall take effect, until an election of the Representatives shall have intervened. *Del.*, 118.

—The sum of two dollars per day for the first forty-two days' attendance, and one dollar per day for each day's attendance thereafter, and ten cents for each necessary mile's travel, going to and returning from the seat of government, shall be allowed to the members of the General Assembly, as a compensation for their services, and no more. The Speaker of the House of Representatives shall be allowed the sum of one dollar per day, in addition to his per diem as a member. *Ill.*, 153.

—Bills making appropriations for the pay of the members and officers of the General Assembly, and for the salaries of the officers of the government, shall not contain any provision on any other subject. *Ill.*, 153.

—The per diem and mileage allowed to each member of the General Assembly, shall be certified by the Speakers of their respective Houses, and entered on the journal, and published at the close of each session. *Ill.*, 153.

—Each member of the first General Assembly under this Constitution shall receive three dollars per diem while in session; and the further sum of three dollars for every twenty miles' travel in going to and returning from the place where such session is held, by the nearest traveled route; after which they shall receive such compensation as shall be fixed by law; but no General Assembly shall have the power to increase the compensation of its own members. And when convened in extra session they shall receive the same mileage and per diem compensation as fixed by law for the regular session, and none other. *Iowa*, 186.

—The members of the Legislature shall receive 'as compensation for their services the sum of three dollars for each day's actual service at any regular or special session, and fifteen cents for each mile traveled by the usual route in going to and returning from the place of meeting; but such compensation shall not in the aggregate exceed the sum of two hundred and forty dollars for each member as per diem allowance for the first session held under this Constitution, nor more than one hundred and fifty dollars for each session thereafter, nor more than ninety dollars for any special session. *Kan.*, 199.

—The members of the General Assembly shall severally receive from the public treasury a compensation for their services, which shall be three dollars a day during their attendance on, and twelve and a half cents per mile for the necessary travel in going to, and returning from, the sessions of their respective houses; *Provided*, That the same may be increased or diminished by law; but no alteration shall take effect during the session at which such alteration shall be made; nor shall a session of the General Assembly continue beyond sixty days, except by a vote of two-thirds of all the members elected to each House, but this shall not apply to the first session held under this Constitution. *Ky.*, 211.

—The members of the General Assembly shall receive from the public treasury a compensation for their services, which shall be eight dollars per day, during their attendance, going to and returning from the sessions of their respective Houses. The com-

pensation may be increased or diminished by law, but no alteration shall take effect during the period of service of the members of the House of Representatives by whom such alteration shall have been made. No session shall extend to a period beyond sixty days, to date from its commencement, and any legislative action had after the expiration of the said sixty days, shall be null and void. This provision shall not apply to the first Legislature which is to convene after the adoption of this Constitution. *La.*, 228.

—The Senators and Representatives shall receive such compensation as shall be established by law, but no law increasing their compensation shall take effect during the existence of the Legislature which enacted it. The expenses of the members of the House of Representatives, in traveling to the Legislature and returning therefrom, once in each session, and no more, shall be paid by the State, out of the public treasury, to every member who shall seasonably attend, in the judgment of the House, and does not depart therefrom without leave. *Me.*, 244.

—The General Assembly shall continue its session so long as in its judgment the public interest may require, and each member thereof shall receive a compensation of five dollars per diem for every day he shall attend the sessions, but shall receive no per diem when absent, unless absent on account of sickness; *Provided, however,* That no member shall receive any other or larger sum than four hundred dollars. When the General Assembly shall be convened by proclamation of the Governor, the session shall not continue longer than thirty days, and in such case the compensation shall be at the rate of five dollars per diem. *Md.*, 261.

—The compensation of the members of the Legislature shall be three dollars a day for actual attendance and when absent on account of sickness for the first sixty days of the session of the year one thousand eight hundred and fifty-one, and for the first forty days of every subsequent session, and nothing thereafter. When convened in extra session their compensation shall be three dollars a day for the first twenty days, and nothing thereafter; and they shall legislate on no other subjects than those expressly stated in the Governor's proclamation, or submitted to them by special message. They shall be entitled to ten cents and no more for every mile actually traveled, going to and returning from the place of meeting, on the usually traveled route; and for stationery and newspapers not exceeding five dollars for each member during any session. Each member shall be entitled to one copy of the laws, journals and documents of the Legislature of which he was a member; but shall not receive at the expense of the State, books newspapers, or other perquisites of office, not expressly authorized by this Constitution. *Mich.*, 302.

—The President of the Senate and the Speaker of the House of Representatives shall be entitled to the same per diem compensation and mileage as members of the Legislature and no more. *Mich.*, 302.

—The compensation of Senators and Representatives shall be three dollars per diem, during the first session, but may afterwards be prescribed by law. But no increase of compensation shall be prescribed which shall take effect during the period for which the members of the existing House of Representatives may have been elected. *Minn.*, 321.

—Each member of the Legislature shall receive for his services three dollars for each day's attendance during the session, and ten cents for every mile he shall travel in going to and returning from the place of the meeting of the Legislature, on the most usual route. *Neb.*, 372.

Provided, however, That they shall not receive pay for more than forty days at any one session.

—The Speaker of the Assembly, and Lieutenant-Governor, and President of the Senate, shall each, during the time of their actual attendance as such presiding officers, receive an additional allowance of two dollars per diem. *Nev.*, 383.

--The members of both Houses of the Legislature shall be compensated for their services out of the treasury of the State, by a law made for that purpose; such members attending seasonably, and not departing without license. *N. H.*, 902.

—Members of the Senate and General Assembly shall receive a compensation for their services, to be ascertained by law, and paid out of the treasury of the State; which compensation shall not exceed the sum of three dollars per day for the period of forty days from the commencement of the session; and shall not exceed the sum of one dollar and fifty cents per day for the remainder of the session. When convened in extra session by the Governor, they shall receive such sum as shall be fixed for the first forty days of the ordinary session. They shall also receive the sum of one dollar for every ten miles they shall travel in going to and returning from their place of meeting, on the most usual route. The President of the Senate and the Speaker of the House of Assembly shall, in virtue of their offices, receive an additional compensation, equal to one-third of their per diem allowance as members. *N. J.*, 414.

—The General Assembly, in cases not provided for in this Constitution, shall fix the term of office and the compensation of all officers; but no change therein shall affect the salary of any officer during his existing term, unless the office be abolished. *Ohio*, 437.

—The members and officers of the General Assembly shall receive a fixed compensation, to be prescribed by law, and no other allowance or perquisites, either in the payment of postage or otherwise; and no change in their compensation shall take effect during their term of office. *Ohio*, 435.

—The members of the Legislative Assembly shall receive for their services a sum not exceeding three dollars a day from the commencement of the session; but such pay shall not exceed in the aggregate one hundred and twenty dollars for per diem allowance for any one session. *Or.*, 452.

—When convened in extra session by the Governor, they shall receive three dollars per day; but no extra session shall continue for a longer period than twenty days. They shall also receive the sum of three dollars for every twenty miles they shall travel in going to and returning from their place of meeting, on the most usual route. The presiding officers of the Assembly shall, in virtue of their office, receive an additional compensation equal to two-thirds of their per diem allowance as members. *Or.*, 452.

—The Senators and Representatives shall receive a compensation for their services to be ascertained by law, and paid out of the treasury of the Commonwealth. *Pa.*, 462.

—The Senators and Representatives shall receive the sum of one dollar for every day of attendance, and eight cents per mile for traveling expenses in going to or returning from the General Assembly. The General Assembly shall regulate the compensation of the Governor and all other officers; subject to the limitations contained in the Constitution. *R. I.*, 476.

—The members of the General Assembly, who shall meet under this Constitution, shall be entitled to receive out of the public treasury, for their expenses during their attendance on, going to, and returning from, the General Assembly, four dollars for each day's attendance, and twenty cents for every mile of the ordinary route of travel between the residence of the member and the capital or other place of sitting of the General Assembly, both going and returning; and the same may be increased or diminished by law, if circumstances shall require; but no alteration shall be made to take effect during the existence of the General Assembly which shall make such alteration. *S. C.*, 484.

—The sum of four dollars per day, and four dollars for every twenty-five miles traveling to and from the seat of government, shall be allowed to the members of the first General Assembly, as a compensation for their services. The compensation of the members of the succeeding Legislatures shall be ascertained by law; but no law increasing the compensation of the

members shall take effect until the commencement of the next regular session after such law shall have been enacted. *Tenn.*, 493.

—Senators and Delegates shall receive for their services a compensation not exceeding three dollars a day during the session of the Legislature, and also ten cents for every mile they shall travel in going to and returning from the place of meeting, by the most direct route. The President of the Senate and Speaker of the House shall, respectively, receive an additional compensation of two dollars a day. *W. Va.*, 551.

—Each member of the Legislature shall receive for his services, two dollars and fifty cents for each day's attendance during the session, and ten cents for every mile he shall travel in going to and returning from the place of the meeting of the Legislature, on the most usual route. *Wis.*, 563.

—The members of the Legislature shall, at their first session hereafter, receive from the Treasury of the State, as their compensation, eight dollars for each day they shall be in attendance, and eight dollars for each twenty-five miles in traveling to and from the seat of government. The above rates of compensation shall remain till changed by law. *Tex.*, 509.

TIME OF MEETING OF LEGISLATURE—LIMITATION OF SESSIONS.

—The General Assembly shall meet annually, on such day as may be by law prescribed; and shall not remain in session longer than thirty days, unless by a vote of two-thirds of each House. *Ala.*, 76.

—The General Assembly shall meet every two years, on the first Monday in November, at the seat of government, until changed by law, except that the General Assembly for the year 1864, shall meet on the second Monday in April of that year. *Ark.*, 85.

--The sessions of the Legislature shall be annual, and shall commence on the first Monday of January next ensuing the election of its members, unless the Governor of the State shall, in the interim, convene the Legislature by proclamation. *Cal.*, 93.

—There shall be one stated session of the General Assembly, to be holden in each year, alternately at Hartford and New Haven, on the first Wednesday of May, and at such other times as the General Assembly shall judge necessary; the first session to be holden at Hartford; but the person administering the office of Governor may, on special emergencies, convene the General Assembly at either of said places, at any other time. And in case of danger from the prevalence of contagious diseases in either of said places, or other circumstances, the person administering the office of Governor, may by proclamation, convene said Assembly at any other place in this State. *Ct.*, 108.

—The General Assembly shall meet on the first Tuesday of January next, and shall not be within the amended provision respecting biennial sessions, which biennial sessions shall commence with the session of the General Assembly on the first Tuesday of January in the year of our Lord one thousand eight hundred and thirty-three. *Del.*, 126.

—The General Assembly shall meet on the first Tuesday of January, biennially, unless sooner convened by the Governor. *Del.*, 118.

—The session of the General Assembly shall not extend in duration over thirty days, unless it be deemed expedient by a concurrent majority of two-thirds of the members of each House; and no member shall receive pay from the State for his services after the expiration of sixty days continuously from the commencement of the session. *Fla.*, 133.

--The first meeting of the General Assembly, under this Constitution, shall be on the first Monday in December next, after which, it shall meet annually on the first Thursday in November, or on such other day as the General Assembly may prescribe. *Ga.*, 143.

—No session of the General Assembly, after the first

above mentioned, shall continue longer than forty days, unless prolonged by a vote of two-thirds of each branch thereof. *Ga.*, 143.

—The first session of the General Assembly shall commence on the first Monday of January, one thousand eight hundred and forty-nine ; and forever after, the General Assembly shall meet on the first Monday of January next ensuing the election of the members thereof, and at no other period, unless as provided by this Constitution. *Ill.*, 152.

—The sessions of the General Assembly shall be held biennially at the capital of the State, commencing on the Thursday next after the first Monday of January, in the year one thousand eight hundred and fifty-three, and on the same day of every second year thereafter, unless a different day or place shall have been appointed by law. But if in the opinion of the Governor the public welfare shall require it, he may at any time, by proclamation, call a special session. *Ind.*, 173.

—No session of the General Assembly, except the first under this Constitution, shall extend beyond the term of sixty-one days, nor any special session beyond the term of forty days. *Ind.*, 174.

— The sessions of the General Assembly shall be biennial, and shall commence on the second Monday in January next ensuing the election of its members ; unless the Governor of the State shall, in the mean time, convene the General Assembly by proclamation. *Iowa*, 185.

—All sessions of the Legislature shall be held at the State capital, and all regular sessions shall commence annually on the second Tuesday of January. *Kan.*, 200.

—The General Assembly shall convene on the first Monday in November, after the adoption of this Constitution, and again on the first Monday in November, 1851, and on the same day of every second year thereafter, unless a different day be appointed by law, and their sessions shall be held at the seat of government. *Ky.*, 211.

—The General Assembly shall meet annually on the first Monday in January, unless a different day be appointed by law, and their sessions shall be held at the seat of government. *La.*, 225.

—The Legislature shall convene on the first Wednesday of January, annually, and shall have full power to make and establish all reasonable laws and regulations for the defense and benefit of the people of this State, not repugnant to this Constitution, nor to that of the United States. *Me.*, 243.

—The annual meeting of the Legislature shall be on the first Wednesday of January, in each year; and the Governor and other State officers elected for the political year commencing on the second Wednesday of May, in the year of our Lord one thousand eight hundred and fifty-one, shall hold their offices till the first Wednesday of January, in the year of our Lord one thousand eight hundred and fifty-two. *Me.*, 253.

—That for the redress of grievances, and for amending, strengthening and preserving the laws, the Legislature ought to be frequently convened. *Md.*, 254.

—The General Assembly shall meet on the first Wednesday of January, eighteen hundred and sixty-five, and on the same day in every second year thereafter, and at no other time, unless convened by the proclamation of the Governor. *Md.*, 261.

—The Legislature ought frequently to assemble for the redress of grievances, for correcting, strengthening and confirming the laws, and for making new laws, as the common good may require. *Mass.*, 282.

—The Legislature shall meet at the seat of government on the first Wednesday in February next, and on the first Wednesday in January of every second year thereafter, and at no other place or time, unless as provided in this Constitution. *Mich.*, 303.

— Shall meet at the seat of government of the State, at such time as shall be prescribed by law. *Minn.*, 321.

—The first session of the Legislature of the State of Minnesota shall commence on the first Wednesday of December next, and shall be held at the capitol in the city of St. Paul. *Minn.*, 330.

—The Legislature shall convene on the first Monday of November, 1857, and biennially thereafter, but may be specially convoked by the Governor at other times. *Miss.*, 344.

—The General Assembly, elected in the year one thousand eight hundred and sixty-six, shall meet on the first Wednesday of January, one thousand eight hundred and sixty-seven; and thereafter the General Assembly shall meet, in regular session, once in every two years; and such meeting shall be on the first Wednesday of January, unless a different day be fixed by law. *Mo.*, 354.

—The first session of the Legislature under this Constitution shall be held on the fourth day of July, one thousand eight hundred and sixty-six; and all regular sessions thereafter shall commence on the first Thursday after the first Monday in January, biennially. But the Legislature may, on extraordinary occasions, be convened by proclamation of the Governor, and when so convened shall transact no business, except such as relates to the objects for which they were so convened, to be stated in the proclamation of the Governor. *N.b.*, 372.

—The sessions of the Legislature shall be biennial, and shall commence on the first Monday of January next ensuing the election of members of the Assembly, unless the Governor of the State shall, in the interim, convene the Legislature by proclamation. *Neb.*, 381.

—The first regular session of the Legislature under the Constitution may extend to ninety days, but no subsequent regular session shall exceed sixty days, nor any special session convened by the Governor exceed twenty days. *Nev.*, 383.

—The restriction of the pay of members of the Legislature, after forty days from the commencement of the session, shall not be applied to the first Legislature convened under this Constitution. *N. J.*, 421.

—The General Assembly which shall convene in December, eighteen hundred and thirty-eight, shall continue its session, as heretofore, notwithstanding the provision in the eleventh section of the first article, and shall at all times be regarded as the first General Assembly under the amended Constitution. *Pa.*, 469.

—The Senate and House shall assemble every year, on the first Wednesday in June, and at such other times as they may judge necessary ; and shall dissolve and be dissolved seven days next preceding the first said Wednesday of June, and shall be styled the General Court of New Hampshire. *N. H.*, 401.

—The General Assembly shall meet biennially, and at each biennial session shall elect, by joint vote of the two Houses, a Secretary of State, Treasurer and Council of State, who shall continue in office for the term of two years. *N. C.*, 428.

—All regular sessions of the General Assembly shall commence on the first Monday of January, biennially. The first session, under this Constitution, shall commence on the first Monday of January, one thousand eight hundred and fifty-two. *Ohio*, 435.

—The sessions of the Legislative Assembly shall be held biennially at the capital of the State, commencing on the second Monday of September in the year eighteen hundred and fifty-eight, and on the same day of every second year thereafter, unless a different day shall have been appointed by law. *Or.*, 450.

—The General Assembly shall meet on the first Tuesday of January in every year, unless sooner convened by the Governor. *Pa.*, 462.

—There shall be two sessions of the General Assembly, holden annually ; one at Newport, on the first Tuesday of May, for the purpose of election and other business ; the other on the last Monday of October, which last session shall be holden at South Kingstown once in two years, and the intermediate years alternately at Bristol and East Greenwich ; and an adjournment from the October session shall be holden annually at Providence. *R. I.*, 475.

—There shall be one session of the General Assembly holden annually, commencing on the last Tuesday in

64

1   § 7. No Member of the Legislature shall receive any civil appointment

2   within this State, or to the Senate of the United States, from the Governor,

3   the Governor and Senate, or from the Legislature during the time for which

4   he shall have been elected ; and all such appointments and all votes given for

5   any such member for any such office or appointment shall be void.

May, at Newport, and an adjournment from the same shall be holden annually at Providence. *R. I.*, 481.
—The first session of the General Assembly shall commence on the first Monday in October, one thousand eight hundred and thirty-five; and forever thereafter the Generl Assembly shall meet on the first Monday in October next ensuing the election. *Tenn.*, 493.
[Legislature meet second Tuesday of October.] *Vt.*, 523.
—The General Assembly shall meet annually and not oftener, unless convened by the Governor in the manner prescribed in this Constitution. *Va.*, 536.
—No session of the General Assembly, after the first under this Constitution, shall continue longer than sixty days, without the concurrence of three-fifths of the members elected to each House, in which case the session may be extended for a further period, not exceeding thirty days. *Va.*, 536.
—The Legislature shall meet once in every year, and not oftener, unless convened by the Governor. The regular sessions shall begin on the third Tuesday of January. *W. Va.*, 551.
—When, for any cause, the Legislature, in the opinion of the Governor, cannot safely meet at the seat of government, the Governor, by proclamation, may convene them at another place. *W. Va.*, 551.
—No session of the Legislature, after the first, shall continue longer than forty-five days, without the concurrence of three-fourths of the members elected to each branch. *W. Va.*, 551.
—The Legislature shall meet at the seat of government, at such time as shall be provided by law, once in each year, and not oftener, unless convened by the Governor. *Wis.*, 563.

LEGISLATORS TO HOLD NO OTHER OFFICE—NON-ACCOUNTING HOLDERS OF PUBLIC MONEY NOT ELIGIBLE.

—No member of the Legislature shall receive any civil appointment from the Governor and Senate, or from the Legislature during the term for which he shall have been elected. *N. Y.* (1821), 36.
—No person being a member of Congress, or holding any judicial or military office under the United States, shall hold a seat in the Legislature. And if any person shall, while a member of the Legislature, be elected to Congress, or appointed to any office, civil or military, under the government of the United States, his acceptance thereof shall vacate his seat. *N. Y.* (1821), 36.
—No person who holds any lucrative office under the United States, or under this State, or under any other State or government (except Postmasters, officers in the militia to whose office no annual salary is attached, Justices of the Peace, Members of the Court of County Commissioners, Notaries Public and Commissioners of Deeds, excepted), no person who has been convicted of having given or offered any bribe to procure his election; no person who has been convicted of bribery, forgery, perjury, or other high crime or misdemeanor which may be by law declared to disqualify him; and no person who has been a collector of public moneys and has failed to account for and pay over into the treasury all sums for which he may be by law accountable, shall be eligible to the General Assembly. *Ala.*, 75.

—No Senator or Representative shall, during the term for which he was elected, be appointed to any civil office of profit under this State, except such offices as may be filled by elections by the people. *Ala.*, 76.
—No person who now is, or shall be hereafter, a collector or holder of public money, nor any assistant or deputy of such holder or collector of public money, shall be eligible to a seat in either House of the General Assembly, nor to any office of trust or. profit; until he shall have accounted for and paid over all sums for which he may have been liable. *Ark.*, 86; *Ky.*, 212; *Ky.*, 261.
—No Senator or Representative shall, during the term for which he shall have been elected, be appointed to any civil office under this State which shall have been created, or the emoluments of which shall have been increased during his continuance in office, except to such office as shall be filled by the election of the people. *Ark.*, 86; (nearly similar), *Cal.*, 98; *Fla.*, 136; *Ind.*, 174; *Iowa*, 186; *Ky.*, 211; *Miss.*, 338; *Mo.*, 353; *Or.*, 452; *Va.*, 536.
—No Judge of the Supreme, Circuit, or inferior courts of law, or equity, Secretary of State, Attorney-General of the State, District Attorneys, State Auditor or Treasurer, Register or Recorder, Clerk of any court of record, Sheriff, Coroner or Member of Congress, or any other person holding any lucrative office under the United States or this State (militia officers, Justices of the Peace, Postmasters and Judges of the county court excepted), shall be eligible to a seat in either House of the General Assembly. *Ark.*, 86.
—No judge of the superior court, and of the supreme court of errors; no member of Congress; no person holding any office under the authority of the United States; no person holding the office of Treasurer, Secretary or Comptroller; no Sheriff or Sheriff's deputy, shall be a member of the General Assembly. *Ct.*, 113.
—*Provided*, That this prohibition shall not extend to members of the first Legislature. *Me.*, 244.
—No Senator or Representative shall, during the time for which he shall have been elected, be appointed to any civil office under this State, which shall have been created, or the emoluments of which shall have been increased, during such time. No person concerned in any army or navy contracts, no member of Congress, nor any person holding any office under this State or the United States, except the Attorney-General, officers usually appointed by the Courts of justice respectively, Attorneys at law, and officers in the militia, holding no disqualifying office, shall, during his continuance in Congress or in office, be a Senator or Representative. *Del.*, 118.
—No person elected to the General Assembly shall receive any civil appointment within this State, or to the Senate of the United States, from the Governor, the Governor and Senate, or from the General Assembly, during the term for which he shall have been elected; and all such appointments, and all votes given for any such member for any such office or appointment shall be void; nor shall any member of the General Assembly be interested, either directly or indirectly, in any contract with the State, or any county thereof, authorized by any law passed during the time for which he shall have been elected, or during one year after the expiration thereof. *Ill.*, 152; *Mich.*, 302.

1   § 8. No person being a Member of Congress, or holding any judicial or

2 military office under the United States, shall hold a seat in the Legislature.

3 And if any person shall, after his election as a Member of the Legislature, be

4 elected to Congress, or appointed to any office, civil or military, under the

5 Government of the United States, his acceptance thereof shall vacate his seat.

—No member of Congress, nor person holding or exercising any office of trust or profit under the United States, or either of them, or under any foreign power, shall be eligible as a member of the General Assembly of this Commonwealth, or hold or exercise any office of trust and profit under the same. *Ky.*, 220; *La.*, 233.

—No Senator or Representative shall, during the term for which he was elected, nor for one year thereafter, be appointed to any civil office of profit under this State, which shall have been created, or the emoluments of which shall been increased during the time such Senator or Representative was in office, except to such offices as may be filled by the election of the people. *La.*, 229; *Nev.*, 382.

—No person who, at any time, may have been a collector of taxes, whether State, parish or municipal, or who may have been otherwise intrusted with public money, shall be eligible to the General Assembly, or to any office of profit or trust, under the State government, until he shall have obtained a discharge for the amount of such collections, and for all public moneys with which he may have been intrusted. *La.*, 229.

—No Senator or Delegate, after qualifying as such, notwithstanding he may thereafter resign, shall, during the whole period of time for which was elected, be eligible to any office which shall have been created, or the salary or profits of which shall have been increased during such term, or shall, during said whole period of time, be appointed to any civil office by the Executive or General Assembly. *Md.*, 262.

—No person holding any civil office of profit or trust under this State, except Justices of the Peace, shall be eligible to the office of Senator or Delegate. *Md.*, 261.

—No person holding the office of Judge of the Supreme Judicial Court, Secretary, Attorney-General (Solicitor-General), Treasurer or Receiver-General, Judge of Probate, Commissary-General—President, Professor or Instructor of Harvard College—Sheriff, Clerk of the House of Representatives, Register of Probate, Register of Deeds, Clerk of the Supreme Judicial Court—(Clerk of the Inferior Court of Common Pleas) or officer of the customs, including, in this description, naval officers—shall, at the same time, have a seat in the Senate or House of Representatives; but their being chosen or appointed to, and accepting the same, shall operate as a resignation of their seat in the Senate or House of Representatives; and the place so vacated shall be filled up.

And the same rule shall take place in case any Judge of the said Supreme Judicial Court, or Judge of Probate, shall accept a seat in Council; or any Councillor shall accept of either of those offices or places. *Mass.*, 292.

—No person holding any office under the United States (or this State), or any county office, except Notaries Public, officers of the militia and officers elected by townships, shall be eligible to or have a seat in either House of the Legislature, and all votes given for any such person shall be void. *Mich.*, 301.

—No Senator or Representative shall, during the time for which he is elected, hold any office under the authority of the United States, or the State of Minnesota, except that of postmaster; and no Senator or Representative shall hold an office under the State, which had been created, or the emoluments of which had been increased during the session of the Legislature of which he was a member, until one year

after the expiration of his term of office in the Legislature. *Minn.*, 321.

—No member of either House of the Legislature shall, after the commencement of the first session of the Legislature after his election, and during the remainder of the term for which he is elected, be eligible to any office or place, the appointment to which may be made in whole or in part by either branch of the Legislature. *Miss.*, 338.

—No member of the Legislature shall, during the term for which he was elected, be appointed or elected to any civil office in the State which shall have been created, or the emoluments of which shall have been increased, during the term for which he was elected. *Neb.*, 372; (nearly similar), *N. J.*, 414; *Pa.*, 462; *Wis.*, 563.

—No Justice of the Supreme Court, nor judge of any other court, Sheriff, Justice of the Peace, nor any person or persons possessed of any office of profit under the government of this State, shall be entitled to a seat either in the Senate or in the General Assembly; but on being elected and taking his seat, his office shall be considered vacant; and no person holding any office of profit under the government of the United States shall be entitled to a seat in either house. *N. J.*, 414.

—That no Judge of the Supreme Court of law or equity, or Judge of Admiralty, shall have a seat in the Senate, House of Commons or Council of State. *N. C.*, 425.

—No person who shall hold any office or place of trust or profit under the United States, or any department thereof, or under this State, or any other State or Government, shall hold or exercise any other office or place of trust or profit under the authority of this State, or be eligible to a seat in either House of the General Assembly; *Provided*, That nothing herein contained shall extend to officers in the militia or Justices of the Peace. *N. C.*, 430.

—No person holding office under the authority of the United States, or any lucrative office under the authority of this State, shall be eligible to, or have a seat in the General Assembly; but this provision shall not extend to township officers, Justices of the Peace, Notaries Public, or officers of the militia. *Ohio*, 433.

—No Senator or Representative shall, during the term for which he shall have been elected, or for one year thereafter, be appointed to any civil office under this State which shall be created, or the emoluments of which shall have been increased during the term for which he shall have been elected. *Ohio*, 434.

—And no member of Congress or other person holding any office (except of attorney at law and in the militia), under the United States or this Commonwealth, shall be a member of either House during his continuance in Congress or in office. *Pa.*, 462.

—No judge of any court of law or equity, Secretary of State, Attorney-General, Register, Clerk of any Court of Record, or person holding any office under the authority of the United States, shall have a seat in the General Assembly; nor shall any person in this State hold more than one lucrative office at the same time; *Provided*, That no appointment in the militia, or to the office of Justice of the Peace, shall be considered a lucrative office, or operate as a disqualification to a seat in either House of the General Assembly. *Tenn.*, 494.

—No Senator or Representative shall during the time for which he was elected, be eligible to any

1 § 9. The elections of Senators and Members of Assembly, pursuant to the

2 provisions of this Constitution, shall be held on the Tuesday succeeding the first

3 Monday of November, unless otherwise directed by the Legislature.

office or place of trust, the appointment to which is vested in the executive or the General Assembly, except to the office of trustee of a literary institution. *Tenn.*, 493.

—No person shall be eligible to a seat in the General Assembly whilst he holds any office of profit or trust under this State, the United States of America, or any of them, or under any other power, except officers in the militia, army or navy of this State, magistrates, or justices of inferior courts, while such justices receive no salaries; nor shall any contractor of the army or navy of this State, the United States of America, or any of them, or the agents of such contractor, be eligible to a seat in either House. And if any member shall accept or exercise any of said disqualifying offices, he shall vacate his seat. *S. C.*, 484.

—No Senator or Representative shall, during the term for which he may be elected, be eligible to any office of profit under this State, which shall have been created or the emoluments of which may have been increased during such term; and no member of either House of the Legislature shall, during the term for which he is elected [although he may resign his seat as such member, shall] be eligible to any office or place, the appointment to which may be made, in whole or in part, by either branch of the Legislature; [nor shall members of either House vote for a member of their own body, though he resign his seat in the same, for Senator in the Congress of the United States;] nor shall members thereof be capable of voting for a member of their own body, for any office whatever, except it be [for Speaker of the House of Representatives and President for the time being of the Senate, who shall be elected from their respective bodies]. *Tex.*, 508.

—No minister of the Gospel, priest of any religious denomination, or salaried officer of any banking corporation or company, and no attorney for the Commonwealth, shall be capable of being elected a member of either House of the General Assembly. The removal of any person elected to either branch of the General Assembly from the city, county, town or district for which he was elected, shall vacate his office. *Va.*, 536.

—No person holding an office of profit under this State or the United States, shall be a member of the Legislature. *W. Va.*, 550.

—No person being a member of Congress, or holding any military or civil office under the United States, shall be eligible to a seat in the Legislature; and if any person shall, after his election as a member of the Legislature, be elected to Congress, or be appointed to any office, civil or military, under the government of the United States, his acceptance thereof shall vacate his seat. *Wis.*, 563.

VACANCIES IN OFFICE OF MEMBER OR SENATOR.

—When vacancies happen in either house, the Governor, or the person exercising the powers of Governor for the time being, shall issue writs of election to fill such vacancies. *Ala.*, 76; (nearly similar,) *Ark.*, 86; *Cal.*, 98; *Del.*, 28; *Ga.*, 147; *Ill.*, 153; *Ind.*, 175; *Iowa*, 185; *Ky.*, 212; *Mich.*, 305; *Minn.*, 322; *Miss.*, 337; *Mo.*, 353; *Neb.*, 373; *Nev.*, 382; *N. H.*, 402; *N. C.*, 428; *Or.*, 453; *Tex.*, 508; *Wis.*, 563.

—If the office of Representative, or the office of Senator become vacant before the regular expiration of the term thereof, a Representative or Senator shall be elected to fill such vacancy, and shall hold the office for the residue of said term. *Del.*, 118.

—When there is a vacancy in either house of the General Assembly, and the General Assembly is not in session, the Governor shall have power to iss c a writ of election to fill such vacancy; which writ · hall be executed as a writ issued by a speaker of either House in case of vacancy. *Del.*, 118.

—Any vacancy in the Senate shall be filled by election by the people of the unrepresented district, upon the order of a majority of the Senators elected. *Mass.*, 300.

—Whenever the seat of a member shall be vacated, by death, resignation, or otherwise, the vacancy may be filled by a new election. *Me.*, 242.

—When vacancies happen in either House, the Speaker shall issue writs of election to fill such vacancies. *Pa.*, 462.

—Vacancies from any cause, in the Senate or House of Representatives may be filled by a new election. *R. I.*, 479; (nearly similar.) *Kan.*, 199.

—And should the Governor fail to issue a writ of election to fill such vacancies, the returning officer for the district or county shall be authorized to order an election for that purpose. *Tex.*, 508.

—The General Assembly shall make provision by law for filling vacancies that may occur in either House by the death, resignation (or otherwise) of any of its members. *Fl.*, 122.

—All vacancies which may happen in either House shall, for the unexpired term, be filled by election, as shall be directed by law. *Ohio*, 434.

—Each House shall direct writs of election for supplying vacancies occasioned by death, resignation, or otherwise; but if vacancies occur during the recess of the Legislature, the writs may be issued by the Governor, under such regulations as may be prescribed by law. *N. J.*, 414.

—If any election district shall neglect to choose a member or members on the day of election, or if any person chosen a member of either House shall refuse to qualify and take his seat, or shall resign, die, depart the State, accept any disqualifying office, or become otherwise disqualified to hold his seat, a writ of election shall be issued by the President of the Senate, or Speaker of the House of Representatives, as the case may be, for the purpose of filling the vacancy thereby occasioned, for the remainder of the term for which the person so refusing to qualify, resigning, dying, departing the State, or becoming disqualified, was elected to serve, or the defaulting election district ought to have chosen a member or members. *S. C.*, 484.

—When vacancies happen in either House, writs of election shall be issued by the Speakers respectively, or in cases of necessity, in such other manner as shall be provided by law; and the persons thereupon chosen shall hold their seats as long as those in whose stead they are elected might have done, if such vacancies had not happened. *Del.*, 118.

—The General Assembly shall regulate by law, by whom and in what manner writs of election shall be issued to fill the vacancies which may happen in either branch thereof. *La.*, 229.

—When, during a recess of the Legislative Assembly, a vacancy shall happen in any office the appointment to which is vested in the Legislative Assembly, or when at any time a vacancy shall have occurred in any other State office, or in the office of judge of any court, the Governor shall fill such vacancy by appointment, which shall expire when a successor shall have been elected and qualified. *Or.*, 453.

—If any member of the Senate or General Assembly shall be elected to represent this State in the Senate or House of Representatives of the United States, and shall accept thereof, or shall accept of

1 § 10. A majority of each House shall constitute a quorum to do business.

2 Each House shall determine the rules of its own proceedings, and be the judge

3 of the elections, returns and qualifications of its own members; shall choose

4 its own officers; and the Senate shall choose a temporary president, when the

5 Lieutenant-Governor shall not attend as president, or shall act as Governor.

any office or appointment under the government of the United States, his seat in the Legislature of this State shall thereby be vacated. *N. J.*, 413.
—The two Houses shall direct writs of election for supplying intermediate vacancies. *N. C.*, 424.
—And in case the elections required by this Constitution on the first Wednesday of January, annually, by the two Houses of the Legislature, shall not be completed on that day, the same may be adjourned from day to day until completed, in the following order: The vacancies in the Senate shall first be filled; the Governor shall then be elected, if there be no choice by the people; and afterwards, the two Houses shall elect the Council. *Me.*, 247.
—The members of the House of Representatives, and such Senators as shall be declared elected shall take the names of such persons as shall be found to have the highest number of votes in such district, and not elected, amounting to twice the number of Senators wanting, if there be so many voted for, and out of these shall elect by ballot a number of Senators sufficient to fill up the vacancies in such district; and in this manner all such vacancies shall be filled up in every district of the Commonwealth; and in like manner all vacancies in the Senate, arising by death, removal out of the State or otherwise, shall be supplied as soon as may be after such vacancies shall happen. *Mass.*, 285.
—Each House shall settle its own rules of proceeding, and direct writs of election for supplying intermediate vacancies, but if vacancies shall occur during the recess of the General Assembly, such writs may be issued by the Governor, under such regulations as may be prescribed by law. *Va.*, 536.

.

NUMBER FORMING A QUORUM.

—A majority of the said members shall, from time to time, constitute a House to proceed upon business. *N. Y.* (1777), 28; (1821,) 35.
—Each House shall determine the rules of its own proceedings, and be the judge of the qualifications of its own members. Each House shall choose its own officers; and the Senate shall choose a temporary President, when the Lieutenant-Governor shall not attend as President, or shall act as Governor. *N. Y.* (1821), 35.
—A majority of each House shall constitute a quorum to do business; but a smaller number may adjourn from day to day, and may compel the attendance of absent members, in such manner, and under such penalties, as each house may provide. *Ala.*, 76; *Cal.*, 98; *Ct.*, 109; *Fl.*, 132; *Ga.*, 143; *Iowa*, 185; *Kan.*, 199; *Md.*, 262; *Mich.*, 302; *Min.*, 321; *Mo.*, 353; *Neb.*, 372; *Nev.*, 382; *N. J.*, 414; *Ohio*, 433; *Pa.*, 412; *R. I.*, 476; *Vt.*, 528; *Va.*, 536; *W. Va.*, 551; *Wis.*, 562; *Miss.*, 337; *S. C.*, 483.
—Two-thirds of each House shall constitute a quorum to do business, but a smaller number may adjourn from day to day, and compel the attendance of absent members, in such manner and under such penalties as each house shall provide. *Ark.*, 86; *Ill.*, 152; *Ind.*, 173; *Or.*, 460; *Tenn.*, 493; *Tex.*, 508.
—Each House shall judge of the elections, returns, and qualifications of its own members; and a majority

of each shall constitute a quorum to do business; but a smaller number may adjourn from day to day, and shall be authorized to compel the attendance of absent members, in such manner, and under such penalties as shall be deemed expedient. *Del.*, 118; *Me.*, 243.
—A quorum being in attendance, if either House fail to effect an organization within the first five days thereafter, the members of the House so failing shall be entitled to no compensation from the end of the said five days until an organization shall have been effected. *Ind.*, 173.
—Not less than a majority of the members of each House of the General Assembly shall constitute a quorum to do business, but a smaller number may adjourn from day to day, and shall be authorized by law to compel the attendance of absent members, in such manner and under such penalties as may be prescribed thereby. *Ky.*, 211; *La.*, 228.
—Not less than one hundred members of the House of Representatives shall constitute a quorum for doing business; but a less number may organize temporarily, adjourn from day to day, and compel the attendance of absent members. *Mass.*, 292.
—Not less than sixteen members of the Senate shall constitute a quorum for doing business. *Mass.*, 285.
—A majority of the members of the House of Representatives shall be a quorum for doing business; but when less than two-thirds of the Representatives elected shall be present, the assent of two-thirds of those members shall be necessary to render their acts and proceedings valid. *N. H.*, 403; *Or.*, 460.
—That neither House of the General Assembly shall proceed upon public business, unless a majority of all the members of such House are actually present. *N. C.*, 426.
—The mode of organizing the House of Representatives, at the commencement of each regular session, shall be prescribed by law. *Neb.*, 372; *Ohio*, 434.
—The organization of the two Houses may be regulated by law, subject to the limitations contained in this Constitution. *R. I.*, 476.

POWERS OF THE LEGISLATURE—ORGANIZATION·AND BUSINESS OF THE TWO HOUSES.

—That the Senate and House of Commons, when met, shall each have power to choose a Speaker, and their other officers; be judges of the qualifications and elections of their members; sit upon their own adjournments from day to day; and prepare bills to be passed into laws. The two Houses shall direct writs of election, for supplying intermediate vacancies; and shall also jointly, by ballot, adjourn themselves to any future day and place. *N. C.*, 424
—The presiding officer shall be styled the President of the Senate, and shall be elected *viva voce* from their own body. *Ga.*, 144.
—The presiding officer of the House of Representatives shall be styled the Speaker, and shall be elected *viva voce* from their own body. *Ga.*, 145.
—The Senate shall appoint their president and other officers, and determine their own rules of proceedings. And not less than seven members of the Senate shall make a quorum for doing business; and

when less than eight Senators shall be present, the assent of five, at least, shall be necessary to render their acts and proceedings valid. *N. H.*, 404.

—Each House shall have all powers necessary for a branch of the legislative department of a free and independant State. *Ind.*, 173; *Or.*, 451.

—The General Assembly shall continue to exercise the powers they have hitherto exercised, unless prohibited by the Constitution. *R. I.*, 476.

—*B: it ordained*, That the Legislature of this State shall have full and complete, ample and plenary power and right to ascertain, adjust and settle, any and all pecuniary liability and indebtedness of this State, or the citizens thereof, to the government of the United States of America, under and by reason of the revenue laws of the latter, either past, present or future; and to provide by law or otherwise, in such way and manner, and on such terms as the Legislature may in its opinion, deem or declare to be most wise, judicious and expedient, for the ascertainment, adjustment and present or ultimate settlement and payment of the same; hereby intending to confer, and actually conferring upon the Legislature of this State, full and absolute power, and right to pledge and use the faith and credit of the State, and to do and perform whatever is or may be necessary, proper or expedient in the premises aforesaid.

Adopted, August 24, 1865. *Miss.*, 345.

—And further, full power and authority are hereby given and granted to the said General Court from time to time, to make, ordain and establish all manner of wholesome and reasonable orders, laws, statutes and ordinances, directions and instructions, either with penalties or without, so as the same be not repugnant or contrary to this Constitution, as they shall judge to be for the good and welfare of this Commonwealth, and for the government and ordering thereof, and of the subjects of the same, and and for the necessary support and defense of the government thereof; and to name and settle annually, or provide by fixed laws, for the naming and settling all civil officers within the said Commonwealth, the election and constitution of whom are not hereafter in this form of government otherwise provided for; and to set forth the several duties, powers and limits of the several civil and military officers of this Commonwealth, and the forms of such oaths or affirmations as shall be respectively administered unto them for the execution of their several offices and places so as the same be not repugnant or contrary to this Constitution; and to impose and levy proportional and reasonable assessments, rates and taxes upon all the inhabitants of, and persons resident, and estates lying within the said Commonwealth; and also to impose and levy reasonable duties and excises upon any produce, goods, wares, merchandise and commodities whatsoever, brought into, produced, manufactured, or being within the same, to be issued and disposed of by warrant, under the hand of the Governor of this commonwealth, for the time being, with the advice and consent of the Council, for the public service, in the necessary defense and support of the government of the said Commonwealth, and the protection and preservation of the subjects thereof, according to such acts as are or shall be in force within the same. *Mass.*, 283.

—They may administer oaths and affirmations in matters depending before them; redress grievances, impeach State criminals, grant charters of incorporation, constitute towns, boroughs, cities and counties; they may annually, on their first session after their election [in conjunction with the Council] (or oftener if need be), elect judges of the Supreme [and several County and Probate] Courts, [Sheriffs and Justices of the Peace,] and also [with the Council] may elect Major-Generals and Brigadier Generals, from time to time, as often as there shall be occasion; and they shall have all other powers necessary for the Legislature of a free and sovereign State. But they shall have no power to add to, alter, abolish or infringe any part of this Constitution. *Vt.*, 523.

DECISIONS UPON QUALIFICATION OF MEMBERS—PUNISHMENT FOR DISORDERLY CONDUCT.

—Each House may determine the rules of its own proceedings, punish members for disorderly behavior, and, with the consent of two-thirds, expel a member, but not a second time for the same offense; and shall have all other powers necessary for a branch of the Legislature of a free and independent State. *Ala.*, 76; *Ct.*, 10J; *Del.*, 118; *Iowa*, 185; *Miss.*, 337; *Neb.*, 372; *Pa.*, 462; *Tenn.*, 493.

—Each House may, during the session, punish by imprisonment any person, not a member, for disrespectful or disorderly behavior in its presence [*Tenn.*, 493], or for obstructing any of its proceedings; *Provided*, That such imprisonment shall not, at any one time, exceed forty-eight hours. *Ala.*, 76; *Miss.*, 337; *Tex.*, 508.

—And each House may punish, by fine and imprisonment, any person not a member, who shall be guilty of disrespect to the House, by any disorderly or contemptuous behavior in their presence during their session, but such imprisonment shall not extend beyond the final adjournment of that session. *Ark.*, 86.

—Each House, during the session, may punish, by imprisonment, any person not a member, for disrespectful or disorderly behavior in its presence, or for obstructing any of its proceedings, provided such imprisonment shall not extend beyond the end of the session. *Fl.*, 132.

—Each House shall determine the rules of its own proceedings, and may, with the concurrence of two-thirds of all the members elected, expel a member. *Cal.*, 98.

—Each House may determine the rules of its own proceedings, punish its members for disorderly behavior, and, with the consent of two-thirds, expel a member, but not a second time for the same cause. *Fl.*, 132; *Ind.*, 173; *Ky.*, 211; *La.*, 228; *Ark.*, 86; *Me.*, 243; *Md.*, 262; *Or.*, 451; *R. I.*, 475; *W. Va.*, 551; *Va.*, 536; *Wis.*, 562; *Tex.*, 508.

—Each House shall be the judge of the election returns and qualifications of its own members; and shall have power to punish them for disorderly behavior or misconduct, by censure, fine, imprisonment or expulsion; but no member shall be expelled except by a vote of two-thirds of the House from which he is expelled. *Ga.*, 145.

—Each House may punish, by imprisonment, not extending beyond the session, any person not a member, who shall be guilty of a contempt by any disorderly behavior in its presence; or who, during the session, shall threaten injury to the person or estate of any member, for anything said or done in either House; or who shall assault or arrest any witness going to or returning from, or who shall rescue, or attempt to rescue, any person arrested by either House. *Ga.*, 145.

—Each House may determine the rules of its proceedings, punish its members for disorderly behavior, and with the concurrence of two-thirds of all the members elected, expel a member, but not a second time for the same cause; and the reason for such expulsion shall be entered upon the journal, with the names of the members voting on the question. *Ill.*, 152.

—Each House may punish, by imprisonment, during its session, any person not a member, who shall be guilty of disrespect to the House, by any disorderly or contemptuous behavior in their presence: *Provided*, such imprisonment shall not, at any one time, exceed twenty-four hours. *Ill.*, 153; *Ind.*, 173; *Or.*, 451; *Min.*, 322.

—Each House of the General Assembly shall judge of the qualifications, elections, and returns of its members; but a contested election shall be determined in such manner as shall be directed by law. *Ky.*, 211; *La.*, 228; *Pa.*, 262.

—Each House may punish, by imprisonment, any person not a member, for disrespectful and disorderly behavior in its presence, or for obstructing any of its proceedings. Such imprisonment shall not exceed ten days for any one offense. *La.*, 228.

—Each House may punish, by imprisonment during the session of the General Assembly, any person not a member, for disrespectful or disorderly behavior in its presence, or for obstructing any of its proceedings, or any of its officers in the execution of their duties; provided such imprisonment shall not, at any one time, exceed ten days. *Md.*, 262; (similar except term of imprisonment which may not extend beyond the period of session) *Me.*, 243; *Nev.*, 382.

—The House of Representatives shall be the judge of the returns, elections and qualifications of its own members, as pointed out in the Constitution; shall choose their own Speaker, appoint their own officers, and settle the rules and order of proceeding in their own House. They shall have authority to punish by imprisonment, every person, not a member, who shall be guilty of disrespect to the House, by any disorderly or contemptuous behavior in its presence; or who, in the town where the General Court is sitting, and during the time of its sitting, shall threaten harm to the body or estate of any of its members, for anything said or done in the House; or who shall assault any of them therefor; or who shall assault or arrest any witness, or other person, ordered to attend the House, in his way in going or returning; or who shall rescue any person arrested by the order of the House. *Mass.*, 286.

—The Senate shall have the same powers in the like cases; and the Governor and Council shall have the same authority to punish in like cases; *Provided,* That no imprisonment, on the warrant or order of the Governor, Council, Senate, or House of Representatives, for either of the above described offenses, be for a term exceeding thirty days. *Mass.*, 286.

—Each House shall be a judge of the election returns, and eligibility of its own members. *Cal.*, 98; *Mass.*, 286; *Minn.*, 321; *W. Va.*, 551.

—Each House may determine the rules of its proceedings, sit upon its own adjournment, punish its members for disorderly behavior, and, with the concurrence of two-thirds, expel a member, but no member shall be expelled a second time for the same offense. *Minn.*, 321.

—Each House shall choose its own officers, determine the rules of its proceedings, and judge of the qualifications, election and return of its members, and may, with the concurrence of two-thirds of all the members elected, expel a member. No member shall be expelled a second time for the same cause, nor for any cause known to his constituents antecedent to his election. The reason for such expulsion shall be entered upon the journal, with the names of the members voting on the question. *Mich.*, 302.

—Each House shall appoint its own officers; shall judge of the qualifications, elections and returns of its own members, may determine the rules of its proceedings; may arrest and punish, by fine, not exceeding three hundred dollars, or by imprisonment in a county jail not exceeding ten days, or both, any person, not a member, who shall be guilty of disrespect to the House, by any disorderly or contemptuous behavior in its presence during its session; may punish its members for disorderly behavior, and, with the concurrence of two-thirds of its members elected, may expel a member; but no member shall be expelled a second time for the same cause. *Mo.*, 353.

—Each House shall choose its own officers, determine the rules of its proceedings, punish its members for disorderly behavior, and, with the concurrence of two-thirds, may expel a member. *N. J.*, 414.

—Each House shall judge of the qualifications, elections and returns of its own members, choose its own officers (except the President of the Senate), determine the rules of its proceedings, and may punish its members for disorderly conduct, and, with the concurrence of two-thirds of all the members elected, expel a member. *Nev.*, 382.

—The House of Representatives shall choose their own Speaker, appoint their own officers, and settle

the rules of proceedings in their own House; and shall be judge of the returns, elections and qualifications of its members, as pointed out in this Constitution. They shall have authority to punish by imprisonment every person who shall be guilty of disrespect to the House in its presence by any disorderly and contemptuous behavior, or by threatening or ill-treating any of its members; or by obstructing its deliberations; every person guilty of a breach of its privileges in making arrests for debt, or by assaulting any member during his attendance at any session; in assaulting or disturbing any one of its officers in the execution of any order or procedure of the House; in assaulting any witness or other person ordered to attend, by and during his attendance of the House, or in rescuing any person arrested by order of the House, knowing them to be such. *N. H.* 403.

— The Senate, Governor and Council shall have the same power in like cases; provided that no imprisonment by either, for any offense, exceed ten days. *N. H.*, 403.

—The Senate shall be final judges of the elections, returns and qualifications of their own members, as pointed out in this Constitution. *N. H.* 404.

— Each House, when assembled, shall choose its own officers; judge of the election, qualifications, and returns of its own members; determine its own rules of proceeding, and sit upon its own adjournments. *Or.*, 450.

—Each House, except as otherwise provided in this Constitution, shall choose its own officers, may determine its own rules of proceeding, punish its members for disorderly conduct, and, with the concurrence of two-thirds, expel a member, but not the second time for the same cause; and shall have all other powers necessary to provide for its safety and the undisturbed transaction of its business. *Ohio*, 434.

—Each House shall choose its own officers, determine its rules of proceeding, punish its members for disorderly behavior, and, with the concurrence of two-thirds, expel a member, but not a second time for the same cause. *S. C.*, 483.

—Each House may punish, by imprisonment, during its sitting, any person, not a member, who shall be guilty of disrespect to the House by any disorderly or contemptuous behavior in its presence; or who, during the time of its sitting, shall threaten harm to the body or estate of any member for anything said or done in either House, or who shall assault any of them therefor, or who shall assault or arrest any witness or other person ordered to attend the House, in his going thereto, or returning therefrom, or who shall rescue any person arrested by order of the House. *S. C.*, 484; *Mass.*, 286.

—They shall have power to choose their Speaker, their Clerk and other necessary officers of the House; sit on their own adjournments; prepare bills and enact them into laws; judge of the elections and qualifications of their own members; they may expel members, but not for causes known to their constituents antecedent to their election. *Vt.*, 523.

—Each House shall judge of the election, qualification and returns of its members, may punish them for disorderly behavior, and, with the concurrence of two-thirds, expel a member, but not a second time for the same offense. *Vt.*, 536.

—Each branch shall have the power necessary to provide for its own safety, and the undisturbed transaction of its business, and may punish, by imprisonment, any person, not a member, for disrespectful behavior in its presence; obstructing any of its proceedings, or any of its officers in the discharge of his duties; or for any assault, threatening or abuse of a member for words spoken in debate. But such imprisonment shall not extend beyond the termination of the session, and shall not prevent the punishment of any offense by the ordinary course of law. *W. Va.*, 551.

—Each House shall be the judge of the elections, returns and qualifications of its own members. *Ark.*, 86; *Neb.*, 373; *N. J.*, 414; *Ohio*, 433; *Fl.*, 132; *Wis.*, 562; *Ill.*, 152; *Iowa*, 185; *Miss.*, 337; *S. C.*, 483.

18

1   § 11. Each House shall keep a journal of its proceedings, and publish the

2 same, except such parts as may require secrecy. The doors of each House

3 shall be kept open, except when the public welfare shall require secrecy.

4 Neither House shall, without the consent of the other, adjourn for more than

5 two days.

—Each House shall establish its own rules, and shall be judge of the elections, returns and qualifications of its own members. *Kan.,* 199.

EACH HOUSE MAY CHOOSE ITS OWN OFFICERS.

—That the Assembly, thus constituted, shall choose their own speaker, be judges of their own members, and enjoy the same privileges, and proceed in doing business, in like manner, as the assemblies of the colony of New York of right formerly did. *N. Y.,* (1777), 21.

—At the first regular called session after each general election for Representatives, the Senate shall choose a President and its other officers, and the House of Representatives shall choose a Speaker and its other officers; and the officers so chosen shall be entitled to hold their respective offices until the next general election for Representatives. Each House shall judge of the qualifications, elections, and returns of its own members; but a contested election shall be determined in such manner as may be by law provided. *Ala.,* 76.

—The House of Representatives, when assembled, shall choose a Speaker, Clerk, and other officers. The Senate shall choose its Clerk and other officers, except the President. *Ct.,* 109.

- Each House shall choose its Speaker and other officers; and also each House whose Speaker shall exercise the office of Governor, may choose a Speaker *pro tempore. Fl.,* 132.

—The Senate and House of Representatives, when assembled, shall each choose a Speaker and other officers (the Speaker of the Senate excepted). Each House shall judge of the qualifications and election of its members, and sit upon its own adjournments. *Ind.,* 173; *Ill.,* 152.

—The House of Representatives shall choose its Speaker and other officers. *Ky.,* 210.

--The House of Representatives shall choose their Speaker, Clerk, and other officers. *Me.,* 242; *Mass.,* 286.

—The Senate shall choose their President, Secretary, and other officers. *Me.,* 242.

—The Senate shall choose its own President, appoint its own officers, and determine its own rules of proceedings. *Mass.,* 285.

—The House of Representatives shall elect its presiding officer, and the Senate and House of Representatives shall elect such other officers as may be provided by law. *Min.,* 321.

—The House of Representatives shall choose their own Speaker, appoint their own officers, and settle the rules of proceedings in their own House. *N. H.,* 403.

—Each House shall choose its Speaker and other officers, and the Senate shall also choose a Speaker *pro tempore,* when the Speaker shall exercise the office of Governor. *Pa.,* 462.

—The House of Representatives shall have authority to elect its Speaker, Clerks, and other officers. The senior member from the town of Newport, if any be present, shall preside in the organization of the House. *R. I.,* 477.

—The House of Delegates shall choose its own Speaker, and in the absence of the Lieutenant-Governor, or when he shall exercise the office of Governor, the Senate shall choose from their own body a President *pro tempore,* and each House shall appoint its own officers. *Va.,* 536.

—The House of Representatives, when assembled, shall elect a Speaker and its other officers, and the Senate shall choose a President for the time being and its other officers. Each House shall judge of the qualifications and elections of its own members, but contested elections shall be determined in such manner as shall be directed by law. *Tex.,* 509.

--The Senate shall choose from their own body a President, and the House of Delegates one of their own number as Speaker. Each branch shall appoint its own officers and remove them at pleasure; and shall determine its own rules of proceeding. *W. Va.,* 551.

—Each House shall choose its own officers, and the Senate shall choose a temporary President, when the Lieutenant-Governor shall not attend as President, or shall not as Governor. *Wis.,* 562.

—The elective officers of the Legislature, other than the Presiding officers, shall be a Chief Clerk and a Sergeant-at-Arms, to be elected by each House. *Wis.,* 571.

--The Senate and House of Representatives, when assembled, shall each choose a Speaker and its other officers, be judges of the qualifications and election of its members, and sit upon its own adjournments from day to day. *Tenn.,* 493.

—The Senate shall have the like powers to decide on the election and qualifications of, and to expel any of its members; make its own rules, and appoint its own officers, as are incident to, or are possessed by, the House of Representatives. *Vt.,* 528.

JOURNAL OF PROCEEDINGS— RIGHT OF RECORDING PROTEST.

—And the journals of all their proceedings shall be kept in the manner heretofore accustomed by the General Assembly of the colony of New York; and (except such parts as they shall, as aforesaid, respectively determine not to be made public), be, from day to day (if the business of the Legislature will permit) published. *N. Y.* (1777), 28.

—Each House shall keep a journal of its proceedings, and publish the same, except such parts as may require secrecy. The doors of each House shall be kept open, except when the public welfare shall require secrecy. Neither House shall, without the consent of the other, adjourn for more than two days. *N. Y.* (1821), 35.

—Each House shall keep a journal of its own proceedings, and cause the same to be published immediately after its adjournment, excepting such parts as, in its judgment, may require secrecy; and the yeas and nays of the members of either House, on any question, shall, at the desire of any two members present, be entered on the journals. Any member of either House shall have liberty to dissent from, and protest against, any act or resolution which he may think injurious to the public or to an individual, and have the reasons of his dissent entered on the journals. *Ala.,* 76.

—They shall each, from time to time, publish a journal of their proceedings, except such parts as may require secrecy; and the yeas and nays upon any question shall be entered on the journal at the desire of any five members. *Ark.*, 80 (nearly similar) *Md.*, 252.

—Each House shall keep a journal of its own proceedings, and publish the same; and the yeas and nays of the members of either House on any question shall, at the desire of any three members present, be entered on the journal. *Cal.*, 98; *Miss.*, 337; *Nev.*, 382; *Tex.*, 508; (similar, except request of *two* members), *Ill.*, 152.

—Each House shall keep a journal of its proceedings, and publish the same, when required by one-fifth of its members, except such parts as, in the judgment of a majority, require secrecy. The yeas and nays of the members of either House shall, at the desire of one-fifth of those present, be entered on the journals. *Ct.*, 109; *Me.*, 243; (nearly similar), *Mch.*, 302.

—Each House shall keep a journal of its proceedings, and publish them immediately after every session, except such parts as may require secrecy, and the yeas and nays of the members on any question shall, at the desire of any member, be entered on the journal. *Del.*, 118.

—Each House shall keep a journal of its proceedings, and cause the same to be published immediately after its adjournment; and the yeas and nays of the members of each House shall be taken and entered upon the journals upon the final passage of every bill, and may by any two members, be required upon any other question; and any member of either House shall have liberty to dissent from or protest against any act or resolution which he may think injurious to the public, or an individual, and have the reasons of his dissent entered on the journal. *Fl.*, 132.

—Each House shall keep a journal of its proceedings and publish them immediately after its adjournment. The yeas and nays of the members, on any question, shall, at the desire of one-fifth of the members present, be entered on the journals. The original journals shall be preserved (after publication) in the office of the Secretary of State; but there shall be no other record thereof. *Ga.*, 145.

—Whenever this Constitution requires an act to be passed by two-thirds of both Houses, the yeas and nays on the passage thereof, shall be entered on the journals of each. *Ga.*, 145.

—Any two members of either House shall have liberty to dissent and protest against any act or resolution which they may think injurious to the public, or to any individual. and have the reasons of their dissent entered on the journals. *Ill.*, 152; *Min.*, 312.

—Any member of either House shall have the right to protest, and to have his protest, with his reasons for dissent, entered on the journal. *Ind.*, 174; (nearly similar,) *Mich.*, 302; *N. C.*, 426; *Or.* 451.

—Each House shall keep a journal of its proceedings, and publish the same. The yeas and nays on any question shall, at the request of any two members, be entered, together with the names of the members demanding the same, on the journal; *Provided*, That, on a motion to adjourn, it shall require one-tenth of the members present to order the yeas and nays. *Ind.*, 173.

—Every member of the General Assembly shall have the liberty to dissent from or protest against any act or resolution which he may think injurious to the public or any individual, and have the reasons for his dissent entered on the journals; and the yeas and nays of the members of either House, on any question, shall, at the desire of any two members present, be entered on the journals. *Iowa*, 185.

—Each House shall sit upon its own adjournment, keep a journal of its proceedings, and publish the same. *Iowa*, 185; *Min.*, 321.

—Each House shall keep and publish a journal of its proceedings. The yeas and nays shall be taken and entered immediately on the journal, upon the final passage of every bill or joint resolution. Neither House, without the consent of the other, shall adjourn for more than two days, Sundays excepted. *Kan.*, 199.

—Any member of either House shall have the right to protest against any act or resolution; and such protest shall, without delay or alteration, be entered on the journal. *Kan.*, 199.

—Each House of the General Assembly shall keep and publish, weekly, a journal of its proceedings, and the yeas and nays of the members on any question shall, at the desire of any two of them, be entered on their journal. *Ky.*, 211; *La.*, 226.

—Each House shall, from time to time, publish a journal of its proceedings, except such parts thereof as may, in its opinion, require secrecy; and the yeas and nays on any question shall be taken and entered on the journal, at the desire of any two members. Whenever the yeas and nays are demanded the whole list of members shall be called, and the names of absentees shall be noted, and published with the journal. *Mo.*, 353.

—Each House shall keep a correct journal of its proceedings, which shall be published. At the desire of any three members in the Senate, or any five members in the House, the ayes and nays shall be entered upon the journal and on the passage of every bill, in either House, the vote shall be taken by yeas and nays, and entered upon the journal, and no law shall be passed in either House without the concurrence of a majority of all the members elected thereto. *Neb.*, 372.

—Upon a motion made and seconded, the yeas and nays, upon any question, shall be taken and entered on the journals; and that the journals of the proceedings of both Houses of the General Assembly shall be printed and made public, immediately after their adjournment. *N. C.*, 426.

—The journals of the proceedings, and all public acts of both Houses of the Legislature, shall be printed and published immediately after every adjournment or prorogation; and upon motion made by any one member, the yeas and nays upon any question shall be entered upon the journal; and any member of the Senate or House of Representatives shall have a right, on motion made at the same time for that purpose, to have his protest or dissent, with the reasons, against any vote, resolve or bill passed, entered on the journal. *N. H.*, 403.

—Each House shall keep a journal of its proceedings, and from time to time publish the same; and the yeas and nays of the members of either House on any question shall, at the desire of one-fifth of those present, be entered on the journal. *N. J.*, 414.

—Any member of either House shall have the right to protest against any act or resolution thereof; and such protest, and the reasons therefor, shall, without alteration, commitment, or delay, be entered upon the journal. *Ohio*, 434.

—Each House shall keep a correct journal of its proceedings, which shall be published. At the desire of any two members the yeas and nays shall be entered upon the journal; and, on the passage of every bill, in either House, the vote shall be taken by yeas and nays and entered upon the journal; and no law shall be passed, in either House, without the concurrence of a majority of all the members elected thereto. *Ohio*, 434.

—Each House shall keep a journal of its proceedings. The yeas and nays on any question shall, at the request of any two members, be entered, together with the names of the members demanding the same, on the journal; *Provided*, That, on a motion to adjourn, it shall require one-tenth of the members present to order the yeas and nays. *Or.*, 450.

—Each House shall keep a journal of its proceedings, and publish them weekly, except such part as may require secrecy; and the yeas and nays of the members on any question shall, at the desire of any two of them, be entered on the journals. *Pa.*, 402.

—Each House shall keep a journal of its proceedings. The yeas and nays of the members of either House shall, at the desire of one-fifth of those present, be entered on the journal. *R. I.*, 476.

—Any member of either House of the General Assembly shall have liberty to dissent from, and protest against, any act or resolve which he may think injurious to the public or to any individual, and to have the reasons for his dissent entered on the journals. *Tenn.*, 494.

—The votes and proceedings of the General Assembly shall be printed (when one-third of the members think it necessary) as soon as convenient after the end of each session, with the yeas and nays on any question, when required by any member (except where the vote shall be taken by ballot), in which case every member shall have a right to insert the reason of his vote upon the minutes. *Vt.*, 524.

—Each House of the General Assembly shall keep a journal of its proceedings, which shall be published from time to time, and the yeas and nays of the members of either House, on any question, shall, at the desire of one-fifth of those present, be entered on the journal. No bill shall become a law until it has been read on three different days of the session in the House in which it originated, unless two-thirds of the members elected to that House shall otherwise determine. *Va.*, 537.

—On the passage of every act which imposes, continues or revives a tax, or creates a debt or charge. or makes, continues or revives any appropriation of public or trust money or property, or releases, discharges or commutes any claim or demand of the State, the vote shall be determined by yeas and nays, and the names of the persons voting for and against the same shall be entered on the journals of the respective Houses, and a majority of all the members elected to each House shall be necessary to give it the force of a law. *Va.*, 538.

—On the passage of every bill, the votes shall be taken by yeas and nays, and be entered on the journal; and no bill shall be passed by either branch without the affirmative vote of a majority of the members elected thereto. *W. Va.*, 551.

—Each branch shall keep a journal of its proceeding, and cause the same to be published from time to time; and the yeas and nays on any question, if called for by one-fifth of those present, shall be entered on the journal. *W. Va.*, 551.

—The yeas and nays of the members of either House, on any question, shall, at the request of one-sixth of those present, be entered on the journal. *Wis.*, 563.

—Each House shall keep a journal of its proceedings, and publish the same, except such parts as require secrecy. The doors of each House shall be kept open except when the public welfare shall require secrecy. Neither House shall, without consent of the other, adjourn for more than three days. *Wis.*, 562.

SESSIONS TO BE OPEN UNLESS THE PUBLIC WELFARE REQUIRES SECRECY.

—That the doors, both of the Senate and Assembly, shall at all times be kept open to all persons, except when the welfare of the State shall require their debates to be kept secret. *N. Y.* (1777), 28.

—The doors of each House shall be kept open, except on such occasions as in the opinion of the House may rebuire secrecy. *Ala.*, 76; *Cal.*, 98; *Ct.*, 109; *Del.*, 118; *Fl.*, 133; *Ind.*, 173; *Iowa*, 185; *Md.*, 262; *Mich.*, 302; *Min.*, 322; *Mo.*, 353; *Nev.*, 382; (except the Senate in Executive Session,) *Nev.*, 382.

—The doors of each House shall be open, except on such occasions of great emergency as in the opinion of the House may require secrecy. *Miss.*, 337.

—The doors of the galleries of each House of the Legislature shall be kept open to all persons who behave decently, except when the welfare of the State, in the opinion of either branch, shall require secrecy. *N. H.*, 402.

—The proceedings of both Houses shall be public, except in cases which, in the opinion of two-thirds of those present, require secrecy. *Ohio*, 434.

—The doors of each House and of committees of the whole shall be kept open, except in such cases as, in the opinion of either House, may require secrecy. *Ark.*, 86; *Ill.*, 153; *Or.*, 451; *Pa.*, 426; *Tenn.*, 493.

—The doors of each House shall be kept open. *Tex.*, 508.

—The doors of the house in which the General Assembly of this Commonwealth shall sit, shall be open for the admission of all persons who behave decently, except only when the welfare of the State may require them to be shut. *Vt.*, 524.

ADJOURNMENTS BY THE LEGISLATURE.

—Neither House shall, without the consent of the other, adjourn for more than three days, nor to any other place than that in which they may be sitting. *Ala.*, 76; *Cal.*, 98; *Del.*, 118; *Fl.*, 133; *Ga.*, 145; *Iowa*, 185; *Ind.*, 173; *Mich.*, 302; *Ky.*, 211; *La.*, 228; *Miss.*, 337; *Nev.*, 382; *N. Y.*, 414; *Or.*, 450; *Pa.*, 462; *S. C.*, 484; *Tenn.*, 493; *Tex.*, 508; *Vt.*, 528; *Va.*, 536.

[Adjournments limited to two days.] *Me.*, 244; *Mass.*, 286; *Kan.*, 199; *Mo.*, 354; *R. I.*, 475; *N. H.*, 404; *W. Va.*, 551.

—Neither House shall, without the consent of the other, adjourn for more than three days at any one time, nor to any other place than that in which the House shall be sitting, without the concurrent vote of two-thirds of the members present. *Md.*, 262.

—The Legislature, on the day of final adjournment, shall adjourn at twelve o'clock at noon. *Mich.*, 303.

—Neither House shall, during a session of the Legislature, adjourn for more than three days (Sundays excepted), nor to any other place than that in which the two Houses shall be assembled, without the consent of the other House. *Minn.*, 321.

—That neither the Assembly nor the Senate shall have the power to adjourn themselves, for any longer time than two days, without the mutual consent of both. *N. Y.* (1777), 28.

—Neither House shall, without the consent of the other, adjourn for more than two days, Sundays excluded; nor to any other place than that, in which the two Houses shall be in session. *Ohio*, 437; *Ill.*, 153.

ADJOURNMENTS BY THE GOVERNOR— POWER OF EXECUTIVE TO PROROGUE THE LEGISLATURE.

—In case of a disagreement between the two Houses with respect to the time of adjournment, the Governor shall have power to adjourn the Legislature to such time as he may think proper; provided it be not beyond the next time fixed for the meeting of the next Legislature. *Ala.*, 79; *Ark.*, 89; *Cal.*, 100; *Ct.*, 110; *Fl.*, 131; *Ill.*, 158; *Iowa*, 188; *Miss.*, 341; *Tex.*, 513.

—And in case of disagreement between the two Houses, with respect to the time of adjournment, he may adjourn them to such time as he shall think proper, not exceeding four months. *Ky.*, 213; *La.*, 235; *Pa.*, 463.

—In case of disagreement between the two Houses, on a question of adjournment, the Governor may adjourn them. *Ga.*, 145.

—In case of disagreement between the two Houses in respect to the time of adjournment, he may adjourn the Legislature to such time as he may think proper, not beyond its regular meeting. *Kan.*, 198.

—The Governor, with advice of Council, shall have full power and authority, during the session of the General Court, to adjourn or prorogue the same at any time the two Houses shall desire; [and to dissolve the same on the day next preceding the last Wednesday in May; and, in the recess of the said court, to prorogue the same from time to time, not exceeding ninety days in any one recess;] and to call it together sooner than the time to which it may be adjourned or prorogued, if the welfare of the Commonwealth shall require the same; and in case of any infectious distemper prevailing in the place where the said court is next at any time to convene, or any other cause happening whereby danger may arise to the health or lives of the members from their attendance, he may direct the session to be held at some other the most convenient place within the State.

[And the Governor shall dissolve the said General Court on the day next preceding the last Wednesday in May.] *Mass.*, 287.

—In cases of disagreement between the two Houses, with regard to the necessity, expediency or time of adjournment or prorogation, the Governor, with advice of the Council, shall have a right to adjourn or prorogue the General Court, not exceeding ninety days; as he shall determine the public good shall require. *Mass.*, 287.

—In case of disagreement between the two Houses in respect to the time of adjournment, he shall have power to adjourn the Legislature to such time as he may think proper, but not beyond the regular meetings thereof. *Neb.*, 374.

—In case of a disagreement between the two Houses with respect to the time of adjournment, the Governor shall have the power to adjourn the Legislature to such time as he may think proper; *Provided*, It be not beyond the time fixed for the meeting of the next Legislature. *Nev*, 385.

—In cases of disagreement between the two Houses with regard to the time or place of adjournment or prorogation, the Governor, with advice of Council, shall have a right to adjourn or prorogue the General Court, not exceeding ninety days at any one time, as he may determine the public good may require, and he shall dissolve the same seven days before the said first Wednesday of June. And in case of any infectious distemper prevailing in the place where the said court at any time is to convene, or any other cause whereby dangers may arise to the health or lives of the members, from their attendance, the Governor may direct the session to be holden at some other, the most convenient place within the State. *N. H.*, 405.

—The Governor, with the advice of the Council, shall have full power and authority, in recess of the General Court, to prorogue the same from time to time, not exceeding ninety days in any one recess of said court; and, during the sessions of said court, to adjourn or prorogue it to any time the two Houses may desire, and call it together sooner than the time to which it may be adjourned or prorogued, if the welfare of the State should require the same. *N. H.*, 406.

—In case of disagreement between the two Houses in respect to the time of adjournment, he shall have power to adjourn the General Assembly to such time as he may think proper, but not beyond the regular meetings thereof. *Ohio*, 436.

—In case of disagreement between the two Houses of the General Assembly respecting the time or place of adjournment, certified to him by either, he may adjourn them to such time and place as he shall think proper; *Provided*, That the time of adjournment shall not extend beyond the day of the next stated session. *R. I.*, 477.

—And in case of disagreement between the two Houses, with respect to adjournment, the Governor may adjourn them to such time as he shall think proper. *Vt.*, 528.

[The Governor had power under the N. Y. Constitution of 1777, to prorogue the Legislature for any period not to exceed sixty days in a year.] 224.

—He may, on extraordinary occasions, convene the Legislature; and, in case of disagreement between the two Houses with respect to the time of adjournment, adjourn them to such time as he shall think proper, not beyond the day of the next annual meeting; and if, since their last adjournment, the place where the Legislature were next to convene shall have become dangerous from an enemy, or contagious sickness, may direct the session to be held at some other convenient place within the State. *Me.*, 245.

—He may, on extraordinary occasions, convene the General Assembly, and should either House remain without a quorum for three days, or in case of disagreement between the two Houses with respect to

the time of adjournment, may adjourn them to such time as he shall think proper, not beyond the fourth Monday of November then next ensuing. *S. C.*, 485.

POWER OF EXECUTIVE TO CONVENE LEGISLATURE.

—He may, by proclamation, on extraordinary occasions, convene the General Assembly at the seat of government, or at a different place, if, since their last adjournment, that shall have become dangerous, from an enemy, or from contagious disorders. *Ala.*. 79 ; *Fl.*, 131 ; *Ky.*, 213 ; *La.*, 235 ; *Miss.*, 341 ; *Tex.*, 513.

—He may, on extraordinary occasions, convene the Legislature by proclamation, and shall state to both Houses, when assembled, the purpose for which they shall have been convened. *Cal.*, 100.

—He may, on extraordinary occasions, convene the General Assembly, and in case of disagreement between the two Houses with respect to the time of adjournment, adjourn them to such time as he shall think proper, not exceeding three months. *Del.*, 120.

—Shall have power to convene the General Assembly on extraordinary occasions; and shall give them, from time to time, information of the state of the republic, and recommend to their consideration such measures as he may deem necessary and expedient. *Ga.*, 147.

—He may, on extraordinary occasions, convene the General Assembly, by proclamation, and shall state to both Houses, when assembled, the purpose for which they shall have been convened. *Iowa*, 188 ; *Ill.*, 158.

—And the General Assembly shall enter on no legislative business, except that for which they were especially called together. *Ill.*, 158.

—He may, on extraordinary occasions, convene the Legislature. *N. Y.* (1777), 24 ; *S. C.*, 481 ; *Pa.*, 463 ; *Me.*, 245 ; *Mich.*, 304 ; *Miss.*, 341.

—The Governor may convene the General Assembly, or the Senate alone, on extraordinary occasions; and whenever, from the presence of an enemy, or from any other cause, the seat of government shall become an unsafe place for the meeting of the General Assembly, he may direct their sessions to be held at some other convenient place. *Md.*, 260.

—He may convene the Legislature at some other place when the seat of government becomes dangerous from disease or a common enemy. *Mich.*, 305.

—On extraordinary occasions he may convene the General Assembly by proclamation; wherein he shall state specifically each matter concerning which the action of that body is deemed necessary; and the General Assembly shall have no power when so convened, to act upon any matter not so stated in the proclamation. *Mo.*, 355.

—He may, on extraordinary occasions, convene the Legislature by proclamation, and shall state to both Houses, when assembled, the purpose for which they have been convened. *Neb.*, 374; *Ohio*, 436; *Or.*, 452; *Tenn.*, 495.

—The Governor may, on extraordinary occasions convene the Legislature by proclamation, and shall state to both Houses, when organized, the purpose for which they have been convened, and the Legislature shall transact no legislative business except that for which they were specially convened, or such other legislative business as the Governor may call to the attention of the Legislature while in session. *Nev.*, 385.

—He shall have power to convene the Legislature (or the Senate only), on extraordinary occasions. He shall communicate by message to the Legislature, at every session, the condition of the State, and recommend such matters to them as he shall judge expedient. *N. Y.* (1821), 38.

—Shall have power to convene the Legislature whenever, in his opinion, public necessity requires it ; he shall communicate by message to the Legislature at the opening of each session, and at such other times as he may deem necessary, the condition of the State,

1   § 12. For any speech or debate in either House of the Legislature, the

2   members shall not be questioned in any other place.

and recommend such measures as he may deem expedient; and grant, under the great seal of the State, commissions to all such officers as shall be required to be commissioned. *N. J.*, 416.

—He may, on extraordinary occasions, convene the General Assembly at any town or city in this State, at any time not provided for by law; and in case of danger from the prevalence of epidemic or contagious disease, in the place in which the General Assembly are, by law, to meet, or to which they may have been adjourned, or for other urgent reasons, he may, by proclamation, convene said Assembly at any other place within this State. *R. I.*, 477.

—And convene the General Assembly on application of a majority of the members of both Houses thereof, or when, in his opinion, the interest of the Commonwealth may require it. *Va.*, 539.

—He shall have power to convene the Legislature on extraordinary occasions; and in case of invasion, or danger from the prevalence of contagious diseases at the seat of government, he may convene them at any other suitable place within the State. *Wis.*, 564.

—The Governor may convene the Legislature by proclamation, whenever in his opinion, the public safety or welfare shall require it. It shall be his duty to convene them on application of a majority of the members elected to each branch. *W. Va.*, 551.

—Should the seat of government become dangerous from disease or a common enemy, he may convene the General Assembly at any other place. *Ind.*, 175.

—That Annapolis be the place for the meeting of the Legislature, and the Legislature ought not to be convened or held at any other place but for evident necessity. *Md.*, 254.

PRIVILEGE FROM ARREST OR SERVICE OF CIVIL PROCESS—FREEDOM OF DEBATE.

—Senators and Representatives shall, in all cases except treason, felony or breach of the peace, be privileged from arrest, during the session of the General Assembly, and in going to and returning from the same, allowing one day for every twenty miles such member may reside from the place at which the General Assembly is convened; nor shall any member be liable to answer for anything spoken in debate in either House, in any court or place elsewhere. *Ala.*, 76; *Fl.*, 132; *Or.*, 450.

—The Senators and Representatives shall, in all cases except treason, felony or breach of the peace, be privileged from arrest during the session of the General Assembly, and for fifteen days before the commencement and after the termination of each session; and for any speech or debate in either House, they shall not be questioned in any other place. *Ark.*, 86.

—Members of the Legislature shall, in all cases except treason, felony and breach of the peace, be privileged from arrest, and they shall not be subject to any civil process during the session of the Legislature, nor for fifteen days next before the Commencement and after the termination of each session. *Cal.*, 93; *Wis.*, 563.

—The Senators and Representatives shall, in all cases of civil process, be privileged from arrest during the session of the General Assembly, and for four days before the commencement and after the termination of any session thereof. And for any speech or debate in either House they shall not be questioned in any other place. *Ct.*, 109.

—The members of both Houses shall be free from arrest during their attendance on the General Assembly, and in going to and returning therefrom; except for treason, felony, or breach of the peace. And no member shall be liable to answer in any other place for anything spoken in debate in either House. *Ga.*, 145.

—Senators and Representatives in all cases except treason, felony or breach of the peace, shall be privileged from arrest during the session of the General Assembly, and in going to and returning from the same. *Iowa*, 185.

—For any speech or debate in either House the members shall not be questioned elsewhere. No member of the Legislature shall be subject to arrest, except for felony and breach of the peace, in going to and returning from the place of meeting, or during the continuance of the session; neither shall he be subject to the service of any civil process during the session, nor for fifteen days previous to its commencement. *Kan.*, 200.

—The members of the General Assembly shall, in all cases except treason, felony, breach or surety of the peace, be privileged from arrest during their attendance at the sessions of their respective Houses, and in going to and returning from the same; and for any speech or debate in either House, they shall not be questioned in any other place. *Del.*, 118; *Ill.*, 153; *Ky.*, 211; *La.*, 228; *Me.*, 244; *Min.*, 321; *Mo.*, 353; *N. J.*, 414; *Ohio*, 434; *Pa.*, 462; *Tenn.*, 493.

—That freedom of speech and debate, or proceedings in the Legislature, ought not to be impeached in any court of judicature. *Md.*, 254.

——No Senator or Delegate shall be liable, in any civil action or criminal prosecution whatever, for words spoken in debate. *Md.*, 262.

—No member of the House of Representatives shall be arrested, or held to bail on mesne process, during his going unto, returning from, or his attending the General Assembly. *Mass.*, 286.

—Senators and Representatives shall, in all cases, except treason, felony, or breach of the peace, be privileged from arrest. They shall not be subject to any civil process during the session of the Legislature, or for fifteen days next before the commencement and after the termination of each session. They shall not be questioned in any other place for any speech in either House. *Mich.*, 301; *Ind.*, 172.

—Senators and Representatives shall in all cases, except treason, felony, or breach of the peace, be privileged from arrest during the session of the Legislature, and in going to and returning from the same, allowing one day for every twenty miles such member may reside from the place at which the Legislature is convened. *Miss.*, 337.

—Members of the Legislature shall in all cases, except treason, felony, or breach of the peace, be privileged from arrest, nor shall they be subject to any civil process, during the session of the Legislature, nor for fifteen days next before the commencement, and after the termination of each session. *Neb.*, 372.

——No member of the Legislature shall be liable in any civil action or criminal prosecution whatever, for words spoken in debate. *Neb.*, 372; *Wis.*, 563.

—Members of the Legislature shall be privileged from arrest on civil process during the session of the Legislature, and for fifteen days next before the commencement of each session. *Nev.*, 382.

—The freedom of deliberation, speech and debate, in either House of the Legislature, is so essential to the rights of the people, that it cannot be the foundation of any accusation or prosecution, action or complaint, in any other court or place whatsoever. *Mass.*, 282; *N. H.*, 400; *Vt.*, 522.

—No member of the House of Representatives or Senate shall be arrested or held to bail on mesne process, during his going to, returning from, or attendance upon the Court. *N. H.*, 403.

—The person of every member of the General Assembly shall be exempt from arrest, and his estate from attachment, in any civil action, during the session

1 § 13. Any bill may originate in either House of the Legislature, and all

2 bills passed by one House may be amended by the other.

1 § 14. The enacting clause of all bills shall be "The People of the State of

2 New York, represented in Senate and Assembly, do enact as follows," and no

3 law shall be enacted except by bill.

of the General Assembly, and two days before the commencement, and two days after the termination thereof, and all process served contrary hereto, shall be void. For any speech in either House, no member shall be questioned in any other place. *R. I.*, 476.

—The members of both Houses shall be protected in their persons and estates during their attendance on, going to, and returning from the General Assembly, and ten days previous to the sitting, and ten days after the adjournment thereof. But these privileges shall not be extended so as to protect any member who shall be charged with treason, felony or breach of the peace. *S. C.*, 484.

—The Senators and Representatives shall, in all cases, except in treason, felony or breach of the peace, be privileged from arrest during the session of the Legislature, and in going to and returning from the same, allowing one day for every twenty miles such member may reside from the place at which the Legislature is convened. *Tex.*, 568.

—For words spoken in debate, or any report, motion, or proposition made, in either branch, a member shall not be questioned in any other place. *W. Va.*, 551.

—Members of the Legislature shall, in all cases except treason, felony, and breach of the peace, be privileged from arrest during the session, and for ten days before and after the same. *W. Va.*, 551.

ORIGIN OF BILLS.

—Any bill may originate in either House of the Legislature; and all bills passed by one House may be amended by the other. *N. Y.* (1821), 36; *Kan.*, 199; (nearly similar), *Ala.*, 76; *Ark.*, 86; *Cal.*, 98; *Fl.*, 133; *Ill.*, 153; *Iowa*, 185; *Mich.*, 302; *Miss.*, 337; *Mo.*, 351; *Neb.*, 373; *Nev.*, 382; *Ohio*, 434; *Tenn.*, 499; *Tex.*, 508; *Va.*, 537; *W. Va.*, 551; *Wis.*, 563.

—All bills for raising revenue shall originate in the House of Representatives; but the Senate may propose or concur with amendments as on other bills. *U. S.*, 11.

—All bills for raising revenue shall originate in the House of Representatives, but may be amended or rejected by the Senate as other bills. *Ala.*, 76; (nearly similar), *Mass.*, 286; *Min.*, 321; *Miss.*, 339; *N. H.*, 403; *N. J.*, 414; *Pa.*, 462; *S. C.*, 484; *Vt.*, 528.

—All bills for raising revenue shall originate in the House of Representatives, but the Senate may propose alterations, as on other bills, and no bill from the operations of which when passed into a law revenue may incidentally arise, shall be accounted a bill for raising revenue; nor shall any matter or clause whatever, not immediately relating to and necessary for raising revenue, be in any manner blended with or annexed to a bill for raising revenue *Del.*, 118.

—Bills may originate in either House, but may be amended or rejected in the other, except that bills for raising revenue shall originate in the House of Representatives. *Ind.*, 173; *Or.*, 431.

—All bills for raising revenue shall originate in the House of Representatives, but the Senate may propose amendments, as in other bills; *Provided*, That they shall not introduce any new matter, under color of amendment, which does not relate to raising revenue. *Ky.*, 212; *La.*, 229.

—Bills, orders or resolutions may originate in either House, and may be altered, amended or rejected in the other; but all bills for raising revenue shall

originate in the House of Representatives, but the Senate may propose amendments, as in other cases; *Provided*, That they shall not, under color of amendment, introduce any new matter, which does not relate to raising a revenue. *Me.*, 244.

—Any bill may originate in either House of the General Assembly, and be altered, amended or rejected by the other; but no bill shall originate in either House during the last ten days of the session, nor become a law until it be read on three different days of the session in each House, unless three-fourths of the members of the House where such bill is pending shall so determine. *Md.*, 262.

—No new bill shall be introduced into either House of the Legislature after the first fifty days of the session shall have expired. *Mich.*, 303.

—After a bill has been rejected, no bill containing the same substance shall be passed into a law during the same session. *Tenn.*, 493.

—After a bill or resolution has been rejected, by either branch of the Legislature, no bill or resolution containing the same substance shall be passed into a law during the same session. *Tex.*, 509.

STYLE OF LAWS.

—That the style of all laws shall be as follows, to wit: "*Be it enacted by the People of the State of ——, represented in Senate and Assembly.*" *N. Y.* (1777), 31; (nearly similar), *Nev.*, 383.

—The style of the laws of this State shall be: "*Be it enacted by the General Assembly of the State of ——.*" *Ark.*, 87; *Ind.*, 172; *Iowa*, 185; *Md.*, 262; *Tenn.*, 443.

—The style of their laws shall be: "*Be it enacted by the Senate and House of Representatives, in General Assembly convened.*" *Ct.*, 108.

—The style of the laws shall be: "*Be it enacted by the Senate and House of Representatives of the State of ——, in General Assembly convened.*" *Ala.*, 75; *Fl.*, 132.

—The style of the laws of this State shall be: "*Be it enacted by the People of the State of ——, represented in the General Assembly.*" *Ill.*, 153.

—The enacting clause of all laws shall be, "*Be it enacted by the Legislature of the State of ——.*" *Kan.*, 200; *Min.*, 322; *Miss.*, 336; *Neb.*, 371; *W. Va.*, 549; *Tex.*, 507.

—The enacting style, in making and passing all acts, statutes and laws, shall be: "*Be it enacted by the Senate and House of Representatives, in General Court assembled, and by authority of the same.*" *Mass.*, 293.

—The style of their acts and laws shall be: "*Be it enacted by the Senate and House of Representatives, in Legislature assembled.*" *Me.*, 241.

—The style of the laws of this State shall be: "*Be it enacted by the General Assembly of the State of ——, as follows:*" *Mo.*, 351; *Ohio*, 434.

—The enacting style in making and passing acts, statutes and laws shall be: "*Be it enacted by the Senate and House of Representatives, in General Court convened.*" *N. H.*, 404.

—The laws of this State shall begin in the following style: "*Be it enacted by the Senate and General Assembly of the State of ——.*" *N. J.*, 415.

—The style of every bill shall be: "*Be it enacted by the Legislative Assembly of the State of ——.*" *Or.*, 440.

1 § 15. No bill shall be passed unless by the assent of a majority of all the
2 members elected to each branch of the Legislature, and the question upon the
3 final passage shall be taken immediately upon its last reading, and the yeas
4 and nays entered on the journal.

—The style of their laws shall be: " *It is enacted by the General Assembly as follows.*" *R. I.*, 475.
—The style of the laws of this State, in future to be passed, shall be: " *It is hereby enacted by the General Assembly of the State of* ———." *Vt.*, 524.
—The style of the laws of this State shall be: "*The People of the State of* ———, *represented in Senate and Assembly, do enact as follows.*" *Wis.*, 563; *Cal.*, 97.
—And no law shall be enacted except by bill. *Ind.*, 172; *Kan.*, 200; *Or.*, 449.

PASSAGE OF BILLS.

—No bill shall have the force of law, until on three several days it be read in each House, and free discussion be allowed thereon, unless in cases of urgency, four-fifths of the House in which the same shall be depending, may deem it expedient to dispense with the rule; and every bill having passed both Houses, shall be signed by the Speaker and President of their respective Houses. *Ala.*, 76; *Fl.*, 133.
—Every bill for an act shall be read three times before each House, twice at length, and in no case shall a bill be read more than twice on one day; and the vote upon the passage of any law shall, in all cases, be taken by yeas and nays, and by recording the same; and every bill having passed both Houses, shall be signed by the President of the Senate and the Speaker of the House of Representatives. *Ark.*, 86.
—Every bill, before it shall pass, shall be read three times, and on three separate and distinct days in each House, unless in cases of actual invasion or insurrection. *Ga.*, 145.
—Every bill shall be read on three different days in each House, unless in case of urgency, three-fourths of the House where such bill is so depending, shall deem it expedient to dispense with this rule; and every bill having passed both Houses, shall be signed by the Speakers of their respective Houses. *Ill.*, 153.
—On the final passage of all bills, the vote shall be by ayes and noes, and shall be entered on the journal; and no bill shall become a law without the concurrence of a majority of all the members elect in each House. *Ill.*, 153.
— Every bill shall be read by sections on three several days in each House, unless, in case of emergency, two-thirds of the House where such bill may be depending shall, by a vote of yeas and nays, deem it expedient to dispense with this rule; but the reading of a bill by sections, on its final passage, shall in no case be dispensed with; and the vote on the passage of every bill or joint resolution shall be taken by yeas and nays. *Ind.*, 173.
—Every act and joint resolution shall be plainly worded, avoiding as far as practicable the use of technical terms. *Ind.*, 173; *Or.*, 451.
—No bill shall be passed unless by the assent of a majority of all the members elected to each branch of the General Assembly, and the question upon the final passage shall be taken immediately upon its last reading, and the yeas and nays entered on the journal. *Iowa*, 186; *Mo.*, 354.
—Every bill shall be read on three separate days in each House, unless in case of emergency. Two-thirds of the House where such bill is pending may, if deemed expedient, suspend the rules; but the reading of the bill by sections, on its final passage, shall in no case be dispensed with. *Kan.*, 199; (nearly similar), *Min.*, 322.

—No bill shall have the force of a law, until, on three several days, it be read over in each House of the General Assembly, and free discussion allowed thereon, unless, in cases of urgency, four-fifths of the House where the bill shall be depending, may deem it expedient to dispense with this rule. *Ky.*, 212; *La.*, 229; *Miss.*, 337.
—No bill shall become a law unless it be passed in each House by a majority of the whole number of members elected, and on its final passage the ayes and noes be recorded. *Md.*, 262.
—Every bill and joint resolution shall be read three times in each House, before the final passage thereof. No bill or joint resolution shall become a law without the concurrence of a majority of all the members elected to each House. On the final passage of all bills, the vote shall be by ayes and nays, and entered on the journal. *Mich.*, 303.
—No bill shall be passed by either House of the Legislature upon the day prescribed for the adjournment of the two Houses. But this section shall not be so construed as to preclude the enrollment of a bill, or the signature and passage from one House to the other, or the reports thereon from committees, or its transmission to the executive for his signature. *Minn.*, 322.
—No law shall be passed unless voted for by a majority of all the members elected to each branch of the Legislature, and the vote entered upon the journal of each House. *Minn.*, 322.
—Every bill shall be fully and distinctly read on three different days, unless, in case of urgency, three-fourths of the House in which it shall be pending, shall dispense with this rule. *Neb.*, 372; *Ohio*, 434.
—Every bill shall be read by sections, on three several days, in each House, unless, in case of emergency, two-thirds of the House, where such bill may be pending, shall deem it expedient to dispense with this rule; but the reading of a bill by sections on its final passage shall, in no case, be dispensed with, and the vote of the final passage of every bill, or joint resolution, shall be taken by yeas and nays, to be entered on the journals of each House; and a majority of all the members elected to each House shall be necessary to pass every bill or joint resolution, and all bills or joint resolutions so passed, shall be signed by the presiding officers of the respective Houses, and by the Secretary of the Senate and Clerk of the Assembly. *Nev.*, 382.
—All bills and joint resolutions shall be read three times in each House, before the final passage thereof; and no bill or joint resolution shall pass, unless there be a majority of all the members of each body personally present and agreeing thereto; and the yeas and nays of members voting on such final passage shall be entered on the journal. *N. J.*, 414.
—Every bill shall be read by sections, on three several days, in each House, unless, in case of emergency, two-thirds of the House where such bill may be depending, by a vote of yeas and nays, deem it expedient to dispense with this rule; but the reading of a bill by sections on its final passage shall in no case be dispensed with, and the vote on the passage of every bill or joint resolutions shall be taken by yeas and nays. *Or.*, 451.
—No bill shall be passed by the Legislature granting any powers, or privileges, in any case, where the authority to grant such powers, or privileges, has been, or may hereafter be, conferred upon the courts of this Commonwealth. *Pa.*, 472.
—No bill shall have the force of law until it shall have been read three times, and on three several

1 § 16. No private or local bill, which may be passed by the Legislature,

2 shall embrace more than one subject, and that shall be expressed in the title.

days, in each House, has had the seal of the State affixed to it, and has been signed in the Senate House by the President of the Senate and the Speaker of the House of Representatives. *S. C.*, 484.

—No bill shall become a law until it has been fully and distinctly read on three different days in each branch; unless in cases of emergency, three-fourths of the members present dispense with this rule. *W. Va.*, 551.

—That whenever the Assembly and Senate disagree, a conference shall be held, in the preference of both, and be managed by committees, to be by them respectively chosen by ballot. *N. Y.* (1777), 28.

SIGNATURE OF BILLS.

—Every bill having passed both Houses, shall be carefully enrolled, and shall be signed by the presiding officer of each House. Any presiding officer refusing to sign a bill which shall have previously passed both Houses, shall thereafter be incapable of holding a seat in either branch of the Legislature, or hold any other office of honor or profit in the State, and in case of such refusal, each House shall, by rule, provide the manner in which such bill shall be properly certified for presentation to the Governor. *Minn.*, 322.

—The presiding officer of each branch shall sign, before the close of the session, all bills and joint resolutions passed by the Legislature. *W. Va.*, 551.

—The presiding officer of each House shall sign publicly, in the presence of the House over which he presides, while the same is in session and capable of transacting business, all bills and joint resolutions passed by the Legislature. *Neb.*, 372; *Ohio*, 434.

—That all bills shall be read three times in each House, before they pass into laws, and be signed by the Speakers of both Houses. *N. C.*, 424.

—Every bill, when passed by the General Assembly, and sealed with the great seal, shall be presented to the Governor, who shall sign the same in the presence of the Presiding Officers and Chief Clerks of the Senate and House of Delegates. Every law shall be recorded in the office of the Court of Appeals, and, in due time, be printed, published and certified under the great seal to the several courts, in the same manner as has been heretofore usual in this State. *Md.*, 263.

—And every bill having passed both Houses shall be signed by the Speaker and President of their respective Houses. *Iowa*, 185.

—All acts shall be signed by the President of the Senate and the Speaker of the House of Representatives; and no bill, ordinance or resolution intended to have the effect of law, which shall have been rejected by either House, shall be again proposed under the same or any other title, without the consent of two-thirds of the House, by which the same was rejected. *Ga.*, 145.

—On the passage in either House of the Legislature of any law, which imposes, continues or renews a tax, or creates a debt or charge, or makes, continues or renews an appropriation of public or trust money, or releases, discharges or commutes a claim or demand of the State, the question shall be taken by yeas and nays, which shall be duly entered on the journal; and three-fifths of all the members elected to such House, shall in all cases be required to constitute a quorum therein. *Va.*, 568.

—Every bill shall be read once on three different days, and be passed each time in the House where it originated, before transmission to the other. No bill shall become a law, until it shall be read and passed on three different days in each House, and be signed by their respective speakers. *Tenn.*, 493.

20

—Every bill shall be read on three different days in each House, unless two-thirds of the House, where the same is pending, shall dispense with this rule; and every bill, having passed both Houses, shall be signed by the Speaker of the House of Representatives, and by the President of the Senate. *Mo.*, 354 (nearly similar), *Tx.*, 508.

—A majority of all the members elected to each House shall be necessary to pass every bill or joint resolution; and all bills and joint resolutions so passed shall be signed by the presiding officers of the respective Houses. *Ind.*, 174; *Or.*, 451.

—A majority of all the members elected to each House, voting in the affirmative, shall be necessary to pass any bill or joint resolution. *Kan.*, 199.

—No law shall be enacted except by bill. *Wis.*, 563; *Nev.*, 383.

—All laws shall be passed by original bill. *Md.*, 262; *Kan.*, 200.

LAWS TO EMBRACE BUT ONE SUBJECT.

—Each law enacted by the Legislature shall embrace but one subject, and matter properly connected therewith, which subject shall be briefly expressed in the title. *Nev.*, 392.

—Every act or resolution having the force of law shall relate to but one subject, and that shall be expressed in the title. *S. C.*, 484.

—No law shall embrace more than one subject, which shall be expressed in its title. *Minn.*, 323; (nearly similar) *Kan.*, 199; *Md.*, 262; *Ky.*, 212; *Mich.*, 303; *Neb.*, 372; *Ohio*, 434; *Pa.*, 472; *La.*, 234; *Tex.*, 516.

—No private or local bill, which may be passed by the Legislature, shall embrace more than one subject, and that shall be expressed in the title. *Wis.*, 563; *Ill.*, 153.

—Nor shall any law or ordinance pass, which refers to more than one subject matter, or contains matter different from what is expressed in the title thereof. *Ga.*, 145.

—Every act shall embrace but one subject and matters properly connected therewith; which subject shall be expressed in the title. But if any subject shall be embraced in an act which shall not be expressed in the title, such act shall be void only as to so much thereof as shall not be expressed in the title. *Ind.*, 173; *Iowa*, 186.

—Each law shall embrace but one subject, which shall be described in the title; and no law, nor any section of any law, shall be revised or amended by reference only to its title and number, but the law or section revised or amended shall itself be set forth at full length. *Ala.*, 75.

—To avoid improper influences which may result from intermixing in one and the same act such things as have no proper relation to each other, every law shall embrace but one object, and that shall be expressed in the title. *N. J.*, 415.

—Every law enacted by the Legislature shall embrace but one object, and that shall be expressed in the title; and no law shall be revised or amended by reference to its title; but in such case, the act revised, or section amended, shall be re-enacted and published at length. *Cal.*, 99.

—No law, enacted by the General Assembly, shall relate to more than one subject, and that shall be expressed in the title; but if any subject embraced in an act be not expressed in the title, such act shall be void only as to so much thereof as is not so expressed. *Mo.*, 354.

RESTRICTIONS UPON LEGISLATION—GEN-
ERAL LAWS.

—The General assembly shall not pass special laws divorcing any named parties; or declaring any named person of age; or authorizing any named minor to sell, lease, or incumber his or her property; or providing for the sale of the real estate of any named minor or other person, laboring under legal disability, by any executor, administrator, guardian, trustee, or other person; or changing the name of any person; or establishing, locating, altering the course, or affecting the construction of roads, or the building or repairing of bridges; or establishing, altering, or vacating any street, avenue, or alley in any city or town; or extending the time for the assessment or collection of taxes, or otherwise relieving any assessor or collector of taxes from the due performance of his official duties; or giving effect to informal or invalid wills or deeds; or legalizing, except as against the State, the unauthorized or invalid acts of any officer; or granting to any individual or company the right to lay down railroad tracks in the streets of any city or town; or exempting any property of any named person or corporation from taxation. The General Assembly shall pass no special law for any case for which provision can be made by a general law; but shall pass general laws providing, so far as it may deem necessary, for the cases enumerated in this section, and for all other cases where a general law can be made applicable. *Mo.*, 354.

—The General Assembly shall not pass local or special laws in the following cases:

For the assessment and collection of taxes for State, county or road purposes;

For laying out, opening and working roads or highways;

For changing the names of persons;

For the incorporation of cities and towns;

For vacating roads, town plats, streets, alleys or public squares;

For locating or changing county seats.

In all the cases above enumerated, and in all other cases where a general law can be made applicable, all laws shall be general and of uniform operation throughout the State; and no law changing the boundary lines of any county shall have effect until, upon being submitted to the people of the counties affected by the change, at a general election, it shall be approved by a majority of the votes in each county, cast for or against it. *Iowa*, 186.

—The Legislative Assembly shall not pass special or local laws in any of the following enumerated cases; that is to say —

Regulating the jurisdiction and duties of Justices of the Peace and of Constables;

For the punishment of crimes and misdemeanors;

Regulating the practice in courts of justice;

Providing for changing the venue in civil and criminal cases;

Granting divorces;

Changing the names of persons;

For laying, opening and working on highways, and for the election or appointment of Supervisors;

Vacating roads, town plats, streets, alleys and public squares;

Summoning and empanneling grand and petit jurors;

For the assessment and collection of taxes for State, county, township or road purposes;

Providing for supporting common schools, and for the preservation of school funds;

In relation to interest on money;

Providing for opening and conducting elections of State, county, or township officers, and designating the places of voting;

Providing for the sale of real estate belonging to minors, or other persons laboring under legal disabilities, by executors, administrators, guardians, or trustees. *Or.*, 451; (nearly similar) *Nev.*, 383; *Ind.*, 174; *Md.*, 263.

—The Legislature shall not audit nor allow any private claim or account. *Mich.*, 303.

[In addition to the list of most of restrictions above recited, the Constitution of Maryland has the following: Giving effect to informal or invalid deeds or wills; refunding money paid into the State Treasury, or releasing persons from their debts or obligations to the State, unless recommended by the Governor or officers of the Treasury Department; or establishing, locating, or affecting the construction of roads, and the repairing or building of bridges. And the General Assembly shall pass no special law for any case for which provision has been made by an existing general law. The General Assembly, at its first session after the adoption of this Constitution, shall pass general laws providing for the cases enumerated in this section, and for all other cases where a general law can be made applicable]. *Md.*, 263.

—In all cases enumerated in the preceding section, and in all other cases where a general law can be made applicable, all laws shall be general, and of uniform operation throughout the State. *Nev.*, 383; *Ind.*, 174.

—All laws of a general nature shall have a uniform operation throughout the State; nor shall any act, except such as relates to public schools, to be passed take effect upon the approval of any other authority than the General Assembly, except as otherwise provided in this Constitution. *Ohio*, 435.

—In all cases where a general rule can be made applicable, no special law shall be enacted. *Kan.*, 200.

—The General Assembly shall not pass any private law, unless it shall be made to appear that thirty days' notice of application to pass such law shall have been given, under such directions and in such manner as shall be provided by law. *N. C.*, 428.

—The General Assembly shall not have power to pass any private law or alter the name of any person, or to legitimate any persons not born in lawful wedlock, or to restore to the rights of citizenship any person convicted of any infamous crime; but shall have power to pass general laws regulating the same. *N. C.*, 428.

—All laws of a general nature shall have a uniform operation. *Cal.*, 96; *Kan.*, 200.

—All laws of a general nature shall have a uniform operation; the General Assembly shall not grant to any citizen or class of citizens privileges or immunities which upon the same terms shall not equally belong to all citizens. *Iowa*, 183.

—Every statute shall be a public law, unless otherwise declared in the statute itself. *Ind.*, 174; *Or.*, 451.

—No special law shall be enacted for the benefit of individuals or corporations, in cases which are provided for by a general law, or where the relief sought can be given by any court of this State. *Ala.*, 78.

—The General Assembly shall pass a general law prescribing the manner in which names of persons may be changed, but no special law for such purpose shall be passed; and no law shall be made allowing minors to contract, or manage their estates. *Fl.*, 133.

—No private or special law shall be passed authorizing the sale of any lands belonging in whole or in part to a minor or minors, or other persons who may at the time be under any legal disability to act for themselves. *N. J.*, 415.

—The Legislature shall have no power to grant leave of absence to a judicial officer, and any such officer who shall absent himself from the State for more than ninety consecutive days, shall be deemed to have vacated his office. *Nev.*, 388.

SUSPENSION OF LAWS.

—That no power of suspending laws shall be exercised, except by the General Assembly, or by its authority. *Ala.*, 73; *Ky.*, 223.

—No law of a general nature, unless otherwise provided for, shall be enforced until sixty days after the passage thereof. *Miss.*, 342.

1   § 17. The Legislature may confer upon the boards of supervisors of the

2 several counties of the State, such further powers of local legislation and

3 administration as they shall from time to time prescribe.

—The Legislature shall have no power to suspend any general law for the benefit of any particular individual, nor to pass any law for the benefit of individuals inconsistent with the general laws of the land; nor to pass any law granting to an individual or individuals, rights, privileges, immunities, or exemptions, other than such as may be, by the same law, extended to any member of the community, who may be able to bring himself within the provisions of such law; *Provided always*, The Legislature shall have power to grant such charters of corporation as they may deem expedient for the public good. *Tenn.*, 499.

—And no public act of the General Assembly shall take effect or be in force, until the expiration of sixty days from the end of the session at which the same may be passed, unless, in case of emergency, the General Assembly shall otherwise direct. *Ill.*, 153.

RE-ENACTMENT OF LAWS.

—No act shall ever be revised or amended by mere reference to its title; but the act revised, or section amended, shall be set forth and published at full length. *Ind.*, 173; *La.*, 234; *Nev.*, 382; *Or.*, 451; *Tex.*, 516; *Va.*, 537.

—And no law shall be revived or amended unless the new act contain the entire act revived, or the section or sections amended, and the section or sections so amended shall be repealed. *Kan.*, 199; *Neb.*, 172; *Ohio*, 434.

—And no law nor section of a law shall be revised or amended by reference to its title or section only, and it shall be the duty of the General Assembly, in amending any article or section of the code of laws of this State, to enact the same as the said article or section would read when amended; and whenever the General Assembly shall enact any public general law, not amendatory of any section or article in the said code, it shall be the duty of the General Assembly to enact the same in articles and sections, in the same manner as the said code is arranged, and to provide for the publication of all additions and alterations which may be made to the code. *Md.*, 262.

—No law shall be revived, altered or amended by reference to its title only; but the act revised, and the section or sections of the act altered or amended, shall be re-enacted and published at length. *Mich.*, 303.

—No act shall be revised or re-enacted by mere reference to the title thereof; nor shall any act be amended by providing that designated words thereof shall be struck out, or that designated words shall be struck out and others inserted in lieu thereof; but in every such case the act revived or re-enacted, or the act, or part of act, amended, shall be set forth and published at length, as if it were an original act or provision. *Mo.*, 354.

MEMBERS OF LEGISLATURE FORBIDDEN TO ACT AS COUNSEL.

—No Governor, member of Congress, or of the General Assembly of this State, shall receive a fee, be engaged as counsel, agent or attorney in any civil case or claim against this State, or to which this State shall be a party, during the time he shall remain in office. *Fl.*, 136.

—No member of the General Court shall take fees, be of counsel, or act as advocate in any cause before either branch of the Legislature, and upon due proof thereof, such member shall forfeit his seat in the Legislature. *N. H.*, 402.

—No member of the General Assembly shall take any fee, or be of counsel in any case pending before either House of the General Assembly, under penalty of forfeiting his seat, upon proof thereof to the satisfaction of the House of which he is a member. *R. I.*, 476.

—No member of the [Council] (*Senate*), or House of Representatives shall directly or indirectly receive any fee or reward to bring forward or advocate any bill, petition, or other business to be transacted in the Legislature, or advocate any cause as counsel in either House of Legislation, except when employed in behalf of the State. *Vt.*, 525.

PUBLIC PRINTING;—STATE PAPER.

—All public printing shall be let on contract, to the lowest responsible bidder, by such executive officers, and in such manner, as shall be prescribed by law. *Kan.*, 206.

—The printing and binding the laws and journals, all blanks, paper and printing for the executive departments, and all other printing ordered by the Legislature, shall be let by contract to the lowest bidder or bidders, who shall give adequate and satisfactory security for the performance thereof. The Legislature shall prescribe by law the manner in which the State printing shall be executed, and the accounts rendered therefor; and shall prohibit all charges for constructive labor. They shall not rescind nor alter such contract, nor release the person or persons taking the same, or his or their sureties, from the performance of any of the conditions of the contract. No member of the Legislature, nor officer of the State, shall be interested directly or indirectly in any such contract. *Mich.*, 303.

—The Legislature shall not establish a State paper. Every newspaper in the State which shall publish all the general laws of any session within forty days of their passage, shall be entitled to receive a sum not exceeding fifteen dollars therefor. *Mich.*, 304.

—The printing of the laws, journals, bills, legislative documents, and papers for each branch of the General Assembly, with the printing required for the Executive and other departments of State, shall be let on contract, to the lowest responsible bidder, by such executive officers, and in such manner as shall be prescribed by law. *Ohio*, 443.

—There shall be elected by the qualified electors of the State, at the same times and places of choosing members of the Legislative Assembly, a State Printer, who shall hold his office for the term of four years.

He shall perform all the public printing for the State which may be provided by law. The rates to be paid to him for such printing shall be fixed by law, and shall neither be increased nor diminished during the term for which he shall have been elected. He shall give such security for the performance of his duties as the Legislative Assembly may provide. *Or.*, 457.

—There shall be published by the Treasurer, in at least one newspaper printed at the seat of government, during the first week of January in each year, and in the next volume of the acts of the Legislature, detailed statements of all moneys drawn from the treasury during the preceding year, for what purposes, and to whom paid, and by what law authorized, and also of all moneys received, and by what authority, and from whom. *Minn.*, 327.

ARTICLE IV.

1   SECTION 1. The executive power shall be vested in a Governor, who shall

2   hold his office for two years; a Lieutenant-Governor shall be chosen at the

3   same time and for the same term.

—The General Assembly shall provide, by law, that the fuel and stationery furnished for the use of the State, the copying, printing, binding, and distributing the laws and journals, and all other printing ordered by the General Assembly, shall be let, by contract, to the lowest responsible bidder; and that no member of the General Assembly, or other officer of the State, shall be interested, either directly or indirectly, in any such contract; *Provided*, That the General Assembly may fix a maximum price. *Ill.*, 154.

EXPENSES OF THE LEGISLATURE.

—The General Assembly shall provide, by law, that the fuel and stationery furnished for the use of the State, the copying, printing, binding, and distributing the laws and journals, and all other printing ordered by the General Assembly, shall be let by contract, to the lowest responsible bidder; and that no member of the General Assembly, or other officer of the State, shall be interested, either directly or indirectly, in any such contract; *Provided*, That the General Assembly may fix a maximum price. *Ill.*, 154.
—No book or other printed matter not appertaining to the business of the session shall be purchased or subscribed for, for the use of the members of the General Assembly, or be distributed among them at the public expense. *Md.*, 262.
—The Legislature may provide by law for the payment of postage on all mailable matter received by its members and officers during the sessions of the Legislature, but not on any sent or mailed by them. *Mich.*, 302.
—The Legislature shall provide by law that all stationery required for the use of the State, and all printing authorized and required by them to be done for their use, or for the State, shall be let by contract to the lowest bidder; but the Legislature may establish a maximum price. No member of the Legislature, or other State officer, shall be interested either directly or indirectly, in any such contract. *Neb.*, 373.
—All stationery required for the use of the State shall be furnished by the lowest responsible bidder, under such regulations as may be prescribed by law; but no State officer or member of the Legislative Assembly shall be interested in any bid or contract for furnishing such stationery. *Or.*, 456.
—The Legislature shall provide by law that all stationery required for the use of the State, and all printing authorized and required by them to be done for their use, or for the State, shall be let by contract to the lowest bidder; but the Legislature may establish a maximum price. No member of the Legislature, or other State officer, shall be interested, either directly or indirectly, in any such contract. *Wis.*, 563.
—That an appropriation may be made for the payment of such actual expenses as the members of the Legislature may incur for postage, express charges, newspapers, and stationery, not exceeding the sum of sixty dollars for any general or special session, to each member. *Nev.*, 383.

LEGISLATION BY SUPERVISORS.

[Limited powers conferred upon Boards of Supervisors.] *Kan.*, 200; *Mich.*, 304, 309; *W. Va.*, 554; *Wis.*, 563.

CHOICE OF UNITED STATES SENATORS.

—In the year in which a regular election for a Senator of the United States is to take place, the members of the General Assembly shall meet in the hall of the House of Representatives on the second Monday following the meeting of the Legislature, and proceed to said election. *La.*, 229.
—Members of the Senate of the United States from this State shall be elected by the two Houses of the Legislature in joint convention, at such times and in such manner as may be provided by law. *Minn.*, 323.
—In all elections for United States Senators, such elections shall be held in joint convention of both Houses of the Legislature. It shall be the duty of the Legislature which convenes next preceding the expiration of the term of such Senator, to elect his successor. If a vacancy in such senatorial representation from any cause occur, it shall be the duty of the Legislature then in session or at the succeeding session thereof, to supply such vacancy. If the Legislature shall at any time, as herein provided, fail to unite in a joint convention within twenty days after the commencement of the session of the Legislature for the election of such Senator, it shall be the duty of the Governor, by proclamation, to convene the two Houses of the Legislature in joint convention, within not less than five days, nor exceeding ten days from the publication of his proclamation, and the joint convention, when so assembled, shall proceed to elect the Senator, as herein provided. *Nev.*, 384.
—And in the election of United States Senators, and in these cases the vote shall be taken " *viva voce.*" *Ohio*, 435.
—It shall be the duty of the two Houses, upon the request of either, to join in grand committee, for the purpose of electing Senators in Congress, at such times and in such manner as may be prescribed by law for said elections. *R. I.*, 476.
[The Legislature shall proceed as early as practicable to elect Senators to represent this State in the Senate of the United States, and also provide for the election of Representatives to the Congress of the United States.] *Tex.*, 509.

EXECUTIVE POWER—HOW VESTED.

—The supreme executive power of this State shall be vested in a Governor. *N. Y.* (1777), 28; *Del.*, 119; *Ct.*, 100; *Ga.*, 146; *Ill.*, 157; *Ind.*, 174; *Kan.*, 198; *Me.*, 244; *Mass.*, 286; *Mich.*, 304; *Miss.*, 340; *Neb.*, 374; *N. J.*, 415; *Ohio*, 435; *Or.*, 452; *Pa.*, 463; *Tenn.*, 491; *R. I.*, 477; *Va.*, 539; *W. Va.*, 551; *Wis.*, 563.
—The supreme executive power of this State shall be vested in a chief magistrate, who shall be styled "the Governor of ——." *Ala.*, 78; *Ark.*, 88; *Cal.*, 100; *Fl.*, 130; *Iowa*, 187; *Ky.*, 213; *La.*, 229; *Mo.*, 355; *N. H.*, 405; *Nev.*, 384; *S. C.*, 485; *Tex.*, 512.
—And whose title shall be, His Excellency. *N. H.*, 405.
—Who shall be styled, *the Governor of the Commonwealth of Massachusetts;* and whose title shall be, His Excellency. *Mass.*, 286.
—The supreme executive power shall be vested in a Governor, or, in his absence, a Lieutenant-Governor and Council. *Vt.*, 523.
—The Executive Department shall consist of a Governor, Secretary of State, Auditor and Treasurer, who

1 § 2. No person except a citizen of the United States shall be eligible to
2 the office of Governor, nor shall any person be eligible to that office, who shall
3 not have attained the age of thirty years, and who shall not have been five
4 years next preceding his election, a resident within this State.

shall be chosen by the electors of the State on the second Tuesday of October, and at the places of voting for members of the Legislature. *Neb.*, 373.
—The Executive Department shall consist of a Governor, Lieutenant-Governor, Secretary of State, Auditor, Treasurer and an Attorney-General, who shall be chosen by the electors of the State (*Miss.*, 323), on the second Tuesday of October, and at the places of voting for members of the General Assembly. *Ohio*, 435.
—The Supreme Executive power of the State, shall be exercised by the Governor, or, in case of his absence or disability, by the Lieutenant-Governor; who shall have all the powers and perform all the duties vested in, and enjoined upon, the Governor and Council, by the eleventh and twenty-seventh sections of the second chapter of the Constitution, as at present established, excepting that he shall not sit as a judge in case of impeachment, nor grant reprieve or pardon in any such case; nor shall he command the forces of the State in person, in time of war or insurrection, unless by the advice and consent of the Senate; and no longer than they shall approve thereof. The Governor may have a Secretary of civil and military affairs, to be by him appointed during pleasure, whose services he may at all times command; and for whose compensation, provision shall be made by law. *Vt.*, 529.
—The Executive power of the State shall be vested in a Governor, whose term of office shall commence on the second Wednesday of January next ensuing his election, and continue for four years, and until his successor shall have qualified, but the Governor chosen at the first election under this Constitution shall not enter upon the discharge of the duties of the office until the expiration of the term for which the present incumbent was elected, unless the said office shall become vacant by death, resignation, removal from the State, or other disqualification of said incumbent. *Md.*, 258.
—The Executive Department shall consist of a Governor, Lieutenant-Governor, Secretary of State, Auditor, Treasurer, Attorney-General and Superintendent of Public Instruction, who shall be chosen by the electors of the State at the time and place of voting for members of the Legislature, and shall hold their offices for the term of two years from the second Monday of January next after their election, and until their successors are elected and qualified. *Kan.*, 197.

QUALIFICATIONS OF GOVERNOR.

Citizenship: Native of the United States. *Ala.*, 78; *Me.*, 244; *Va.*, 539.
Citizen of the United States 2 years. *Cal.*, 100; *Iowa*, 188. 5 years: *Ind.*, 174; *Md.*, 259; *Mich.*, 304. 10 years: *Fl.*, 130; *S. C.*, 485. 12 years: *Del.*, 119; *Ga.*, 147. 14 years: *Ill.*, 158. 20 years: *Mass.*, 340; *N. J.*, 416. Time not specified: *Ky.*, 213; *Miss.*, 323; *Mo.*, 355; *Or.*, 452; *Tenn.*, 494; *Tex.*, 512; *Wis.*, 564. Citizens of State. *La.*, 329; *Miss.*, 320; *Tenn.*, 494; *Pa.*, 463; *Va.*, 539.
Residence: Resident of State (actual), *Me.*, 244. 1 year: *Min.*, 323. 2 years: *Cal.*, 100; *Iowa*, 188; *Mich.*, 304; *Nev.*, 384. 3 years: *Or.*, 452. 4 years: *Ala.*, 78; *Ark.*, 88; *Vt.*, 526. 5 years: *Fl.*, 130; *Ind.*, 174; *La.*, 229; *Min.*, 340. 6 years: *Del.*, 119; *Ga.*, 147; *Ky.*, 213; *Tex.*, 512. 7 years: *Mo.*, 355;

N. H., 405; *N. J.*, 416; *Pa.*, 463; *Tenn.*, 494. 10 years: *Ill.*, 154; *S. C.*, 485.
Age: At least 25 years: *Cal.*, 100; *Min.*, 323; *Nev.*, 384. 30 years: *Ala.*, 78; *Ark.*, 88; *Ct.*, 107; *Del.*, 119; *Fl.*, 130; *Ga.*, 147; *Ind.*, 174; *Iowa*, 188; *Me.*, 244; *Md.*, 259; *Mich.*, 304; *Miss.*, 340; *N. H.*, 405; *N. J.*, 416; *Pa.*, 463; *S. C.*, 485; *Tenn.*, 494; *Tex.*, 512; *Va.*, 539. At least 35 years: *Ill.*, 158; *Ky.*, 213; *La.*, 229; *Mo.*, 355.
Color and sex: Must be a white male. *Mo.*, 355.
Freehold qualifications: To the value of £1,000. *Mass*, 286.

GOVERNOR TO HOLD NO OTHER OFFICE.

—No member of Congress or person holding any office under the United States, or this State, shall execute the office of Governor. *Del.*, 119; *Ind.*, 175; *La.*, 229; *Mich.*, 305; *Pa.*, 436; *Tenn.*, 495; except as herein provided, *Cal.*, 100; *Iowa*, 188; *Kan.*, 198; *Neb.*, 374; *Nev.*, 385; *Ohio*, 436; *Or.*, 452.
—And no person shall hold the office of Governor, and any other office or commission, civil or military (except in the militia), under this State or the United States, or any of them, or any other power, at one and the same time. *S. C.*, 485.
—Neither the Governor nor Lieutenant-Governor shall be eligible to any other office during the term for which he shall have been elected. *Ind.*, 176.
—The person acting as Governor shall not be elected or appointed to any other office during his term of service. *W. Va.*, 551.
—No person holding the office of Governor shall hold any other office or commission, civil or military. *Tex.*, 514.
—No person elected Governor or Lieutenant-Governor shall be eligible to any office or appointment from the Legislature, or either House thereof, during the time for which he was elected. All votes for either of them for any such office shall be void. *Mich.*, 305.
—No person shall at one and the same time hold the office of Governor and any other office or commission, civil or military, either under this State, the United States, or any other State or Government. *Ala.*, 79.
—No person shall hold the office of Governor or Lieutenant-Governor, and any other office or commission, civil or military, either in this State or under any State, or the United States, or any other power, at one and the same time. *Ark.*, 90.
—No Governor, Lieutenant-Governor, or Judge of the Supreme Judicial Court, shall hold any other office or place under the authority of this Commonwealth, except such as by the Constitution they are admitted to hold, saving that the judges of the said court may hold the offices of Justices of the Peace through the State; nor shall they hold any other place or office, or receive any pension or salary from any other State, or government, or power, whatever. *Mass.*, 292.
—No person shall hold the office of Governor and any other office or commission, civil or military, either in this State, or under any State, or the United States, or any other power, at one and the same time, except the Lieutenant-Governor or the Speaker of the House of Representatives, when he shall hold the office as aforesaid. *Fl.*, 130.

21

1 § 3. The Governor and Lieutenant-Governor shall be elected at the times

2 and places for choosing members of the Assembly. The persons respectively

3 having the highest number of votes for Governor and Lieutenant-Governor,

4 shall be elected; but in case two or more shall have an equal and the highest

5 number of votes for Governor, or for Lieutenant-Governor, the two Houses of

6 the Legislature, at its next annual session, shall, forthwith, by joint ballot,

7 choose one of the said persons so having an equal and the highest number of

8 votes for Governor or Lieutenant-Governor.

TERM OF GOVERNOR.

One year: *Ct.*, 109; *Me.*, 244; *Mass.*, 286; *N. H.*, 405; *R. I.*, 477; *Vt.*, 522. Two years: *N. Y.*, (1821), 37; *Ala.*, 78; *Ga.*, 146; *Iowa*, 188; *Kan.*, 197; *Mich.*, 304; *Minn.*, 323; *Miss.*, 340; *Mo.*, 355; *Neb.*, 373; *N. C.*, 429; *Ohio*, 435; *W. Va.*, 551; *Wis.*, 563. Three years: *N. Y.*, (1777), 24; *N. J.*, 416; *Pa.*, 463. Four years: *Ark.*, 88; *Cal.*, (amendment of 1862); *Del.*, 119; *Fl.*, 130; *Ill.*, 152; *Ind.*, 175; *Ky.*, 213; *La.*, 229; *Md.*, 258; *Nev.*, 384; *Or.*, 452; *S. C.*, 485; *Tenn.*, 494; *Tex.*, 512; *Va.*, 539.

ELIGIBILITY TO SUBSEQUENT TERMS.

Ineligible for next term: *Del.*, 119; *Ga.*, 146; *Ky.*, 213; *N. J.*, 416; *S. C.*, 485; *Va.*, 539. May hold 8 years in 12: *Ark.*, 88; *Or.*, 452; *Tex.*, 512. 4 years in 8: *Ill.*, 192; *Ind.*, 174. 4 years in 6: *Ala.*, 78; *Me.*, 358; *Miss.*, 340; *N. C.*, 429. 6 years in 9: *Pa.*, 463. 6 years in 8: *Tenn.*, 494.

COMMENCEMENT OF GOVERNOR'S TERM.

1st day of January: *Mich.*, 318; *N. Y.* (1821), 44; *N. C.*, 429. 1st Monday of January: *Neb.*, 373. 2d Monday of January: *Ill.*, 152; *Iowa*, 188; *Ind.*, 175; *La.*, 229. 1st Wednesday of January: *Me.*, 244. 3d Tuesday of January: *N. J.*, 415; *Pa.*, 463; *Del.*, 119. 1st Thursday after organization of Legislature, or as soon thereafter as practicable: *Tex.*, 512. 4th day of March: *W. Va.*, 551. 1st Wednesday of May: *Ct.*, 109. 3d Monday of November: *Miss.*, 344. 5th Tuesday after election: *Ky.*, 213. 1st Monday of December: *Cal.*, (amendment of 1862). Time to be fixed by law: *Or.*, 452.
—The term of office of the Governor, Lieutenant-Governor, and Treasurer of the State, respectively, shall commence when they shall be chosen and qualified, and shall continue for the term of one year, or until their successors shall be chosen and qualified, or to the adjournment of the session of the Legislature, at which, by the Constitution and laws, their successors are required to be chosen, and not after such adjournment. *Vt.*, 530.

GOVERNOR'S POWERS AS COMMANDER-IN-CHIEF.

—The Governor shall be general and Commander-in-Chief of all the militia, and admiral of the navy of the State. *N. Y.* (1821), 38.
—The Governor shall be Commander-in-Chief of the militia, the army and navy of this State. *Cal.*, 100; (nearly similar), *Fl.*, 130; *Ga.*, 147; *Iowa*, 188; *N. J.*, 416.
—He shall be Commander-in-Chief of the army of this State, and of the militia thereof, except when they shall be called into the service of the United States. *Ark.*, 89; *Ct.*, 110; *Del.*, 119; *Ill.*, 158; *La.*, 230; *Miss.*, 341; *Mo.*, 355; *Neb.*, 374; *Nev.*, 384; *Ohio*, 436; *Pa.*, 463; *Me.*, 244; *R. I.*, 477; *S. C.*, 485; *Tenn.*, 494; *Tex.*, 512.
—The Governor shall be Commander-in-Chief of the military and naval forces, and may call out such forces to execute the laws, to suppress insurrections and to repel invasions. *Mich.*, 304; *Min.*, 323; *Or.*, 452; *Ind.*, 175; *Kan.*, 203.
—He shall be Commander-in-Chief of the land and naval forces of the State; have power to embody the militia to repel invasion, suppress insurrection, and enforce the execution of the laws. *Va.*, 539.
—But he need not command in person, unless advised to do so by a resolution of the General Assembly. *Mo.*, 355.
—He shall have power to call forth the militia to execute the laws of the State, to suppress insurrections, and to repel invasions; and shall appoint his Aid-de-Camp. *Ala.*, 79.
- The Governor, for the time being, shall be Captain-General and Commander-in-Chief of the militia; and in the recess of the General Assembly, shall have power, by and with the advice of the Council of State, to embody the militia for the public safety. *N. C.*, 424.
—The Governor shall be Commander-in-Chief of the land and naval forces of the State, and may call out the militia to repel invasions, suppress insurrections, and enforce the execution of the laws; but shall not take the command in person without the consent of the General Assembly. *Md.*, 259.
—He shall be Commander-in-Chief of the army and navy of this Commonwealth, and of the militia thereof, except when they shall be called into the service of the United States; but he shall not command personally in the field, unless advised so to do by a resolution of the General Assembly. *Ky.*, 213.
—He shall be Commander-in-Chief of the army and navy of this State, and of the militia thereof, except when they shall be called into the service of the United States; and when acting in the service of the United States, the General Assembly shall fix his rank. *Ala.*, 79.
—But he shall not march nor convey any of the citizens out of the State without their consent, or that of the Legislature, unless it shall become necessary, in order to march or transport them from one part of the State to another, for the defense thereof. *Me.*, 244.
—The Governor of this Commonwealth, for the time being, shall be the Commander-in-Chief of the army and navy, and of all the military forces of the State, by sea and land; and shall have full power, by himself or by any commander, or other officer or officers, from time to time, to train, instruct, exercise and govern the militia and navy; and, for the special defense and safety of the Commonwealth, to assemble in martial array and put in warlike posture the inhabitants thereof, and to lead and conduct them, and with them to encounter, repel, resist, expel and pursue, by force of arms, as well by sea as by land, within or without the limits of this Commonwealth,

1 § 4. The Governor shall be Commander-in-Chief of the military and naval

2 forces of the State. He shall have power to convene the Legislature (or the

3 Senate only) on extraordinary occasions. He shall communicate by message

4 to the Legislature, at every session, the condition of the State, and recommend

5 such matters to them as he shall judge expedient. He shall transact all neces-

6 sary business with the officers of government, civil and military. He shall

and also to kill, slay and destroy, if necessary, and conquer, by all fitting ways, enterprises and means whatsoever, all and every such person and persons as shall, at any time hereafter, in a hostile manner, attempt or enterprise the destruction, invasion, detriment or annoyance of this Commonwealth; and to use and exercise, over the army and navy, and over the militia in actual service, the law martial, in time of war or invasion, and also in time of rebellion, declared by the Legislature to exist, as occasion shall necessarily require; and to take and surprise, by all ways and means whatsoever, all and every such person or persons, with their ships, arms, ammunition and other goods as shall, in a hostile manner, invade or attempt the invading, conquering or annoying this Commonwealth; and that the Governor be intrusted with all these and other powers incident to the offices of Captain-General and Commander-in-Chief, and Admiral, to be exercised agreeably to the rules and regulations of the Constitution, and the laws of the land, and not otherwise.

Provided, That the said Governor shall not, at any time hereafter, by virtue of any power by this Constitution granted, or hereafter to be granted to him by the Legislature, transport any of the inhabitants of this Commonwealth, or oblige them to march out of the limits of the same, without their free and voluntary consent, or the consent of the General Court; except so far as may be necessary to march or transport them by land or water, for the defense of such parts of the State to which they cannot otherwise conveniently have access. *Mass.*, 287 (nearly similar), *N. II.*, 406.

—The Governor shall be Commander-in-Chief of the military forces of the State; shall have power to call out the militia to repel invasion, suppress insurrection and enforce the execution of the laws; shall conduct in person or in such manner as may be prescribed by law, all intercourse with other States; and during the recess of the Legislature, shall fill temporarily all vacancies in office, not provided for by this Constitution or the Legislature, by commissions, to expire at the end of thirty days after the commencement of the succeeding session of the Legislature. He shall take care that the laws be faithfully executed; communicate to the Legislature at each session thereof the condition of the State, and recommend to their consideration such measures as he may deem expedient. He shall have power to remit fines and penalties in such cases and under such regulations as may be prescribed by law; to commute capital punishment, and, except when the prosecution has been carried on by the House of Delegates, to grant reprieves and pardons after conviction; but he shall communicate to the Legislature, at each session, the particulars of every case of fine or penalty remitted, of punishment commuted, and of reprieve or pardon granted, with his reasons for remitting, commuting or granting the same. *W. Va.*, 552.

—The Governor shall be Captain-General and Commander-in-Chief of the forces of the State; but shall not command in person, except advised thereto by the Council, and then only so long as they shall approve thereof. And the Lieutenant-Governor shall, by virtue of his office, be Lieutenant-General of all the forces of the State. *Va.*, 524.

—When the Governor shall be out of the State in

time of war, at the head of a military force thereof, he shall continue Commander-in-Chief of all the military forces of the State. *Mich.*, 305.

—But when the Governor shall, with the consent of the Legislature, be out of the State in time of war, and at the head of any military force thereof, he shall continue Commander-in-Chief of the military forces of the State. *Nev.*, 385.

GOVERNOR TO COMMUNICATE BY MESSAGE.

—That it shall be the duty of the Governor to inform the Legislature, at every session, of the condition of the State, so far as may respect his department; to recommend such matters to their consideration as shall appear to him to concern its good government, welfare and prosperity, to correspond with the Continental Congress, and other States; to transact all necessary business with the officers of government, civil and military; to take care that the laws are faithfully executed, to the best of his ability, and to expedite all such measures as may be resolved upon by the Legislature. *N. Y.* (1777), 29.

—He shall from time to time give to the General Assembly information of the State of the Government, and recommend to their consideration such measures as he may deem expedient. *Ala.*, 79; *Ark.*, 89; *Cal.*, 100; *Ct.*, 110; *Del.*, 120; *Fl.*, 131; *Ill.*, 158; *Ind.*, 175; *Iowa*, 189; *Kan.*, 198; *Ky.*, 213; *La.*, 230; *Me.*, 245; *Md.*, 260; *Mich.*, 304; *Min.*, 323; *Miss.*, 341; *Mo.*, 355; *Neb.*, 374; *Nev.*, 386; *Ohio*, 436; *Or.*, 452; *Pa.*, 463; *S. C.*, 485; *Tenn.*, 495; *Tex.*, 513; *Va.*, 539; *W. Va.*, 552; *Wis.*, 564.

GOVERNOR TO TRANSACT BUSINESS WITH OTHER STATES—HE MAY REQUIRE REPORTS FROM PUBLIC OFFICERS.

—He may require from the Secretary of State the Comptroller of Public Accounts, and the State Treasurer, information in writing on any subject relating to the duties of their respective offices. *Ala.*, 79.

—He shall transact all necessary business with officers of government, and may require information in writing from the officers of the Executive department upon any subject relating to the duties of their respective offices. *Cal.*, 100; *Ind.*, 175; *Iowa*, 189; *Mich.*, 304; *Nev.*, 384; *Or.*, 453; *Wis.*, 564.

—He may require any information, in writing, from the officers of the Executive department on any subject relating to the duties of their respective offices. *Ark.*, 89; *Ct.*, 110; *Del.*, 120; *Fl.*, 130; *Ill.*, 158; *Kan.*, 198; *Ky.*, 213; *La.*, 230; *Me.*, 245; *Miss.*, 341; *Neb.*, 374; *Ohio*, 435; *Pa.*, 463; *S. C.*, 485; *Tenn.*, 495; *Tex.*, 513.

—Conduct, either in person or in such other manner as shall be prescribed by law, all intercourse with other and foreign States. *Va.*, 539.

—The officers of the Executive department, and of all public State institutions, shall at least ten days preceding each regular session of the Legislature, severally report to the Governor, who shall transmit such reports to the Legislature. *Kan.*, 198; (ten days before shall transmit, &c.,) *Ohio*, 436.

—It shall be the duty of the Governor semi-annually,

84

7 expedite all such measures as may be resolved upon by the Legislature, and

8 shall take care that the laws are faithfully executed. He shall, at stated

9 times, receive for his services a compensation to be established by law, which

10 shall neither be increased nor diminished after his election or during his con-

11 tinuance in office.

and oftener if he deem it expedient, to examine the bank book, account books and official proceedings of the Treasurer and Comptroller of the State. *Md.*, 260.

—He may require the opinion, in writing, of the principal officer in each of the Executive departments, upon any subject relating to the duties of their respective offices. *Ind.*, 175; *Minn.*, 323; *Vt.*, 540; *W. Va.*, 552.

—And may also require the opinion in writing of the Attorney-General upon any question of law connected with his official duties. *Va.*, 540; *W. Va.*, 552.

—He shall transact all necessary business with the officers of government, civil and military. He shall expedite all such measures as may be resolved upon by the Legislature, and shall take care that the laws are faithfully executed. He shall at stated times receive for his services, a compensation which shall neither be increased nor diminished during the term for which he shall have been elected. *N. Y.* (1821), 38.

[The Governor and Council.] Are to correspond with other States, transact business with officers of Government, civil and military, and to prepare such business as may appear to them necessary to lay before the General Assembly.

APPOINTING POWER OF GOVERNOR.

—He shall appoint all officers whose offices are established by this Constitution, or shall be established by law, and whose appointments are not herein otherwise provided for. *Del.*, 119.

—The Governor shall nominate, and, by and with the advice and consent of the Senate (a majority of all the Senators concurring), appoint all officers whose offices are established by this Constitution, or which may be created by law, and whose appointments are not otherwise provided for; and no such officer shall be appointed or elected by the General Assembly. *Ill.*, 158.

—The appointing power shall remain as heretofore, and all officers in the appointment of the Executive Department shall continue in the exercise of the duties of ther respective offices until the Legislature shall pass such laws as may be required by the eighth section of the sixth article of the amended Constitution, and until appointments shall be made under such laws; unless their commissions shall be superseded by new appointments, or shall sooner expire by their own limitations, or the said offices shall become vacant by death or resignation, and such laws shall be enacted by the first Legislature under the amended Constitution. *Pa.*, 469.

—The Senate shall vote on the confirmation or rejection of the officers to be appointed by the Governor with the advice and consent of the Senate, by yeas and nays; and the names of the Senators voting for and against the appointments, respectively, shall be entered on a journal to be kept for that purpose, and made public at the end of each session, or before. *La.*, 229.

—All civil officers appointed by the Governor and Senate shall be nominated to the Senate within fifty days from the commencement of each regular session

of the General Assembly, and their term of office, except in cases otherwise provided for in this Constitution, shall commence on the first Monday of May next ensuing their appointment, and continue for two years (unless sooner removed from office), and until their successors respectively qualify according to law. *Md.*, 259.

—A person once rejected by the Senate shall not be re-appointed by the Governor to the same office during the same session or the recess thereafter. [*Ga.*, 147; *Md.*, 259.]

—Unless at the request of the Senate. *Md.*, 259.

—He shall nominate, and by and with the advice and consent of the Senate, appoint all officers whose offices are established by the Constitution, and whose appointments are not herein otherwise provided for; *Provided, however,* That the Legislature shall have a right to prescribe the mode of appointment to all other offices established by law. *La.*, 230; *Md.*, 259.

—The Governor, and in his absence the Lieutenant-Governor [with the Council (the major part of whom including the Governor or Lieutenant-Governor, shall be a quorum to transact business)], shall have power to commission all officers, and also to appoint officers except where provision is or shall be otherwise made by law, or this frame of government; and shall supply every vacancy in any office occasioned by death or otherwise, until the office can be filled in the manner directed by law, or this Constitution. *Vt.*, 529.

—He shall have power, by and with the advice and consent of the Senate, to appoint a State Librarian and Notary Public, and such other officers as may be provided by law. He shall have power to appoint commissioners to take the acknowledgment of deeds, or other instruments in writing, to be used in this State. *Min.*, 323.

—He shall have power to fill all vacancies that may happen in such judicial offices during the recess of the Senate, by granting commissions, which shall expire at the end of their next session; *Provided,* That in acting on executive nominations the Senate shall sit with open doors, and in confirming or rejecting the nominations of the Governor the vote shall be taken by yeas and nays. *Pa.*, 463.

—Nominations to fill all vacancies that may have occurred during the recess, shall be made to the Senate during the first ten days of its session. And should any nomination so made be rejected, the same individual shall not again be nominated during the session to fill the same office; and should the Governor fail to make nominations to fill any vacancy during the session of the Senate, such vacancy shall not be filled by the Governor until the next meeting of the Senate. *Tex.*, 514.

—The Governor and Council shall have a negative on each other, both in the nominations and appointments. Every nomination and appointment shall be signed by the Governor and Council, and every negative shall be also signed by the Governor or Council, who made the same. *N. H.*, 406.

—And this Convention do further, in the name and by the authority of the people of this State, ordain, determine and declare, That by the true construction of the twenty-third article of the Constitution of this State, the right to nominate all officers other than those who by the Constitution are directed to be otherwise appointed, is vested concurrently in the person administering the government of this State for the time being and in each of the members of the Council of Appointment.

GENERAL POWERS OF GOVERNOR.

—The Governor shall have power, and it shall be his
duty, except at such times as the Legislature may be
in session, to examine into the condition and administration of any public office, and the acts of any public
officer, elective or appointed; to remove from office
for gross neglect of duty, or for corrupt conduct in
office, or any other misfeasance or malfeasance therein,
either of the following officers, to wit: The Attorney-
General, State Treasurer, Commissioner of the Land
Office, Secretary of State, Auditor-General, Superintendent of Public Instruction, or members of the State
Board of Education, or any other officer of the
State, except legislative and judicial, elective or
appointed; and to appoint a successor for the remainder of their respective unexpired terms of office, and
report the causes of such removal to the Legislature
at its next session. *Mich.*, 310.
—The Governor, for the time being, shall have power
to draw for and apply such sums of money as shall be
voted by the General Assembly, for the contingencies
of government, and be accountable to them for the
same. He also may, by and with the advice of
the Council of State, lay embargoes, or prohibit
the exportation of any commodity, for any term not
exceeding thirty days, at any one time in the recess
of the General Assembly; and shall have the power
of granting pardons and reprieves, except where the
prosecution shall be carried on by the General
Assembly, or the law shall otherwise direct; in which
case, he may, in the recess, grant a reprieve until the
next sitting of the General Assembly; and he may
exercise all the other executive powers of government, limited and restrained, as by this Constitution
is mentioned, and according to the laws of the State.
And, on his death, inability, or absence from the
State, the Speaker of the Senate, for the time being,
and in case of his death, inability, or absence from the
State, the Speaker of the House of Commons shall
exercise the powers of Government after such death,
or during such absence or inability of the Governor,
or Speaker of the Senate, or until a new nomination
is made by the General Assembly. *N. C.*, 424.
—He shall take care that the laws be faithfully executed. *Ala.*, 79; *Ark.*, 89; *Cal.*, 100; *Ct.*, 110; *Del.*,
120; *Fl.*, 131; *Ind.*, 175; *Iowa*, 188; *Kan.*, 196; *Ky.*,
213; *La.*, 230; *Md.*, 259; *Me.*, 245; *Mich*, 304; *Min.*,
323; *Miss.*, 341; *Mo.*, 355; *Neb.*, 434; *Nev.*, 384; *Ohio*,
435; *Or.*, 452; *N. J.*, 416; *Pa.*, 463; *R. I.*, 477;
S. C., 485; *Tenn.*, 495; *Tex.*, 513; *Va.*, 539; *W. Va.*,
552; *Wis.*, 564.
—To take care that the laws be distributed. *Mo.*, 355;
—And shall be a conservator of peace throughout the
State. *Mo.*, 355.

SALARY OF GOVERNOR.

—He shall, at stated times, receive a compensation
for his services, which shall not be increased or diminished during the term for which he shall have
been elected; nor shall he receive, within that period,
any other emolument from the United States, or any
one of them, or from any foreign power. *Ark.*, 89.
—The Governor and Council shall be compensated for
their services, from time to time by such grants as
the General Court shall think reasonable. *N. H.*,
407.
—As the public good requires that the Governor
should not be under the undue influence of any of
the members of the General Court, by a dependence
on them for his support—that he should, in all cases,
act with freedom for the benefit of the public—that
he should not have his attention necessarily diverted
from that object to his private concerns—and that he
should maintain the dignity of the Commonwealth in
the character of its Chief Magistrate—it is necessary
that he should have an honorable stated salary, of a
fixed and permanent value, amply sufficient for those
purposes, and established by standing laws; and it
shall be among the first acts of the General Court,

22

after the commencement of this Constitution, to establish such salary by law accordingly. *Mass.*, 288.
—He shall, at stated times, receive a compensation
for his services, which shall not be either increased
or diminished during the term for which he shall have
been elected. *Ala.*, 78; *Del.*, 119; *Ind.*, 176; *Fl.*,
130; *Ky.*, 213; *Me.*, 244; *Miss.*, 341; *Mo.*, 355; *N.
J.*, 416; *Pa.*, 463; *R. I.*, 477; *S. C.*, 585; *Tenn.*, 495.
—The compensation of the Governor, Lieutenant-
Governor, Senators and Representatives shall be
established by law, and shall not be varied so as to
take effect until after an election, which shall next
succeed the passage of the law establishing said compensation. *Ct.*, 110.
—The Lieutenant-Governor, Secretary of State,
Comptroller, Treasurer, Attorney-General and Surveyor-General, shall each, at stated times during their
continuance in office, receive for their services a compensation, which shall not be increased or diminished
during the term for which they shall have been
elected; but neither of these officers shall receive for
his own use any fees for the performance of his official duties. *Cal.*, 101.
—Salary $1,000. *Mich.*, 308; *Neb.*, 374.
do 1,250. *Wis.*, 564.
do 1,500. *Ill.*, 158; *Or.*, 457.
do 2,000. *W. Va.*, 552.
do 2,500. *Minn.*, 323.
do 3,000. (Minimum.) *Fl.*, 130.
do 4,000. *Md.*, 260; *Nev.*, 393; *Tex.*, 512.
do 5,000. *Va.*, 539.
do 8,000. *La.*, 230.
do 10,000. *Cal.*, 106.
—The President of the Senate and the Speaker of
the House of Representatives shall, during the time
they respectively administer the government, receive
the same compensation which the Governor would
have received if he had been employed in the duties
of his office. *Ala.*, 80.
—The Lieutenant-Governor shall while he acts as
President of the Senate, receive for his services the
same compensation which shall be allowed to the
Speaker of the House of Representatives and no
more; and during the time he administers the government as Governor shall receive the same compensation which the Governor would have received had
he been employed in the duties of his office and no
more. The President for the time being of the Senate shall, during the time he administers the government, receive in like manner the same compensation
which the Governor would have received had he
been employed in the duties of his office. If the
Lieutenant-Governor shall be required to administer
the Government, and shall, whilst in such administration die, resign, or be absent from the State, during the recess of the Legislature, it shall be the duty
of the Secretary of State to convene the Senate, for
the purpose of choosing a President for the time
being. *Tex.*, 513.
—The Governor shall have a competent salary, which
shall not be increased nor diminished during the time
for which he shall have been elected; neither shall
he receive within that time any other emolument
from the United States, or either of them, nor from
any foreign power. *Ga.*, 146.
—During his continuance in office shall receive no
other emolument from this or any other government.
Va., 539; *W. Va.*, 552.
—The Governor shall reside at the seat of Government, and receive a salary of fifteen hundred dollars
per annum, which shall not be increased or diminished; and he shall not during the time for which he
shall have been elected, receive any emolument from
the United States, or either of them. *IV.*, 153.
—Until the Legislature shall otherwise direct, in accordance with the provisions of this Constitution, the
salary of the Governor shall be ten thousand dollars
per annum; and the salary of the Lieutenant-Governor shall be double the pay of a State Senator; and
the pay of members of the Legislature shall be sixteen dollars per diem while in attendance, and sixteen
dollars for every twenty miles travel by the usual

1 § 5. The Governor shall have the power to grant reprieves, commutations

2 and pardons, after conviction, for all offenses except treason and cases of

3 impeachment, upon such conditions and with such restrictions and limitations

4 as he may think proper, subject to such regulations as may be provided by

5 law relative to the manner of applying for pardons. Upon conviction for

6 treason, he shall have power to suspend the execution of the sentence until

route from their residences, to the place of holding the session of the Legislature, and in returning therefrom. And the Legislature shall fix the salaries of all officers, other than those elected by the people at the first election. *Cal.*, 106.

(1) *N. Y.* (1821), 38.

PARDONING POWER.

—He shall have power to remit fines and forfeitures, and grant reprieves and pardons, except in cases of impeachment. *Pa.*, 463; *Tenn.*, 494.

— He shall have power to grant reprieves and pardons, after conviction, for offenses against the State, except in cases of impeachment. *Min.*, 323.

—He shall have power to grant reprieves after conviction, in all cases except those of impeachment, until the end of the next session of the General Assembly (*R. I.*, 477) and no longer. *Ct.*, 110.

—The pardoning power shall be vested in the Governor, under regulations and restrictions prescribed by law. *Kan.*, 198.

—He shall have power, with the advice and consent of the Council, to remit, after conviction, all forfeiture and penalties, and grant reprieves and pardons, except in cases of impeachment. *Me.*, 245.

—In all criminal and penal cases (except of impeachment), after conviction, he shall have power to grant reprieves and pardons, and remit fines and forfeitures, under such rules and regulations as shall be prescribed by law. *Fl.*, 131.

— He shall have power to grant reprieves for offenses against the State, except in cases of impeachment, and to grant pardons, or to remit any part of a sentence, in all cases after conviction, except for treason, murder, or other capital offenses, in which cases he may respite the execution, and make report thereof to the next General Assembly. *Ga.*, 147.

—The Governor or person administering the government shall have power to suspend the collection of fines and forfeitures, and to grant reprieves to extend until the expiration of a time not exceeding ninety days after conviction; but this power shall not extend to cases of impeachment. *N. J.*, 416.

—The Governor, Justices of the Supreme Court, and Attorney-General, or a major part of them, of whom the Governor shall be one, may, upon such conditions and with such limitations and restrictions as they may think proper, remit fines and forfeitures, commute punishments, and grant pardons after convictions in all cases, except treason and impeachments, subject to such regulations as may be provided by law relative to the manner of applying for pardons. *Nev.*, 385.

—In all criminal and penal cases, except those of treason and impeachment, he shall have power to grant reprieves and pardons, and to remit fines and forfeitures, under such rules and regulations as may be prescribed by law; and in cases of treason, he shall have power, by and with the advice and consent of the Senate, to grant reprieves and pardons, and in

the recess of the Senate he may respite the sentence until the end of the next session of the General Assembly. *Ala.*, 79; *Ark.*, 89; *Tex.*, 513; *Miss.*, 341.

—The Governor shall have the power to grant reprieves, commutations and pardons, after conviction, for all offenses except treason and cases of impeachment, upon such conditions and with such restrictions and limitations as he may think proper, subject to such regulations as may be provided by law relative to the manner of applying for pardons. He shall, at each session of the General Assembly, communicate to that body each case of reprieve, commutation or pardon granted; stating the name of the convict, the crime of which he was convicted, the sentence and its date, the date of the commutation, pardon or reprieve, and the reasons for granting the same [*Mo.*, 355; *Or.*, 453 (nearly similar), *Ill.*, 158; *Cal.*, 100; *Ind.*, 175; *Iowa*, 188; *Mich.*, 305; *Nev.*, 385; *Ohio.* 436; *Wis.*, 564], and also the names of all persons in whose favor remission of fines and forfeitures shall have been made, and the several amounts remitted; *Provided, however,* That the General Assembly may, by law, constitute a council, to be composed of officers of State, without whose advice and consent the Governor shall not have power to grant pardons in any case, except such as may by law be left to his sole power. *Ind.*, 175.

—Upon conviction for treason, he shall have the power to suspend the execution of the sentence until the case shall be reported to the Legislature at its next meeting, when the Legislature shall either pardon, or commute the sentence, direct the execution of the sentence, or grant a further reprieve. *Cal.*, 100; *Ill.*, 158; *Ind.*, 175; *Wis.*, 564; *Iowa*, 188; *Mich.*, 305; *Nev.*, 385; *Or.*, 453; *Ohio*, 436.

—He shall have power to remit fines and forfeitures, under such regulations as may be prescribed by law; and shall report to the General Assembly at its next meeting, each case of reprieve, commutation, or pardon granted, and the reasons therefor; and also all persons in whose favor remission of fines and forfeitures shall have been made and the several amounts remitted. *Iowa*, 188; *Or.*, 453.

—He shall have power to grant reprieves and pardons, except in cases of impeachment, and in cases in which he is prohibited by other articles of this Constitution, and to remit fines and forfeitures for offenses against the State; but shall not remit the principal or interest of any debt due to the State, except in cases of fines and forfeitures; and before granting a *nolle prosequi*, or pardon, he shall give notice in one or more newspapers of the application made for it, and of the day on or after which his decision will be given; and in every case in which he exercises this power, he shall report to either branch of the General Assembly whenever required, the petitions, recommendations and reasons which influenced his decision. *Md.*, 260.

—He shall have power to grant reprieves and pardons after conviction (except in cases of impeachment), in such manner, on such terms and under such restrictions as he shall think proper, and he shall have power to remit fines and forfeitures, unless otherwise directed by law. It shall be his duty to report to the General Assembly at the next regular session thereafter all pardons granted by him, with a full statement of each case and the reason moving him thereunto. *S. C.*, 485.

7 the case shall be reported to the Legislature at its next meeting, when the

8 Legislature shall either pardon or commute the sentence, direct the execution

9 of the sentence, or grant a further reprieve. He shall annually communicate

10 to the Legislature each case of reprieve, commutation or pardon granted;

11 stating the name of each convict, the crime of which he was convicted, the

12 sentence and its date, and the date of the commutation, pardon or reprieve.(')

—He shall have power to remit fines and forfeitures and to grant reprieves and pardons, except in cases of impeachment. He shall set forth in writing, fully, the grounds of all reprieves, pardons and remissions, to be entered in the register of his official acts, and laid before the General Assembly at their next session. *Del.*, 120.

—The Governor, or person administering the government, the Chancellor, and the six Judges of the Court of Errors and Appeals, or a major part of them, of whom the Governor, or person administering the government shall be one, may remit fines and forfeitures and grant pardons, after conviction, in all cases except impeachment. *N. J.*, 416.

—The Governor shall have power to grant reprieves for all offenses against the State, and except in cases of impeachment, shall, with the consent of the Senate, have power to grant pardons, remit fines and forfeitures, after conviction. In cases of treason he may grant reprieves until the end of the next session of the General Assembly, in which the power of pardoning shall be vested. *La.*, 230.

—The power of pardoning offenses, except such as persons may be convicted of before the Senate by impeachment of the House, shall be in the Governor, by and with the advice of Council; but no charter of pardon granted by the Governor, with advice of Council, before conviction, shall avail the party pleading the same, notwithstanding any general or particular expressions contained therein descriptive of the offense or offenses intended to be pardoned. *N. H.*, 406.

—He shall have power to remit fines and forfeitures, grant reprieves and pardons, except in cases of impeachment. In cases of treason, he shall have power to grant reprieves until the end of the next session of the General Assembly, in which the power of pardoning shall be vested; but he shall have no power to remit the fees of the clerk, sheriff, or Commonwealth's attorney, in penal or criminal cases. *Ky.*, 213.

—The power of pardoning offenses, except such as persons may be convicted of before the Senate, by an impeachment of the House, shall be in the Governor, by and with the advice of council; but no charter or pardon granted by the Governor, with advice of the council, before conviction, shall avail the party pleading the same, notwithstanding any general or particular expressions contained therein, descriptive of the offense or offenses intended to be pardoned. *Mass.*, 287.

—He shall have power, after conviction, to grant reprieves, commutations and pardons, for all crimes and offenses except treason and cases of impeachment, upon such conditions as he may think proper; subject, however, to such regulations as to the manner of applying for pardon as may be prescribed by law. *Neb.*, 374.

—He shall communicate to the Legislature at every regular session each case of reprieve, commutation or pardon granted; stating the name and crime of the convict, the sentence, its date and the date of the commutation, pardon or reprieve, with his reasons therefor. *Neb.*, 374.

—The Governor, by and with the advice and consent of the Senate, shall hereafter exclusively exercise the pardoning power, except in cases of impeachment, to the same extent as such power is now exercised by the General Assembly. *R. I.*, 481.

—He shall have power to remit fines and penalties in such cases and under such rules and regulations as may be prescribed by law; and, except when the prosecution has been carried on by the House of Delegates, or the law shall otherwise particularly direct, to grant reprieves and pardons after conviction, and to commute capital punishment; but he shall communicate to the General Assembly, at each session, the particulars of every case of fine or penalty remitted, of reprieve or pardon granted, and of punishment commuted, with his reasons for remitting, granting or commuting the same. *Va.*, 539.

—And, at his discretion, to grant reprieves and pardons to persons convicted of crimes, other than treason or murder, in which he may suspend the execution of the sentence, until it shall be reported to the Legislature at their subsequent meeting; and they shall either pardon or direct the execution of the criminal, or grant a further reprieve. *N. Y.* (1777), 24.

—The General Assembly shall have power, by a vote of two-thirds of each branch, to grant pardons in cases of final conviction for treason, and to pardon or commute after final conviction in capital cases. *Ga.*, 146.

—The Governor and Council shall have power to grant pardons and remit fines, in all cases whatsoever, except in treason and murder, in which they shall have power to grant reprieves, but not to pardon until after the end of the next session of Assembly; an l except in cases of impeachment, in which there shall be no remission or mitigation of punishment, but by act of legislation. *Va.*, 524.

88

1   § 6. In case of the impeachment of the Governor, or his removal from

2 office, death, inability to discharge the powers and duties of the said office,

3 resignation or absence from the State, the powers and duties of the office shall

4 devolve upon the Lieutenant-Governor for the residue of the term, or until the

5 disability shall cease. But when the Governor shall, with the consent of the

6 Legislature, be out of the State in time of war, at the head of a military force

7 thereof, he shall continue Commander-in-Chief of all the military force of the

8 State.

VACANCIES IN THE OFFICE OF GOVERNOR.

—Whenever the chair of the Governor shall become vacant by reason of his death, absence from the State, or otherwise, the President of the Senate shall, during such vacancy, have and exercise all the powers and authorities which, by this Constitution, the Governor is vested with when personally present; but when the President of the Senate shall exercise the office of Governor, he shall not hold his office in the Senate. *N. H.*, 406.

—And in case of his absence, or impeachment, or when he shall exercise the office of Governor, the Senate shall choose a president *pro tempore. Ohio*, 436; *Iowa*, 188.

—The Senate shall choose a President *pro tempore*, to preside in case of his absence or impeachment, or when he shall hold the office of Governor. *Kan.*, 193; (nearly similar), *Ind*, 175; *New.*, 385; *Min.*, 324; *Md.*, 259; *La.*, 230; *S. C.*, 485.

—If, by reason of death, resignation, absence or other cause, there be no Governor or Lieutenant-Governor present to preside in the Senate, the Senate shall elect one of their own members to preside during such absence or vacancy; and until such election is made by the Senate, the Secretary of State shall preside. *R. I*, 477.

—During a vacancy in the office of Governor, if the Lieutenant-Governor die, resign, be impeached, displaced, be incapable of performing the duties of his office, or absent from the State, the President *pro tempore* of the Senate shall act as Governor until the vacancy be filled or the disability cease. *Mich.*, 305.

—If the Lieutenant-Governor shall be called upon to administer the government, and shall, while in such administration, resign, die or be absent from the State during the recess of the General Assembly, it shall be the duty of the Secretary of State, for the time being, to convene the Senate for the purpose of choosing a Speaker. *Ky.*, 214.

—A member of the Senate or of the House of Representatives being chosen, and acting as Governor or Lieutenant-Governor, shall thereupon vacate his seat, and another person shall be elected in his stead. *S. C.*, 485.

—In case of the impeachment of the Governor, his removal from office, death, resignation, or absence from the State, the powers and duties of the office shall devolve upon the Secretary of State, until such disability shall cease, or the vacancy be filled. *Neb.*, 374.

—If, during the vacancy of the office of Governor, the Secretary of State shall be impeached, displaced, resign, die, or be absent from the State, the powers and duties of the office of Governor shall devolve upon the President of the Senate, and should a vacancy occur by impeachment, death, resignation, or absence from the State of the President of the Senate, the Speaker of the House of Representatives shall act as Governor till the vacancy be filled. *Neb.*, 374.

—In case of a vacancy in the office of Governor from any other cause than those herein enumerated, or in case of the death of the Governor elect, before he is qualified into office, the powers, duties and emoluments of the office shall devolve upon the President of the Senate or Speaker of the House of Assembly, as above provided for; until a new Governor be elected and qualified. *N. J.*, 417; *Ill.*, 159.

—When the Government shall be administered by the Lieutenant-Governor, or he shall be unable to attend as President of the Senate, the Senate shall elect one of their members as President *pro tempore. And if*, during the vacancy of the office of Governor, the Lieutenant-Governor shall die, resign, refuse to serve, or be removed from office, or if he shall be impeached, or absent from the State, the President of the Senate *pro tempore* shall, in like manner, administer the government, until he be superseded by a Governor or Lieutenant-Governor. *Ct.*, 110.

—Whenever the government shall be administered by the Lieutenant-Governor, or he shall be unable to attend as Speaker of the Senate, the Senators shall elect one of their own number as Speaker for that occasion; and if, during the vacancy of the office of Governor, the Lieutenant-Governor should be impeached, removed from office, refuse to qualify, or resign, or die, or be absent from the State, the Speaker of the Senate shall, in like manner, administer the government. *Ill.*, 158; *Ark.*, 90; (nearly similar, *N. Y.* (1777), 30.

—In case of the death, resignation, or disability of the Governor, the President of the Senate shall exercise the executive powers of the government until such disability be removed, or a successor is elected and qualified. And in case of the death, resignation, or disability of the President of the Senate, the Speaker of the House of Representatives shall exercise the executive power of the government until the removal of the disability or the election and qualification of a Governor. *Ga.*, 147; (nearly similar), *W. Va.*, 552.

—Whenever the government shall be administered by the Lieutenant-Governor, or he shall fail to attend as Speaker of the Senate, the Senators shall elect one of their own members as Speaker for that occasion. And if, during the vacancy of the office of Governor, the Lieutenant-Governor shall be impeached, removed from office, refuse to qualify, resign, die, or be absent from the State, the Speaker of the Senate shall, in like manner, administer the government; *Provided*, That whenever a vacancy shall occur in the office of Governor, before the first two years of the term shall have expired, a new election for Governor shall take place, to fill such vacancy. *Ky.*, 213.

—When either the President or Speaker of the House of Representatives shall so exercise said office, he shall receive the compensation of Governor only, and his duties as President or Speaker shall be suspended, and the Senate or House of representatives, as the case may be, shall fill the vacancy until his duties as Governor shall cease. *Miss.*, 341.

—In case of a vacancy during the recess of the Sen-

89

ate, in any office which the Governor has power to fill, he shall appoint some suitable person to said office, whose commission shall continue in force till the end of the next session of the General Assembly, or till some other person is appointed to the same office, whichever shall first occur, and the nomination of the person thus appointed during the recess, or of some other person in his place, shall be made to the Senate within thirty days after the next meeting of the General Assembly. *Md.*, 259.

—In case of the removal of the Governor from office, or of his death, resignation, or inability to discharge the duties of the office, the same shall devolve on the Secretary of State; and in case of the removal from office, death, resignation, or inability both of the Governor and Secretary of State, the President of the Senate shall act as Governor until the disability be removed or a Governor elected. *Or.*, 452.

—In case of the impeachment of the Governor, his absence from the State, or inability to discharge the duties of his office, the powers, duties and emoluments of the office shall devolve upon the Lieutenant-Governor; and in case of his death, resignation, or removal, then upon the Speaker of the Senate for the time being, until the Governor, absent or impeached, shall return or be acquitted; or until the disqualification or inability shall cease; or until a new Governor shall be elected and qualified. *Ill.*, 159.

—If the Lieutenant-Governor shall be called upon to administer the government, and shall, while in such administration, resign, die, or be absent from the State, during the recess of the General Assembly, it shall be the duty of the Secretary of State for the time being, to convene the Senate for the purpose of choosing a Speaker. *Ill.*, 159.

—In case of the removal of the Governor from office, or of his death, or resignation, the powers and duties of the office shall devolve upon the Speaker of the Senate; and in case of the death, removal from office, or resignation of the Speaker of the Senate, the powers and duties of the office shall devolve on the Speaker of the House of Representatives. *Ten.*, 495.

—Whenever the office of Governor shall become vacant by death, resignation, removal from office, or otherwise, the President of the Senate shall exercise the office of Governor until another Governor shall be duly qualified; and in case of the death, resignation, removal from office, or other disqualification of the President of the Senate so exercising the office of Governor, the Speaker of the House of Representatives shall exercise the office, until the President of the Senate shall have been chosen; and when the office of Governor, President of the Senate, and Speaker of the House shall become vacant, in the recess of the Senate, the person acting as Secretary of State for the time being, shall, by proclamation convene the Senate, that a President may be chosen to exercise the office of Governor. *Miss.*, 341; (nearly similar), *Me.*, 245; *Mo.*, 356; *Tex.*, 513; *Del.*, 120.

—In case of the impeachment of the Governor, his removal from office, death, refusal to qualify, resignation, or absence from the State, the President of the Senate shall exercise all the power and authority appertaining to the office of Governor, until the time appointed by the Constitution for the election of Governor shall arrive (unless the General Assembly shall provide by law for the election of a Governor to fill such vacancy), or until the Governor who is absent or impeached shall return or be acquitted; and if, during such vacancy in the office of Governor, the President of the Senate shall be impeached, removed from office, refuse to qualify, die, resign, or be absent from the State, the Speaker of the House of Representatives shall, in like manner, administer the government. *Ala.*, 79.

—If the trial of a contested election shall continue longer than until the third Tuesday of January next ensuing the election of a Governor, the Governor of the last year, or the Speaker of the Senate, or of the House of Representatives, who may then be in the exercise of the Executive authority, shall continue

therein until a determination of such contested election. The Governor shall not be removed from his office for inability, but with the concurrence of two-thirds of all the members of each branch of the Legislature. *Del.*, 120.

—In case of the death or resignation of the Governor, or his removal from office, the Speaker of the Senate shall exercise the office of Governor until another Governor shall be duly qualified; but in such case another Governor shall be chosen at the next annual election of Representatives, unless such death, resignation or removal shall occur within three calendar months immediately preceding such next annual election, in which case a Governor shall be chosen at the second succeeding annual election of Representatives. And if the trial of a contested election shall continue longer than until the third Monday of January next ensuing the election of Governor, the Governor of the last year, or the Speaker of the Senate who may be in the exercise of the executive authority, shall continue therein until the determination of such contested election, and until a Governor shall be duly qualified as aforesaid. *Pa.*, 463.

—If the Lieutenant-Governor, while acting as Governor, shall be impeached, displaced, resign or die, or otherwise become incapable of performing the duties of the office, the President *pro tempore* of the Senate shall act as Governor until the vacancy is filled, or the disability removed; and if the President of the Senate, for any of the above causes, shall be rendered incapable of performing the duties pertaining to the office of Governor, the same shall devolve upon the Speaker of the House of Representatives. *Iowa*, 180.

—In case of the death, resignation or removal from office of the Governor, the powers, duties and emoluments of the office shall devolve upon the President of the Senate, and in case of his death, resignation or removal, then upon the Speaker of the House of Assembly, for the time being, until another Governor shall be elected and qualified; but in such case another Governor shall be chosen at the next election for members of the State Legislature, unless such death, resignation or removal shall occur within thirty days immediately preceding such next election in which case a Governor shall be chosen at the second succeeding election for members of the Legislature. *N. J.*, 417.

—And the Legislature shall provide, by general law, declaring what officer shall act as Governor whenever there shall be a vacancy in both the offices of Governor and Lieutenant-Governor, occasioned by a failure to elect, or by the removal from office, or by the death, resignation or inability of both Governor and Lieutenant-Governor, to exercise the powers and discharge the duties of the office of the Governor; and such officer, so designated, shall exercise the powers and discharge the duties appertaining to the office of Governor, accordingly, until the disability shall be removed, or a Governor shall be elected. *Vt.*, 530.

—In case of the impeachment of the Governor, his removal from office, death, refusal to qualify, resignation, or absence from the State, the Lieutenant-Governor shall exercise all the power and authority appertaining to the office of Governor, until the Governor absent or impeached, shall return, or be acquitted, or until the Governor next regularly elected shall be duly qualified, as the case may be; and for the time the Lieutenant-Governor shall occupy the office of Governor, he shall receive the same compensation as shall be allowed by law to the regularly elected Governor. *Fla.*, 131.

—In case of the impeachment of both the Governor and Lieutenant-Governor, their removal from office, death, refusal to qualify, resignation, or absence from the State, the Speaker of the House of Representatives shall in like manner administer the Government, unless the General Assembly shall otherwise provide; and for the time he shall occupy the office of Governor, he shall receive the same compensation as shall be allowed by law to the Governor. *Fl.*, 131.

23

1 § 7. The Lieutenant-Governor shall possess the same qualifications of

2 eligibility for office as the Governor. He shall be the President of the Senate,

3 but shall only have a casting vote therein. If during a vacancy of the office

4 of Governor, the Lieutenant-Governor shall be impeached, displaced, resign,

5 die, or become incapable of performing the duties of his office, or he be absent

6 from the State, the President of the Senate shall act as Governor, until the

7 vacancy shall be filled, or the disability shall cease.

—If the Lieutenant-Governor, while holding the office of Governor, shall be impeached or displaced, or shall resign or die, or otherwise become incapable of performing the duties of the office, the President of the Senate shall act as Governor until the vacancy is filled, or the disability removed; and if the President of the Senate, for any of the above causes, shall be rendered incapable of performing the duties pertaining to the office of Governor, the same shall devolve upon the Speaker of the House of Representatives. *Kan.*, 198.

—In case of the death, impeachment, resignation, removal, or other disability of the Governor, the power and duties of the office for the residue of the term, or until the disability shall be removed, shall devolve upon the President of the Senate. *Kan.*, 198.

—In case of impeachment of the Governor, his removal from office, death, refusal or inability to qualify, resignation or absence from the State, the powers and duties of the office shall devolve upon the Lieutenant-Governor for the residue of the term, or until the Governor, absent or impeached, shall return or be acquitted. The Legislature may provide by law, for the case of removal, impeachment, death, resignation, disability or refusal to qualify, of both the Governor and the Lieutenant-Governor, declaring what officer shall act as Governor, and such officer shall act accordingly, until the disability be removed, or for the remainder of the term. *La.*, 230.

—In case of the impeachment of the Governor, his removal from office, death, inability, resignation, or absence from the State, the powers and duties of the office shall devolve upon the Lieutenant-Governor for the residue of the term, or until the disability censes. *Mich.*, 305; *Nev.* 385.

—In case of the impeachment of the Governor, his absence from the State, or inability to discharge the duties of his office, the powers, duties, and emoluments of the office shall devolve upon the President of the Senate; and in case of his death, resignation or removal, then upon the Speaker of the House of Assembly, for the time being, until the Governor, absent or impeached, shall return or be acquitted, or until the disqualification or inability shall cease, or until a new Governor be elected and qualified. *N. J.*, 417.

—If the Lieutenant-Governor, while executing the office of Governor, shall be impeached, displaced, resign or die, or otherwise become incapable of performing the duties of the office, the President of the Senate shall act as Governor until the vacancy is filled, or the disability removed; and if the President of the Senate, for any of the above causes, shall be rendered incapable of performing the duties pertaining to the office of Governor, the same shall devolve upon the Speaker of the House of Representatives. *Ohio*, 436.

—If the offices of Governor and Lieutenant-Governor be both vacant by reason of death, resignation, impeachment, absence or otherwise, the person entitled to preside over the State for the time being, shall in like manner fill the office of Governor during such absence or vacancy. *R. I.*, 477.

LIEUTENANT-GOVERNOR TO BE ELECTED.

—That a Lieutenant-Governor shall, at every election of a Governor (and as often as the Lieutenant-Governor shall die, resign or be removed from office), be elected in the same manner with the Governor, to continue in office until the next election of a Governor; and such Lieutenant-Governor shall, by virtue of his office, be President of the Senate, and, upon an equal division, have a casting voice in their decisions, but not vote on any other occasion. And in case of the impeachment of the Governor, or his removal from office, death, resignation or absence from the State, the Lieutenant-Governor shall exercise all the power and authority appertaining to the office of Governor until another be chosen, or the Governor, absent or impeached, shall return or be acquitted. *Provided*, That where the Governor shall with the consent of the Legislature, be out of the State, in time of war, at the head of a military force thereof, he shall still continue in his command of all the military forces of the State, both by sea and land. *N. Y.* (1777), 29.

—A Lieutenant-Governor shall be elected at the same time and for the same term as the Governor, and his qualification and the manner of his election in all respects shall be the same. *Va.*, 540; (nearly similar), *Cal.*, 100; *Ct.*, 114; *Fl.*, 130; *Mo.*, 256; *S. C.*, 485; *Wis.*, 563.

—A Lieutenant-Governor shall be chosen at every election of Governor, in the same manner, continue in office for the same time, and possess the same qualifications. In voting for Governor and Lieutenant-Governor, the electors shall distinguish whom they vote for as Governor, and whom as Lieutenant-Governor. *Ill.*, 158; (nearly similar), *Ark.*, 89; *Iowa*, 187; *Ky.*, 213; *Md.*, 259; *Tenn.*, 563.

—The Lieutenant Governor and President of the Senate *pro tempore*, when performing the duties of Governor, shall receive the same compensation as the Governor. *Mich.*, 305.

—There shall be annually elected a Lieutenant-Governor of the Commonwealth of Massachusetts, whose title shall be—His Honor; and who shall be qualified, in point of religion, property and residence in the Commonwealth, in the same manner with the Governor; and the day and manner of his election, and the qualifications of the electors, shall be the same as are required in the election of a Governor. The return of the votes for this officer, and the declaration of his election, shall be in the same manner; [and if no one person shall be found to have a majority of all the votes returned, the vacancy shall be filled by the Senate and House of Representatives, in the same manner as the Governor is to be elected, in case no one person shall have a majority of the votes of the people to be Governor.] *Mass.*, 289.

—There shall be a Lieutenant-Governor, who shall hold his office during four years. *Ind.*, 174.

—And during the time he administers the government, as Governor, shall receive the same compensation which the Governor would have received, had he been employed in the duties of his office. *Ky.*, 214; (nearly similar), *La.*, 230.

1 § 8. The Lieutenant-Governor shall, while acting as such, receive a com-

2 pensation which shall be fixed by law, and which shall not be increased or

3 diminished during his continuance in office.

—At the annual meetings of the electors, immediately after the election of Governor, there shall also be chosen, in the same manner as hereinbefore provided for the election of Governor, a Lieutenant-Governor who shall continue in office for the same time, and possess the same qualifications. *Ct.*, 110.

POWERS AND DUTIES OF LIEUTENANT-GOVERNOR.

—In case of the impeachment of the Governor, or his removal from office, death, resignation, or absence from the State, the powers and duties of the office shall devolve upon the Lieutenant-Governor, for the residue of the term, or until the Governor absent or impeached, shall return or be acquitted. But when the Governor shall, with the consent of the Legislature, be out of the State, in time of war, at the head of a military force thereof, he shall continue commander-in-chief of all the military force of the State. *N. Y.* (1821), 38; *Cal.*, 101; *Wis.*, 564.

—Whenever the office of the Governor and Lieutenant-Governor shall be vacant by reason of death, absence, or otherwise, then the Council, or the major part of them, shall, during such vacancy, have full power and authority, to do and execute, all and every such acts, matters and things, as the Governor or the Lieutenant-Governor might or could, by virtue of this Constitution, do or execute, if they, or either of them, were personally present. *Mass.*, 289.

—In case of the removal of the Governor from office, or of his death, failure to qualify, resignation, removal from the State, or inability to discharge the powers and duties of the office, the said office, with its compensation, shall devolve upon the Lieutenant-Governor; and the General Assembly shall provide by law for the discharge of the executive functions in other necessary cases. *Va.*, 540.

—Whenever the chair of the Governor shall be vacant, by reason of his death, or absence from the Commonwealth, or otherwise, the Lieutenant-Governor, for the time being, shall, during such vacancy, perform all the duties incumbent upon the Governor, and shall have and exercise all the powers and authorities, which, by this Constitution, the Governor is vested with, when personally present. *Mass.*, 289.

—In case of vacancy in the office of Governor, or of his inability to serve, impeachment, or absence from the State, the Lieutenant-Governor shall fill the office of Governor and exercise the powers and authority appertaining thereto, until a Governor is qualified to act, or until the office is filled at the next annual election. *R. I.*, 477; (nearly similar), *Ky.*, 213; *Iowa*, 188; *Ohio*, 436; *Ark.*, 90; *Ct.*, 113; *Tex.*, 513.

—Unless the General Assembly shall provide by law for the election of Governor to fill such vacancy. *Ark.*, 90.

—And the General Assembly shall by law provide for the case of removal from office, death, resignation, or inability, both of the Governor and Lieutenant-Governor, declaring what officer shall then act as Governor and such officer shall act accordingly, until the disability be removed, or a Governor be elected. *Ind.*, 175.

—In case of the impeachment of the Governor, or his removal from office, death, resignation, disqualification, disability, or removal from the State, the Lieutenant-Governor shall succeed to his office, and in case of the impeachment of the Lieutenant-Governor, or his removal from office, death, resigna-

tion, disqualification, disability, or removal from the State, the President *pro tempore* of the Senate shall succeed to his office; and when the offices of the Governor, Lieutenant-Governor and President *pro tempore* of the Senate shall become vacant in the recess of the Senate, the Secretary of State, for the time being, shall by proclamation, convene the Senate, that a President *pro tempore* may be chosen to exercise the office of Governor for the unexpired term. *S. C.*, 485; (nearly similar). *Md.*, 259.

—If the Lieutenant-Governor shall be required to administer the Government, and shall while in such administration die or resign during the recess of the General Assembly, it shall be the duty of the Secretary for the time being to convene the Senate for the purpose of choosing a President *pro tempore. Ct.*, 110.

—The Lieutenant-Governor, while acting as Governor, shall receive the same pay as provided for Governor; and while presiding in the Senate shall receive, as compensation therefor the same mileage and double the per diem pay provided for a Senator, and none other. *Iowa*, 188.

The Lieutenant-Governor shall be President of the Senate, but shall have only a casting vote therein. If, during a vacancy of the office of Governor, the Lieutenant-Governor shall be impeached, displaced, resign, die, or be absent from the State, the President of the Senate shall act as Governor, until the vacancy shall be filled, or the disability shall cease. *Cal.*, 100; *N. Y.* (1821), 38; *Wis.*, 564.

—The Governor, and in his absence the Lieutenant-Governor, shall preside in the Senate and in grand committee. The presiding officer of the Senate and grand committee, shall have a right to vote in case of equal division, but not otherwise. *R. I.*, 477.

—He shall, by virtue of his office, be Speaker of the Senate, have a right, when in committee of the whole, to debate and vote on all subjects, and when the Senate are equally divided, to give the casting vote. *Ky.*, 213.

—The Lieutenant-Governor shall, by virtue of his office, be President of the Senate, and whenever the Senate are equally divided, shall have the right to give the casting vote. *Md.*, 259; (nearly similar) *Fl.*, 130; *Iowa*, 188; *Kan.*, 198; *La.*, 230; *Nev.*, 382; *Ohio*, 436; *S. C.*, 485.

—He shall, by virtue of his office, be President of the Senate, have a right, when in committee of the whole, to debate, and whenever the Senate are equally divided, shall give the casting vote. *Iowa*, 90; (nearly similar) *Ct.*, 110; *Ill.*, 158; *Mich.*, 305; *Ind.*, 176; *Mo.*, 356; *Tenn.*, 513.

[And may also vote in joint vote of both Houses.] *Mo.*, 356.

[Allowed no vote.] *Va.*, 540.

—The Lieutenant-Governor, while he acts as President of the Senate, shall receive for his services the same compensation which shall for the same period be allowed to the Speaker of the House, and no more. *Md.*, 259; (nearly similar), *Ark.*, 90; *Ill.*, 158; *Ky.*, 214; *Mo.*, 356; *Va.*, 540.

—The Lieutenant-Governor shall receive double the per diem allowance of members of the Senate, for every day's attendance as President of the Senate, and the same mileage as shall be allowed to members of the Legislature. *Wis.*, 564.

[Compensation double that of a State Senator.] *Min.*, 324.

—And during the time he administers the government, as Governor, he shall receive the same compensation which the Governor would have received had he been employed in the duties of his office. *Ark.*, 90.

1 § 9. Every bill which shall have passed the Senate and Assembly, shall

2 before it becomes a law, be presented to the Governor; if he approve, he shall

3 sign it; but if not, he shall return it with his objections to that House in which

4 it shall have originated, who shall enter the objections at large on their journal

5 and proceed to reconsider it. If, after such consideration, two-thirds of the

6 members present shall agree to pass the bill, it shall be sent, together with the

7 objections, to the other House, by which it shall likewise be reconsidered; and

8 if approved by two-thirds of all the members present, it shall become a law,

—The Lieutenant-Governor shall receive for his services a salary of five thousand dollars per annum, to be paid quarterly. *La.*, 230.

—The Lieutenant-Governor, while he shall act as President of the Senate, shall receive for his services the same compensation as the Speaker of the House of Representatives; and any person acting as Governor shall receive the compensation attached to the office of Governor. *Ind.*, 176.

—The Lieutenant-Governor shall be President of the Senate, except when he shall exercise the office of Governor, or when his office shall be vacant, or in his absence; in which cases the Senate shall appoint one of its own members to be President of the Senate *pro tempore*. And the President of the Senate shall have a casting vote, but no other. *Vt.*, 528.

VETO POWER.

[The New York Constitution of 1846, followed the language used in 1821. It is nearly like that of United States, but differs in using the word "present," in speaking of the return of bills with objections. The veto power under the Constitution of 1777, was entrusted to the Council of Revision, and was as follows:]

—And whereas, laws, inconsistent with the spirit of this constitution, or with the public good, may be hastily and unadvisedly passed: Be it ordained, that the Governor, for the time being, the Chancellor, and the Judges of the Supreme Court—or any two of them, together with the Governor—shall be, and hereby are, constituted a Council, to revise all bills about to be passed into laws by the Legislature; and for that purpose shall assemble themselves from time to time, when the Legislature shall be convened: for which, nevertheless, they shall not receive any salary or consideration, under any pretense whatever. And that all bills, which have passed the Senate and Assembly, shall, before they become laws, be presented to the said Council, for their revisal and consideration: and if, upon such revision, and consideration, it should appear improper to the said Council, or a majority of them, that the said bill should become a law of this State, that they return the same, together with their objections thereto in writing, to the Senate or House of Assembly (in whichsoever the same shall have originated) who shall enter the objections, sent down by the Council, at large in their minutes, and proceed to reconsider the said bill. But if, after such reconsideration, two-thirds of the said Senate or House of Assembly, shall, notwithstanding the said objections, agree to pass the same, it shall, together with the objections, be sent to the other branch of the Legislature, where it shall also be reconsidered, and if approved by two-thirds of the members present, shall be a law.

—And in order to prevent any unnecessary delays, be it further ordained, that if any bill shall not be returned by the Council within ten days after it shall have been presented, the same shall be a law, unless the Legislature shall, by their adjournment, render a return of the said bill, within ten days, impracticable; in which case the bill shall be returned on the first day of the meeting of the Legislature, after the expiration of the said ten days. *N. Y.* (1777), 26.

—Every bill, which shall have passed both Houses of the General Assembly, shall be presented to the Governor; if he approve, he shall sign it, but if not, he shall return it, with his objections, to the House in which it originated, who shall enter the objections at large upon the journals, and proceed to reconsider it; if, after such reconsideration, a majority of the whole number elected to that House shall agree to pass the bill, it shall be sent, with the objections, to the other House, by whom it shall likewise be reconsidered, and if approved by a majority of the whole number elected to that House, it shall become a law; but, in such cases, the votes of both Houses shall be determined by yeas and nays, and the names of the members voting for or against the bill shall be entered on the journals of each House, respectively. If any bill shall not be returned by the Governor within five days (Sundays excepted), after it shall have been presented to him, the same shall be a law, in like manner as if he had signed it; unless the General Assembly, by their adjournment, prevent its return, in which case it shall not be a law. *Ala.*, 79; *N. J.*, 416; *Vt.*, 529; (nearly similar, except time for return) *Ark.*, 89; *Ct.*, 110; *Ill.*, 159; *Ind.*, 175; *Ky.*, 214; *Miss.*, 341; *Mo.*, 355; *S. C.*, 486.

—Every order, resolution, or vote, to which the concurrence of both Houses may be necessary (except on questions of adjournment, and for bringing on elections by the two Houses), shall be presented to the Governor, and, before it shall take effect, be approved by him, or, being disapproved, shall be re-passed by both Houses, according to the rules and limitations prescribed in the case of a bill. *Ala.*, 79; (nearly similar), *Ark.*, 89; *Fl.*, 131; *Ga.*, 147; *Ky.*, 214; *La.*, 230; *Minn.*, 322; *Miss.*, 341; *Mo.*, 355; *Pa.*, 462; *Tex.*, 514.

—Every resolve shall be presented to the Governor, and, before the same shall take effect, shall be approved by him; or, being disapproved by him, shall be re-passed by the Senate and House of Representatives, according to the rules and limitations prescribed in the case of a bill. *N. H.*, 405.

COUNCIL.

[A Council of Revision, consisting of Governor, Chancellor, and Judges of the Supreme Court, created by the N. Y. Constitution of 1777], 26.

[A Council of Appointment, consisting of the Governor and four Senators, was created by the N. Y. Constitution of 1777], 30, 32, 34.

—There shall be a Council, to consist of seven persons, citizens of the United States, and residents of this State, to advise the Governor in the executive part of the government, whom the Governor shall have full power, at his discretion, to assemble; and

9 notwithstanding the objections of the Governor. But in all such cases, the
10 votes of both Houses shall be determined by yeas and nays, and the names of
11 the members voting for and against the bill shall be entered on the journal of
12 each House respectively. If any bill shall not be returned by the Governor
13 within ten days (Sundays excepted), after it shall have been presented to him,
14 the same shall be a law, in like manner as if he had signed it, unless the Legis-
15 lature shall, by their adjournment, prevent its return; in which case it shall
16 not be a law.

he, with the Counsellors or a majority of them, may, from time to time, hold and keep a Council, for ordering and directing the affairs of state according to law. *Me.*, 245.

—The Counsellors shall be chosen annually, on the first Wednesday of January, by joint ballot of the Senators and Representatives in Convention; and vacancies which shall afterward happen shall be filled in the same manner; but not more than one Counsellor shall be elected from any district prescribed for the election of Senators; and they shall be privileged from arrest in the same manner as Senators and Representatives. *Me.*, 245.

—The resolutions and advice of Council shall be recorded in a register, and signed by the members agreeing thereto, which may be called for by either House of the Legislature; and any Counsellor may enter his dissent to the resolution of the majority. *Me.*, 245.

[The Governor and Council fill certain civil and military offices.] *Me.*, 244.

—Eight Councillors shall be annually chosen by the inhabitants of this Commonwealth, qualified to vote for Governor. The election of Councillors shall be determined by the same rule that is required in the election of Governor. The Legislature, at its first session after this amendment shall have been adopted, and at its first session after the next State census shall have been taken, and at its first session after each decennial State census thereafterwards, shall divide the Commonwealth into eight districts of contiguous territory, each containing a number of inhabitants as nearly equal as practicable, without dividing any town or ward of a city, and each entitled to elect one Councillor; *Provided, however,* That if, at any time, the Constitution shall provide for the division of the Commonwealth into forty senatorial districts, then the Legislature shall so arrange the councillor districts that each district shall consist of five contiguous senatorial districts, as they shall be, from time to time, established by the Legislature. No person shall be eligible to the office of Councillor who has not been an inhabitant of the Commonwealth for the term of five years immediately preceding his election. The day and manner of election, the return of the votes and the declaration of the said elections, shall be the same as are required in the election of Governor. Whenever there shall be a failure to elect the full number of Councillors, the vacancies shall be filled in the same manner as is required for filling vacancies in the Senate; and vacancies occasioned by death, removal from the State, or otherwise, shall be filled in like manner, as soon as may be after such vacancies shall have happened. *Mass.*, 297.

—The Governor, and in his absence the Lieutenant-Governor, shall be President of the Council, but shall have no voice in Council, and the Lieutenant-Governor shall always be a member of the Council, except when the chair of the Governor shall be vacant. *Mass.*, 289.

—The Councillors in the civil arrangements of the Commonwealth, shall have rank next after the Lieutenant-Governor. *Mass.*, 289.

—The Governor shall have authority, from time to time, at his discretion, to assemble and call together the Councillors of this Commonwealth for the time being, and the Governor, with the said Councillors, or five of them, at least, shall and may, from time to time, hold and keep a Council for the ordering and directing the affairs of the Commonwealth, agreeably to the Constitution and the laws of the land. *Mass.*, 287.

—The resolutions and advice of the Council shall be recorded in a register and signed by the members present; and this record may be called for, at any time, by either House of the Legislature; and any member of the Council may insert his opinion, contrary to the resolution of the majority. *Mass.*, 289.

—In case of a vacancy in the Council, from a failure of election or other cause, the Senate and House of Representatives shall by concurrent vote, choose some eligible person from the people of the district wherein such vacancy occurs, to fill that office. If such vacancy shall happen when the Legislature is not in session, the Governor, with the advice and consent of the Council, may fill the same by the appointment of some eligible person. *Mass.*, 300.

—There shall be annually elected by ballot five Councillors, for advising the Governor in the executive part of government. The freeholders and other inhabitants of each county, qualified to vote for Senators, shall, some time in the month of March, give in their votes for one Councillor; which votes shall be received, sorted, counted, certified and returned to the Secretary's office, in the same manner as the votes for Senators, to be by the Secretary laid before the Senate and House of Representatives on the first Wednesday of June. *N. H.,* 407.

—And the person having a majority of votes in any county shall be considered as duly elected a Councillor, but if no person shall have a majority of votes in any county, the Senate and House of Representatives shall take the names of the two persons who have the highest number of votes in each county, and not elected, and out of those two shall elect by joint ballot the Councillor wanted for such county; and the qualifications for Councillor shall be the same as for Senators. *N. H.,* 407.

—If any person thus chosen a Councillor shall be elected Governor, or member of either branch of the Legislature, and shall accept the trust; or if any person elected a Councillor shall refuse to accept the office; or in case of death, resignation, or removal of any Councillor out of the State, the Governor may issue a precept for the election of a new Councillor in that county where such vacancy shall happen; and the choice shall be in the same manner as before directed; and the Governor shall have full power and authority to convene the Council, from time to time, at his discretion; and with them, or the majority of them, may and shall, from time to time, hold a Council for ordering and directing the affairs of this State, according to the laws of the land. *N. H.,* 407.

—The resolutions and advice of the Council shall be recorded by the Secretary in a register, and signed

24

by all the members present agreeing thereto; and this record may be called for at any time by either House of the Legislature, and any member of the Council may enter his opinion contrary to the resolution of the majority, with the reasons for such opinion. *N. H.*, 407.

—The Legislature may, if the public good shall hereafter require it, divide the State into five districts, as nearly equal as may be, governing themselves by the number of ratable polls and proportion of pubic taxes; each district to elect a Councillor; and in case of such division, the manner of the choice shall be conformable to the present mode of election in counties. *N. H.*, 407.

—*And whereas*, The elections appointed to be made by this Constitution on the first Wednesday of June, annually, by the two Houses of the Legislature, may not be completed on that day, the said elections may be adjourned from day to day, until the same be completed. And the order of the elections shall be as follows: The vacancies of the Senate, if any, shall be first filled up: the Governor shall then be elected, provided there should be no choice of him by the people, and afterward the two Houses shall proceed to fill up the vacancy, if any, in the Council. *N. H.*, 407.

—That the Senate and House of Commons, jointly, at their first meeting, after each annual election, shall, by ballot, elect seven persons to be a Council of State for one year; who shall advise the Governor in the execution of his office; and that four members shall be a quorum; their advice and proceedings shall be entered in a journal, to be kept for that purpose only, and signed by the members present; to any part of which any member present may enter his dissent. And such journal shall be laid before the General Assembly when called for by them. *N. C.*, 424.

—That no member of the Council of State shall have a seat either in the Senate or House of Commons. *N. C.*, 425.

—The Supreme Executive Council of this State shall consist of a Governor, Lieutenant-Governor, and twelve persons chosen in the following manner, to wit:— the freemen of each town shall, on the day of election for choosing Representatives to attend the General Assembly, bring in their votes for Governor, with his name fairly written, to the Constable, who shall seal them up, and write on them, " Votes for Governor," and deliver them to the Representative chosen to attend the General Assembly. And at the opening of the General Assembly there shall be a committee appointed out of the Council and Assembly, who, after being duly sworn to the faithful discharge of their trust, shall proceed to receive, sort and count the votes for the Governor, and declare the person who has the major part of the votes to be Governor for the year ensuing. And if there be no choice made, then the Council and General Assembly, by their joint ballots, shall make choice of a Governor. The Lieutenant-Governor and Treasurer shall be chosen in the manner above directed. And each freeman shall give in twelve votes for twelve Councillors in the same manner, and the twelve highest in nomination shall serve for the ensuing year as Councillors. *Vt.*, 523.

[A Council of Censors, elected septennially.] *Vt.*, 527.

—[Detailed powers granted to Governor and Council, see *Va.*, 524. Among them are the following:] They are to take care that the laws be faithfully executed; are to expedite the execution of such measures as as may be resolved upon by the General Assembly; and they may draw upon the treasury for such sums as may be appropriated by the House of Representatives; they may lay embargoes, or prohibit the exportation of any commodity for any time not exceeding thirty days, in the recess of the House only. They may grant such licenses as shall be directed by law; and shall have power to call together the General Assembly, when necessary, before the day to which they shall stand adjourned. The Gov-

ernor or Lieutenant-Governor and the Council, shall meet at the time and place with the General Assembly; [the Lieutenant-Governor shall, during the presence of the Commander-in-Chief, vote and act as one of the Council; and the Governor, and in his absence the Lieutenant-Governor shall, by virtue of their offices, preside in Council, and have a casting, but no other vote. Every member of the Council shall be a Justice of the Peace for the whole State, by virtue of his office. The Governor and Council shall have a Secretary, and keep fair books of their proceedings, wherein any Councillor may enter his dissent, with his reasons to support it. And the Governor may appoint a Secretary for himself and his Council. *Va.*, 524.

—Every bill which may have passed the Legislature shall, before it becomes a law, be presented to the Governor. If he approve it he shall sign it, but if not, he shall return it with his objections, to the House in which it originated, which shall enter the same upon the journal, and proceed to reconsider it. If, after such reconsideration, it again pass both Houses by yeas and nays, by a majority of two-thirds of the members of each House present, it shall become a law, notwithstanding the Governor's objections. If any bill shall not be returned within ten days after it shall have been presented to him (Sundays excepted), the same shall be a law, in like manner as if he had signed it, unless the Legislature, by adjournment, prevent such return. *Cal.*, 98; (nearly similar), *Mich.*, 302; *La.*, 230; *Nev.*, 384; *Or.*, 453; *Pa.*, 462; (nearly similar except in time,) *Fl.*, 131; *Iowa*, 185; *Me.*, 243; *Neb.*, 374; *N. H.*, 405; *Tex.*, 513; *Wis.*, 564.

—The Governor shall have the revision of all bills passed by both Houses, before the same shall become laws, but two-thirds of each House may pass a law notwithstanding his dissent; and if any bill should not be returned by the Governor within five days (Sundays excepted) after it has been presented to him, the same shall be law, unless the General Assembly by their adjournment, shall prevent its return. He may approve any appropriation, and disapprove any other appropriation in the same bill, and the latter shall not be effectual unless passed by two-thirds of each House. *Ga.*, 147.

—If any bill shall not be returned by the Governor within ten days (Sundays excepted), after it shall have been presented to him, the same shall be a law, in like manner as if he had signed it, unless the General Assembly shall, by their adjournment, prevent its return, in which case the said bill shall be returned on the first day of the meeting of the General Assembly, after the expiration of said ten days, or be a law. *Ill.*, 159.

—If any bill shall not be returned by the Governor within three days (Sundays excepted), after it shall have been presented to him, it shall be a law without his signature, unless the general adjournment shall prevent its return, in which case it shall be a law, unless the Governor, within five days next after such adjournment, shall file such bill, with his objections thereto, in the office of the Secretary of State, who shall lay the same before the General Assembly at its next session, in like manner as if it had been returned by the Governor. But no bill shall be presented to the Governor within two days next previous to the final adjournment of the General Assembly. *Ind.*, 175.

—Any bill submitted to the Governor for his approval during the last three days of a session of the General Assembly, shall be deposited by him in the office of the Secretary of State within thirty days after the adjournment, with his approval if approved by him, and with his objections if he disapproves thereof. *Iowa*, 185.

—Every bill and joint resolution passed by the House of Representatives and Senate shall, within two days thereafter, be signed by the presiding officers and presented to the Governor; if he approve, he shall sign it; but if not, he shall return it to the House of Representatives, which shall enter the objections, at large, upon its journal, and proceed to reconsider the same. If, after such reconsideration, two-thirds of the members elected shall agree to pass the bill or resolution, it shall be sent, with the objections, to the Senate, by which it shall likewise be reconsidered; and if approved by two-thirds of all the members elected, it shall become a law. But in all such cases the vote shall be taken by yeas and nays, and entered upon the journals of each House. If any bill shall not be returned within three days (Sundays excepted) after it shall have been presented to the Legislature, it shall become a law in like manner as if he had signed it, unless the Legislature, by its adjournment, prevent its return, in which case it shall not become a law. *Kan.,* 199.

[A recent amendment of the Constitution of Kansas allows bills to originate in either House, and modifies the section last quoted.]

—No bill or resolve of the Senate or House of Representatives shall become a law, and have force as such, until it shall have been laid before the Governor for his revisal; and if he, upon such revision, approve thereof, he shall signify his approbation by signing the same. But if he have any objection to the passing of such bill or resolve, he shall return the same together with his objections thereto, in writing, to the Senate or House of Representatives, in whichsoever the same shall have originated, who shall enter the objections sent down by the Governor, at large, on their records, and proceed to reconsider the said bill or resolve; but if, after such reconsideration, two-thirds of the said Senate or House of Representatives shall, notwithstanding the said objections, agree to pass the same, it shall, together with the objections, be sent to the other branch of the Legislature, where it shall also be reconsidered, and if approved by two-thirds of the members present, shall have the force of law; but in all such cases, the vote of both Houses shall be determined by yeas and nays; and the names of the persons voting for or against the said bill or resolve shall be entered upon the public records of the Commonwealth.

And in order to prevent unnecessary delays if any bill or resolve shall not be returned by the Governor within five days after it shall have been presented, the same shall have the force of law. *Mass.,* 283.

—If any bill or resolve shall be objected to, and not approved by the Governor; and if the General Court shall adjourn within five days after the same shall have been laid before the Governor for his approbation, and thereby prevent his returning it with his objections, as provided by the Constitution, such bill or resolve shall not become a law, nor have force as such. *Mass.,* 294.

—Every bill which shall have passed the Senate and House of Representatives, in conformity to the rules of each House, and the joint rules of the two Houses, shall, before it becomes a law, be presented to the Governor of the State. If he approve, he shall sign and deposit it in the office of the Secretary of State for preservation, and notify the House where it originated of the fact. But if not, he shall return it with his objections, to the House in which it shall have originated, when such objections shall be entered at large on the journal of the same; and the House shall proceed to reconsider the bill. If, after such reconsideration, two-thirds of that House shall agree to pass the bill, it shall be sent, together with the objections, to the other House, by which it shall likewise be reconsidered, and if it be approved by two-thirds of that House it shall become a law. But in all such cases the votes of both Houses shall be determined by yeas and nays, and the names of the persons voting for or against the bill shall be entered on the journal of each House, respectively. If any bill shall not be returned by the Governor within three days (Sundays excepted), after it shall have been presented to him, the same shall be a law in like manner as if he had signed it, unless the Legislature, by adjournment within that time, prevent its return, in which case it shall not be a law. The Governor may approve, sign nd file in the office of the Secretary of State, within three days after the adjournment of the Legislature, any act passed during the three last days of the session, the same shall become a law. *Min.,* 321.

—The Governor shall have a negative upon all laws passed by the Legislature, under such rules and limitations as are in this Constitution prescribed. *Min.,* 223.

—If any bill shall not be returned by the Governor within ten days (Sundays excepted) after it shall have been presented to him, the same shall become a law, in like manner as if the Governor had signed it, unless the General Assembly, by its adjournment, shall prevent its return, in which case it shall not become a law, unless the Governor, after such adjournment, and within ten days after the bill was presented to him (Sundays excepted) shall sign and deposit the same in the office of the Secretary of State; in which case it shall become a law, in like manner as if it had been signed by him during the session of the General Assembly. *Mo.,* 355.

— If any bill shall not be returned within five days after it shall have been presented to him (Sunday excepted), exclusive of the day on which he received it, the same shall be a law 'in like manner as if he had signed it, unless the Legislature, by its final adjournment, prevent such return, in which case it shall be a law, unless the Governor, within ten days next after the adjournment (Sundays excepted), shall file such bill, with his objections thereto, in the office of the Secretary of State, who shall lay the same before the Legislature at its next session, in like manner as if it had been returned by the Governor; and if the same shall receive the vote of two-thirds of the members elected to each branch of the Legislature, upon a vote taken by yeas and nays, to be entered upon the journals of each House, it shall become a law. *Nev.,* 384.

—If any bill shall not be returned by the Governor within five days, Sundays excepted, after it shall have been presented to him, it shall be a law without his signature, unless the general adjournment shall prevent its return; in which case it shall be a law, unless the Governor, within five days next after the adjournment, Sundays excepted, shall file such bill, with his objections thereto, in the office of the Secretary of State, who shall lay the same before the Legislative Assembly at its next session, in like manner as if it had been returned by the Governor. *Or.,* 453.

—If any bill shall not be returned by the Governor within ten days, Sunday excepted, after it shall have been presented to him, it shall be a law in like manner as if he had signed it, unless the General Assembly, by their adjournment prevented its return, in which case it shall be a law, unless sent back within three days after their next meeting. *Pa.,* 462.

—And, that time may be always allowed the Governor to consider bills passed by the General Assembly, neither House shall read any bill on the last day of its session, except such bills as have been returned by the Governor as herein provided. *S. C.,* 486.

—Every bill presented to the Governor one day previous to the adjournment of the Legislature, and not returned to the House in which it originated before its adjournment, shall become a law, and have the same force and effect as if signed by the Governor. The Governor may approve any appropriation, and disapprove any other appropriation in the same bill. In such case, he shall, in signing the bill designate the appropriations disapproved, and shall return a copy of such appropriations, with his objections to the House in which the bill shall have originated; and the same proceedings shall then be had as in the case of other bills disapproved by the Governor; but if the Legislature has adjourned before the bill is returned to the House, he shall return the same to the Secretary of State, with his objections, and also to the next session of the Legislature. *Tex.,* 513.

—To the end that laws, before they are enacted, may be more maturely considered, and the inconvenience of hasty determinations as much as possible prevented, all bills which originate in the Assembly, shall be laid before the Governor and Council, for their revision and concurrence, or proposals of amendment, who shall return the same to the Assembly, with their proposals of amendment, if any, in writing; and if the same are not agreed to by the Assembly, it shall be in the power of the Governor and Council to suspend the passing of such bills until the next session of the Legislature; *Provided,* That if the Governor and Council shall neglect or refuse to return any such bill to the Assembly, with written proposals of amendment, within five days, or before the rising of the Legislature, the same shall become a law.] *Vt.,* 525.

[The Constitutions of Ohio, Rhode Island, Tennessee, Virginia, and West Virginia give no veto power to the executive.]

Summary of votes required to pass bills over veto. Majority of whole number elected: *Ala.,* 79; *Ark.,* 89; *Ind.,* 175; *Ky.,* 214; *Mo.,* 355; *N. J.,* 416; *S. C.,* 486.

Majority of members: *Ill.,* 159; *Vt.,* 529.

Majority of two-thirds present: *Cal.,* 98; *Me.,* 243; *Mass.,* 283; *Neb.,* 374; *Or.,* 453; *Tex.,* 513; *Wis.,* 564.

Majority of two-thirds voting: *Ct.,* 110.

Majority of two-thirds of members: *U. S.,* 11; *Iowa,* 185; *Min.,* 321; *Miss.,* 341; *N. H.,* 405; *Pa.,* 462.

Majority of two-thirds of members elected : *Kan.,* 199; *La.,* 230; *Mich.,* 302; *Nev.,* 384.

Summary of time allowed for return of bills. Two days: *S. C.,* 486.

Three days : *Ark.,* 89; *Ct.,* 110; *Ind.,* 175; *Iowa,* 185; *Kan.,* 199; *Min,* 321; *Neb.,* 374; *Wis.,* 564.

Five days : *Ala.,* 79; *Fla.,* 131; *Me.,* 243; *Mass.,* 283, 294; *Nev.,* 384; *N. H.* 405; *N. J.,* 416; *Or.,* 453; *Tex.,* 513; *Vt.,* 529.

Six days : *Miss.,* 341.

Ten days : *U. S.,* 11; *Cal.,* 98; *Ill.,* 159; *Ky.,* 217; *La.,* 230; *Mich.,* 302; *Mo.,* 355; *Pa.,* 462.

THE GREAT SEAL, AND ITS USES.

—There shall be a seal of this State, which shall be kept by the Governor, and used by him officially. *Ark.,* 89.

—That there shall be a seal of this State, which shall be kept by the Governor, and used by him as occasion may require, and shall be called "the great seal of the State of North Carolina," and shall be affixed to all grants and commissions. *N. C.,* 424.

—There shall be a seal of this State, which shall be kept by the Governor, and used by him officially, and shall be called "the great seal of the State." *Tenn.,* 495; (nearly similar,) *Cal.,* 100; *Ind.,* 181; *Iowa,* 189; *Kan.,* 198; *Miss.,* 341; *Neb.,* 374; *Nev.,* 385; *N. J.,* 420; *Ohio,* 433; *Or.,* 450.

—There shall be a seal of the State, which shall be kept by the Secretary of State, and be used by him officially, and shall be called by him the great seal of the State of Minnesota, and shall be attached to all official acts of the Governor (his signature to acts and resolves of the Legislature excepted,) requiring authentication. The Legislature shall provide for an appropriate device and motto for said seal. *Min.,* 320.

—The great seal of the State shall be deposited in the office of the Secretary of State, and shall not be affixed to any instrument of writing, but by order of the Governor or General Assembly, and that used previously to the year 1861, shall be the great seal of the State. *Ga.,* 148.

—The State Seal last heretofore used (until altered by the General Assembly), shall continue to be the Great Seal of the State, and shall be kept by the Governor for the time being, and used by him officially. *Fl.,* 131.

—There shall be a great seal of the State, which shall be kept and used by the Governor officially; and the seal now in use shall continue to be the great seal of the State, until another shall have been adopted by the General Assembly. *Ala.,* 79.

—There shall be a seal of the State, which shall be kept by the Governor, and used by him officially, the said seal shall be a star of five points encircled by an olive and live oak branches, and the words "The State of Texas." *Tex.,* 513.

—The Secretary of State shall be the custodian of the seal of State, and shall authenticate therewith all official acts of the Governor, his approbation of laws excepted. The said seal shall be called the "*great seal of the State of Missouri*;" and the emblems and devices thereof heretofore prescribed by law shall not be subject to change. *Mo.,* 356.

—All commissions shall be in the name of the State, shall be sealed with the great seal, and be signed and tested by the Governor. *Del.,* 119.

—That all commissions and grants shall run in the name of the State of North Carolina, and bear test, and be signed by the Governor. *N. C.,* 426.

—All grants and commissions shall be in the name and by the authority of the State of ——, be sealed with the State seal, and signed by the Governor. *Tenn.,* 4; (nearly similar,) *La.,* 231; *Pa.,* 466; *S. C.,* 487.

—All Commissions shall be in the name and by the authority of the State; shall be sealed with the great seal of the State, signed by the Governor, and attested by the Secretary of State. *Ala.,* 81; (nearly similar,) *Ark.,* 89; *Cal.,* 100; *Ct.,* 110; *Fla.,* 131; *Ill.,* 159; *Iowa,* 189; *Kan.,* 198; *Mich.,* 305; *Miss.,* 341; *Neb.,* 379; *Nev.,* 385; *Ohio,* 436; *Or.,* 459; *Tex.,* 513.

—All communications shall be in the name and by authority of the State of Rhode Island and Providence Plantations; shall be sealed with the State seal, signed by the Governor, and attested by the Secretary. *R. I.,* 477.

—All Commissions shall be in the name of the Commonwealth, signed by the Governor, and attested by the Secretary or his deputy, and have the great seal of the Commonwealth affixed thereto. *Mass.,* 293; (nearly similar,) *N. H.,* 409.

—Commissions and grants shall run in the name of the Commonwealth of Virginia, and be attested by the Governor, with the seal of the Commonwealth annexed. *Va.,* 540.

—All commissions shall be in the name of the State, signed by the Governor, attested by the Secretary or his deputy, and have the seal of the State thereto affixed. *Me.,* 247.

—All official acts of the Governor, his approval of the laws excepted, shall be authenticated by the great seal of the State, which shall be kept by the Secretary of State. *Mich.,* 305.

—The Governor shall commission all officers not otherwise provided by law. All commissions shall run in the name and by the authority of the State of ——, be sealed by the State seal, signed by the Governor, and attested by the Secretary of State. *Mo.,* 357.

—All public commissions and grants shall run thus: "The State of Maryland," &c., and shall be signed by the Governor, with the seal of the State annexed; all writs and process shall run to the same style, and be tested, sealed and signed as usual; and all indictments shall conclude "against the peace, government and dignity of the State." *Md.,* 267.

—All commissions shall be in the name of the freemen of the State of Vermont, sealed with the State seal, signed by the Governor, and in his absence, the Lieutenant-Governor, and attested by the Secretary; which seal shall be kept by the Governor. *Vt.,* 526.

—It shall be the duty of the Legislature to provide a great seal for the State, which shall be kept by the Secretary of State; and all official acts of the Governor, his approbation of the laws excepted, shall be thereby authenticated. *Wis.,* 571.

—All grants and commissions shall be in the name and by the authority of the State of New Jersey sealed with the great seal, signed by the Governor o person administering the government, and counter

ARTICLE V.

1   SECTION 1. The Secretary of State, Comptroller, Treasurer and Attorney-

2 General, shall be chosen at a general election, and shall hold their offices for

3 two years. Each of the officers in this article named (except the Speaker of

4 the Assembly), shall at stated times, during his continuance in office, receive

5 for his services a compensation, which shall not be increased or diminished

6 during the term for which he shall have been elected; nor shall he receive, to

7 his use, any fees or perquisites of office, or other compensation.

signed by the Secretary of State, and shall run "The State of New Jersey to ———, greeting." *N. J.*, 420.

—The Governor shall use his private seal until a State seal is provided. *Kan.*, 207.

—He shall commission all officers of the State. *S. C.*, 485.

—All civil officers elected or appointed pursuant to the provisions of this Constitution, shall be commissioned by the Governor. *N. J.*, 419.

—And the Governor shall issue commissions to the Auditor, Register, Treasurer, President of the Board of Internal Improvement, Superintendent of Public Instruction, and such other officers as he may be directed by law to commission, as soon as he has ascertained the result of the election of those officers respectively. *Ky.*, 221.

STATE OFFICERS.

—The Secretary of State, Comptroller, Treasurer, Attorney-General, Surveyor-General and Commissary-General shall be appointed as follows: The Senate and Assembly shall each openly nominate one person for the said offices respectively; after which they shall meet together, and if they shall agree in their nominations, the person so nominated shall be appointed to the office for which he shall be nominated. If they shall disagree, the appointment shall be made by the joint ballot of the Senators and members of Assembly. The Treasurer shall be chosen annually. The Secretary of State, Comptroller, Attorney-General, Surveyor-General and Commissary-General shall hold their offices for three years, unless sooner removed by concurrent resolution of the Senate and Assembly. *N. Y.* (1821), 39.

—A Secretary of State, a Comptroller of Public Accounts, and a State Treasurer, shall be elected by a joint vote of both Houses of the General Assembly, each of whom shall continue in office during the term of two years, shall perform all the duties that may be required of him by law, and receive such compensation as may be by law provided. *Ala.*, 81.

—There shall be elected a Secretary of State by the qualified voters of the State, who shall continue in office during the term of four years, and until his successor in office be duly qualified; he shall keep a fair register of all official acts and proceedings of the Governor, and shall, when required, lay the same, and all papers, minutes and vouchers relative thereto, before the General Assembly, and shall perform such other duties as may be required by law. *Ark.*, 89; *Fl.*, 131.

—A Secretary of State, a Comptroller, a Treasurer, an Attorney General, and a Surveyor General, shall be elected at the same time and places, and in the same manner as the Governor and Lieutenant-Governor, and whose term of office [four years] shall be the same as the Governor. *Cal.*, (amendment of 1862.)

—The Secretary of State shall keep a fair record of the official acts of the legislative and executive departments of the Government, and shall, when required, lay the same, and all matters relative thereto, before either branch of the Legislature, and shall perform such other duties as shall be assigned him by law; and that no inconvenience may result to the public service from the taking effect of the amendments proposed to said Art. V., by the Legislature of 1861, no officer shall be superseded or suspended thereby, until the election and qualification of the several officers provided for in said amendments. *Cal.*, (amendment of 1862.)

—The Comptroller, Treasurer, Attorney-General and Surveyor-General shall be chosen by joint vote of the two Houses of the Legislature, at their first session under this Constitution, and thereafter shall be elected at the same time and places, and in the same manner as the Governor and Lieutenant-Governor. *Cal.* (Amendment of 1862.).

—A Secretary shall be chosen next after the Treasurer, and in the same manner; and the votes for Secretary shall be returned to, and counted, canvassed and declared by the Treasurer and Comptroller. He shall have the safe keeping and custody of the public records and documents, and particularly the acts, resolutions and orders of the General Assembly, and record the same; and perform all such duties as shall be prescribed by law. He shall be the keeper of the seal of the State, which shall not be altered. *Ct.*, 111, 114.

—A Secretary shall be appointed and commissioned during the Governor's continuance in office, if he shall so long behave himself well. He shall keep a fair register of all the official acts and proceedings of the Governor, and shall, when required by either branch of the Legislature, lay the same, and all papers, minutes, and vouchers, relative thereto, before them, and shall perform such other duties as shall be enjoined on him by law. He shall have a compensation for his services to be fixed by law. *Del.*, 120.

—There shall be a Secretary of State, a Comptroller-General, a Treasurer, and Surveyor-General, elected by the General Assembly, and they shall hold their offices for the like period as the Governor, and shall have a competent salary, which shall not be increased or diminished during the period for which they shall have been elected. The General Assembly may at any time consolidate any two of these offices, and require all the duties to be discharged by one officer. *Ga.*, 148.

—There shall be elected by the qualified electors of this State, at the same time of the election for Governor, a Secretary of State, whose term of office shall be the same as that of the Governor, who shall keep a fair register of the official acts of the Governor, and, when required, shall lay the same, and all papers, minutes and vouchers, relative thereto, before either branch of the General Assembly, and shall perform such other duties as shall be assigned him by law, and shall receive a salary of eight hundred dollars per annum, and no more, except fees; *Provided,*

That if the office of Secretary of State should be vacated by death, resignation, or otherwise, it shall be the duty of the Governor to appoint another, who shall hold his office until another Secretary shall be elected and qualified. *Ill.*, 159.

—There shall be elected by the voters of the State, a Secretary, an Auditor, and a Treasurer of State, who shall severally hold their offices for two years. They shall perform such duties as may be enjoined by law; and no person shall be eligible to either of said offices more than four years in any period of six years. *Ind.*, 176.

—The Governor and the Secretary, Auditor and Treasurer of State, shall, severally reside, and keep the public records, books and papers in any manner relating to their respective offices, at the seat of government. *Ind.*, 176.

—The Secretary of State, Auditor of State, and Treasurer of State, shall be elected by the qualified electors, who shall continue in office two years, and until their successors are elected and qualified; and perform such duties as may be required by law. *Iowa,* 180.

—The Executive Department shall consist of a Governor, Lieutenant-Governor, Secretary of State, Auditor, Treasurer, Attorney-General, and Superintendent of Public Instruction, who shall be chosen by the electors of the State, at the time and place of voting for members of the Legislature, and shall hold their offices for the term of two years from the second Monday of January, next after their election, and until their successors are elected and qualified. *Kan.*, 197.

—Should either the Secretary of State, Auditor, Treasurer, Attorney-General, or Superintendent of Public Instruction, become incapable of performing the duties of his office for any of the causes specified in the thirteenth section of this article, the Governor shall fill the vacancy until the disability is removed, or a successor is elected and qualified. Every such vacancy shall be filled by election at the first general election that occurs more than thirty days after it shall have happened; and the person chosen shall hold the office for the unexpired term. *Kan.*, 198.

—The Governor shall nominate, and by and with the advice and consent of the Senate, appoint a Secretary of State, who shall be commissioned during the term for which the Governor was elected, if he shall so long behave himself well. He shall keep a fair register, and attest all the official acts of the Governor, and shall, when required, lay the same, and all papers, minutes and vouchers relative thereto, before either House of the General Assembly; and shall perform such other duties as may be required of him by law. *Ky.*, 214.

—The General Assembly shall direct by law, how persons who now are, or who may hereafter become securities for public officers, may be relieved or discharged on account of such securityship. *Ky.*, 220.

—There shall be a Secretary of State, who shall hold his office during the term for which the Governor shall have been elected. The records of the State shall be kept and preserved in the office of the Secretary; he shall keep a fair register of the official acts and proceedings of the Governor, and when necessary shall attest them; he shall, when required, lay the said register, and all papers, minutes and vouchers relative to his office before either House of the General Assembly, and shall perform such other duties as may be enjoined on him by law. *La.*, 231.

—The Secretary of State, Treasurer of State and Auditor of Public Accounts, shall be elected by the qualified electors of the State; and in case of any vacancy caused by the resignation, death or absence of the Secretary, Treasurer or Auditor, the Governor shall order an election to fill said vacancy. *La.*, 231.

—The Secretary of State, the Treasurer and the Auditor shall receive a salary of five thousand dollars per annum each. *La.*, 231.

—The General Assembly shall have the right of abolishing the office of State Engineer, by a majority vote of all the members elected to each branch, and of substituting a Board of Public Works in lieu thereof, should they deem it necessary. *La.*, 236.

—The Secretary of State shall be chosen annually, at the first session of the Legislature, by joint ballot of the Senators and Representatives in Convention. *Me.*, 245.

—The records of the State shall be kept in the office of the Secretary, who may appoint his deputies, for whose conduct he shall be accountable. *Me.*, 245.

—He shall attend the Governor and Council, Senate and House of Representatives, in person, or by his deputies, as they shall respectively require. *Me.*, 245.

—He shall carefully keep and preserve the records of all the official acts and proceedings of the Governor and Council, Senate and House of Representatives, and when required, lay the same before either branch of the Legislature, and perform such other duties as are enjoined by this Constitution, or shall be required by law. *Me.*, 246.

—A Secretary of State shall be appointed by the Governor, by and with the advice and consent of the Senate, who shall continue in office, unless sooner removed by the Governor, till the end of the official term of the Governor from whom he received his appointment, and shall receive an annual salary of one thousand dollars. *Md.*, 260.

—The Secretary of State shall carefully keep and preserve a record of all official acts and proceedings which may at all times be inspected by a committee of either branch of the General Assembly, and shall perform such other duties as are now or may hereafter be prescribed by law, or as may properly belong to his office. *Md.*, 260.

—The Secretary, Treasurer, and Receiver-General, Auditor, and Attorney-General, shall be chosen annually, on the day in November prescribed for the choice of Governor; and each person then chosen as such, duly qualified in other respects, shall hold his office for the term of one year from the third Wednesday in January next thereafter, and until another is chosen and qualified in his stead. The qualification of the voters, the manner of the election, the return of the votes, and the declaration of the election, shall be such as are required in the election of Governor. In case of a failure to elect either of said officers on the day of November aforesaid, or in case of the decease, in the meantime, of the person elected as such, such officer shall be chosen on or before the third Wednesday in January next thereafter, from the two persons who had the highest number of votes for said offices on the day in November aforesaid, by joint ballot of the Senators and Representatives in one room; and in case the office of Secretary, or Treasurer and Receiver-General, or Auditor, or Attorney-General shall become vacant, from any cause, during an annual or special session of the General Court, such vacancy shall in like manner be filled by choice from the people at large; but if such vacancy shall occur at any other time, it shall be supplied by the Governor by appointment, with the advice and consent of the Council. The person so chosen or appointed, duly qualified in other respects, shall hold his office until his successor is chosen and duly qualified in his stead. In case any person chosen or appointed to either of the offices aforesaid, shall neglect, for the space of ten days after he could otherwise enter upon his duties, to qualify himself in all respects to enter upon the discharge of such duties, the office to which he has been elected or appointed shall be deemed vacant. No person shall be eligible to either of said offices unless he shall have been an inhabitant of this Commonwealth five years next preceding his election or appointment. *Mass.*, 292.

—The records of the Commonwealth shall be kept in the office of the Secretary, who may appoint his deputies, for whose conduct he shall be accountable; and he shall attend the Governor and Council, the Senate and House of Representatives in person, or by his deputies, as they shall respectively require. *Mass.*, 293.

—There shall be elected at each general biennial election a Secretary of State, a Superintendent of Public Instruction, a State Treasurer, a Commissioner of the

Land Office, an Auditor-General, and an Attorney-General, for the term of two years. They shall keep their offices at the seat of government, and shall perform such duties as may be prescribed by law. *Mich.*, 308.

—Their term of office shall commence on the first day of January, one thousand eight hundred and fifty-three, and of every second year thereafter. *Mich.*, 308.

—The Secretary of State, State Treasurer, and Commissioner of the State Land Office shall constitute a Board of State Auditors to examine and adjust all claims against the State, not otherwise provided for by general law. They shall constitute a Board of State Canvassers to determine the result of all elections for Governor, Lieutenant-Governor, and State officers, and of such other officers as shall by law be referred to them. *Mich.*, 308.

—The Executive Department shall consist of a Governor, Lieutenant-Governor, Secretary of State, Auditor, Treasurer, and Attorney-General, who shall be chosen by the electors of the State. *Min.*, 323.

—The official term of the Secretary of State, Treasurer, and Attorney-General shall be two years. The official term of the Auditor shall be three years, and each shall continue in office until his successor shall have been elected and qualified. *Min.*, 323.

—The salary of the Secretary of State for the first term shall be fifteen hundred dollars per annum. The Auditor, Treasurer, and Attorney-General shall each, for the first term, receive a salary of one thousand dollars per annum. And the further duties and salaries of said executive officers shall each thereafter be prescribed by law. *Min.*, 323.

—The Governor shall have power to fill any vacancy that may occur in the office of Secretary of State, Treasurer, Auditor, Attorney-General, and such other State and district officers as may be hereafter created by law, until the next annual election, and until their successors are chosen and qualified. *Min.*, 323.

—The Secretary of State shall be elected by the qualified electors of the State, and shall continue in office during the term of two years. He shall keep a fair register of all the official acts and proceedings of the Governor, and shall, when required, lay the same, and all papers, minutes, and vouchers relative thereto, before the Legislature, and shall perform such other duties as may be required of him by law. *Miss.*, 341.

—A State Treasurer and Auditor of Public Accounts shall be elected by the qualified electors of the State, who shall hold their offices for the term of two years, unless sooner removed. *Miss.*, 342.

—The official term of Secretary of State, Auditor of Public accounts, State Treasurer and Attorney-General shall commence on the first Monday of January next after their election; but the Attorney-General shall hold his office as heretofore, for the term of four years. On the first Monday of October, 1858, and biennially thereafter, an election shall be held for all county, district and ministerial officers, except officers who may then be entitled to hold over after January, 1859, or until the time of holding another election, and the official terms of all such officers then and thereafter elected shall commence on the first Monday of January next after this election; but all such officers elected in 1855, or previously, whose official terms, in the absence of this provision, would expire in November, 1857, shall continue in office until the first Monday of January, 1859. *Miss.*, 344.

—There shall be a Secretary of State, a State Auditor, a State Treasurer, and an Attorney-General, who shall be elected by the qualified voters of the State, at the same time in the same manner, and for the same term of office as the Governor. No person shall be eligible to either of said offices, unless he be a white male citizen of the United States, and at least twenty-five years old, and shall have resided in this State five years next before his election. The Secretary of State, the State Auditor, the State Treasurer, and the Attorney-General, shall keep their respective offices at the seat of government, and shall perform such duties as may be required of them by law. *Mo.*, 356.

—The Secretary of State shall keep a register of the official acts of the Governor, and when necessary, shall attest them, and shall lay copies of the same, together with copies of all papers relating thereto, before either House of the General Assembly, whenever required to do so. *Mo.*, 356.

—Contested elections of Secretary of State, State Auditor, State Treasurer, and Attorney-General, shall be decided before such tribunal, and in such manner as may be by law provided. *Mo.*, 356.

—The Secretary, Auditor and Treasurer of State, shall severally perform such duties as shall be prescribed by law. *Neb.*, 374.

—The Secretary of State and Treasurer shall hold their offices for two years, and the Auditor for four years. Their terms of office shall commence on the second Monday of January next after their election and continue until their successors are elected and qualified. *Neb.*, 373.

—The Secretary of State shall receive during his continuance in office an annual compensation of six hundred dollars; the State Treasurer, four hundred dollars; and the State Auditor, eight hundred dollars. *Neb.*, 374.

—A Secretary of State, a Treasurer, a Controller, a Surveyor-General, and an Attorney-General shall be elected at the same time and places, and in the same manner as the Governor. The term of office of each shall be the same as is prescribed for the Governor. Any elector shall be eligible to either of said offices. *Nev.*, 385.

—The Secretary of State shall keep true records of the official acts of the Legislature and Executive Department of the government, and shall, when required, lay the same, and all matters relative thereof, before either branch of the Legislature. *Nev.*, 385.

—The Secretary of State, State Treasurer, State Controller, Surveyor-General, Attorney-General, and Superintendent of Public Instruction, shall perform such other duties as may be prescribed by law. *Nev.*, 386.

—The salary of the Secretary of State shall be three thousand six hundred dollars per annum; the salary of the State Controller shall be three thousand six hundred dollars per annum the; salary of the State Treasurer shall be three thousand six hundred dollars per annum; the salary of the Surveyor-General shall be one thousand dollars per annum; the salary of the Attorney-General shall be two thousand five hundred dollars per annum; the salary of the Superintendent of Public Instruction shall be two thousand dollars per annum; the salary of each Judge of the Supreme Court shall be seven thousand dollars per annum; the salaries of the foregoing officers shall be paid quarterly out of the State treasury. The pay of State Senators and members of Assembly shall be eight dollars per day for each day of actual service, and forty cents per mile for mileage going to and returning from the place of meeting. No officer mentioned in this section shall receive any fee or perquisites to his own use, for the performance of any duty connected with his office, or for the performance of any additional duty imposed upon him by law. *Nev.*, 393.

—The Secretary, Treasurer and Commissary-General shall be chosen by joint ballot of the Senators and Representatives, assembled in one room. *N. H.*, 408.

—The records of the State shall be kept in the office of the Secretary; and he shall attend the Governor and Council, the Senate and Representatives, in person or by Deputy, as they may require. *N. H.*, 408.

—The Secretary of State shall at all times have a Deputy, to be by him appointed; for whose conduct in office he shall be responsible; and in case of the death, removal, or inability of the Secretary, his Deputy shall exercise all the duties of the office of Secretary of State, until another shall be appointed. *N. H.*, 408.

—The Secretary, before he enters upon the business of his office, shall give bond, with sufficient sureties, in a reasonable sum, for the use of the State, for the punctual performance of his trust. *N. H.*, 408.

—The State Treasurer and the Keeper and Inspectors of the State prison shall be appointed by the Senate and General Assembly, in joint-meeting.

They shall hold the offices for one year, and until their successor shall be qualified into office. *N. J.*, 419.

—The Secretary of State shall be *ex officio* an auditor of the accounts of the Treasurer, and, as such, it shall be his duty to assist the Legislature in the annual examination and settlement of said accounts, until otherwise provided by law. *N. J.*, 419.

—The Secretary of State shall be the Register of the Prerogative Court, and shall perform the duties required of him by law in that respect. *N. J.*, 418.

—The Secretary of State shall be the Clerk of the Court of Errors and Appeals. *N. J.*, 417.

—That the General Assembly shall, by joint ballot of both Houses triennially, appoint a Secretary for this State. *N. C.*, 425.

—That no Secretary of this State, Attorney-General, or Clerk of any Court of Record shall have a seat in the Senate, House of Commons, or Council of State. *N. C.*, 425.

—The Executive Department shall consist of a Governor, Lieutenant-Governor, Secretary of State, Auditor, Treasurer, and an Attorney-General, who shall be chosen by the electors of the State, on the second Tuesday of October, and at the places of voting for members of the General Assembly.

—The Governor, Lieutenant-Governor, Secretary of State, Treasurer and Attorney-General shall hold their offices for two years; and the Auditor for four years. Their terms of office shall commence on the second Monday of January next after their election, and continue until their successors are elected and qualified. *Ohio*, 435.

—There may be established in the Secretary of State's Office, a Bureau of Statistics, under such regulations as may be prescribed by law. *Ohio*, 444.

—Should the office of Auditor, Treasurer, Secretary, or Attorney-General, become vacant, for any of the causes specified in the fifteenth section of this article, the Governor shall fill the vacancy until the disability is removed, or a successor elected and qualified. Every such vacancy shall be filled by election, at the first general election that occurs more than thirty days after it shall have happened; and the person chosen shall hold the office for the full term fixed in the second section of this article. *Ohio*, 436.

—There shall be elected by the qualified electors of the State, at the times and places of choosing members of the Legislative Assembly, a Secretary and Treasurer of State, who shall severally hold their offices for the term of four years; but no person shall be eligible to either of said offices more than eight in any period of twelve years. *Or.*, 453.

—The Secretary of State shall keep a fair record of the official acts of the Legislative Assembly and Executive Department of the State, and shall, when required, lay the same and all matters relative thereto before either branch of the Legislative Assembly. He shall be, by virtue of his office, Auditor of Public Accounts, and shall perform such other duties as shall be assigned him by law. *Or.*, 453.

—The Governor shall appoint a Secretary of the Commonwealth during pleasure. *Pa.*, 463.

—The Secretary of the Commonwealth shall keep a fair register of all the official acts and proceedings of the Governor, and shall, when required, lay the same, and all papers, minutes and vouchers relative thereto, before either branch of the Legislature, and shall perform such other duties as shall be enjoined him by law. *Pa.*, 464.

[The Secretary of State, Attorney-General and General Treasurer elected annually.] *R. I.*, 478.

—In case an election of the Secretary of State, Attorney-General, or General Treasurer, should fail to be made by the electors at the annual election, the vacancy or vacancies shall be filled by the General Assembly in grand committee, from the two candidates for such office having the greatest number of votes of the electors. Or, in case of a vacancy in either of said offices from other causes, between the sessions of the General Assembly, the Governor shall appoint some person to fill the same until a successor, elected by the General Assembly, is qualified to act; and in such case, and also in all other cases of vacancies not otherwise provided for the General Assembly may fill the same in any manner they may deem proper. *R. I.*, 478.

—The Secretary of State shall, by virtue of his office, be Secretary of the Senate, unless otherwise provided by law; and the Senate may elect such other officers as they may deem necessary. *R. I*, 477.

—The duties and powers of the Secretary, Attorney-General, and General Treasurer, shall be the same under the Constitution as are now established, or as from time to time may be prescribed by law. *R. I.*, 477.

—The Treasurer and the Secretary of State shall be elected by the General Assembly in the House of Representatives, shall hold their offices for four years, and shall not be eligible for the next succeeding term. *S. C.*, 487.

—The Secretary of State shall hold his office and reside at the seat of government. *S. C.*, 488.

—A Secretary of State shall be appointed by joint vote of the General Assembly, and commissioned during the term of four years; he shall keep a fair register of all the official acts and proceedings of the Governor, and shall, when required, lay the same, and all papers, minutes, and vouchers relative thereto, before the General Assembly, and shall perform such other duties as shall be enjoined by law. *Tenn*, 495.

—There shall be a Secretary of State, who shall be appointed by the Governor, by and with the advice and consent of the Senate, and shall continue in office during the term of service of the Governor elect. He shall keep a fair register of all official acts and proceedings of the Governor, and shall, when required, lay the same, and all papers, minutes and vouchers relative thereto, before the Legislature, or either House thereof, and shall perform such other duties as may be required of him by law. *Tex.*, 513.

—The Secretary of State and all officers whose elections are not otherwise provided for, and who, under the existing provisions of the Constitution, are elected by the Council and House of Representatives, shall hereafter be elected by the Senate and House of Representatives, in joint assembly, at which the presiding officer of the Senate shall preside, and such presiding officer, in such joint assembly, shall have a casting vote, and no other. *Vt.*, 529.

—A Secretary of the Commonwealth, Treasurer and an Auditor of Public Accounts shall be elected by the joint vote of the two Houses of the General Assembly, and continue in office for the term of two years, unless sooner removed. *Va.*, 540.

—The Secretary shall keep a record of the official acts of the Governor, which shall be signed by the Governor and attested by the Secretary; and when required, he shall lay the same, and any papers, minutes and vouchers pertaining to his office, before either House of the General Assembly; and shall perform such other duties as may be prescribed by law. *Va.*, 540.

—A Secretary of State, a Treasurer and an Auditor shall be elected at the same time and for the same term as the Governor. Their duties shall be prescribed by law. The Secretary of State shall receive thirteen hundred, the Treasurer fourteen hundred, and the Auditor fifteen hundred dollars per annum. *W. Va.*, 552.

—There shall be chosen by the qualified electors of the State, at the times and places of choosing the members of the Legislature, a Secretary of State, Treasurer, and an Attorney-General, who shall severally hold their offices for the term of two years. *Wis.*, 565.

—The Secretary of State shall keep a fair record of the official acts of the Legislature and executive department of the State, and shall, when required, lay the same and all matters relative thereto before either branch of the Legislature. He shall be *ex officio* Auditor, and shall perform such other duties as shall be assigned him by law. He shall receive as a compensation for his services, yearly, such sum as shall be provided by law, and shall keep his office at the seat of government. *Wis.*, 565.

—The powers, duties, and compensation of the Treasurer and Attorney-General shall be prescribed by law. *Wis*, 565.

FINANCIAL OFFICERS OF THE STATE.

—The Treasurer of this State shall be appointed by act of the Legislature, to originate with the Assembly. *Provided*, That he shall not be elected out of either branch of the Legislature. *N. Y.* (1777), 30.

[The Comptroller and Treasurer under the Constitution of 1821 were appointed by the Legislature. The mode prescribed in Art. IV, § 6, p. 39.]

[A Comptroller of Public Accounts and State Treasurer, elected by joint ballot of both Houses for a term of two years]. *Ala.*, 81.

—There shall be elected, by the qualified voters of this State, an Auditor and Treasurer for this State, who shall hold their offices for the term of two years, and until their respective successors are elected and qualified, unless sooner removed; and shall keep their respective offices at the seat of government, and perform such duties as shall be prescribed by law; and in case of vacancy by death, resignation, or otherwise, such vacancy shall be filled by the Governor as in other cases. *Ark.*, 90.

—A Secretary of State, a Comptroller, a Treasurer, an Attorney-General, and Surveyor-General, shall be chosen in the manner provided in this Constitution; and the term of office and eligibility of each shall be the same as are prescribed for the Governor and Lieutenant-Governor. *Cal.*, 101.

—A Comptroller of Public Accounts shall be annually chosen by the electors, in their meeting in April, and in the same manner as the Treasurer and Secretary are chosen, and the votes for Comptroller shall be returned to and counted, canvassed and declared by the Treasurer and Secretary. *Ct.*, 115.

—The State Treasurer shall be appointed biennially by the House of Representatives, with the concurrence of the Senate. In case of vacancy in the office of State Treasurer in the recess of the General Assembly, either through omission of the General Assembly to appoint, or by death, removal out of the State, resignation, or inability of State Treasurer, or his failure to give security, the Governor shall fill the vacancy by appointment, to continue until the next meeting of the General Assembly. The State Treasurer shall settle his accounts annually with the General Assembly, or a Committee thereof, which shall be appointed at every biennial session. No person who hath served in the office of State Treasurer shall be eligible to a seat in either House of the General Assembly until he shall have made a final settlement of his accounts as Treasurer, and discharged the balance, if any, due thereon. . *Del.*, 119.

—A State Treasurer and Comptroller of Public Accounts shall be elected by the qualified electors of the State at the same time, and who shall continue in office for the same term of years as the Governor of the State, and until their successors shall have been duly commissioned and qualified. *Fl.*, 132.

—There shall be chosen, by the qualified electors throughout the State, an Auditor of Public Accounts, who shall hold his office for the term of four years, and until his successor is qualified, and whose duty shall be regulated by law, and who shall receive a salary, exclusive of clerk hire, of one thousand dollars per annum for his services, and no more. *Ill.*, 159.

—There shall be elected, by the qualified electors throughout the State, a State Treasurer, who shall hold his office for two years, and until his successor is qualified; whose duties may be regulated by law,

and who shall receive a salary of eight hundred dollars per annum, and no more. *Ill.*, 159.

—There shall be elected by the voters of the State, a Secretary, an Auditor, and a Treasurer of State, who shall severally hold their offices for two years. They shall perform such duties as may be enjoined by law; and no person shall be eligible to either of said offices more than four years in any period of six years. *Ind.*, 176.

—The Secretary of State, Auditor of State, and Treasurer of State, shall be elected by the qualified electors, who shall continue in office two years, and until their successors are elected and qualified, and perform such duties as may be required by law. *Iowa*, 189.

[State Auditor and Treasurer elected for term of two years] *Kan.*, 197; *Min.*, 323; *Neb.*, 372; *Wis.*, 565.

—A Treasurer shall be elected by the qualified voters of the State, for the term of two years; and an Auditor of Public Accounts, Register of the Land Office, and Attorney-General, for the term of four years. The duties and responsibilities of these officers shall be prescribed by law; *Provided*, That inferior State officers, not specially provided for in this Constitution, may be appointed or elected in such manner as shall be prescribed by law, for a term not exceeding four years. *Ky.*, 214.

—There shall be a Treasurer of the State, and an Auditor of Public Accounts, who shall hold their respective offices during the term of four years. *La.*, 231.

—The Treasurer shall be chosen annually, at the first session of the Legislature, by joint ballot of the Senators and Representatives in Convention, but shall not be eligible for more than five years successively. *Me.*, 246.

—The Treasurer shall, before entering on the duties of his office, give a bond to the State, with sureties, to the satisfaction of the Legislature, for the faithful discharge of his trust. *Me.*, 246.

—The Treasurer shall not, during his continuance in office, engage in any business of trade or commerce, or as a broker, nor as an agent or factor for any merchant or trader. *Me.*, 246.

—The Treasury Department of this State shall consist of a Comptroller and a Treasurer. *Md.*, 272.

—The Comptroller shall be chosen by the qualified electors of the State at each regular election for members of the General Assembly. He shall hold his office for two years, commencing on the second Wednesday in January next ensuing his election, and shall receive an annual salary of twenty-five hundred dollars, but shall not be allowed, nor shall he receive any fees, commissions or perquisites of any kind, in addition thereto, for the performance of any official duty or service. He shall keep his office at the seat of government, and shall take such oath, and enter into such bond for the faithful performance of his duty as are now or may hereafter be prescribed by law. A vacancy in the office of Comptroller shall be filled by the Governor for the residue of the term. The first election for Comptroller under this Constitution shall be held on the Tuesday next after the first Monday in the month of November, in the year eighteen hundred and sixty-four, but the Comptroller then elected shall not enter upon the discharge of the duties of his office until the expiration of the term of the present incumbent, unless the said office shall sooner become vacant. *Md.*, 272.

—The Comptroller shall have the general superintendence of the fiscal affairs of the State; he shall digest and prepare plans for the improvement and management of the revenue, and for the support of the public credit; prepare and report estimates of the revenue and expenditures of the State; superintend and enforce the collection of all taxes and revenue; adjust, settle, and preserve all public accounts; decide on the forms of keeping and stating accounts; grant, under regulations prescribed by law, all warrants for moneys to be paid out of the treasury in pursuance of appropriations by law, prescribe the formalities of the transfer of stock or other evidences of the State debt, and countersign the same, without which such evidences shall not be valid; he shall make full reports of all h's proceedings and of the state of the Treasury Department, within ten days after the commencement of each session of the General Assembly, and perform such other duties as are now or may hereafter be prescribed by law. *Md.*, 272.

—The Treasurer shall be elected on joint ballot by the two Houses of the General Assembly at each regular session thereof. He shall hold his office for two years, and shall receive an annual salary of twenty-five hundred dollars, but shall not be allowed, nor shall he receive any fees, commissions, or perquisites of any kind in addition thereto, for the performance of any official duty or service. He shall keep his office at the seat of government, and shall take such oath, and enter into such bond for the faithful discharge of his duty as are now or may hereafter be prescribed by law; a vacancy in the office of Treasurer shall be filled by the Governor for the residue of the term. The General Assembly at its first session after the adoption of this Constitution shall elect a Treasurer, but the Treasurer then elected shall not enter upon the discharge of the duties of his office until the expiration of the term of the present incumbent, unless the said office shall sooner become vacant. *Md.*, 272.

—The Treasurer shall receive and keep the moneys of the State, and disburse the same upon warrants drawn by the Comptroller and not otherwise; he shall take receipts for all moneys paid by him, and all receipts for moneys received by him shall be indorsed upon warrants signed by the Comptroller, without which warrants, so signed, no acknowledgment of money received into the Treasury shall be valid; and upon warrants issued by the Comptroller, he shall make arrangements for the payment of the interest of the public debt, and for the purchase thereof, on account of the sinking fund. Every bond, certificate or other evidence of the debt of the State shall be signed by the Treasurer and countersigned by the Comptroller, and no new certificate or other evidence intended to replace another shall be issued until the old one shall be delivered to the Treasurer, and authority executed in due form for the transfer of the same shall be filed in his office, and the transfer accordingly made on the books thereof, and the certificate or other evidence canceled; but the General Assembly may make provision for the loss of certificates or other evidence of the debt. *Md.*, 272.

—The Treasurer shall render his accounts quarterly to the Comptroller, and on the third day of each regular session of the General Assembly he shall submit to the Senate and House of Delegates fair and accurate copies of all accounts by him from time to time rendered and settled with the Comptroller. He shall at all times submit to the Comptroller the inspection of the moneys in his hands, and perform all other duties that are now or may hereafter be prescribed by law. *Md.*, 272.

—The Secretary, Treasurer and Receiver-General, Auditor and Attorney-General, shall be chosen annually, on the day in November prescribed for the choice of Governor; and each person then chosen as such, duly qualified in other respects, shall hold his office for the term of one year from the third Wednesday in January next thereafter, and until another is chosen and qualified in his stead. The qualifications of the voters, the manner of the election, the return of the votes, and the declaration of the election, shall be such as are required in the election of Governor. In case of a failure to elect either of said officers on the day in November aforesaid, or in case of the decease in the meantime, of the person elected as such, such officer shall be chosen on or before the third Wednesday in January next thereafter, from the two persons who had the highest number of votes for said offices on the day in November aforesaid, by joint ballot of the Senators and Representatives, in one room; and in case the office of Secretary, or Treasurer and Receiver-General, or Auditor, or Attorney-General, shall become vacant, from any cause, during an annual

or special session of the General Court, such vacancy shall in like manner be filled by choice from the people at large; but if such vacancy shall occur at any other time, it shall be supplied by the Governor by appointment, with the advice and consent of the Council. The person so chosen or appointed, duly qualified in other respects, shall hold his office until his successor is chosen and duly qualified in his stead. In case any person chosen or appointed to either of the offices aforesaid, shall neglect, for the space of ten days after he could otherwise enter upon his duties, to qualify himself in all respects to enter upon the discharge of such duties, the office to which he has been elected or appointed shall be deemed vacant. No person shall be eligible to either of said offices unless he shall have been an inhabitant of this Commonwealth five years next preceding his election or appointment. *Mass.*, 293.

—There shall be elected at each general biennial election a Secretary of State, a Superintendent of Public Instruction, a State Treasurer, a Commissioner of the Land Office, an Auditor-General, and an Attorney-General, for the term of two years. They shall keep their offices at the seat of government, and shall perform such duties as may be prescribed by law.

Their term of office shall commence on the first day of January, one thousand eight hundred and fifty-three, and of every second year thereafter.

Whenever a vacancy shall occur in any of the State offices, the Governor shall fill the same by appointment, by and with the advice and consent of the Senate, if in session.

The Secretary of State, State Treasurer, and Commissioner of the State Land Office shall constitute a Board of State Auditors to examine and adjust all claims against the State, not otherwise provided for by general law. They shall constitute a Board of State Canvassers to determine the result of all elections for Governor, Lieutenant-Governor, and State officers, and of such other officers as shall by law be referred to them. *Mich.*, 308.

—A State Treasurer and Auditor of Public Accounts shall be elected by the qualified electors of the State, who shall hold their offices for the term of two years, unless sooner removed. *Miss.*, 342.

—There shall be a Secretary of State, a State Auditor, a State Treasurer, and an Attorney-General, who shall be elected by the qualified voters of the State, at the same time, in the same manner, and for the same term of office as the Governor. No person shall be eligible to either of said offices, unless he be a white male citizen of the United States, and at least twenty-five years old, and shall have resided in this State five years next before his election. The Secretary of State, the State Auditor, the State Treasurer, and the Attorney-General, shall keep their respective offices at the seat of government, and shall perform such duties as may be required of them by law. *Mo.*, 356.

—Contested elections of Secretary of State, State Auditor, State Treasurer, and Attorney-General, shall be decided before such tribunal, and in such manner as may be by law provided. *Mo.*, 356.

—A Secretary of State, a Treasurer, a Controller, a Surveyor-General, and an Attorney-General shall be elected at the same time and places, and in the same manner as the Governor. The term of office of each shall be the same as is prescribed for the Governor. Any elector shall be eligible to either of said offices. *Nev.*, 385.

—The Secretary of State, State Treasurer, State Controller, Surveyor-General, Attorney-General, and Superintendent of Public Instruction, shall perform such other duties as may be prescribed by law. *Nev.*, 385.

—The Secretary, Treasurer, and Commissary-General, shall be chosen by joint ballot of the Senators and Representatives, assembled in one room. *N. H.*, 408.

—The State Treasurer and the Keeper and Inspectors of the State prison shall be appointed by the Senate and General Assembly, in joint meeting.

They shall hold the offices for one year, and until their successors shall be qualified into office. *N. J.*, 419.

—That the General Assembly, shall, by joint ballot of both Houses, annually, appoint a Treasurer or Treasurers for this State. *N. C.*, 425.

—That no Treasurer shall have a seat either in the Senate, House of Commons, or Council of State, during his continuance in that office, or before he shall have finally settled his accounts with the public for all the moneys which may be in his hands, at the expiration of his office, belonging to the State, and hath paid the same into the hands of the succeeding Treasurer. *N. C.*, 425.

—[State Treasurer elected for two years, and Auditor for four years.] *Ohio*, 435.

[A Treasurer of State elected for term of four years but is not eligible more than eight years in twelve.] *Or.*, 453.

—The power and duties of the Treasurer of State shall be such as may be prescribed by law. *Or.*, 453.

[Salary of Treasurer of State, $800.] *Or.*, 457.

—A State Treasurer shall be elected annually, by joint vote of both branches of the Legislature. *Pa.*, 466.

[A general Treasurer, elected annually.] *R. I.*, 478.

—If an election fail, he is appointed by the General Assembly in grand committee. *R. I.*, 478.

—The business of the treasury shall be conducted by one Treasurer, who shall hold his office and reside at the seat of government. *S. C.*, 488.

—There shall be a Treasurer or Treasurers appointed for the State, by the joint vote of both Houses of the General Assembly, who shall hold his or their offices for two years. *Tenn.*, 497.

—There shall be elected, by the qualified electors of this State, in the manner prescribed by law, a Comptroller of Public Accounts and a State Treasurer, each of whom shall hold his office for the term of four years; and in case of a vacancy in either of said offices, the Governor shall have power to fill the same by appointment, which shall continue in force until the office can be filled at the next general election for State and county officers, and the successor duly qualified. *Tex.*, 514.

[Treasurer elected]. *Vt.*, 523.

—The Treasurer of the State shall, before entering upon the duties of his office, give sufficient security to the Secretary of State, in behalf of the State of Vermont, before the Governor of the State, or one of the Judges of the Supreme Court. And Sheriffs and High Bailiffs, before entering upon the duties of their respective offices, shall give security to the Treasurer of their respective counties, before one of the Judges of the Supreme Court, or the two assistant judges of the County Court of their respective counties, in such manner and in such sums as shall be directed by the Legislature. *Vt.*, 530.

—The Treasurer's account shall be annually audited, and a fair statement thereof be laid before the General Assembly, at their session in October. *Vt.*, 526.

—And in case there shall be a vacancy in the office of Treasurer, by reason of any of the causes enumerated, the Governor shall appoint a Treasurer for the time being, who shall act as Treasurer until the disability shall be removed, or a new election shall be made. *Vt.*, 530.

—A Secretary of the Commonwealth, Treasurer and an Auditor of Public Accounts shall be elected by the joint vote of the two Houses of the General Assembly, and continue in office for the term of two years, unless sooner removed.

—The powers and duties of the Treasurer and Auditor shall be such as now are, or may be hereafter prescribed by law. *Va.*, 540.

—A Secretary of State, a Treasurer and an Auditor shall be elected at the same time and for the same term as the Governor. Their duties shall be prescribed by law. The Secretary of the State shall receive thirteen hundred, the Treasurer fourteen hundred, and the Auditor fifteen hundred dollars per annum. *W. Va.*, 552.

[The powers, duties and compensation of the Treasurer to be prescribed by law.] *Wis.*, 565.

ATTORNEY-GENERAL.

—An Attorney-General, and as many solicitors as there are judicial circuits in the State, shall be elected by a joint vote of both houses of the General Assembly, each of whom shall hold his office for the term of four years, shall perform all the duties that may be required of him by law, and shall receive such compensation for his services as may be by law provided, which shall not be diminished during his continuance in office. *Ala.*, 81.

—The qualified voters thereof shall elect an Attorney for the State, for each judicial circuit established by law, who shall continue in office two years, and until his successor is elected and qualified and reside within the circuit for which he was elected at the time of, and during his continuance in office. In all cases where an Attorney for the State, of any circuit, fails to attend and prosecute, according to law, the court shall have power to appoint any Attorney *pro tempore*. *Ark.*, 92.

—The qualified voters of this State shall elect an Attorney-General, whose salary shall be the same as that of Circuit Judge, who shall be learned in the law; who shall be at least thirty years of age, and shall hold his office for the term of four years from the date of his commission, and until his successor is elected and qualified; and whose duty it shall be to prosecute the State's pleas before the Supreme Court, and give his opinion, in writing, on all questions of law or equity, when required by the Governor or other officer of the State, and perform such other duties as may be prescribed by law. *Ark.*, 32.

—The Attorney-General, the State's attorneys, and Clerks of the Supreme and Circuit Courts, and Courts of Chancery, if any such be established, shall receive for their services such salaries, fees and perquisites of office, as shall, from time to time be fixed by law. *Ark.*, 91.

—There shall be an Attorney-General for the State, who shall reside at the seat of government, and he shall perform such duties as may be prescribed by law; he shall be elected by the qualified voters of the State, at the same time and in the same manner that the Comptroller, Secretary of State and Treasurer are elected, and his term of office shall be the same; but he may be removed by the Governor, or the address of a majority of the two Houses of the General Assembly, and shall receive for his services a compensation to be fixed by law. *Fl.*, 135.

—There shall be a State's Attorney and Solicitors elected in the same manner as the Judges of the Superior Court, and commissioned by the Governor, who shall hold their offices for the term of four years, or until their successors shall be appointed and qualified, unless removed by sentence on impeachment, or by the Governor, on the address of two-thirds of each branch of the General Assembly. They shall have salaries adequate to their services fixed by law, which shall not be increased or diminished during their continuance in office. *Ga.*, 149.

—The General Assembly shall provide, by law, for the election of an Attorney-General by the people, whose term of office shall be two years, and until his successor is elected. *Iowa*, 190.

—There shall be elected in each judicial circuit, by the voters thereof, a Prosecuting Attorney, who shall hold his office for two years. *Ind.*, 177.

—When a vacancy shall happen in the office of Attorney-General, Auditor of Public Accounts, Treasurer, Register of the Land office, President of the Board of Internal Improvement, or Superintendent of Public Instruction, the Governor, in the recess of the Senate, shall have power to fill the vacancy by granting commissions which shall expire at the end of the next session, and shall fill the vacancy for the balance of the time by and with the advice and consent of the Senate. *Ky.*, 221.

—A Commonwealth's Attorney for each judicial district shall be elected. *Ky.*, 218.

—The Commonwealth's Attorney and Circuit Court Clerk shall be elected at the same time as the Circuit

Judge; the Commonwealth's Attorney by the qualified voters of the district, the Circuit Court Clerk by the qualified voters of the county. The County Attorney, Clerk, Surveyor, Coroner and Jailor shall be elected at the same time and in the same manner as the Presiding Judge of the County Court. *Ky.*, 218.
—There shall be an Attorney-General for the State, and as many District Attorneys as the Legislature shall find necessary. The Attorney-General shall be elected every four years by the qualified voters of the State. He shall receive a salary of five thousand dollars per annum, payable on his own warrant, quarterly. The District Attorneys shall be elected by the qualified voters of their respective districts for a term of four years. They shall receive such salaries as shall be provided by the Legislature. *La.*, 232.

[The Attorney-General is appointed by Governor and Council.] *Me.*, 244.
—There shall be an Attorney-General elected by the qualified voters of the State, on general ticket, on the Tuesday next after the first Monday in the month of November, in the year eighteen hundred and sixty-four, and on the same day in every fourth year thereafter, who shall hold his office for four years from the first Monday of January next ensuing his election, and until his successor shall be elected and qualified, and shall be re-eligible thereto, and shall be subject to removal for incompetency, wilful neglect of duty, or misdemeanor in office, on conviction in a court of law. *Md.*, 270.
—All elections for Attorney-General shall be certified to, and returns made thereof by the Clerks of the Circuit Courts for the several counties, and the Clerk of the Superior Court of Baltimore city, to the Governor of the State, whose duty it shall be to decide upon the election and qualifications of the person returned, and in case of a tie between two or more persons to designate which of said persons shall qualify as Attorney-General, and to administer the oath of office to the person elected. *Md.*, 271.
—It shall be the duty of the Attorney-General to prosecute and defend, on the part of the State, all cases which at the time of his election and qualification, and which thereafter may be depending in the Court of Appeals, or in the Supreme Court of the United States, by or against the State, or wherein the State may be interested; and he shall give his opinion in writing whenever required by the General Assembly, or either branch thereof. the Governor, the Comptroller, the Treasurer, or any State's Attorney, on any matter or subject depending before them, or either of them, and when required by the Governor or the General Assembly he shall aid any State's Attorney in prosecuting any suit or action brought by the State in any court of this State; and he shall commence and prosecute or defend any suit or action in any of said courts, on the part of the State, which the General Assembly or the Governor, acting according to law, shall direct to be commenced, prosecuted or defended; and he shall receive for his services an annual salary of twenty-five hundred dollars; but he shall not be entitled to receive any fees, perquisites or rewards whatever in addition to the salary aforesaid for the performance of any official duty, nor have power to appoint any agent, representative or deputy, under any circumstances whatever. *Md.*, 271.
—No person shall be eligible to the office of Attorney-General who has not resided and practiced law in this State for at least seven years next preceding his election. *Md.*, 271.
—In case of a vacancy in the office of Attorney-General, occasioned by death, resignation, or his removal from the State, or his conviction, as hereinbefore specified, the said vacancy shall be filled by the Governor for the residue of the term thus made vacant. *Md.*, 271.
—There shall be an Attorney for the State in each county and the city of Baltimore, to be styled "The State's Attorney," who shall be elected by the voter's thereof, respectively, on the Tuesday next after the

first Monday in the month of November, eighteen hundred and sixty-seven, and on the same day every fourth year thereafter, and shall hold his office for four years from the first Monday in January next ensuing his election, and until his successor shall be elected and qualified, and shall be re-eligible thereto, and be subject to removal therefrom for incompetency, willful neglect of duty or misdemeanor in office, on conviction in a court of law. *Md.*, 271.

All elections for the State's Attorney shall be certified to and returns made thereof by the Clerks of the said counties and city to the judges having criminal jurisdiction respectively, whose duty it shall be to decide upon the elections and qualifications of the persons returned, and in case of a tie between two or more persons, to designate which of said persons shall qualify as State's Attorney, and to administer the oaths of office to the persons elected. *Md.*, 271.
—No person shall be eligible to the office of State's Attorney who has not been admitted to practice law in this State, and who has not resided for at least one year in the county or city in which he may be elected. *Md.*, 271.
—The Attorney-General of the State is required to prepare and report to the Legislature, at the commencement of the next session, such changes and modifications in existing laws as may be deemed necessary to adapt the same to this Constitution, and as may be best calculated to carry into effect its provisions; and he shall receive no additional compensation therefor. *Mich.*, 316.
—There shall be an Attorney-General elected by the qualified electors of the State; and a competent number of District Attorneys shall be elected by the qualified voters of their respective districts, whose compensation and term of service shall be prescribed by law. *Miss*, 340.
—The Attorney-General, Prosecutors of Pleas, Clerk of the Supreme Court, Clerk of the Court of Chancery, and Secretary of State, shall be nominated by the Governor, and appointed by him, with the advice and consent of the Senate.

They shall hold their offices five years. *N. J.*, 419.
—The General Assembly, at its first session after the year one thousand eight hundred and thirty-nine, and from time to time thereafter, shall appoint an Attorney-General, who shall be commissioned by the Governor, and shall hold his office for the term of four years; but if the General Assembly should hereafter extend the term during which solicitors of the State shall hold their offices, then they shall have power to extend the term of office of the Attorney-General to the same period. *N. C.*, 429.
—An Attorney-General for the State shall be elected by the qualified voters of the State at large, and the Attorney for the State for any circuit or district to which a judge of an inferior court may be assigned, shall be elected by the qualified voters within the bounds of such district or circuit, in the same manner that members of the General Assembly are elected; all said Attorneys, both for the State and circuit or district, shall hold their offices for the term of six years. In all cases where the Attorney for any district fails or refuses to attend and prosecute according to law, the court shall have power to appoint an Attorney *pro tempore*. *Ten.*, 503.
—An Attorney-General shall be elected by the people, who shall reside at the capital of the State during his continuance in office, whose duties shall be prescribed by law, who shall hold his office for four years, and who, in addition to perquisites, shall receive an annual salary of three thousand dollars, which shall not be increased or diminished during his term of office. *Tex.*, 511.
—At every election of a Governor, an Attorney-General shall be elected by the voters of the Commonwealth for the term of four years. He shall be commissioned by the Governor, shall perform such duties and receive such compensation as may be prescribed by law, and be removable in the manner prescribed for the removal of judges. *Va.*, 543.
—At every election of a Governor, an Attorney-

1 § 2. A State Engineer and Surveyor shall be chosen at a general election,

2 and shall hold his office two years, but no person shall be elected to said office

3 who is not a practical engineer.

1 § 3. Three Canal Commissioners shall be chosen at the General election

2 which shall be held next after the adoption of this Constitution, one of

3 whom shall hold his office for one year, one for two years, and one for three

4 years. The Commissioners of the Canal Fund shall meet at the Capitol on the

5 first Monday of January, next after such election and determine by lot which

6 of said Commissioners shall hold his office for one year, which for two, and

7 which for three years; and there shall be elected annually, thereafter, one

8 Canal Commissioner, who shall hold his office for three years.

1 § 4. Three Inspectors of State Prisons shall be elected at the general

2 election which shall be held next after the adoption of this Constitution, one

3 of whom shall hold his office for one year, one for two years, and one for three

4 years. The Governor, Secretary of State and Comptroller shall meet at the

5 Capitol on the first Monday of January next succeeding such election, and

6 determine by lot which of said inspectors shall hold his office for one year,

7 which for two, and which for three years; and there shall be elected annually

8 thereafter, one Inspector of State Prisons, who shall hold his office for three

9 years; said inspectors shall have the charge and superintendence of the State

10 Prisons and shall appoint all the officers therein. All vacancies in the office

11 of such inspector shall be filled by the Governor till the next election.

General shall be elected. He shall be commissioned by the Governor; shall perform such duties and receive such compensation as may be prescribed by law, and be removable in the same manner as the judges. *W. Va.*, 554.

COMMISSIONERS OF FUNDS.

—The Auditor of State, Secretary of State and Attorney-General are hereby created a Board of Commissioners, to be styled "The Commissioners of the Sinking Fund." *Ohio*, 439.
—The Commissioners of the Sinking Fund shall, immediately preceding each regular session of the General Assembly, make an estimate of the probable amount of the fund provided for in the seventh section of this article, from all sources except from taxation, and report the same, together with all their proceedings relative to said fund and the public debt, to the Governor, who shall transmit the same, with his regular message, to the General Assembly, and the General Assembly shall make all necessary provision for raising and disbursing said Sinking Fund, in pursuance of the provisions of this article. *Ohio*, 439.
27

—It shall be the duty of the said commissioners faithfully to apply said fund, together with all moneys that may be, by the General Assembly, appropriated to that object, to the payment of the interest, as it becomes due, and the redemption of the principal of the public debt of the State, excepting only the school and trust funds held by the State. *Ohio*, 440.
—The said Commissioners shall, semi-annually, make a full and detailed report of their proceedings to the Governor, who shall immediately cause the same to be published, and shall also communicate the same to the General Assembly, forthwith, if it be in session, and if not, then at its first session after such report shall be made. *Ohio*, 440.

INVIOLABILITY OF FUNDS.

—The principal of all funds arising from the sale or other disposition of lands or other property, granted or entrusted to this State for educational and religious purposes, shall forever be preserved inviolate and undiminished; and the income arising therefrom shall be faithfully applied to the specific objects of the original grants or appropriations. *Ohio*, 438.

1 § 5. The Lieutenant-Governor, Speaker of the Assembly, Secretary of State
2 Comptroller, Treasurer, Attorney-General, and State Engineer and Surveyor,
3 shall be the Commissioners of the Land Office. The Lieutenant-Governor,
4 Secretary of State, Comptroller, Treasurer, and Attorney-General shall be the
5 Commissioners of the Canal Fund. The Canal Board shall consist of the
6 Commissioners of the Canal Fund, the State Engineer and Surveyor, and
7 the Canal Commissioners.

1 § 6. The powers and duties of the respective boards, and of the several
2 officers in this article mentioned, shall be such as now are or hereafter may be
3 prescribed by law.

1 § 7. The Treasurer may be suspended from office by the Governor, during
2 the recess of the Legislature, and until thirty days after the commencement
3 of the next session of the Legislature, whenever it shall appear to him that
4 such Treasurer has, in any particular, violated his duty. The Governor shall
5 appoint a competent person to discharge the duties of the office, during such
6 suspension of the Treasurer.

1 § 8. All offices for the weighing, gauging, measuring, culling or inspecting
2 any merchandise, produce, manufacture or commodity whatever, are hereby
3 abolished, and no such office shall hereafter be created by law; but nothing
4 in this section contained, shall abrogate any office created for the purpose of
5 protecting the public health or the interests of the State in its property, reve-
6 nue, tolls or purchases, or of supplying the people with correct standards of
7 weights and measures, or shall prevent the creation of any office for such
8 purposes hereafter.

ARTICLE VI.

1   SECTION 1. The Assembly shall have the power of impeachment, by the vote

2 of the majority of all the members elected. The court for the trial of

3 impeachments shall be composed of the President of the Senate, the Senators,

4 or a major part of them, and the Judges of the Court of Appeals, or the

5 major part of them. On the trial of an impeachment against the Governor,

6 the Lieutenant-Governor shall not act as a member of the court. No judicial

7 officer shall exercise his office after he shall have been impeached, until he

8 shall have been acquitted. Before the trial of an impeachment, the members

9 of the court shall take an oath or affirmation truly and impartially to try the

10 impeachment according to evidence, and no person shall be convicted without

11 the concurrence of two-thirds of the members present. Judgment in cases

12 of impeachment shall not extend further than to removal from office, or

13 removal from office and disqualification to hold and enjoy any office of honor,

14 trust or profit under this State ; but the party impeached shall be liable to

15 indictment and punishment according to law.

IMPEACHMENT.

—A court shall be instituted, for the trial of impeachments and the correction of errors, under the regulations which shall be established by the Legislature ; and to consist of the President of the Senate, for the time being, and the Senators, Chancellor, and Judges of the Supreme Court, or the major part of them ; except that when an impeachment, shall be prosecuted against the Chancellor, or either of the Judges of the Supreme Court, the person, so impeached, shall be suspended from exercising his office, until his acquittal ; and, in like manner, when an appeal, from a decree in equity, shall be heard, the Chancellor shall inform the court, of the reasons of his decree, but shall not have a voice in the final sentence. And if the cause to be determined, shall be brought up by a writ of error, on a question of law, on a judgment in the Supreme Court, the judges of that court shall assign the reasons of such their judgment, but shall not have a voice for its affirmance or reversal. *N. Y.* (1777), 31.

—The power of impeaching all officers of the State, for mal and corrupt conduct in their respective offices, be vested in the representatives of the people in Assembly ; but that it shall always be necessary that two-third parts of the members present shall consent to and agree in such impeachment. That previous to the trial of every impeachment, the members of the said court shall respectively be sworn, truly and impartially to try and determine the charge in question, according to evidence ; and that no judgment of the said court shall be valid unless it be assented to by two-third parts of the members then present; nor shall it extend farther, than to removal from office, and disqualification to hold and enjoy any place of honor, trust, or profit, under this State. But the party so convicted shall be, nevertheless, liable and subject to indictment, trial, judgment and punishment, according to the laws of the land. *N. Y.* (1777), 31.

—*And it is further ordained*, that in every trial on impeachment, or indictment for crimes or misdemeanors, the party impeached or indicted, shall be allowed counsel, as in civil actions. *Y. N.* (1777), 31.
—The court for the trial of impeachments, and the correction of errors, shall consist of the President of the Senate, the Senators, the Chancellor, and the justices of the Supreme Court, or the major part of them ; but when an impeachment shall be prosecuted against the Chancellor, or any justice of the Supreme Court, the person so impeached shall be suspended from exercising his office until his acquittal, and when an appeal from a decree in chancery shall be heard, the Chancellor shall inform the court of the reasons of his decree, but shall have no voice in the final sentence ; and when a writ of error shall be brought on a judgment of the Supreme Court, the justices of that court shall assign the reasons for their judgment, but shall not have a voice for its affirmance or reversal. *N. Y.* (1821), 40.
—The Assembly shall have the power of impeaching all civil officers of this State for mal and corrupt conduct in office, and for high crimes and misdemeanors: but a majority of all the members elected shall concur in an impeachment. Before the trial of an impeachment the members of the court shall take an oath or affirmation truly and impartially to try and determine the charge in question, according to evidence ; and no person shall be convicted, without the concurrence of two-thirds of the members present. Judgment in cases of impeachment, shall not extend farther than the removal from office and disqualification to hold and enjoy any office of honor, trust or profit, under this State ; but the party convicted shall be liable to indictment and punishment, according to law. *N. Y.* (1821). 40.
—The House of Representatives shall have the sole power of preferring impeachments ; all impeachments shall be tried by the Senate ; the Senators, when sitting for that purpose, shall be on oath or affirmation; and no person shall be convicted under an impeachment without the concurrence of two-thirds

of the Senators present. *Ala.*, 76; (nearly similar), *Cal.*, 98; *Ct.*, 113; *Del.*, 121; *Iowa*, 186; *Kan.*, 200; *Mo.*, 360; *Neb.*, 373; *Ohio*, 434.
—All civil officers of the State, whether elected by the people or by the General Assembly, or appointed by the Governor, shall be liable to impeachment for any misdemeanor in office; but judgment in such cases shall not extend further than removal from office, and disqualification to hold any office of honor, trust or profit under the State; but the party convicted shall, nevertheless, be liable and subject to indictment, trial and punishment according to law. *Ala.*, 81.
—The Governor, Lieutenant-Governor, Secretary of State, Auditor, Treasurer, and all Judges of the Supreme, Circuit and interior Courts of law and equity, and the prosecuting attorneys for the State, shall be liable to impeachment for any malpractice or misdemeanor in office, but judgment in such cases shall not extend further than removal from office, and disqualification to hold any office of trust or profit under this State. The party impeached, whether convicted or acquitted, shall nevertheless be liable to be indicted, tried and punished according to law. *Ark.*, 87; (nearly similar,) *Cal.*, 98; *Mo.*, 359.
—The House of Representatives shall have the sole power of impeachment, and all impeachments shall be tried by the Senate; and when sitting for that purpose, the Senators shall be on oath or affirmation to do justice according to law and evidence. When the Governor shall be tried, the Chief Justice of the Supreme Court shall preside, and no person shall be convicted without the concurrence of two-thirds of all the Senators elected; and for reasonable cause which shall not be sufficient ground for impeachment, the Governor shall, on the joint address of two-thirds of each branch of the Legislature, remove from office the Judges of the Supreme and inferior Courts; *Provided*, The cause or causes of removal be spread on the journals, and the party charged be notified of the same, and heard by himself and counsel before the vote is finally taken and decided. *Ark.*, 87.
—The Governor and all other executive and judicial officers shall be liable to impeachment; but judgments in such cases shall not extend further than to removal from office and disqualification to hold any office of honor, trust, or profit under this State. The party convicted shall nevertheless be liable and subject to indictment, trial and punishment according to law. *Ct.*, 113; *Del.*, 121; *Fl.*, 136; *Ill.*, 153; *Kan.*, 200; *Ky.*, 218; *Miss.*, 342; *Ohio*, 434; *R. I.*, 480.
—When the Governor is impeached the Chief Justice shall preside. [*Ct.*, 113;] but have no vote thereon. *N. H.*, 405.
—The power of impeachment shall be vested in the House of Representatives. *Fl.*, 136; *La.*, 232.
—All impeachments shall be tried by the Senate; when sitting for that purpose the Senators shall be upon oath or affirmation; and no person shall be convicted without the concurrence of two-thirds of the members present. *Fl.*, 136; *Ga.*, 144; *Ky.*, 218; *Me.*, 243; *Miss.*, 342; *Pa.*, 464; *S. C.*, 487; *Tex.*, 518; *Vt.*, 529.
— Judgment in cases of impeachment, shall not extend further than removal from office, and disqualification to hold and enjoy any office of honor, profit or trust, within this State; but the party convicted shall, nevertheless, be liable and subject to indictment, trial, judgment and punishment according to law. *Ga.*, 144; *La.*, 232; *Me.*, 243; *N. H.*, 405; *N. J.*, 419; *N. C.*, 429; *Pa.*, 464; *Tex.*, 518; *Vt.*, 529; *W. Va.*, 548; *Wis.*, 565.
— The House of Representatives shall have the sole power of impeaching; but a majority of all the members elected, must concur in an impeachment. All impeachments shall be tried by the Senate; and when sitting for that purpose, the Senators shall be upon oath, or affirmation, to do justice according to law and evidence. No person shall be convicted without the concurrence of two-thirds of the Senators elected. *Ill.*, 153.

—The Governor and all other civil officers shall be liable to impeachment for misdemeanor in office during their continuance in office, and for two years thereafter. *Ill.*, 159; *N. J.*, 416.
—All State officers shall, for crime, incapacity, or negligence, be liable to be removed from office, either by impeachment by the House of Representatives, to be tried by the Senate, or by a joint resolution of the General Assembly, two-thirds of the members elected to each branch voting in either case therefor. *Ind.*, 176.
—All State, county, township, and town officers may be impeached or removed from the office in such manner as may be prescribed by law. *Ind.*, 176.
—The Governor, Judges of the Supreme and District Courts, and other State officers, shall be liable to impeachment for any misdemeanor or malfeasance in office; but judgment in such cases shall extend only to removal from office, and disqualification to hold any office of honor, trust or profit under this State; but the party convicted or acquitted shall, nevertheless, be liable to indictment, trial and punishment according to law. All other civil officers shall be tried for misdemeanors and malfeasance in office, in such manner as the General Assembly may provide. *Iowa*, 187.
—The judges of all courts shall be liable to impeachment; but for any reasonable cause, which shall not be sufficient ground for impeachment, the Governor shall remove any of them, on the address of a majority of the members elected to each House of the General Assembly. In every such case the cause or causes for which such removal may be required shall be stated at length in the address, and inserted in the journal of each House. *La.*, 232.
—Impeachments of the Governor, Lieutenant-Governor, Attorney-General, Secretary of State, State Treasurer, Auditor of Public Accounts, and the Judges of the Inferior Courts, Justices of the Peace excepted, shall be tried by the Senate; the Chief Justice of the Supreme Court, or the senior judge thereof, shall preside during the trial of such impeachment. Impeachments of the Judges of the Supreme Court shall be tried by the Senate. When sitting as a court of impeachment, the Senators shall be upon oath or affirmation, and no person shall be convicted without the concurrence of a majority of the Senators elected. *La.*, 233.
—The House of Representatives shall have the sole power of impeachment. *Ky.*, 218; *Me.*, 242; *Miss.*, 342; *Pa.*, 464; *R. I.*, 480; *Tenn.*, 495.
—They [the House] shall have the sole power to impeach all persons who have been or may be in office. *Ga.*, 145.
—All officers against whom articles of impeachment may be preferred shall be suspended from the exercise of their functions during the pendency of such impeachment; the appointing power may make a provisional appointment to replace any suspended officer until the decision of the impeachment. *La.*, 232; *Tex.*, 518.
—Every person holding any civil office under this State, may be removed, by impeachment, for misdemeanor in office; and every person holding any office may be removed by the Governor, with the advice of the Council, on the address of both branches of the Legislature. But, before such address shall pass either House, the causes of removal shall be stated and entered on the journal of the House in which it originated, and a copy thereof served on the person in office, that he may be admitted to a hearing in his defense. *Me.*, 247.
—The House of Delegates shall have the sole power of impeachment in all cases, but a majority of all the members elected must concur in an impeachment; all impeachments shall be tried by the Senate, and when sitting for that purpose, the Senators shall be on oath or affirmation to do justice according to the law and evidence, but no person shall be convicted without the concurrence of two-thirds of all the Senators elected. *Md.*, 262.
—The House of Representatives shall be the grand inquest of this Commonwealth; and all impeach-

ments made by them shall be heard and tried by the Senate. *Mass.*, 286; *N. H.*, 403.

—The Senate shall be a court, with full authority to hear and determine all impeachments made by the House of Representatives, against any officer or officers of the Commonwealth, for misconduct and maladministration in their offices; but previous to the trial of every impeachment, the members of the Senate shall, respectively, be sworn truly and impartially to try and determine the charge in question, according to evidence. Their judgment, however, shall not extend further than to removal from office, and disqualification to hold or enjoy any place of honor, trust or profit, under this Commonwealth; but the paty so convicted shall be, nevertheless, liable to indictment, trial, judgment and punishment, according to the laws of the land. *Mass.*, 285.

—The House of Representatives shall have the sole power of impeaching civil officers for corrupt conduct in office, or for crimes or misdemeanors; but a majority of the members elected shall be necessary to direct an impeachment. *Mich.*, 309.

—Every impeachment shall be tried by the Senate. When the Governor or Lieutenant-Governor is tried, the Chief Justice of the Supreme Court shall preside. When an impeachment is directed, the Senate shall take an oath or affirmation truly and impartially to try and determine the same according to the evidence. No person shall be convicted without the concurrence of two-thirds of the members elected. Judgment in case of impeachment, shall not extend further than removal from office; but the party convicted shall be liable to punishment according to law. *Mich.*, 310.

—When an impeachment is directed, the House fo Representatives shall elect from their own body three members, whose duty it shall be to prosecute such impeachment. No impeachment shall be tried until the final adjournment of the Legislature, when the Senate shall proceed to try the same. *Mich.*, 310 *Tenn.*, 495.

—No Judicial officer shall exercise his office after an impeachment is directed, until he is acquitted. *Mich.*, 310.

—The Governor may make a provisional appointment to fill a vacancy occasioned by the suspension of an officer until he shall be acquitted, or until after the election and qualification of a successor. *Mich.*, 310.

—For reasonable cause, which shall not be sufficient ground for the impeachment of a judge, the Governor shall remove him on a concurrent resolution of two-thirds of the members elected to each House of the Legislature; but the cause for which such removal is required shall be stated at length in such resolution. *Mich.*, 310.

—The House of Representatives shall have the sole power of impeachment, through a concurrence of a majority of all the members elected to seats therein. All impeachments shall be tried by the Senate; and when sitting for that purpose, the Senators shall be upon oath or affirmation to do justice according to law and evidence. No person shall be convicted without the concurrence of two-thirds of the members present. *Min.*, 322.

—The Governor, Secretary of State, Treasurer, Auditor, Attorney-General, and the Judges of the Supreme and District Courts, may be impeached for corrupt conduct in office, or for crimes and misdemeanors; but judgment in such case shall not extend further than removal from office and disqualification to hold and enjoy any office of honor, trust or profit in this State. The party convicted thereof shall nevertheless be liable and subject to indictment, trial, judgment, and punishment according to law. *Min.*, 329; *Neb.*, 373.

—No officer shall exercise the duties of his office after he shall have been impeached, and before his acquittal. *Min.*, 329.

—On the trial of an impeachment against the Governor, the Lieutenant-Governor shall not act as a member of the court. *Min.*, 329.

—No person shall be tried on impeachment before he

shall have been served with a copy thereof at least twenty days previous to the day set for trial. *Min.*, 329.

—The Assembly shall have the sole power of impeachment. The concurrence of a majority of all the members elected shall be necessary to an impeachment. All impeachments shall be tried by the Senate, and when sitting for that purpose, the Senators shall be upon oath or affirmation to do justice according to law and evidence. The Chief Justice of the Supreme Court shall preside over the Senate while sitting to try the Governor or Lieutenant-Governor upon impeachment. No person shall be convicted without the concurrence of two-thirds of the Senators elected. *Nev.*, 388.

—The Governor and other State and Judicial officers, except Justices of the Peace, shall be liable to impeachment for misdemeanor or malfeasance in office, but judgment in such case shall not extend further than removal from office and disqualification to hold any office of honor, profit, or trust under this State. The party, whether convicted or acquitted, shall nevertheless be liable to indictment, trial, judgment, and punishment according to law. *Nev.*, 388.

—The Senate shall be a court, with full power and authority to hear, try and determine all impeachments made by the House of Representatives against any officer or officers of the State for bribery, corruption, mal-practice or mal-administration in office; with full power to issue summons or compulsory process, convening witnesses before them; but previous to the trial of any such impeachment, the members of the Senate shall respectively be sworn, truly and impartially to try and determine the charge in question according to evidence. And every officer impeached for bribery, corruption, mal-practice or mal-administration in office shall be served with an attested copy of the impeachment and order of the Senate thereon, with such citation as the Senate may direct, setting forth the time and place of their sitting to try the impeachment; which service shall be made by the Sheriff, or such other sworn officer as the Senate may appoint, at least fourteen days previous to the time of trial; and such citation being duly served and returned, the Senate may proceed in the hearing of the impeachment, giving the person impeached, if he shall appear, full liberty of producing witnesses and proofs, and of making his defense by himself and counsel; and may, also, upon his refusing or negecting to appear, hear the proofs in support of the impeachment, and render judgment thereon, his nonappearance notwithstanding; and such judgment shall have the same force and effect as if the person impeached had appeared and pleaded in the trial. *N. H.*, 404.

—The members of the Council may be impeached by the House and tried by the Senate for bribery, corruption, mal-practice or mal-administration. *N. H.*, 407.

—*Provided, nevertheless,* That whenever they [the Senate] shall sit on the trial of any impeachment, they may adjourn to such time and place as they may think proper, although the Legislature be not assembled on such day or at such place. *N. H.*, 404.

—Any judicial officer impeached shall be suspended from exercising his office until his acquittal. *N. J.*, 417.

—The House of Assembly shall have the sole power of impeaching, by a vote of a majority of all the members; and all impeachments shall be tried by the Senate; the members when sitting for that purpose to be on oath or affirmation "truly and impartially to try and determine the charge in question according to evidence;" and no person shall be convicted without the concurrence of two-thirds of all the members of the Senate. *N. J.*, 417.

—The House of Commons shall have the sole power of impeachment. The Senate shall have the sole power to try all impeachments. No person shall be convicted upon any impeachment, unless two-thirds of the Senators present shall concur in such conviction; and before the trial of any impeachment,

28

1 · § 2. There shall be a Court of Appeals, composed of eight judges, of whom

2 four shall be elected by the electors of the State for eight years, and four

3 selected from the class of Justices of the Supreme Court having the shortest

4 time to serve. Provision shall be made by law for designating one of the

5 number elected as Chief Judge, and for selecting such Justices of the Supreme

6 Court, from time to time, and for so classifying those selected, that one shall

7 be elected every second year.

the members of the Senate shall take an oath or affirmation truly and impartially to try and determine the charge in question, according to evidence. *N. C.*, 429.

— The Governor, Judges of the Supreme Court, and Judges of the Superior Courts, and all other officers of this State (except Justices of the Peace and militia officers), may be impeached for willfully violating any article of the Constitution, mal-administration or corruption. *N. C.*, 429.

—That the Governor and other officers offending against the State, by violating any part of this Constitution, maladministration, or corruption, may be prosecuted, on the impeachment of the General Assembly, or presentment of the Grand Jury of any court of supreme jurisdiction in this State. *N. C.*, 425.

—Public officers shall not be impeached; but incompetency, corruption, malfeasance, or delinquency in office may be tried in the same manner as criminal offenses, and judgment may be given of dismissal from office, and such further punishment as may have been prescribed by law. *Or.*, 455.

—The Governor, and all other civil officers under this Commonwealth, shall be liable to impeachment for any misdemeanor in office. *Pa.*, 464.

—A vote of two-thirds of all the members elected shall be required for an impeachment of the Governor. Any officer impeached shall thereby be suspended from office until judgment in the case shall have been pronounced. *R. I.*, 480.

—All impeachments shall be tried by the Senate; and when sitting for that purpose, they shall be under oath or affirmation. No person shall be convicted except by vote of two-thirds of the members elected. When the Governor is impeached, the Chief or Presiding Justice of the Supreme Court for the time being, shall preside, with a casting vote in all preliminary questions. *R. I.*, 480.

—The Governor, Lieutenant-Governor and all civil officers shall be liable to impeachment for high crimes and misdemeanors, for any misbehavior in office, for corruption in procuring office, or for any act which shall degrade their official character. But judgment in such cases shall not extend further than to removal from office, and disqualification to hold any office of honor, trust or profit under this State. The party convicted shall, nevertheless, be liable to indictment, trial, judgment and punishment according to law. *S. C.*, 487.

—The House of Representatives shall have the sole power of impeaching, but no impeachment shall be made unless with the concurrence of two-thirds of the House of Representatives. *S. C.*, 487.

—All impeachments shall be tried by the Senate; when sitting for that purpose, the Senators shall be upon oath or affirmation. No person shall be convicted without the concurrence of two-thirds of the Senators sworn to try the officer impeached. *Tenn.*, 493.

—The Governor, Judges of the Supreme Court, Judges of Inferior Courts, Chancellors, Attorneys for the State, and Secretary of State, shall be liable to impeachment, whenever they may, in the opinion of the House of Representatives, commit any crime in

their official capacity, which may require disqualification; but judgment shall only extend to removal from office and disqualification to fill any office thereafter. The party shall, nevertheless, be liable to indictment, trial, judgment, and punishment, according to law. *Tenn.*, 496.

—Impeachments of the Governor, Lieutenant-Governor, Attorney-General, Secretary of State, Treasurer, Controller, and of the Judges of the District Court, shall be tried by the Senate. *Tex.*, 518.

—Impeachment of Judges of the Supreme Court shall be tried by the Senate; when sitting as a Court of Impeachment, the Senators shall be upon oath or affirmation; and no person shall be convicted without the concurrence of two-thirds of the Senators present. *Tex.*, 518.

—The Governor, Lieutenant-Governor, Judges and all others offending against the State by mal-administration, corruption, neglect of duty, or other high crime or misdemeanor, shall be impeachable by the House of Delegates, and be prosecuted before the Senate, which shall have the sole power to try impeachments. *Va.*, 537.

—Every officer of State, whether judicial or executive, shall be liable to be impeached by the General Assembly, either when in office or after his resignation or removal for maladministration. *Vt.*, 529.

[The right to impeach State criminals is enumerated among the powers of the House]. *Vt.*, 523.

—The Senate may sit during the recess of the Legislature for the trial of impeachments. *W. Va.*, 548.

—Any officer of the State may be impeached for maladministration, corruption, incompetence, neglect of duty, or any high crime or misdemeanor. The House of Delegates shall have the sole power of impeachment. The Senate shall have the sole power to try impeachments. When sitting for that purpose, the Senators shall be on oath or affirmation; and no person shall be convicted without the concurrence of two-thirds of the members present. *W. Va.*, 548.

—The court for the trial of impeachments shall be composed of the Senate. The House of Representatives shall have the power of impeaching all civil officers of this State for corrupt conduct in office, or for crimes and misdemeanors; but a majority of all the members elected shall concur in an impeachment. On the trial of an impeachment against the Governor, the Lieutenant-Governor shall not act as a member of the court. No judicial officer shall exercise his office after he shall have been impeached, until his acquittal. Before the trial of an impeachment, the members of the court shall take an oath or affirmation truly and impartially to try the impeachment according to evidence; and no person shall be convicted without the concurrence of two-thirds of the members present. *Wis.*, 565.

JUDICIAL POWER—HOW VESTED.

—The judicial power of this State shall be vested in one Supreme Court, Circuit Courts to be held in each county of the State, and such inferior courts of law and equity, to consist of not more than five members as the General Assembly may, from time to time, direct, ordain and establish. *Ala.*, 80.

—The judicial power of this State shall be vested in one Supreme Court, in County Courts, and in Justices of the Peace. The General Assembly may also vest such jurisdiction as may be deemed necessary in Corporation Courts, and when they deem it expedient, may establish Courts of Chancery. *Ark.*, 80.

—The judicial power of this State shall be vested in a Supreme Court, in District Courts, in County Courts, in Probate Courts, and in Justices of the Peace, and in such Recorders' and other inferior courts as the Legislature may establish in any incorporated city or town. *Cal.*, (as amended in 1862).

—The judicial power of the State shall be vested in a Supreme Court of Errors, a Superior Court, and such Inferior Courts as the General Assembly shall, from time to time, ordain and establish, the powers and jurisdiction of which courts shall be defined by law. *Ct.*, 111.

—The judicial power of this State shall be vested in a Court of Errors and Appeals, a Superior Court, a Court of Chancery, an Orphan's Court, a Court of Oyer and Terminer, a Court of General Sessions of the Peace and Jail Delivery, a Register's Court, Justices of the Peace, and such other courts as the General Assembly, with the concurrence of two-thirds of all the members of both Houses shall from time to time establish. *Del.*, 121.

—To compose the said courts there shall be five Judges in the State. One of them shall be Chancellor of the State; he shall also be President of the Orphan's Court; he may be appointed in any part of the State. The other four Judges shall compose the Superior Court, the Court of Oyer and Terminer, and the Court of General Sessions of the Peace and Jail Delivery, as hereinafter prescribed. One of them shall be Chief Justice of the State, and may be appointed in any part of it. The other three Judges shall be Associate Judges, and one of them shall reside in each county. *Del.*, 121.

—The judicial power of this State, both as to matters of law and equity, shall be vested in a Supreme Court, Courts of Chancery, Circuit Courts, and Justices of the Peace, provided the General Assembly may also vest such civil or criminal jurisdiction as may be necessary in Corporation Courts, and such other courts as the General Assembly may establish : but such jurisdiction shall not extend to criminal cases. *Fl.*, 133.

—The judicial powers of this State shall be vested in a Supreme Court for the Correction of Errors, a Superior, Inferior, Ordinary and Justices' Court, and in such other courts as have been, or may be, established by law. *Ga.*, 148.

—The judicial power of this State shall be, and is hereby, vested in one Supreme Court, in Circuit Courts, in County Courts and in Justices of the Peace; *Provided*, That inferior local courts, of civil and criminal jurisdiction, may be established by the General Assembly in the cities of this State, but such courts shall have a uniform organization and jurisdiction in such cities. *Ill.*, 159.

—The judicial power of the State shall be vested in a Supreme Court, in Circuit Courts, and in such inferior courts as the General Assembly may establish. *Ind.* 176.

—The judicial power shall be vested in a Supreme Court, District Courts and such other courts, inferior to the Supreme Court, as the General Assembly may from time to time establish. *Iowa*, 189.

—The judicial power of this State shall be vested in a Supreme Court, District Courts, Probate Courts, Justices of the Peace and such other courts, inferior to the Supreme Court, as may be provided by law; and all Courts of Record shall have a seal to be used in the authentication of all process. *Kan.*, 200.

—The judicial power of this Commonwealth, both as to matters of law and equity, shall be vested in one Supreme Court (to be styled the Court of Appeals), the courts established by this Constitution, and such courts, inferior to the Supreme Court, as the General Assembly may, from time to time, erect and establish. *Ky.*, 214.

—The judiciary power shall be vested in a Supreme Court, in such inferior courts as the Legislature may, from time to time, order and establish, and in Justices of the Peace. *La.*, 231.

—The judicial power of this State shall be vested in a Supreme Judicial Court, and such other courts as the Legislature shall, from time to time, establish. *Me.*, 246.

—The judicial power of this State shall be vested in a Court of Appeals, Circuit Courts, Orphans' Courts, such Courts for the city of Baltimore as may be hereinafter prescribed or provided for, and Justices of the Peace; all said Courts shall be Courts of Record, and each shall have a seal, to be used in the authentication of all process issuing from them. The process and official character of Justices of the Peace shall be authenticated as hath heretofore been practiced in this State, or may hereafter be prescribed by law. *Md.*, 265.

—The judicial power is vested in one Supreme Court, in Circuit Courts, in Probate Courts, and in Justices of the Peace. Municipal courts of civil and criminal jurisdiction may be established by the Legislature in cities. *Mich.*, 305.

—The judicial power of the State shall be vested in a Supreme Court, District Courts, Courts of Probate, Justices of the Peace, and such other courts, inferior to the Supreme Court, as the Legislature may from time to time establish by a two-third vote. *Min.*, 324.

—The judicial power of this State shall be vested in one High Court of Errors and Appeals, and such other courts of law and equity as are hereinafter provided for in this Constitution. *Miss.*, 338.

—The judicial power, as to matters of law and equity, shall be vested in a Supreme Court, in District Courts, in Circuit Courts, and in such inferior tribunals as the General Assembly may, from time to time, establish. *Mo.*, 357.

—The judicial power of this State shall be vested in a Supreme Court, District Courts, Probate Courts, Justices of the Peace, and such inferior courts as the Legislature may from time to time establish. *Neb.*, 375.

—The judicial power of this State shall be vested in a Supreme Court, District Courts, and in Justices of the Peace. The Legislature may also establish courts for municipal purposes only, in incorporated cities and towns. *Nev.*, 386.

—The judicial power shall be vested in a Court of Errors and Appeals in the last resort in all causes, as heretofore; a Court for the trial of Impeachments, a Court of Chancery, a Prerogative Court, a Supreme Court, Circuit Courts, and such inferior courts as now exist, and as may be hereafter ordained and established by law; which inferior courts the Legislature may alter or abolish, as the public good shall require. *N. J.*, 417.

—The judicial power of the State shall be vested in a Supreme Court, in District Courts, Courts of Common Pleas, Courts of Probate, Justices of the Peace, and in such other courts, inferior to the Supreme Court, in one or more counties, as the General Assembly may from time to time establish. *Ohio*, 436.

—The judicial power of the State shall be vested in a Supreme Court, Circuit Courts, and County Courts, which shall be courts of record, having general jurisdiction, to be defined, limited, and regulated by law, in accordance with this Constitution. Justices of the Peace may also be invested with limited judicial powers, and Municipal Courts may be created to administer the regulations of incorporated towns and cities. *Or.*, 454.

—The Judicial power of this Commonwealth shall be vested in a Supreme Court, in Courts of Oyer and Terminer and General Jail Delivery, in a Court of Common Pleas, Orphans' Court, Register's Court, and a Court of Quarter Sessions of the Peace, for each county; in Justices of the Peace, and in such other courts as the Legislature may from time to time establish. *Pa.*, 464.

—The Judicial power of this State shall be vested in one Supreme Court, and in such inferior courts as the General Assembly may, from time to time, ordain and establish. *R. I.*, 479.

—The Judicial power shall be vested in such Superior and Interior Courts of Law and Equity as the General Assembly shall, from time to time direct and establish. *S. C.*, 486.

—The Judges shall meet and sit at Columbia, at such time as the General Assembly may by act prescribe, for the purpose of hearing and determining all motions for new trials and in arrest of judgment, and such points of law as may be submitted to them; and the General Assembly may by act appoint such other places for such meetings as in their discretion may seem fit. *S. C.*, 486.

—The Judicial power of this State shall be vested in one Supreme Court, in such Inferior Courts as the Legislature shall, from time to time, ordain and establish, and the Judges thereof, and in Justices of the Peace. The Legislature may also vest such jurisdiction as may be deemed necessary in Corporation Courts. *Tenn.*, 495.

—The judicial power of this State, shall be vested in one Supreme Court, in District Courts, in County Courts, and in such Corporation Courts, and other inferior courts or tribunals as the Legislature may from time to time ordain and establish. The Legislature may establish criminal courts, in the principal cities within this State, with such criminal jurisdiction, co-extensive with the limits of the county wherein such city may be situated and under such regulations as may be prescribed by law, and the judge therein, may preside over the courts of one or more cities, as the Legislature may direct. *Tex.*, 510.

—There shall be a Supreme Court of Appeals, District Courts, and Circuit Courts. The jurisdiction of these tribunals and of the judges thereof, except so far as the same is conferred by this Constitution, shall be regulated by law. The judges shall be chosen by the joint vote of the two Houses of the General Assembly, from persons nominated by the Governor. *Va.*, 541.

—The judicial power of the State shall be vested in a Supreme Court of Appeals and Circuit Courts, and such inferior tribunals as are herein authorized. *W. Va.*, 552.

—The judicial power of this State, both as to matters of law and equity, shall be vested in a Supreme Court, Circuit Courts, Courts of Probate, and Justices of the Peace. The Legislature may also vest such jurisdiction as shall be deemed necessary in Municipal Courts, and shall have power to establish inferior courts in the several counties, with limited civil and criminal jurisdiction; *Provided*, That the jurisdiction which may be vested in Municipal Courts shall not exceed in their respective municipalities, that of Circuit Courts, in their respective circuits, as prescribed in this Constitution; and that the Legislature shall provide as well for the election of Judges of the Municipal Courts as of the judges of inferior courts, by the qualified electors of the respective jurisdictions. The term of office of the judges of the said municipal and inferior courts shall not be longer than that of the judges of the Circuit Court. *Wis.*, 565.

COURTS OF ERROR AND OF APPEAL.

—When the Superior Court consider that a question of law ought to be decided before all the judges, they shall have power, upon the application of either party, to direct it to be heard in the Court of Errors and Appeals; and in that case the Chancellor and four judges shall compose the Court of Errors and Appeals, the Chancellor presiding, and any four of them being a quorum; and in the absence of the Chancellor the Chief Justice shall preside. The Superior Court, in exercising this power, may direct a cause to be proceeded into verdict and judgment in that Court, or to be otherwise proceeded in, as shall be best for expediting justice. *Del.*, 121.

—Upon appeal from the Court of Chancery, the Court of Errors and Appeals shall consist of the Chief Justice and three Associate Judges; any of them shall be a quorum. *Del.*, 122.

—The Court of Errors and Appeals shall have jurisdiction to issue writs of error to the Superior Court, and to receive appeals from the Court of Chancery, and to determine finally all matters in error in the judgments and proceedings of said Superior Court, and all matters of appeal in the interlocutory or final decrees and proceedings in chancery. The Court of Errors and Appeals, upon a writ of error to the Superior Court, shall consist of three judges at least, that is to say, the Chancellor who shall preside, the Associate Judge, who could not, on account of his residence, sit in the cause below, and one of the judges who did sit in the said cause. [The order in which the Judges of Superior Court are to preside in detail.] *Del.*, 121.

—The Court of Appeals shall have appellate jurisdiction only, which shall be co-extensive with the State, under such restrictions and regulations, not repugnant to this Constitution, as may, from time to time, be prescribed by law. *Ky.*, 214.

—The Judges of the Court of Appeals shall, after their first term, hold their offices for eight years, from and after their election, and until their successors shall be duly qualified, subject to the conditions hereinafter prescribed; but for any reasonable cause, the Governor shall remove any of them on the address of two-thirds of each House of the General Assembly; *Provided, however,* That the cause or causes for which such removal may be required, shall be stated at length in such address, and on the journal of each House. They shall, at stated times, receive for their services an adequate compensation, to be fixed by law, which shall not be diminished during the time for which they shall have been elected. *Ky.*, 214.

—The Court of Appeals shall consist of four judges, any three of whom may constitute a court for the transaction of business. The General Assembly, at its first session after the adoption of this Constitution, shall divide the State, by counties, into four districts, as nearly equal in voting population, and with as convenient limits as may be, in each of which the qualified voters shall elect one Judge of the Court of Appeals; *Provided,* That whenever a vacancy shall occur in said court, from any cause, the General Assembly shall have the power to reduce the number of judges and districts; but in no event shall there be less than three judges and districts. Should a change in the number of the Judges of the Court of Appeals be made, the term of office and number of districts shall be so changed as to preserve the principle of electing one judge every two years. *Ky.*, 215.

—The Court of Appeals shall hold its sessions at the seat of government unless otherwise directed by law, but the General Assembly may, from time to time, direct that said Court shall hold sessions in any one or more of said districts. *Ky.*, 215.

—The General Assembly shall provide for an additional judge or judges, to constitute, with the remaining judge or judges, a special court for the trial of such cause or causes as may, at any time be pending in the Court of Appeals, on the trial of which a majority of the judges cannot sit, on account of interest in the event of the cause; or on account of their relationship to either party; or when a judge may have been employed in or decided the cause in the inferior Court. *Ky.*, 216.

—The Court of Appeals shall consist of a Chief Justice and four Associate Justices, and for their selection the State shall be divided into five judicial districts; and one of the Justices of the Court of Appeals shall be elected from each of said districts, by the qualified voters of the whole State. The present Chief Justice and Associate Justices of the Court of Appeals shall continue to act as such until the expiration of the term for which they were respectively elected, and until their successors are elected and qualified; and an election for a Justice of the Court of Appeals, to be taken from the fourth judicial district, shall be held on the Tuesday next after the first Monday in the month of November, eighteen hundred and sixty-four. *Md.*, 267.

—The Court of Appeals shall hold its sessions in the city of Annapolis, on the first Monday in April and the first Monday in October of each and every year, or at such other times as the General Assembly may by law direct, and it shall be competent for the justices of said court, sufficient cause appearing to them, temporarily to transfer their sittings elsewhere. *Md.*, 267.

—The jurisdiction of the Court of Appeals shall be co-extensive with the limits of the State, and such as now is or may hereafter be prescribed for it by law, and its sessions shall continue for not less than ten months in the year, if the business before it shall so require. *Md.*, 267.

—Any three of the Justices of the Court of Appeals may constitute a quorum, but no cause shall be decided without the concurrence of at least three justices in the decision; and, in every case decided, an opinion in writing shall be filed within three months after the argument or submission of the cause, and the judgment of the court shall be final and conclusive. *Md.*, 267.

—Provision shall be made by law for publishing reports of all causes argued and determined in the Court of Appeals, which the justices shall designate as proper for publication. *Md.*, 267.

—The High Court of Errors and Appeals shall consist of three judges, any two of whom shall form a quorum. The Legislature shall divide the State into three districts, and the qualified electors of each district shall elect one of said judges for the term of six years. *Miss.*, 338.

—The High Court of Errors and Appeals shall be held at least once in each year, at the seat of government, and at such other place or places in the State as the Legislature may direct. *Miss.*, 339.

—The High Court of Errors and Appeals shall have no jurisdiction, but such as properly belongs to a Court of Errors and Appeals. *Miss.*, 338.

—The Clerk of the High Court of Errors and Appeals shall be appointed by the said Court for the term of four years, and the Clerks of the Circuit, Probate, and other inferior courts, shall be elected by the qualified electors of the respective counties, and shall hold their offices for the term of two years. *Miss.*, 339.

—The Court of Errors and Appeals shall consist of the Chancellor, the Justices of the Supreme Court, and six judges, or a major part of them; which judges are to be appointed for six years. *N. J.*, 417.

—The Supreme Court of Appeals shall consist of three Judges, so chosen, any two of whom may hold a court. It shall have appellate jurisdiction only, except in cases of *habeas corpus, mandamus* and prohibition. It shall not have jurisdiction in civil cases where the matter in controversy, exclusive of costs, is less in value or amount than five hundred dollars, except in controversies concerning the title or boundaries of land, the probate of a will, the appointment or qualification of a personal representative, guardian, committee or curator; or concerning a mill, road, way, ferry or landing, or right of a corporation or of a county to lay tolls or taxes, and except in cases of *habeas corpus, mandamus* and prohibition, or cases involving freedom or the constitutionality of a law. *Va.*, 542.

—Special Courts of Appeals, to consist of not less than three nor more than five Judges, may be formed of the Judges of the Supreme Court of Appeals, and of the Circuit Courts, or any of them, to try any cases being on the dockets of the Supreme Court of Appeals when this Constitution goes into operation; or to try any cases which may be on the dockets of the Supreme Court of Appeals, in respect to which a majority of the judges of said court may be so situated as to make it improper for them to sit on the hearing thereof. And a special Court of Appeals, to consist of not less than three nor more than five judges, may be formed of the Judges of the Circuit Courts, to exercise the jurisdiction and perform the

29

duties of the Supreme Court of Appeals and of the judges thereof, until the Judges of the Supreme Court of Appeals shall have been duly chosen and qualified. *Va.*, 542.

—When a judgment or decree is reversed or affirmed by the Supreme Court of Appeals, the reasons therefor shall be stated in writing, and preserved with the record of the case. *Va.*, 542.

—The Supreme Court of Appeals shall consist of the three judges, any two of whom shall be a quorum. They shall be elected by the voters of the State, and shall hold their offices for the term of twelve years, except that of those first elected, one to be designated by lot in such manner as they may determine, shall hold his office for four years; another to be designated in like manner, for eight years, and the third for twelve years; so that one shall be elected every four years after the first election. *W. Va.*, 553.

—The Supreme Court of Appeals shall have original jurisdiction in cases of *habeas corpus, mandamus* and prohibition. It shall have appellate jurisdiction in civil cases where the matter in controversy, exclusive of costs, is of greater value or amount than two hundred dollars; in controversies concerning the title or boundaries of land, the probate of wills, the appointment or qualification of a personal representative, guardian, committee, or curator, or concerning a mill, road, way, ferry, or landing, or the right of a corporation or county to levy tolls or taxes; and also in cases of *habeas corpus, mandamus* and prohibition, and cases involving freedom, or the constitutionality of a law. It shall have appellate jurisdiction in criminal cases where there has been a conviction for felony or misdemeanor in a Circuit Court, and such other appellate jurisdiction in both civil and criminal cases as may be prescribed by law. *W. Va.*, 553.

—When a judgment or decree is reversed or affirmed by the Supreme Court of Appeals, every point made and distinctly stated in writing in the cause, and fairly arising upon the record of the case, shall be considered and decided, and the reasons therefor shall be concisely and briefly stated in writing and preserved with the records of the case. *W. Va.*, 553.

COURT OF CHANCERY.

[Appointment and powers of Chancellor noticed], *N. Y.* (1777), 26, 30, 31.

—The Chancellor and Justices of the Supreme Court, shall hold their offices during good behavior, or until they shall attain the age of sixty years.

—The Governor shall nominate, and with the consent of the Senate, appoint masters and examiners in chancery; who shall hold their offices for three years, unless sooner removed by the Senate, on the recommendation of the Governor. The registers and assistant registers, shall be appointed by the Chancellor, and hold their offices during his pleasure. *N. Y.* (1821), 40.

—The General Assembly shall have power to establish a court or courts of Chancery, with original and appellate equity jurisdiction; *Provided*, That the Judges of the several Circuit Courts shall have power to issue writs of injunction, returnable into the Courts of Chancery. *Ala.*, 80.

—Until the General Assembly shall deem it expedient to establish Courts of Chancery, the Circuit Courts shall have jurisdiction in matters of equity, subject to appeal to the Supreme Court, in such manner as may be prescribed by law. *Ark.*, 91.

—In matters of Chancery jurisdiction in which the Chancellor is interested, the Chief Justice sitting in the Superior Court without the Associate Judges, shall have jurisdiction, with an appeal to the Court of Errors and Appeals, which shall consist in this case of the three Associate Judges, the senior Associate Judge presiding. *Del.*, 122.

—The Chancellor shall hold the Court of Chancery. This court shall have all the powers vested by the laws of this State in the Court of Chancery. *Del.*, 121.

1 § 3. There shall be a Supreme Court having general jurisdiction in law

2 and equity.

1 § 4. The State shall be divided into eight judicial districts, of which the

2 city of New York shall be one; the others to be bounded by county lines, and

3 to be compact and equal in population as nearly as may be. There shall be

4 four Justices of the Supreme Court in each district, and as many more in the

5 district composed of the city of New York as may from time to time be

—Until the General Assembly shall otherwise provide, the Chancellor shall exercise all the powers which any law of the State vests in the Chancellor besides the general powers of the Court of Chancery; and the Chief Justice and Associate Judges shall each singly exercise all the powers which any law of this State vests in the Judges singly of the Supreme Court or Court of Common Pleas. *Del.*, 123.

—By the death of any party, no suit in Chancery or at law, where the cause of action survives, shall abate, but until the Legislature shall otherwise provide, suggestion of such death being entered of record, the executor or administrator of a deceased petitioner or plaintiff may prosecute the said suit; and if a respondent or defendant dies, the executor or administrator being duly served with a *scire facias*, thirty days before the term thereof, shall be considered as a party to the suit, in the same manner as if he had voluntarily made himself a party; and in any of those cases, the court shall pass a decree, or render judgment for or against the executors or administrators, as to right appertains. But where an executor or administrator of a deceased respondent or defendant becomes a party the court, upon motion, shall grant such a continuance of the cause as to the judges shall appear proper. *Del.*, 124.

—Whenever a person, not being an executor or administrator, appeals from a decree of the Chancellor, or applies for a writ of error, such appeal or writ shall be no stay of proceeding in the Chancery, or the court to which the writ issues, unless the appellant or plaintiff in error shall give sufficient security, to be approved respectively by the Chancellor, or by a judge of the court from which the writ issues, that the appellant or plaintiff in error shall prosecute respectively his appeal or writ to effect, and pay the condemnation money and all costs, or otherwise abide the decree in appeal or the judgment in error, if he fail to make his plea good. *Del.*, 124.

—That whenever the General Assembly shall create a Chancery Court, under the provisions of this Constitution, the Judges thereof shall be elected in the manner provided in the last two sections of this article, and shall hold their offices and be subject to all the provisions of said sections; *Provided, however*, That the said Judges shall be elected by general ticket or by districts, as the General Assembly may direct. *Fla.*, 134.

—The Court of Chancery shall consist of a Chancellor. *N. J.*, 417.

—The Chancellor shall be the Ordinary, or Surrogate-General, and Judge of the Prerogative Court. *N. J.*, 417.

—When an appeal from an order or decree shall be heard, the Chancellor shall inform the Court, in writing, of the reason for his order or decree; but he shall not sit as a member, or have a voice in the hearing or final sentence. *N. J.*, 417.

—A future Legislature may, when they shall conceive the same to be expedient and necessary, erect a Court of Chancery, with such powers as are usually exercised by that court, or as shall appear for the interest of the Commonwealth; *Provided*, They do not constitute themselves the judges of said court. *Vt.*, 523.

—Chancery Courts, with full jurisdiction in all matters of equity, shall be held in each judicial district by the Circuit Judge thereof, at such times and places as may be directed by law. The Superior Court of Chancery, and the several Vice-Chancery Courts shall continue as now organized, until the first Monday in November, 1857, for the disposition of causes now depending therein. The Legislature shall provide by law for the preservation of the records of the said Superior Court of Chancery and of said Vice-Chancery Courts, and also for the transfer of all causes that may remain undetermined therein, to other courts for final decision. *Miss.*, 339.

SUPREME COURT—ORGANIZATION—TERMS AND MISCELLANEOUS PROVISIONS.

—The Supreme Court shall consist of a chief justice, and two justices, any of whom may hold the court. *N. Y.* (1821), 41.

—The Supreme Court shall be held at the seat of government; but, if that shall have become dangerous, from an enemy or from disease, may adjourn to a different place. *Ala.*, 80.

—The Supreme Court shall be composed of three Judges, one of whom shall be styled Chief Justice, any two of whom shall constitute a quorum, and the concurrence of any two of said Judges shall, in every case, be necessary to a decision. *Ark.*, 90.

—The Supreme Court shall consist of a Chief Justice and four assistant Justices. The presence of three Justices shall be necessary for the transaction of business, excepting such business as may be done at chambers; and the concurrence of three Justices shall be necessary to pronounce a judgment. *Cal.*, (as amended in 1862).

—The times and places of holding the terms of the several courts of record shall be provided for by law. *Cal.*, (as amended in 1862).

—The Superior Court shall consist of the Chief Justice and two Associate Judges. The Chief Justice shall preside in every county, and in his absence the Senior Associate Judge sitting in the county shall preside. No Associate Judge shall sit in the county in which he resides. Two of the said judges shall constitute a quorum. One may open and adjourn the court, and make all rules necessary for the expediting of business.

This court shall have jurisdiction of all causes of a civil nature, real, personal, and mixed, at common law, and all other the jurisdiction and powers vested by the laws of this State in the Supreme Court or Court of Common Pleas. *D. l.*, 121.

—The Court of Oyer and Terminer shall consist of all the judges. Three of the said judges shall constitute a quorum. One may open and adjourn the court. This court shall exercise the jurisdiction now vested in the Courts of Oyer and Terminer and General Jail Delivery by the laws of this State. In the absence of the Chief Justice the Senior Associate present shall preside. *Del.*, 121.

—The Supreme Court shall be holden at such times and places as may be prescribed by law; the two Judges of the Circuit Court may be added to the Supreme Court, when in session, at the discretion of

6 authorized by law, but not to exceed in the whole such number, in proportion

7 to its population, as shall be in conformity with the number of such judges in

8 the residue of the State in proportion to its population. They shall be

9 classified so that one of the justices of each district shall go out of office at

10 the end of every two years. After the expiration of their terms under such

11 classification, the term of their office shall be eight years.

the Legislature; and the court so composed shall constitute the Supreme Court of the State, when the Legislature shall so direct. *Fl.*, 133.

—No duty not judicial shall be imposed by law upon the Justices of the Supreme Court, Chancellors or the Judges of the Circuit Courts of this State, except in cases otherwise provided for in this Constitution. *Fl.*, 135.

—The Supreme Court shall hold one term annually in each of the aforesaid grand divisions, at such time and place, in each of said divisions, as may be provided for by law. *Ill.*, 160.

—The Supreme Court shall consist of three judges, two of whom shall form a quorum; and the concurrence of two of said judges shall in all cases be necessary to a decision. *Ill.*, 160.

—The terms of the Supreme Court for the First Division shall be held at Mount Vernon, in Jefferson county; for the Second Division, at Springfield, in Sangamon county; for the Third Division, at Ottawa, in La Salle county; until some other place in either division is fixed by law. *Ill.*, 162.

—The Supreme Court shall consist of not less than three, nor more than five judges, a majority of whom shall form a quorum. They shall hold their offices for six years, if they so long behave well. *Ind.*, 176.

—The Supreme Court shall, upon the decision of every case, give a statement in writing of each question arising in the record of such case, and the decision of the court thereon. *Ind.*, 177.

—The Supreme Court shall consist of three judges, two of whom shall constitute a quorum to hold court. *Iowa*, 189.

—The Supreme Court shall consist of one Chief Justice and two Associate Justices, a majority of whom shall constitute a quorum. *Kan.*, 200.

—The Supreme Court shall be composed of one Chief Justice and four Associate Justices, a majority of whom shall constitute a quorum. *La.*, 231.

—No judgment shall be rendered by the Supreme Court without the concurrence of a majority of the judges comprising the court. Whenever the majority cannot agree, in consequence of the recusation of any member of the court, the judges not recused shall have power to call upon any judge or judges of the inferior courts, whose duty it shall be when so called upon, to sit in the place of the judge or judges recused, and to aid in determining the case. *La.*, 231.

—The Legislature shall provide for the removal of all causes now pending in the Supreme Court or other courts of the State under the Constitution of 1852, to courts created by or under this Constitution. *La.*, 237.

—For the term of six years, and thereafter, until the Legislature otherwise provide, the Judges of the several Circuit Courts shall be Judges of the Supreme Court, four of whom shall constitute a quorum. A concurrence of three shall be necessary to a final decision. After six years the Legislature may provide by law for the organization of a Supreme Court, with the jurisdiction and powers prescribed in this Constitution, to consist of one Chief Justice and three Associate Justices, to be chosen by the electors of the State. Such Supreme Court, when so organized, shall not be changed or discontinued by the Legislature for eight years thereafter. The Judges thereof shall be so classified that but one of them shall go out

of office at the same time. Their term of office shall be eight years. *Mich.*, 305.

—Four terms of the Supreme Court shall be held annually, at such times and places as may be designated by law. *Mich.*, 305.

—The Supreme Court shall, by general rules, establish, modify and amend the practice in such court and in the Circuit Courts, and simplify the same. The Legislature shall, as far as practicable, abolish distinctions between law and equity proceedings. The office of master in chancery is prohibited. *Mich.*, 305.

—On the first day of January, in the year one thousand eight hundred and fifty-two, the jurisdiction of all suits and proceedings then pending in the present Supreme Court, shall become vested in the Supreme Court established by this Constitution, and shall be finally adjudicated by the court where the same may be pending. The jurisdiction of all suits and proceedings at law and equity, then pending in the Circuit Courts and County Courts for the several counties, shall become vested in the Circuit Courts of the said counties, and District Court for the Upper Peninsula. *Mich.*, 316.

—The Supreme Court, the Circuit and Probate Courts of each county, shall be courts of record, and shall each have a common seal. *Mich.*, 306.

—The Supreme Court shall consist of one Chief Justice and two Associate Justices, but the number of Associate Justices may be increased to a number not exceeding four, by the Legislature by a two-thirds vote, when it shall be deemed necessary. *Min.*, 324.

—It shall hold one or more terms in each year, as the Legislature may direct, at the seat of government, and the Legislature may provide by a two-thirds vote that one term in each year shall be held in each or any judicial district. *Min.*, 324.

—The Supreme Court shall consist of three judges, any two of whom shall be a quorum; and the said judges shall be conservators of the peace throughout the State. *Mo.*, 357.

—If, in regard to any cause pending in the Supreme Court, the judges sitting shall be equally divided in opinion, no judgment shall be entered therein, based on such division; but the parties to the cause may agree upon some person, learned in the law, who shall act as special judge in the cause, and who shall therein sit with the court, and give decision, in the same manner and with the same effect as one of the judges. If the parties cannot agree upon a special judge the court shall appoint one. *Mo.*, 357.

—The Legislature may, after the year one thousand eight hundred seventy-five, increase the number of Justices of the Supreme Court, and the judicial districts of the State. *Neb.*, 375.

—The Supreme Court, the District Court, and such other courts as the Legislature shall designate shall be courts of record. *Nev.*, 387.

—The Supreme Court shall consist of a Chief Justice and two Associate Justices, a majority of whom shall constitute a quorum; *Provided*, That the Legislature, by a majority of all the members elected to each branch thereof, may provide for the election of two additional Associate Justices, and if so increased, three shall constitute a quorum. The concurrence of a majority of the whole court shall be necessary to render a decision. *Nev.*, 386.

—The terms of holding the Supreme Court and District Courts, shall be as fixed by law. The terms of the Supreme Court shall be held at the seat of government, and the District Courts shall be held at the county seats of their respective counties; *Provided,* That in case any county shall hereafter be divided into two or more districts, the Legislature may by law designate the places of holding courts in such districts. *Nev.,* 387.

—The terms of the Supreme Court shall, until provision be made by law, be held at such times as the Judges of the said courts, or a majority of them, may appoint. The first terms of the several District Courts (except as hereinafter mentioned) shall commence on the first Monday of December, A. D., eighteen hundred and sixty-four; the first term of the District Court in the Fifth Judicial District shall commence on the first Monday of December, A. D., eighteen hudred and sixty-four, in the county of Nye, and shall commence on the first Monday of January, A. D., eighteen hundred and sixty-five, in the county of Churchill. The terms of the Fourth Judicial District Court shall, until otherwise provided by law, be held at the county seat of Washoe county, and the first term thereof be held on the first Monday of December, A. D., eighteen hundred and sixty-four. *Nev.,* 395.

— There shall be but one form of civil action, and law and equity may be administered in the same action. *Nev.,* 387.

—The Supreme Court shall consist of a Chief Justice and four Associate Justices. The number of Associate Justices may be increased or decreased by law, but shall never be less than two. *N. J.,* 418.

—The Supreme Court shall consist of five judges, a majority of whom shall be necessary to form a quorum, or to pronounce a decision. *Ohio,* 437.

—It shall hold at least one term in each year at the seat of government, and such other terms, at the seat of government, or elsewhere, as may be provided by law. The Judges of the Supreme Court shall be elected by the electors of the State at large. *Ohio,* 437.

—Suits pending in the Supreme Court in banc shall be transferred to the Supreme Court provided for in this Constitution, and be proceeded in according to law. *Ohio,* 445.

—The Supreme Court shall consist of four justices, to be chosen in districts by the electors thereof, who shall be citizens of the United States, and who shall have resided in the State at least three years next preceding their election, and after their election to reside in their respective districts. *Or.,* 454.

—The number of justices and districts may be increased, but shall not exceed five until the white population of the State shall amount to one hundred thousand, and shall never exceed seven; and the boundaries of districts may be changed, but no change of district shall have the effect to remove a judge from office, or require him to change his residence without his consent. *Or.,* 454.

—The judge who has the shortest term to serve, or the oldest of several having such shortest terms, and not holding by appointment, shall be the Chief Justice. *Or.,* 454.

—The terms of the Supreme Court shall be appointed by law; but there shall be one term at the seat of government annually. And at the close of each term the judges shall file with the Secretary of State, concise written statements of the decisions made at that term. *Or.,* 454.

—Until otherwise directed by law, the Courts of Common Pleas shall continue as at present established. Not more than five counties shall at any time be included in one judicial district organized for said courts. *Pa.,* 465.

—The Supreme Court shall be composed of three judges, one of whom shall reside in each of the grand divisions of the State; the concurrence of two of said judges shall in every case be necessary to a decision.

—The Supreme Court shall consist of five Justices, any three of whom shall constitute a quorum. They shall be elected by the qualified voters of the State at a general election for State or county officers, and they shall elect from their own number a presiding officer, to be styled the Chief Justice. *Tex.,* 510.

—The testimony in causes in equity. shall be taken in like manner as in cases at law; and the office of Master in Chancery is hereby prohibited. *Wis.,* 567.

—The Supreme Court shall hold at least one term annually, at the seat of government of the State, at at such time as shall be provided by law, and the Legislature may provide for holding other terms, and at other places, when they may deem it necessary. A Circuit Court shall be held at least twice in each year, in each county in this State, organized for judicial purposes. The Judge of the Circuit Court may hold courts for each other, and shall do so when required by law. *Wis.,* 566.

CIRCUIT COURTS.

—The State shall be divided, by law, into a convenient number of circuits, not less than four, nor exceeding eight, subject to alteration, by the Legislature, from time to time, as the public good may require; for each of which, a circuit judge shall be appointed, in the same manner, and hold his office by the same tenure, as the justices of the Supreme Court; and who shall possess the powers of a justice of the Supreme Court at chambers, and in the trial of issues joined in the Supreme Court; and in Courts of Oyer and Terminer, and gaol delivery. And such equity powers may be vested in the said circuit judges, or in the County Courts, or in such other subordinate courts as the Legislature may by law direct, subject to the appellate jurisdiction of the chancellor. *N. Y.* (1821) 41.,

—The State shall be divided into convenient circuits, each of which shall contain not less than three, nor more than six counties; and for each circuit there shall be appointed a judge, who shall, after his appointment, reside in the circuit for which he may be appointed. *Ala.,* 80.

—A Circuit Court shall be held in each county in the State, at least twice in every year; and the judges of the several circuits may hold courts for each other when they deem it expedient, and shall do so when directed by law. *Ala.,* 80.

—The Circuit Courts shall exercise a superintending control over the County Courts. and over Justices of the Peace in each county, in their respective circuits, and shall have power to issue all the necessary writs to carry into effect their general and specific powers. *Ark.,* 91.

—Judges of the Circuit Courts may temporarily exchange circuits, or hold courts for each other, under such regulations as may be pointed out by law. *Ark.,* 91.

—A Circuit Court shall be held in such counties and at such times and places therein as may be prescribed by law; and the judges of the several Circuit Courts may hold courts for each other, either for the entire circuit or for a portion thereof, and they shall do so when required, by order of the Governor or Chief Justice of the Supreme Court; and they may exercise jurisdiction in cases of writs of habeas corpus in any Judicial Circuit in which the judge may happen to be at the time the case arises. *Fl.,* 134.

—The General Assembly shall have power to establish and organize a separate court or courts of original equity jurisdiction; but until such court or courts shall be established and organized, the Circuit Courts shall exercise such jurisdiction. *Fl.,* 134.

—There shall be two more terms of the Circuit Court held, annually, in each county of this State, at such times as shall be provided by law; and said courts shall have jurisdiction in all cases at law and equity, and in all cases of appeal from all inferior courts. *Ill.,* 160.

—The Circuit Courts shall each consist of one Judge, and shall have such civil and criminal jurisdiction as may be prescribed by law. *Ind.,* 177.

1 § 5. The Legislature shall have the same powers to alter and regulate the
2 jurisdiction and proceedings in law and equity as they have heretofore
3 possessed.

1 § 6. Provision may be made by law for designating from time to time one
2 or more of the said justices, who is not a judge of the Court of Appeals, to

—The General Assembly may provide by law that the Judge of one circuit may hold the courts of another circuit, in cases of necessity or convenience; and in case of temporary inability of any judge, from sickness or other cause, to hold the courts in his circuit, provision shall be made by law for holding such courts. *Ind.*, 177.

—A Circuit Court shall be established in each county, now existing, or which may hereafter be erected in this Commonwealth. *Ky.*, 216.

—The Circuit Court shall be held twice, at least, in each year, in each county organized for judicial purposes, by one of the Justices of the Supreme Court, at times to be appointed by law; and at such other times as may be appointed by the judges severally in pursuance of law. *Or.*, 454.

—For each circuit, the thirteenth excepted, there shall be one Judge, who shall be styled Circuit Judge, who, during his term of office, shall reside in one of the counties composing the circuit for which he may be elected; the said judges shall hold a term of their courts in each of the counties comprising their respective circuits at such times as now are or may hereafter be fixed by law, such terms to be never less than two in each year in each county; special terms may be held by said judges in their discretion, whenever the business of their several counties renders such terms necessary. *Md.*, 268.

—The Judges of the respective Circuit Courts of this State, and of the courts of Baltimore city, shall render their decisions, in all cases argued before them, or submitted to their judgment, within two months after the same shall have been so argued or submitted. *Md.*, 268.

—A Circuit Court shall be held at least twice in each year in every county organized for judicial purposes, and four times in each year in counties containing ten thousand inhabitants. Judges of the Circuit Court may hold courts for each other, and shall do so when required by law. *Mich.*, 306.

—A Circuit Court shall be held in each county of this State, at least twice in each year; and the Judges of said courts, shall interchange circuits with each other, in such manner as may be prescribed by law, and shall receive for their services a compensation to be fixed by law, which shall not be diminished during their continuance in office. *Miss.*, 329.

—The Circuit Courts shall be held in every county of this State, by one or more of the justices of the Supreme Court, or a judge appointed for that purpose; and shall, in all places within the county, except in those of a criminal nature, have common law jurisdiction concurrent with the Supreme Court, and any final judgment of a Circuit Court may be docketted in the Supreme Court and shall operate as a judgment obtained in the Supreme Court from the time of such docketing. *N. J.*, 418.

—District Courts shall be composed of the Judges of the Courts of Common Pleas of the respective districts, and one of the Judges of the Supreme Court, any three of whom shall be a quorum, and shall be held in each county therein, at least once in each year; but if it shall be found inexpedient to hold such court annually, in each county of any district, the General Assembly may, for such district, provide that said court shall hold at least three annual sessions therein, in not less than three places; *Provided*, That the General Assembly may, by law, authorize the judges of each district to fix the times of holding the courts therein. *Ohio*, 437.
30

—The District Courts shall, in their respective counties, be the successors of the present Supreme Court, and all suits, prosecutions, judgments, records and proceedings, pending and remaining in said Supreme Court, in the several counties of any district, shall be transferred to the respective District Courts of such counties, and be proceeded in as though no change had been made in said Supreme Court. *Ohio*, 445.

—The General Assembly shall provide by law for holding Circuit Courts, when, for any cause, the judge shall fail to attend, or, if in attendance, cannot properly preside. *Ky.*, 217.

—A Circuit Court shall be held at least twice a year by the judge of each circuit, in every county and corporation thereof, wherein a Circuit Court is now or may hereafter be established. But the judges in the same district may be required or authorized to hold the courts of their respective circuits alternately, and a judge of one circuit to hold a court in any other circuit. *Va.*, 542.

—A District Court shall be held at least once a year in every district, by the judges of the circuits constituting the section and the Judge of the Supreme Court of Appeals for the section of which the district forms a part, any three of whom may hold a court; but no judge shall sit or decide upon an appeal taken from his own decision. The Judge of the Supreme Court of Appeals of one section may sit in District Courts of another section, when required or authorized by law to do so. *Va.*, 542.

—A Circuit Court shall be held in every county at least four times a year, unless otherwise provided by law, in pursuance of the third section of this article. The judges may be required or authorized to hold the courts of their respective circuits alternately, and a judge of one circuit to hold a court in any other circuit. *W. Va.*, 553.

JURISDICTION OF COURTS.

—The Judges of the Supreme Court shall, by virtue of their offices, be conservators of the peace throughout the State; as also the Judges of the Circuit Courts within their respective circuits, and the Judges of the Inferior courts within their respective counties. *Ala.*, 81.

—The Circuit Court shall have original jurisdiction in all matters, civil and criminal, within this State, not otherwise excepted in this Constitution: but in civil cases only, where the matter or sum in controversy exceeds fifty dollars. *Ala.*, 80.

—Except in cases otherwise directed in this Constitution, the Supreme Court shall have appellate jurisdiction only, which shall be co-extensive with the State, under such restrictions and regulations, not repugnant to this Constitution, as may from time to time be prescribed by law. *Provided*, That said court shall have power to issue writs of injunction, *mandamus, quo warranto, habeas corpus*, and such other remedial and original writs as may be necessary to give it a general superintendence and control of inferior jurisdictions. *Ala.*, 80.

—The Supreme Court, except in cases otherwise directed by this Constitution, shall have appellate jurisdiction only, which shall be co-extensive with the State, under such restrictions and regulations as may, from time to time be prescribed by law. *Ark.*, 90.

—It shall have a general superintending control over all inferior and other courts of law and equity. It

3 preside at the general term of the said court to be held in the several districts.

4 Any three or more of the said justices, of whom one of the said justices so

5 designated shall always be one, may hold such general terms. And any one

6 or more of the justices may hold special terms and Circuit Courts, and any

7 one of them may preside in Courts of Oyer and Terminer in any county.

shall have power to issue writs of error, supersedeas, certiorari and habeas corpus, mandamus and quo warranto, and other remedial writs, and to hear and determine the same. Said judges shall be conservators of the peace throughout the State, and shall have power to issue any of the aforesaid writs. *Ark.*, 90.
—The Circuit Court shall have original jurisdiction over all criminal cases which shall not be otherwise provided for by law; and exclusive original jurisdiction of all crimes amounting to felony at the common law, and original jurisdiction of all civil cases which shall not be cognizable before Justices of the Peace, until otherwise directed by the General Assembly; and original jurisdiction in all matters of contract, where the sum in controversy is over two hundred dollars. It shall hold its terms at such place in each county as may be by law directed. *Ark.*, 91.
—The Supreme Court shall have appellate jurisdiction in all cases in equity, also in all cases at law which involve the title or possession of real estate, or the legality of any tax, impost, assessment, toll, or municipal fine, or in which the demand, exclusive of interest, or the value of the property in controversy amounts to $300; also in all cases arising in the probate courts; and also in all criminal cases amounting to felony, on questions of law alone. The Court shall also have power to issue writs of mandamus, certiorari, prohibition, and habeas corpus, and also all writs necessary or proper to the complete exercise of its appellate jurisdiction. Each of the justices shall have power to issue writs of habeas corpus to any part of the State, upon petition on behalf of any person held in actual custody, and may make such writs returnable before himself, or the Supreme Court, or before any District Court, or any County Court in the State, or before any judge of said courts. *Cal,* (as amended in 1862.)
—The District Courts shall have original jurisdiction in all cases in equity; also in all cases at law which involve the title or possession of real property, or the legality of any tax, impost, assessment, toll or municipal fine, and in all other cases in which the demand, exclusive of interest, or the value of the property in controvery amounts to $300; and also in all criminal cases not otherwise provided for. The District Courts and their judges shall have power to issue writs of *habeas corpus*, on petition by or on behalf of any person held in actual custody in their respective districts. *Cal.,* (amended in 1862.)
—Said [County] Courts shall also have power to issue naturalization papers. *Cal.,* (amended in 1862.)
—The County Courts shall have original jurisdiction of actions of forcible entry and detainer, of proceedings of insolvency, of actions to prevent or abate a nuisance, and of all such special cases and proceedings as are not otherwise provided for; and also such criminal jurisdiction as the Legislature may prescribe. They shall also have appellate jurisdiction in all cases arising in courts held by Justices of the Peace and Recorders, and in such inferior courts as may be established in pursuance of section one of this article, in their respective counties. The County Judges shall also hold in their several counties Probate Courts, and perform such duties as Probate Judges as may be prescribed by law. The County Courts and their Judges shall have power to issue writs of *habeas corpus*, on petition or on behalf of any person in actual custody, in their respective counties. *Cal.,* (amended in 1862.)
—The Supreme Court, the District Courts, County

Courts, and Probate Courts, and such other courts as the Legislature shall prescribe, shall be courts of record. *Cal,* (amended in 1862).
—The Legislature shall fix by law the jurisdiction of Recorders' or other inferior municipal courts, which may be established in pursuance of section one of this article, and shall fix by law the powers, duties, and responsibilities of the judges thereof. *Cal,* (amended in 1862).
—The General Assembly, notwithstanding anything contained in this article, shall have power to repeal or alter any act of the General Assembly, giving jurisdiction to the Courts of Oyer and Terminer and General Jail Delivery, or to the Supreme Court, or the Court of Common Pleas, or the Court of General Quarter Sessions of the Peace and General Jail Delivery, or the Orphans' Court, or to the Court of Chancery, in any matter, or giving any power to either of said courts. Until the General Assembly shall otherwise direct, there shall be an appeal to the Court of Errors and Appeals in all cases in which there is an appeal, according to an act of the General Assembly, to the High Court of Errors and Appeals. *Del.* 123.
—The members of the Senate and House of Representatives, the Chancellor, the Judges, and the Attorney-General shall, by virtue of their offices, be conservators of the peace throughout the State; and the Treasurer, Secretary, Prothonotaries, Registers, Recorders, Sheriffs, and Coroners shall, by virtue of their offices, be conservators thereof within the counties respectively in which they reside. *Del.,* 125.
—The jurisdiction of each of the aforesaid courts, Superior Court, Chancery and Orphans' Court, shall be co-extensive with the State. Process may be issued out of each court, in either county, into every county. *Del.,* 122.
—The General Assembly may by law give to any inferior courts by them to be established, or to one or more Justices of the Peace, jurisdiction of the criminal matters following, that is to say, assaults and batteries, keeping without license a public house of entertainment, tavern, inn, ale house, ordinary or victualing house, retailing or selling without license wine, rum, brandy, gin, whiskey, or spirituous or mixed liquors contrary to law, disturbing camp-meetings held for the purpose of religious worship, disturbing other meetings for the purpose of religious worship, nuisances, horse-racing, cock-fighting and shooting matches, larcenies committed by negroes or mulattoes, and the offense of knowingly buying, receiving or concealing by negroes or mulattoes, of stolen goods and things the subject of larceny, and of any negro or mulatto being accessary to any larceny. The General Assembly may by law regulate this jurisdiction, and provide that the proceedings shall be with or without indictment by grand jury, or trial by petit jury, and may grant or deny the priviledge of appeal to the Court of General Sessions of the Peace. The matters within this section shall be and the same hereby are excepted and excluded from the provision of the Constitution, that—"No person shall for an indictable offense be proceeded against criminally by information," and also from the provision of the Constitution concerning trial by jury. *Del.,* 123.
—In civil causes when pending, the Superior Court shall have the power, before judgment, of directing upon such terms as they shall deem reasonable, amendments in pleadings and legal proceedings, so

that by error in any of them, the determination of causes, according to their real merits, shall not be hindered; and also of directing the examination of witnesses that are aged, very infirm, or going out of the State. upon interrogatories *de bene esse*, to be read in evidence, in case of the death or departure of the witnesses before the trial, or inability by reason of age, sickness, bodily infirmity or imprisonment, then to attend; and also the power of obtaining evidence from places not within this State. *Del.*, 123.

—The Supreme Court, except in cases otherwise directed in this Constitution, shall have appellate jurisdiction only, which shall be co-extensive with the State, under such restrictions and regulations, not repugnant to this Constitution, as may from time to time be prescribed by law, provided that the said court shall always have power to issue writs of injunction, *mandamus*, *quo warranto*, *habeas corpus*, and such other original and remedial writs as may be necessary to give it a general superintendence and control of all other courts. *Fl.*, 133.

—The Justices of the Supreme Court, Chancellors and Judges of the Circuit Courts, shall, by virtue of their offices, be conservators of the peace throughout the State. *Fl.*, 135.

—The Circuit Courts shall have original jurisdiction in all matters, civil and criminal, not otherwise excepted in this Constitution. *Fl.*, 134.

—The General Assembly shall by law authorize the Circuit Court to grant licenses for building toll-bridges, and to establish ferries, and to regulate the tolls of both, to construct dams across streams not navigable; to ascertain and declare what streams are navigable; but no special law for such purpose shall be made. *Fl.*, 133.

—The said [Supreme] court shall have no original jurisdiction, but shall be a court alone for the trial and correction of errors in law and equity' from the Superior Courts of the several circuits, and from the City Courts of the cities of Savannah and Augusta, and such other like courts as may be here-after established in other cities; and shall sit "at the seat of government" at such time or times in each year, as the General Assembly shall prescribe, for the trial and determination of writs of error from said courts. *Ga.*, 148.

—The said [Supreme] Court shall dispose of and finally determine every case on the docket of such court, at the first or second term after such writ of error brought, and in case the plaintiff in error shall not be prepared at the first term of such court, after error brought, to prosecute the case, unless precluded by some providential cause from such prosecution, it shall be stricken from the docket, and the judgment below affirmed. And in any case that may occur, the court may, in its discretion, withhold its judgment, until the term next after the argument thereon. *Ga.*, 148.

—The Superior Courts shall also have exclusive jurisdiction in all criminal cases, except as relates to fines for neglect of duty, contempts of court, violation of road laws, obstructions of water-courses, and in all other minor offenses which do not subject the offender or offenders to loss of life, limb or member, or to confinement in the penitentiary; jurisdiction of all such cases shall be vested in such County or Corporation Courts, or such other courts, judicatures, or tribunals as now exist, or may hereafter be constituted, under such rules and regulations as the Legislature may have directed, or may hereafter by law direct. *Ga.*, 148.

—The Superior Court shall have exclusive jurisdiction in all cases of divorce, both total and partial; but no total divorce shall be granted except on the concurrent verdicts of two special juries. In each divorce case the court shall regulate the rights and disabilities of the parties. *Ga.*, 148.

—The Superior Court shall have exclusive jurisdiction in all cases respecting titles to land, which shall be tried in the county where the land lies; and also in all equity causes which shall be tried in the county where one or more of the defendants reside, against whom substantial relief is prayed. *Ga.*, 148.

—It shall have appellate jurisdiction in all such cases as may be provided by law. *Ga.*, 149.

—It shall have power to issue writs of *mandamus*, prohibition, *scire facias*, and all other writs which may be necessary for carrying its powers fully into effect. *Ga.*, 149.

—The Superior Court shall have jurisdiction in all other civil cases, and in them the General Assembly may give concurrent jurisdiction to the inferior court, or such other County Courts as they may hereafter create, which cases shall be tried in the county where the defendant resides. *Ga.*, 149.

—In cases of joint obligors, or joint promisors or co-partners, or joint trespassers residing in different counties the suit may be brought in either county. *Ga.*, 149.

—In case of a maker and indorser, or indorsers of promissory notes residing in different counties in this State, the same may be sued in the county where the maker resides. *Ga.*, 149.

—The Supreme Court may have original jurisdiction in cases relative to the revenue, in cases of *mandamus*, *habeas corpus*, and in such cases of impeachment as may be by law directed to be tried before it, and shall have appellate jurisdiction in all other cases. *Ill.*, 160.

—On the first Monday of December, one thousand eight hundred and forty-eight, jurisdiction of all suits and proceedings, then pending in the present Supreme Court, shall become vested in the Supreme Court established by this Constitution, and shall be finally adjudicated by the Court where the same may be pending. The jurisdiction of all suits and proceedings then pending in Circuit Courts of the several counties shall be vested in the Circuit Courts of said counties. *Ill.*, 168.

—The Judges of the Supreme Court, elected as aforesaid, shall have and exercise the powers and jurisdiction conferred upon the present Judges of that Court; and the said Judges of the Circuit Courts shall have and exercise the powers and jurisdictions conferred upon the Judges of those Courts, subject to the provisions of this Constitution. *Ill.*, 168.

—The Supreme Court shall have jurisdiction co-extensive with the limits of the State, in appeals and writs of error, under such regulations and restrictions as may be prescribed by law. It shall also have such original jurisdiction as the General Assembly may confer. *Ind.*, 177.

—All judicial officers shall be conservators of the peace in their respective jurisdictions. *Ind.*, 177; (nearly similar), *Ky.*, 215; *La.*, 231; *Md.*, 266; *Mich.*, 306; *Tex.*, 511.

—The Supreme Court shall have appellate jurisdiction only in all cases in chancery, and shall constitute a Court for the Correction of Errors at law, under such restrictions as the General Assembly may, by law, prescribe; and shall have power to issue all writs and process necessary to secure justice to parties, and exercise a supervisory control over all inferior judicial tribunals throughout the State. *Iowa*, 189.

—The Judges of the Supreme and District Courts shall be conservators of the peace throughout the same. *Iowa*, 189.

—The District Court shall be a court of law and equity, which shall be distinct and separate jurisdictions, and have jurisdiction in civil and criminal matters arising in their respective districts, in such manner as shall be prescribed by law. *Iowa*, 189.

—The Supreme Court shall have original jurisdiction in proceedings in *quo warranto*, *mandamus*, and *habeas corpus*; and such appellate jurisdiction as may be provided by law. It shall hold one term each year at the seat of government, and such other terms at such places as may be provided by law, and its jurisdiction shall be co-extensive with the State. *Kan.*, 200.

—The District Courts shall have such jurisdiction in their respective districts as may be provided by law. *Kan.*, 201.

—The several Justices and Judges of the Courts of record in this State shall have such jurisdiction at chambers as may be provided by law. *Kan.*, 201.

—The jurisdiction of said [Circuit] Court shall be and remain as now established, hereby giving to the General Assembly the power to change or alter it. *Ky.*, 216.

—The Supreme Court, except in cases hereafter provided, shall have appellate jurisdiction only; which jurisdiction shall extend to all cases when the matter in dispute shall exceed three hundred dollars; to all cases in which the constitutionality or legality of any tax, toll or impost whatsoever, or of any fine, forfeiture or penalty imposed by a municipal corporation, shall be in contestation; and to all criminal cases on questions of law alone, whenever the offense charged is punishable with death or imprisonment at hard labor, or when a fine exceeding three hundred dollars is actually imposed. *La.*, 231.

—The Supreme Court, and each of the Judges thereof, shall have power to issue writs of *habeas corpus*, at the instance of all persons in actual custody under process, in all cases in which they may have appellate jurisdiction. *La.*, 231.

—The Legislature shall have power to vest in clerks of courts authority to grant such orders, and do such acts as may be deemed necessary for the furtherance of the administration of justice, and in all cases the powers thus granted shall be specified and determined. *La.*, 232.

—The judge or judges of any court of this State, except the Court of Appeals, shall order and direct the record of proceedings in any suit of action, issue or petition, presentment or indictment pending in such court, to be transmitted to some other court in the same or any adjoining circuit having jurisdiction in such cases, whenever any party to such cause, or the counsel of any party shall make it satisfactorily appear to the court that such party cannot have a fair and impartial trial in the court in which such suit or action, issue or petition, presentment or indictment is pending; and the General Assembly shall make such modifications of existing law as may be necessary to regulate and give force to this provision. *Md.*, 266.

—The several courts, except as herein otherwise provided, shall continue with like powers and jurisdiction, both at law and in equity, as if this Constitution had not been adopted, and until the organization of the Judicial Department provided by this Constitution. *Md.*, 276.

—The trial by jury of all issues of fact in civil proceedings in the several courts of law in this State, where the amount in controversy exceeds the sum of five dollars, shall be inviolably preserved. *Md.*, 277.

—One court shall be held in each county of the State: the said courts shall be called Circuit Courts for the county in which they may be held, and shall have and exercise all the power, authority and jurisdiction, original and appellate, which the present Circuit Courts of this State now have and exercise, or which may hereafter be prescribed by law. *Md.*, 267.

—The Circuit Courts shall have original jurisdiction in all matters civil and criminal, not excepted in this Constitution, and not prohibited by law; and appellate jurisdiction from all inferior courts and tribunals, and a supervisory control of the same. They shall also have power to issue writs of *habeas corpus, mandamus*, injunctions, *quo warranto, certiorari*, and other writs necessary to carry into effect their orders, judgments, and decrees, and give them a general control over inferior courts and tribunals within their respective jurisdictions. *Mich.*, 306.

—The Supreme Court shall have a general superintending control over all inferior courts, and shall have power to issue writs of error, *habeas corpus, mandamus, quo warranto, procedendo*, and other original and remedial writs, and to hear and determine the same. In all other cases it shall have appellate jurisdiction only. *Mich.*, 305.

—The Supreme Court shall have original jurisdiction in such remedial cases as may be prescribed by law, and appellate jurisdiction in all cases, both in law and equity, but there shall be no trial by jury in said court. *Min.*, 324.

—The District Courts shall have original jurisdiction in all civil cases, both in law and equity, where the amount in controversy exceeds one hundred dollars, and in all criminal cases where the punishment shall exceed three months' imprisonment, or a fine of more than one hundred dollars, and shall have such appellate jurisdiction as may ,be prescribed by law. The Legislature may provide by law that the judge of one district may discharge the duties of the judge of any other district not his own, when convenience or the public interest may require it. *Min.*, 324.

—The Circuit Court shall have original jurisdiction in all matters, civil and criminal, within this State; but in civil cases only when the principal of the sum in controversy exceeds fifty dollars. *Miss.*, 339.

—The judges of all the courts of the State, and also the members of the Board of County Police, shall in virtue of their offices be conservators of the peace, and shall be by law vested with ample powers in this respect. *Miss.*, 340.

—The Supreme Court, except in cases otherwise directed by this Constitution, shall have appellate jurisdiction only, which shall be co-extensive with the State, under the restrictions and limitations in this Constitution provided. *Mo.*, 357.

—The Supreme Court shall have a general superintending control over all inferior courts of law. It shall have power to issue writs of *habeas corpus, mandamus, quo warranto, certiorari*, and other original remedial writs, and to hear and determine the same. *Mo.*, 357.

—The Circuit Court shall have jurisdiction over all criminal cases, which shall not be otherwise provided for by law; and exclusive original jurisdiction in all civil cases, which shall not be cognizable before Justices of the Peace, until otherwise directed by the General Assembly. It shall hold its terms at such time and place in each county, as may be by law directed. *Mo.*, 358.

—The Circuit Court shall exercise a superintending control over all such inferior tribunals as the General Assembly may establish, and over Justices of the Peace in each county in their respective circuits. *Mo.*, 359.

—The jurisdiction of the several courts herein provided for, both appellate and original, shall be as fixed by law; *Provided*, That Probate Courts, Justices of the Peace or any inferior court that may be established by the Legislature shall not have jurisdiction in any matter wherein the title or boundaries of land may be in dispute. Nor shall either of the courts mentioned in this proviso have power to order or decree the sale or partition of real estate; *And, provided further*, That Justices of the Peace and such inferior courts as may be established by the Legislature, shall not have jurisdiction when the debt or sum claimed shall exceed one hundred dollars; and the jurisdiction of the District and Probate Courts, and Justices of the Peace shall be uniform throughout the State. *Neb.*, 379.

—The Supreme Court shall have appellate jurisdiction only except in cases relating to revenue, mandamus, *quo warranto, habeas corpus*, and such cases of impeachment as may be required to be tried before it; and both the Supreme and District Courts shall have both chancery and common law jurisdiction. *Neb.*, 375.

—The Supreme Court shall have appellate jurisdiction in all cases in equity; also in all cases at law in which is involved the title or right of possession to, or the possession of real estate or mining claims, or the legality of any tax, impost, assessment, toll, or municipal fine, or in which the demand, exclusive of interest or the value of the property in controversy, exceeds three hundred dollars; also in all other civil cases not included in the general subdivisions of law and equity, and also on questions of law alone in all criminal cases in which the offense charged amounts to felony. The court shall also have power to issue writs of *mandamus, certiorari*, prohibition, *quo warranto, habeas corpus*, and also all writs necessary or proper to the complete exercise of its appellate jurisdiction. Each of the justices shall have power to issue writs of *habeas corpus* to any part of the State upon petition by or on behalf of any person held in actual custody, and may make such writs returnable before himself or the Supreme Court, or before any district court of the State or before any judge of said courts. *Nev.*, 386.

—The District Courts in the several judicial districts of this State shall have original jurisdiction in all cases in equity; also, in all cases at law which involve the title, or the right of possession to, or the possession of real property or mining claims, or the legality of any tax, impost, assessment, toll or municipal fine, and in all other cases in which the demand, exclusive of interest, or the value of the property in controversy exceeds three hundred dollars; also, in all cases relating to estate of deceased persons, and the persons and estates of minors and insane persons, and of the action of forcible entry and unlawful detainer; and also in all criminal cases not otherwise provided for by law. They shall also have final appellate jurisdiction in cases arising in Justices' Courts, and such other inferior tribunals as may be established by law. The District Courts, and the judges thereof, shall have power to issue writs of *mandamus*, injunction, *quo warranto*, *certiorari*, and all other writs proper and necessary to the complete exercise of their jurisdiction, and also shall have power to issue writs of *habeas corpus* on petition by, or on behalf of, any person held in actual custody in their respective districts. *Nev.*, 387.

—The Legislature may vest in the Circuit Courts or Courts of Common Pleas, within the several counties of this State, chancery powers, so far as relates to the foreclosure of mortgages and sale of mortgaged premises. *N. Y.*, 415.

—The several Judges of the Supreme Court, of the Common Pleas, and of such other courts as may be created, shall, respectively, have and exercise such power and jurisdiction, at chambers, or otherwise, as may be directed by law. *Ohio*, 438.

—It [the Supreme Court] shall have original jurisdiction in *quo warranto*, *mandamus*, *habeas corpus* and *procedendo*, and such appellate jurisdiction as may be provided by law. *Ohio*, 437.

—The District Court shall have like original jurisdiction with the Supreme Court, and such appellate jurisdiction as may be provided by law. *Ohio*, 437.

—The jurisdiction of the Courts of Common Pleas, and of the Judges thereof, shall be fixed by law. *Ohio*, 437.

—The General Assembly shall have no power to pass, but may, by general laws, authorize courts to carry into effect, upon such terms as shall be just and equitable, the manifest intention of parties, and officers, by curing omissions, defects and errors, in instruments and proceedings, arising out of their want of conformity with the laws of this State. *Ohio*, 435.

—The Supreme Court shall have jurisdiction only to revise the final decisions of the Circuit Courts; and every cause shall be tried, and every decision shall be made by those judges only, or a majority of them, who did not try the cause, or make the decision in Circuit Court. *Or.*, 454.

—All judicial power, authority and jurisdiction not vested by this Constitution, or by laws consistent therewith, exclusively in some other court, shall belong to the Circuit Courts; and they shall have appellate jurisdiction, and supervisory control over the County Courts, and all other inferior courts, officers and tribunals. *Or.*, 454.

—The jurisdiction of the Supreme Court shall extend over the State, and the judges thereof shall, by virtue of their offices, be Justices of Oyer and Terminer and General Jail Delivery, in the several counties. *Pa.*, 465.

—The Supreme Court, and the several Courts of Common Pleas, shall, beside the powers heretofore usually exercised by them, have the powers of a Court of Chancery, so far as relates to the perpetuating of testimony, the obtaining of evidence from places not within the State, and the care of the persons and estates of those who are *non compotes mentis*. And

the Legislature shall vest in the said courts such other powers to grant relief in equity, as shall be found necessary; and may, from time to time, enlarge or diminish those powers or vest them in such other courts as they shall judge proper, for the due administration of justice. *Pa.*, 465.

—The President of the Court in each circuit within such circuit, and the Judges of the Court of Common Pleas within their respective counties, shall be Justices of the Peace, so far as relates to criminal matters. *Pa.*, 465.

—The several courts shall have such jurisdiction as may, from time to time, be prescribed by law. Chancery powers may be conferred on the Supreme Court, but on no other court to any greater extent than is now provided by law. *R. I.*, 479.

—The Supreme Court, established by this Constitution, shall have the same jurisdiction as the Supreme Judicial Court at present established, and shall have jurisdiction of all causes which may be appealed to, or pending in the same; and shall be held at the same time and places, and in each county, as the present Supreme Judicial Court, until otherwise prescribed by the General Assembly. *R. I.*, 481.

—The jurisdiction of this [the Supreme Court], shall be appellate only, under such restrictions and regulations as may from time to time be prescribed by law; but it may possess such other jurisdiction as is now conferred by law on the present Supreme Court. Said courts shall be held at one place, and at one place only, in each of the three grand divisions in the State. *Tenn.*, 496.

—Judges shall not charge juries with respect to matters of fact, but may state the testimony and declare the law. *Tenn.*, 496.

—The jurisdiction of such inferior courts, as the Legislature may from time to time establish, shall be regulated by law. *Tenn.*, 496.

—The Legislature shall have the right to vest such powers in the courts of justice, with regard to private and local affairs, as may be deemed expedient. *Tenn.*, 499.

—The Supreme Court shall have appellate jurisdiction only, which shall be co-extensive with the limits of the State; but in criminal cases below the grade of felony, and in appeals from interlocutory judgments, with such exceptions and under such regulations as the Legislature shall make; and the Supreme Court and the judges thereof, shall have power to issue the writ of *habeas corpus*, and under such regulations as may be prescribed by law, the said court and the Judges thereof, may issue the writ of *mandamus*, and such other writs as may be necessary to enforce its own jurisdiction. The Supreme Court shall also have power upon affidavit, or otherwise, as by the court may be thought proper, to ascertain such matters of fact as may be necessary to the proper exercise of its jurisdiction. The Supreme Court shall sit for the transaction of business, from the first Monday of October until the last Saturday of June of every year, at the capital, and at not more than two other places in the State. *Tex.*, 510.

—The District Court shall have original jurisdiction of all criminal cases; of all suits in behalf of the State to recover penalties, forfeitures and escheats; of all cases of divorce; of all suits to recover damages for slander or defamation of character; of all suits for the trial of title of land; of all suits for the enforcement of liens; of all suits for the trial of the right of property, levied on by virtue of any writ of execution, sequestration or attachment, when the property levied on shall be equal to, or exceed in value one hundred dollars; and of all suits, complaints or pleas whatever, without regard to any distinction between law and equity, when the matter in controversy shall be valued at, or amount to, one hundred dollars, exclusive of interest; and the said courts and the judges thereof shall have power to issue writs of injunction, *certiorari*, and all other writs necessary to enforce their own jurisdiction, and to give them a general superintendence and control over inferior tribunals. The District Courts shall

31

have appellate jurisdiction in cases originating in inferior courts, which may be final in such cases as the Legislature may prescribe; and original and appellate jurisdiction and general control over the County Court established in each county, for appointing guardians, granting letters testamentary and of administration; for settling the accounts of executors, administrators and guardians, and for the transaction of business appertaining to estates; and original jurisdiction and general control over executors, administrators, guardians and minors, under such regulations as may be prescribed by law. *Tex.,* 510.

—The District Courts shall not have original jurisdiction, except in cases of *habeas corpus, mandamus* and prohibition. *Va.,* 542.

—The Circuit Courts shall have the supervision and control of all proceedings before justices and other inferior tribunals, by *mandamus,* prohibition *or certiorari.* They shall, except in cases confided exclusively by this Constitution to some other tribunal, have original and general jurisdiction of all matters at law, where the amount in controversy, exclusive of interest, exceeds twenty dollars, and of all cases in equity, and of all crimes and misdemeanors. They shall have appellate jurisdiction in all cases, civil and criminal, where an appeal, writ of error or *supersedeas* may be allowed to the judgment or proceedings of any inferior tribunal. They shall also have such other jurisdiction, whether supervisory, original, appellate or concurrent, as may be prescribed by law. *W. Va.,* 553.

—The Circuit Courts shall have power, under such general regulations as may be prescribed by law, to grant divorces, change the names of persons, and direct the sales of estates belonging to infants and other persons under legal disabilities, but relief shall not be granted by special legislation in such cases. *W. Va.,* 557.

—The Supreme Court, except in cases otherwise provided in this Constitution, shall have appellate jurisdiction only, which shall be co-extensive with the State; but in no case removed to the Supreme Court, shall a trial by jury be allowed. The Supreme Court shall have a general superintending control over all inferior courts; it shall have power to issue writs of *habeas corpus, mandamus, injunction, quo warranto, certiorari,* and other original and remedial writs, and to hear and determine the same. *Wis.,* 565.

—The Circuit Courts shall have original jurisdiction in all matters, civil and criminal, within this State, not excepted in this Constitution, and not hereafter prohibited by law, an appellate jurisdiction from all inferior courts and tribunals, and a supervisory control over the same. They shall also have the power to issue writs of *habeas corpus, mandamus, injunction, quo warranto, certiorari,* and all other writs necessary to carry into effect their orders, judgments and decrees, and give them a general control over inferior courts and jurisdictions. *Wis.,* 566.

JUDGES TO GIVE OPINIONS.

—The judges of all courts within the State, shall, as often as it may be advisable so to do, in every definite judgment refer to the particular law in virtue of which such judgment may be rendered, and in all cases adduce the reasons on which their judgment is founded. *La.,* 231.

—They shall be obliged to give their opinion upon important questions of law, and upon solemn occasions, when required by the Governor, Council, Senate, or House of Representatives. *Me.,* 246.

—Each branch of the Legislature, as well as the Governor and Council, shall have authority to require the opinions of the Justices of the Supreme Judicial Court, upon important questions of law, and upon solemn occasions. *Mass.,* 290; *N. H.,* 403.

—The Judges of the Supreme Court shall give their opinion upon important questions of Constitutional

law, and upon solemn occasions, when required by the Governor, the Senate or the House of Representatives; and all such opinions shall be published in connection with the reported decisions of said court. *Mo.,* 358.

JUDGES TO CHARGE JURIES.

—Judges shall not charge juries with regard to matter of fact, but may state the testimony and declare the law. *Ark.,* 91; *Cal.,* 102; *Nev.,* 382.

—The Judges of the Supreme Court shall, in all trials, instruct the jury in the law. They shall also give their written opinion upon any question of law whenever requested by the Governor, or by either House of the General Assembly. *R. I.,* 479.

CHANGE OF VENUE.

—The General Assembly shall not change the venue in any criminal or penal prosecution, but shall provide for the same by general laws. *Ky.,* 212.

—The Legislature shall provide by law for all change of venue in civil and criminal cases. *La.,* 234.

—The General Assembly shall provide by law for the indictment and trial of persons charged with the commission of any felony in any county other than that in which the offense was committed, whenever, owing to prejudice, or any other cause, an impartial grand or petit jury cannot be impanneled in the county in which such offense was committed. *Mo.,* 302.

—The Legislature shall provide for a change of venue in civil and criminal cases, and for the erection of a penitentiary at as early a day as practicable. *Tex.,* 316.

—All criminal cases shall be tried in the county where the crime was committed, except in cases where a jury cannot be obtained. *Ga.,* 148.

COSTS.

—No costs shall be paid by a person accused on a bill being returned ignoramus, nor on acquittal by a jury. *Del.,* 125.

—At any time pending an action for debt or damages, the defendant may bring into court a sum of money for discharging the same, and the costs then accrued, and the plaintiff not accepting thereof, it shall be delivered for his use to the Clerk or Prothonotary of the court; and if, upon the final decision of the cause, the plaintiff shall not recover a greater sum than that so paid into court for him, he shall not recover any costs accruing after such payment, except where the plaintiff is an executor or administrator. *Del.,* 123.

—The Legislature shall by law provide that on the entry or commencement of any suit in the District Court, the party so commencing or entering such suit, shall, before the same is commenced or entered, pay to the Clerk of the District Court the sum of five dollars; and in like manner on the entry or commencement of any suit in the Supreme Court, shall pay the sum of ten dollars to the clerk thereof, which money so paid, shall be for the use of the State, and shall be paid by said clerks to the proper offices designated by law, as by law may be required; which money so received shall be held and esteemed as a judiciary fund, and to be applied in payment of the salaries of the Justices of the Supreme Court. Which amounts so paid shall be taxed as costs against the unsuccessful party, and collected as other costs; *Provided,* the Legislature may provide, by law for dispensing with the payment of said sums of money in cases where the party so commencing or entering suit shall be really unable to pay the same, and the amount shall in all cases be taxed and collected as other costs; *Provided, also,* That the Legislature shall have power whenever the amount so received shall exceed the salaries of the Judges of the Supreme Court, to reduce the amount to be paid so that the gross amount will not exceed such salaries. *Neb.,* 375.

1   § 7. The judges of the Court of Appeals and justices of the Supreme

2 Court shall severally receive at stated times, for their services, a compensation

3 to be established by law, which shall not be increased or diminished during

4 their continuance in office.

1   § 8. They shall not hold any other office or public trust. All votes for

2 either of them, for any elective office (except that of justice of the Supreme

3 Court, or judge of the Court of Appeals), given by the Legislature or the

4 people, shall be void. They shall not exercise any power of appointment to

5 public office. Any male citizen of the age of twenty-one years, of good moral

6 character, and who possesses the requisite qualifications of learning and

7 ability, shall be entitled to admission to practice in all the courts of this State.

SALARIES OF JUDGES — PROHIBITION AGAINST FEES.

—The judges of the Supreme Court, Circuit Courts and Courts of Chancery, shall, at stated times, receive for their services a compensation, which shall be fixed by law, and which shall not be diminished during their continuance in office; but they shall receive no fees or perquisites of office, nor hold any office of profit or trust under this State, the United States, or any other power. *Ala.*, 80.

—The Judges of the Supreme Courts and Circuit Courts shall, at stated times, receive a compensation for their services, to be ascertained by law, which shall not be diminished during the time for which they are elected. *Ark.*, 91.

—The presiding Judge of the Probate and County Court, and Justices of the Peace, shall receive for their services such compensation and fees as the General Assembly may from time to time by law direct. *Ark.*, 91.

—No judicial officer except a Justice of the Peace, Recorders and Commissioners, shall receive to his own use any fees or perquisites of office. *Cal.* (as amended in 1862.)

—The Justices of the Supreme Court, District Judges, and County Judges, shall severally, at stated times during their continuance in office, receive for their services a compensation, which shall not be increased or diminished during the term for which they shall have been elected; *Provided*, That County Judges shall be paid out of the county treasury of their respective counties. *Cal.* (as amended in 1862.)

—And receive for their services a compensation which shall be fixed by law and paid quarterly, and shall not be less than the following sums, that is to say :— the annual salary of the Chief Justice shall not be less than the sum of one thousand two hundred dollars; and the annual salary of the Chancellor shall not be less than the sum of one thousand one hundred dollars; and the annual salaries of the Associate Judges, respectively, shall not be less than the sum of one thousand dollars each. *Del.*, 123.

—The judges shall have salaries adequate to their services fixed by law, which shall not be diminished nor increased during their continuance in office; but shall not receive any other perquisites or emoluments whatever, from parties or others, on account of any duty required of them. *Ga.*, 149.

—The Judges of the Supreme Court shall receive a salary of twelve hundred dollars per annum, payable quarterly, and no more. The Judges of the Circuit Courts shall receive a salary of one thousand dollars

per annum, payable quarterly, and no more. *Ill.*, 160.

—The Judges of the Supreme Court, and Circuit Courts shall at stated times, receive a compensation, which shall not be diminished during their continuance in office. *Ind.*, 177; *Mo.*, 359.

—The salary of each Judge of the Supreme Court shall be two thousand dollars per annum; and that of each District Judge, sixteen hundred dollars per annum, until the year 1860, after which time they shall severally receive such compensation as the General Assembly may by law prescribe; which compensation shall not be increased or diminished during the term for which they shall have been elected. *Iowa*, 189.

—The Justices of the Supreme Court and Judges of the District Courts shall, at stated times, receive for their services such compensation as may be provided by law, which shall not be increased during their respective terms of office; *Provided*, Such compensation shall not be less than fifteen hundred dollars to each justice or judge, each year. *Kan.*, 201.

—The Judges of the Circuit Courts shall, at stated times, receive for their services an adequate compensation, to be fixed by law, which shall be equal and uniform throughout the State, and which shall not be diminished during the time for which they were elected. *Ky.*, 216.

—The Chief Justice shall receive a salary of seven thousand five hundred dollars, and each of the Associate Justices a salary of seven thousand dollars annually, until otherwise provided by law. The court shall appoint its own clerks. *La.*, 231.

—The judges, both of the Supreme and Inferior Courts, shall receive a salary, which shall not be diminished during their continuance in office; and they are prohibited from receiving any fees of office or other compensation than their salaries for any civil duties performed by them. *La.*, 232.

—The Justices of the Supreme Judicial Court shall, at stated times, receive a compensation, which shall not be diminished during their continuance in office, but they shall receive no other fee or reward. *Me.*, 246.

—The salary of the Justices of the Court of Appeals shall be three thousand dollars each per annum, payable quarterly. *Md.*, 267.

—The salary of each Judge of the Circuit Court shall be twenty-five hundred dollars per annum, payable quarterly, and shall not be increased or diminished during his continuance in office. *Md.*, 268.

—And no fees or perquisites, commission or reward of any kind, shall be allowed to any judge in this State, besides his annual salary or fixed per diem for the discharge of any official duty. *Md.*, 266.

—Permanent and honorable salaries shall also be established by law for the Justices of the Supreme Judicial Court. *Mass.*, 289; (nearly similar), *N. H.*, 407.

—And if it shall be found that any of the salaries aforesaid, so established, are insufficient, they shall, from time to time, be enlarged, as the General Court shall judge proper. *Mass.*, 289.

—The Judges of the Circuit Court shall each receive an annual salary of one thousand five hundred dollars; the State Treasurer shall receive an annual salary of one thousand dollars; the Auditor-General shall receive an annual salary of one thousand dollars; the Superintendent of Public Instruction shall receive an annual salary of one thousand dollars; the Secretary of State shall receive an annual salary of eight hundred dollars; the Commissioner of the Land Office shall receive an annual salary of eight hundred dollars; the Attorney-General shall receive an annual salary of eight hundred dollars. They shall receive no fees or perquisites whatever, for the performance of any duties connected with their offices. It shall not be competent for the Legislature to increase the salaries herein provided. *Mich.*, 308.

—Each of the Judges of the Circuit Court shall receive a salary payable quarterly. *Mich.*, 306.

—The Judges of the Supreme and District Courts shall be men learned in the law, and shall receive such compensation, at stated times, as may be prescribed by the Legislature, which compensation shall not be diminished during their continuance in office, but they shall receive no other fee or reward for their services. *Minn.*, 324.

—The judges of said court shall receive for their services a compensation to be fixed by law, which shall not be diminished during their continuance in office. *Miss.*, 339.

—The salary of the Justices of the Supreme Court shall be two thousand dollars each per annum and no more; and all other judicial officers shall be paid for their services in fees to be prescribed by law. *N. J.*, 376.

—No judicial officer, except Justice of the Peace and City Recorders, shall receive to his own use any fees or perquisites of office. *Nev.*, 387.

—The Justices of the Supreme Court and District Judges shall each receive quarterly, for their services, a compensation to be fixed by law, and which shall not be increased or diminished during the term for which they shall have been elected, unless a vacancy occurs, in which case a successor of the former incumbent shall receive only such salary as may be provided by law at the time of his election or appointment; and provision shall be made by law for setting apart from each year's revenue a sufficient amount of money to pay such compensation; *Provided*, That District Judges shall be paid out of the treasuries of the counties composing their respective districts. *Nev.*, 387.

—The Judges of the several District Courts of this State shall be paid as hereinbefore provided, salaries at the following rates per annum: First Judicial District (each judge), $6,000; Second Judicial District, $4,000; Third Judicial District, $5,000; Fourth Judicial District, $5,000; Fifth Judicial District, $3,600; Sixth Judicial District, $4,000; Seventh Judicial District, $6,000; Eighth Judicial District, $3,600; Ninth Judicial District, $5,000. *Nev.*, 395.

—The salary of any Judge in said judicial districts may, by law, be altered or changed, subject to the provisions contained in this Constitution. *Nev.*, 395.

—Such of the six judges as shall attend the court shall receive, respectively, a per diem compensation, to be provided by law. *N. J.*, 417.

—That the Governor, Judges of the Supreme Court of law and equity, Judges of Admiralty, and Attorney-General, shall have adequate salaries during their continuance in office. *N. C.*, 425.

—The Judges of the Supreme Court and of the Court of Common Pleas, shall, at stated times, receive for their services such compensation as may be provided by law, which shall not be diminished or

increased during their term of office, but they shall receive no fees or perquisites. *Ohio*, 431.

—The Judges of the Supreme Court shall each receive an annual salary of two thousand dollars. They shall receive no fees or perquisites whatever for the performance of any duties connected with their respective offices, and the compensation of officers, if not fixed by this Constitution, shall be provided by law. *Or.*, 457.

—The Judges of the Supreme Court shall receive a compensation for their services, which shall not be diminished or increased during their continuance in office. *R. I.*, 480.

—The Judges of the Supreme and inferior courts shall, at stated times, receive a compensation for their services, to be ascertained by law, which shall not be increased or diminished during the time for which they are elected. They shall not be allowed any fees or perquisites of office, nor hold any other office of trust or profit under this State or the United States. *Tenn.*, 496.

—Judges shall be commissioned by the Governor, and shall receive fixed and adequate salaries, which shall not be diminished during their continuance in office. The salary of a Judge of the Supreme Court of Appeals shall not be less than three thousand dollars, and that of a Judge of the Circuit Court not less than two thousand dollars per annum, except that of the Judge of the fifth circuit, which shall not be less than fifteen hundred dollars per annum, and each shall receive a reasonable allowance for necessary travel. *Va.*, 542.

—Judges shall be commissioned by the Governor. The salary of a Judge of the Supreme Court of Appeals shall be two thousand, and that of a Judge of a Circuit Court eighteen hundred dollars per annum, and each shall receive the same allowance for necessary travel as members of the Legislature. *W. Va.*, 553.

—Each of the Judges of the Supreme and Circuit Courts shall receive a salary, payable quarterly, of not less than one thousand five hundred dollars annually. *Wis.*, 566.

TERM OF OFFICE OF JUDGES.

—The Chancellor, the Judges of the Supreme Court, and first Judge of the County Court in every county, hold their offices during good behavior, or until they shall have respectively attained the age of sixty years.

—The Chancellor and Justices of the Supreme Court shall hold their offices during good behavior, or until they shall attain the age of sixty years. *N. Y.* (1821), 40.

—The Judges of the several Courts of this State shall hold their offices for the term of six years; and the right of any judge to hold his office for the full term hereby prescribed shall not be affected by any change hereafter made by law in any circuit or district, or in the mode or time of election.

Immediately after such election by the people, the Lieutenant-Governor and Speaker of the House of Representatives shall proceed, by lot, to divide the judges into three classes. The commission of the first class shall expire at the end of four years; of the second class, at the end of six years; and of the third class at the end of eight years; so that one-third of the whole number shall be chosen every four, six and eight years. *Ark.*, 91.

—The District Judges shall hold their offices for the term of six years from the first day of January next after their election. The Legislature shall have no power to grant leave of absence to a judicial officer and any such officer who shall absent himself from the State for upwards of thirty consecutive days, shall be deemed to have forfeited his office. *Cal.*, (as amended in 1862.)

—The County Judges shall hold their offices for the term of four years from the first day of January next after their election. *Cal.*, (as amended in 1862.)

—In order that no inconvenience may result to the public service from the taking effect of the amendments proposed to said article six by the Legislature of 1861, no officer shall be superceded thereby, nor shall the organization of the several courts be changed thereby, until the election and qualification of the several officers provided for in said amendments. *Cal.*, (as amended in 1862.)

—The Chancellor and Judges shall respectively hold their offices during good behavior. *Del.*, 123.

—On the first Monday in December, one thousand eight hundred and forty-eight, the term of office of Judges of the Supreme Court, State's Attorneys, and of the Clerks of the Supreme and Circuit Courts, shall expire; and on the said day, the term of office of the Judges, State's Attorneys, and Clerks elected under the provisions of this Constitution, shall commence. *Ill.*, 168.

—All judicial officers shall hold their offices until their successors shall have qualified. *Kan.*, 201.

—The Judges first elected shall serve as follows, to wit: one shall serve until the first Monday in August, 1852; one until the first Monday in August, 1854; one until the first Monday in August, 1856, and one until the first Monday in August, 1858. The judges, at the first term of the court succeeding their election, shall determine, by lot, the length of time which each one shall serve; and at the expiration of the service of each, an election in the proper district shall take place to fill the vacancy. The judge having the shortest time to serve shall be styled the Chief Justice of Kentucky. *Ky.*, 215.

—The Judges of the Circuit Court shall, after their first term, hold their office for the term of six years from the day of their election. They shall be commissioned by the Governor, and continue in office until their successors be qualified, but shall be removable from office in the same manner as the Judges of the Court of Appeals; and the removal of a Judge from his district shall vacate his office. *Ky.*, 216.

—The first election of County Court Judges shall take place at the same time of the election of Judges of the Circuit Court. The Presiding Judge, first elected, shall hold his office until the first Monday in August, 1854. The Associate Judges shall hold their offices until the first Monday in August, 1852, and until their successors be qualified; and afterwards elections shall be held on the first Monday in August, in the years in which vacancies regularly occur. *Ky.*, 217.

—All judicial officers now in office, or who may be hereafter appointed, shall, from and after the first day of March in the year 1840, hold their offices for the term of seven years from the time of their respective appointments, unless sooner removed by impeachment or by address of both branches of the Legislature to the Executive, and no longer, unless re-appointed thereto. *Me.*, 252.

—The present Judges of the Circuit Courts shall continue to act as Judges of the respective Circuit Courts within the judicial circuits in which they respectively reside, until the expiration of the term for which they were respectively elected, and until their successors are elected and qualified, viz.: the present judges of the first, second, third, fourth, sixth and eighth judicial circuits, as organized at the time of the adoption of this Constitution, shall continue to act as judges respectively of the first, second, fourth, fifth, ninth and twelfth judicial circuits as organized under the Constitution; and an election of judges of the third, sixth, seventh, eighth, tenth and eleventh judicial circuits shall be held on the Tuesday next after the first Monday in the month of November, in the year eighteen hundred and sixty-four. *Md.*, 269.

—On the first day of January, in the year one thousand eight hundred and fifty-two, the terms of office of the Judges of the Supreme Court, under existing laws, and of the Judges of the County Courts, and of the Clerks of the Supreme Court, shall expire on the said day. *Mich.*, 316.

—The Judges of the Supreme Court shall be elected by the electors of the State at large, and their term of office shall be seven years, and until their successors are elected and qualified. *Minn.*, 324.

—The office of one of said Judges shall be vacated in two years, and of one in four years, and of one in six years, so that at the expiration of every two years, one of said judges shall be elected as aforesaid. *Miss.*, 338.

—The Judges of the Supreme Court shall hold office for the term of six years, and until their successors shall be duly elected and qualified, except as hereinafter provided. *Mo.*, 357.

—The Judges of the Supreme Court and District Judges provided to be elected at the first election under this Constitution, shall qualify and enter upon the duties of their respective offices on the first Monday of December succeeding their election. *Nev.*, 395.

—The tenure that all commissioned officers shall have by law in their offices shall be expressed in their respective commissions. All judicial officers, duly appointed, commissioned and sworn, shall hold their offices during good behavior, excepting those concerning whom there is a different provision made in this Constitution. *N. H.*, 408.

—It is essential to the preservation of the rights of every individual, his life, liberty, property and character, that there be an impartial interpretation of the laws and administration of justice. It is the right of every citizen to be tried by judges as impartial as the lot of humanity will admit. It is, therefore, not only the best policy, but for the security of the rights of the people, that the Judges of the Supreme Judicial Court should hold their offices so long as they behave well; subject, however, to such limitations on account of age as may be provided by the Constitution of the State; and that they should have honorable salaries, ascertained and established by standing laws. *N. H.*, 401.

—The Justices of the Supreme Court and Chancellor shall hold their offices for the term of seven years; shall, at stated times, receive for their services a compensation, which shall not be diminished during the term of their appointment; and they shall hold no other office under the government of this State or of the United States. *N. J.*, 419.

—Immediately after the court shall first assemble, the six judges shall arrange themselves in such manner that the seat of one of them shall be vacated every year, in order that thereafter one judge may be annually appointed. *N. J.*, 417.

—They [the Judges of the Court of Common Pleas], shall hold their offices for five years; but when appointed to fill vacancies, they shall hold for the unexpired term only. *N. J.*, 419.

—The Judges of the Supreme Court shall, immediately after the first election under this Constitution, be classified by lot, so that one shall hold for the term of one year, one for two years, one for three years, one for four years and one for five years; and at all subsequent elections, the term of each of said judges shall be for five years. *Ohio*, 437.

—The Judges of the Courts of Common Pleas shall, while in office, reside in the district for which they are elected; and their term of office shall be for five years. *Ohio*, 437.

—The judges first chosen under this Constitution shall allot among themselves their terms of office, so that the term of one of them shall expire in two years, one in four years, and two in six years; and thereafter one or more shall be chosen every two years, to serve for the term of six years. *Or.*, 454.

—The Judges of the Supreme Court, of the several Courts of Common Pleas, and of such other courts of record as are or shall be established by law, shall be nominated by the Governor, and by and with the consent of the Senate appointed and commissioned by him. The Judges of the Supreme Court shall hold their offices for the term of fifteen years, if they shall so long behave themselves well. *Pa.*, 464.

—The Associate Judges of the Courts of Common

Pleas shall hold their offices for the term of five years, if they shall so long behave themselves well. *Pa.*, 464.

—The commissions of the Judges of the Supreme Court who may be in office on the first day of January next, shall expire in the following manner:—The commission which bears the earliest date shall expire on the first day of January, Anno Domini one thousand eight hundred and forty-two; the commission next dated shall expire on the first day of Jaunary, Anno Domini one thousand eight hundred and forty-five; the commission next dated shall expire on the first day of January, Anno Domini one thousand eight hundred and forty-eight; the commission next dated shall expire on the first day of January, Anno Domini one thousand eight hundred and fifty-one; and the commission last dated shall expire on the first day of January, Anno Domini one thousand eight hundred and fifty-four. *Pa.*, 469.

—The commissions of the President Judges of the several judicial districts, and of the Associate Law Judges of the First Judicial District shall expire as follows:—The commissions of one-half of those who shall have held their offices ten years or more, at the adoption of the amendments to the Constitution, shall expire on the twenty-seventh day of February, one thousand eight hundred and forty-nine; the commissions of the other half of those who shall have held their offices ten years or more, at the adoption of the amendments to the Constitution, shall expire on the twenty-seventh day of February, one thousand eight hundred and forty-two; the first half to embrace those whose commissions shall bear the oldest date. The commissions of all the remaining judges who shall not have held their offices for ten years at the adoption of the amendments to the Constitution, shall expire on the twenty-seventh day of February next after the end of ten years from the date of their commissions. *Pa.*, 469.

—The Legislature, at its first session under the amended Constitution, shall divide the other Associate Judges of the State into four classes. The commissions of those of the first class shall expire on the twenty-seventh day of February, eighteen hundred and forty; of those of the second class on the twenty-seventh day of February, eighteen hundred and forty-one; of those of the third class on the twenty-seventh day of February, eighteen hundred and forty-two; and of those of the fourth class on the twenty-seventh day of February, eighteen hundred and forty-three. The said classes, from the first to the fourth, shall be arranged according to the seniority of the commissions of the several judges. *Pa.*, 469.

—For each circuit a judge shall be chosen in the manner hereinbefore provided, who shall hold his office for the term of eight years unless sooner removed in the manner prescribed by this Constitution. He shall, at the time of being chosen, be at least thirty years of age, and shall have resided in the State one year next preceding his election, and during his continuance in office shall reside in the circuit of which he is judge. *Va.*, 541.

—For each section a judge shall be chosen in the manner hereinbefore provided, who shall hold his office for the term of twelve years unless sooner removed in the manner prescribed by this Constitution. He shall, at the time of his being chosen be at least thirty years of age, and shall have resided in the State one year next preceding his election, and during his continuance in office he shall reside in the section for which he is chosen. *Va.*, 542.

—Judges and all other officers, whether elected or appointed, shall continue to discharge the duty of their offices after their terms of service have expired, until their successors are qualified. *Va.*, 543.

—For each circuit a judge shall be elected by the voters thereof, who shall hold his office for the term of six years. During his continuance in office he shall reside in the circuit of which he is judge. *W. Va.*, 553.

JUDGES MAY HOLD NO OTHER OFFICE.

—That the Chancellor, and Judges of the Supreme Court shall not, at the same time, hold any other office, excepting that of delegate to the General Congress, upon special occasions; and that the first Judges of the County Courts, in the several counties, shall not, at the same time, hold any other office, excepting that of Senator, or Delegate to the General Congress. But if the Chancellor, or either of the said judges, be elected or appointed to any other office, excepting as is before excepted, it shall be at his option in which to serve. *N. Y.* (1777), 30.

—Neither the Chancellor nor Justices of the Supreme Court, nor any circuit judge, shall hold any other office or public trust. All votes for any elective office, given by the Legislature or the people, for the Chancellor or a Justice of the Supreme Court, or Circuit Judge, during his continuance in judicial office shall be void. *N. Y.* (1821), 41.

—They shall not be allowed any fees or perquisites of office, nor hold any other office or trust or profit under this State or the United States. *Ark.*, 91.

—The Justices of the Supreme Court and the District Judges and County Judges, shall be ineligible to any other office than a judicial office during the term for which they shall have been elected. *Cal.*, (as amended in 1862.)

—They shall hold no other office of profit, nor receive any fees or perquisites in addition to their salaries for business done by them. *Del.*, 123

—The Judges of the Supreme and Circuit Courts shall not be eligible to any other office or public trust, of profit in this State or the United States, during the term for which they are elected, nor for one year thereafter. All votes for either of them for any elective office (except that of Judge of the Supreme or Circuit Courts), given by the General Assembly, or the people, shall be void. *Ill.*, 160.

—No person elected to any judicial office shall, during the term for which he shall have been elected, be eligible to any office of trust or profit under the State, other than a judicial office. *Ind.*, 177.

—And such justices or judges shall receive no fees or perquisites, nor hold any other office of profit or trust under the authority of the State, or of the United States, during the term of office for which such justices and judges shall be elected, nor practice law in any of the courts in the State during their continuance in office. *Kan.*, 201.

—The Justices of the Supreme Judicial Court shall hold no office under the United States, nor any State nor any other office under this State, except that of Justice of the Peace. *Me.*, 246.

—No person holding the office of Justice of the Supreme Judicial Court, or of any inferior court, Attorney-General, County Attorney, Treasurer of the State, Adjutant-General, Judge of Probate, Register of Probate, Register of Deeds, Sheriffs or their deputies, Clerks of the Judicial Courts, shall be a member of the Legislature; and any person holding either of the foregoing offices, elected to and accepting a seat in the Congress of the United States, shall thereby vacate said office; and no person shall be capable of holding or exercising, at the same time, within this State, more than one of the offices before mentioned. *Me.*, 247.

—No judge of any court of this Commonwealth (except the Court of Sessions), and no person holding any office under the authority of the United States (Postmasters excepted), shall, at the same time hold the office of Governor, Lieutenant-Governor or Councillor, or have a seat in the Senate or House of Representatives of this Commonwealth; and no judge of any court in this Commonwealth (except the Court of Sessions), nor the Attorney-General [Solicitor-General, County Attorney], Clerk of any court, Sheriff, Treasurer and Receiver-General, Register of Probate, nor Register of Deeds, shall continue to hold his said office after being elected a member of the Congress of the United States, and accepting that trust; but the acceptance of such trust by any of the officers aforesaid, shall be deemed and taken to be a resignation of his said office; [and Judges of the Courts of Common Pleas shall hold no other office under the government of this Commonwealth, the office of Justice of the Peace and militia officers excepted.] *Mass.*, 295.

—They shall be ineligible to any other than a judicial office during the term for which they are elected, and one year thereafter. All votes for any person elected such judge for any office other than judicial, given either by the Legislature or the people, shall be void. *Mich.*, 306.

—The Justices of the Supreme Court and the District Courts, shall hold no office under the United States, nor any other office under this State. And all votes for either of them for any elective office under this Constitution, except a judicial office, given by the Legislature or the people, during their continuance in office shall be void. *Minn.*, 325.

—No Judge of any court of law or equity, Secretary of State, Attorney-General, Clerk of any Court of Record, Sheriff or Collector, or any person holding a lucrative office under the United States or this State, shall be eligible to the Legislature; *Provided*, That officers in the militia, to which there is attached no annual salary, and the office of Justice of the Peace shall not be deemed lucrative. *Miss.*, 338.

—The Justices of the Supreme Court and the District Judges shall be ineligible to any office, other than a judicial office, during the term for which they shall have been elected, and all elections or appointments of any such judges, by the people, Legislature, or otherwise, during said period, to any office other than judicial, shall be void. *Nev.*, 387.

—Nor hold any other office of profit or trust, under the authority of this State, or the United States. All votes for either of them. for any elective office, except a judicial office, under the authority of this State, given by the General Assembly, or the people, shall be void. *Ohio*, 437.

—No Judge of any court of law or equity, Secretary of State, Attorney-General, Clerk of any court of record, Sheriff or Collector, or any person holding a lucrative office under the United States, or this State, or any foreign government, shall be eligible to the Legislature, nor shall at the same time hold or exercise any two offices, agencies or appointments of trust or profit under this State; *Provided*, That offices of the militia, to which there is attached no annual salary the office of Notary Public and the office of Justice of the Peace shall not be deemed lucrative, and that one person may hold two or more county offices, if so provided by the Legislature. *Tex.*, 509.

—No judge, during his term of service, shall hold any other office, appointment, or public trust; nor the acceptance thereof shall vacate his judicial office; nor shall he, during such term, or within one year thereafter, be eligible to any political office. *Va.*, 542.

—No judge, during his term of office, shall hold any other office, appointment, or public trust, under this or any other government, and the acceptance thereof shall vacate his judicial office; nor shall he, during his continuance therein, be eligible to any political office. *W. Va.*, 553.

—They shall hold no office or public trust, except a judicial office, during the term for which they are respectively elected; and all votes for them for any office except a judicial office given by the Legislature or the people, shall be void. *Wis.*, 566.

QUALIFICATION OF JUDGES.

—No person who shall have arrived at the age of seventy years shall be appointed or elected to, or shall continue in the office of judge in this State. *Ala.*, 81.

—The qualified voters of this State shall elect the Judges of the Supreme Court; the Judges of the

Supreme Court shall be at least thirty years of age; they shall hold their offices during the term of eight years from the date of their commissions, and until their successors are elected and qualified. *Ark.*, 91.

—The qualified voters of each judicial district shall elect a Circuit Judge. The Judges of the Circuit Court shall be at least twenty-five years of age and shall be elected for the term of four years from the date of their commissions, and shall serve until their successors are elected and qualified. *Ark.*, 91.

—No person shall be eligible to the office of judge of any court of this State who is not a citizen of the United States, and who shall not have resided in this State five years next preceding his election, and who shall not for two years next preceding his election have resided in the division, circuit, or county, in which he shall be elected; nor shall any person be elected Judge of the Supreme Court who shall be, at the time of his election, under the age of thirty-five years; and no person shall be eligible to the office of Judge of the Circuit Court until he shall have attained the age of thirty years. *Ill.*, 160.

—No person shall be eligible to the office of Judge of the Court of Appeals, who is not a citizen of the United States, a resident of the district for which he may be a candidate two years next preceding his election, at least thirty years of age, and who has not been a practicing lawyer eight years, or whose service upon the bench of any Court of record, when added to the time he may have practiced law, shall not be equal to eight years. *Ky.*, 215.

—No person shall be eligible as Judge of the Circuit Court who is not a citizen of the United States, a resident of the district for which he may be a candidate two years next preceding his election, at least thirty years of age, and who has not been a practicing lawyer eight years, or whose service upon the bench of any court of record, when added to the time he may have practiced law, shall not be equal to eight years. *Ky.*, 216.

—All judicial officers, except Justices of the Peace, shall hold their offices during good behavior, but not beyond the age of seventy years. *Me.*, 246.

—The Judges of the several Courts, except the Judges of the Orphans' Courts, shall be citizens of the United States, and residents of this State, not less than five years next preceding their election, or appointment by the Executive in case of a vacancy; and not less than one year next preceding their election or appointment, residents in the judicial district or circuit, as the case may be, for which they may be elected or appointed; they shall not be less than thirty years of age at the time of their election and selected from those who have been admitted to practice law in this State, and who are most distinguished for integrity, wisdom and sound legal knowledge. *Md.*, 265.

—No person shall be eligible to the office of Judge of the High Court of Errors and Appeals, who shall not have attained, at the time of his election, the age of thirty years. *Miss.*, 338.

—No person shall be eligible to the office of Judge of the Circuit Court, who shall not at the time of his election, have attained the age of twenty-six years. *Miss.*, 339.

—No person shall be elected or appointed a Judge of the Supreme Court, nor of a Circuit Court, before he shall have attained to the age of thirty years, and have been a citizen of the United States five years, and a qualified voter of this State three years. *Me.*, 359.

—No person shall hold the office of judge of any court, or Judge of Probate. or Sheriff of any county after he has attained the age of seventy years. *N. H.*, 408.

—The President Judges of the several Courts of Common Pleas, and of such other courts of record as are or shall be established by law, and all other judges, required to be learned in the law, shall hold their offices for the term of ten years, if they shall so long behave themselves. *Pa.*, 464.

—Judges of the Supreme Court shall be thirty-five years of age, and shall be elected for the term of eight years. *Tenn.*, 503.

—The judges of such inferior courts as the Legislature may establish, shall be thirty years of age, and shall be elected for the term of eight years. *Tenn.*, 503.

—They shall have arrived at the age of thirty-five years at the time of election; shall hold their offices for the term of ten years, and each of them shall receive an annual salary of at least four thousand five hundred dollars, which shall not be increased or diminished during his term of office. *Tex.*, 510.

—Judges must have attained the age of thirty-five years, the Governor the age of thirty years, and the Attorney-General and Senators the age of twenty-five years, at the beginning of their respective terms of service, and must have been citizens of the State for five years next preceding, or at the time this Constitution goes into operation. *W. Va.*, 548.

—No person shall be eligible to the office of judge who shall not, at the time of his election, be a citizen of the United States, and have attained the age of twenty-five years, and be a qualified elector within the jurisdiction for which he may be chosen. *Wis.*, 566.

ATTORNEYS—SUITORS MAY SELECT THEIR COUNSEL.

—And that all attorneys, solicitors, and counsellors at law hereafter to be appointed, be appointed by the court, and licensed by the first judge of the court in which they shall respectively plead or practice; and be regulated by the rules and orders of the said courts. *N. Y.* (1777), 30.

—Attorneys at law, all inferior officers of the Treasury Department, election officers, officers relating to taxes, to the poor, and to highways, Constables and hundred officers, shall be appointed in such manner as is or may be directed by law. *Del.*, 125.

—Every person of good moral character, being a voter, shall be entitled to admission to practice law in all courts of justice. *Ind.*, 177.

—Any suitor in any court of this State shall have the right to prosecute or defend his suit, either in his own proper person, or by an attorney or agent of his choice. *Mich.*, 307; *Wis.*, 563.

—Every person being a citizen of the United States shall be permitted to appear to and try his own case in all the courts of this State. *Md.*, 266.

PROSECUTING ATTORNEYS.

—There shall be one Solicitor for each circuit, who shall reside therein, to be elected by the qualified electors of the circuit, who shall his office for the term of four years, and shall receive for his services a compensation to be fixed by law. *Fl.*, 135.

—There shall be elected in each of the Judicial Circuits of this State, by the qualified electors thereof, one State's Attorney, who shall hold his office for the term of four years, and until his successor shall be commissioned and qualified; who shall perform such duties and receive such compensation as may be prescribed by law; *Provided*, That the General Assembly may hereafter provide by law for the election, by the qualified voters of each county in this State, of one County Attorney for each county, in lieu of the State's Attorneys provided for in this section; the term of office, duties, and compensation, of which County Attorneys shall be regulated by law. *Ill.*, 161.

—The qualified electors of each judicial district shall at the time of election of District Judge, elect a District Attorney, who shall be a resident of the district for which he is elected, and shall hold his office for the term of four years, and until his successor shall have been elected and qualified. *Iowa*, 190.

—The State's Attorney shall perform such duties and receive such fees and commissions as are now or may hereafter be prescribed by law, and if any State's Attorney shall receive any other fee or reward than such as is or may be allowed by law, he shall, on conviction thereof be removed from office; *Provided*, That the State's Attorney from Baltimore city shall have power to appoint one deputy, at a salary of not more than fifteen hundred dollars per annum, to be paid by the State's Attorney out of the fees of his office, as has heretofore been practiced. *Md.*, 271.

—In case of vacancy in the office of State's Attorney, or of his removal from the county or city in which he shall have been elected, or on his conviction as herein specified, the said vacancy shall be filled by the judge of the county or city, respectively, having criminal jurisdiction in which said vacancy shall occur, for the residue of the term thus made vacant. *Md.*, 271.

—There shall be elected by districts composed of one or more counties, a sufficient number of prosecuting attorneys, who shall be the law officers of the State, and of the counties within their respective districts, and shall perform such duties pertaining to the administration of law and general police as the Legislative Assembly may direct. *Or.*, 455.

—The Legislature shall elect Attorneys for the State, by joint vote of both Houses of the General Assembly, who shall hold their offices for the term of six years. In all cases where an attorney for any district fails or refuses to attend and prosecute according to law, the court shall have the power to appoint an attorney *pro tempore.* *Tenn.*, 496.

—There shall be a District Attorney for each judicial district in the State, elected by the qualified electors of the district, who shall reside in the district for which he shall be elected; shall hold his office for four years; and, together with the perquisites prescribed by law, shall receive an annual salary of one thousand dollars, which shall not be increased or diminished during his term of office. *Tex.*, 511.

—The Attorney for the Commonwealth, elected for a county or corporation wherein a Circuit Court is directed to be held, shall be Attorney for the Commonwealth for that court; but in case a Circuit Court is held for a city, or for a county and a city, there shall be an Attorney for the Commonwealth for such, to be elected by the voters of such city, or county and city, and to continue in office for the term of four years. The duties and compensation of these officers, and the mode of removing them from office, shall be prescribed by law. *Va.*, 543.

—State's Attorneys shall be elected by the freemen of their respective counties. *Vt.*, 529.

NOTARIES PUBLIC.

[Appointed by Governor and Council.] *Me.*, 244.

—Notaries Public shall be appointed by the Governor, in the same manner as judicial officers are appointed, and shall hold their offices during seven years, unless sooner removed by the Governor, with the consent of the Council, upon the address of both Houses of the Legislature. *Mass.*, 294.

—The Governor, by and with the advice and consent of two-thirds of the Senate, shall appoint a convenient number of Notaries Public, not exceeding six for each county; who, in addition to such duties as are prescribed by law, shall discharge such other duties as the Legislature may, from time to time, prescribe. *Tex.*, 514.

1 § 9. The classification of the justices of the Supreme Court, the times and

2 place of holding the terms of the Court of Appeals, and of the general

3 and special terms of the Supreme Court within the several districts, and the

4 Circuit Courts and Courts of Oyer and Terminer within the several counties,

5 shall be provided for by law.

1 § 10. The testimony in equity cases shall be taken in like manner as in

2 cases at law.

1 § 11. Justices of the Supreme Court and judges of the Court of Appeals

2 may be removed by concurrent resolution of both Houses of the Legislature,

3 if two-thirds of all the members elected to the Assembly, and a majority of

REMOVAL OF JUDGES.

—For any willful neglect of duty, or any other reasonable cause, which shall not be sufficient ground of impeachment, the Governor shall remove any judge, on the address of two-thirds of each House of the General Assembly: *Provided,* That the cause, or causes for which said removal may be required, shall be stated at length in such address, and entered on the journals of each House. *And provided further,* that the Judge intended to be removed shall be notified of such cause or causes, and shall be admitted to a hearing in his own defense, before any vote for such address; and in all such cases, the vote shall be taken by yeas and nays, and be entered on the journals of each House respectively. *Ala.,* (nearly similar) *Tex.,* 511.

—The Judges of the Supreme Court of Errors and of the Superior Court, appointed in the year 1855, and thereafter, shall hold their offices for the term of eight years, but may be removed by impeachment, and the Governor shall also remove them on the address of two-thirds of each house of the General Assembly. No Judge of the Supreme Court of Errors, or of the Superior Court, shall be capable of holding office, after he shall have arrived at the age of seventy years. *Ct.,* 115.

—The Judges of the Supreme Court and of the Superior Court shall hold their offices during good behavior, but may be removed by impeachment; and the Governor shall also remove them, on the address of two-thirds of the members of each House of the General Assembly; all other Judges and Justices of the Peace shall be appointed annually. No Judge or Justice of the Peace shall be capable of holding his office after he shall have arrived at the age of seventy years. *Ct.,* 111.

—The Governor may, for any reasonable cause, in his discretion, remove any of them on the address of two-thirds of all the members of each branch of the General Assembly. In all cases where the Legislature shall so address the Governor, the cause of removal shall be entered on the journals of each House. The Judge against whom the Legislature may be about to proceed, shall receive notice thereof, accompanied with the causes alleged for his removal, at least five days before the day on which either House of the General Assembly shall act thereupon. *Del.,* 123.

—For any reasonable cause, to be entered on the journals of each House, which shall not be sufficient ground for impeachment, both Justices of the Supreme Court, and Judges of the Circuit Court, shall be removed from office, on the vote of two-thirds of the members elected to each branch of the General Assembly; *Provided, always,* That no member of either House of the General Assembly shall be eligible to fill the vacancy occasioned by such removal; *Provided, also,* That no removal shall be made unless the Justice or Judge complained of shall have been served with a copy of the complaint against him, and shall have an opportunity of being heard in his defense. *Ill.,* 100.

—Any Judge or Prosecuting Attorney who shall have been convicted of corruption or other high crime, may, on information in the name of the State, be removed from office by the Supreme Court, or in such other manner as may be prescribed by law. *Ind.,* 177.

—Justices of the Supreme Court and Judges of the District Courts may be removed from office by resolution of both Houses if two-thirds of the members of each House concur. But no such removal shall be made except upon complaint, the substance of which shall be entered upon the journal, nor until the party charged shall have had notice and opportunity to be heard. *Kan.,* 201; (nearly similar), *Ohio,* 438.

—That the independency and uprightness of judges are essential to the impartial administration of justice, and a great security to the rights and liberties of the people; wherefore the judges shall not be removed, except for misbehavior, on conviction in a court of law, or by the Governor, upon the address of the General Assembly; *Provided,* That two-thirds of all the members of each House concur in such address. No judge shall hold any other office, civil or military, or political trust or employment of any kind whatsoever, under the Constitution or laws of this State, or of the United States, or any of them, or receive fees or perquisites of any kind for the discharge of his official duties. *Md.,* 255.

—Any judge shall be removed from office by the Governor on conviction in a court of law, of incompetency, of willful neglect of duty, of misbehavior in office, or on any other crime; or on impeachment according to this Constitution, or the laws of the State; or on the address of the General Assembly, two-thirds of each House concurring in such address, and the accused having been notified of the charges against him, and had opportunity of making his defense. *Md.,* 266.

—Judges of the County Court and Justices of the Peace, Sheriffs, Coroners, Surveyors, Jailors, County Assessor, Attorney for the County, and Constables, shall be subject to indictment or presentment for malfeasance or misfeasance in office, or willful neglect in the discharge of their official duties, in such mode as may be prescribed by law, subject to appeal to the Court of Appeals; and, upon conviction, their offices shall become vacant. *Ky.,* 217.

—The Legislature of this State may provide for the removal of inferior officers from office, for malfeasance or nonfeasance in the performance of their duties. *Min.,* 329.

4 all the members elected to the Senate concur therein. All judicial officers,

5 except those mentioned in this section, and except justices of the peace, and

6 judges and justices of inferior courts not of record, may be removed by the

7 Senate on the recommendation of the Governor; but no removal shall be

8 made by virtue of this section, unless the cause thereof be entered on the

9 journals, nor unless the party complained of shall have been served with a

10 copy of the complaint against him, and shall have had an opportunity of

11 being heard in his defense. On the question of removal the ayes and noes

12 shall be entered on the journals.

—The judges of the several courts of this State, for willful neglect of duty or other reasonable cause, shall be removed by the Governor on the address of two-thirds of both Houses of the Legislature; the address to be by joint vote of both Houses. The cause or causes for which such removal shall be required, shall be stated at length in such address, and on the journals of each House. The judge so intended to be removed shall be notified and admitted to a hearing in his own defense before any vote for such address shall pass; the vote on such address shall be taken by yeas and nays, and entered on the journals of each House. *Miss.*, 340.

—Judges of Probate, Clerks, Sheriffs and other county officers, for willful neglect of duty, or misdemeanor in office, shall be liable to presentment or indictment by a grand jury, and trial by a petit jury, and upon conviction shall be removed from office. *Miss.*, 340.

—Any Judge of the Supreme Court or the Circuit Court, may be removed from office, on the address of two-thirds of each House of the General Assembly to the Governor for that purpose; but each House shall state, on its respective journal, the cause for which it shall wish the removal of such judge, and give him notice thereof; and he shall have the right to be heard in his defense, in such manner as the General Assembly shall by law direct; but no judge shall be removed in this manner for any cause for which he might have been impeached. *Mo.*, 359.

—For any reasonable cause to be entered on the journals of each House, which may or may not be sufficient grounds for impeachment, the Chief Justice and Associate Justices of the Supreme Court, and Judges of the District Courts, shall be removed from office on the vote of two-thirds of the members elected to each branch of the Legislature, and the justice or judge complained of shall be served with a copy of the complaint against him, and shall have an opportunity of being heard in person or by counsel in his defense; *Provided*, That no member of either branch of the Legislature shall be eligible to fill the vacancy occasioned by such removal. *Nev.*, 388.

—No judicial officer shall be superseded, nor shall the organization of the several Courts of the Territory of Nevada be changed until the election and qualification of the several officers provided for in this article. *Nev.*, 388.

—The Governor, with consent of the Council, may remove judges, upon the address of both Houses of the Legislature. *N. H.*, 408.

—Any Judge of the Supreme Court, or of the Superior Courts, may be removed from office for mental or physical inability, upon a concurrent resolution of two-thirds of both branches of the General Assembly. The Judge, against whom the Legislature may be about to proceed, shall receive notice thereof, accompanied by a copy of the cause alleged for his removal, at least twenty days before the day on which either branch of the General Assembly shall act thereon. *N. C.*, 429.

—The salaries of the Judges of the Supreme Court, or of the Superior Courts, shall not be diminished during their continuance in office. *N. C.*, 429.

—The Governor may remove from office a Judge of the Supreme Court, or prosecuting attorney, upon the joint resolution of the Legislative Assembly, in which two-thirds of the members elected to each House shall concur, for incompetency, corruption, malfeasance, or delinquency in office, or other sufficient cause, stated in such resolution. *Or.*, 495.

—Judges and Attorneys for the State, may be removed from office by a concurrent vote of both Houses of the General Assembly, each House voting separately; but two-thirds of all the members elected to each House must concur in such vote; the vote shall be detrmined by ayes and noes, and the names of the members voting for or against the judge or attorney for the State, together with the cause or causes of removal, shall be entered on the journals of each House respectively. The judge or attorney for the State, against whom the Legislature may be about to proceed, shall receive notice thereof, accompanied with a copy of the causes alleged for his removal, at least ten days before the day on which either House of the General Assembly shall act thereupon. *Tenn.*, 496.

—For any reasonable cause which shall not be sufficient grounds of impeachment, the Governor shall remove any of them on the address of two-thirds of each branch of the Legislature. *Pa.*, 470.

—Judges may be removed from office by a concurrent vote of both Houses of the General Assembly, but a majority of all the members elected to each House must concur in such vote; and the cause of removal shall be entered on the journal of each House. The judge against whom the General Assembly may be about to proceed, shall receive notice thereof, accompanied by a copy of the causes alleged for his removal, at least twenty days before the day on which either House of the General Assembly shall act thereupon. *Va.*, 542.

—Judges may be removed from office for misconduct, incompetence, or neglect of duty, or on conviction of an infamous offense, by the concurrent vote of a majority of all the members elected to each branch of the Legislature, and the cause of removal shall be entered on the journals. The judge against whom the Legislature may be about to proceed, shall receive notice thereof, accompanied by a copy of the causes alleged for his removal, at least twenty days before the day on which either branch of the Legislature shall act thereon. *W. Va.*, 553.

—Any judge of the Supreme or Circuit Court may be removed from office by address of both Houses of the Legislature, if two-thirds of all the members elected to each House concur therein, but no removal shall be made by virtue of this section, unless the judge complained of shall have been served with a copy of the charges against him, as the ground of address, and shall have had an opportunity of being heard in

1   § 12. The judges of the Court of Appeals shall be elected by the electors

2 of the State, and the justices of the Supreme Court by the electors of the

3 several judicial districts, at such times as may be prescribed by law.

1   § 13. In case the office of any judge of the Court of Appeals, or justice

2 of the Supreme Court shall become vacant before the expiration of the regular

3 term for which he was elected, the vacancy may be filled by appointment by

4 the Governor, until it shall be supplied at the next general election of judges,

5 when it shall be filled by election for the residue of the unexpired term.

his defense. On the question of removal, the ayes and noes shall be entered on the journals. *Wis*, 567.
—Every person appointed a Justice of the Peace shall hold his office for four years, unless removed by the County Court, for causes particularly assigned by the judges of the said court. And no Justice of the Peace shall be removed, until he shall have notice of the charges made against him, and an opportunity of being heard in his defense. *N. Y.* (1821), 39.

ELECTION OR APPOINTMENT OF JUDGES.

—The Governor shall nominate, by message in writing, and with the consent of the Senate shall appoint all judicial officers, except justices of the peace. *N. Y.* (1821), 39.
—Judges of the Supreme Court and Chancellors, shall be elected by a joint vote of both Houses of the General Assembly; Judges of the Circuit and Probate Courts, and of such other inferior courts as may be by law established, shall be elected by the qualified electors of the respective counties, cities, or districts, for which such courts may be established. Elections of judges by the people shall be held on the first Monday in May, or such other day as may be by law prescribed, not within a less period than two months of the day fixed by law for the election of Governor, members of the General Assembly, or members of Congress. *Ala.*, 80.
—The Justices of the Supreme Court shall be elected by the qualified electors of the State, at special elections, to be provided by law, at which elections no officer other than judicial shall be elected, except a Superintendent of Public Instruction. The first election for Justices of the Supreme Court shall be held in the year 1863. The justices shall hold their offices for the term of ten years from the first day of January next after their election, except those elected at the first election, who, at their first meeting shall so classify themselves by lot, that one justice shall go out of office every two years. The justice having the shortest term to serve shall be chief justice. *Cal.*, (amendment of 1862.)
—The Judges of the Supreme Court of Errors, of the Superior and Inferior Courts, and all Justices of the Peace, shall be appointed by the General Assembly, in such manner as shall by law be prescribed. *Ct.*, 111.
—The Judges of Probate shall be appointed by the electors residing in the several probate districts, and qualified to vote for representatives therein, in such manner as shall be prescribed by law. *Ct.*, 115.
—The Justices of the Peace for the several towns in this State shall be appointed by the electors in such towns; and the time and the manner of their election, the number for each town, and the period for which they shall hold their offices, shall be prescribed by law. *Ct.*, 115.
--[Judges appointed by Governor.] *Del.*, 119.
—The Attorney-General, Registers in Chancery, Prothonotaries, Registers, Clerks of the Orphans' Court and of the Peace, shall respectively be com-

missioned for five years, if so long they shall behave themselves well; but may be removed by the Governor within that time on conviction of misbehavior in office, or on the address of both Houses of the Legislature. Prothonotaries, Registers in Chancery, Clerks of the Orphans' Court, Registers, Recorders, and Sheriffs, shall keep their offices in the town or place in each each county in which the Superior Court is usually held. *Del.*, 125.
—The Governor shall have power to commission a Judge *ad litem* to decide any cause in which there is a legal exception to the Chancellor or any judge, so that such appointment is necessary to constitute a quorum in either court. The commission in such case shall confine the office to the cause, and it shall expire on the determination of the cause. The Judge so appointed shall receive a reasonable compensation, to be fixed by the General Assembly. A Member of Congress, or any person holding or exercising an office under the United States, shall not be disqualified from being appointed a Judge *ad litem*]. *Del.*, 122.
—There shall be appointed by the Governor, by and with the advice and consent of the Senate, a Chief Justice and two Associate Justices of the Supreme Court of this State, who shall reside in this State, and hold their office for the term of six years from their appointment and confirmation, unless sooner removed under the provisions of this Constitution, for the removal of judges by address or impeachment; and for willful neglect of duty or other reasonable cause, which shall not be sufficient ground for impeachment, the Governor shall remove any of them on the address of two-thirds of the General Assembly; *Provided, however,* That the cause or causes shall be notified to the judge so intended to be removed, and he shall be admitted to a hearing in his own defense, before any vote for such removal shall pass, and in such case, the vote shall he taken by yeas and nays, and entered on the journal of each House respectively; and in case of the appointment to fill a vacancy in said offices, the person so appointed shall only hold office for the unexpired term of his predecessor. *Fl.*, 134.
—There shall be elected, at the time and places prescribed by law, by the qualified electors of each of the respective Judicial Circuits of this State, one Judge of the Circuit Court, who shall reside in the circuit for which he may be elected, and the said Circuit Judges shall continue in office for the term of six years from the date of their respective elections, unless sooner removed, under the provisions in this Constitution for the removal of Judges by address or impeachment; and for willful neglect of duty, or other reasonable cause, which shall not be sufficient for impeachment, the Governor shall remove any of them on the address of two-thirds of the General Assembly; *Provided, however,* That the cause or causes shall be stated at length in such address and entered on the journal of each House; *And provided, further,* That the cause or causes shall be notified to such judge so intended to be removed, and he

shall be admitted to a hearing in his own defense before any vote or votes for such removal shall pass; and in such cases the vote shall be taken by yeas and nays, and entered on the journals of each House, respectively. *Fl.*, 134.

—The appointment of Chief Justice and Associate Justices of the Supreme Court shall be made every sixth year after their first appointment, and the election of Judges of the Circuit Court, and Judges or Chancellors of the Chancery Court, when established, shall be held in every sixth year after their first election, at the same time and places as the elections for members of the General Assembly. *Ky.*, 134.

—The Judges of the Superior Courts shall be duly elected on the first Wednesday in January, until the Legislature shall otherwise direct, immediately before the expiration of the term for which they or either of them may have been appointed or elected, from the circuits in which they are to serve, by a majority vote of the people of the circuit qualified to vote for members of the General Assembly, for the term of four years—vacancies to be filled as is provided by the laws of force prior to January 1, 1861—and shall continue in office until their successors shall be elected and qualified; removable by the Governor on the address of two-thirds of each branch of the General Assembly, or by impeachment and conviction thereon. *Ga.*, 148.

—The Supreme Court shall consist of three judges, who shall be elected by the General Assembly, for such term of years—not less than six—as shall be prescribed by law, and shall continue in office until their successors shall be elected and qualified; removable by the Governor on the address of two-thirds of each branch of the General Assembly, or by impeachment and conviction thereon. *Ga.*, 148.

—The first election for Justices of the Supreme Court and Judges of the Circuit Courts shall be held on the first Monday of September, 1848. *Ill.*, 160.

—The second election for one Justice of the Supreme Court shall be held on the first Monday of June, 1852; and every three years thereafter an election shall be held for one Justice of the Supreme Court. *Ill.*, 160.

—On the first Monday of June, 1855, and every sixth year thereafter, an election shall be held for Judges of the Circuit Courts; *Provided*, whenever an additional circuit is created, such provision may be made as to hold the second election of such additional judge at the regular election herein provided. *Ill.*, 160.

—All Judges and State's Attorneys shall be commissioned by the Governor. *Ill.*, 161.

—Elections of Judges of the Supreme and Circuit Courts shall be subject to be contested. *Ill.*, 169.

— That at the first election fixed by this Constitution for the election of Judges, there shall be elected one Circuit Judge in each of the nine judicial circuits now established in this State. *Ill.*, 167.

—The State shall be divided into as many districts as there are judges of the Supreme Court; and such districts shall be formed of contiguous territory, as nearly equal in population as, without dividing a county, the same can be made. One of said judges shall be elected from each district, and reside therein; but said judges shall be elected by the electors of the State at large. *Ind.*, 176.

—The Judges of the Supreme Court shall be elected by the qualified voters of the State, and shall hold their court at such time and place as the General Assembly may prescribe. The Supreme Judges so elected shall be classified so that one Judge shall go out of office every two years; and the Judge holding the shortest term of office under such classification, shall be Chief Justice of the court during his term, and so on in rotation. After the expiration of their terms of office, under such classification, the term of each Judge of the Supreme Court shall be six years, and until his successor shall have been elected and qualified. The Judges of the Supreme Court shall be ineligible to any other office in the State, during the term for which they shall have been elected. *Iowa*, 189.

—The first election for Judges of the Supreme Court,

and such county officers as shall be elected at the August election, in the year one thousand eight hundred and fifty-seven, shall be held on the second Tuesday of October, in the year one thousand eight hundred and fifty-nine. *Iowa*, 195.

—The District Court shall consist of a single judge, who shall be elected by the qualified voters of the district in which he resides. The Judge of the District Court shall hold his office for the term of four years, and until his successor shall have been elected and qualified, and shall be ineligible to any other office, except that of Supreme Judge, during the term for which he was elected. *Iowa*, 189.

—The Judges of the Supreme and District Courts shall be chosen at the general election, and the term of office of each judge shall commence on the first day of January next after his election. *Iowa*, 190.

—The Chief Justice and two Associate Justices shall be elected by the electors of the State at large, and whose term of office, after the first, shall be for six years. At the first election a Chief Justice shall be chosen for six years, one Associate Justice for four years, and one for two years. *Kan.*, 200.

—All the judicial officers provided for by this article shall be elected at the first election under this Constitution, and shall reside in their respective townships, counties or districts, during their respective terms of office.

—The first election of the Judges and Clerks of the Court of Appeals shall take place on the second Monday in May, 1851, and thereafter, in each district as a vacancy may occur, by the expiration of the term of office; and the judges of the said court shall be commissioned by the Governor. *Ky.*, 215.

—The General Assembly shall provide by law the manner of conducting and making due return of all elections of Judges of the County Court and Justices of the Peace, and for determining contested elections, and provide the mode of filling vacancies in these offices. *Ky.*, 217.

—They shall be commissioned by the Governor. *Ky.*, 217.

—The first election of Judges of the Circuit Court shall take place on the second Monday in May, 1851; and afterwards on the first Monday in August, 1856, and on the first Monday in August every sixth year thereafter. *Ky.*, 216.

—All persons qualified to vote for members of the General Assembly, in each district, shall have the right to vote for judges. *Ky.*, 216.

—The Judges of the Supreme Court shall be appointed by the Governor, by and with the advice and consent of the Senate, for a term of eight years; the judges of the inferior courts for a term of six years. *La.*, 232.

[Judges appointed by the Governor and Council.] *Me.*, 244.

—The Judges of the Court of Appeals shall be elected by the qualified voters of the State; and the Governor, by and with the advice and consent of the Senate, shall designate the Chief Justice; and the judges of the judicial circuits shall be elected by the qualified voters of their respective circuits; each Judge of the Court of Appeals and of each judicial circuit shall hold his office for the term of fifteen years from the time of his election, or until he shall have attained the age of seventy years whichever may first happen, and be re-eligible thereto until he shall have attained the age of seventy years, and not after. *Md.*, 265.

—All election of judges and other officers, provided for this Constitution, State's Attorneys excepted, shall be certified and the returns made by the Clerks of the respective counties to the Governor, who shall issue commissions to the different persons for the offices to which they shall have been respectively elected; and in all such elections, the person having the greatest number of votes shall be declared to be elected. *Md.*, 266.

—If in any case of election for Judges, Clerks of the Courts of Law, and Registers of Wills, the opposing candidates shall have an equal number of votes, it shall be the duty of the Governor to order a new election: and in case of any contested election the Governor shall send the return to the House of Delegates, who shall judge of the election and qualification of the candidates at such election. *Md.*, 266.

—The judges of the several courts of this State, except the Judges of the Orphans' Court, shall be elected at the regular election, whether for State or County officers, as the case may be, immmediately preceding the expiration of the term of the incumbent whose place is to be filled. *Md.*, 277.

—All judicial officers, the Attorney-General, the Solicitor-General, all Sheriffs, Coroners and Registers of Probate, shall be nominated and appointed by the Governor, by and with the advice and consent of the Council; and every such nomination shall be made by the Governor, and made at least seven days prior to such appointment. *Mass.*, 288.

—Judicial officers of cities and villages shall be elected, and all other officers shall be elected or appointed at such time and in such manner as the Legislature may direct. *Mich.*, 313.

—The first election of Judges of the Circuit Courts shall be held on the first Monday in April, one thousand eight hundred and fifty-one, and every sixth year thereafter. Whenever an additional circuit is created, provision shall be made to hold the subsequent election of such additional judges at the regular elections herein provided. *Mich.*, 306.

—All judges other than those provided for in this Constitution shall be elected by the electors of the judicial district, county, or city, for which they shall be created, nor for a longer term than seven years. *Minn.*, 325.

—There shall be elected in each county where a District Court shall be held, one clerk of said court, whose qualifications, duties and compensation shall be prescribed by law, and whose term of office shall be four years. *Minn.*, 325.

—The High Court of Errors and Appeals shall consist of three judges, any two of whom shall form a quorum. The Legislature shall divide the State into three districts, and the qualified electors of each district shall elect one of said judges for the term of six years. *Miss.*, 339.

—The Secretary of State, on receiving all the official returns of the first election, shall proceed, forthwith, in the presence and with the assistance of two Justices of the Peace, to determine by lot among the three candidates having the highest number of votes, which of said judges elect shall serve for the term of two years, and which shall serve for the term of four years, and which shall serve for the term of six years, and having so determined the same, it shall be the duty of the Governor to issue commissions accordingly. *Miss.*, 339.

—The Judges of the Circuit Court shall be elected by the qualified electors of each Judicial District, and hold their offices for the term of four years, and reside in their respective districts. *Miss.*, 339.

—The Legislature shall provide by law for determining contested elections of Judges of the High Court of Errors and Appeals, of the Circuit and Probate Courts, and other officers. *Miss.*, 340.

—At the general election in the year one thousand eight hundred and sixty-eight, all the Judges of the Supreme Court shall be elected by the qualified voters of the State, and shall enter upon their office on the first Monday of January next ensuing. At the first session of the court thereafter the judges shall, by lot, determine the duration of their several terms of office, which shall be respectively two, four, and six years; and shall certify the result to the Secretary of State. At the general election every two years after said first election, one judge of said court shall be elected, to hold office for the period of six years from the first Monday of January next ensuing. The judge having at any time the shortest term to serve shall be the Presiding Judge of the court. *Mo.*, 357.

—The State shall be divided into convenient circuits, of which the county of St. Louis shall constitute one,

for each of which, except as in the next succeeding section specified, a judge shall be elected by the qualified voters of the respective circuits, and except as hereinafter provided, shall be elected for the term of six years; but may continue in office until his successor shall be elected and qualified; and the judge of each circuit, after his election or appointment, as hereinafter provided, shall reside in, and bo a conservator of the peace within the circuit for which he shall be elected or appointed; and if any vacancy shall happen in the office of any circuit judge, by death, resignation, or removal out of his circuit, or by any other disqualification, the Governor shall, upon being satisfied that a vacancy exists, issue a writ of election to fill such vacancy; provided that said vacancy shall happen at least six months before the next general election for said judge; but if such vacancy shall happen within six months of the general election aforesaid. the Governor shall appoint a judge for such circuit; but every election or appointment, to fill a vacancy shall be for the residue of the term only. And the General Assembly shall provide, by law, for the election of said judges in their respective circuits; and in case of a tie, or contested election between the candidates, the same shall be determined in the manner to be prescribed by law. And the General Assembly shall provide, by law for the election of said judges, in their respective circuits to fill any vacancy which shall occur at any time at least six months before a general election for said judges. At the general election in the year one thousand eight hundred and sixty-eight, and at the general election every sixth year thereafter, except as hereinafter provided, all the circuit judges shall be elected, and shall enter upon their offices on the first Monday of January next ensuing. No judicial circuit shall be altered or changed at any session of the General Assembly next preceding the general election for said judges. *Mo.*, 358.

—From and after the first day of January, one thousand eight hundred and sixty-six, the Circuit Court of the county of St. Louis shall be composed of three judges, each of whom shall try causes separately, and all, or a majority of whom, shall constitute a court in bank, to decide questions of law, and to correct errors occurring in trials; and, from and after that day, there shall not be in said county any other court of record having civil jurisdiction, except a Probate Court and a County Court. The additional Judges of the Circuit Court of the county of St. Louis, authorized by this section, shall be appointed by the Governor, with the advice and consent of the Senate, and shall hold their offices until the next general election of Judges of Circuit Courts, when the whole number of the judges of said court shall be elected. At the first session of said court after the judges thereof who may be elected in the year one thousand eight hundred and sixty-eight shall have assumed office, the said judges shall by lot determine the duration of their several terms of office, which shall be respectively two, four and six years; and shall certify the result to the Secretary of State. At the general election, every two years, after the election in that year, one judge of said court shall be elected, to hold office for the term of six years from the first Monday of January next ensuing. The General Assembly shall have power to increase the number of the judges of said court, from time to time, as the public interest may require. Any additional judges authorized shall hold office for the term of six years, and be elected at a general election, and enter upon their office on the first Monday of January next ensuing. *Mo.*, 358.

—The Supreme Court shall consist of a Chief Justice and two Associate Justices, any two of whom shall constitute a quorum, and shall hold a term of the Supreme Court at the seat of government of the State, annually. Said Supreme Judges shall be elected by the qualified electors of the State, at such time and in such manner as may be provided by law. Said Justices of the Supreme Court shall hold their office for the term of six years from the time of

3½

134

their election, and until their successors shall have been elected and qualified. *Neb.*, 375.

—Probate Judges, Justices of the Peace, and persons holding inferior courts, herein authorized to be established by the Legislature, shall be elected by the electors of the several districts for which they may be elected in the manner and time fixed by law. *Neb.*, 375.

—The Justices of the Supreme Court shall be elected by the qualified electors of the State, at the general election, and shall hold office for the term of six years, from and including the first Monday of January next succeeding their election; *Provided*, That there shall be elected, at the first election under this Constitution, three Justices of the Supreme Court, who shall hold office from and including the first Monday of December, A. D., eighteen hundred and sixty-four, and continue in office thereafter two, four and six years respectively from and including the first Monday of January next succeeding their election. They shall meet as soon as practicable after their election and qualification, and at their first meeting shall determine by lot the term of office each shall fill, and the Justice drawing the shortest term shall be Chief Justice, after which the senior Justice in commission shall be Chief Justice. And in case the commission of any two or more of said Justices shall bear the same date, they shall determine by lot who shall be Chief Justice. *Neb.*, 386.

—At the first general election under this Constitution there shall be elected, in each of the respective districts (except as in the section hereinafter otherwise provided), one District Judge, who shall hold office from and including the first Monday of December, A. D., eighteen hundred and sixty-four, and until the first Monday of January, A. D., eighteen hundred and sixty-seven; after the said first election, there shall be elected at the general election which immediately precedes the expiration of the term of his predecessor, one District Judge in each of the respective judicial districts (except in the first district as in the section hereinafter provided.) The District Judges shall be elected by the qualified electors of their respective districts, and shall hold office for the term of four years (excepting those elected at said first election), from and including the first Monday of January next succeeding their election and qualification: *Provided*, That the first judicial district shall be entitled to, and shall have, three District Judges, who shall possess co-extensive and concurrent jurisdiction, and who shall be elected at the same times, in the same manner, and shall hold office for the like terms as herein prescribed in relation to the judges in other judicial districts. Any one of said judges may preside on the impanneling of grand juries, and the presentment and trial and indictments under such rules and regulations as may be prescribed by law. *Nev.*, 386.

—All Judicial officers, the Attorney-General, Solicitors, all Sheriffs, Coroners, Registers of Probate, and all officers of the navy, and general and field officers of the militia, shall be nominated and appointed by the Governor and Council; and every such nomination shall be made at least three days prior to such appointment, and no appointment shall take place unless a majority of the Council agree thereto. *N. H.*, 405.

—Justices of the Supreme Court, Chancellor, and Judges of the Court of Errors and Appeals shall be nominated by the Governor, and appointed by him, with the advice and consent of the Senate. *N. J.*, 419.

—Judges of the Courts of Common Pleas shall be appointed by the Senate and General Assembly in joint meeting. *N. J.*, 419.

—There shall be no more than five Judges of the Inferior Court of Common Pleas, in each of the counties in this State after the terms of the judges of said court now in office shall terminate. One judge for each county shall be appointed every year, and no more, except to fill vacancies, which shall be for the unexpired term only. *N. J.*, 418.

—The first election for Judges of the Supreme Court, Courts of Common Pleas, and Probate Courts, and the Clerks of the Courts of Common Pleas, shall be held on the second Tuesday of October, one thousand eight hundred and fifty-one, and the official term of said judges and clerks, so elected, shall commence on the second Monday of February, one thousand eight hundred and fifty-two. Judges and Clerks of the Courts of Common Pleas and Supreme Court, in office on the first day of September, one thousand eight hundred and fifty-one, shall continue in office with their present power and duties, until the second Monday of February, one thousand eight hundred and fifty-two. No suit or proceeding, pending in any of the Courts of this State, shall be affected by the adoption of this Constitution. *Ohio*, 444.

—All judges, other than those provided for in this Constitution, shall be elected by the electors of the judicial district for which they may be created, but not for a longer term of office than five years. *Ohio*, 437.

—The General Assembly may increase or diminish the number of the Judges of the Supreme Court, the number of the districts of the Court of Common Pleas, the number of judges in any district, change the districts, or the subdivisions thereof, or establish other courts, whenever two-thirds of the members elected to each House shall concur therein; but no such change, addition, or diminution, shall vacate the office of any judge. *Ohio*, 438.

—When the white population of the State shall amount to two hundred thousand, the Legislative Assembly may provide for the election of Supreme and Circuit Judges in distinct classes, one of which classes shall consist of three Justices of the Supreme Court, who shall not perform circuit duty; and the other class shall consist of the necessary number of Circuit Judges, who shall hold full terms without allotment, and who shall take the same oath as the Supreme Judges. *Or.*, 454.

—The Judges of the Supreme Court of the several Courts of Common Pleas, and of such other courts of record as are or shall be established by law, shall be elected by the qualified electors of the Commonwealth in the manner following, to wit: The Judges of the Supreme Court, by the qualified electors of Commonwealth at large. The President Judges of the several Courts of Common Pleas and of such other courts of record as are or shall be established by law, and all other judges required to be learned in the law, by the qualified electors of the respective districts over which they are to preside or act as judges. And the Associate Judges of the Courts of Common Pleas by the qualified electors of the counties respectively. The Judges of the Supreme Court shall hold their offices for the term of fifteen years, if they shall so long behave themselves well, subject to the allotment hereinafter provided for, subsequent to the first election. The President Judges of the several Courts of Common Pleas, and of such other courts of record as are or shall be established by law, and all other judges required to be learned in the law, shall hold their offices for the term of ten years, if they shall so long behave themselves well. The Associate Judges of the Courts of Common Pleas shall hold their offices for the term of five years, if they shall so long behave themselves well: all of whom shall be commissioned by the Governor, but for any reasonable cause, which shall not be sufficient grounds of impeachment, the Governor shall remove any of them on the address of two-thirds of each branch of the Legislature. The first election shall take place at the general election of this Commonwealth next after the adoption of this amendment, and the commissions of all the judges who may be then in office shall expire on the first Monday of December following, when the terms of the new judges shall commence. The persons who shall then be elected Judges of the Supreme Court shall hold their offices as follows: one of them for three years, one for six years, one for nine years, one for twelve years, and one for fifteen years, the term of each to be decided by lot by the said judges, as soon after the election as convenient, and the result certified by them to the Governor, that the commissions may be issued in accordance thereto. The judge whose commission will first expire shall be Chief Justice. during his term, and thereafter each judge whose commission shall first expire shall in turn be the Chief Justice,' and if two or more commissions shall expire on the same day, the judges holding them shall decide by lot which shall be the Chief Justice. Any vacancies happening by death, resignation, or otherwise, in any of the said courts, shall be filled by appointment by the Governor, to continue till the first Monday of December succeeding the next general election. The Judges of the Supreme Court and the Presidents of the several Courts of Common Pleas shall at stated times, receive for their service an adequate compensation, to be fixed by law, which shall not be diminished during their continuance in office, but they shall receive no fees or perquisites of office, nor hold any other office of profit under this Commonwealth, or under the government of the United States, or any other State of this Union. The Judges of the Supreme Court during their continuance in office shall reside within this Commonwealth, and the other judges during their continuance in office shall reside within the district or county for which they were respectively elected. *Pa.*, 470.

—The Judges of the Supreme Court shall be elected by the two Houses in grand committee. Each judge shall hold his office until his place be declared vacant by a resolution of the General Assembly to that effect; which resolution shall be voted for by a majority of all the members elected to the House in which it may originate, and be concurred in by the same majority of the other House. Such resolution shall not be entertained at any other than the annual session for the election of public officers; and in default of the passage thereof at said session, the judge shall hold his place as is herein provided. But a judge of any court shall be removed from office, if upon impeachment, he shall be found guilty of any official misdemeanor. *R. I.*, 479.

—The Judges of the Superior Courts shall be elected by the General Assembly, shall hold their offices during good behavior, and shall at stated times, receive a compensation for their services, which shall neither be increased nor diminished during their continuance in office; but they shall receive no fees or perquisites of office, nor hold any other office of profit or trust under this State, the United States of America, or any of them, or any other power. The General Assembly shall, as soon as possible, establish for each district in the State an inferior court or courts, to be styled the "District Court," the judge whereof shall be resident in the district while in office, shall be elected by the General Assembly for four years and shall be re-eligible, which court shall have jurisdiction of all civil causes wherein one or both of the parties are persons of color, and of all criminal cases wherein the accused is a person of color; and the General Assembly is empowered to extend the jurisdiction of the said court to other subjects. *S. C.*, 486.

—The Judges of the Supreme Court shall be elected by the qualified voters of the State at large, and the judges of such inferior courts as the Legislature may establish shall be elected by the qualified voters residing within the bounds of any district or circuit to which such inferior judge or judges, either of law or equity, may be assigned, by ballot, in the same manner that members of the General Assembly are elected. *Tenn.*, (amendment).

—The General Assembly shall, by joint vote of both Houses, appoint judges of several courts in law and equity; but courts may be established to be holden by Justices of the Peace. *Tenn.*, 496.

—The Legislature shall appoint a day for holding the election of Judges and Attorneys-General, separate and apart from the days already prescribed, or hereafter to be prescribed by the Legislature for holding the elections for State and county officers. *Tenn.*, 503.

—For each section a judge shall be chosen in the manner hereinbefore provided, who shall hold his office for the term of twelve years unless sooner removed in the manner prescribed by this Constitution. He shall, at the time of his being chosen be at least thirty years of age, and shall have resided in the State one year next preceding his election, and during his continuance in office he shall reside in the section for which he is chosen. *Va.*, 542.

—Judges shall be commissioned by the Governor. *Va.*, 542.

—For each circuit a judge shall be elected by the voters thereof, who shall hold his office for the term of six years. During his continuance in office he shall reside in the circuit of which he is judge. *W. Va.*, 553.

—The Supreme Court of Appeals shall consist of three judges, any two of whom shall be a quorum. They shall be elected by the voters of the State, and shall hold their offices for the term of twelve years; except that of those first elected, one, to be designated by lot in such manner as they may determine, shall hold his office for four years; another, to be designated in like manner, for eight years, and the third, for twelve years; so that one shall be elected every four years after the first election. *W. Va.*, 553.

—For each circuit there shall be a judge chosen by the qualified electors therein, who shall hold his office as is provided in this Constitution, and until his successor shall be chosen and qualified; and after he shall have been elected, he shall reside in the circuit for which he was elected. One of said judges shall be designated as Chief Justice, in such manner as the Legislature shall provide. And the Legislature shall, at its first session, provide by law, as well for the election of, as for classifying the Judges of the Circuit Court, to be elected under this Constitution, in such manner that one of said judges shall go out of office in two years, one in three years, one in four years, one in five years, and one in six years, and thereafter the judge elected to fill the office shall hold the same for six years. *Wis.*, 566.

VACANCIES IN OFFICE OF JUDGES.

—Vacancies in the office of Circuit Judge, Probate Judge, or Judge of any other inferior court established by law, shall be filled by the Governor; and the person appointed by him shall hold office until the next election day by law appointed for the election of judges, and until his successor shall have been elected and qualified. *Ala.*, 80.

—That should a vacancy occur either in the Chancery or Circuit Courts, by death, removal, resignation or otherwise, it shall be the duty of the Governor to issue a writ of election to fill such vacancy, and he shall give at least sixty days' notice thereof by proclamation: and the Judge so elected to fill said vacancy, shall continue in office from the time he qualifies under his commission, until the expiration of the term of his predecessor: *Provided, however,* That should it become necessary to fill any such vacancy before an election can be held under the provisions of this Constitution, the Governor shall have power to fill such vacancy by appointment, and the person so appointed shall hold his office from the date of his commission until his successor shall be duly elected and qualified. *Fl.*, 135.

—The office of one of said judges shall be vacated, after the first election held under this article, in three years; of one, in six years; and of one in nine years; to be decided by lot, so that one of said judges shall be elected once in every three years. The judge having the longest term to serve shall be the first Chief Justice; after which, the judge having the oldest commission shall be Chief Justice. *Ill.*, 160.

—All vacancies in the Supreme and Circuit Courts shall be filled by election as aforesaid; *Provided, however,* That if the unexpired term does not exceed one year, such vacancy may be filled by executive appointment. *Ill.*, 160.

—In case of vacancy in any judicial office, it shall be filled by appointment of the Governor until the next regular election that shall occur more than thirty days after such vacancy shall have happened. *Kan.*, 201.

—County and district officers shall vacate their offices by removal from the district or county in which they shall be appointed. *Ky.*, 217.

—If a vacancy shall occur in the office of Judge of the Circuit Court, the Governor shall issue a writ of election to fill such vacancy, for the residue of the term: *Provided*, That if the unexpired term be less than one year, the Governor shall appoint a judge to fill such vacancy. *Ky.*, 216.

—In case of the death, resignation, removal or other disqualification of a judge of any court of this State, except of the Orphans' Courts, the Governor, by and with the advice and consent of the Senate, shall thereupon appoint a person duly qualified to fill said office until the next general election thereafter, whether for members of General Assembly or county officers, whichever shall first occur, at which time an election shall be held as herein prescribed for a judge, who shall hold said office for the term of fifteen years, and until the election and qualification of his successor. *Md.*, 266.

—In case of the death, resignation, removal or other disqualification of a judge of an Orphans' Court, the Governor, by and with the advice and consent of the Senate, shall appoint a person duly qualified to fill said office for the residue of the term thus made vacant. *Md.*, 270.

—When a vacancy occurs in the office of Judge of the Supreme Circuit or Probate Court, it shall be filled by appointment of the Governor, which shall continue until a successor is elected and qualified. When elected, such successor shall hold his office the residue of the unexpired term. *Mich.*, 306.

—Whenever a judge shall remove beyond the limits of the jurisdiction for which he was elected, or a Justice of the Peace from the township in which he was elected, or by a change in the boundaries of such township shall be placed without the same, they shall be deemed to have vacated their respective offices. *Mich.*, 307.

—In case the office of any judge shall become vacant before the expiration of the regular term for which he was elected, the vacancy shall be filled by appointment by the Governor, until a successor is elected and qualified. And such successor shall be elected at the first annual election that occurs more than thirty days after the vacancy shall have happened. *Min.*, 325.

—The provisions contained in this article, requiring an election to be held to fill a vacancy in the office of Judges of the Supreme and Circuit Courts, shall have relation to vacancies occurring after the year one thousand eight hundred and sixty-eight, up to which time any such vacancy shall be filled by appointment by the Governor. *Mo.*, 359.

—If a vacancy shall happen in the office of any Judge of the Supreme Court, by death, resignation, removal out of the State, or other disqualification, the Governor shall appoint a suitable person to fill the vacancy, until the next general election occurring more than three months after the happening of such vacancy, when the same shall be filled by election, by the qualified voters of the State, for the residue of the term. *Mo.*, 357.

—If there be a vacancy in the office of judge of any circuit, or if he be sick, absent, or from any cause unable to hold any term of court of any county of his circuit, such term of court may be held by a judge of any other circuit, and at the request of the judge of any circuit, any term of court in his circuit may be held by the judge of any other circuit. *Mo.*, 359.

—In case the office of any Justice of the Supreme Court, District Judge, or other State officer shall become vacant before the expiration of the regular term, for which he was elected, the vacancy may be filled by appointment by the Governor until it shall be filled by election for the residue of the unexpired term. *Nev.*, 395.

—In case the office of any judge shall become vacant before the expiration of the regular term for which he was elected, the vacancy shall be filled by appointment by the Governor, until a successor is elected and qualified; and such successor shall be elected for the unexpired term, at the first annual election that occurs more than thirty days after the vacancy shall have happened. *Ohio*, 437.

—Every vacancy in the office of Judge of the Supreme Court shall be filled by election for the remainder of the vacant term, unless it would expire at the next election; and until so filled, or when it would so expire, the Governor shall fill the vacancy by appointment. *Or.*, 454.

—In case of vacancy by death, resignation, removal from the State or from office, refusal or inability to serve, of any Judge of the Supreme Court the office may be filled by the grand committee, until the next annual election, and the judge then elected shall hold his office as before provided. In cases of impeachment, or temporary absence or inability, the Governor may appoint a person to discharge the duties of the office during the vacancy caused thereby. *R. I.*, 479.

—In case of a vacancy in the offices of Justice of the Supreme Court, Judges of the District Court, Attorney General, and District Attorneys, the Governor of the State shall have power to fill the same by appointment, which shall continue in force until the office can be filled at the next general election for State or county officers, and the successor duly qualified. *Tex.*, 511.

—When a vacancy shall happen in the office of Judge of the Supreme or Circuit Courts, such vacancy shall be filled by an appointment of the Governor, which shall continue until a successor is elected and qualified; and when elected, such successor shall hold his office the residue of the unexpired term. There shall be no election for a judge or judges at any general election for State or county officers, nor within thirty days either before or after such election. *Wis.*, 566.

1 § 14. There shall be elected in each of the counties of this State, except

2 the city and county of New York, one County Judge, who shall hold his

3 office for four years. He shall hold the County Court, and perform the duties

4 of the office of Surrogate. The County Court shall have such jurisdiction in

5 cases arising in Justices' Courts, and in special cases, as the Legislature may

6 prescribe; but shall have no original civil jurisdiction, except in such special

7 cases. The County Judge, with two justices of the peace to be designated

8 according to law, may hold courts of sessions, with such criminal jurisdiction

9 as the Legislature shall prescribe, and perform such other duties as may be

10 required by law. The County Judge shall receive an annual salary, to be

COUNTY COURTS.

—There shall be in each of the organized counties of the State, a County Court, for each of which a County Judge shall be elected by the qualified electors of the county, at the special judicial elections to be held as provided for the election of Justices of the Supreme Court, by section three of this article. *Cal.*, (as amended in 1862.)

—The Legislature may also provide for the appointment by the several district courts, of one or more commissioners in the several counties of their respective districts, with authority to perform chamber business of the Judges of the District Courts and County Courts, and also to take depositions, and to perform such other business connected with the administration of justice as may be prescribed by law. *Cal.*, (as amended in 1862.)

—The Court of General Sessions of the Peace and Jail Delivery shall be composed in each county of the same judges and in the same manner as the Superior Court. Two shall constitute a quorum. One may open and adjourn the Court. This court shall have all the jurisdiction and powers vested by the laws of this State in the Court of General Quarter Sessions of the Peace and Jail Delivery. *Del.*, 121.

—The Prothonotary of the Superior Court may issue process, take recognizances of bail and enter judgments, according to law and the practices of the court. No judgment in one county shall bind lands or tenements in another, until a *testatum fieri facias* being issued, shall be entered of record in the office of the Prothonotary of the county wherein the lands or tenements are situated. *Del.*, 124.

—The Registers of the several counties shall respectively hold the Registers' Courts in each county. Upon the litigation of a cause, the depositions of the witnesses examined shall be taken at large in writing, and make part of the proceedings in the cause. This court may issue process throughout the State, to compel the attendance of witnesses. Appeals may be made from the Registers' Court to the Superior Court, whose decision shall be final. In cases where a Register is interested in questions concerning the probate of wills, the granting letters of administration, or executors, administrators, or guardians' accounts, the cognizance thereof shall belong to the Orphan's Court, with an appeal to the Superior Court, whose decision shall be final. *Del.*, 124.

—There shall be in each county a court to be called a County Court. *Ill.*, 161.

—One County Judge shall be elected by the qualified voters of each county, who shall hold his office for four years, and until his successor is elected and qualified. *Ill.*, 161.

- -The jurisdiction of said court shall extend to all

probate and such other jurisdiction as the General Assembly may confer in civil cases, and such criminal cases as may be prescribed by law, where the punishment is by fine only, not exceeding one hundred dollars. *Ill.*, 161.

—The County Judge, with such Justices of the Peace in each county as may be designated by law, shall hold terms for the transaction of county business, and shall perform such other duties as the General Assembly shall prescribe; *Provided*, the General Assembly may require that two Justices, to be chosen by the qualified electors of each county, shall sit with the County Judge in all cases; and there shall be elected, quadrennially, in each county, a Clerk of the County Court, who shall be *ex officio* Recorder, whose compensation shall be fees; *Provided*, the General Assembly may, by law, make the Clerk of the Circuit Court *ex officio* Recorder, in lieu of the County Clerk. *Ill.*, 161.

—The General Assembly shall provide for the compensation of the County Judge. *Ill.*, 161.

—A County Court shall be established in each county now existing, or which may hereafter be erected within this Commonwealth, to consist of a Presiding Judge and two Associate Judges, any two of whom shall constitute a court for the transaction of business; *Provided*, The General Assembly may at any time abolish the office of the Associate Judges, whenever it shall be deemed expedient; in which event they may associate with said court, any or all of the Justices of the Peace for the transaction of business. *Ky.*, 216.

—The Judges of the County Court shall be elected by the qualified voters in each county, for the term of four years, and shall continue in office until their successors be duly qualified, and shall receive such compensation for their services as may be provided by law. *Ky.*, 216.

—No person shall be eligible to the office of presiding or associate Judge of the County Court, unless he be a citizen of the United States, over twenty-one years of age, and shall have been a resident of the county in which he shall be chosen, one year next preceding the election. *Ky.*, 217.

—The jurisdiction of the County Court shall be regulated by law; and, until changed, shall be the same now vested in the County Courts of this State. *Ky.*, 217.

—The Legislature may provide by law for the election of one or more persons in each organized county, who may be vested with judicial powers, not exceeding those of a Judge of the Circuit Court at chambers. *Mich.*, 306.

—The Legislature may provide for the election of one person in each organized county in this State, to be called a Court Commissioner, with judicial power and jurisdiction not exceeding the power and juris-

35

11 fixed by the Board of Supervisors, which shall be neither increased or diminu-

12 ished during his continuance in office. The Justices of the Peace, for services

13 in Courts of Sessions, shall be paid a per diem allowance out of the county

14 treasury. In counties having a population exceeding forty thousand, the Leg-

15 islature may provide for the election of a separate officer to perform the

16 duties of the office of Surrogate. The Legislature may confer equity juris-

17 diction in special cases upon the County Judge. Inferior local courts, of civil

18 and criminal jurisdiction, may be established by the Legislature in cities; and

19 such courts, except for the cities of New York and Buffalo, shall have an

20 uniform organization and jurisdiction in such cities.

diction of a Judge of the District Court at chambers; or the Legislature may, instead of such election, confer such powers and jurisdiction upon Judges of Probate in the State. *Minn.*, 325.
—Inferior tribunals, to be known as County Courts, shall be established in each county for the transaction of all county business. In such courts, or in such other tribunals inferior to the Circuit Courts, as the General Assembly may establish, shall be vested the jurisdiction of all matters appertaining to probate business, to granting letters testamentary and of administration, to settling the accounts of executors, administrators and guardians, and to the appointment of guardians, and such other jurisdiction as may be conferred by law. *Mo.*, 359.
—Judges of the County Courts, and recorders of cities, shall hold their offices for five years, but may be removed by the Senate, on the recommendation of the Governor, for causes to be stated in such recommendation. *N. Y.* (1821), 41.
—The commissions for the appointments of judges of said court [Inferior Court of Common Pleas] shall bear date and take effect on the first day of April next; and all subsequent commissions for judges of said court, shall bear date and take effect on the first day of April in every successive year, except commissions to fill vacancies, which shall bear date and take effect when issued. *N. J.*, 418.
—The said Courts of Common Pleas, shall be the successors of the present Courts of Common Pleas in the several counties, except as to probate jurisdiction; and all suits, prosecutions, proceedings, records, and judgments pending or being in said last-mentioned courts, except as aforesaid, shall be transferred to the Courts of Common Pleas created by this Constitution, and proceeded in as though the same had been therein instituted. *Ohio*, 445.
—There shall be elected in each county, for the term of four years, a County Judge, who shall hold the County Court at times to be regulated by law. *Or.*, 454.
—The County Court shall have the jurisdiction pertaining to Probate Courts and Boards of County Commissioners, and such other powers and duties and such civil jurisdiction not exceeding the amount or value of five hundred dollars, and such criminal jurisdiction not extending to death or imprisonment in the penitentiary, as may be prescribed by law. But the Legislative Assembly may provide for the election of two commissioners to sit with the County Judge whilst transacting county business in any or all the counties, or may provide a separate board for transacting such business. *Or.*, 455.
—The County Judge may grant preliminary injunctions, and such other writs as the Legislative Assembly may authorize him to grant, returnable to the Circuit Court, or otherwise, as may be provided by

law; and may hear and decide questions arising upon *habeas corpus*, provided such decisions be not against the authority or proceedings of a court, or judge of equal or higher jurisdiction. *Or.*, 455.
—The counties having less than ten thousand white inhabitants shall be reimbursed, wholly or in part, for the salary and expenses of the County Court, by fees, per centage, and other equitable taxation of the business done in said court and in the office of the County Clerk. *Or.*, 455.
—The Judges of the Court of Common Pleas of each county, any two of whom shall be a quorum, shall compose the Court of Quarter Sessions of the Peace, and Orphans' Court thereof; and the Register of Wills, together with the said judges, or any two of them, shall compose the Register's Court of each county. *Pa.*, 465.
—The Judges of the Court of Common Pleas, in each county, shall, by virtue of their offices, be Justices of Oyer and Terminer and General Jail Delivery, for the trial of capital and other offenders therein; any two of said judges, the president being one, shall be a quorum: but they shall not hold a Court of Oyer and Terminer, or Jail Delivery, in any county, when the Judges of the Supreme Court, or any of them shall be sitting in the same county. The party accused, as well as the Commonwealth, may, under such regulations as shall be prescribed by law, remove the indictment and proceedings, or a transcript thereof, into the Supreme-Court. *Pa.*, 465.
—The Superior Court shall sit in each county not less than twice in every year, at such stated times as have been or may be appointed by the General Assembly, and the Inferior and County Court at such times as the General Assembly may direct. *Ga.*, 149.
—Courts of justice shall be maintained in every county in this State, and also in new counties when formed, which courts shall be open for the trial of all causes proper for their cognizance, and justice shall be therein impartially administered without corruption or unnecessary delay. The Judges of the Supreme Court shall be Justices of the Peace throughout the State, and the several Judges of the County Courts in their respective counties, by virtue of their office, except in the trial of such cases as may be appealed to the County Court. *Vt.*, 523.
—The Assistant Judges of the County Court shall be elected by the freemen of their respective counties. *Vt.*, 520.
—There shall be established in each county in the State, an inferior tribunal styled the County Court; and there shall be elected by the persons in each county, who are qualified to vote for members of the Legislature, a Judge of the County Court, who shall be a conservator of the peace, who shall hold his office for four years, and who shall

1 § 15. The Legislature may, on application of the Board of Supervisors,
2 provide for the election of local officers, not to exceed two in any county, to
3 discharge the duties of County Judge and of Surrogate, in cases of their
4 inability or of a vacancy, and to exercise such other powers in special cases as
5 may be provided by law.

receive such compensation as may be prescribed by law, and who may be removed from office for neglect of duty, incompetency, or malfeasance, in such manner as may be prescribed by law. *Tex.*, 511.

—The County Court shall have jurisdiction of all misdemeanors and petty offenses, the same are now, or may hereafter be defined by law; of such civil cases where the matter in controversy shall not exceed five hundred dollars, exclusive of interest, under such regulations, limitations, and restrictions as may be prescribed by law, without regard to any distinction between law and equity; to probate wills, to appoint guardians of minors, idiots, lunatics, and persons *non compos mentis*; to grant letters testamentary and of administration; to settle the accounts of executors, anministrators and guardians; to transact all business appertaining to the estates of deceased persons, minors, idiots, lunatics, and persons *non compos mentis*, including the settlement, partition and distribution of such estates; and to apprentice minors under such regulations as may be prescribed by law. One term of the County Court shall be held in each county at least once in every two months, and the Legislature may provide for the appointment of a County Attorney to represent the State and county in said court, whose term of office, duties and compensation shall be such as may be prescribed by law. *Tex.*, 511.

—The Legislature may provide for the appointment of one or more persons in each organized county, and may vest in such persons such judicial powers as shall be prescribed by law: *Provided*, That said power shall not exceed that of a Judge of the Circuit Court at chambers. *Wis.*, 567.

—There shall be in each county of the Commonwealth a County Court, which shall be held monthly, by not less than three nor more than five justices, except when the law shall require the presence of a greater number. *Va.*, 543.

—The jurisdiction of the said courts shall be the same as that of the existing County Courts, except so far as it is modified by this Constitution, or may be changed by law. *Va.*, 543.

PROBATE COURTS.

—The General Assembly shall have power to establish, in each county within this State, a Court of Probate, for the granting of letters testamentary, and of administration, and for orphans' business. *Ala.*, 80.

—The qualified voters of each county shall choose a County and Probate Judge, who shall hold his office for two years, and until his successor is elected and qualified. He shall, in addition to the duties that may be required of him by law, as a presiding Judge, of the County Court, be a Judge of the Court of Probate, and have such jurisdiction in matters relating to the estates of deceased persons, executors, administrators and guardians, as may be prescribed by law, until otherwise directed by the General Assembly. *Ark.*, 91.

—The County Judges shall also hold in their several Counties Probate Courts, and perform such other duties as Probate Judge, as may be prescribed by law. In the city and county of San Francisco, the Legislature may separate the office of Probate Judge

from that of County Judge, and may provide for the election of a Probate Judge, who shall hold his office for the term of four years. *Cal.*, (amendment of 1862.)

—The Judges of Probate shall be appointed by the electors residing in the several probate districts, and qualified to vote for representatives therein, in such manner as shall be prescribed by law. *Ct.*, 115.

—The Orphans' Court in each county shall be held by the Chancellor and the Associate Judge residing in the county; the Chancellor being present. Either of them, in the absence of the other, may hold the court. When they concur in opinion, there shall be no appeal from their decision except in matter of real estate. When their opinions are opposed, or when a decision is made by one of them, and in all matters involving a right to real estate, or the appraised value or other value thereof, there shall be an appeal to the Superior Court of the county, which shall have final jurisdiction in every such case. This court shall have all the jurisdiction and powers vested by the laws of this State in the Orphans' Court. *Del.*, 122.

—An executor, administrator, or guardian shall file every account with the Register for the county, who shall, as soon as conveniently may be, carefully examine the particulars with the proofs thereof, in the presence of such executor, administrator or guardian, and shall adjust and settle the same, according to the very right of the matter and the law of the land; which account so settled shall remain in his office for inspection; and the executor, administrator, or guardian shall, within three months after such settlement, give due notice in writing to all persons entitled to shares of the estate, or to their guardians respectively, if residing within the State, that the account is lodged in the said office for inspection. Exceptions may be made by persons concerned, to both sides of every such account, either denying the justice of the allowances made to the accountant, or alleging further charges against him; and the exceptions shall be heard in the Orphans' Court for the county; and thereupon the account shall be adjusted and settled according to the right of the matter and the law of the land. *Del.*, 124.

—There shall be elected in each county of this State, by the qualified voters, an officer to be styled the Judge of Probate, to take probate of wills to grant letters testamentary, of administration and guardianship, to attend to the settlement of the estates of decedents and minors, and to discharge the duties usually appertaining to courts of ordinary, and such other duties as may be required by law; subject to the direction and supervision of the Circuit Courts, as may be provided by law. *Fl.*, 134.

—The powers of a Court of Ordinary and of Probate shall be vested in an Ordinary for each county, from whose decisions there may be an appeal to the Superior Court, under regulations prescribed by law. The Ordinary shall be *ex officio* clerk of said court, and may appoint a deputy clerk. The Ordinary, as clerk, or his deputy, may issue citations, and grant temporary letters of administration, to hold until permanent letters are granted; and said Ordinary, as clerk, or his deputy, may grant marriage licenses. The Ordinaries, in and for the respective counties, shall be elected, as other county officers are, on the first Wednesday in January, 1868, and every fourth year thereafter, and shall be commissioned by the Governor for the term of four years. In case of any

140

vacancy of said office of Ordinary, from any cause, the same shall be filled by election, as is provided in relation to other county officers, and until the same is filled, the Clerk of the Superior Court, for the time being, shall act as Clerk of said Court of Ordinary. *Ga.*, 149.

[County Courts possess probate jurisdiction.] *Ill.*, 161 ; *Mo.*, 359; *Or.*, 454.
—There shall be a Probate Court in each county, which shall be a Court of Record, and have such probate jurisdiction and care of estates of deceased persons, minors, and persons of unsound minds, as may be prescribed by law, and shall have jurisdiction in cases of *habeas corpus*. This court shall consist of one judge, who shall be elected by the qualified voters of the county, and hold his office two years. He shall be his own clerk, and shall hold court at such times and receive for compensation such fees as may be prescribed by law. *Kan.*, 201.

[Registers of Probate appointed by the Governor and Council.] *Me.*, 244.
—The Orphan's Courts shall have all the powers now vested by law in the Orphan's Courts of this State, subject to such changes as the General Assembly may prescribe, and shall have such other jurisdiction as may from time to time be provided by law. *Md.*, 270.
—The General Assembly shall provide a simple and uniform system of charges in the offices of Clerks of Courts and Registers of Wills, in the counties of this State and the city of Baltimore, and for the collection thereof; provided the amount of compensation to any of said officers shall not exceed the sum of twenty-five hundred dollars a year, over and above office expenses, and compensation to assistants; and provided further, that such compensation of Clerks, Registers, assistants and office expenses, shall always be paid out of the fees or receipts of the offices respectively. *Md.*, 264.
—There shall be a Register of Wills in each county of the State and in the city of Baltimore, to be elected by the legal and qualified voters of said counties and city respectively, who shall hold his office for six years from the time of his election, and until his successor is elected and qualified; he shall be re-eligible and subject at all times to removal for willful neglect of duty or misdemeanor in office in the same manner that clerks of courts are removable. In the event of any vacancy in the office of Register of Wills, said vacancy shall be filled by the Judges of the Orphan's Court in which such vacancy occurs, until the next general election for county officers, when a register shall be elected to serve for six years thereafter. *Md.*, 270.
—The Judges of Probate of wills, and for granting letters of administration, shall hold their courts at such place or places, on fixed days, as the convenience of the people shall require; and the Legislature shall, from time to time, hereafter, appoint such times and places; until which appointments the said courts shall be holden at the times and places which the respective judges shall direct. *Mass.*, 209.
—In each of the counties organized for judicial purposes, there shall be a Court of Probate. The judge of such court shall be elected by the electors of the county in which he resides, and shall hold his office for four years, and until his successor is elected and qualified. The jurisdiction, powers, and duties of such court, shall be prescribed by law. *Mich.*, 306.
—The Supreme Court, the Circuit and Probate Courts of each county, shall be courts of record, and shall each have a common seal. *Mich.*, 306.
The first election of Judges of the Probate Courts shall be held on the Tuesday succeeding the first Monday of November, one thousand eight hundred and fifty-two, and every fourth year thereafter. *Mich.*, 306.
—There shall be established in each organized county in the State a Probate Court, which shall be a Court of record, and be held at such times and places as may be prescribed by law. It shall be held by one judge, who shall be elected by the voters of the

county, for the term of two years. He shall be a resident of such county at the time of his election, and reside therein during his continuance in office, and his compensation shall be provided by law. He may appoint his own clerk, where none has been elected, but the Legislature may authorize the election by the electors of any county, of one Clerk or Register of Probate for such county, whose powers, duties, term of office and compensation shall be prescribed by law. A Probate Court shall have jurisdiction over the estates of deceased persons, and persons under guardianship, but no other jurisdiction, except as prescribed by this Constitution. *Minn.*, 325.
—A Court of Probate shall be established in each county of this State, with jurisdiction in all matters testamentary and of administration in minors' business and the allotment of dower in cases of idiotcy and lunacy, and of persons *non compos mentis*. The judge of said court shall be elected by the qualified electors of the respective counties for the term of two years. *Miss.*, 339.
—The jurisdiction of the several courts herein provided for, both appellate and original shall be as fixed by law : *Provided*, That Probate Courts, Justices of the Peace or any inferior court that may be established by the Legislature shall not have jurisdiction in any matter wherein the title or boundaries of land may be in dispute. Nor shall either of the courts mentioned in this proviso have power to order or decree the sale or partition of real estate. *Neb.*, 375.
—Probate Judges, Justices of the Peace, and persons holding inferior courts, herein authorized to be established by the Legislature, shall be elected by the electors of the several districts for which they may be elected in the manner and time fixed by law. *Neb.*, 375.
—All cases, both civil and criminal, which may be pending and undetermined in the Probate Courts of the several counties at the time when, under the provisions of this Constitution, said Probate Courts are to be abolished, shall be transferred to and determined by the District Courts of such counties respectively. *Nev.*, 395.
—All matters relating to the probate of wills and granting letters of administration shall be exercised by the Judges of Probate, in such manner as the Legislature have directed, or may hereafter direct; and the Judges of Probate shall hold their courts at such place or places, on such fixed days as the convenience of the people may require, and the Legislature from time to time appoint. *N. H.*, 408.
—The Chancellor shall be the Ordinary, or Surrogate General, and Judge of the Prerogative Court.
—All persons aggrieved by any order, sentence or decree of the Orphans' Court, may appeal from the same or from any part thereof, to the Prerogative Court; but such order, sentence, or decree shall not be removed into the Supreme or Circuit Court, if the subject-matter thereof be within the jurisdiction of the Orphan's Court. *N. J.*, 418.
—There shall be established in each county a Probate Court, which shall be a court of record, open at all times, and holden by one judge, elected by the voters of the county, who shall hold his office for the term of three years, and shall receive such compensation payable out of the county treasury, or by fees, or both, as shall be provided by law. *Ohio*, 437.
—The Probate Court shall have jurisdiction in probate and testamentary matters, the appointment of administrators and guardians, the settlement of the accounts of executors, administrators and guardians, and such jurisdiction in *habeas corpus*, the issuing of marriage licenses, and for the sale of land by executors, administrators, and guardians, and such other jurisdiction in any county or counties, as may be provided by law. *Ohio*, 437.
—The Probate Courts provided for in this Constitution, as to all matters within the jurisdiction conferred upon said courts, shall be the successors, in the several counties, of the present Courts of Common Pleas; and the records, files and papers, business and proceedings appertaining to said jurisdiction shall be

transferred to said Courts of Probate, and be there proceeded in according to law. *Ohio*, 445.

—The Judges of the Court of Common Pleas of each county, any two of whom shall be a quorum, shall compose the Court of Quarter Sessions of the Peace, and Orphans' Court thereof; and the Register of Wills, together with the said judges, or any two of them, shall compose the Register's Court of each county. *Pa.*, 465.

—A Register's office, for the probate of wills and granting letters of administration, and an office for the recording of deeds, shall be kept in each county. *Pa.*, 465.

—To probate wills, to appoint guardians of minors, idiots, lunatics, and persons *non compos mentis;* to grant letters testamentary and of administration; to settle the accounts of executors, administrators and guardians; to transact all business appertaining to the estates of deceased persons, minors, idiots, lunatics, and persons *non compos mentis*, including the settlement, partition and distribution of such estates; and to apprentice minors under such regulations as may be prescribed by law. *Tex.*, 512.

—Judges of Probate shall be elected by the freemen of their respective districts. *Vt.*, 520.

—The Recorder, in addition to the duties incident to the recording of inventories, and other papers relating to estates, and of deeds and other writings, the registering of births, marriages and deaths, and the issuing of marriage licenses, shall have authority, under such regulations as may be prescribed by law, to receive proof of wills and admit them to probate, to appoint and qualify personal representatives, guardians, committees and curators, to administer oaths, take acknowledgments of deeds and other writings, and relinquishments of dowers. *W. Va.*, 554.

—There shall be chosen in each county by the qualified electors thereof, a Judge of Probate, who shall hold his office for two years, and until his successor shall be elected and qualified, and whose jurisdiction, powers and duties, shall be prescribed by law; *Provided, however,* That the Legislature shall have power to abolish the office of Judge of Probate in any county, and to confer probate powers upon such inferior courts as may be established in said county. *Wis.*, 567.

ERECTION OF NEW COURTS.

—The General Court shall forever have full power and authority to erect and constitute judicatories and courts of record or other courts, to be held in the name of the Commonwealth, for the hearing, trying and determining of all manner of crimes, offenses, pleas, processes, plaints, actions, matters, causes and things whatsoever, arising or happening within the Commonwealth, or between or concerning persons inhabiting or residing, or brought within the same; whether the same be criminal, or civil, or whether the said crimes be capital or not capital, and whether the said pleas be real, personal or mixed; and for the awarding and making out of execution thereupon; to which courts and judicatories are hereby given and granted full power and authority from time to time, to administer oaths or affirmations, for the better discovery of truth in any matter in controversy, or depending before them. *Mass.*, 283.

—The General Court shall forever have full power and authority to erect and constitute judicatories and courts of record, or other courts, to be holden in the name of the State, for the hearing, trying and determining all manner of crimes, offenses, pleas, processes, plaints, actions, causes, matters and things whatsoever, arising and happening within this State, or between or concerning persons inhabiting or residing or brought within the same, whether the same be criminal or civil, or whether the crimes be capital or not capital, and whether the said pleas be real, personal or mixed; and for the awarding and issuing execution thereon. To which courts and judicatories are hereby given and granted full power and authority, from time to time, to administer oaths or affirmations for the better discovery of truth in any matter in controversy, or depending before them. *N. H.*, 401.

—And farther, full power and authority are hereby given and granted to the said General Court, from time to time, to make, ordain and establish all manner of wholesome and reasonable orders, laws, statutes, ordinances, directions and instructions, either with penalties or without, so as the same be not repugnant or contrary to this Constitution, as they may judge for the benefit and welfare of this State, and for the governing and ordering thereof, and of the subjects of the same, for the necessary support and defense of the government thereof; and to name and settle annually, or provide by fixed laws, for the naming and settling of all civil officers within this State; such officers excepted, the election and appointment of whom are hereafter in this form of government otherwise provided for; and to set forth the several duties, powers and limits of the several civil and military officers of this State, and the forms of such oaths or affirmations as shall be respectively administered unto them for the execution of their several offices and places, so as the same be not repugnant or contrary to this Constitution; and also to impose fines, mulcts, imprisonments and other punishments; and to impose and levy proportional and reasonable assessments, rates and taxes, upon all the inhabitants of, and residents within the said State, and upon all estates within the same; to be issued and disposed of by warrant under the hand of the Governor of this State for the time being, with the advice and consent of the Council, for the public service in the necessary defense and support of the government of this State, and the protection and preservation of the subjects thereof, according to such acts as are or shall be in force within the same. *N. H.*, 401.

—The Legislature may, from time to time, establish such other inferior courts as may be deemed necessary, and to abolish the same whenever they shall deem it expedient. *Miss.*, 340.

[The Legislature may erect new courts.] *Mass.*, 283; *Miss.*, 370; *N. H.*, 402.

—The Legislature shall have power, if they should think it expedient and necessary, to provide by law for the organization of a separate Supreme Court, with the jurisdiction and powers prescribed in this Constitution, to consist of one Chief Justice and two Associate Justices, to be elected by the qualified electors of the State, at such time and in such manner as the Legislature may provide. The separate Supreme Court, when so organized, shall not be changed or discontinued by the Legislature; the judges thereof shall be so classified that but one of them shall go out of office at the same time, and their term of office shall be the same as is provided for the Judges of the Circuit Court. And whenever the Legislature may consider it necessary to establish a separate Supreme Court, they shall have power to reduce the number of Circuit Court judges to four, and subdivide the judicial circuits, but no such subdivision or reduction shall take effect until after the expiration of the term of some of the said judges, or till a vacancy occur by some other means. *Wis.*, 565.

JUDICIAL DISTRICTS.

—The State shall be divided into convenient circuits, each to consist of not less than five nor more than seven counties contiguous to each other, for each of which a judge shall be elected, who, during his continuance in office, shall reside and be a conservator of the peace, within the circuit for which he shall have been elected. *Ark.*, 91.

—The State shall be divided by the Legislature of 1863, into fourteen judicial districts, subject to such alteration from time to time, by a two-thirds vote of the

1 § 16. The Legislature may reorganize the judicial districts at the first ses-
2 sion after the return of every enumeration under this Constitution, in the
3 manner provided for in the fourth section of this article, and at no other time ;
4 and they may, at such session, increase or diminish the number of districts,
5 but such increase or diminution shall not be more than one district at any one
6 time. Each district shall have four Justices of the Supreme Court ; but no
7 diminution of the districts shall have the effect to remove a judge from office.

members elected to both Houses, as the public good may require ; in each of which there shall be a District Court, and for each of which a District Judge shall be elected by the qualified electors of the district, at the special judicial elections to be held as provided for the election of Justices of the Supreme Court by section three of this article. *Cal.*, (as amended in 1862).

—The State shall be divided into convenient circuits; and for each circuit there shall be a Judge, who shall, after his election or appointment, reside in the circuit for which he has been elected or appointed ; and shall, as well as Justices of the Supreme Court, receive for his services a salary of not less than twenty-five hundred dollars per annum, which shall not be diminished during his continuance in office, but the judges shall receive no fees, perquisites of office, nor hold any other office of profit under the State, the United States, or any other power. *Fl.*, 133.

—The State shall be divided into three grand divisions, as nearly equal as may be, and the qualified electors of each division shall elect one of the said judges for the term of nine years ; *Provided*, That after the first election of such judges the ·General Assembly may have the power to provide by law for their election by the whole State, or by divisions, as they may deem most expedient. *Ill.*, 160.

—The State shall be divided into nine judicial districts, in each of which one circuit judge shall be elected by the qualified electors thereof, who shall hold his office for the term of six years, and until his successor shall be commissioned and qualified ; *Provided*, That the General Assembly may increase the number of circuits to meet the future exigencies of the State. *Ill.*, 160.

—The foregoing districts may, after the taking of each census by the State, be altered, if necessary, to equalize the said districts in population, but such alteration shall be made by adding to such district such adjacent county or counties as will make said district nearest equal in population ; *Provided*, no such alteration shall affect the office of any judge then in office. *Ill.*, 162.

—The State shall be divided into as many districts as there are judges of the Supreme Court, and such districts shall be formed of contiguous territory, as nearly equal in population as, without dividing a county, the same can be made. One of said judges shall be elected from each district, and reside therein ; but said judges shall be elected by the electors of the State at large. *Ind.*, 176.

—The State shall from time to time be divided into judicial circuits, and a judge for each circuit shall be elected by the voters thereof. He shall reside within the circuit, and shall hold his office for the term of six years, if he so long behave well. *Ind.*, 177.

—The State shall be divided into eleven judicial districts, and after the year 1860, the General Assembly may reorganize the judicial districts, and increase or diminish the number of districts, or the number of judges of the said court, and may increase the number of judges of the Supreme Court ; but such increase or diminution shall not be more than one district, or one judge of either court at any one ses-

sion ; and no reorganization of the districts or diminution of the judges, shall have the effect of removing a judge from office. Such reorganization of the districts, or any change in the boundaries thereof, or increase or diminution of the number of judges shall take place every four years thereafter, if necessary, and at no other time. *Iowa*, 189.

—The General Assembly, at the first session under this Constitution, shall district the State into eleven judicial districts, for District Court purposes, and shall also provide for the apportionment of the members of the General Assembly, in accordance with the provisions of this Constitution. *Iowa*, 195.

—The State shall be divided into five judicial districts, in each of which there shall be elected, by the electors thereof, a district judge, who shall hold his office for the term of four years. District Courts shall be held at such times and places as may be provided by law. *Kan.*, 200.

—New or unorganized counties shall by law be attached for judicial purposes to the most convenient judicial district. *Kan.*, 201.

—Provision may be made by law for the increase of the number of judicial districts whenever two-thirds of the members of each House shall concur. Such districts shall be formed of compact territory and bounded by county lines, and such increase shall not vacate the office of any judge. *Kan.*, 201.

—The General Assembly, if they deem it necessary, may establish one additional district every four years, but the judicial districts shall not exceed sixteen, until the population of this State shall exceed one million five hundred thousand. *Ky.*, 216.

—At the first session after the adoption of this Constitution, the General Assembly shall divide the State into twelve judicial districts, having due regard to business, territory, and population : *Provided*, That no county shall be divided. *Ky.*, 216.

—They shall, at the same time the judicial districts are laid off, direct elections to be held in each district, to elect a judge for said district, and shall prescribe in what manner the election shall be conducted. *Ky.*, 216.

—The judicial districts of this State shall not be changed, except at the first session after an enumeration, unless when a new district may be established. *Ky.*, 216.

—The State shall be divided into eight judicial circuits ; in each of which the electors thereof shall elect one Circuit Judge, who shall hold his office for the term of six years, and until his successor is elected and qualified. *Mich.*, 306.

—The Legislature may alter the limits of circuits, or increase the number of the same. No alteration or increase shall have the effect to remove a judge from office. In every additional circuit established the judge shall be elected by the electors of such circuit, and his term of office shall continue as provided in this Constitution for Judges of the Circuit Court. *Mich.*, 306.

—The Legislature may at any time change the number of judicial districts or their boundaries, when it shall be deemed expedient, but no such change shall vacate the office of any judge. *Minn.*, 325.

1 § 17. The electors of the several towns shall, at their annual town meeting,

2 and in such manner as the Legislature may direct, elect Justices of the Peace,

3 whose term of office shall be four years. In case of an election to fill a

4 vacancy occurring before the expiration of a full term they shall hold for the

5 residue of the unexpired term. Their number and classification may be regu-

—The State shall be divided by the Legislature into six judicial districts, which shall be composed of contiguous territory, be bounded by county lines and contain a population as nearly equal as may be practicable. In each judicial district, one judge shall be elected by the electors thereof, who shall constitute said court, and whose term of office shall be seven years. Every District Judge shall, at the time of his election, be a resident of the district for which he shall be elected, and shall reside therein during his continuance in office. *Minn.*, 324.

—The State shall be divided into convenient districts, and each district shall contain not less than three nor more than twelve counties. *Miss.*, 339.

—The State, except the county of St. Louis, shall be divided into not less than five districts, each of which shall embrace at least three judicial circuits; and in each district a court, to be known as the District Court, shall be held, at such times and places as may be provided by law. Each District Court shall be held by the Judges of the Circuit Courts embraced in the district, a majority of whom shall be a quorum. The District Courts shall, within their respective districts, have like original jurisdiction with the Supreme Court, and appellate jurisdiction from the final judgments of the Circuit Courts, and of all inferior courts of record within the district, except Probate and County Courts. After the establishment of such District Courts, no appeal or writ of error shall lie from any Circuit Court, or inferior court of record, to the Supreme Court, but shall be prosecuted to the District Court, from the final judgment of which an appeal or writ of error may be taken to the Supreme Court, in such cases as may be provided by law. *Mo.*, 358.

— The State shall be divided into convenient districts, not to exceed four, in each of which the Supreme Court shall be held, at such time and place as the General Assembly may appoint; and when sitting in either district, it shall exercise jurisdiction over causes originating in that district only; but the General Assembly may direct, by law, that the said court shall be held in one place only. *Mo.*, 357.

—The State shall be divided into three judicial districts, and the District Courts shall be held at such times and places as may be provided by law, and the Legislature shall, by law, assign the Justices to hold District Courts in the several districts; *Provided*, That until the Legislature shall have provided by law, the Governor shall have authority to make such assignment. *Neb.*, 375.

—The State is hereby divided into nine judicial districts. The Legislature may, however, provide, by law, for an alteration in the boundaries or division of the districts herein prescribed, and also for increasing or diminishing the number of judicial districts and judges therein. But no such change shall take effect except in case of a vacancy or the expiration of a term of an incumbent of the office. *Nev.*, 386.

—The State shall be divided into nine common pleas districts, of which the county of Hamilton shall constitute one, of compact territory, and bounded by county lines; and each of said districts, consisting of three or more counties, shall be subdivided into three parts, of compact territory, bounded by county lines, and as nearly equal in population as practicable; in each of which one Judge of the Court of Common Pleas for said district, and residing therein, shall be elected by the electors of said subdivision. Courts of Common Pleas shall be held by one or more of these judges in every county in the district, as often as may be provided by law; and more than one court, or sitting thereof, may be held at the same time in each district. *Ohio*, 437.

—The boundaries of the several judicial and election districts shall remain as they are now established. *S. C.*, 482.

—The State shall be divided into convenient judicial districts. For each district there shall be elected by the qualified voters thereof, at a general election for State or county officers a judge who shall reside in the same; shall hold his office for the term of eight years; shall receive an annual salary of not less than three thousand five hundred dollars, which shall not be increased or diminished during his term of service, and shall hold the courts at one place in each county in the district at least twice in each year, in such manner as may be prescribed by law. *Tex.*, 510.

—Each judicial district in the State shall constitute one election district, except Charleston district, which shall be divided into two election districts; one consisting of the late parishes of St. Philip and St. Michael, to be designated the election district of Charleston; the other, consisting of all that part of the judicial district which is without the limits of the said parishes, to be known as the election district of Berkeley. *S. C.*, 482.

—The State shall be divided into sixteen judicial circuits, seven districts, and three sections. *Va.*, 541.

—The General Assembly may at the end of five years after the adoption of this Constitution, and thereafter at intervals of ten years, re-arrange the said circuits, districts and sections, and place any number of circuits in a district and of districts in a section; but each circuit shall be altogether in one district and each district in one section; and there shall not be less than two districts and four circuits in a section, and the number of sections shall not be diminished. *Va.*, 591.

—The Legislature may from time to time, re-arrange the circuits; and after the expiration of five years from the time this Constitution goes into operation, and thereafter, at periods of ten years, may increase or diminish the number of circuits, or the number of courts in a year, as necessity may require. *W. Va.*, 552.

—The State shall be divided into five judicial circuits. *Wis.*, 566.

—The Legislature may alter the limits, or increase the number of circuits, making them as compact and convenient as practicable, and bounding them by county lines, but no such alteration or increase shall have the effect to remove a judge from office. In case of an increase of circuits, the judge or judges shall be elected as provided in this Constitution, and receive a salary not less than that herein provided for Judges of the Circuit Court. *Wis.*, 566.

JUSTICES OF THE PEACE.

—[Under the first Constitution of New York, Justices were appointed by the Council of Appointment. In 1821, they were appointed by Supervisors and Judges, but in 1826 an amendment was adopted, directing their election for a term of four years]. 39, 44.

—A competent number of Justices of the Peace shall be appointed in and for each county, in such mode, and for such term of office, as the General Assembly

6 lated by law. Justices of the Peace and judges or justices of inferior courts
7 not of record, and their clerks, may be removed after due notice and an
8 opportunity of being heard in their defense by such county, city or State
9 courts as may be prescribed by law, for causes to be assigned in the order of
10 removal.

may by law direct; whose jurisdiction, in civil cases, shall be limited to causes in which the amount in controversy shall not exceed one hundred dollars; and in all cases tried by a Justice of the Peace, the right of appeal shall be secured, under such rules and regulations, as may be prescribed by law. *Ala.*, 80.
—The qualified voters residing in each township shall elect the Justices of the Peace for each township. For every one hundred voters there may be elected one Justice of the Peace; *Provided,* That each township, however small, shall have two Justices of the Peace. Justices of the Peace shall be elected for the term of two years, and shall hold their offices until their successors are elected and qualified; shall be commissioned by the Governor, and shall reside in the township for which they are elected during their continuance in office. The first election for Justices of the Peace shall take place on the second Monday in March, 1864, and the second election on the first Monday in August, one thousand eight hundred and sixty-six, *and at the regular elections thereafter.* Justices of the Peace, individually, or two or more of them jointly, shall have original jurisdiction in cases of bastardy, and in all matters of contract, and actions for the recovery of fines and forfeiture where the amount claimed does not exceed two hundred dollars, and concurrent jurisdiction with Circuit Courts where the amount claimed exceeds one hundred dollars, and does not exceed two hundred dollars, and such jurisdiction as may be provided by law in actions *ex delicto,* where the damages claimed do not exceed one hundred dollars; and prosecutions for assault and battery and other penal offenses less than felony, punishable by fine only. Every action cognizable before a Justice of the Peace, instituted by summons or warrant, shall be brought before some Justice of the Peace of the township where the defendant resides. They may also sit as examining courts, and commit, discharge, or recognize any person charged with any crime of any grade. For the forgoing purposes they shall have power to issue all necessary process. They shall also have power to bind to keep the peace, or for good behavior. *Ark.*, 92.
—There shall be established in each county in the State, a court to holden by the Justices of the Peace, a court called the County Court, which shall have jurisdiction in all matters relating to taxes, disbursements of money for county purposes, and in every other case that may be necessary to the internal improvement and local concerns of the respective counties. *Ark.*, 91.
—The Legislature shall determine the number of Justices of the Peace to be elected in each city and township of the State, and fix by law their powers, duties, and responsibilities; *Provided,* such powers shall not in any case trench upon the jurisdiction of the several courts of record. *Cal.,* (as amended in 1862).
—There shall be appointed in each county, a sufficient number of Justices of the Peace, with such jurisdiction in civil and criminal cases as the General Assembly may prescribe. *Ct.,* 111.
—The Governor shall appoint a competent number of persons to the office of Justice of the Peace, not exceeding twelve in each county, until two-thirds of both Houses of the Legislature shall by law direct an addition to the number, who shall be commissioned for seven years, if so long they shall behave themselves well, but may be removed by the Governor within that time on conviction of misbehavior in

office, or on the address of both Houses of the Legislature. *Del.,* 124.
—A competent number of Justices of the Peace shall be from time to time elected in and for each county, in such mode and for such term of office as the General Assembly may direct, and shall possess such jurisdiction as may be prescribed by law; and in cases tried before a Justice of the Peace, the right of appeal shall be secured under such rules and regulations as may be prescribed by law. *Fl.,* 134.
—The Justice or Justices of the Inferior Court and the Judge of such other County Court as may by law be created, shall be elected in each county by the persons entitled to vote for members of the General Assembly. *Ga.,* 149.
—The Justice of the Peace shall be elected in each district by the persons entitled to vote for members of the General Assembly. *Ga.,* 149.
—A competent number of Justices of the Peace shall be elected by the voters in each township in the several counties. They shall continue in office four years, and their powers and duties shall be prescribed by law. *Ind.,* 177.
—The jurisdiction of Justices of the Peace shall extend to all civil cases (except cases in chancery and cases where the question of title to any real estate may arise), where the amount in controversy does not exceed one hundred dollars, and by the consent of parties may be extended to any amount not exceeding three hundred dollars. *Iowa,* 193.
—There shall be elected in each county in this State, in such districts as the General Assembly may direct, by the qualified electors thereof a competent number of Justices of the Peace, who shall hold their offices for the term of four years, and until their successors shall have been elected and qualified, and who shall perform such duties, receive such compensation, and exercise such jurisdiction, as may be prescribed by law. *Ill.,* 161.
—Two Justices of the Peace shall be elected in each township, whose term of office shall be two years, and whose powers and duties shall be prescribed by law. The number of Justices of the Peace may be increased in any township by law. *Kan.,* 201.
—Each county in this State shall be laid off into districts of convenient size, as the General Assembly may, from time to time, direct. Two Justices of the Peace shall be elected in each district, by the qualified voters therein, at such time and place as may be prescribed by law, for the term of four years, whose jurisdiction shall be co-extensive with the county; no person shall be eligible as a Justice of the Peace, unless he be a citizen of the United States, twenty-one years of age, and a resident of the district in which he may be candidate. *Ky.,* 217.
—The General Assembly may provide by law, that the Justices of the Peace in each county shall sit at the Court of Claims and assist in laying the county levy and making appropriations only. *Ky.,* 217.
—A Constable shall be elected in every Justice's district, who shall be chosen for two years, at such time and place as may be provided by law, whose jurisdiction shall be co-extensive with the county in which he may reside. *Ky.,* 218.
—The jurisdiction of Justices of the Peace shall not exceed in civil cases the sum of one hundred dollars, exclusive of interest, subject to appeal in such cases as shall be provided for by law. They shall be elected by the qualified voters of their several districts, and shall hold their office during a term of two years.

They shall have such criminal jurisdiction as shall be provided by law. *La.*, 232.

—Justices of the Peace and Notaries Public shall hold their offices during seven years, if they so long behave themselves well, at the expiration of which term they may be re-appointed, or others appointed as the public interest may require. *Me.*, 246.

—Judges of the County Court, and Justices of the Peace, shall be conservators of the peace. *Ky.*, 217.

—The Governor, by and with the advice and consent of the Senate, shall appoint such number of Justices of the Peace, and the County Commissioners of the several counties, and the Mayor and City Council of Baltimore, shall appoint such number of Constables for the several election districts of the counties and wards of the city of Baltimore, as are now or may hereafter be prescribed by law; and Justices of the Peace and Constables so appointed, shall be subject to removal by the judge having criminal jurisdiction in the county or city, for incompetency, willful neglect of duty, or misdemeanor in office, on conviction in a court of law. The Justices of the Peace and Constables so appointed and commissioned shall be conservators of the peace, shall hold their office for two years, and shall have such jurisdiction, duties and compensation, subject to such right of appeal in all cases, from the judgment of Justices of the Peace, as hath been heretofore exercised, or shall be hereafter prescribed by law. *Md.*, 270.

—In the event of a vacancy in the office of a Justice of the Peace, the Governor shall appoint a person to serve as Justice of the Peace for the residue of the term, and in case of a vacancy in the office of Constable, the County Commissioners of the county in which the vacancy occurs, or the Mayor and City Council of Baltimore, as the case may be, shall appoint a person to serve as Constable for the residue of the term. *Md.*, 270.

—In order that the people may not suffer from the long continuance in place of any Justice of the Peace, who shall fail of discharging the important duties of his office with ability or fidelity, all commissions of Justices of the Peace shall expire and become void in the term of seven years from their respective dates; and upon the expiration of any commission, the same may, if necessary, be renewed, or another person appointed, as shall most conduce to the well being of the Commonwealth. *Mass.*, 290.

—In civil cases, Justices of the Peace shall have exclusive jurisdiction to the amount of one hundred dollars, and concurrent jurisdiction to the amount of three hundred dollars, which may be increased to five hundred dollars, with such exceptions and restrictions as may be provided law. They shall also have such criminal jurisdiction, and perform such duties as shall be prescribed by the Legislature. *Mich.*, 306.

—There shall be, not exceeding four Justices of the Peace in each organized township. They shall be elected by the electors of the townships, shall hold their offices for four years, and until their successors are elected and qualified. At the first election in any township, they shall be classified as prescribed by law. A justice elected to fill a vacancy shall hold his office for the residue of the unexpired term. The Legislature may increase the number of justices in cities. *Mich.*, 306.

—The Legislature shall provide for the election of a sufficient number of Justices of the Peace in each county, whose term of office shall be two years, and whose duties and compensation shall be prescribed by law: *Provided*, That no Justice of the Peace shall have jurisdiction of any civil cause where the amount in controversy shall exceed one hundred dollars, nor in a criminal cause where the punishment shall exceed three months imprisonment, or a fine of over one hundred dollars, nor in any cause involving the title to real estate. *Minn.*, 325.

—A competent number of Justices of the Peace and Constables shall be chosen in each county by the qualified electors thereof, by districts, who shall hold their offices for the term of two years. The jurisdiction of Justices of the Peace shall be limited to causes

in which the principal of the amount in controversy shall not exceed the amount of fifty dollars. In all causes tried by a Justice of the Peace, the right of appeal shall be secured under such rules and regulations as shall be prescribed by law. *Miss.*, 340.

—In each county there shall be appointed, or elected, as many Justices of the Peace as the public good may be thought to require. Their powers and duties, and their duration in office, shall be regulated by law. *Mo.*, 359.

—The Legislature shall determine the number of Justices of the Peace, to be chosen in each city and township of the State, and shall fix by law their powers, duties and responsibilities: *Provided*, That such Justices' Courts shall not have jurisdiction of the following cases, viz.: *First*, Of cases in which the matter in dispute is a money demand or personal property, and the amount of demand exclusive of interest or the value of the property exceeds three hundred dollars. *Second*, Of cases wherein the title to real estate, or mining claims, or questions of boundaries to land is or may be involved; or of cases that in any manner shall conflict with the jurisdiction of the several courts of record in this State: *And, Provided, further,* That Justices' Courts shall have such criminal jurisdiction as may be prescribed by law; and the Legislature may confer upon said courts jurisdiction concurrent with the District Courts of actions to enforce mechanics' liens, wherein the amount, exclusive of interest, does not exceed three hundred dollars; and also, of actions for the possession of lands and tenements, where the relation of landlord and tenant exists, or where such possession has been unlawfully or fraudulently obtained or withheld. *Nev.*, 387.

—In order that the people may not suffer from the long continuance in place of any Justice of the Peace who shall fail in discharging the important duties of his office with ability and fidelity, all commissions of Justices of the Peace shall become void at the expiration of five years from their respective dates; and upon the expiration of any commission, the same may, if necessary, be renewed, or another person appointed, as shall most conduce to the well being of the State. *N. H.*, 408.

—The General Court are empowered to give to Justices of the Peace jurisdiction in civil causes, when the damages demanded shall not exceed four pounds, and title of real estate is not concerned; but with the right of appeal to either party to some other court, so that a trial by jury in the last resort may be had. *N. H.*, 408.

—Justices of the Peace shall be elected by ballot, at the annual meetings of the townships in the several counties of the State, and of the wards in the cities that may vote in wards, in such manner, under such regulations, as may be hereafter provided by law.

They shall be commissioned for the county, and their commissions shall bear date and take effect on the first day of May next after their election.

They shall hold their offices for five years; but when elected to fill vacancies, they shall hold for the unexpired term only: *Provided*, That the commission of any Justice of the Peace shall become vacant upon his ceasing to reside in the township in which he was elected.

The first election for Justices of the Peace shall take place at the next annual town meetings of the townships in the several counties of the State, and of the wards in cities that may vote in wards. *N. J.*, 419.

—There may be elected under this Constitution two, and not more than five Justices of the Peace in each of the townships of the several counties of this State, and in each of the wards, in cities that may vote in wards. When a township or ward contains two thousand inhabitants or less, it may have two justices; when it contains more than two thousand inhabitants, and not more than four thousand, it may have four justices; and when it contains more than four thousand inhabitants, it may have five justices: *Provided*, That whenever any township not voting in wards, contains more than seven thousand inhabitants, such township may have an additional justice for each additional three thousand inhabitants above four thousand. *N. J.*, 418.

—Upon the conviction of any Justice of the Peace of any infamous crime, or of corruption or malpractice in office, the commission of such justice shall be thereby vacated, and he shall be forever disqualified from holding such appointment. *N. C.*, 429.

—That the Justices of the Peace, within their respective counties in this State, shall in future be recommended to the Governor, for the time being, by the Representatives in General Assembly, and the Governor shall commission them accordingly, and the justices, when so commissioned, shall hold their offices during good behavior, and shall not be removed from office by the General Assembly, unless for misbehavior, absence or inability. *N. C.*, 425.

—A competent number of Justices of the Peace shall be elected by the electors, in each township in the several counties. Their term of office shall be three years, and their powers and duties shall be regulated by law. *Ohio*, 437.

—Justices of the Peace, and county and township officers may be removed, in such manner and for such cause, as shall be prescribed by law. *Ohio*, 440.

—Justices of the Peace may also be invested with limited judicial powers. *Or.*, 454.

—Justices of the Peace or Aldermen, shall be elected in the several wards, boroughs and townships, at the same time of the election of Constables by the qualified voters thereof, in such number as shall be directed by law, and shall be commissioned by the Governor for a term of five years. But no township, ward or borough, shall elect more than two Justices of the Peace or Aldermen without the consent of a majority of the qualified electors within such township, ward or borough. *Pa.*, 466.

—Justices of the Peace and other civil officers, not hereinbefore mentioned, for crimes or misdemeanors in office, shall be liable to indictment in such courts as the Legislature may direct; and upon conviction, shall be removed from office, by said court, as if found guilty on impeachment; and shall be subject to such other punishment as may be prescribed by law. *Tenn.*, 496.

—There shall be elected a convenient number of Justices of the Peace, who shall have such civil and criminal jurisdiction as shall be provided by law, where the matter in controversy shall not exceed, in value, one hundred dollars, exclusive of interest; also one Sheriff, one Coroner, and a sufficient number of Constables, who shall hold their offices for four years, to be elected by the qualified voters of the district, or county, as the Legislature may direct. Justices of the Peace, Sheriffs and Coroners shall be commissioned by the Governor. The Sheriff shall not be eligible more than eight years in every twelve. *Tex.*, 512.

—Justices of the Peace shall be elected by the freemen of their respective towns; and towns having less than one thousand inhabitants may elect any number of Justices of the Peace not exceeding *five;* towns having one thousand, and less than two thousand inhabitants, may elect *seven ;* towns having two thousand, and less than three thousand inhabitants, may elect *ten ;* towns having three thousand, and less than five thousand inhabitants, may elect *twelve ;* and towns having five thousand, or more, inhabitants, may elect *fifteen* Justices of the Peace. *Vt.*, 529.

—The Justices of the Peace for the several towns in this State shall be appointed by the electors in such towns; and the time and the manner of their election, the number for each town, and the period for which they shall hold their offices, shall be prescribed by law. *Ct.*, 115.

—The power and jurisdiction of Justices of the Peace

within their respective counties shall be prescribed by law. *Va.*, 543.

—Each county shall be laid off into districts as nearly equal as may be in territory and population. Such districts as now laid off by law shall continue, subject to such changes as may hereafter be made by the General Assembly. In each district there shall be elected, by the voters thereof, four Justices of the Peace, who shall be commissioned by the Governor, reside in their respective districts, and hold their offices for the term of four years. The justices so elected shall choose one of their own body, who shall be the presiding justice of the County Court, and whose duty it shall be attend each term of said court. The other justices shall be classified by law for the performance of their duties in court. *Va.*, 543.

—The Justices of the Peace, Sheriffs, Attorneys for the Commonwealth, Clerks of the Circuit and County Courts, and all other county officers, shall be subject to indictment for malfeasance, misfeasance or neglect of official duty; and upon conviction thereof, their offices shall become vacant. *Va.*, 544.

—The civil jurisdiction of a justice shall extend to actions of assumpsit, debt, detinue and trover, if the amount claimed, exclusive of interest, does not exceed one hundred dollars, when the defendant resides, or, being a non-resident of the State, is found, or has effects or estate within his township, or when the cause of action arose therein; but any other justice of the same county may issue a summons to the defendant to appear before the justice of the proper township, which may be served by a Constable of either township. In case of a vacancy in the office of Justice or Constable in any township having but one, or of the disability to act of the incumbent, any other Justice or Constable of the same county may discharge the duties of their respective offices within the said township. The manner of conducting the aforesaid actions, and of issuing summonses and executions, and of executing and making return of the same, shall be prescribed by law; and the Legislature may give to Justices and Constables such additional civil jurisdiction and powers, within their respective townships, as may be deemed expedient. *W. Va.*, 555.

—Every Justice and Constable shall be a conservator of the peace throughout his county, and have such jurisdiction and powers in criminal cases therein as may be prescribed by law. Jurisdiction of all misdemeanors and breaches of the peace, punishable by fine not exceeding ten dollars, or by imprisonment for not more than thirty days, may be, by law, vested in the justices. *W. Va.*, 555.

—Either party to a civil suit brought before a justice where the value in controversy, or the damages claimed, exceeds twenty dollars, and the defendant, in such cases of misdemeanor or breach of the peace as may be made by law cognizable by a single justice, when the penalty is imprisonment or a fine exceeding five dollars, shall be entitled to a trial by six jurors, if demanded, under such regulations as may be prescribed by law. *W. Va.*, 555.

—The electors of the several towns, at their annual town meetings, and the electors of cities and villages, at their charter elections, shall in such manner as the Legislature may direct, elect Justices of the Peace, whose term of office shall be for two years, and until their successors in office shall be elected and qualified. In case of an election to fill a vacancy occurring before the expiration of a full term, the justice elected shall hold for the residue of the unexpired term. Their number and classification shall be regulated by law. And the tenure of two years shall in no wise interfere with the classification in the first instance. The justices thus elected shall have such civil and criminal jurisdiction as shall be prescribed by law. *Wis.*, 567.

1   § 18. All judicial officers of cities and villages, and all such judicial officers

2   as may be created therein by law, shall be elected at such times and in such

3   manner as the Legislature may direct.

1   § 19. Clerks of the several counties of this State shall be clerks of the

2   Supreme Court, with such powers and duties as shall be prescribed by law. A

3   clerk of the Court of Appeals, to be *ex officio* clerk of the Supreme Court, and

4   to keep his office at the seat of government, shall be chosen by the electors of

5   the State; he shall hold his office for three years, and his compensation shall

6   be fixed by law and paid out of the public treasury.

MUNICIPAL AND LOCAL COURTS.

—The special justices, and the assistant justices and their clerks, in the city of New York, shall be appointed by the Common Council of the said city; and shall hold their offices for the same term that the justices of the peace in the other counties of this State, hold their offices, and shall be removable in like manner. *N. Y.* (1821), 40.

—Provision shall be made by law prescribing the powers, duties and responsibilities of any municipal court that may be established in pursuance of section 1, of this article; and also fixing by law the jurisdiction of said court so as not to conflict with that of the several courts of record. *Nev.*, 387.

—The Recorders of the several Mayors' Courts in this Commonwealth, shall be appointed for the same time and in the same manner, as the President Judges of the several judicial districts; of those now in office, the commission oldest in date shall expire on the twenty-seventh day of February, one thousand eight hundred and forty-one, and the others every two years thereafter, according to their respective dates; those oldest in date expiring first. *Pa.*, 469.

—The General Assembly may vest such jurisdiction as shall be deemed necessary, in Corporation Courts, and in the magistrates who may belong to the corporate body. *Va.*, 544.

—The Legislature may establish courts of limited jurisdiction within any incorporated town or city, subject to appeal to the Circuit Courts. *W. Va.*, 559.

—The Legislature shall impose a tax on all civil suits commenced or prosecuted in the Municipal, Inferior, or Circuit Courts, which shall constitute a fund to be applied toward the payment of the salary of judges. *Wis.*, 567.

OFFICERS AND REPORTERS OF COURTS.

--*And be it further ordained*, That the Register and Clerks in Chancery, be appointed by the Chancellor; the Clerks of the Supreme Court by the Judges of the said court; the Clerk of the Court of Probate, by the judge of said court; and the Register and Marshal of the Court of Admiralty, by the Judge of the Admiralty. The said marshal, registers and clerks to continue in office during the pleasure of those by whom they are appointed, as aforesaid. *N. Y.* (1777), 30.

—The Clerk of the Court of Oyer and Terminer, and General Sessions of the Peace in and for the city and county of New York, shall be appointed by the Court of General Sessions of the Peace in said city, and hold his office during the pleasure of said court; and such clerks and other officers of courts, whose appointment is not herein provided for, shall be appointed for several years, or by the Governor, with the consent of the Senate, as may be directed by law. *N. Y.* (1821), 40.

—Clerks of the Circuit Courts, and of such inferior courts as may be by law established, shall be elected by the qualified electors in each county, for the term of four years; and may be removed from office for such causes and in such manner as may be by law prescribed. Vacancies in the office of clerk shall be filled by the Judge of the Court, and the person so appointed shall hold office until the next general election, and until his successor is elected and qualified; *Provided*, That the General Assembly shall have power to annex the duties of clerk to the office of judge of any inferior court by law established. *Ala.*, 81.

—The Supreme Court shall appoint its own Clerk or Clerks, for the term of four years. The qualified voters of each county shall elect a Clerk of the Circuit Court for the respective counties, who shall hold his office for the term of two years, and until his successor is elected and qualified, and Courts of Chancery, if any be established, shall appoint their own Clerks. *Ark.*, 91.

—The Legislature shall provide for the election of a Clerk of the Supreme Court, County Clerks, District Attorneys, Sheriffs, and other necessary officers, and shall fix by law their duties and compensation. *Cal.*, (as amended in 1862).

—The Legislature shall provide for the speedy publication of such opinions of the Supreme Court as it may deem expedient; and all opinions shall be free for publication by any person. *Cal.*, (as amended in 1862.)

—The Clerks of the Circuit Courts of the several circuits of this State, shall be elected by the qualified voters in their several counties at such times and places as are now or may be provided by law : *Provided, however*, That the Chief Justice of the Supreme Court and the Chancellors of the Court of Chancery, when such courts shall be established, shall have the power to appoint the Clerks of their respective courts. *Fl.*, 135.

—The qualified voters of each county in this State shall elect a Clerk of the Circuit Court, who shall hold his office for the term of four years, and until his successor shall have been elected and qualified, who shall perform such duties and receive such compensation as may be prescribed by law. The Clerks of the Supreme court shall be elected in each division, by the qualified electors thereof, for the term of six years, and until their successors shall have been elected and qualified; whose duties and compensation shall be provided by law. *Ill.*, 161.

—The General Assembly shall provide by law for the speedy publication of the decisions of the Supreme Court made under this Constitution; but no judge shall be allowed to report such decision. *Ind.*, 177.

—There shall be elected by the voters of the State, a Clerk of the Supreme Court, who shall hold his office four years, and whose duties shall be prescribed by law. *Ind.*, 177.

—There shall be appointed, by the Justices of the

Supreme Court, a Reporter and Clerk of said court, who shall hold their offices two years, and whose duties shall be prescribed by law. *Kan.*, 200.

—There shall be elected, by the qualified voters of this State, a Clerk of the Court of Appeals, who shall hold his office, from the first election, until the first Monday in August, 1858, and thereafter for the term of eight years from and after his election; and should the General Assembly provide for holding the Court of Appeals in any one or more of said districts, they shall also provide for the election of a Clerk by the qualified voters of such district, who shall hold his office for eight years, possess the same qualifications, and be subject to removal in the same manner as the Clerk of the Court of Appeals; but if the General Assembly shall, at its first or any other session, direct the Court of Appeals to hold its sessions in more than one district, a Clerk shall be elected by the qualified voters of such district. And the Clerk, first provided for in this section, shall be elected by the qualified voters of the other district or districts. The same principle shall be observed whenever the Court shall be directed to hold its sessions in either of the other districts. Should the number of Judges be reduced, the term of the office of Clerk shall be six years. *Ky.*, 215.

—No person shall be eligible to the office of Clerk of the Court of Appeals, unless he be a citizen of the United States, a resident of the State two years next preceding his election, of the age of twenty-one years, and have a certificate from a Judge of the Court of Appeals, or a Judge of a Circuit Court, that he has been examined by the Clerk of his Court, under his supervision, and that he is qualified for the office for which he is a candidate. *Ky.*, 215.

—Should a vacancy occur in the office of the Clerk of the Court of Appeals, the Governor shall issue a writ of election, and the qualified voters of the State, or of the district in which the vacancy may occur, shall elect a Clerk of the Court of Appeals, to serve until the end of the term for which such Clerk was elected; *Provided,* That when a vacancy shall occur from any cause, or the Clerk be under charges upon information, the Judges of the Court of Appeals shall have power to appoint a Clerk, *pro tem.,* to perform the duties of clerk until such vacancy shall be filled, or the Clerk acquitted; *And, provided further,* That no writ of election shall issue to fill a vacancy unless the unexpired term exceed one year. *Ky.*, 216.

—No person shall be eligible to the office of Clerk unless he shall have procured from a Judge of the Court of Appeals, or a Judge of the Circuit Court a certificate that he has been examined by the Clerk of his Court, under his supervision, and that he is qualified for the office for which he is a candidate. *Ky.*, 218.

—The Clerks of the Court of Appeals, Circuit, and County Courts, shall be removable from office by the Court of Appeals, upon information and good cause shown. The Court shall be judges of the fact as well as the law. Two-thirds of the members present must concur in the sentence. *Ky.*, 217.

—Circuit Court Clerk for each county, shall be elected, whose term of office shall be the same as that of the Circuit Judges; also, a County Court Clerk, an Attorney, Surveyor, Coroner, and Jailer, for each county, whose term of office shall be the same as that of the Presiding Judge of the County Court. *Ky.*, 218.

—The Clerks of the Inferior Courts shall be elected by the qualified voters of their several districts, and shall hold their offices during a term of four years. *La.*, 232.

—The Court of Appeals shall appoint its own clerk, who shall hold his office for six years, and may be re-appointed at the end thereof; he shall be subject to removal by the court for incompetency, neglect of duty, misdemeanor in office, or such other cause or causes as may be prescribed by law. *Md.*, 267.

—The clerks of the several courts created or continued by this Constitution shall have charge and custody of the records and other papers; shall perform all the duties and be allowed the fees which appertain to their several offices as the same now are or may hereafter be regulated by law. *Md.*, 266.

—There shall be a Clerk of the Circuit Court for each county, who shall be selected by a plurality of the qualified voters of said county; he shall hold his office for the term of six years from the time of his election, and until a new election is held and his successor duly qualified; he shall be re-eligible at the end of his term, and shall at any time be subject to removal for willful neglect of duty, or other misdemeanor in office, on conviction in a court of law. In the event of any vacancy in the office of the clerk of any of the circuit courts, said vacancy shall be filled by the judge of said circuit in which said vacancy occurs, until the next general election for county officers, when a Clerk of said Circuit Court shall be elected to serve for six years thereafter. *Md.*, 268.

—The Clerk of the Court of Common Pleas shall have authority to issue within said city all marriage and other licenses required by law, subject to such provisions as the General Assembly have now or may hereafter prescribe, and the Clerk of the Superior Court of said city shall receive and record all deeds, conveyances and other papers which are required by law to be recorded in said city. He shall also have custody of all papers connected with the proceedings on the law or equity side of Baltimore County Court, and of the dockets thereof, so far as the same have relation to the city of Baltimore. *Md.*, 269.

—The Supreme Court may appoint a reporter of its decisions. The decisions of the Supreme Court shall be in writing, and signed by the judges concurring therein. Any judge dissenting therefrom, shall give the reasons of such dissent in writing, under his signature. All such opinions shall be filed in the office of the Clerk of the Supreme Court. The judges of the Circuit Court, within their respective jurisdictions, may fill vacancies in the office of County Clerk and of Prosecuting Attorney; but no Judge of the Supreme Court or Circuit Court shall exercise any other power of appointment to public office. *Mich.*, 306.

—It shall be the duty of such Supreme Court to appoint a reporter of its decisions. There shall be chosen by the qualified electors of the State, one Clerk of the Supreme Court, who shall hold his office for the term of three years, and until his successor is duly elected and qualified; and the Judges of the Supreme Court, or a majority of them, shall have the power to fill any vacancy in the office of Clerk of the Supreme Court, until an election can be regularly had. *Min.*, 324.

—The Supreme Court and the District Courts shall appoint their respective clerks. Clerks of all other courts of record shall be elected by the qualified voters of the county, at a general election, and shall hold office for the term of four years from and after the first Monday in January next ensuing, and until their successors are duly elected and qualified. The first election of such clerks, after the adoption of this Constitution, shall be at the general election in the year one thousand eight hundred and sixty-six; any existing law of this State to the contrary notwithstanding. *Mo.*, 359.

—No clerk of any court, established by this Constitution, or by any law of this State, shall apply to his own use, from the fees and emoluments of his office, a greater sum than two thousand five hundred dollars for each year of his official term, after paying out of such fees and emoluments such amounts for deputies and assistants in his office as the court may deem necessary and may allow; but all surplus of such fees and emoluments over that sum, after paying the amounts so allowed, shall be paid into the county treasury for the use of the county. The General Assembly shall pass such laws as may be necessary to carry into effect the provisions of this section. *Mo.*, 359.

—The judges of courts (those of probate excepted) shall appoint their respective clerks, to hold their office during pleasure; and no such clerk shall act as an attorney, or be of counsel in any cause in the court of which he is clerk, nor shall he draw any writ originating a civil action. *N. H.*, 409.

—The law reporter shall be appointed by the Justices of the Supreme Court, or a majority of them, and the chancery reporter shall be appointed by the Chancellor. They shall hold their offices for five years. *N. J.*, 419.

—The officers of the Supreme Court of Appeals and of the District Courts shall be appointed by the said courts respectively, or by the judges thereof in vacation. Their duties, compensation, and tenure of office shall be prescribed by law. *Va.*, 543.

—The judge or judges of any court may appoint such officers for their respective courts as may be found necessary, and it shall be the duty of the General Assembly to prescribe by law a fixed compensation for all such officers. *Md.*, 266.

—The Clerks of the Supreme and Circuit Courts and States' Attorneys shall be elected at the first special election for Judges. The second election for Clerks of the Supreme Court shall be held on the first Monday of June, 1855, and every sixth year thereafter. The second election for Clerks of the Circuit Courts, and State's Attorneys, shall be held on the Tuesday next after the first Monday of November, 1852, and every fourth year thereafter. *Ill.*, 161.

—Prothonotaries of the Supreme Court shall be appointed by the said court for the term of three years, if they so long behave themselves well. Prothonotaries and Clerks of the several other courts, Recorders of Deeds and Registers of Wills, shall at the times and places of election of Representatives, be elected by the qualified electors of each county, or the districts over which the jurisdiction of said courts extends, and shall be commissioned by the Governor. They shall hold their offices for three years, if they so long behave themselves well, and until their successors shall be duly qualified. The Legislature shall provide by law the number of persons in each county who shall hold said offices, and how many and which of said offices shall be filled by one person. Vacancies in any of the said offices shall be filled by appointments to be made by the Governor, to continue until the next general election, and until successors shall be elected and qualified as aforesaid. *Pa.*, 466.

—Prothonotaries, clerks of the several courts, except of the Supreme Court, Recorders of Deeds and Registers of Wills, shall be first elected under the amended Constitution, at the election of Representatives, in the year eighteen hundred and thirty-nine, in such manner as may be prescribed by law. *Pa.*, 460.

—Judges of the Supreme Court shall appoint their clerks, who shall hold their offices for the period of six years. Chancellors, if Courts of Chancery shall be established, shall appoint their clerks and masters, who shall hold their offices for the period of six years. Clerks of such inferior courts as may be hereafter established, which shall be required to be holden in the respective counties of this State, shall be elected by the qualified voters thereof, for the term of four years; they shall be removed from office for malfeasance, incompetency or neglect of duty, in such manner as may be prescribed by law. *Tenn.*, 497.

—The Supreme Court shall appoint its own clerks, who shall give bonds in such manner as is now, or may hereafter be required by law; shall hold their offices for four years, and shall be subject to removal by the said court for good cause, entered on record of the minutes of said court. *Tex.*, 510.

—When a vacancy shall occur in the office of clerk of any court (except it be a County or Corporation Court), such court or the judges thereof, in vacation, may appoint a clerk *pro tempore*, who shall discharge the duties of the office until the vacancy is filled; when such vacancy shall occur in the office of a clerk of a County or Corporation Court (if in vacation), the presiding justice thereof may appoint the clerk *pro tempore*, who shall discharge the duties of the office until the next term, and then the court shall appoint a *pro tempore* clerk to serve until the vacancy shall be filled. *Va.*, 593.

38

—There shall be a Clerk of the Circuit Court chosen in each county organized for judicial purposes, by the qualified electors thereof, who shall hold his office for two years, subject to removal as shall be provided by law. In case of a vacancy, the Judge of the Circuit Court shall have the power to appoint a clerk, until the vacancy shall be filled by an election. The clerk thus elected or appointed, shall give such security as the Legislature may require; and when elected, shall hold his office for a full term. The Supreme Court shall appoint its own clerk, and the Clerk of a Circuit court may be appointed Clerk of the Supreme Court. *Wis.*, 566.

—The officers of the Supreme Court of Appeals shall be appointed by the court, or by the judges thereof in vacation. Their duties, compensation and tenure of office shall be prescribed by law. *W. Va.*, 553.

—The voters of each county shall elect a Clerk of the Circuit Court, whose term of office shall be four years. His duties and compensation, and the mode of removing him from office, shall be prescribed by law; and when a vacancy shall occur in the office, the Judge of the Circuit Court shall appoint a clerk, who shall discharge the duties of the office until the vacancy is filled. In any case, in respect to which the clerk shall be so situated as to make it improper for him to act, the court shall appoint a substitute. *W. Va.*, 553.

COUNTY CLERKS—CLERKS OF COUNTY
COURTS.

[County Clerks elected. Their duties and compensation fixed by law.] County Clerks shall be ex-officio Clerks of the Courts of Record in and for their respective counties. *Cal.*, (as amended in 1862.)

—The Clerk of each county organized for judicial purposes shall be the Clerk of the Circuit Court of such county, and of the Supreme Court, when held within the same. *Mich.*, 306.

—The election of Clerks and Surrogates in those counties where the term of office of the present incumbent shall expire previous to the general election of eighteen hundred and forty-five, shall be held at the general election next ensuing the adoption of this Constitution; the result of which election shall be ascertained in the manner now provided by law for the election of Sheriffs. *N. J.*, 421.

—Clerks of counties 'shall be clerks of the inferior courts of common pleas and quarter sessions of the several counties, and perform the duties and be subject to the regulations now required of them by law, until otherwise ordained by the Legislature. *N. J.*, 421.

—There shall be elected in each county, by the electors thereof, one Clerk of the Court of Common Pleas, who shall hold his office for the term of three years, and until his successor shall be elected and qualified. He shall, by virtue of his office, be clerk of all other courts of record held therein; but the General Assembly may provide by law, for the election of a clerk, with a like term of office, for each or any other of the courts of record, and may authorize the Judge of the Probate Court to perform the duties of clerk for his court, under such regulations as may be directed by law. Clerks of courts shall be removable for such cause, and in such manner, as shall be prescribed by law. *Ohio*, 438.

—A County Clerk shall be elected in each county for the term of two years, who shall keep all the public records, books, and papers of the county, record conveyances, and perform the duties of Clerk of the Circuit and County Courts, and such other duties as may be prescribed by law; but whenever the number of voters in the county shall exceed twelve hundred, the Legislative Assembly may authorize the election of one person as Clerk of the Circuit Court, one person as Clerk of the County Court, and one person Recorder of Conveyances. *Or.*, 455.

1 § 20. No judicial officer, except Justices of the Peace, shall receive to his

2 own use, any fees or perquisites of office.

1 § 21. The Legislature may authorize the judgments, decrees and decisions

2 of any local inferior court of record of original civil jurisdiction, established

3 in a city, to be removed for review directly into the Court of Appeals.

—There shall be a Clerk of the District Court for each county, who shall be elected by the qualified voters for members of the Legislature, and who shall hold his office for four years, subject to removal by information or by indictment of a grand jury, and conviction by a petit jury. In case of vacancy, the Judge of the District Court shall have the power to appoint a clerk, until a regular election can be held. *Tex.*, 511.

—The voters of each county or corporation in which a Circuit Court is held shall elect a clerk of such court, whose term of office shall be six years. *Va.* 543.

—The records, books, papers, seals and other property and appurtenances of the former Circuit and County Courts, within the State of West Virginia, shall be transferred to, and remain in, the care and custody of the Circuit Courts of the respective counties, to which all process outstanding at the time this Constitution goes into operation shall be returned, and by which new process in suits then pending, or previously determined, in the said former courts, may be issued in proper cases. Copies and transcripts of the records and proceedings of the said former courts shall be made and certified by the courts having the care and custody of such records and proceedings, or the proper officers thereof, and shall have the same force and effect as if they had been heretofore properly made and certified by the said former courts. *W. Va.*, 558.

JUDGES NOT TO TRY CERTAIN CAUSES,

NOR RECEIVE FEES.

—No Judge shall preside on the trial of any cause in the event of which he may be interested, or where either of the parties shall be connected with him by affinity or consanguinity, within such degrees as may be prescribed by law, or in which he may have been counsel, or have presided in any inferior court, except by consent of all the parties. In case all or any of the Judges of the Supreme Court shall be thus disqualified from presiding on any cause or causes, the Court or Judges thereof, shall certify the same to the Governor of the State, and he shall immediately commission, specially, the requisite number of men of law knowledge, for the trial and determination thereof. The same course shall be pursued in the Circuit and inferior courts as prescribed in this section for cases of the Supreme Court. *Ark.*, 91.

—Provision shall be made by law for the selection, by the bar, of a *pro tem.* judge of the district court, when the judge is absent or otherwise unable or disqualified to sit in any case. *Kan.*, 201.

—No judge shall sit in any case wherein he may be interested, or where either of the parties may be connected with him by affinity or consanguinity within such degrees as now are or may hereafter be prescribed by law, or where he shall have been of counsel in the case. *Md.*, 266.

—No judge shall sit on the trial of any cause when the parties or either of them shall be connected with him by affinity or consanguinity, or when he may be interested in the same, except by consent of the judge and of the parties; and whenever a quorum of said court are situated as aforesaid, the Governor of the State shall in such case specially commission two or more men of law knowledge for the determination thereof *Miss.*, 339.

—No Judge of the Supreme or inferior courts shall preside on the trial of any cause in the event of which he may be interested, or where either of the parties shall be connected with him by affinity or consanguinity within such degrees as may be prescribed by law, or in which he may have been of counsel, or in which he may have presided in any inferior court, except by consent of all the parties. In case all or any of the Judges of the Supreme Court shall be thus disqualified from presiding on the trial of any cause or causes, the court or the judges thereof shall certify the same to the Governor of the State, and he shall forthwith specially commission the requisite number of men of law knowledge, for the trial and determination thereof. In case of sickness of any of the judges of the Supreme or inferior courts, so that they or any of them are unable to attend, the Legisture shall be authorized to make provision by the general laws, that special judges may be appointed to attend said courts. *Tenn.*, 496.

—No judge shall sit in any case wherein he may be interested, or where either of the parties may be connected with him by affinity or consanguinity within such degrees as may be prescribed by law, or where he shall have been of counsel in the case. *Tex.*, 511.

—When the Supreme Court, or any three of its members, shall be thus disqualified to hear and determine any case or cases in said court, or when no judgment can be rendered in any case or cases in said court, by reason of the equal division of opinion of said judges, the same shall be certified to the Governor of the State, who shall immediately commission the requisite number of persons, learned in the law, for the trial and determination of said case or cases. When a Judge of the District Court is thus disqualified, the parties may, by consent, appoint a proper person to try the said case; or, upon their failing to do so, a competent person shall be appointed to try the same in the county where it is pending, in such manner as may be prescribed by law. And the District Judges may exchange districts, or hold courts for each other, when they may deem it expedient, and shal l do so when directed by law. The disqualification of judges of inferior tribunals shall be remedied, and vacancies in their offices shall be filled as prescribed by law. *Tex.*, 511.

—No Justice of the Supreme Court shall sit as a judge or take part in the Appellate Court on the trial or hearing of any case which shall have been decided by him in the court below. *Fl.*, 135.

—In all cases heard before the Supreme Court, as an appellate court, the justice who may have tried such cause in the court below, shall not participate in the decision thereof until the other two justices, if present, shall have failed to agree in the decision of such cause. *Neb.*, 375.

—When any Judge of the Court of Appeals is so situated in regard to any case pending before it, as to make it improper for him to aid in the trial of the same, or is under any other disability, the remaining judges may call to their assistance a Judge of the Circuit Court, who shall act as a Judge of the Court of Appeals in the cases to which such disability relates. *W. Va.*, 553.

1   § 22. The Legislature shall provide for the speedy publication of all statute

2 laws, and of such judicial decisions as it may deem expedient. And all laws

3 and judicial decisions shall be free for publication by any person.

1   § 23. Tribunals of conciliation may be established, with such powers and

2 duties as may be prescribed by law; but such tribunals shall have no power

3 to render judgment to be obligatory on the parties, except they voluntarily

4 submit their matters in difference and agree to abide the judgment, or assent

5 thereto, in the presence of such tribunal, in such cases as shall be prescribed

6 by law.

PUBLICATION OF THE LAWS.

— The Legislature shall provide for the speedy publication of all statute laws, and of all judicial decisions as it may deem expedient; and all laws and judicial decisions shall be free for publication by any person. *Cal.*, 102; *Mich.*, 304; *Wis.*, 567.

—All laws, decrees, regulations, and provisions, which from their nature require publication, shall be published in English and Spanish. *Cal.*, 105.

—That all laws of the State and all official writings, and the executive, legislative, and judicial proceedings, shall be conducted, preserved and published in no other than the English language. *Ill.*, 168.

—No act shall take effect until the same shall have been published and circulated in the several counties of the State by authority, except in cases of emergency, which emergency shall be declared in the preamble or in the body of the law. *Ind.*, 174.

—No law of the General Assembly, passed at a regular session, of a public nature; shall take effect until the 4th day of July next after the passage thereof. Laws passed at a special session shall take effect ninety days after the adjournment of the General Assembly by which they were passed. If the General Assembly shall deem any law of immediate importance, they may provide that the same shall take effect by publication in the newspapers in the State. *Iowa*, 186.

—The Legislature shall prescribe the time when its acts shall be in force, and shall provide for the speedy publication of the same: and no law of a general nature shall be in force until the same be published. *Kan.*, 200.

—The laws, public records, and the written judicial and legislative proceedings of the State, shall be conducted, promulgated, and preserved in the English language. *Mich.*, 314.

—No law passed by the General Assembly shall take effect until the first day of June next after the session at which it may be passed, unless it be otherwise expressly declared therein; and in case any public law is made to take effect before the said first day of June, the General Assembly shall provide for the immediate publication of the same. *Md.*, 203.

—No public act shall take effect or be in force until the expiration of ninety days from the end of the session at which the same is passed, unless the Legislature shall otherwise direct, by a two-thirds vote of the members elected to each House. *Mich.*, 303.

—No act shall take effect until ninety days from the end of the session at which the same shall have been passed, except in case of emergency; which emergency shall be declared in the preamble or in the body of the law. *Or.*, 451.

TRIBUNALS OF CONCILIATION. COURTS

OF ARBITRATION.

—It shall be the duty of the General Assembly to pass such laws as may be necessary and proper to decide differences by arbitrators to be appointed by the parties who may choose that summary mode of adjustment. *Ala.*, 77; *Ky.*, 220; *La.*, 233.

—Tribunals for conciliation may be established, with such powers and duties as may be prescribed by law; but such tribunals shall have no power to render judgment to be obligatory on the parties, except they voluntarily submit their matters in difference, and agree to abide the judgment, or assent thereto in the presence of such tribunal, in such cases as shall be prescribed by law. *Cal.*, 102; (nearly similar), *Ind.*, 177.

—The Legislature may establish Courts of Conciliation, with such powers and duties as shall be prescribed by law. *Mich.*, 307.

—The General Assembly may establish Courts of Conciliation, and prescribe their powers and duties; but such courts shall not render final judgment, in any case, except upon submission, by the parties, of the matter in dispute, and their agreement to abide such judgment. *Ohio*, 438.

—It shall be the duty of the Legislature to pass such laws as may be necessary and proper to decide differences by arbitration, when the parties shall elect that mode of trial. *Tex.*, 516.

—The Legislature shall pass laws for the regulation of tribunals of conciliation, defining their powers and duties. Such tribunals may be established in and for any township, and shall have power to render judgment, to be obligatory on the parties, when they shall voluntarily submit their matter in difference to arbitration, and agree to abide the judgment, or assent thereto in writing. *Wis.*, 567.

1 § 24. The Legislature, at its first session after the adoption of this Constitu-
2 tion, shall provide for the appointment of three Commissioners, whose duty it
3 shall be to revise, reform, simplify, and abridge the rules of practice, pleadings,
4 forms and proceedings of the courts of record of this State, and to report
5 thereon to the Legislature, subject to their adoption and modification from
6 time to time.

1 § 25. The Legislature, at its first session after the adoption of this Constitu-
2 tion, shall provide for the organization of the Court of Appeals, and for trans-
3 ferring to it the business pending in the Court for the Correction of Errors,
4 and for the allowance of writs of error and appeals to the Court of Appeals,
5 from the judgments and decrees of the present Court of Chancery and Supreme
6 Court, and of the courts that may be organized under this Constitution.

CODE.

—It shall be the duty of the General Assembly, from time to time, as circumstances may require, to frame and adopt a Penal Code, founded on principles of reformation. *Ala.*, 77.

—It shall be the duty of the General Assembly to provide for the carrying into effect of this article, and to provide for a general system of practice in all the courts of this State. *Iowa*, 190.

—The General Assembly, at its first session after the adoption of this Constitution, shall provide for the appointment of three commissioners, and prescribe their tenure of office, compensation, and the mode of filling vacancies in said commission. *Ohio*, 443.

—The said commissioners shall revise, reform, simplify and abridge the practice, pleadings, forms, and proceedings of the Courts of record of this State; and, as far as practicable and expedient, shall provide for the abolition of the distinct forms of action at law, now in use, and for the administration of justice by a uniform mode of proceeding, without reference to any distinction between law and equity. *Ohio*, 443.

—The proceedings of the Commissioners shall, from time to time, be reported to the General Assembly, and be subject to the action of that body. *Ohio*, 443.

APPEALS—CERTIORARI.

—The General Assembly may authorize the judgments, decrees, and decisions, of any local, inferior court of record, of original, civil, or criminal jurisdiction, established in a city, to be removed, for revision, directly into the Supreme Court. *Ill.*, 162.

—Appeals and writs of error may be taken from the Circuit Court of any county to the Supreme Court held in the division which includes such county, or, with the consent of all the parties in the cause, to the Supreme Court in the next adjoining division. *Ill.*, 162.

—All appeals from Probate Courts and Justices of the Peace shall be to the District Court. *Kan.*, 201.

—The right to appeal or sue out a writ of error to the Court of Appeals shall remain as it now exists, until altered by law, hereby giving to the General Assembly the power to change, alter, or modify said ight. *Ky.*, 216.

—The Legislature, at its first session, and from time o time thereafter, shall provide by law that upon the institution of each civil action and other proceedings, and also upon the perfecting of an appeal in any civil action or proceeding in the several courts of record in this State, a special court fee or tax shall be advanced to the clerks of said courts respectively by the party or parties bringing such action or proceeding, or taking such appeal, and the money so paid in, shall be accounted for by such clerks, and applied toward the payment of the compensation of the judges of said courts as shall be directed by law. *Nev.*, 388.

—Final judgments in any Circuit Court may be brought by writ of error into the Supreme Court, or directly into the Court of Errors and Appeals. *N. J.*, 418.

—The Judges of the Courts of Common Pleas shall, within their respective counties, have like powers with the Judges of the Supreme Court, to issue writs of *certiorari* to the Justices of the Peace, and to cause their proceedings to be brought before them, and the like right and justice to be done. *Pa.*, 465.

—The judges or justices of such inferior courts of law as the Legislature may establish, shall have power, in all civil cases, to issue writs of *certiorari*, to remove any cause or transcript thereof, from any inferior jurisdiction, into said court on sufficient cause supported by oath or affirmation. *Tenn.*, 496.

—In all cases an appeal shall lie, under such regulations as may be prescribed by law, from the judgment or proceedings of a Justice or Recorder, to the Circuit Court of the county, excepting judgments of Justices in assumpsit, debt, detinue, and trover, and for fines, where the amount does not exceed ten dollars, exclusive of interest and costs, and where the case does not involve the freedom of a person, the validity of a law, or the right of corporation or county to levy tolls or taxes. *W. Va.*, 555.

—It [the Superior court] shall have power to correct errors in inferior judicatories by writ of *certiorari*, and to grant new trials in the Superior Court on proper and legal grounds. *Ga.*, 149.

—All suits, pleas, plaints, and other proceedings pending in any Court of Record, or Justice's Court, may be prosecuted to final judgment and execution; and all appeals, writs of error, certiorari, injunctions, or other proceedings whatever, may progress and be carried on as if this Constitution had not been adopted, and the Legislature shall direct the mode in which such suits, pleas, plaints, prosecutions and other proceedings, and all papers, records, books, and documents connected therewith, may be removed to the courts established by this Constitution. *Kan.*, 207.

WRITS OF ERROR.

—No writ of error shall be brought upon any judgment heretofore confessed, entered, or rendered, but within five years from this time; nor upon any judgment hereafter to be confessed, entered, or rendered, but within five years after the confessing, entering, or rendering thereof; unless the person entitled to such writ be an infant, feme covert, *non compos mentis*, or a prisoner, and then within five years exclusive of the time of such disability. *Del.*, 124.

—The General Assembly may pass laws authorizing writs of error in criminal or penal cases, and regulating the right of challenge of jurors therein. *Ky.*, 212.

—When a writ of error shall be brought, no justice who has given a judicial opinion, in the cause, in favor of or against any error complained of, shall sit as a member, or have a voice on the hearing, or for its affirmance or reversal; but the reasons for such opinion shall be assigned to the court in writing. *N. J.*, 417.

STYLE OF WRITS, PROCESS AND PROCEEDINGS

—And that all writs and other proceedings shall run in the name of *The People of the State of New York*, and be tested in the name of the chancellor, or chief judge of the court from whence they shall issue. *N. Y.* (1777), 31.

—The style of all process shall be, *The State of* ——; and all prosecutions shall be carried on in the name, and by the authority of the State of ——, and shall conclude, *against the peace and dignity of the same. Ala.*, 81; *Ia.*, 231; (nearly similar,) *Ky.*, 215.

—All writs and other process shall run in the name of the "State of ——," and bear test and be signed by the Clerks of the respective courts from which they issue. Indictments shall conclude "against the peace and dignity of the State of ——." *Ark.*, 92.

—The style of all process shall be, "The People of the State of ——," all the prosecutions shall be conducted in the name and by the authority of the same. *Cal.*, 102; *Iowa*, 189; (nearly similar,) *Kan.*, 201.

—The style in all process and public acts shall be, "*The State of* ——." Prosecutions shall be carried on in the name of the State. *Del.*, 124; *Miss.*, 339; *Nev.*, 387; *Wis.*, 567.

—The style of all process shall be "The State of ——," and all criminal prosecutions shall be carried on in the name of the State, and all indictments shall conclude, "against the peace and dignity of the same." *A a.*, 135; (nearly similar,) *Ohio*, 439; *S. C.*, 486; *Tex.*, 511.

—All process, writs, and other proceedings, shall run in the name of "*The People of the State of* ——." All prosecutions shall be carried on "*In the name and by the authority of the People of the State of* ——," and conclude "*against the peace and dignity of the same.*" *Ill.*, 161.

—All criminal prosecutions shall be carried on in the name and by the authority of the State, and the style of all process shall be, "The State of ——." *Ind.*, 177.

—All writs issuing out of the clerk's office in any of the courts of law, shall be in the name of the Commonwealth of ——; they shall be under the seal of the court from whence they issue; they shall bear test of the first justice of the court to which they shall be returnable who is not a party, and be signed by the clerk of such court. *Mass.*, 293.

—The style of all process shall be, "In the name of the People of the State of ——." *Mich.*, 307.

—Legal pleadings and proceedings in the courts of this State shall be under the direction of the Legislature. The style of all process shall be "The State of ——," and all indictments shall conclude "against the peace and dignity of the State of Minnesota." *Min.*, 325.

—All writs and process shall run, and all prosecutions shall be conducted, in the name of the "State of ——;" all writs shall be tested by the clerk of the court from which they shall be issued; and all indictments shall conclude "against the peace and dignity of the State." *Mo.*, 359.

—All process, writs, and other proceedings shall run in the name of "*The People of the State of* ——." *Neb.*, 375.

—All writs issuing out of the clerk's office in any of the courts of law, shall be in the name of the State of ——; shall be under the seal of the court whence they issue, and bear teste of the chief, first or senior justice of the court; but when such justice shall be interested, then the writ shall bear the teste of some other justice of the court, to which the same shall be returnable; and be signed by the clerk of such court. *N. H.*, 409.

—All indictments, presentments and informations shall conclude against the peace and dignity of the State. *N. H.*, 409.

—All writs shall be in the name of the State; and all indictments shall conclude in the following manner, viz.: "against the peace of this State, the government and dignity of the same." *N. J.*, 420.

—All writs shall run in the same manner, and bear test, and be signed by the clerks of the respective courts. Indictments shall conclude *against the peace and dignity of the State. N. C.*, 426., *Tenn.*, 497.

—The style of all process shall be "The Commonwealth of ——." All prosecutions shall be carried on in the name and by the authority of the Commonwealth of ——, and conclude, "against the peace and dignity of the same." *Pa.*, 465.

—All prosecutions shall commence, *By the authority of the State of* ——; all indictments shall conclude with these words: *against the peace and dignity of the State;* and all fines shall be proportioned to the offences. *Vt.*, 526.

—Writs shall run in the name of the Commonwealth of ——, and be attested by the clerks of the several courts. Indictments shall conclude, "against the peace and dignity of the Commonwealth." *Va.*, 543.

—Writs, grants and commissions, issued under State authority, shall run in the name of, and official bonds shall be made payable to "The State of ——." Indictments shall conclude "against the peace and dignity of the State of ——." *W. Va.*, 546.

ARTICLE VII.

1   § 1. After paying the expenses of collection, superintendence and ordinary
2 repairs, there shall be appropriated and set apart in each fiscal year, out of
3 the revenues of the State canals, in each year, commencing on the first day
4 of June, one thousand eight hundred and forty-six, the sum of one million
5 and three hundred thousand dollars, until the first day of June, one thousand
6 eight hundred and fifty-five, and from that time the sum of one million and
7 seven hundred thousand dollars in each fiscal year, as a sinking fund to pay
8 the interest and redeem the principal of that part of the State debt called the
9 canal debt, as it existed at the time first aforesaid, and including three hun-
10 dred thousand dollars then to be borrowed, until the same shall be wholly
11 paid; and the principal and income of the said sinking fund shall be sacredly
12 applied to that purpose.

1   § 2. After complying with the provisions of the first section of this article,
2 there shall be appropriated and set apart out of the surplus revenues of the
3 State canals, in each fiscal year, commencing on the first day of June, one
4 thousand eight hundred and forty-six, the sum of three hundred and fifty
5 thousand dollars, until the time when a sufficient sum shall have been appro-
6 priated and set apart, under the said first section, to pay the interest and
7 extinguish the entire principal of the canal debt; and after that period, then
8 the sum of one million and five hundred thousand dollars in each fiscal year,
9 as a sinking fund, to pay the interest and redeem the principal of that part of
10 the State debt called the general fund debt, including the debt for loans of the
11 State credit to railroad companies which have failed to pay the interest
12 thereon, and also the contingent debt on State stocks loaned to incorporated
13 companies which have hitherto paid the interest thereon, whenever and as far
14 as any part thereof may become a charge on the treasury or general fund,
15 until the same shall be wholly paid; and the principal and income of the said
16 last mentioned sinking fund shall be sacredly applied to the purpose aforesaid;
17 and if the payment of any part of the moneys to the said sinking fund shall
18 at any time be deferred, by reason of the priority recognized in the first sec-
19 tion of this article, the sum so deferred, with quarterly interest thereon, at

20 the then current rate, shall be paid to the last mentioned sinking fund, as soo
21 as it can be done consistently with the just rights of the creditors holding said
22 canal debt.

1   § 3. After paying the said expenses of collection, superintendence and
2 repairs of the canals, and the sums appropriated by the first and second sec-
3 tions of this article, there shall be appropriated and set apart in each fiscal year
4 out of the surplus revenues of the canals, as a sinking fund, a sum sufficient
5 to pay the interest as it falls due, and extinguish the principal within eighteen
6 years, of any loan made under this section ; and if the said sinking fund shall
7 not be sufficient to redeem any part of the principal at the stipulated times
8 of payment, or to pay any part of the interest of such loans as stipulated,
9 the means to satisfy any such deficiency shall be procured on the credit of the
10 said sinking fund. After complying with the foregoing provisions, there shall
11 be paid annually out of said revenues, into the treasury of the State, two
12 hundred thousand dollars, to defray the necessary expenses of government.
13 The remainder shall, in each fiscal year, be applied to meet the appropriations
14 for the enlargement and completion of the canals mentioned in this section,
15 until the said canals shall be completed. In each fiscal year thereafter the
16 remainder shall be disposed of in such manner as the Legislature may direct ;
17 but shall at no time be anticipated or pledged for more than one year in
18 advance. The Legislature shall, annually, during the next four years, appro-
19 priate to the enlargement of the Erie, the Oswego, the Cayuga and Seneca
20 canals, and to the completion of the Black River and Genesee Valley canals,
21 and for the enlargement of the locks of the Champlain canal, whenever, from
22 dilapidation or decay, it shall be necessary to rebuild them, a sum not exceed-
23 ing two millions two hundred and fifty thousand dollars. The remainder of
24 the revenues of the canals, for the current fiscal year in which such appro-
25 priation is made, shall be applied to meet such appropriation ; and if the same
26 shall be deemed insufficient, the Legislature shall, at the same session, provide
27 for the deficiency by loan. The Legislature shall also borrow one million and
28 five hundred thousand dollars, to refund to the holders of the canal revenue
29 certificates issued under the provisions of chapter four hundred and eighty-

30 five of the laws of the year one thousand eight hundred and fifty-one, the
31 amount received into the treasury thereon ; but no interest to accrue after
32 July first, one thousand eight hundred and fifty-five, shall be paid on such
33 certificates. The provisions of section twelve of this article, requiring every
34 law for borrowing money to be submitted to the people, shall not apply to the
35 loans authorized by this section. No part of the revenues of the canals, or
36 of the funds borrowed under this section, shall be paid or applied upon or in
37 consequence of any alleged contract made under chapter four hundred and
38 eighty five of the laws of the year one thousand eight hundred and fifty-one,
39 except to pay for work done or materials furnished prior to the first day of
40 June, one thousand eight hundred and fifty-two. The rates or toll on persons
41 and property transported on the canals shall not be reduced below those for
42 the year one thousand eight hundred and fifty-two, except by the Canal
43 Board, with the concurrence of the Legislature. All contracts for work or
44 materials on any canal shall be made with the person who shall offer to do or
45 provide the same at the lowest price, with adequate security for their
46 performance.

1 § 4. The claims of the State against any incorporated company to pay the
2 interest and redeem the principal of the stock of the State loaned or advanced
3 to such company, shall be fairly enforced, and not released or compromised ;
4 and the moneys arising from such claims shall be set apart and applied as part
5 of the sinking fund, provided in the second section of this article. But the
6 time limited for the fulfillment of any condition of any release or compromise
7 heretofore made or provided for may be extended by law.

1 § 5. If the sinking funds, or either of them provided in this article, shall
2 prove insufficient to enable the State, on the credit of such fund, to procure
3 the means to satisfy the claims of the creditors of the State as they become
4 payable, the Legislature shall, by equitable taxes, so increase the revenues
5 of the said funds as to make them, respectively, sufficient perfectly to preserve
6 the public faith. Every contribution or advance to the canals, or their debt,
7 from any source other than their direct revenues, shall, with quarterly interest,
8 at the rates then current, be repaid into the treasury, for the use of the State,

9 out of the canal revenues, as soon as it can be done consistently with the just
10 rights of the creditors holding the said canal debt.

1 § 6. The Legislature shall not sell, lease or otherwise dispose of any of the
2 canals of the State; but they shall remain the property of the State and
3 under its management forever.

1 § 7. The Legislature shall never sell or dispose of the Salt Springs belong-
2 ing to this State. The lands contiguous thereto, and which may be necessary
3 and convenient for the use of the Salt Springs, may be sold by authority of
4 law, and under the direction of the Commissioners of the Land Office, for the
5 purpose of investing the moneys arising therefrom in other lands alike con-
6 venient; but by such sale and purchase, the aggregate quantity of these
7 lands shall not be diminished.

1 § 8. No moneys shall ever be paid out of the treasury of this State, or any
2 of its funds, or any of the funds under its management, except in pursuance
3 of an appropriation by law; nor unless such payment be made within two
4 years next after the passage of such appropriation act; and every such law,
5 making a new appropriation or continuing or reviving an appropriation,
6 shall distinctly specify the sum appropriated, and the object to which it
7 is to be applied; and it shall not be sufficient for such law to refer to any
8 other law to fix such sum.

1 § 9. The credit of the State shall not, in any manner, be given or loaned
2 to or in aid of any individual association or corporation.

INTERNAL IMPROVEMENTS.

—Internal improvement shall be encouraged by the government of this State, and it shall be the duty of the General Assembly, as soon as may be, to make provision by law for ascertaining the proper objects of improvement in relation to roads, canals, and navigable waters; and it shall also be their duty to provide by law for an equal, systematic, and economical application of the funds which may be appropriated to these objects. *Ark.*, 93.

—A liberal system of internal improvements, being essential to the development of the resources of the State, shall be encouraged by the government of this State; and it shall be the duty of the General Assembly, as soon as practicable, to ascertain by law proper objects for the extension of internal improvements in relation to roads, canals, and navigable streams, and to provide for a suitable application of such funds as may have been, or may hereafter be appropriated by said General Assembly for such improvements. *Ft.*, 138.

—The General Assembly shall encourage internal improvements, by passing liberal general laws of incorporation for that purpose. *Ill.*, 164.

—The State shall never be a party in carrying on any works of internal improvement. *Kan.*, 205.

—So long as the Board of Internal Improvement shall be continued, the President thereof shall be elected by the qualified voters of this Commonwealth, and hold the office for the term of four years, and until another be duly elected and qualified. The election shall be held at the same time and be conducted in the same manner, as the election of Governor of this Commonwealth under this Constitution; but nothing herein contained shall prevent the General Assembly from abolishing said Board of Internal Improvement, or the office of President thereof. *Ky.*, 221.

—There shall be appointed by the Governor a State Engineer, skilled in the theory and practice of his profession, who shall hold his office at the seat of government for the term of four years. He shall have the superintendence and direction of all public works in which the State may be interested, except

40

those made by joint stock companies or such as may be under the parochial or city authorities exclusively and not in conflict with the general laws of the State. He shall communicate to the General Assembly, through the Governor, annually, his views concerning the same; report upon the condition of the public works in progress, recommend such measures as in his opinion the public interest of the State may require, and shall perform such other duties as may be prescribed by law. His salary shall be five thousand dollars per annum, until otherwise provided by law. The mode of appointment, number and salary of his assistants shall be fixed by law. The State Engineer and assistants shall give bonds for the performance of their duties as shall be prescribed by law. *La.*, 236.

—The Legislature may establish the price and pay of foremen, mechanics, laborers and others employed on the public works of the State or parochial or city governments; *Provided*, That the compensation to be paid all foremen, mechanics, cartmen and laborers employed on the public works, under the government of the State of Louisiana, City of New Orleans, and the police juries of the various parishes of the State, shall not be less than as follows, viz.: Foremen, $3.50 per day; mechanics, $3.00 per day; cartmen, $3.50 per day; laborers, $2.00 per day. *La.*, 235.

—Nine hours shall constitute a day's labor for all mechanics, artisans and laborers employed on public works. *La.*, 235.

—The General Assembly may create internal improvement districts, composed of one or more parishes, and may grant a right to the citizens thereof to tax themselves for their improvements. Said internal improvement districts, when created, shall have the right to select Commissioners, shall have power to appoint officers, fix their pay and regulate all matters relative to the improvements of their districts, provided such improvements will not conflict with the general laws of the State. *La.*, 236.

—The Governor, the Comptroller of the Treasury and the Treasurer shall constitute the Board of Public Works in this State; they shall keep a journal of their proceedings, and shall hold regular sessions in the city of Annapolis on the first Wednesday in January, April, July and October in each year, and oftener if necessary, at which sessions they shall hear and determine such matters as affect the public works of the State, and as the General Assembly may confer upon them the power to decide. *Md.*, 273.

—The Governor, Comptroller, and Treasurer, shall receive no additional salary for services rendered by them as members of the Board of Public Works. *Md.*, 273.

—They shall exercise a diligent and faithful supervision of all public works in which the State may be interested as stockholder or creditor, and shall appoint the directors in every railroad or canal company in which the State has the legal power to appoint directors, which said directors shall represent the State in all meetings of the stockholders of every railroad or canal company in which the State is a stockholder; they shall require the directors of all public works from time to time, and as often as there shall be any change in the rates of toll on any of said works, to furnish said Board of Public Works a schedule of such modified rates of toll, and shall use all legal powers which they may possess to obtain the establishment of rates of toll which may prevent an injurious competition with each other to the detriment of the interests of the State; and so to adjust them as to promote the agricultural interests of the State; they shall report to the General Assembly at each regular session, and recommend such legislation as they shall deem necessary and requisite to promote or protect the interests of the State in the said public works; they shall perform such other duties as may be hereafter prescribed by law, and a majority of them shall be competent to act. *Md.*, 293.

—The General Assembly shall have power to receive from the United States any grant or donation of land, money or securities, for any purpose designated by the United States, and shall administer or distribute the same, according to the conditions of said grant. *Md.*, 264.

—No money from the Treasury shall be appropriated to objects of internal improvement unless a bill for that purpose be approved by two-thirds of both branches of the Legislature; and a regular statement and account of the receipts and expenditures of public moneys shall be published annually. *Miss.*, 343.

—So long as this State shall have public works which require superintendence, there shall be a Board of Public Works, to consist of three members, who shall be elected by the people, at the first general election after the adoption of this Constitution; one for the term of one year, one for the term of two years, and one for the term of three years; and one member of said Board shall be elected annually thereafter, who shall hold his office for three years. *Ohio*, 440.

— The powers and duties of said Board of Public Works and its several members, and their compensation, shall be such as now are, or may be prescribed by law. *Ohio*, 440.

—A well regulated system of internal improvement is calculated to develope the resources of the State, and promote the happiness and prosperity of her citizens, therefore it ought to be encouraged by the General Assembly. *Tenn.*, 499.

—A well regulated system of internal improvement is calculated to develope the resources of the State, and promote the happiness and prosperity of her citizens. Therefore the Legislature shall have power and it shall be its duty to encourage the same; and the Legislature shall have power to guarantee the bonds of railroad companies to any amount not exceeding in any case the sum of fifteen thousand dollars per mile; *Provided*, That in no case shall the State guarantee the payment of the bonds of any railroad company until such company shall have previously graded and prepared at least twenty-five miles of its roadway, ready to lay the iron rails thereon, and so on, continuously, on each additional section of ten miles, so graded and prepared after the preceding section has been finished and in operation, until the whole road shall be completed; *Further provided*, That the Legislature shall require that the company or companies which receive aid from the State, shall use the same exclusively for the purchase of iron rails, fastening and rolling stock, and placing the same upon the road, and upon the failure to do so, shall forfeit all their rights under this provision, together with their property and franchises; and it shall be declared a felony for any officer or agent of any railroad company to misappropriate any funds granted under the provisions of this section, or any other funds or property of the company. The State shall always be secured for all bonds guaranteed for any railroad company, by a first lien or mortgage upon the road, rolling stock, depots and franchises of the corporation, whose bonds may be guaranteed. The Legislature shall provide by law, that the managers of railroad companies shall make reports periodically, of their acts, and the condition of the corporation affairs, which shall be officially published for public information. And in no case shall the State guarantee the bonds of railroad companies, as herein provided, except by a vote of two-thirds of both Houses of the Legislature; provided the Legislature shall have no power, directly or indirectly, to release any railroad company from the payment in specie, of the principal or interest of the obligations or debts due to the school fund or to the State. An act entitled "An act supplemental and amendatory of an act to regulate railroad companies, approved February 7th, 1853," approved 21st December, 1857, be and the same is hereby repealed, and of no further effect; and the franchise or corporate privileges of any incorporated company shall not be sold under judgments, except for the foreclosure of mortgages or liens, created in the manner prescribed by law. The

Comptroller of the State is authorized to take possession of any railroad, in default of paying any bonds which may be guaranteed by the State, under such regulations as may be prescribed by law. *Tex.*, 517.

—There shall be a Board of Public Works, to consist of three Commissioners. The State shall be divided into three districts containing as nearly as may be equal number of voters, and the voters of each district shall elect one Commissioner, whose term of office shall be six years; but of those first elected, one to be designated by lot, shall remain in office for two years only, and one other, to be designated in like manner, shall remain in office for four-years only. *Va.*, 540.

—The General Assembly shall provide for the election and compensation of the Commissioners, and the organization of the Board. The Commissioners first elected shall assemble on a day to be appointed by law, and decide by lot the order in which their term of service shall expire. *Va.*, 540.

—The Board of Public Works shall appoint all officers employed on the public works, and all persons representing the interest of the Commonwealth in works of internal improvement, and shall perform such other duties as may be prescribed by law. *Va.*, 540.

—The members of the Board of Public Works may be removed by the concurrent vote of a majority of all the members elected to each House of General Assembly; but the cause of removal shall be entered on the journal of each House. *Va.*, 540.

—The General Assembly shall have power, by a vote of three-fifths of the members elected to each House, to abolish said Board whenever in their opinion a Board of Public Works shall no longer be necessary; and until the General Assembly shall direct an election of a Board of Public Works, after the adoption of this Constitution, and such Board shall have been duly elected and qualified, the Governor, Auditor, and Treasurer of the Commonwealth shall constitute said Board, and shall exercise the authority and discharge the duties thereof, and the Secretary of the Commonwealth shall discharge the duties of the clerk of said Board. *Va.*, 540.

CANAL FUND.

—Rates of toll, not less than those agreed to by the Canal Commissioners, and set forth in their report to the Legislature of the twelfth of March, one thousand eight hundred and twenty-one, shall be imposed on and collected from all parts of the navigable communications between the great western and northern lakes and the Atlantic ocean, which now are, or hereafter shall be made and completed; and the said tolls, together with the duties on the manufacture of all salt, as established by the act of the fifteenth of April, one thousand eight hundred and seventeen; and the duties on goods sold at auction, excepting therefrom the sum of thirty-three thousand five hundred dollars, otherwise appropriated by the said act; and the amount of the revenue, established by the act of the Legislature of the thirtieth of March, one thousand eight hundred and twenty, in lieu of the tax upon steamboat passengers; shall be and remain inviolably appropriated and applied to the completion of such navigable communications, and to the payment of the interest, and reimbursement of the capital of the money already borrowed, or which hereafter shall be borrowed, to make and complete the same. And neither the rates of toll on the said navigable communications; nor the duties on the manufacture of salt aforesaid; nor the duties on goods sold at auction, as established by the act of the fifteenth of April, one thousand eight hundred and seventeen; nor the amount of the revenue, established by the act of March the thirtieth, one thousand eight hundred and twenty, in lieu of the tax upon steamboat passengers; shall be reduced or diverted, at any time before the full and complete payment of the principal and interest of the money borrowed, or to be borrowed,

as aforesaid. And the Legislature shall never sell or dispose of the salt springs belonging to this State, nor the lands contiguous thereto, which may be necessary or convenient for their use, nor the said navigable communications, or any part or section thereof; but the same shall be and remain the property of this State. *N. Y.* (1821), 42.

—That the duties on the manufacture of salt, as established by the act of the fifteenth of April, one thousand eight hundred and seventeen, and by the tenth section of the seventh article of the Constitution of this State, may, at any time hereafter, be reduced by an act of the Legislature of this State; but shall not, while the same is appropriated and pledged by the said section, be reduced below the sum of six cents upon each and every bushel; and the said duties shall remain inviolably appropriated and applied as is provided by the said tenth section. And that so much of the said tenth section of the seventh article of the Constitution of this State as is inconsistent with this amendment, be abrogated. *N. Y.* (1821), 45.

EXTRA PAYMENT TO CONTRACTORS.

—The General Assembly shall never grant or authorize extra compensation to any public officer, agent, servant or contractor, after the service shall have been rendered, or the contract entered into. *Ill.*, 154; (nearly similar), *Mich.*, 303; *Neb.*, 373; *Wis.*, 563; *Iowa*, 187; *Ohio*, 439; *Md.*, 263.

LOAN OF STATE CREDIT—ASSUMPTION OF LOCAL DEBTS.

—Nor shall the debts or liabilities of any corporation, person, or persons or other State, be guaranteed nor any money, credit, or other thing, be loaned or given away, except by a like concurrence of each House; and the votes shall in each case, be taken by yeas and nays, and be entered on the journals. *Ala.*, 78.

—The credit of the State shall not be directly or indirectly loaned in any case. *Me.*, 253; *Md.*, 263; *N. J.*, 414.

—The credit of the State shall not in any manner be given or loaned to, or in aid of any individuals, association, or corporation; nor shall the State directly or indirectly become a stockholder in any association or corporation. *Cal.*, 104; *Iowa*, 190; *Ohio*, 439.

—The General Assembly shall not pledge the faith and credit of the State to raise funds in the aid of any corporation whatever. *Fl.*, 139; *Ill.*, 154; *Min.*, 327.

—The credit of this Commonwealth shall never be given or loaned in aid of any person, association, municipality, or corporation. *Ky.*, 212.

—The credit of the State shall not be granted to, or in aid of any person, association, or corporation. *Mich.*, 312; *Neb.*, 376; *Wis.*, 563; *Or.*, 457.

—The State shall not be a party to, or interested in any work of internal improvement, nor engaged in carrying on any such work, except in the expenditure of grants to the State or land or other property. *Mich.*, 312.

—The credit of the State shall not be given or loaned in aid of any person, association, or corporation; nor shall the State hereafter become a stockholder in any corporation or association, except for the purpose of securing loans heretofore extended to certain railroad corporations by the State. *Mo.*, 362.

—The State shall never assume the debts of any county, town, city or other corporation whatever, unless such debts have been created to repel invasion, suppress insurrection, or to provide for the public defense. *Nev.*, 389; (nearly similar), *Pa.*, 471; *W. Va.*, 556.

—The State shall never assume the debts of any county, city, town or township, or of any corporation whatever, unless such debt shall have been crented to repel invasion, suppress insurrection, or defend the State in war. *Ohio*, 439; *Or.*, 457.

—The State shall never contract any debt for purposes of internal improvement. *Ohio*, 443.

—Hereafter the State shall not become a stockholder in any bank. If the State become a stockholder in any association or corporation for purposes of internal improvement, such stock shall be paid for at the time of subscribing, or a tax shall be levied for the ensuing year, sufficient to pay the subscription in full. *W. Va.*, 556.

—The credit of the State shall not be granted to, or in aid of, any county, city, town, township, corporation or person, nor shall the State ever assume or become responsible for the debts or liabilities of any county, city, town, township, corporation or person, unless incurred in time of war or insurrection for the benefit of the State. *W. Va.*, 556.

—The credit of the Commonwealth shall not in any manner or event be pledged or loaned to any individual, company, corporation, or association; nor shall the Commonwealth hereafter become a joint owner or stockholder in any company, association, or corporation. *Pa.*, 471.

-- The State shall not donate or loan money on its credit, or subscribe to, or be interested in the stock of any company, association, or corporation, except corporations formed for educational or charitable purposes. *Nev.*, 389.

—The Legislature shall not have power to grant aid to companies or associations of individuals, except to charitable associations, and to such companies or associations as are and shall be formed for the exclusive purpose of making works of internal improvement, wholly or partially within the State, to the extent only of one-fifth of the capital of such companies, by subscription in stock or loan in money or public bonds; but any aid thus granted shall be paid to the company only in the same proportion as the remainder of the capital shall be actually paid in by the stockholders of the company; and in case of loan such adequate security shall be required as the Legislature may seem proper. No corporation or individual association, receiving the aid of the State, as herein provided, shall possess banking or discounting privileges. *La.*, 234.

—Nor shall the General Assembly ever, on behalf of the State, assume the debts of any county, city, town or township, nor of any corporation whatever. *Ind.*, 179.

—The State shall not become a stockholder in any corporation, nor shall it assume or pay the debt or liability of any corporation, unless incurred in time of war, for the benefit of the State. *Iowa*, 191.

—The General Assembly shall have no power for any purpose whatever, to release the lien held by the State upon any railroad. *Mo.*, 362.

—No county shall create any debts or liabilities which shall singly, or in the aggregate, exceed the sum of five thousand dollars, except to suppress insurrection or repel invasion; but the debts of any county at the time this constitution takes effect, shall be disregarded in estimating the sum to which such county is limited. *Or.*, 457.

TAXATION—REVENUES.

—All lands liable to taxation in this State, shall be taxed in proportion to their value. *Ala.*, 78; *Mo.*, 348.

—No power to levy taxes shall be delegated to individuals or private corporations. *Ala.*, 78.

—All revenue shall be raised by taxation to be fixed by law. *Ark.*, 93.

—All property subject to taxation shall be taxed according to its value, that value to be ascertained in such manner as the General Assembly shall direct, making the same equal and uniform throughout the State. No one species of property, from which a tax may be collected, shall be taxed higher than another species of property of equal value: *Provided*, The

General Assembly shall have the power to tax merchants, hawkers, peddlers and privileges, in such manner as may from time to time be prescribed by law: *And provided further*, That no other or greater amount of revenue shall at any time be levied than required for the necessary expenses of the government unless by a concurrence of two-thirds of both Houses of the General Assembly. *Ark.*, 93.

—No other or greater tax shall be levied on the production or labor of the country than may be required for expenses of inspection. *Ark.*, 93.

—Taxation shall be equal and uniform throughout the State. All property in this State shall be taxed in proportion to its value, to be ascertained as directed by law; but Assessors and Collectors of town, county, and State taxes shall be elected by the qualified electors of the district, county, or town in which the property taxed for State, county, or town purposes, is situated. *Cal.*, 104.

—The General Assembly shall devise and adopt a system of revenue, having regard to an equal and uniform mode of taxation throughout the State. *Fla.*, 137; (nearly similar), *Kan.*, 214.

—No other or greater amount of tax or revenue shall at any time be levied, than may be required for the necessary expenses of the government. *Fla.*, 137.

—The specification of the objects and subjects of taxation shall not deprive the General Assembly of the power to require other objects or subjects to be taxed in such manner as may be consistent with the principles of taxation fixed in this Constitution. *Ill.*, 164.

—The General Assembly shall provide for levying a tax by valuation, so that every person and corporation shall pay a tax in proportion to the value of his or her property; such value to be ascertained by some person or persons to be elected or appointed in such manner as the General Assembly shall direct, and not otherwise; but the General Assembly shall have power to tax peddlers, auctioneers, brokers, hawkers, merchants, commission merchants, showmen, jugglers, innkeepers, grocery keepers, toll-bridges and ferries, and persons using and exercising franchises and privileges, in such manner as they shall from time to time direct. *Ill.*, 163.

—The property of the State and counties, both real and personal, and such other property as the General Assembly may deem necessary for school, religious and charitable purposes, may be exempted from taxation. *Ill.*, 163.

—The General Assembly shall provide by law for a uniform and equal rate of assessment and taxation, and shall prescribe such regulations as shall secure a just valuation for taxation of all property, both real and personal, excepting such only for municipal, educational, literary, scientific, religious, or charitable purposes as may be specially exempted by law. *Ind.*, 178.

—Every law which imposes, continues, or revives a tax, shall distinctly state the tax, and the object to which it is applied; and it shall not be sufficient to refer to any other law to fix such tax or object. *Iowa*, 191.

—No tax shall be levied except in pursuance of a law, which shall distinctly state the object of the same; to which object only such tax shall be applied. *Kan.*, 204.

—A county assessor shall be elected in each county at the same time and for the same term that the Presiding Judge of the County Court is elected, until otherwise provided for by law. He shall have power to appoint such assistants as may be necessary and proper. *Ky.*, 219.

—Taxation shall be equal and uniform throughout the State. All property shall be taxed in proportion to its value, to be ascertained as directed by law. The General Assembly shall have power to exempt from taxation property actually used for church, school, or charitable purposes. The General Assembly shall levy an income tax upon all persons pursuing any occupation, trade or calling, and all such persons shall obtain a license, as provided by law. All tax on income shall be pro rata on the amount of income or business done. *La.*, 234.

—And while the public charges of government, or any part thereof, shall be assessed on polls and estates, in the manner that has hitherto been practiced, in order that such assessments may be made with equality, there shall be a valuation of estates within the Commonwealth, taken anew once in every ten years at least, and as much oftener as the General Court shall order. *Mass.*, 283.

—While the public expenses shall be assessed on polls and estates, a general valuation shall be taken at least once in ten years. *Me.*, 248.

—All taxes upon real estate, assessed by authority of this State, shall be apportioned and assessed equally, according to the just value thereof. *Me.*, 248.

—The State may continue to collect all specific taxes accruing to the treasury under existing laws. The Legislature may provide for the collection of specific taxes, from banking, railroad, plankroad, and other corporations hereafter created. *Mich.*, 312.

—The Legislature shall provide an uniform rule of taxation, except on property paying specific taxes, and taxes shall be levied on such property as shall be prescribed by law. *Mich.*, 312.

—All assessments hereafter authorized shall be on property at its cash value. *Mich.*, 312.

—The Legislature shall provide for an equalization by a State board, in the year one thousand eight hundred and fifty-one, and every fifth year thereafter, of assessments on all taxable property, except that paying specific taxes. *Mich.*, 312.

—Every law which imposes, continues, or revives a tax, shall distinctly state the tax, and the object to which it is to be applied; and it shall not be sufficient to refer to any other law to fix such tax or object. *Mich.*, 312.

—All taxes to be raised in this State shall be as nearly equal as may be, and all property on which taxes are to be levied shall have a cash valuation, and be equalized and uniform throughout the State. *Min.*, 326.

—The Legislature shall provide for an annual tax, sufficient to defray the estimated expenses of the State for each year; and whenever it shall happen that such ordinary expenses of the State for any year shall exceed the income of the State for such year, the Legislature shall provide for levying a tax for the ensuing year sufficient, with other sources of income, to pay the deficiency of the preceding year, together with the estimated expenses of such ensuing year. *Min.*, 326.

—No property, real or personal, shall be exempt from taxation, except such as may be used exclusively for public schools, and such as may belong to the United States, to this State, to counties, or to municipal corporations within this State, *Mo.*, 362.

—The Legislature shall provide for an annual tax, sufficient to defray the estimated expenses of the State for each year, and whenever the expenses of any year shall exceed the income, the Legislature shall provide for levying a tax for the ensuing year, sufficient, with other sources of income, to pay the deficiency, as well as the expenses of such ensuing year. *Neb.*, 376; (nearly similar, except the term is two years,) *Mec.*, 389.

—The Legislature shall provide by law for a uniform and equal rate of assessment and taxation, and shall prescribe such regulations as shall secure a just valuation for taxation of all property, real, personal or possessory, except mines and mining claims, the proceeds of which alone shall be taxed, and also excepting such property as may be exempted by law for municipal, educational, literary, scientific, religious, or charitable purposes. *Nev.*, 389.

—And while the public charges of government, or any part thereof, shall be assessed on polls and estates in the manner that has heretofore been practiced, in order that such assessments may be made with equality, there shall be a valuation of the estates within the State, taken anew once in every five years at least, and as much oftener as the General Court shall order. *N. H.*, 402.

—And the inhabitants of plantations and places unincorporated, qualified as this Constitutions provides, who are or shall be required to assess taxes upon themselves toward the support of government, or shall be taxed therefor, shall have the same privilege of voting for Senators in the plantations and places where they reside, as the inhabitants of the respective towns and parishes aforesaid have. And the meetings of such plantations and places for that purpose shall be holden annually in the month of March, at such places respectively therein as the assessors thereof shall direct, which assessors shall have like authority for notifying the electors, collecting and returning the votes as the selectmen and town clerks have in their several towns, by this Constitution. *N. H.*, 404.

—The General Assembly shall provide for raising revenue, sufficient to defray the expenses of the State, for each year, and also a sufficient sum to pay the interest on the State debt. *Ohio*, 442.

—No tax shall be levied, except in pursuance of law; and every law imposing a tax, shall state, distinctly, the object of the same, to which only it shall be applied. *Ohio*, 443; *Or.*, 456.

—The Legislative Assembly shall provide by law for a uniform and equal rate of assessment and taxation, and shall prescribe such regulations as shall secure a just valuation for taxation of all property, both real and personal, excepting such only for municipal, educational, literary, scientific, religious, or charitable purposes, as may be specially exempted by law. *Or.*, 456.

—Whenever the expenses of any fiscal year shall exceed the income, the Legislative Assembly shall provide for levying a tax for the ensuing fiscal year, sufficient, with other sources of income, to pay the deficiency, as well as the estimated expense of the ensuing fiscal year. *Or.*, 456.

—The General Assembly shall, from time to time, provide for making new valuations of property for the assessment of taxes, in such manner as they may deem best. A new estimate of such property shall be taken before the first direct State tax, after the adoption of this Constitution, shall be assessed. *R. I.*, 476.

—All taxes upon property, real or personal, shall be laid upon the actual value of the property taxed, as the same shall be ascertained by an assessment made for the purpose of laying such tax. In the first apportionment which shall be made under this Constitution, the amount of taxes shall be estimated from the average of the two years next preceding such apportionment; but in every subsequent apportionment, from the average of the ten years then next preceding. *S. C.*, 483.

—All lands liable to taxation, held by deed, grant or entry, town lots, bank stock, slaves between the ages of twelve and fifteen years, and such other property as the Legislature may from time to time deem expedient, shall be taxable. All property shall be taxed according to its value; that value to be ascertained in such manner as the Legislature shall direct, so that the same shall be equal and uniform throughout the State. No one species of property from which a tax may be collected shall be taxed higher than any other species of property of equal value. But the Legislature shall have power to tax merchants, peddlers, and privileges, in such manner as they may, from time to time, direct. *Tenn.*, 494.

—No article manufactured of the produce of this State shall be taxed otherwise than to pay inspection fees. *Tenn.*, 499.

—Taxation shall be equal and uniform throughout the State. All property in this State shall be taxed in proportion to its value, to be ascertained as directed by law, except such property as two-thirds of both Houses of the Legislature may think proper to exempt from taxation. The Legislature shall have power to lay an income tax, and to tax all persons pursuing any occupation, trade or profession; *Provided*, That the term occupation shall not be construed to apply to pursuits, either agricultural or mechanical. *Tex.*, 516.

41

1   § 10. The State may, to meet casual deficits or failures in revenues, or for

2 expenses not provided for, contract debts, but such debts, direct and contingent,

3 singly or in the aggregate, shall not at any time exceed one million of dollars,

4 and the moneys arising from the loans creating such debts shall be applied to

5 the purpose for which they were obtained or to repay the debt so contracted,

6 and to no other purpose whatever.

—The assessor and collector of taxes shall be appointed in such manner, and under such regulations as the Legislature may direct. *Tex.,* 516.

—The General Assembly may levy a tax on incomes, salaries and licenses; but no tax shall be levied on property from which any income so taxed is derived, or the capital invested in trade or business in respect to which the license so taxed is issued. *Va.,* 538.

—Taxation shall be eqal and uniform throughout the Commonwealth, and all property shall be taxed in proportion to its value, which shall be ascertained in such manner as may be prescribed by law. *Va.,* 538.

—Taxation shall be equal and uniform throughout the State, and all property, both real and personal, shall be taxed in proportion to its value, to be ascertained as directed by law. No one species of property from which a tax may be collected, shall be taxed higher than any other species of property of equal value; but property used for educational, literary, scientific, religious or charitable purposes, and public property, may, by law, be exempted from taxation. *W. Va.,* 556.

—The Legislature shall provide for an annual tax, sufficient to defray the estimated expenses of the State for each year; and whenever the ordinary expenses of any year shall exceed the income, shall levy a tax for the ensuing year, sufficient, with other sources of income, to pay the deficiency, as well as the estimated expenses of such year. *W. Va.,* 556.

—The Legislature shall provide for an annual tax sufficient to defray the estimated expenses of the State for each year; and whenever the expenses of any year shall exceed the income, the Legislature shall provide for levying a tax for the ensuing year, sufficient, with other sources of income, to pay the deficiency, as well as the estimated expenses of such ensuing year. *Wis.,* 503.

—The rule of taxation shall be uniform, and taxes shall be levied upon such property as the Legislature shall prescribe. *Wis.,* 567.

—[Minute provisions relating to the sale of lands for taxes]. *Ill.,* 163.

—The property of all corporations for pecuniary profit now existing, or hereafter created, shall be subject to taxation, the same as that of individuals. *Iowa,* 191.

—The Legislature shall provide for taxing the notes and bills discounted or purchased, moneys loaned, and other property, effects, or dues of every description (without deduction), of all banks now existing, or hereafter to be created, and of all bankers; so that all property employed in banking shall always bear a burden of taxation equal to that imposed upon the property of individuals. *Kan.* 204.

—The Legislature shall provide, each year, for raising revenue sufficient to defray the current expenses of the State. *Kan.,* 204.

—Laws shall be passed taxing all moneys, credits, investments in bonds, stocks, joint-stock companies, or otherwise, and also all real and personal property, according to its true value in money; but public burying-grounds, public school-houses, public hospitals, academies, colleges, universities, and all seminaries of learning, all churches, church property used for religious purposes, and houses of worship, institutions of purely public charity, public property used exclusively for any public purpose, and personal property to an amount not exceeding in value two hundred dollars for each individual, shall, by general law be exempt from taxation. *Min.* 326.

—Laws shall be passed for taxing the notes and bill discounted or purchased, moneys loaned, and all other property, effects, or dues of every description, of all banks, and of all bankers; so that all property employed in banking shall always be subject to a taxation equal to that imposed on the property of individuals. *Min.* 327.

—No municipal corporations, except cities, shall be created by special act; and no city shall be incorporated with less than five thousand permanent inhabitants, nor unless the people thereof, by a direct vote upon the question, shall have decided in favor of such corporation. *Mo.,* 360.

—The property of corporations, now existing or hereafter created, shall forever be subject to taxation, the same as the property of individuals. *Neb.,* 377.

—All real property or possessory rights to the same, as well as personal property in this State, belonging to corporations now existing or hereafter created, shall be subject to taxation the same as property of individuals: *Provided,* That the property of corporations formed for municipal, charitable, religious or educational purposes, may be exempted by law. *Nev.,* 388.

—Laws shall be passed taxing, by a uniform rule, all moneys, credits, investments in bonds, stocks, joint stock companies, or otherwise; and also all real and personal property, according to its true value in money; but burying grounds, public school houses, houses used exclusively for public worship, institutions of purely public charity, public property used exclusively for any public purpose; and personal property, to an amount not exceeding in value two hundred dollars for each individual, may, by general laws, be exempted from taxation; but, all such laws shall be subject to alteration or repeal, and the value of all property so exempted shall from time to time be ascertained and published, as may be directed by law. *Ohio,* 442.

—The property of corporations, now existing or hereafter created, shall forever be subject to taxation the same as the p operty of individuals. *Ohio,* 443.

—The General Assembly shall provide by law for taking the notes and bills discounted or purchased, moneys loaned, and all other property, effects or dues of every description (without deduction), of all banks now existing or hereafter created, and of all bankers, so that all property employed in banking shall always bear a burden of taxation equal to that imposed on the property of individuals. *Ohio,* 442.

STATE DEBTS.

—The General Assembly shall not borrow or raise money on the credit of the State (except for purposes of military defense against actual or threatened invasion, rebellion, or insurrection), without the concurrence of two-thirds of the members of each House. *Ala.,* 73.

—*Be it ordained by the People of the State of Arkansas,* That the Provisional Governor who may be elected by this Convention, be authorized to negotiate a loan not exceeding $150,000 for the State of Arkansas, for the purposes of government, till such time as

1 § 11. In addition to the above limited power to contract debts, the State
2 may contract debts to repel invasion, suppress insurrection, or defend the
3 State in war, but the money arising from the contracting of such debts, shall
4 be applied to the purpose for which it was raised or to repay such debts, and
5 to no other purpose whatever.

there may be funds in the treasury from the ordinary sources of revenue, and that he have full authority to pledge therefor the faith and credit of the State. *Ark.*, 95.

—The Legislature shall not in any manner create any debt or debts, liability or liabilities, which shall singly or in the aggregate, with any previous debts or liabilities, exceed the sum of three hundred thousand dollars, except in case of war, to repel invasion or suppress insurrection, unless the same shall be authorized by some law for some single object or work, to be distinctly specified therein, which law shall provide ways and means, exclusive of loans, for the payment of the interest of such debt or liability as it falls due, and also pay and discharge the principal of such debt or liability within twenty years from the time of the contracting thereof, and shall be irrepealable until the principal and interest thereon shall be paid and discharged; but no such law shall take effect until, at a general election, it shall have been submitted to the people, and have received a majority of all the votes cast for and against it at such election; and all money raised by authority of such law shall be applied only to the specific object therein stated, or to the payment of the debt thereby created; and such law shall be published in at least one newspaper in each judicial district, if one be published therein throughout the State, for three months next preceding the election at which it is submitted to the people. *Cal.*, 102; *Ill.*, 154.

—The General Assembly shall provide for the publication of said law for three months at least before the vote of the people shall be taken upon the same, and provision shall be made, at the time, for the payment of the interest annually, as it shall accrue, by a tax levied for the purpose, or from other sources of revenue; which law, providing for the payment of such interest by such tax, shall be irrepealable until such debt is paid: *And provided, further*, That the law levying the tax shall be submitted to the people with the law authorizing the debt to be contracted. *Ill.*, 154.

—There shall be annually assessed and collected, in the same manner as other State revenue may be assessed and collected, a tax of two mills upon each dollar's worth of taxable property, in addition to all other taxes, to be applied as follows, to wit: The fund so created shall be kept separate, and shall, annually, on the first day of January, be apportioned and paid over, *pro rata*, upon all such State indebtedness, other than the canal and school indebtedness, as may, for that purpose, be presented by the holders of the same, to be entered as credits upon, and, to that extent, in extinguishment of the principal of said indebtedness. *Ill.*, 167.

—All the revenues derived from the sale of any of the public works belonging to the State, and from the net annual income thereof, and any surplus that may, at any time, remain in the treasury derived from taxation for general State purposes, after the payment of the ordinary expenses of the government, and of the interest on bonds of the State, other than bank bonds, shall be annually applied, under the direction of the General Assembly, to the payment of the principal of the public debt. *Ind.*, 178.

—No law shall authorize any debt to be contracted on behalf of the State, except in the following cases: To meet casual deficits in the revenue; to pay the interest on the State debt; to repel invasion, suppress

insurrection, or if hostilities be threatened, provide for the public defense. *Ind.*, 179.

—The State may contract debts to supply casual deficits or failures in revenues, or to meet expenses not otherwise provided for; but the aggregate amount of such debts, direct and contingent, whether contracted by virtue of one or more acts of the General Assembly, or at different periods of time, shall never exceed the sum of two hundred and fifty thousand dollars; and the money arising from the creation of such debts shall be applied to the purpose for which it was obtained, or to repay the debts so contracted, and to no other purpose whatever. *Iowa*, 190.

—In addition to the above limited power to contract debts, the State may contract debts to repel invasion, suppress insurrection, or defend the State in war; but the money arising from the debts so contracted shall be applied to the purpose for which it was raised, or to repay such debts, and to no other purpose whatever. *Iowa*, 190; (nearly similar,) *Kan.*, 205; *Mich.*, 312; *Min.*, 327; *N b.*, 376; *Pa.*, 471; *Wis.*, 568.

—Except the debts herein before specified in this article, no debt shall be hereafter contracted by, or on behalf of this State, unless such debt shall be authorized by some law for some single work or object, to be distinctly specified therein; and such law shall impose and provide for the collection of a direct annual tax, sufficient to pay the interest on such debt, as it falls due, and also to pay and discharge the principal of such debt, within twenty years from the time of the contracting thereof; but no such law shall take effect until at a general election it shall have been submitted to the people, and have received a majority of all the votes cast for or against it at such election; and all the money raised by authority of such law, shall be applied only to the specific object therein stated, or to the payment of the debt created thereby; and such law shall be published in at least one newspaper in each county, if one is published therein, throughout the State, for three months preceding the election at which it is submitted to the people. *Iowa*, 190.

—The Legislature may at any time after the approval of such law by the people, if no debt shall have been contracted in pursuance thereof, repeal the same; and may at any time forbid the contracting of any further debt or liability under such law; but the tax imposed by such law, in proportion to the debt or liability which may have been contracted in pursuance thereof shall remain in force and be irrepealable, and be annually collected, until the principal and interest are fully paid. *Iowa*, 191.

—For the purpose of defraying extraordinary expenses and making public improvements, the State may contract public debts; but such debts shall never, in the aggregate, exceed one million dollars, except as hereinafter provided. Every such debt shall be authorized by law for some purpose specified therein, and the vote of a majority of all the members elected to each House, to be taken by the yeas and nays, shall be necessary to the passage of such law; and every such law shall provide for levying an annual tax sufficient to pay the annual interest of such debt, and the principal thereof, when it shall become due; and shall specifically appropriate the proceeds of such taxes to the payment of such principal and interest; and such appropriation shall not be repealed, nor the taxes postponed or diminished, until the interest and principal of such debts shall have been wholly paid. *Kan.*, 204.

—No debt shall be contracted by the State except as herein provided, unless the proposed law for creating such debt shall first be submitted to a direct vote of the electors of the State at some general election; and if such proposed law shall be ratified by a majority of all the votes cast at such general election, then it shall be the duty of the Legislature next after such election to enact such law and create such debt, subject to all the provisions and restrictions provided in the preceding section of this article. *Kan.*, 204.

—The General Assembly shall have no power to pass laws to diminish the resources of the sinking fund, as now established by law, until the debt of the State be paid, but may pass laws to increase them; and the whole resources of said fund, from year to year, shall be sacredly set apart and applied to the payment of the interest and principal of the State debt, and to no other use or purpose, until the whole debt of the State is fully paid and satisfied. *Ky.*, 212.

—The General Assembly may contract debts to meet casual deficits or failures in the revenue, but such debts, direct or contingent, singly or in the aggregate, shall not, at any time, exceed five hundred thousand dollars; and the moneys arising from loans creating such debts shall be applied to the purposes for which they were obtained, or to repay such debts; *Provided*, That the State may contract debts to repel invasion, suppress insurrection, or, if hostilities are threatened, provide for the public defense. *Ky.*, 212.

—No act of the General Assembly shall authorize any debt to be contracted on behalf of the Commonwealth, except for the purposes mentioned in the thirty-fifth section of this article, unless provision be made therein to lay and collect an annual tax sufficient to pay the interest stipulated, and to discharge the debt within thirty years; nor shall such act take effect until it shall have been submitted to the people at a general election, and shall have received a majority of all the votes cast for or against it: *Provided*, That the General Assembly may contract debts, by borrowing money to pay any part of the debt of the State, without submission to the people, and without making provision in the act authorizing the same for a tax to discharge the debt so contracted, or the interest thereon. *Ky.*, 212.

—The General Assembly shall have no power to pass any act or resolution, for the appropriation of any money, or the creation of any debt, exceeding the sum of one hundred dollars, at any one time, unless the same, on its final passage, shall be voted for by a majority of all the members then elected to each branch of the General Assembly; and the yeas and nays thereon entered on the journal. *Ky.*, 212.

—No liability shall be contracted by the State as above mentioned, unless the same be authorized by some law for some single object or work, to be distinctly specified therein, which shall be passed by a majority of the members elected to both Houses of the General Assembly; and the aggregate amount of debts and liabilities incurred under this and the preceding article shall never, at any time, exceed eight millions of dollars. *La.*, 234.

—Whenever the Legislature shall contract a debt exceeding in amount the sum of one hundred thousand dollars, unless in case of war, to repel invasion, or suppress insurrection, they shall, in the law creating the debt, provide adequate ways and means for the payment of the current interest and of the principal when the same shall become due. And the said law shall be irrepealable until principal and interest are fully paid and discharged, or unless the repealing law contains some other adequate provisions for the payment of the principal and interest of the debt. *La.*, 234.

—The Legislature shall not create any debt or debts, liability or liabilities on behalf of the State, which shall singly, or in the aggregate, with previous debts and liabilities hereafter incurred at any one time,

exceed three hundred thousand dollars, except to suppress insurrection, to repel invasion, or for purposes of war; but this amendment shall not be construed to refer to any money that has been, or may be deposited with this State by the government of the United States, or to any fund which the State shall hold in trust for any Indian tribe. *Me.*, 253.

—No debt shall be hereafter contracted by the General Assembly unless such debts shall be authorized by a law providing for the collection of an annual tax or taxes, sufficient to pay the interest on such debt as it falls due, and also to discharge the principal thereof within fifteen years from the time of contracting the same, and the taxes laid for this purpose shall not be repealed or applied to any other object until the said debt and interest thereon shall be fully discharged. The credit of the State shall not in any manner be given or loaned to or in aid of any association or corporation, nor shall the General Assembly have the power in any mode to involve the State in the construction of works of internal improvement, nor in any enterprise which shall involve the faith or credit of the State, nor make any appropriations therefor; and they shall not use or appropriate the proceeds of the internal improvement companies, or of the State tax now levied, or which may hereafter be levied, to pay off the public debt, to any other purpose, until the interest and debt are fully paid, or the sinking fund shall be equal to the amount of the outstanding debt; but the General Assembly may, without laying a tax, borrow an amount, never to exceed fifty thousand dollars, to meet temporary deficiencies in the treasury, and may contract debts to any amount that may be necessary for the defense of the State. *Md.*, 263.

—The Legislature shall provide by law a sinking fund of at least twenty thousand dollars a year, to commence in eighteen hundred and fifty-two, with compound interest at the rate of six per cent per annum, and an annual increase of at least five per cent, to be applied solely to the payment and extinguishment of the principal of the State debt, other than the amounts due to educational funds, and shall be continued until the extinguishment thereof. The unfunded debt shall not be funded or redeemed at a value exceeding that established by law in one thousand eight hundred and forty-eight. *Mich.*, 311.

—The State may contract debts to meet deficits in revenue. Such debts shall not in the aggregate at any one time exceed fifty thousand dollars. The moneys so raised shall be applied to the purposes for which they were obtained, or to the payment of the debts so contracted. *Mich.*, 311.

—No scrip, certificate, or other evidence of State indebtedness shall be issued except for the redemption of stock previously issued, or for such debts as are expressly authorized in this Constitution. *Mich.*, 312.

—For the purpose of defraying extraordinary expenditures, the State may contract public debts, but such debts shall never, in the aggregate, exceed two hundred and fifty thousand dollars; every such debt shall be authorized by law, for some single object to be distinctly specified therein; and no such law shall take effect until it shall have been passed by the vote of two-thirds of the members of each branch of the Legislature, to be recorded by yeas and nays on the journals of each House, respectively; and every such law shall levy a tax annually sufficient to pay the annual interest of such debt, and also a tax sufficient to pay the principal of such debt within ten years from the final passage of such law, and shall specially appropriate the proceeds of such taxes to the payment of such principal and interest; and such appropriation and taxes shall not be repealed, postponed or diminished until the principal and interest of such debt shall have been wholly paid. [*Neb.*, 376; *Wis.*, 568, except limit is $100,000.] The State shall never contract any debts for works of internal improvement; or be a party in carrying on such works, except in cases where grants of land or other property shall have been made to the State, especially dedicated by the grant to specific purposes, and in such cases the State shall devote thereto the avails of such grants, and may pledge or appropriate the revenues derived from such works in aid of their completion. *Min.*, 327.

—All debts authorized by the preceding section shall be contracted by loan on State bonds of amounts not less than five hundred dollars each, on interest, payable within ten years after the final passage of the law authorizing such debt; and such bonds shall not be sold by the State under par. A correct registry of all such bonds shall be kept by the Treasurer, in numerical order, so as always to exhibit the number and amount unpaid, and to whom severally made payable. *Min.*, 327.

—The money arising from any loan made, or debt or liability contracted, shall be applied to the object specified in the act authorizing such debt or liability, or to the repayment of such debt or liability, and to no other purpose whatever. *Min.*, 327.

—No law shall ever be passed to raise a loan of money upon the credit of the State, or to pledge the faith of the State or the payment or redemption of any loan or debt, unless such law be proposed in the Senate or House of Representatives, and be agreed to by a majority of the members of each House, and entered on their journals with the yeas and nays taken thereon, and be referred to the next succeeding Legislature, and published for three months previous to the next regular election, in three newspapers of the State; and unless a majority of each branch of the Legislature, so elected, after such publication, shall agree to, and pass such law; and in such case the yeas and nays shall be taken, and entered on the journals of each House; *Provided*, That nothing in this section shall be so construed as to prevent the Legislature from negotiating a further loan of one and a half million of dollars, and vesting the same in stock reserved to the State by the charter of the Planters' Bank of the State of Mississippi. *Miss.*, 343.

—The State shall never contract any debt for works of internal improvement, or be a party in carrying on such works; but whenever grants of lands or other property shall have been made to the State, especially dedicated by the grant to particular works of internal improvement, the State may carry on such particular works, and shall devote thereto the avails of such grants, and may pledge or appropriate the revenues derived from such works in aid of their completion. *Neb.*, 376; *Wis.*, 568.

—The Legislature shall not authorize the borrowing of money or the issuance of State bonds for any sum exceeding in the aggregate fifty thousand dollars, without submitting a proposition therefor to a vote of the people for their approval or rejection, except in case of war, to repel invasion, or suppress insurrection. *Neb.*, 373.

—For the purpose of enabling the State to transact its business upon a cash basis from its organization, the State may contract public debts; but such debts shall never, in the aggregate, exclusive of interest, exceed the sum of three hundred thousand dollars, except for the purpose of defraying extraordinary expenses as hereinafter mentioned. Every such debt shall be authorized by law for some purpose or purposes, to be distinctly specified therein; and every such law shall provide for levying an annual tax sufficient to pay the interest semi-annually, and the principal within twenty years from the passage of such law, and shall specially appropriate the proceeds of said taxes to the payment of said principal and interest; and such appropriation shall not be repealed, nor the taxes postponed or diminished until the principal and interest of said debts shall have been wholly paid. Every contract of indebtedness entered into or assumed by or on behalf of the State, when all its debts and liabilities amount to said sum before mentioned, shall be void and of no effect, except in cases of money borrowed to repel invasion or suppress insurrection, defend the State in time of war, or, if hostilities be threatened, to provide for public defense. *Neb.*, 389.

—For the first three years after the adoption of this

Constitution, the Legislature shall not levy a tax for State purposes exceeding one per cent per annum, on the taxable property in the State; *Provided*, The Legislature may levy a special tax, not exceeding one-fourth of one per cent per annum, which shall be appropriated to the payment of the indebtedness of the Territory of Nevada, assumed by the State of Nevada, and for that purpose only, until all of said indebtedness is paid. *Nev.*, 395.

—The Legislature shall not, in any matter, create any debt or debts, liability or liabilities, of the State, which shall singly or in the aggregate, with any previous debts or liabilities, at any time exceed one hundred thousand dollars, except for purposes of war, or to repel invasion, or to suppress insurrection, unless the same shall be authorized by a law for some single object or work, to be distinctly specified therein; which law shall provide the ways and means, exclusive of loans, to pay the interest of each debt or liability as it falls due, and also to pay and discharge the principal of such debt or liability within thirty-five years from the time of the contracting thereof, and shall be irrepealable until such debt or liability, and the interest thereon, are fully paid and discharged; and no such law shall take effect until it shall, at a general election, have been submitted to the people, and have received the sanction of a majority of all the votes cast for and against it at such election; and all money to be raised by the authority of such law shall be applied only to the specific object stated therein, and to the payment of the debt thereby created. This section shall not be construed to refer to any money that has been or may be deposited with this State by the government of the United States. *N. J.*, 415.

—The State may contract debts to supply casual deficits or failures in revenues, or to meet expenses not otherwise provided for; but the aggregate amount of such debts, direct and contingent, whether contracted by virtue of one or more acts of the General Assembly, or at different periods of time, shall never exceed seven hundred and fifty thousand dollars; and the money arising from the creation of such debts shall be applied to the purposes for which it was obtained, or to repay the debts so contracted, and to no other purpose whatever. *Ohio*, 439; *Pa.*, 471.

—In addition to the above limited power, the State may contract debts to repel invasion, suppress insurrection, defend the State in war or to redeem the present outstanding indebtedness of the State; but the money arising from the contracting of such debts, shall be applied to the purpose for which it was raised, or to repay such debts, and to no other purpose whatever; and all debts incurred to redeem the present outstanding indebtedness of the State shall be so contracted as to be payable by the sinking fund, hereinafter provided for, as the same shall accumulate. *Ohio*, 439.

—Except the debts above specified, no debt whatever shall hereafter be created by or on behalf of the State. *Ohio*, 439.

—The faith of the State being pledged for the payment of its public debt, in order to provide therefor, there shall be created a sinking fund, which shall be sufficient to pay the accruing interest on such debt, and annually to reduce the principal thereof, by a sum not less than one hundred thousand dollars, increased yearly, and each and every year, by compounding, at the rate of six per cent. per annum. The said sinking fund shall consist of the net annual income of the public works and stocks owned by the State, of any other funds or resources that are, or may be, provided by law, and of such further sum, to be raised by taxation, as may be required for the purposes aforesaid. *Ohio*, 439.

—The Legislative Assembly shall not, in any manner, create any debt or liabilities, which shall singly, or in the aggregate, with previous debts or liabilities, exceed the sum of fifty thousand dollars, except in case of war, or to repel invasion, or suppress insurrection; and every contract of indebtedness entered into, or assumed by or on behalf of the State, when all its

42

1 § 12. Except the debts specified in the tenth and eleventh sections of this

2 article, no debt shall be hereafter contracted by or on behalf of this State,

3 unless such debt shall be authorized by a law, for some single work or object, to

4 be distinctly specified therein; and such law shall impose and provide for

5 the collection of a direct annual tax to pay, and sufficient to pay the interest

6 on such debt as it falls due, and also to pay and discharge the principal of

7 such debt within eighteen years from the time of the contracting thereof.

8 No such law shall take effect until it shall at a general election have been

liabilities and debts amount to said sum, shall be void, and of no effect. *Or.*, 457.

—The General Assembly shall have no power, hereafter, without the express consent of the people, to incur State debts to an amount exceeding fifty thousand dollars, except in time of war, or in case of insurrection or invasion; nor shall they, in any case, without such consent, pledge the faith of the State for the payment of the obligations of others. This section shall not be construed to refer to any money that may be deposited with this State by the Government of the United States. *R. I.*, 476.

—The Legislative Assembly shall provide for raising revenue sufficient to defray the expenses of the State for each fiscal year, and also a sufficient sum to pay the interest on the State debt, if there be any. *Or.*, 456.

—Except the debts above specified in sections one and two of this article, no debt whatever shall be created by or on behalf of the State. *Pa.*, 471.

—To provide for the payment of the present debt, and any additional debt contracted as aforesaid, the Legislature shall, at its first session after the adoption of this amendment, create a sinking fund which shall be sufficient to pay the accruing interest on such debt, and annually to reduce the principal thereof by a sum not less than two hundred and fifty thousand dollars, which sinking fund shall consist of the net annual income of the public works, from time to time owned by the State, or the proceeds of the sale of the same or any part thereof, and of the income or proceeds of sale of stocks owned by the State, together with other funds or resources that may be designated by law. The said sinking fund may be increased from time to time by assigning to it any part of the taxes or other revenues of the State not required for the ordinary and current expenses of government, and unless in case of war, invasion or insurrection, no part of the said sinking fund shall be used or applied otherwise than in extinguishment of the public debt, until the amount of such debt is reduced below the sum of five millions of dollars. *Pa*, 471.

—The aggregate amount of debts hereafter contracted by the Legislature, shall never exceed the sum of one hundred thousand dollars, except in case of war, to repel invasion, or suppress insurrections. And in no case shall any amount be borrowed, except by a vote of two-thirds of both Houses of the Legislature. *Tex.*, 517.

—No debt shall be contracted by this State except to meet casual deficits in the revenue, to redeem a previous liability of the State or to suppress insurrection, repel invasion or defend the State in time of war. If the State becomes a stockholder in any association or corporation for purposes of internal improvements, such stock shall be paid for at the time of subscription, or a tax shall be levied for the ensuing year sufficient to pay the subscription in full. *Va.*, 538.

—The liability to the State of any incorporated company or institution to redeem the principal and pay the interest of any loan heretofore made or which may hereafter be made by the State to such com-

pany or institution, shall not be released; and the General Assembly shall not pledge the faith of the State, or bind it in any form for the debt or obligation of any company or corporation. *Va.*, 538.

—The General Assembly may at any time direct the sale of the stocks held by the Commonwealth in internal improvements and other companies located within the limits of this Commonwealth, but the proceeds of such sale, if made before the payment of the public debt, shall be appropriated to the payment thereof. *Va.*, 538.

—The Legislature may at any time direct a sale of the stocks owned by the State in banks and other corporations, but the proceeds of such sale shall be applied to the liquidation of the public debt. *W. Va.*, 556.

—No debt shall be contracted by this State, except to meet casual deficits in the revenue, to redeem a previous liability of the State, to suppress insurrection, repel invasion, or defend the State in time of war. *W. Va.*, 556.

—The State shall never contract any public debt, except in the cases and manner herein provided. *Wis.*, 568.

—No liability, either State, parochial or municipal, shall exist for any debts contracted for, or in the interest of the rebellion against the United States government. *La.*, 235.

—The Legislature shall not provide for the payment of any bonds now held by rebels in arms against the State or United States government. *Va.*, 538.

—It shall not provide for the payment of any debt or obligation created in the name of the State of Virginia by the usurped and pretended State authorities at Richmond. And it shall not allow any county, city or corporation, to levy or collect any tax for the payment of any debt created for the purpose of aiding any rebellion against the State or the United States. *Va.*, 538.

TAXATION BY COUNTIES, CITIES, VILLAGES AND TOWNS—RESTRICTIONS UPON THEIR CREDIT.

—It shall be the duty of the Legislature, and they are hereby empowered to provide for the organization of cities and incorporated villages, and to restrict their power of taxation, assessment, borrowing money, contracting debts, and loaning their credit, so as to prevent abuses in assessments and taxation, and in contracting debts by such municipal corporations. *Wis.*, 570.

—The General Assembly shall provide for the organization of cities, incorporated villages, by general laws; and restrict their power of taxation, assessment, borrowing money, contracting debts, and loaning their credit, so as to prevent the abuse of such power. *Ohio*, 443.

—Acts of the Legislative Assembly, incorporating towns and cities, shall restrict their powers of taxation, borrowing money, contracting debts, and loaning their credit. *Or.*, 457.

167

9 submitted to the people, and have received a majority of all the votes cast for

10 and against it, at such election. On the final passage of such bill in either

11 house of the Legislature, the question shall be taken by ayes and noes, to be

12 duly entered on the journals thereof, and shall be : "Shall this bill pass, and

13 ought the same to receive the sanction of the people?" The Legislature may

14 at any time, after the approval of such law by the people, if no debt shall

15 have been contracted in pursuance thereof, repeal the same; and may at any

16 time, by law, forbid the contracting of any further debt or liability under

17 such law; but the tax imposed by such act, in proportion to the debt and

18 liability which may have been contracted, in pursuance of such law, shall

19 remain in force and be irrepealable, and be annually collected, until the

20 proceeds thereof shall have made the provision herein before specified to pay

21 and discharge the interest and principal of such debt and liability. The

22 money arising from any loan or stock creating such debt or liability shall be

23 applied to the work or object specified in the act authorizing such debt or

—The General Assembly shall have power to authorize the several counties and incorporated towns in this State, to impose taxes for county and corporation purposes respectively, in such manner as shall be prescribed by law ; and all property shall be taxed according to its value, upon the principles established in regard to State taxation. *Tenn.*, 494 ; (nearly similar), *Fl.*, 137.

The commissioners of counties, the trustees of townships, and similar boards, shall have such power of local taxation, for police purposes, as may be prescribed by law. *Ohio*, 440.

—The corporate authorities of counties, townships, school-districts, cities, towns and villages, may be vested with power to assess and collect taxes for corporate purposes; such taxes to be uniform in respect to persons and property within the jurisdiction of the body imposing the same. And the General Assembly shall require that all the property within the limits of municipal corporations belonging to individuals shall be taxed for the payment of debts contracted under authority of law. *Ill.*, 164.

—The Legislature shall provide for the organization of cities and incorporated villages by general laws; and restrict their power of taxation, assessment, borrowing money, contracting debts and loaning their credit, so as to prevent the abuse of such power. *Neb.*, 377.

—The Legislature shall provide for the incorporation and organization of cities and villages, and shall restrict their powers of taxation, borrowing money, contracting debts and loaning their credit. *Mich.*, 313.

—It shall be the duty of the Legislature to provide for the organization of cities and incorporated villages, and to restrict their power of taxation, assessment, borrowing money, contracting debts and loaning their credit, so as to prevent abuses in assessments and in contracting debts by such municipal corporations. *Cal.*, 100.

—No county shall subscribe for stock in any incorporated company, unless the same be paid for at the time of such subscription; nor shall any county loan its credit to any incorporated company, nor borrow money for the purpose of taking stock in any such company. *Ind.*, 179.

—The General Assembly shall never authorize any county, city, town, or township, by vote of its citizens or otherwise, to become a stockholder in any joint stock company, corporation, or association whatever; or to raise money for, or to loan its credit in aid of any such company, corporation, or association. *Ohio*, 439.

—No law shall be passed by which a citizen shall be compelled, directly or indirectly, to become a stockholder in, or contribute to a railroad, or other work of internal improvement, without his consent, except the inhabitants of a corporate town or city. This provision shall not be construed to deny the power of taxation for the purpose of making levees or dams to prevent the overflow of rivers. *Ga.*, 146.

—No county, city, town, or other municipal corporation, shall become a stockholder in any joint-stock company, corporation or association whatever, or loan its credit in aid of any such company, corporation, or association, except railroad corporations, companies, or associations. *Nev.*, 389.

—No political or municipal corporation shall become a stockholder in any banking corporation, directly or indirectly. *Iowa*, 191.

—The General Assembly shall not authorize any county, city or town to become a stockholder in, or to loan its credit to any company, association or corporation, unless two-thirds of the qualified voters of such county, city or town, at a regular or special election to be held therein, shall assent thereto *Mo.*, 362.

—The Legislature shall not authorize any county, city, borough, township, or corporate district, by virtue of a vote of its citizens, or otherwise, to become a stockholder in any company, association, or corporation; or to obtain money for, or loan its credit to, any corporation, association, institution or party. *Pa.*, 471.

—No county, city, town or other municipal corporation, by vote of its citizens or otherwise, shall become a stockholder in any joint stock company, corporation or association whatever, or raise money for or loan its credit to, or in aid of any such company, corporation or association. *Or.*, 457.

24 liability, or for the repayment of such debt or liability, and for no other
25 purpose whatever. No such law shall be submitted to be voted on within
26 three months after its passage, or at any general election when any other law,
27 or any bill, or any amendment to the Constitution shall be submitted to be
28 voted for or against.

1 § 13. Every law which imposes, continues or revives a tax, shall distinctly
2 state the tax and the object to which it is to be applied; and it shall not be
3 sufficient to refer to any other law to fix such tax or object.

1 § 14. On the final passage, in either House of the Legislature, of every act
2 which imposes, continues or revives a tax or creates a debt or charge, or
3 makes, continues or revives any appropriation of public or trust money, or
4 property; or releases, discharges or commutes any claim or demand of the
5 State, the question shall be taken by ayes and noes, which shall be duly
6 entered on the journals, and three-fifths of all the members elected to either
7 House shall, in all such cases, be necessary to constitute a quorum therein.

—Provision shall be made by general law for the organization of cities, towns and villages; and their power of taxation, assessment, borrowing money, contracting debts, and loaning their credit, shall be so restricted as to prevent the abuse of such power. *Kan.*, 205.

—No county or other political or municipal corporation shall be allowed to become indebted in any manner, or for any purpose, to an amount in the aggregate exceeding five per centum on the value of the taxable property within such county or corporation, to be ascertained by the last State and county tax lists, previous to the incurring of such indebtedness. *Iowa*, 199.

—No money shall be drawn from any county or township treasury, except by authority of law. *Min.*, 328.

—Any county and township organization shall have such powers of local taxation as may be prescribed by law. *Min.*, 328.

—The Legislature shall provide for the organization of cities and towns by general laws; and restrict the power of taxation, assessment, borrowing money, contracting debts, and loaning their credit, except for procuring supplies of water. *Nev.*, 389.

—The Board of Supervisors of any county may borrow or raise by tax one thousand dollars, for constructing or repairing public buildings, highways, or bridges; but no greater sum shall be borrowed or raised by tax for such purpose in any one year, unless authorized by a majority of the electors of such county voting thereon. *Mich.*, 309.

CAPITATION TAXES.

—No capitation or other direct tax shall be laid, unless in proportion to the census. *U. S.*, 13.

—The Legislature shall provide by law for the payment of an annual poll-tax of not less than two nor exceeding four dollars from each male person resident in the State between the age of twenty-one and sixty-years, uncivilized American Indians excepted, one-half to be applied for State and one-half for county purposes; and the Legislature may, in its discretion, make such payment a condition to the right of voting. *Nev.*, 381.

—All free males over the age of twenty-one years, and under the age of forty-five years, and all slaves over the age of twelve years, and under the age of fifty years, shall be subject to capitation tax, and no other person shall be subject to such tax; *Provided*, That nothing herein contained shall prevent exemptions of taxable polls, as heretofore prescribed by law, in cases of bodily infirmity. *N. C.*, 430.

—The levying of taxes, by the poll, is grievous and oppressive; therefore the General Assembly shall never levy a poll-tax, for county or State purposes. *Ohio*, 442.

—Poll-tax of $1.00 to be levied for benefit of schools. *R. I.*, 475.

—The General Assembly, whenever a tax is laid upon land, shall, at the same time, impose a capitation tax, which shall not be less upon each poll than one-fourth of the tax laid on each hundred dollars' worth of the assessed value of the land taxed; excepting, however, from the operation of such capitation tax all such classes of persons, as from disability or otherwise, ought, in the judgment of the General Assembly, to be exempted. *S. C.*, 488.

—A capitation tax, equal to the tax assessed on land of the value of two hundred dollars, shall be levied on every white male inhabitant who has attained the age of twenty-one years; and one equal moiety of the capitation tax upon white persons shall be applied to the purposes of education in primary and free schools; but nothing herein contained shall prevent exemptions of taxable polls in cases of bodily infirmity. *Va.*, 538.

—A capitation tax of one dollar, shall be levied upon each white male inhabitant who has attained the age of twenty-one years. *W. Va.*, 556.

—The assessors of each town or city shall annually assess upon every person whose name shall be registered, a tax of one dollar, or such sum as with his other taxes shall amount to one dollar, which registry tax shall be paid into the treasury of such town or city, and be applied to the support of public schools therein. *R. I.*, 475.

—A tax on white polls shall be laid in such manner and of such an amount as may be prescribed by law. *Tenn.*, 494.

·ARTICLE VIII.

1 Section 1. Corporations may be formed under general laws; but shall not

2 be created by special act, except for municipal purposes, and in cases where

3 in the judgment of the Legislature, the objects of the corporation cannot be

4 attained under general laws.   All general laws and special acts passed

5 pursuant to this section, may be altered from time to time, or repealed.

FORMATION OF CORPORATIONS.

—Corporations may be formed under general laws, but shall not be created by special act, except for municipal purposes. All general laws and special acts passed pursuant to this section may be altered from time to time, or repealed. *Cal.,* 99; *Mich.,* 312; *Mo.,* 360; *Or.,* 457.

-No act of incorporation, except for the renewal of existing corporations, shall be hereafter enacted without the concurrence of two-thirds of each branch of the Legislature, and with a reserved power of revocation, by the Legislature; and no act of incorporation which may be hereafter enacted shall continue in force for a longer period than twenty years, without the re-enactment of the Legislature, unless it be an incorporation for public improvement. *Del.,* 119.

—The General Assembly shall pass no act of incorporation, nor make any alteration in one, unless with the assent of at least two thirds of each House, and unless public notice in one or more newspapers in the State shall have been given for at least three months immediately preceding the session at which the same may be applied for. *Fl.,* 159.

—No act incorporating any railroad, banking, insurance, commercial or financial corporation shall be introduced into the General Assembly, unless the person or persons applying for such corporation shall have deposited with the Treasurer the sum of one hundred dollars as a bonus to the State. *Fl.,* 133.

—The General Assembly shall pass no act of incorporation, nor make any alteration in one, unless with the assent of at least two-thirds of each House, and unless public notice in one or more newspapers in the State shall have been given for at least three months immediately preceding the session at which the same may be applied for. *Fl.,* 138.

—The General Assembly shall have no power to grant corporate powers and privileges to private companies, except to banking, insurance, railroad, canal, plank-road, navigation, mining, express, lumber, manufacturing, and telegraph companies; nor to make or change election precincts; nor to establish bridges and ferries; nor to change names, or legitimate children; but shall by law prescribe the manner in which such power shall be exercised by the courts. But no bank charter shall be granted or extended, and no act passed authorizing the suspension of specie payment by any chartered bank, except by a vote of two-thirds of each branch of the General Assembly. *Ga.,* 146.

—Corporations not possessing banking powers or privileges, may be formed under general laws, but shall not be created by special acts, except for municipal purposes, and in cases where, in the judgment of the General Assembly, the objects of the corporation cannot be attained under general laws. *Ill.,* 164.

—Corporations other than banking, shall not be created by special act, but may be formed under general law. *Ind.,* 179.

—Subject to the provisions of this article, the General Assembly shall have power to amend or repeal all laws for the organization or creation of corporations, or granting of special or exclusive privileges or immunities, by a vote of two thirds of each branch of the General Assembly; and no exclusive privilege, except as in this article provided, shall ever be granted. *Iowa,* 191.

—No corporation shall be created by special laws, but the General Assembly shall provide, by general laws, for the organization of all corporations hereafter to be created, except as hereinafter provided. *Iowa,* 191.

—The Legislature shall pass no special act conferring corporate powers. Corporations may be created under general laws, but all such laws may be amended or repealed. *Kan.,* 205; *Nev.,* 388.

—The General Assembly shall pass a general law for the incorporation of towns, religious, literary, scientific, benevolent, military and other associations, not commercial, industrial, or financial; but no special act incorporating any such association shall be passed. *Fl.,* 133.

—The title to all property of religious corporations shall vest in trustees, whose election shall be by the members of such corporations. *Kan.,* 205.

—Corporations shall not be created in this State by special laws except for political or municipal purposes; but the Legislature shall provide by general law for the organization of all other corporations, except corporations with banking or discounting privileges, the creation, renewal or extension of which is hereby prohibited. *La.,* 234.

—Corporations may be formed under general laws, but shall not be created by special act, except for municipal purposes, and in cases where, in the judgment of the General Assembly, the object of the corporation cannot be attained under general laws. All laws and special acts, pursuant to this section, may be altered from time to time, or repealed: *Provided,* Nothing herein contained shall be construed to alter, change or amend in any manner, the section in relation to banks. *Md.,* 265.

—The Legislature shall pass no law altering or amending any act of incorporation heretofore granted without the assent of two-thirds of the members elected to each House, nor shall any such act be renewed or extended.   This restriction shall not apply to municipal corporations. *Mich.,* 312.

—No corporation shall hold any real estate hereafter acquired for a longer period than ten years, except such real estate as shall be actually occupied by such corporation in the exercise of its franchises. *Mich.,* 313.

—Previous notice of any application for an alteration of the charter of any corporation shall be given in such manner as may be prescribed by law. *Mich.,* 313.

—No corporation shall be formed under special acts, except for municipal purposes. *Min.,* 328.

—No law shall be passed reviving or re-enacting any act heretofore passed creating any private corporation, where such corporation shall not have been organized and commenced the transaction of its business within one year from the time such act took effect, or within such other time as may have been prescribed in such act for such organization and commencement of business. *Mo.,* 360.

—The Legislature shall pass no special act conferring corporate powers. *Neb.,* 376; *Ohio,* 443.

—Corporations may be formed under general laws. *Neb.,* 376.

—Corporations created by or under the laws of the

1   § 2. Dues from corporations shall be secured by such individual liability

2 of the corporators and other means as may be prescribed by law.

1   § 3. The term corporation, as used in this article, shall be construed to

2 include all associations and joint-stock companies having any of the powers

3 and privileges of corporations not possessed by individuals or partnerships.

4 And all corporations shall have the right to sue and shall be subject to be

5 sued in all courts in like cases as natural persons.

Territory of Nevada shall be subject to the provisions of such laws until the Legislature shall pass laws regulating the same, in pursuance of the provisions of this Constitution. *Nev.,* 388.

—Corporations may be formed under general laws; but all such laws may, from time to time, be altered or repealed. *Ohio,* 443.

—The Legislature shall have the power to alter, revoke or annul any charter of incorporation hereafter conferred by or under any special or general law, whenever in their opinion it may be injurious to the citizens of the Commonwealth; in such manner, however, that no injustice shall be done to the corporators. *Pa.,* 472.

—Hereafter, when any bill shall be presented to either House of the General Assembly, to create a corporation, for any other than religious, literary or charitable purposes, or for military or fire company, it shall be continued until another election of members of the General Assembly shall have taken place, and such public notice of the pendency thereof shall be given as may be required by law. *R. I.,* 476.

—No private corporation shall be created, unless the bill creating it shall be passed by two-thirds of both Houses of the Legislature; and two thirds of the Legislature shall have power to revoke and repeal all private corporations by making compensation for the franchise. And the State shall not be part owner of the stock, or property, belonging to any corporation. *Tex.,* 516.

—The Legislature shall pass general laws whereby any number of persons associated for mining, manufacturing, insuring, or other purpose useful to the public, excepting banks of circulation and the construction of works of internal improvement, may become a corporation on complying with the terms and conditions thereby prescribed; and no special act incorporating, or granting peculiar privileges to any joint stock company or association, not having in view the issuing of bills to circulate as money or the construction of some work of internal improvement, shall be passed. No company or association, authorized by this section, shall issue bills to circulate as money. No charter of incorporation shall be granted under such general laws, unless the right be reserved to alter or amend such charter, at the pleasure of the Legislature, to be declared by general law. *W. Va.,* 558.

—Corporations without banking powers or privileges may be formed under general laws, but shall not be created by special act, except for municipal purposes, and in cases where, in the judgment of the Legislature, the objects of the corporation cannot be attained under general laws. All general laws or special acts enacted under the provisions of this section may be altered or repealed by the Legislature at any time after their passage. *Wis.,* 569.

—No corporation, except for municipal purposes, or for the construction of railroads, plank-roads, and canals, shall be created for a longer time than thirty years. *Mich.,* 313.

DEFINITION OF TERM CORPORATION.

—The term corporations as used in this article shall be construed to include all associations and joint-stock companies having any of the powers or privileges of corporations not possessed by individuals or partnerships. And all corporations shall have the right to sue, and shall be subject to be sued in all courts in like cases as natural persons. *Cal.,* 99; *Kan.,* 205; *Mich.,* 313; *Min.,* 323.

PRIVATE PROPERTY TAKEN BY CORPORATIONS.

—The property of no person shall be taken by any corporation for public use without compensation being first made or secured, in such manner as may be prescribed by law. *Mich.,* 313.

—No municipal corporation shall take private property for public use against the consent of the owner, without the necessity thereof being first established by the verdict of a jury. *Wis.,* 570.

—Individuals or private corporations shall not be authorized to take private property for public use, without just compensation first made to the owners. *N. J.,* 415.

—No right of way shall be appropriated to the use of any corporation until full compensation be first made or secured therefor. *Nev.,* 389.

—The Legislature shall not invest any corporate body or individual with the privilege of taking private property for public use, without requiring such corporation or individual to make compensation to the owners of said property, or give adequate security therefor, before such property shall be taken. *Pa.,* 466.

—No right of way shall be appropriated to the use of any corporation until full compensation therefor be first made in money, or secured by a deposit of money, to the owner, irrespective of any benefit from any improvement proposed by such corporation. *Kan.,* 205.

BANKS.

—Not more than one bank shall be established, nor more than one bank charter be renewed at any one session of the General Assembly; nor shall any bank be established, nor any bank charter be renewed, without the concurrence of two-thirds of each House of the General Assembly, and in conformity with the following rules—that is to say:

RULE 2. The remedy for the collection of debts shall be reciprocal for and against the bank.

RULE 3. No bank shall commence operations until one-half of the capital stock subscribed for be actually paid in gold and silver; which amount shall, in no case, be less than one hundred thousand dollars.

RULE 4. If any bank shall neglect or refuse to pay, on demand, any bill, note, or obligation issued by the corporation according to the promise therein expressed,

1 § 4. The Legislature shall have no power to pass any act granting any
2 special charter for banking purposes; but corporations or associations may be
3 formed for such purposes under general laws.

1 § 5. The Legislature shall have no power to pass any law sanctioning in
2 any manner, directly or indirectly, the suspension of specie payments, by any
3 person, association or corporation issuing bank notes of any description.

1 § 6. The Legislature shall provide by law for the registry of all bills or
2 notes issued or put in circulation as money, and shall require ample security
3 for the redemption of the same in specie.

the holder of such bill, note, or obligation shall be entitled to receive and recover interest thereon until paid, or until specie payments are resumed by the bank, at the rate of twelve per centum per annum from the date of such demand; unless the General Assembly shall, by a vote of two-thirds of each House thereof, sanction such suspension of specie payments. *Ala.*, 77.

RULE 5. Whenever any bank suspends specie payments, its charter is thereby forfeited; unless such suspension shall be sanctioned and legalized, at the next session of the General Assembly, by a vote of two-thirds of each House thereof. *Ala.*, 77.

—The Legislature shall have no power to pass any act granting any charter for banking purposes; but associations may be formed under general laws for the deposit of gold and silver, but no such association shall make, issue, or put in circulation, any bill, check, ticket, certificate, promissory note, or other paper, or the paper of any bank, to circulate as money. *Cal.*, 99.

—The Legislature of this State shall prohibit by law, any person or persons, association, company, or corporation, from exercising the privilege of banking, or creating paper to circulate as money. *Cal.*, 99.

—No bank charter, nor any act of incorporation granting exclusive privileges, shall be granted for a longer period than twenty years. *Fl.*, 139.

—Banks chartered by the General Assembly shall be restricted to the business of exchange, discount and deposit, and they shall not deal in real estate, nor in merchandise or chattels, except as security for loans or discounts, or for debts due to such bank; nor shall they be concerned in insurance, manufacturing, exportation, or importation, except of bullion, or specie; nor shall they own real estate or chattels, except such as shall be necessary for their actual use in the transaction of business, or which may be received in payment of previously contracted debts, or purchased at legal sales to satisfy such debts, of which they shall be required to make sale within three years after the acquisition thereof. *Fl.*, 139.

—The capital stock of any bank shall not be less than one hundred thousand dollars, to be paid in suitable installments, and shall be created only by the payment of specie therein. *Fl.*, 139.

—All liabilities of such banks shall be payable in specie, and the circulation of no bank shall exceed three dollars for one of capital actually paid in. *Fl.*, 139.

—No dividends or profits exceeding ten per centum per annum on the capital stock paid in shall be made, but all profits over ten per centum per annum shall be set apart and retained as a safety fund. *Fl.*, 139.

—Stockholders in a bank when an act of forfeiture is committed, or when it is dissolved or has expired, shall be individually and severally liable for the redemption of the outstanding circulation, in proportion to the stock owned by each, and no transfer of stock shall exonerate such stockholders from this lia-

bility, unless such transfer was made at least two years previous to said forfeiture, dissolution or expiration. *Fl.*, 139.

—Banks shall be open to inspection under such regulations as may be prescribed by law, and it shall be the duty of the Governor to appoint a person or persons not connected in any manner with any bank in the State, to examine at least once a year into their state and condition; and the officers of every bank shall make quarterly returns under oath, to the Governor, of its state and condition, and the names of the stockholders and shares held by each. *Fl.*, 139.

—*Non user* for the space of one year, or any act of a corporation, or those having the control or management thereof, or intrusted therewith, inconsistent with, or in violation of the provisions of this Constitution, or of its charter, shall cause its forfeiture, and the General Assembly shall by general law provide a summary process for the sequestration of its effects and assets, and the appointment of officers to settle its affairs, and no forfeited charter shall be restored. *Fl.*, 139.

—No State bank shall hereafter be created, nor shall the State own or be liable for any stock in any corporation or joint stock association for banking purposes, to be hereafter created. *Ill.*, 164.

—No act of the General Assembly, authorizing corporations or associations with banking powers, shall go into effect, or in any manner be in force, unless the same shall be submitted to the people at the general election next succeeding the passage of the same and be approved by a majority of all the votes cast at such election, for and against such law. *Ill.*, 164.

—Nor to revive or extend the charter of the State Bank, or the charter of any other bank heretofore existing in this State, and shall pass laws to prohibit the sale of lottery tickets in this State. *Ill.*, 154.

—The General Assembly shall not have power to establish or incorporate any bank or banking company, or moneyed institution, for the purpose of issuing bills of credit, or bills payable to order or bearer, except under the conditions prescribed in this Constitution. *Ind.*, 179.

—No banks shall be established otherwise than under a general banking law, except as provided in the fourth section of this article. *Ind.*, 179.

—If the General Assembly shall enact a general banking law, such law shall provide for the registry and countersigning by an officer of State of all paper credit designed to be circulated as money, and ample collateral security, readily convertible into specie, or the redemption of the same in gold or silver, shall be required, which collateral security shall be under the control of the proper officer or officers of State. *Ind.*, 179.

—The General Assembly may also charter a bank with branches without collateral security, as required in the preceding section. *Ind.*, 179.

—If the General Assembly shall establish a bank with branches, the branches shall be mutually responsible for each other's liabilities upon all paper credit issued as money. *Ind.*, 179.

—All bills or notes issued as money shall be at all times redeemable in gold or silver; and no law shall be passed sanctioning, directly or indirectly, the suspension by any bank or banking company of specie payments. *Ind.*, 179.

—Holders of bank notes shall be entitled, in case of insolvency, to preference of payment over all other creditors. *Ind.*, 179.

—No bank shall receive, directly or indirectly, a greater rate of interest than shall be allowed by law to individuals loaning money. *Ind.*, 179.

—Every bank or banking company shall be required to cease all banking operations within twenty years from the time of its organization, and promptly thereafter to close its business. *Ind.*, 179.

—The General Assembly is not prohibited from investing the trust funds in a bank with branches; but in case of such investment, the safety of the same shall be guaranteed by unquestionable security. *Ind.*, 179.

—The State shall not be a stockholder in any bank after the expiration of the present bank charter; nor shall the credit of the State ever be given or loaned in aid of any person, association or corporation; nor shall the State hereafter become a stockholder in any corporation or association. *Ind.*, 179.

—No act of the General Assembly, authorizing or creating corporations or associations with banking powers, nor amendments thereto, shall take effect, or in any manner be in force, until the same shall have been submitted separately to the people, at a general or special election, as provided by law, to be held not less than three months after the passage of the act, and shall have been approved by a majority of all the electors voting for and against it at such election. *Iowa.*, 191.

—No act of the General Assembly, authorizing associations with banking powers, shall take effect until it shall be submitted to the people, at the general election next succeeding the passage thereof, and be approved by a majority of all the electors voting at such election. *Ohio*, 443.

—Subject to the provisions of the foregoing section, the General Assembly may also provide for the establishment of a State Bank, with branches. *Iowa*, 191.

—If a State Bank be established, it shall be founded on an actual specie basis, and the branches shall be mutually responsible for each other's liabilities upon all notes, bills, and other issues intended to circulate as money. *Iowa*, 191.

—If a general banking law shall be enacted, it shall provide for the registry and countersigning, by an officer of State, of all bills, or paper credit designed to circulate as money, and require security to the full amount thereof, to be deposited with the State Treasurer, in United States stocks, or in interest paying stocks of States in good credit and standing, to be rated at ten per cent below their average value in the city of New York, for the thirty days next preceding their deposit; and in case of a depreciation of any portion of said stocks, to the amount of ten per cent on the dollar, the bank or banks owning said stocks shall be required to make up said deficiency by depositing additional stocks, and said law shall also provide for the recording of the names of all stockholders in such corporations, the amount of stock held by each, the time of any transfer, and to whom. *Iowa*, 191.

—In case of the insolvency of any banking institution, the bill holders shall have a reference over its other creditors. *Iowa*, 191; *La.*, 234; *Mich.*, 312; *Min.*, 328.

—The suspension of specie payments by banking institutions shall never be permitted or sanctioned. *Iowa*, 191.

—No bank shall be established otherwise than under a general banking law. *Kan.*, 215.

—All banking laws shall require, as collateral security

for the redemption of the circulating notes of any bank organized under their provisions, a deposit with the Auditor of State of the interest-paying bonds of the several States or of the United States, at the cash rates of the New York Stock Exchange, to an amount equal to the amount of circulating notes, which such bank shall be authorized to issue, and a cash deposit in its vaults of ten per cent of such amount of circulating notes; and the Auditor shall register and countersign no more circulating bills of any bank than the cash value of such bonds when deposited. *Kan.*, 205.

—Whenever the bonds pledged as collateral security for the circulation of any bank shall depreciate in value, the Auditor of State shall require additional security, or curtail the circulation of such bank to such extent as will continue the security unimpaired. *Kan.*, 215.

—All circulating notes shall be redeemable in the money of the United States. Holders of such notes shall be entitled, in case of the insolvency of such banks, to preference of payment over all other creditors. *Kan.*, 205.

—The State shall not be a stockholder in any banking institution. *Kan.*, 205.

—All banks shall be required to keep offices and officers for the issue and redemption of their circulation, at a convenient place within the State, to be named on the circulating notes issued by such bank. *Kan.*, 205.

—No banking institution shall issue circulating notes of a less denomination than one dollar. *Kan.*, 205.

—No banking law shall be in force until the same shall have been submitted to a vote of the electors of the State at some general election, and approved by a majority of all the votes cast at such election. *Kan.*, 205.

—Any banking law may be amended or repealed. *Kan.*, 205.

—No banking law, or law for banking purposes, or amendments thereof, shall have effect until the same shall, after its passage, be submitted to a vote of the electors of the State, at a general election, and be approved by a majority of the votes cast thereon at such election. *Mich.*, 312.

—The General Assembly shall grant no charter for banking purposes, nor renew any banking corporation now in existence, except upon the condition that the stockholders shall be liable to the amount of their respective share or shares of stock in such banking institution, for all its debts and liabilities, upon note, bill, or otherwise, and upon the further condition, that no director or other officer of said corporation, shall borrow any money from said corporation, and if any director or other officer shall be convicted upon indictment, of directly or indirectly, violating this section, he shall be punished, by fine or imprisonment, at the discretion of the court. The books, papers, and accounts of all banks shall be open to inspection, under such regulations as may be prescribed by law. *Md.*, 264.

—The Legislature shall provide by law for the registry of all bills or notes issued or put in circulation as money, and shall require security to the full amount of notes and bills so registered in State or United States stocks, bearing interest, which shall be deposited with the State Treasurer, for the redemption of such bills or notes in specie. *Min.*, 328; *Mich.*, 312.

—And in case of a depreciation of said stocks, or any part thereof, to the amount of ten per cent. or more on the dollar, the bank or banks owning said stock shall be required to make up said deficiency by additional stocks. *Min.*, 328.

—The Legislature shall pass no law authorizing or sanctioning the suspension of specie payments by any person, association or corporation. *Mich.*, 312.

—The Legislature may, by a vote of two-thirds of the members elected to each House create a single bank with branches. *Mich.*, 312.

—The Legislature shall have no power to pass any law sanctioning in any manner, directly or indirectly, the suspension of specie payments by any person,

1   § 7. The Stockholders in every corporation and joint stock association for

2 banking purposes, issuing bank notes or any kind of paper credits to circulate

3 as money, after the first day of January, one thousand eight hundred and

4 fifty, shall be individually responsible to the amount of their respective share

5 or shares of stock in any such corporation or association, for all its debts and

6 liabilities of every kind, contracted after the said first day of January, one

7 thousand eight hundred and fifty.

1   § 8. In case of the insolvency of any bank or banking association, the bill-

2 holders thereof shall be entitled to preference in payment over all other creditors

3 of such bank or association.

---

association, or corporation issuing bank notes of any description. *Min.*, 327.

—Any general banking law which may be passed in accordance with this article, shall provide for recording the names of all stockholders in such corporations, the amount of stock held by each, the time of transfer, and to whom transferred. *Min.*, 328.

—The Legislature may, by a two-thirds vote, pass a general banking law, with the following restrictions and requirements. *Min.*, 327.

—No corporate body shall hereafter be created, renewed, or extended, with the privilege of making, issuing, or putting in circulation any notes, bills, or other paper, or the paper of any other bank, to circulate as money; and the General Assembly shall prohibit, by law, individuals and corporations from issuing bills, checks, tickets, promissory notes, or other paper to circulate as money. *Mo.*, 360.

—The General Assembly shall, at its first session after this Constitution goes into effect, enact laws enabling any of the existing banks of issue to reorganize as national banks under the act of Congress; and shall also provide for the sale of the stock owned by this State in the Bank of the State of Missouri, upon such terms and conditions as shall be by law established. *Mo.*, 360.

—No bank notes or paper of any kind shall ever be permitted to circulate as money in this State, except the federal currency and the notes of banks authorized under the laws of Congress. *Nev.* 389.

—The assent of three-fifths of the members elected to each House, shall be requisite to the passage of every law for granting, continuing, altering, amending, or renewing charters for banks or money corporations; and all such charters shall be limited to a term not exceeding twenty years. *N. J.*, 415.

—The Legislative Assembly shall not have the power to establish or incorporate any bank, or banking company, or monied institution whatever; nor shall any bank, company, or institution exist in the State, with the privilege of making, issuing, or putting in circulation any bill, check, certificate, promissory note, or other paper, or the paper of any bank, company, or person, to circulate as money. *Or.*, 457.

—No corporate body shall be hereafter created, renewed or extended with banking or discounting privileges, without six months' previous public notice of the intended application for the same in such manner as shall be prescribed by law. Nor shall any charter for the purposes aforesaid, be granted for a longer period than twenty years, and every such charter shall contain a clause reserving to the Legislature the power to alter, revoke or annul the same, whenever in their opinion it may be injurious to the citizens of the Commonwealth; in such manner, however, that no injustice shall be done to the corpora-

44

tors. No law hereafter enacted, shall create, renew or extend the charter, of more than one corporation. *Pa.*, 463.

—No corporate body shall hereafter be created, renewed, or extended with banking or discounting privileges. *Tex.*, 516.

—The Legislature shall prohibit by law, individuals from issuing bills, checks, promissory notes, or other paper to circulate as money. *Tex.*, 517.

—No act to incorporate any bank of circulation or internal improvement company, or to confer additional privileges on the same, shall be passed, unless public notice of the intended application for such act be given under such regulations as shall be prescribed by law. *W. Va.*, 558.

—The Legislature may submit to the voters at any general election, the question of "bank or no bank," and if at any such election a number of votes equal to a majority of all the votes cast at such election on that subject shall be in favor of banks, then the Legislature shall have power to grant bank charters, or to pass a general banking law, with such restrictions and under such regulations as they may deem expedient and proper, for the security of the billholders; *Provided*, That no such grant or law shall have any force or effect until the same shall have been submitted to a vote of the electors of the State at some general election, and been approved by a majority of the votes cast on that subject at such election. *Wis.*, 570.

—The Legislature shall not have power to create, authorize or incorporate, by any general or special law, any bank or banking power or privilege, or any institution or corporation having any banking power, or privilege whatever, except as provided in this article. *Wis.*, 570.

LIABILITY OF STOCKHOLDERS AND OF CORPORATIONS.

—The stockholders shall be respectively liable for the debts of the bank, in proportion to the amount of their stock. *Ala.*, 77.

—Dues from corporations shall be secured by such individual liability of the corporators, and other means, as may be prescribed by law. *Cal.*, 99.

—Each stockholder of a corporation, or joint-stock association, shall be individually and personally liable for his proportion of all its debts and liabilities. *Cal.*, 99.

—Dues from corporations, not possessing banking powers and privileges, shall be secured by such individual liabilities of the corporators, or other means, as may be prescribed by law. *Ill.*, 164.

—The stockholders in every corporation, or joint-stock association for banking purposes, issuing bank

174

notes, or any kind of paper credits to circulate as money, shall be individually responsible, to the amount of their respective share or shares of stock in any such corporation or association, for all debts and liabilities of every kind. *Ill.*, 164.

—The stockholders in every bank or banking company shall be individually responsible to an amount over and above their stock, equal to their respective shares of stock, for all debts or liabilities of said bank or banking company. *Ind.*, 179.

—Dues from corporations, other than banking, shall be secured by such individual liability of the corporators, or other means, as may be prescribed by law. *Ind.*, 179.

—Every stockholder in a banking corporation or institution shall be individually responsible and liable to its creditors, over and above the amount of stock by him or her held, to an amount equal to his or her respective shares so held, for all its liabilities, accruing while he or she remains such stockholders. *Iowa*, 191.

—Dues from corporations shall be secured by individual liability of the stockholders to an additional amount equal to the stock owned by each stockholder, and such other means as shall be provided by law; but such individual liabilities shall not apply to railroad corporations, nor corporations for religious or charitable purposes. *Kan.*, 215.

—The stockholders of all corporations and joint stock associations shall be individually liable for all labor performed for such corporation or association. *Mich.*, 312.

—Each stockholder in any corporation shall be liable to the amount of the stock held or owned by him. *Min.*, 328.

—Dues from private corporations shall be secured by such means as may be prescribed by law; but in all cases each stockholder shall be individually liable, over and above the stock by him or her owned, and any amount unpaid thereon, in a further sum, at least equal in amount to such stock. *Mo.*, 260.

—Dues from corporations shall be secured by such means as may be prescribed by law; *Provided*, That corporators in corporations formed under the laws of this State, shall not be individually liable for the debts or liabilities of such corporation. *Nev.*, 388.

—Dues from corporations shall be secured, by such individual liability of the stockholders, and other means, as may be prescribed by law; but, in all cases, each stockholder shall be liable, over and above the stock by him or her owned, and any amount unpaid thereon, to a further sum, at least equal in amount to such stock. *Ohio*, 443.

—The stockholders of all corporations and joint-stock companies shall be liable for the indebtedness of said corporation to the amount of their stock subscribed and unpaid, and no more. *Or.*, 457.

—Corporations may sue and be sued in all courts in like manner as individuals. *Nev.*, 389.

—The stockholders in any corporation and joint association for banking purposes, issuing bank notes, shall be individually liable in an amount equal to double the amount of stock owned by them for all the debts of such corporation or association; and such individual liability shall continue for one year after any transfer or sale of stock by any stockholder or stockholders. *Min.*, 329.

—The officers and stockholders of every corporation or association for banking purposes issuing bank notes or paper credits to circulate as money, shall be individually liable for all debts contracted during the time of their being officers or stockholders of such corporation or association. *Mich.*, 312.

STATE INSTITUTIONS.

—It shall be the duty of the General Assembly to provide by law for the support of institutions for the education of the deaf and dumb, and of the blind, and also for the treatment of the insane. *Ind.*, 178.

—The General Assembly shall provide houses of refuge for the correction and reformation of juvenile offenders. *Ind.*, 178.

—Institutions for the benefit of the insane, blind and deaf and dumb, and such other benevolent institutions as the public good may require, shall be fostered and supported by the State, subject to such regulations as may be prescribed by law. Trustees of such benevolent institutions as may be hereafter created shall be appointed by the Governor, by and with the advice and consent of the Senate; and upon all nominations made by the Governor, the question shall be taken by yeas and nays, and entered upon the journal. *Kan.*, 203.

—A penitentiary shall be established, the directors of which shall be appointed or elected, as prescribed by law. *Kan.*, 203.

—The Governor shall fill any vacancy that may occur in the offices aforesaid, until the next session of the Legislature, and until a successor to his appointee shall be confirmed and qualified. *Kan.*, 203.

—Institutions for the benefit of those inhabitants who are deaf, dumb, blind or insane, shall always be fostered and supported. *Mich.*, 311.

—Institutions for the benefit of the insane, blind, and deaf and dumb, and such other benevolent institutions as the public good may require, shall be fostered and supported by the State, subject to such regulations as may be prescribed by law. *Nev.*, 391.

—A State Prison shall be established and maintained in such a manner as may be prescribed by law, and provision may be made by law for the establishment and maintenance of a House of Refuge for juvenile offenders. *Nev.*, 391.

—The respective counties of the State shall provide, as may be prescribed by law, for those inhabitants who, by reason of age and infirmities, or misfortunes, may have claim upon the sympathy and aid of society. *Kan.*, 203; *Nev.*, 391.

—Institutions for the benefit of the insane, blind, and deaf and dumb, shall always be fostered and supported by the State, and be subject to such regulations as may be prescribed by the General Assembly. *Ohio*, 439.

—The Directors of the Penitentiary shall be appointed or elected in such manner as the General Assembly may direct; and the trustees of the benevolent and other State institutions, now elected by the General Assembly, and of such other State institutions as may be hereafter created, shall be appointed by the Governor, by and with the advice and consent of the Senate; and upon all nominations made by the Governor the question shall be taken by yeas and nays and entered upon the journals of the Senate. *Ohio*, 439.

—The Governor, Secretary of State, and Attorney-General shall constitute a Board of State Prison Commissioners, which Board shall have such supervision of all matters connected with the State prison as may be provided by law. They shall also constitute a Board of Examiners, with power to examine all claims against the State, except salaries or compensation of officers fixed by law, and perform such other duties as may be prescribed by law. And no claim against the State except salaries or compensation of officers fixed by law, shall be passed upon by the Legislature without having been considered and acted upon by said Board of Examiners. *Nev.*, 385.

—The four hundred thousand acres of land that have been surveyed and set apart under the provisions of a law approved 30th August, A. D. 1856, for the benefit of a lunatic asylum, a deaf and dumb asylum, a blind asylum, and an orphan asylum, shall constitute a fund for the support of such institutions, one-fourth part for each; and the said fund shall never be diverted to any other purpose. The said lands may be sold, and the funds invested under the same rules and regulations as provided for the lands belonging to the school fund. The income of said fund only shall be applied to the support of such institutions; and until so applied shall be invested in the same manner as the principal. *Tex.*, 520.

1 § 9. It shall be the duty of the Legislature to provide for the organization

2 of cities and incorporated villages, and to restrict their power of taxation,

3 assessment, borrowing money, contracting debts and loaning their credit, so

4 as to prevent abuses in assessments, and in contracting debt by such municipal

5 corporations.

COUNTIES—COUNTY SEATS.

—The General Assembly may, by a vote of two-thirds of both branches thereof, arrange and designate boundaries for the several counties of this State, which boundaries shall not be altered except by a like vote; but no new county shall be hereafter formed of less extent than six hundred square miles, nor shall any existing county be reduced to a less extent than six hundred square miles; and no new county shall be formed not containing a sufficient number of inhabitants to entitle it to one representative under the existing ratio of representation, nor unless the counties from which it is taken shall be left with the required number entitling them to separate representation. *Ala.*, 74.

—No county now established by law shall ever be reduced by the establishment of any new county or counties, to less than six hundred square miles, nor to a less population than its ratio of representation in the House of Representatives; nor shall any county be hereafter established which shall contain less than six hundred square miles, or a less population than would entitle each county to a member in the House of Representatives. *Ark.*, 87.

—The Legislature shall establish a system of county and town governments, which shall be as nearly uniform as practicable throughout the State. *Cal.*, 104; *Wis.*, 563.

—If a new county be established, it shall be added to a district which it adjoins. The Senatorial districts may be changed by the General Assembly, but only at the first session after the taking of each census by the United States Government, and their number shall never be increased. *Ga.*, 144.

—They may alter the boundaries of counties, and establish new counties; but every bill to establish a new county shall be passed by at least two-thirds of the members present in each branch of the General Assembly. *Ga.*, 146.

—No county shall be divided, or have any part stricken therefrom, without submitting the question to a vote of the people of the county, nor unless a majority of all the legal voters of the county, voting on the question, shall vote on the same. *Ill.*, 162.

—There shall be no territory stricken from any county unless a majority of the voters living in such territory shall petition for such division; and no territory shall be added to any county without the consent of the majority of the voters of the county to which it is proposed to be added. *Ill.*, 163.

—All territory which has been or may be stricken off, by Legislative enactment, from any organized county or counties, for the purpose of forming a new county, and which shall remain unorganized after the period provided for such organization, shall be and remain a part of the county or counties from which it was originally taken, for all purposes of county and State government, until otherwise provided by law. *Ill.*, 163.

—No county seat shall be removed until the point to which it is proposed to be removed shall be fixed by law, and a majority of the voters of the county shall have voted in favor of its removal to such point. *Ill.*, 163.

—The General Assembly shall provide, by a general law, for a township organization, under which any county may organize whenever a majority of the voters of such county, at any general election, shall

so determine; and whenever any county shall adopt a township organization, so much of this Constitution as provides for the management of the fiscal concerns of the said county by the County Court may be dispensed with, and the affairs of said county may be transacted in such manner as the General Assembly may provide. *Ill.*, 163.

—No new county shall be formed or established by the General Assembly, which will reduce the county or counties, or either of them, from which it shall be taken, to less contents than four hundred square miles; nor shall any county be formed of less contents; nor shall any line thereof pass within less than ten miles of any county seat of the county or counties proposed to be divided. *Ill.*, 162.

—All lands which have been granted, as a "common," to the inhabitants of any town, hamlet, village, or corporation, by any person, body politic, or corporate, or by any government having power to make such grant, shall forever remain common to the inhabitants of such town, hamlet, village, or corporation; but the said commons, or any of them, or any part thereof, may be divided, leased, or granted in such manner as may hereafter be provided by law, on petition of a majority of the qualified voters interested in such commons or any of them. *Ill.*, 165.

—No county shall be reduced to an area less than four hundred square miles; nor shall any county under that area be further reduced. *Ind.*, 181.

—No new county shall be hereafter created containing less than four hundred and thirty-two square miles; nor shall the territory of any organized county be reduced below that area, except the county of Worth, and the counties west of it, on the Minnesota line, may be organized without additional territory. *Iowa*, 194.

—The Legislature shall provide for organizing new counties, locating county seats, and changing county lines; but no county seat shall be changed without the consent of a majority of the electors of the county, nor any county organized, nor the lines of any county changed, so as to include an area of less than four hundred and thirty-two square miles. *Kan.*, 203.

—When a new county shall be erected, officers for the same, to serve until the next stated election, shall be elected, or appointed in such a way and at such times as the General Assembly may prescribe. *Ky.*, 219.

—The General Assembly may provide for organizing new counties, locating and removing county seats and changing county lines, but no new county shall be organized without the consent of a majority of the legal voters residing within the limits about to form said county, nor shall the lines of any county be changed without the consent of a majority of the legal voters residing within the limits of the lines proposed to be changed, nor shall any new county contain less than four hundred square miles nor less than ten thousand white inhabitants, nor shall any county be reduced below that amount of square miles, nor below that number of white inhabitants. *Md.*, 235.

—The General Assembly shall provide by general law for dividing the counties into townships or permanent municipal corporations, in place of the existing election districts, prescribing their limits and confiding to them all powers necessary for the management of their public local concerns; and whenever

176

the organization of these township corporations shall
be perfected, all officers provided for in this Constitution, but whose official functions shall have been
superseded by such organization shall be dispensed
with, and the affairs of such townships and of the
counties as affected by the action of such townships
shall be transacted in such manner as the General
Assembly may direct. *Md.*, 276.

—The General Court shall have full power and
authority to erect and constitute municipal or city
governments, in any corporate town or towns in this
Commonwealth, and to grant to the inhabitants
thereof such powers, privileges and immunities not
repugnant to the Constitution, as the General Court
shall deem necessary or expedient for the regulation
and government thereof, and to prescribe the manner
of calling and holding public meetings of the inhabitants in wards or otherwise, for the election of
officers under the Constitution, and the manner
of returning the votes given at such meetings; *Provided,* That no such government shall be erected or
constituted in any town not containing twelve thousand inhabitants; nor unless it be with the consent,
and on the application of a majority of the inhabitants of such town present and voting thereon, pursuant to a vote at a meeting duly warned and holden
for that purpose; *And provided, also,* That all by-laws
made by such municipal or city government shall be
subject, at all times, to be annulled by the General
Court. *Mass.*, 294.

—No county seat once established shall be removed
until the place to which it is proposed to be removed
shall be designated by two-thirds of the Board of
Supervisors of the county, and a majority of the
electors voting thereon shall have voted in favor of
the proposed location, in such manner as shall be
prescribed by law. *Mich.*, 309.

—Each organized township shall be a body corporate,
with such powers and immunities as shall be prescribed by law. All suits and proceedings by or
against a township, shall be in the name thereof.
Mich., 309.

—Nor organized county shall ever be reduced by the
organization of new counties to less than sixteen
townships, as surveyed by the United States, unless
in pursuance of law, a majority of electors residing
in each county to be affected thereby shall so decide.
The Legislature may organize any city into a separate county, when it has attained a population of
twenty thousand inhabitants, without reference to
geographical extent, when a majority of the electors
of a county in which such city may be situated,
voting thereon, shall be in favor of a separate organization. *Mich.*, 309.

—Each organized county shall be a body corporate,
with such powers and immunities as shall be established by law. All suits and proceedings by or against
a county shall be in the name thereof. *Mich.*, 309.

—Any territory attached to any county for judicial
purposes, if not otherwise represented, shall be considered as forming a part of such county, so far as
regards elections for the purpose of representation.
Mich., 317.

—The Legislature may organize any city into a
separate county, when it has attained a population of
twenty thousand inhabitants, without reference to
geographical extent, when a majority of the electors
of the county in which such city may be situated,
voting thereon, shall be in favor of a separate organization. *Min.*, 328.

—The Legislature may, from time to time, establish
and organize new counties; but no new county shall
contain less than four hundred square miles; nor shall
any county be reduced below that amount; and all
laws changing county lines in counties already organized, or for removing county seats, shall, before taking
effect, be submitted to the electors of the county or
counties to be affected thereby, at the next general
election after the passage thereof, and be adopted by
a majority of such electors. Counties now established may be enlarged, but not reduced below four
hundred square miles. *Min.*, 328.

—Laws may be passed providing for the organization,
for municipal and other town purposes, of any congressional or fractional townships in the several
counties in the State, provided that when a township is divided by county lines, or does not contain
one hundred inhabitants, it may be attached to one
or more adjacent townships, or parts of townships,
for the purposes aforesaid. *Min.*, 328.

—No new county shall be established by the Legislature, which shall reduce the county or counties, or
either of them, from which it may be taken, to less
contents than five hundred and seventy-six square
miles; nor shall any new county be laid off of less
contents. *Miss.*, 343.

—The General Assembly shall have no power to
establish any new county with a territory of less
than five hundred square miles, or with a population
less than the ratio of representation existing at the
time; nor to reduce any county now established to
less than that area, or to less population than such
ratio. *Mo.*, 354.

—The General Assembly shall have no power to
remove the county seat of any county unless two-
thirds of the qualified voters of the county, at a general election, shall vote in favor of such removal.
No compensation or indemnity for real estate, or for
improvements thereon, affected by such removal,
shall be allowed. *Mo.*, 354.

—And the Legislature, on the application of the
major part of the inhabitants of any county, shall
have authority to divide the same into two districts
for registering deeds, if to them it shall appear necessary; each district to elect a Register of Deeds; and
before they enter upon the business of their offices,
shall be respectively sworn faithfully to discharge the
duties thereof, and shall severally give bond, with
sufficient sureties, in a reasonable sum, for the use of
the county, for the punctual performance of their
respective trusts. *N. H.*, 408.

—The General Assembly shall attach any new counties, that may hereafter be erected, to such districts,
or subdivisions thereof, as shall be most convenient.
Ohio, 442.

—No new county shall contain less than four hundred square miles of territory, nor shall any county
be reduced below that amount; and all laws creating
new counties, changing county lines, or removing
county seats, shall, before taking effect, be submitted
to the electors of the several counties to be affected
thereby, at the next general election after the passage
thereof, and be adopted by a majority of all the
electors voting at such election, in each of said counties; but any county now or hereafter containing
one hundred thousand inhabitants, may be divided,
whenever a majority of the voters, residing in each
of the proposed divisions, shall approve of the law
passed for that purpose; but no town or city within
the same, shall be divided, nor shall either of the
divisions contain less than twenty thousand inhabitants. *Ohio*, 435.

—No county shall be reduced to an area less than
four hundred square miles; nor shall any new county
be established in this State containing a less area, nor
unless such new county shall contain a population of
at least twelve hundred inhabitants. *Or.*, 458.

—The citizens who may be included in any new
county, shall vote with the county or counties from
which they may have been stricken off for members
of Congress, for Governor, and for members of the
General Assembly, until the next apportionment of
members to the General Assembly after the establishment of such new county. *Tenn.*, 498.

—New counties may be established by the Legislature, to consist of not less than three hundred and
fifty square miles, and which shall contain a population of four hundred and fifty qualified voters. No
line of such county shall approach the court-house of
any old county from which it may be taken, nearer
than twelve miles. No part of a county shall be
taken to form a new county or a part thereof, without the consent of a majority of the qualified voters
in such part taken off. And in all cases where an

old county may be reduced for the purpose of forming a new one, the seat of justice in said old county shall not be removed without the concurrence of two-thirds of both branches of the Legislature, nor shall said old county be reduced to less than six hundred and twenty-five square miles.

[Special clauses are inserted in Constitution relative to counties named.] *Tenn.*, 498.

—No county shall be divided by a line cutting off over one tenth of its population (either to form a new county, or otherwise), without the express assent of such county, by a vote of the electors thereof; nor shall any new county be established, containing less than four hundred square miles. *Pa.*, 471.

—The Legislature may, from time to time, abolish new counties for the convenience of the inhabitants of such new county or counties; *Provided*, That no new county shall be established which shall reduce the county or counties, or either of them, from which it shall be taken, to a less area than nine hundred square miles, unless by consent of two-thirds of the Legislature, nor shall any county bo organized of less contents; *Provided further*, That all counties heretofore created are hereby declared to be legally constituted counties. Every new county has the right of suffrage and representation, shall be considered as part of the county or counties from which it was taken until the next apportionment of representation thereafter; *Provided also*, That no new county shall be laid off, when less than one hundred and twenty qualified jurors are at the time resident therein. *Tex.*, 517.

—No new county shall be formed with an area of less than six hundred square miles; nor shall the county or counties from which it is formed be reduced below that area, nor shall any county, having a white population less than five thousand, be deprived of more than one-fifth of such population, nor shall a county having a larger white population be reduced below four thousand. But any county, the length of which is three times its mean breadth, or which exceeds fifty miles in length, may be divided at the discretion of the General Assembly. In all general elections the voters in any county not entitled to separate representation shall vote in the same election district. *Va.*, 539.

—No new county shall be formed having an area of less than four hundred square miles; or if another county be thereby reduced below that area, or if any territory be thereby taken from a county containing less than four hundred square miles. And no new county shall be formed containing a white population of less than four thousand; or if the white population of another county be thereby reduced below that number; or if any county containing less than four thousand white inhabitants be thereby reduced in area. But the Legislature may, at any time, annex any county containing less than four thousand white inhabitants to an adjoining county or counties as a part thereof. *W. Va.*, 555.

—No county with an area of nine hundred square miles or less shall be divided, or have any part stricken therefrom, without submitting the question to a vote of the people of the county, nor unless a majority of all the legal voters of the county, voting on the question, shall vote for the same. *Wis.*, 571.

—No county seat shall be removed until the point to which it is proposed to be removed shall be fixed by law, and a majority of the voters of the county, voting on the question, shall have voted in favor of its removal to such point. *Wis.*, 571.

—The different counties in this State shall be laid off as the General Assembly may direct, into districts of convenient size, so that the whole number in each county shall not be more than twenty-five, or four for every one hundred square miles. There shall be two Justices of the Peace and one Constable elected in each district, by the qualified voters therein, except districts including county towns, which shall elect three Justices and two Constables. The jurisdiction of said officers shall be co-extensive with the county. Justices of the Peace shall be elected for the term of six, and Constables for the term of two years. Upon the removal of either of said officers from the district in which he was elected, his office shall become vacant from the time of such removal. Justices of the Peace shall be commissioned by the Governor. The Legislature shall have power to provide for the appointment of an additional number of Justices of the Peace in incorporated towns. *Tenn.*, 497.

—Each county, town, city, and incorporated village, shall make provision for the support of its own officers, subject to such restrictions and regulations as the Legislature may prescribe. *Cal.*, 104.

—Every county shall be divided into not less than three, nor more than ten townships, laid off as compactly as practicable, with reference to natural boundaries, and containing as nearly as practicable, an equal number of white population, but not less than four hundred. Each township shall be designated, "The Township of —— in the county of ——," by which name it may sue and be sued. *W. Va.*, 557.

—The Board of Supervisors may alter the bounds of a township of their county, or erect new townships therein, with the consent of a majority of the voters of each township interested, assembled in stated township meeting, or in a meeting duly called for the purpose, subject to the provisions of the first section of this article. *W. Va.*, 555.

—Nothing contained in this article shall impair or affect the charter of any municipal corporation, or restrict the power of the Legislature to create or regulate such corporations. *W. Va.*, 555.

ARTICLE IX.

1   SECTION 1. The capital of the Common School Fund, the capital of the

2   Literature Fund, and the capital of the United States Deposit Fund, shall be

3   respectively preserved inviolate. The revenues of the said Common School

4   Fund shall be applied to the support of common schools ; the revenues of the

5   said Literature Fund shall be applied to the support of academies, and the

6   sum of twenty-five thousand dollars of the revenues of the United States

7   Deposit Fund shall each year be appropriated to and made a part of the capital

8   of the said Common School Fund.

SCHOOLS—SCHOOL FUNDS.

—The General Assembly shall from time to time enact necessary and proper laws for the encouragement of schools and the means of education ; shall take proper measures to preserve from waste or damage such lands as have been or may be granted by the United States for the use of schools in each township in this State, and apply the funds which may be raised from such lands in strict conformity with the object of such grant; shall take like measures for the improvement of such lands as have been or may hereafter be granted by the United States to this State for the support of a seminary of learning; and the money which may be raised from such lands by rent, lease or sale, or from any other quarter, for the purpose aforesaid, shall be and forever remain a fund for the exclusive support of a State university for the promotion of the arts, literature, and the sciences; and it shall be the duty of the General Assembly to provide by law effectual means for the improvement and permanent security of the funds of such institution. *Ala.*, 77.

--*Be it ordained*, That no act of the Legislature of this State prohibiting the education of any class of the inhabitants thereof, shall have the force of law. *Ark.*, 95.

—The proceeds of all lands belonging to this State, except such parts thereof as may be reserved or appropriated to public use, or ceded to the United States, which shall hereafter be sold or disposed of, together with the fund denominated the common school fund, shall be and remain a perpetual fund; the interest of which shall be inviolably appropriated and applied to the support of common schools throughout this State. *N. Y.* (1821), 42.

—Knowledge and learning generally diffused throughout a community, being essential to the preservation of a free government, and diffusing the opportunities and advantages of education through the various parts of the State, being highly conducive to this end, it shall be the duty of the General Assembly to provide by law for the improvement of such lands as are or hereafter may be granted by the United States to this State for the use of schools, and to apply any funds which may be raised from such lands, or from any other source, to the accomplishment of the object for which they are or may be intended. The General Assembly shall, from time to time, pass such laws as shall be calculated to encourage intellectual, scientific and agricultural improvement, by allowing rewards and immunities for the promotion and improvement of arts, science, commerce, manufactures, and natural history, and countenance and encourage the principles of humanity, industry and morality. *Ark.*, 92.

—The legislature shall provide for the election by the people of a Superintendent of Public Instruction, who shall hold his office for three years, and whose duties shall be prescribed by law, and who shall receive such compensation as the Legislature may direct. *Cal.*, 103; (nearly similar), *Mich.*, 308; *Nev.*, 389; (nearly similar, but term two years), *Ind.*, 178; nearly similar, but term four years), *Ky.*, 222; *Mo.*, 360.

—The Legislature shall encourage by all suitable means the promotion of intellectual, scientific, moral and agricultural improvement. The proceeds of all land that may be granted by the United States to this State for the support of schools, which may be sold or disposed of, and the five hundred thousand acres of land granted to the new states under an act of Congress, distributing the proceeds of the public lands among the several states of the Union, approved A. D., 1841 ; and all estate of deceased persons who may have died without leaving a will, or heir, and also such per cent as may be granted by Congress on the sale of lands in this State, shall be and remain a perpetual fund, the interest of which, together with all the rents of the unsold lands, and such other means as the Legislature may provide, shall be inviolably appropriated to the support of common schools throughout the State. *Cal.*, 103.

·· The Legislature shall provide for a system of common schools, by which a school shall be kept up and supported in each district at least three months in every year, any district neglecting to keep and support such a school, may be deprived of its proportion of the interest of the public fund during such neglect. *Cal.*, 103.

—The fund called the School Fund shall remain a perpetual fund, the interest of which shall be inviolably appropriated to the support and encouragement of the public or common schools throughout the State, and for the equal benefit of all the people thereof. The value and amount of said fund shall, as soon as practicable, be ascertained in such manner as the General Assembly may prescribe, published and recorded in the Comptroller's office ; and no law shall ever be made authorizing said fund to be diverted to any other use that the encouragement and support of public or common schools, among the several school societies, as justice and equity shall require. *Ct.*, 112.

—The proceeds of all lands for the use of schools and a seminary or seminaries of learning shall be and remain a perpetual fund, the interest of which, together with all moneys accrued from any other source, applicable to the same object, shall be inviolably appropriated to the use of schools and seminaries of learning, respectively, and to no other purpose. *Fl.*, 138.

—The General Assembly shall take such measures as may be necessary to preserve, from waste or damage, all lands so granted and appropriated for the purpose of education. *Fl.*, 138.

—Knowledge and learning, generally diffused throughout a community, being essential to the preservation of a free government, it shall be the duty of the General Assembly to encourage, by all suitable means, moral, intellectual, scientific and agricultural improvement, and to provide by law for a general and uniform system of common schools, wherein tuition shall be without charge, and equally open to all *Ind.*, 177.

—The common school fund shall consist of the congressional township fund, and the lands belonging thereto;

The surplus revenue fund;

The saline fund, and the lands belonging thereto;

The bank tax fund, and the fund arising from the one hundred and fourteenth section of the charter of the State Bank of Indiana;

The fund to be derived from the sale of county seminaries, and the moneys and property heretofore held for such seminaries; from the fines assessed for breaches of the penal laws of the State; and from all forfeitures which may accrue;

All lands and other estate which shall escheat to the State for want of heirs or kindred entitled to the inheritance. *Ind.*, 178.

—All lands that have been, or may hereafter be, granted to the State, where no special purpose is expressed in the grant, and the proceeds of the sales thereof, including the proceeds of the sales of the swamp lands granted to the State of Indiana by the act of Congress of 28th September, 1850, after deducting the expense of selecting and draining the same. *Ind.*, 178.

—Taxes on the property of corporations that may be assessed for common school purposes. *Ind.*, 178.

—The principal of the common school fund shall remain a perpetual fund, which may be increased, but shall never be diminished; and the income thereof shall be inviolably appropriated to the support of common schools, and to no other purpose whatever. *Ind.*, 178.

—The General Assembly shall invest, in some safe and profitable manner, all such portions of the common school fund as have not heretofore been intrusted to the several counties; and shall make provision by law for the distribution among the several counties of the interest thereof. *Ind.*, 178.

—If any county shall fail to demand its proportion of such interest for common school purposes, the same shall be reinvested for the benefit of such county. *Ind.*, 178.

—The several counties shall be held liable for the preservation of so much of the said fund as may be intrusted to them, and for the payment of the annual interest thereon. *Ind.*, 178.

—All trust funds held by the State shall remain inviolate, and be faithfully and exclusively applied to the purposes for which the trust was created. *Ind.*, 178.

—The educational interest of the State, to include common schools and other educational institutions, shall be under the management of a Board of Education, which shall consist of the Lieutenant-Governor, who shall be the presiding officer of the board, and have the casting vote in case of a tie, and one member to be elected from each judicial district in the State. *Iowa*, 191.

—No person shall be eligible as a member of said Board who shall not have attained the age of twenty-five years, and been one year a citizen of the State. *Iowa*, 192.

—One member of said board shall be chosen by the qualified electors of each district, and shall hold the office for the term of four years, and until his successor is elected and qualified. After the first election under this Constitution, the board shall be divided, as nearly as practicable, into two equal classes, and the seats of the first class shall be vacated after the expiration of two years; and one-half of the board shall be chosen every two years thereafter. *Iowa*, 192.

—The first session of the Board of Education shall be held at the seat of government, on the first Monday of December, after their election; after which the General Assembly may fix the time and place of meeting. *Iowa*, 192.

—The session of the board shall be limited to twenty days, and but one session shall be held in any one year, except on extraordinary occasions, when, upon the recommendation of two thirds of the board, the Governor may order a special session. *Iowa*, 192.

—The Board of Education shall appoint a Secretary, who shall be the executive officer of the Board, and perform such duties as may be imposed upon him by the Board and the laws of the State. They shall keep a journal of their proceedings, which shall be published and distributed in the same manner as the journals of the General Assembly. *Iowa*, 192.

—All rules and regulations made by the Board shall be published and distributed to the several counties, townships, and school districts, as may be provided for by the Board, and when so passed, published and distributed, they shall have the force and effect of law. *Iowa*, 192.

—The Board of Education shall have full power and authority to legislate and make all needful rules and regulations in relation to common schools and other educational institutions that are instituted, to receive aid from the school or university fund of this State; but all acts, rules and regulations of said Board may be altered, amended, or repealed by the General Assembly; and when so altered, amended or repealed they shall not be re-enacted by the Board of Education. *Iowa*, 192.

—The Governor of the State shall be *ex officio*, a member of said Board. *Iowa*, 192.

—The Board shall have power to levy taxes, or make appropriations of money. The contingent expenses shall be provided for by the General Assembly. *Iowa*, 192.

—The members of the Board of Education shall provide for the education of all the youths of the State, through a system of common schools. And such schools shall be organized and kept in each school-district at least three months in each year. Any district failing, for two consecutive years, to organize and keep up a school, may be deprived of their portion of the school fund. *Iowa*, 192.

—The members of the Board of Education shall each receive the same per diem during the time of their session, and mileage going to and returning therefrom, as members of the General Assembly. *Iowa*, 192.

—The majority of the Board shall constitute a quorum for the transaction of business; but no rule, regulation or law for the regulation and government of common schools or other educational institutions shall pass without the concurrence of a majority of all the members of the Board, which shall be expressed by the yeas and nays on the final passage. The style of all the acts of the Board shall be, "Be it enacted by the Board of Education of the State of Iowa." *Iowa*, 192.

—At any time after the year of 1863, the General Assembly shall have power to abolish or re-organize said Board of Education, and provide for the educational interest of the State in any other manner that to them shall seem best and proper. *Iowa*, 192.

—The educational and school funds and lands shall be under the control and management of the General Assembly of this State. *Iowa*, 192.

—The General Assembly shall encourage, by all suitable means, the promotion of intellectual, scientific, moral, and agricultural improvement. The proceeds of all lands that have been, or hereafter may be, granted by the United States to this State for the support of schools, which shall hereafter be sold or disposed of, and the five hundred thousand acres of land granted to the new States, under an act of Congress, distributing the proceeds of the public lands among the several States of the Union, approved in the year of our Lord one thousand eight hundred and forty-one, and all estates of deceased persons who may have died without leaving a will or heir, and also such per cent. as may have been granted by Congress, on the sale of lands in this State, shall be, and remain a perpetual fund, the interest of which, together with all the rents of the unsold lands, and such other means as the General Assembly may provide, shall be inviolably appropriated to the support of common schools throughout the State. *Iowa*, 192.

—The money which may have been, or shall be paid by persons as an equivalent for exemption from military duty, and the clear proceeds of all fines collected in the several counties for any breach of the penal laws, shall be exclusively applied, in the several counties in which such money is paid, or fine collected, among the several school-districts of said counties, in proportion to the number of youths subject to enumeration in such districts, to the support of common schools, or the establishment of libraries, as the Board of Education shall from time to time provide. *Iowa*, 193.

—The financial agents of school funds shall be the same that, by law, receive and control the State and county revenue, for other civil purposes, under such regulations as may be provided by law. *Iowa*, 193.

—The money subject to the support and maintenance of common schools shall be distributed to the districts in proportion to the number of youths between the age of five and twenty-one years, in such manner as may be provided by the General Assembly. *Iowa*, 193.

—All losses to the permanent, school or university fund of this State, which shall have been occasioned by the defalcation, mismanagement or fraud of the agents or officers controlling and managing the same, shall be audited by the proper authorities of the State. The amount so audited shall be a permanent funded debt against the State, in favor of the respective fund sustaining the loss, upon which not less than six per cent annual interest shall be paid. The amount of liability so created shall not be counted as a part of the indebtedness authorized by the second section of this article. *Iowa*, 190.

—The State Superintendent of Public Instruction shall have the general supervision of the common school funds and educational interest of the State, and perform such other duties as may be prescribed by law. A Superintendent of Public Instruction shall be elected in each county, whose term of office shall be two years, and whose duties and compensation shall be prescribed by law. *Kan.*, 202.

—The proceeds of all lands that have been or may be granted by the United States to the State for the support of schools, and the five hundred thousand acres of land granted to the new States, under an act of Congress distributing the proceeds of public lands among the several States of the Union, approved September 4, A. D., 1841, and all estates of persons dying without heir or will, and such per cent as may be granted by Congress on the sale of lands in this State, shall be the common property of the State, and shall be a perpetual school fund, which shall not be diminished, but the interest of which, together with all the rents of the lands, and such other means as the Legislature may provide, by tax or otherwise, shall be inviolably appropriated to the support of common schools. *Kan.*, 202.

—The income of the State school funds shall be disbursed annually, by order of the State Superintendent, to the several County Treasurers, and thence to the Treasurer of the several school districts, in equitable proportion to the number of children and youth resident therein between the ages of five and twenty-one years; *Provided*, That no school district in which a common school has not been maintained at least three months in each year, shall be entitled to receive any portion of such funds. *Kan.*, 202.

—The school lands shall not be sold unless such sale shall be authorized by a vote of the people at a general election; but, subject to re-valuation every five years, they may be leased for any number of years not exceeding twenty-five, at a rate established by law. *Kan.*, 202.

—All money which shall be paid by persons as an equivalent for exemption from military duty; the clear proceeds of estrays, ownership of which shall vest in the taker up; and the proceeds of fines for any breach of the penal laws, shall be exclusively applied, in the several counties in which the money

is paid or fines collected, to the support of common schools. *Kan.*, 302.

—No religious sect or sects shall ever control any part of the common school or university funds of the State. *Kan.*, 203.

—The State Superintendent of Public Instruction, Secretary of State and Attorney-General, shall constitute a Board of Commissioners, for the management and investment of the school funds. Any two of said Commissioners shall constitute a quorum. *Kan.*, 203.

—The Legislature, in providing for the formation and regulation of schools, shall make no distinction between the rights of males and females. *Kan.*, 200.

—The capital of the fund called and known as the "Common School Fund," consisting of one million two hundred and twenty-five thousand seven hundred and sixty-eight dollars and forty-two cents, for which bonds have been executed by the State to the Board of Education, and seventy-three thousand five hundred dollars of stock in the Bank of Kentucky; also, the sum of fifty-one thousand two hundred and twenty-three dollars and twenty-nine cents, balance of interest on the school fund for the year 1848, unexpended, together with any sum which may be hereafter raised in the State by taxation, or otherwise, for purposes of education, shall be held inviolate, for the purpose of sustaining a system of common schools. The interest and dividends of said funds, together with any sum which may be produced for that purpose by taxation or otherwise, may be appropriated in aid of common schools, but for no other purpose. The General Assembly shall invest said fifty-one thousand two hundred and twenty-three dollars and twenty-nine cents in some safe and profitable manner; and any portion of the interest and dividends of said school fund, or other money or property raised for school purposes, which may not be needed in sustaining common schools, shall be invested in like manner. The General Assembly shall make provision, by law, for the payment of the interest of said school fund; *Provided*, That each county shall be entitled to its proportion of the income of said fund, and if not called for, for common school purposes, it shall be reinvested from time to time for the benefit of such county. *Ky.*, 222.

—There shall be elected a Superintendent of Public Education, who shall hold his office for the term of four years. His duties shall be prescribed by law, and he shall receive a salary of four thousand dollars per annum until otherwise provided law: *Provided*, That the General Assembly shall have power, by a vote of a majority of the members elected to both Houses, to abolish the said office of Superintendent of Public Education, whenever, in their opinion, said office shall be no longer necessary. *La.*, 236.

—The Legislature shall provide for the education of all children of the State, between the ages of six and eighteen years, by maintenance of free public schools by taxation or otherwise. *La.*, 236.

—The general exercises in the common schools shall be conducted in the English language. *La.*, 236.

—The proceeds of all lands heretofore granted by the United States to this State for the use or purpose of the public schools, and of all lands which may hereafter be granted or bequeathed for that purpose, and the proceeds of the estates of deceased persons to which the state may have become entitled by law, shall be and remain a perpetual fund, on which the State shall pay an annual interest of six per cent, which interest, together with the interest of the trust funds, deposited with the State by the United States, under the act of Congress, approved June 23, 1836, and all the rents of the unsold lands shall be appropriated to the purpose of such schools, and the appropriation shall remain inviolable. *La.*, 236.

—No appropriation shall be made by the Legislature for the support of any private school or institution of learning whatever, but the highest encouragement shall be granted to public schools throughout the State. *La.*, 237.

—The Governor shall, within thirty days after the

ratification by the people of this Constitution, appoint, subject to the confirmation of the Senate, at its first session thereafter, a State Superintendent of Public Instruction, who shall hold his office for four years, and until his successor shall have been appointed and shall have qualified. He shall receive an annual salary of twenty-five hundred dollars, and such additional sum for traveling and incidental expenses as the General Assembly may by law allow; shall report to the General Assembly within thirty days after the commencement of its first session under this Constitution, a uniform system of free public schools, and shall perform such other duties pertaining to his office as may from time to time be prescribed by law. *Md.*, 274.

—There shall be a State Board of Education, consisting of the Governor, the Lieutenant-Governor, and Speaker of the House of Delegates, and the State Superintendent of Public Instruction, which Board shall perform such duties as the General Assembly may direct. *Md.*, 274.

—There shall be in each county such number of School Commissioners as the State Superintendent of Public Instruction shall deem necessary, who shall be appointed by the State Board of Education; shall hold office for four years, and shall perform such duties and receive such compensation as the General Assembly or State Superintendent may direct; the School Commissioners of Baltimore city shall remain as at present constituted, and shall be appointed, as at present, by the Mayor and City Council, subject to such alterations and amendments as may be made from time to time by the General Assembly, or the said Mayor and City Council. *Md.*, 274.

—The General Assembly, at its first session after the adoption of this Constitution, shall provide a uniform system of free public schools, by which a school shall be kept open and supported free of expense for tuition in each school-district, for at least six months in each year; and in case of a failure on the part of the General Assembly so to provide, the system reported to it by the State Superintendent of Public Instruction, shall become the system of free public schools of the State; *Provided*, That the report of the State Superintendent shall be in conformity with the provisions of this Constitution, and such system shall be subject to such alterations, conformable to this article, as the General Assembly may from time to time enact. *Md.*, 274.

—The General Assembly shall levy at each regular session after the adoption of this Constitution an annual tax of not less than ten cents on each one hundred dollars of taxable property throughout the State, for the support of the free public schools, which tax shall be collected at the time and by the same agents as the general State levy; and shall be paid into the treasury of the State, and shall be distributed under such regulations as may be prescribed by law, among the counties and the city of Baltimore, in proportion to their respective population between the ages of five and twenty years; *Provided*, That the General Assembly shall not levy any additional school tax upon particular counties, unless such county express by popular vote its desire for such tax; the city of Baltimore shall provide for its additional school tax as at present, or as may hereafter be provided by the General Assembly, or by the Mayor and City Council of Baltimore. *Md.*, 275.

—The General Assembly shall further provide by law, at its first session after the adoption of this Constitution, a fund for the support of the free public schools of the State, by the imposition of an annual tax of not less than five cents on each one hundred dollars of taxable property throughout the State, the proceeds of which tax shall be known as the public school fund, and shall be invested by the Treasurer, together with its annual interest until such time as said fund shall, by its own increase and any additions which may be made to it from time to time, together with the present school fund amount to six millions of dollars when the tax of ten cents in the hundred dollars authorized by the preceding section, may be

discontinued in whole or in part, as the General Assembly may direct; the principal fund of six millions hereby provided, shall remain forever inviolate as the free public school fund of the State, and the annual interest of said school fund shall be disbursed for educational purposes only, as may be prescribed by law. *Md.*, 275.

—All moneys raised by taxation in the towns and cities for the support of public schools, and all moneys which may be appropriated by the State for the support of common schools, shall be applied to, and expended in, no other schools than those which are conducted according to law, under the order and superintendence of the authorities of the town or city in which the money is to be expended; and such moneys shall never be appropriated to any religious sect for the maintenance, exclusively, of its own school. *Mass.*, 298.

—The Superintendent of Public Instruction shall have the general supervision of public instruction, and his duties shall be prescribed by law. *Mich.*, 310.

—The proceeds from the sales of all lands that have been or hereafter may be granted by the United States to the State for educational purposes, and the proceeds of all lands or other property given by individuals or appropriated by the State for like purposes, shall be and remain a perpetual fund, the interest and income of which, together with the rents of all such lands as may remain unsold, shall be inviolably appropriated and annually applied to the specific objects of the original gift, grant, or appropriation. *Mich.*, 310.

—All lands, the titles to which shall fail from a defect of heirs, shall escheat to the State; and the interest on the clear proceeds from the sales thereof shall be appropriated exclusively to the support of primary schools. *Mich.*, 310.

—The Legislature shall, within five years from the adoption of this Constitution, provide for and establish a system of primary schools, whereby a school shall be kept, without charge for tuition, at least three months in each year, in every school district in the State, and all instruction in said schools shall be conducted in the English language. *Mich.*, 310.

—A school shall be maintained in each school-district at least three months in each year. Any school-district neglecting to maintain such school shall be deprived for the ensuing year of its proportion of the income of the primary school fund, and of all funds arising from taxes for the support of schools. *Mich.*, 310.

—There shall be elected at the general election in the year one thousand eight hundred and fifty-two, three members of a State Board of Education, one for two years, one for four years, and one for six years; and at each succeeding biennial election there shall be elected one member of such Board, who shall hold his office for six years. The Superintendent of Public Instruction shall be *ex officio* a member and Secretary of such Board. The Board shall have the general supervision of the State Normal School, and their duties shall be prescribed by law. *Mich.*, 311.

—All specific State taxes except those received from the mining companies of the Upper Peninsula, shall be applied in paying the interest upon the primary school, university, and other educational funds, and the interest and principal of the State debt, in the order herein recited, until the extinguishment of the State debt, other than the amounts due to educational funds, when such specific taxes shall be added to, and constitute a part of the primary school interest fund. The Legislature shall provide for an annual tax, sufficient, with other resources to pay the estimated expenses of the State Government, the interest of the State debt, and such deficiency as may occur in the resources. *Mich.*, 311.

—Religion, morality, and knowledge being necessary to good government, the preservation of liberty, and the happiness of mankind, schools and means of education, shall forever be encouraged in this State. *Miss.*, 343.

49

—The stability of a republican form of government depending mainly upon the intelligence of the people, it shall be the duty of the Legislature to establish a general and uniform system of public schools. *Min.*, 326.

—The proceeds of such lands as are or hereafter may be granted by the United States for the use of schools within each township in this State, shall remain a perpetual school fund to the State, and not more than one-third of said lands may be sold in two years, one-third in five years and one-third in ten years; but the lands of the greatest valuation shall be sold first; *Provided*, That no portion of said lands shall be sold otherwise than at public sale. The principal of all funds arising from sales or other disposition of lands, or other property, granted or intrusted to this State, in each township for educational purposes, shall forever be preserved inviolate and undiminished; and the income arising from the lease or sale of said school lands shall be distributed to the different townships throughout the State. in proportion to the number of scholars in each township between the ages of five and twenty-one years, and shall be faithfully applied to the specific objects of the original grants or appropriations. *Min.*, 326.

—Suitable laws shall be passed by the Legislature for the safe keeping, transfer, and disbursement of the State school funds, and all officers and other persons charged with the same shall be required to give ample security for all moneys and funds of any kind, to keep an accurate entry of each sum received, and of each payment and transfer; and if any of said officers or other persons shall convert to his own use in any form, or shall loan with or without interest, contrary to law, or shall deposit in banks, or exchange for other funds, any portion of the funds of the State, every such act shall be adjudged to be an embezzlement of so much of the State funds as shall be thus taken, and shall be declared a felony; and any failure to pay over or produce the State or school funds intrusted to such persons, on demand, shall be held and taken to be *prima facie* evidence of such embezzlement. *Min.*, 327.

—The Legislature shall make such provisions, by taxation or otherwise, as, with the income arising from the school fund, will secure a thorough and efficient system of public schools in each township in the State. *Min.*, 326.

—A general diffusion of knowledge and intelligence being essential to the preservation of the rights and liberties of the people, the General Assembly shall establish and maintain free schools for the gratuitous instruction of all persons in this State, between the ages of five and twenty-one years. *Mo.*, 360.

—Separate schools may be established for children of African descent. All funds provided for the support of public schools shall be appropriated in proportion to the number of children, without regard to color. *Mo.*, 360.

—The supervision of public instruction shall be vested in a "Board of Education," whose powers and duties shall be prescribed by law. A Superintendent of Public Schools, who shall be the President of the Board, shall be elected by the qualified voters of the State. He shall possess the qualifications of a State Senator, and hold his office for the term of four years; and shall perform such duties, and receive such compensation, as may be prescribed by law. The Secretary of State and Attorney-General shall be *ex-offi-io* members, and, with the Superintendent, compose said Board of Education. *Mo.*, 360.

—The proceeds of all lands that have been, or hereafter may be, granted by the United States to this State, and not otherwise appropriated by this State or the United States; also, all moneys, stocks, bonds, lands, and other property now belonging to any fund for purposes of education; also, the net proceeds of all sales of lands and other property and effects that may accrue to the State by escheat, or from sales of estrays, or from unclaimed dividends, or distributive shares of the estates of deceased persons, or from fines, penalties and forfeitures; also, any proceeds of

the sales of public lands which may have been, or hereafter may be, paid over to this State, if Congress will consent to such appropriation; also, all other grants, gifts, or devises that have been, or hereafter may be, made to this State, and not otherwise appropriated by the terms of the grant, gift, or devise, shall be securely invested and sacredly preserved as a public school fund; the annual income of which fund, together with so much of the ordinary revenue of the State as may be necessary, shall be faithfully appropriated for establishing and maintaining the free schools and the university in this article provided for, and for no other uses or purposes whatsoever. *Mo.*, 361.

—No part of the public school fund shall ever be invested in the stock, or bonds, or other obligations of any State, or of any county, city, town, or corporation. The stock of the Bank of the State of Missouri now held for school purposes, and all other stocks belonging to any school or university fund, shall be sold, in such manner and at such time as the General Assembly shall prescribe; and the proceeds thereof, and the proceeds of the sales of any lands or other property which now belongs, or may hereafter belong, to said school fund, may be invested in the bonds of the United States. All county school funds shall be loaned upon good and sufficient unincumbered real estate security, with personal security in addition thereto. *Mo.*, 361.

— No township or school-district shall receive any portion of the public school fund, unless a free school shall have been kept therein for not less than three months during the year for which distribution thereof is made. The General Assembly shall have power, to require, by law, that every child, of sufficient mental and physical ability, shall attend the public schools, during the period between the ages of five and eighteen years, for a term equivalent to sixteen months, unless educated by other means. *Mo.*, 361.

—In case the public school fund shall be insufficient to sustain a free school at least four months in every year in each school-district in this State, the General Assembly may provide, by law, for the raising of such deficiency, by levying a tax on all the taxable property in each county, township, or school-district, as they may deem proper. *Mo.*, 361.

—The General Assembly shall, as far as it can be done without infringing upon vested rights, reduce all lands, moneys, and other property, used or held for school purposes, in the various counties of this State, into the public school fund herein provided for; and in making distribution of the annual income of said fund, shall take into consideration the amount of any county or city fund, appropriated for common school purposes, and make such distribution as will equalize the amount appropriated for common schools throughout the State. *Mo.*, 361.

—The principal of all funds arising from the sale, or other disposition of lands or other property granted or intrusted to this State, for educational and religious purposes, shall forever be preserved inviolate and undiminished; and the income arising therefrom shall be faithfully applied to the specific objects of the original grants or appropriations. The Legislature shall make such provisions by taxation or otherwise, as, with the income arising from the school trust fund, will secure a thorough and efficient system of common schools throughout the State; but no religious sect or sects shall ever have any exclusive right to, or control of any part of the school funds of this State. *Neb.*, 376.

—The university lands, school lands, and all other lands which have been acquired by the Territory of Nebraska, or which may hereafter be acquired by the State of Nebraska for educational or school purposes, shall not be aliened or sold for a less sum than five dollars per acre. *Neb.*, 376.

—The Legislature shall encourage, by all suitable means, the promotion of intellectual, literary, scientific, mining, mechanical, agricultural and moral improvement, and also provide for the election by the people, at the general election, of a Superintendent of Public Instruction, whose term of office shall be two years from the first Monday of January, A. D., 18 5, and until the election and qualification of his successor. and whose duties shall be prescribed by law. *Nev.*, 389.

—The Legislature shall provide for a uniform system of common schools, by which a school shall be established and maintained in each school district at least six months in every year, and any school district neglecting to establish and maintain such a scho)l, or which shall allow instruction of a sectarian character therein, may be deprived of its portion of the interest of the public school fund during such a neglect or infraction, and the Legislature may pass such laws as will tend to secure a general attendance of the children in each school district upon said public schools. *Nev.*, 389.

—All lands, including the sixteenth and thirty-sixth sections, in every township, donated for the benefit of public schools, in the act of the thirty-eighth Congress, to enable the people of Nevada Territory to form a State Government, the thirty thousand acres of public lands granted by an act of Congress, approved July second, eighteen hundred and sixty-two, for each Senator and Representative in Congress, and all proceeds of lands that have been or may be hereafter granted or appropriated by the United States to this State, and also the five thousand acres of land granted to the new States under the act of Congress, distributing the proceeds of the public lands among the several States of the Union, approved A. D. eighteen hundred and forty-one; *Provided*, That Congress makes provision for or authorizes such division to be made for the purpose herein contained, all estates that may escheat to the State, all of such per cent. as may be granted by Congress on the sale of land, all fines collected under the penal laws of the State, all property given or bequeathed to the State for educational purposes; and all proceeds derived from any or all of such sources shall be, and the same are hereby, solemnly pledged for educational purposes, and shall not be transferred to any other fund for any other uses, and the interest thereon shall, from time to time, be apportioned among the several counties in proportion to the ascertained numbers of the persons between the ages of six and eighteen years in the different counties; and the Legislature shall provide for the sale of floating land warrants to cover the aforesaid lands, and for the investment of all proceeds derived from any of the above mentioned sources in United States bonds or the bonds of this State; *Provided*, That the interest only of the aforesaid proceeds shall be used for educational purposes, and any surplus interest shall be added to the principal sum; *And, Provided further*, That such portions of said interest as may be necessary may be apportioned for the support of the State University. *Neb.*, 390.

—The Legislature shall have power to establish normal schools, and such different grades of schools, from the primary department to the university, as in their discretion they may deem necessary, and all professors in said university, or teachers in said schools, of whatever grade, shall be required to take and subscribe to the oath as prescribed in article 16, of this Constitution. No professor or teacher who fails to comply with the provisions of any law framed in accordance with the provisions of this section shall be entitled to receive any portion of the public moneys set apart for school purposes. *Nev.*, 390.

—The fund for the support of free schools, and all money, stock and other property, which may hereafter be appropriated for that purpose, or received into the treasury under the provision of any law heretofore passed to augment the said fund, shall be securely invested, and remain a perpetual fund; and the income thereof, except so much as it may be judged expedient to apply to an increase of the capital, shall be annually appropriated to the support of public schools, for the equal benefit of all the people of the State; and it shall not be competent for the Legislature to borrow, appropriate, or use the said

fund, or any part thereof, for any other purpose, under any pretense whatever. *N. J.*, 415.

—That a school or schools shall be established by the Legislature, for the convenient instruction of youth, with such salaries to the masters, paid by the public, as may enable them to instruct at low prices; and all useful learning shall be duly encouraged and promoted in one or more universities. *N. C.*, 426.

—The General Assembly shall make such provisions, by taxation or otherwise, as, with the interest arising from the school trust fund, will secure a thorough and efficient system of common schools throughout the State; but no religious or other sect or sects shall ever have any exclusive right to or control of any part of the school funds of this State. *Ohio*, 433.

—The Governor shall be Superintendent of Public Instruction, and his powers and duties in that capacity shall be such as may be prescribed by law; but after the term of five years from the adoption of this Constitution, it shall be competent for the Legislative Assembly to provide by law for the election of a Superintendent, to provide for his compensation and prescribe his powers and duties. *Or.*, 453.

—The proceeds of all the lands which have been, or hereafter may be, granted to this State for educational purposes (excepting the lands heretofore granted to aid in the establishment of a university), all the moneys and clear proceeds of all property which may accrue to the State by escheat or forfeiture; all moneys which may be paid as exemption from military duty; the proceeds of all gifts, devises and bequests made by any person to the State for common school purposes; the proceeds of all property granted to the State, when the purposes of such grant shall not be stated; all the proceeds of the five hundred thousand acres of land to which this State is entitled by the provision of an act of Congress, entitled "An act to appropriate the proceeds of the sales of the public lands, and to grant pre-emption rights," approved the fourth of September, 1841, and also the five per centum of the net proceeds of the sales of the public lands to which this State shall become entitled on her admission into the Union (if Congress shall assent to such appropriation of the two grants last mentioned), shall be set apart as a separate and irreducible fund, to be called the common school fund, the interest of which, together with all other revenues derived from the school lands mentioned in this section, shall be exclusively applied to the support and maintenance of common schools in each school district, and purchase of suitable libraries and apparatus therefor. *Or.*, 456.

—The Legislative Assembly shall provide by law for the establishment of a uniform and regular system of common schools. *Or.*, 456.

—Provision shall be made by law for the distribution of the income of the common school fund among the several counties of this State, in proportion to the number of children resident therein between the ages of four and twenty years. *Or.*, 456.

—The Legislature shall, as soon as conveniently may be, provide by law for the establishment of schools throughout the State, in such manner that the poor may be taught gratis. *Pa.*, 466.

—The diffusion of knowledge as well as of virtue, among the people being essential to the preservation of their rights and liberties, it shall be the duty of the General Assembly to promote public schools, and to adopt all means which they may deem necessary and proper to secure to the people the advantages and opportunities of education. *R. I.*, 480.

—The money which now is or which may hereafter be appropriated by law for the establishment of a permanent fund for the support of public schools, shall be securely invested, and remain a perpetual fund for that purpose. *R. I.*, 480.

—All donations for the support of public schools or for other purposes of education which may be received by the General Assembly, shall be applied according to the terms prescribed by the donors. *R. I.*, 480.

—The General Assembly shall make all necessary

provisions by law for carrying this article into effect. They shall not divert said money or fund from the aforesaid uses, nor borrow, appropriate, or use the same, or any part thereof, for any other purpose, under any pretense whatsoever. *R. I.*, 480.

—Knowledge, learning, and virtue, being essential to the preservation of republican institutions, and the diffusion of the opportunities and advantages of education throughout the different portions of the State, being highly conducive to the promotion of this end; it shall be the duty of the General Assembly in all future periods of this government, to cherish literature and science. And the fund called the *common school fund*, and all the lands and proceeds thereof, dividends, stocks, and other property of every description whatever, heretofore by law appropriated by the General Assembly of this State for the use of common schools, and all such as shall hereafter be appropriated, shall remain a *perpetual fund*, the principal of which shall never be diminished by legislative appropriation, and the interest thereof shall be inviolably appropriated to the support and encouragement of common schools throughout the State, and for the equal benefit of all the people thereof; and no law shall be made authorizing said fund, or any part thereof, to be diverted to any other use than the support and encouragement of common schools; and it shall be the duty of the General Assembly to appoint a Board of Commissioners, for such term of time as they may think proper, who shall have the general superintendence of said fund, and who shall make a report of the condition of the same from time to time, under such rules, regulations, and restrictions as may be required by law: *Provided*, That if at any time hereafter a division of the public lands of the United States, or of the money arising from the sales of such lands, shall be made among the individual States, the part of such lands, or money coming to this State, shall be devoted to the purposes of education or internal improvement; and shall never be applied to any other purpose. *Tenn.*, 499.

—A general diffusion of knowledge being essential to the preservation of the rights and liberties of the people, it shall be the duty of the Legislature of this State to make suitable provisions for the support and maintenance of public schools. *Tex.*, 519.

—The Legislature shall, as early as practicable, establish a system of free schools throughout the State; and as a basis for the endowment and support of said system, all the funds, lands, and other property, heretofore set apart and appropriated, or that may hereafter be set apart and appropriated for the support and maintenance of public schools, shall constitute the public school fund; and said fund and the income derived therefrom shall be a perpetual fund exclusively for the education of all the white scholastic of this State, and no law shall ever be made appropriating said fund to any use or purpose whatever. And until such time as the Legislature shall provide for the establishment of such system of public schools in the State, the fund thus created and the income derived therefrom, shall remain as a charge against the State, and be passed to the credit of the free common school fund. *Tex.*, 519.

—And all the alternate sections of land reserved by the State out of grants heretofore made, or that may hereafter be made, to railroad companies or other corporations of any nature whatever, for internal improvements, or for the development of the wealth and resources of the State, shall be set apart as a part of the perpetual school fund of the State; *Provided*, That if at any time hereafter any portion of the public domain of this State shall be sold, and by virtue of said sale the jurisdiction over said land shall be vested in the United States government; in such event, one-half of the proceeds derived from said sale shall become a part of the perpetual school fund of the State; and the Legislature shall hereafter appropriate one-half of the proceeds resulting from all sales of the public lands to the perpetual public school fund. *Tex.*, 519.

—The Legislature shall provide from time to time, for the sale of lands belonging to the perpetual public school fund, upon such time and terms as it may deem expedient; *Provided*, That in cases of sale the preference shall be given to actual settlers; *And provided further*, That the Legislature shall have no power to grant relief to purchasers by granting further time for payment, but shall, in all cases, provide for the forfeiture of the land to the State for the benefit of a perpetual public school fund; and that all interest accruing upon such sales shall be a part of the income belonging to the school fund, and subject to appropriation annually for educational purposes. *Tex.*, 519.

—The Legislature shall have no power to appropriate or loan or invest, except as follows, any part of the principal sum of the perpetual school fund for any purpose whatever; and it shall be the duty of the Legislature to appropriate annually the income which may be derived from said fund, for educational purposes, under such system as it may adopt; and it shall, from time to time, cause the principal sum now on hand and arising from sales of land, or from any other source, to be invested in the bonds of the United States of America, or the bonds of the State of Texas, or such bonds as the State may guarantee. *Tex.*, 519.

—All public lands which have been heretofore, or may be hereafter, granted for public schools, to the various counties or other political divisions in this State, shall be under the control of the Legislature, and may be sold on such terms and under such regulations as the Legislature shall by law prescribe; and the proceeds of the sale of said lands shall be added to the perpetual school fund of the State. But each county shall receive the full benefit of the interest arising from the proceeds of the sale of the lands granted to them, respectively: *Provided*, That the lands already patented to the counties shall not be sold without the consent of such county or counties to which the lands may belong. *Tex.*, 519.

—The Legislature may provide for the levying of a tax for educational purposes; *Provided*, The taxes levied shall be distributed from year to year, as the same may be collected; *And provided*, That all the sums arising from said tax which may be collected from Africans, or persons of African descent, shall be exclusively appropriated for the maintenance of a system of public schools for Africans and their children; and it shall be the duty of the Legislature to encourage schools among these people. *Tex.*, 519.

—The Governor, by and with the advice and consent of two-thirds of the Senate, shall appoint an officer to be styled the Superintendent of Public Instruction. His term of office shall be four years, and his annual salary shall not be less than ($2,000) two thousand dollars, payable at stated times; and the Governor, Comptroller and Superintendent of Public Education, shall constitute a Board to be styled a Board of Education, and shall have the general management and control of the perpetual school fund, and common schools, under such regulations as the Legislature may hereafter prescribe. *Tex.*, 520.

—The several counties in this State which have not received their quantum of the lands for the purposes of education, shall be entitled to the same quantity heretofore appropriated by the Congress of the Republic of Texas, and the State, to other counties. And the counties which have not had the lands to which they are entitled for educational purposes, located, shall have a right to contract for the location, surveying and procuring the patents for said lands, and of paying for the same with any portion of said lands so patented, not to exceed one-fourth of the whole amount to be so located, surveyed and patented — to be divided according to quantity, allowing to each part a fair proportion of land, water and timber. *Tex.*, 520.

—Laws for the encouragement of virtue and prevention of vice and immorality ought to be constantly kept in force and duly executed; and a competent number of schools ought to be maintained in each town, for the convenient instruction of youth, and one or more grammar schools be incorporated and properly supported, in each county in this State. And all religious societies or bodies of men that may be hereafter united or incorporated for the advancement of religion and learning, or for other pious and charitable purposes, shall be encouraged and protected in the enjoyment of the privileges, immunities, and estates, which they in justice ought to enjoy under such regulations as the General Assembly of this State shall direct. *Vt.*, 527.

—All money accruing to this State, being the proceeds of forfeited, delinquent, waste and unappropriated lands; and of lands heretofore sold for taxes and purchased by the State of Virginia, if hereafter redeemed, or sold to others than this State; all grants, devises or bequests that may be made to this State for the purposes of education, or where the purposes of such grants, devises or bequests are not specified; this State's just share of the literary fund of Virginia, whether paid over or otherwise liquidated, and any sums of money, stocks or property which this State shall have the right to claim from the State of Virginia for educational purposes; the proceeds of the estates of all persons who may die without leaving a will or heir, and of all escheated lands; the proceeds of any taxes that may be levied on the revenues of any corporation hereafter created; all moneys that may be paid as an equivalent for exemption from military duty, and such sums as may from time to time be appropriated by the Legislature for the purpose, shall be set apart as a separate fund, to be called the school fund, and invested under such regulations as may be prescribed by law, in the interest-bearing securities of the United States, or of this State, and the interest thereof shall be annually applied to the support of free schools throughout the State, and to no other purpose whatever. But any portion of said interest remaining unexpended at the close of the fiscal year shall be added to, and remain a part of the capital of the school fund. *W. Va.*, 557.

—The Legislature shall provide, as soon as practicable, for the establishment of a thorough and efficient system of free schools. They shall provide for the support of such schools by appropriating thereto the interest of the invested school fund; the net proceeds of all forfeitures, confiscations and fines accruing to this State under the laws thereof; and by general taxation on persons and property, or otherwise. They shall also provide for raising, in each township, by the authority of the people thereof, such a proportion of the amount required for the support of free schools therein as shall be prescribed by general laws. *W. Va.*, 557.

—Provision may be made by law for the election and prescribing the powers, duties and compensation of a General Superintendent of Free Schools for the State, whose term of office shall be the same as that of the Governor, and for a County Superintendent for each county, and for the election, in the several townships, by the voters thereof, of such officers, not specified in this Constitution as may be necessary to carry out the objects of this article, and for the organization, whenever it may be deemed expedient, of a State Board of Instruction. *W. Va.*, 557.

—The supervision of public instruction shall be vested in a State Superintendent, and such other officers as the Legislature shall direct. The State Superintendent shall be chosen by the qualified electors of the State, in such manner as the Legislature shall provide; his powers, duties and compensation shall be prescribed by law; *Provided*, That his compensation shall not exceed the sum of twelve hundred dollars annually. *Wis.*, 568.

—The proceeds of all lands that have been, or hereafter may be, granted by the United States to this State, for educational purposes (except the lands heretofore granted for the purposes of a university), and all moneys and the clear proceeds of all property that may accrue to the State by forfeiture or escheat, and all monies which may be paid as an equivalent for exemption from military duty, and the clear pro-

47

ceeds of all fines collected in the several counties for any breach of the penal laws, and all monies arising from any grant to the State, where the purposes of such grant are not specified, and the five hundred thousand acres of land to which the State is entitled by the provisions of an act of Congress entitled "An act to appropriate the proceeds of the sales of the public lands, and to grant pre-emption rights," approved the fourth day of September, one thousand eight hundred and forty-one, and also the five *per centum* of the net proceeds of the public lands to which the State shall become entitled on her admission into the Union (if Congress shall consent to such appropriation of the two grants last mentioned), shall be set apart as a separate fund, to be called the school fund, the interest of which, and all other revenues derived from the school lands, shall be exclusively applied to the following objects, to wit:

1. To the support and maintenance of common schools, in each school-district, and the purchase of suitable libraries and apparatus therefor.

2. The residue shall be appropriated to the support and maintenance of academies and normal schools, and suitable libraries and apparatus therefor.

3. The Legislature shall provide by law for the establishment of district schools, which shall be as nearly uniform as practicable, and such schools shall be free and without charge for tuition to all children between the ages of four and twenty years, and no sectarian instruction shall be allowed therein.

4. Each town and city shall be required to raise by tax, annually, for the support of common schools therein, a sum not less than one-half the amount received by such town or city respectively for school purposes, from the income of the school fund.

5. Provision shall be made by law for the distribution of the income of the school fund among the several towns and cities of the State, for the support of common schools therein, in some just proportion to the number of children and youth resident therein, between the ages of four and twenty years, and no appropriation shall be made from the school fund to any city or town, for the year in which said city or town shall fail to raise such tax, nor to any school-district for the year in which a school shall not be maintained at least three months. *Wis.*, 569.

[The proceeds from the sale of lands, except such parts as might be reserved for public use or ceded to the United States, were declared as belonging to the school fund, by the Constitution of 1821.] *P.* 42.

UNIVERSITIES—PROMOTION OF SCIENCE.

—The General Assembly shall make provision by law for obtaining correct knowledge of the several objects proper for improvement in relation to the roads and navigable waters in this State, and for making a systematic and economical application of the means appropriated to those objects. *Ala.*, 77.

—The Legislature shall take measures for the protection, improvement, or other disposition of such lands as have been, or may hereafter be reserved or granted by the United States or any person or persons, to the State for the use of the university; and the funds accruing from the rents or sale of such lands, or from any other source for the purpose aforesaid, shall be and remain a permanent fund, the interest of which shall be applied to the support of said university, with such branches as the public convenience may demand for the promotion of literature, the arts and sciences, as may be authorized by the terms of such grant. And it shall be the duty of the Legislature, as soon as may be, to provide effectual means for the improvement and permanent security of the funds of said university. *Ct.*, 103.

—The charter of Yale College, as modified by agreement of the corporation thereof, in pursuance of an act of the General Assembly, passed in May, 1792, is hereby confirmed. *Ct.*, 112.

—The General Assembly shall have power to appropriate money for the promotion of learning and science, and to provide for the education of the people; and shall provide for the early resumption of the regular exercises of the University of Georgia, by the adequate endowment of the same. *Ga.*, 146.

—The university lands and the proceeds thereof, and all monies belonging to said fund shall be a permanent fund for the sole use of the State University. The interest arising from the same shall be annually appropriated for the support and benefit of said university. *Iowa*, 192.

—The State University shall be established at one place without branches at any other place, and the university fund shall be applied to that institution, and no other. *Iowa*, 192.

—The General Assembly shall take measures for the protection, improvement, or other disposition of such lands as have been, or may thereafter be reserved, or granted by the United States, or any person or persons, to this State, for the use of a university, and the funds accruing from the rents or sale of such lands, or from any other source for the purpose aforesaid, shall be, and remain a permanent fund, the interest of which shall be applied to the support of the university, for the promotion of literature, the arts and sciences, as may be authorized by the terms of such grant. And it shall be the duty of the General Assembly, as soon as may be, to provide effectual means for the improvement and permanent security of the funds of said University. *Iowa*, 193.

—The Legislature shall encourage the promotion of intellectual, moral, scientific and agricultural improvement, by establishing a uniform system of common schools, and schools of a higher grade, embracing normal, preparatory, collegiate, and university departments. *Kan.*, 202.

—Provision shall be made by law for the establishment, at some eligible and central point, of a State university, for the promotion of literature and the arts and sciences, including a normal and an agricultural department. All funds arising from the sale or rents of lands granted by the United States to the State for the support of a State univerity, and all other grants, donations, or bequests, either by the State or by individuals, for such purpose, shall remain a perpetual fund, to be called the " University fund ;" the interest of which shall be appropriated to the support of the State university. *Kan.*, 203.

—A University shall be established in the city of New Orleans. It shall be composed of four Faculties, to wit: one of Law, one of Medicine, one of the Natural Sciences, and one of Letters; the Legislature shall provide by law for its organization and maintenance. *La.*, 236.

—All moneys arising from the sales which have been, or may hereafter be made of any lands heretofore granted by the United States to this State for the use of a specific seminary of learning, or from any kind of a donation that may hereafter be made for that purpose, shall be and remain a perpetual fund, the interest of which at six per cent. per annum shall be appropriated to the promotion of literature and the arts and sciences, and no law shall ever be made diverting said funds to any other use than to the establishment and improvement of said seminary of learning; and the General Assembly shall have power to raise funds for the organization and support of said Seminary of learning in such manner as it may deem proper. *La.*, 236.

—A general diffusion of the advantages of education being essential to the preservation of the rights and liberties of the people; to promote this important object, the Legislature are authorized, and it shall be their duty to require the several towns to make suitable provision, at their own expense, for the support and maintenance of public schools, and it shall further be their duty, to encourage and suitably endow, from time to time, as the circumstances of the people may authorize, all academies, colleges and seminaries of learning within the State; *Provided*, That no donation, grant, or endowment, shall at any time be made by the Legislature, to any literary institution now established, or which may hereafter be established, unless, at the time of making such endowment, the Legislature of the State shall have the right to grant any further powers to alter, limit or restrain any of the powers vested in any such literary institution as shall be judged necessary to promote the best interests thereof. *Me.*, 247.

—Wisdom and knowledge, as well as virtue, diffused generally among the body of the people, being necessary for the preservation of their rights and liberties; and as these depend on spreading the opportunities and advantages of education in the various parts of the country, and among the different orders of the people, it shall be the duty of the Legislatures and magistrates, in all future periods of this Commonwealth, to cherish the interests of literature and the sciences, and all seminaries of them; especially the university at Cambridge, public schools, and grammar schools in the towns ; to encourage private societies and public institutions, rewards and immunities, for the promotion of agriculture, arts, sciences, commerce, trades, manufactures, and a natural history of the country ; to countenance and inculcate the principles of humanity and general benevolence, public and private charity, industry and frugality, honesty and punctuality in their dealings; sincerity, and good humor, and all social affections and generous sentiments among the people. *Mass.*, 291.

—That the Legislature ought to encourage the diffusion of knowledge and virtue, the extension of a judicious system of general education, the promotion of literature, the arts, science, agriculture, commerce and manufactures, and the general melioration of the condition of the people. *Md.*, 256.

—There shall be elected in the year eighteen hundred and sixty-three, at the time of the election of a Justice of the Supreme Court, eight Regents of the University, two of whom shall hold their office for two years, two for four years, two for six years, and two for eight years. They shall enter upon the duties of their office on the first of January next succeeding their election. At every regular election of a Justice of the Supreme Court thereafter, there shall be elected two Regents, whose term of office shall be eight years. When a vacancy shall occur in the office of Regent, it shall be filled by appointment of the Governor. The Regents thus elected shall constitute the Board of Regents of the University of Michigan. *Mich.*, 311.

—The Regents of the University and their successors in office shall continue to constitute the body corporate, known by the name and title of " The Regents of the University of Michigan." *Mich.*, 311.

—The Regents of the University shall at their first annual meeting, or as soon thereafter as may be, elect a President of the University, who shall be *ex officio* a member of their Board, with the privilege of speaking, but not of voting. He shall preside at the meetings of the Regents, and be the principal executive officer of the University. The Board of Regents shall have the general supervision of the University, and the direction and control of all expenditures from the University interest fund. *Mich.*, 311.

—The Legislature shall encourage the promotion of intellectual, scientific, and agricultural improvement ; and shall, as soon as practicable, provide for the establishment of an agricultural school. The Legislature may appropriate the twenty-two sections of salt spring lands now unappropriated, or the money arising from the sale of the same, where such lands have been already sold, and any land which may hereafter be granted or appropriated for such purpose, for the support and maintenance of such school, and may make the same a branch of the University for instruction in agriculture and the natural sciences connected therewith, and place the same under the supervision of the Regents of the University. *Mich.*, 311.

—The location of the University of Minnesota, as established by existing laws, is hereby confirmed and said institution is hereby declared to be the University of the State of Minnesota. All the rights, immunities, franchises, and endowments heretofore granted or conferred, are hereby perpetuated unto the said University, and all lands which may be granted hereafter by Congress, or other donations, for said University purposes, shall vest in the institution referred to in this section. *Minn.*, 326.

—The General Assembly shall also establish and maintain a State University, with departments for instruction in teaching, in agriculture, and in natural science, as soon as the public school fund will permit. *Mo.*, 360.

—The Legislature shall provide for the establishment of a State University, which shall embrace departments for agriculture, mechanic arts and mining, to be controlled by a Board of Regents, whose duties shall be prescribed by law. *Nev.*, 390.

—The Legislature shall provide a special tax of one-half of one mill on the dollar of all taxable property in the State, in addition to the other means provided for the support and maintenance of said university and common schools : *Provided*, That at the end of ten years they may reduce said tax to one-quarter of one mill on each dollar of taxable property. *Nev.*, 390.

—The Governor, Secretary of State, and Superintendent of Public Instruction shall, for the first four years, and until their successors are elected and qualified, constitute a Board of Regents, to control and manage the affairs of the University and the funds of the same, under such regulations as may be provided by law. But the Legislature shall, at its regular session next preceding the expiration of the term of office of the said Board of Regents, provide for the election of a new Board of Regents and define their duties. *Nev.*, 390.

—The Board of Regents shall, from the interest accruing from the first funds which come under their control, immediately organize and maintain the said mining department in such manner as to make it the most effective and useful ; *Provided*, That all the proceeds of the public lands donated by act of Congress approved July second, eighteen hundred and sixty-two, for a college for the benefit of agriculture, the mechanic arts, and including military tactics, shall be invested by the said Board of Regents in a separate fund, to be appropriated exclusively to the benefit of the first named departments to the University, as set forth in section four above, and the Legislature shall provide that if, through neglect or any other contingency, any portion of the fund so set apart shall be lost or misappropriated, the State of Nevada shall replace said amount so lost or misappropriated in said fund, so that the principal of said fund shall remain forever undiminished. *Nev.*, 390.

—Knowledge and learning, generally diffused through a community, being essential to the preservation of a free government; spreading the opportunities and advantages of education through the various parts of the country being highly conducive to promote this end, it shall be the duty of the Legislatures and magistrates, in all future periods of this government, to cherish the interests of literature and the sciences, and all seminaries and public schools; to encourage private and public institutions, rewards and immunities for the promotion of agriculture, arts, sciences, commerce, trade, manufactures and natural history of the country; to countenance and inculcate the principles of humanity and general benevolence, public and private charity, industry and economy, honesty and punctuality, sincerity, sobriety, and all social affections and generous sentiments among the people. *N. H.*, 400.

—The Governor, Secretary of State and State Treasurer, shall constitute a Board of Commissioners for the sale of school and university lands, and for the investment of the funds arising therefrom, and their powers and duties shall be such as may be prescribed by law ; *Provided*, That no part of the university funds, or of the interest arising therefrom, shall be expended until the period of ten years from the adoption of this Constitution, unless the same shall be otherwise disposed of, by the consent of Congress, for common school purposes. *Or.*, 456.

—The arts and sciences shall be promoted in one or more seminaries of learning. *Pa.*, 466.

—The above provisions shall not be construed to prevent the Legislature from carrying into effect any laws have been passed in favor of the colleges, universities or academies, or from authorizing heirs or distributees to receive and enjoy escheated property, under such rules and regulations as, from time to time, may be prescribed by law. *Tenn.*, 500.

—The moneys and lands heretofore granted to, or which may hereafter be granted for the endowment and support of one or more universities, shall constitute a special fund for the maintenance of said universities, and until the university or universities are located and commenced, the principal and the interest arising from the investment of the principal, shall be vested in like manner, and under the same restrictions as provided for the investment and control of the perpetual public school fund, in section four and five (4 and 5) in this article of the Constitution, and the Legislature shall have no power to appropriate the university fund for any other purpose than that of the maintenance of said universities, and the Legislature shall, at an early day, make such provisions, by law, as will organize and put into operation the university. *Tex.*, 519.

—The Legislature shall foster and encourage moral, intellectual, scientific and agricultural improvement ; they shall, whenever it may be practicable, make suitable provision for the blind, mute and insane, and for the organization of such institutions of learning as the best interests of general education in the State may demand. *W. Va.*, 557.

—Provision shall be made by law for the establishment of a State university, at or near the seat of State government, and for connecting with the same from time to time, such colleges in different parts of the State, as the interests of education may require. The proceeds of all lands that have been or may hereafter be granted by the United States to the State for the support of a university, shall be and remain a perpetual fund, to be called the "university fund," the interest of which shall be appropriated to the support of the State university, and no sectarian instruction shall be allowed in such university. *Wis.*, 569.

—The Secretary of State, Treasurer, and Attorney-General shall constitute a Board of Commissioners for the sale of the school and university lands, and for the investment of the funds arising therefrom. Any two of said Commissioners shall be a quorum for the transaction of all business pertaining to the duties of their office. *Wis.*, 569.

—Provision shall be made by law for the sale of all school and university lands, after they shall have been appraised, and when any portion of such lands shall be sold, and the purchase-money shall not be paid at the time of the sale, the Commissioners shall take security by mortgage upon the land sold for the sum remaining unpaid, with seven per cent interest thereon, payable annually at the office of the Treasurer. The Commissioners shall be authorized to execute a good and sufficient conveyance to all purchasers of such lands, and to discharge any mortgages taken as security, when the sum due thereon shall have been paid. The Commissioners shall have power to withhold from sale any portion of such lands when they shall deem it expedient, and shall invest all moneys arising from the sale of such lands, as well as all other university and school funds, in such manner as the Legislature shall provide, and shall give such security for the faithful performance of their duties as may be required by law. *Wis.*, 569.

LIBRARIES.

—The State Librarian shall be elected by a joint vote of the two branches of the General Assembly for four years, and until his successor shall be elected and qualified. His salary shall be fifteen hundred dollars per annum, and the General Assembly shall pass no law whereby he shall receive any additional compen-

ARTICLE X.

1 SECTION 1. Sheriffs, clerks of counties, including the Register and Clerk of
2 the city and county of New York, Coroners, and District Attorneys, shall be
3 chosen by the electors of the respective counties, once in every three years
4 and as often as vacancies shall happen. Sheriffs shall hold no other office, and
5 be ineligible for the next three years after the termination of their offices.
6 They may be required by law to renew their security from time to time; and
7 in default of giving such new security, their offices shall be deemed vacant.
8 But the county shall never be made responsible for the acts of the Sheriff.
9 The Governor may remove any officer in this section mentioned, within the
10 term for which he shall have been elected; giving to such officer a copy of the
11 charges against him, and an opportunity of being heard in his defense.

sation. He shall perform such duties as are now or may hereafter be prescribed by law. In case of a vacancy in the office of State Librarian from death, resignation or other cause, the Governor shall fill such vacancy until the next meeting of the General Assembly thereafter, and until a successor be elected and qualified. *Md.*, 273.
—The Legislature shall also provide for the establishment of at least one librarian in each county; and all fines assessed and collected in the several counties and townships for any breach of the penal laws, shall be exclusively applied to the support of such libraries. *Mich.*, 311.

COUNTY AND TOWN OFFICERS.

—That town clerks, supervisors, assessors, constables, collectors, and all other officers, heretofore eligible by the people shall always continue to be so eligible, in the manner directed by the present or future acts of the Legislature. *N. Y.* (1777), 31.
[The provisions embraced in section one of article ten are copied from the New York Constitution of 1821.]
- -That loan officers, county treasurers, and clerks of the supervisors, continue to be appointed in the manner directed by the present or future acts of the Legislature. *N. Y.* (1777), 31.
—That sheriffs and coroners be annually appointed; and that no person shall be capable of holding either of the said offices more than four years successively; nor the sheriff of holding any other office at the same time. *N. Y.* (1777), 30.
—The clerks of courts, except those clerks whose appointment is provided for in the preceding section, shall be appointed by the courts of which they respectively are clerks; and district attorneys, by the County Courts. Clerks of courts and district attorneys shall hold their offices for three years, unless sooner removed by the courts appointing them. *N. Y.* (1821), 39.
—So many coroners as the Legislature may direct, not exceeding four in each county, shall be elected in the same manner as sheriffs, and shall hold their offices for the same term, and be removable in like manner. *N. Y.* (1821), 40.
—A Sheriff shall be elected in each county, by the qualified electors thereof, who shall hold his office for the term of three years, unless sooner removed, and shall not be eligible to serve, either as principal or deputy, for any two successive terms. Vacancies in

the office of Sheriff shall be filled by the Governor, as in other cases; and the person so appointed shall continue in office until the next general election in the county for Sheriff as by law provided. *Ala.*, 81.
—The qualified voters of each township shall elect one Constable for the term of two years, who shall hold his office till his successor is elected and qualified, who shall, during his continuance in office, reside in the township for which he was elected. Incorporated towns may have a separate Constable and a separate Magistracy. *Ark.*, 92.
—The qualified voters of each county shall elect one Sheriff, one Coroner, and one County Surveyor, for the term of two years, and until their successors are elected. They shall be commissioned by the Governor, reside in their respective counties during their continuance in office, and be disqualified for the office a second term, if it should appear that they or either of them are in default for moneys collected by virtue of their respective offices. *Ark.*, 97.
—A Sheriff shall be appointed in each county by the electors therein, in such manner as shall be prescribed by law, who shall hold his office for three years, removable by the General Assembly, and shall become bound with sufficient sureties to the Treasurer of the State, for the faithful discharge of the duties of his office. *Ct.*, 115.
—The Sheriff and Coroner of each county shall be chosen by the citizens residing in such county. They shall hold their respective offices for two years, if so long they behave themselves well, and until their successors be duly qualified; but no person shall be twice chosen Sheriff upon election by the citizens in any term of four years. They shall be commissioned by the Governor. The Governor shall fill vacancies in these offices by appointments to continue until the next election, and until successors shall be duly qualified. The Legislature, two-thirds of each branch concurring, may vest the appointment of Sheriffs and Coroners in the Governor; but no person shall be twice appointed Sheriff in any term of six years. *Del.*, 125.
—County Judges, Clerks, Sheriffs, and other county officers, for willful neglect of duty, or misdemeanor in office, shall be liable to presentment or indictment by a grand jury, and trial by a petit jury; and, upon conviction, shall be removed from office. *Ill.*, 161.
—There shall be elected in each county, by the voters thereof, at the time of holding general elections, a Clerk of the Circuit Court, Auditor, Recorder, Treasurer, Sheriff, Coroner, and Surveyor. The Clerk, Auditor, and Recorder, shall continue in office four

1 § 2. All county officers whose election or appointment is not provided for

2 by this Constitution, shall be elected by the electors of the respective counties,

3 or appointed by the Board of Supervisors, or other county authorities, as the

4 Legislature shall direct. All city, town and village officers, whose election or

5 appointment is not provided for by this Constitution, shall be elected by the

6 electors of such cities, towns and villages, or of some division thereof, or

7 appointed by such authorities thereof as the Legislature shall designate for

8 that purpose. All other officers whose election or appointment is not provided

9 for by this Constitution, and all officers whose offices may hereafter be created

10 by law, shall be elected by the people, or appointed as the Legislature may

11 direct.

years; and no person shall be eligible to the office of Clerk, Recorder, or Auditor, more than eight years in any period of twelve years. The Treasurer, Sheriff, Coroner, and Surveyor, shall continue in office two years; and no person shall be eligible to the office of Treasurer or Sheriff more than four years in any period of six years. *Ind.*, 176.

—There shall be elected in each county in this State, by the qualified electors thereof, a Sheriff, who shall hold his office for the term of two years, and until his successor shall have been elected and qualified: *Provided*, no person shall be eligible to the said office more than once in four years. *Ill.*, 163.

—No person shall be elected or appointed as a county officer who shall not be an elector of the county; nor any one who shall not have been an inhabitant thereof during one year next preceding his appointment, if the county shall have been so long organized; but if the county shall not have been so long organized, then within the limits of the county or counties out of which the same shall have been taken. *Ind.*, 176.

—Vacancies in county, township and town offices, shall be filled in such manner as shall be prescribed by law. *Ind.*, 176.

—Such other county and township officers as may be necessary, shall be elected or appointed in such manner as may be prescribed by law. *Ind.*, 176.

—The Legislature shall provide for such county and township officers as may be necessary. *Kan.*, 203.

—All county officers shall hold their offices for the term of two years, and until their successors shall be qualified; but no person shall hold the office of Sheriff or County Treasurer for more than two consecutive terms. *Kan.*, 203.

—All county and township officers may be removed from office, in such manner and for such cause as shall be prescribed by law. *Kan.*, 203.

—There shall be elected in each organized county a Clerk of the District Court, who shall hold his office two years, and whose duties shall be prescribed by law. *Kan.*, 201.

—No person shall be eligible to the offices mentioned in this article, who is not at the time twenty-four years old (except Clerks of County and Circuit Courts, Sheriffs, Constables and County Attorneys, who shall be eligible at the age of twenty-one years), a citizen of the United States, and who has not resided two years next preceding the election, in the State, and one year in the county or district for which he is a candidate. No person shall be eligible to the office of Commonwealth's or county Attorney, unless he shall have been a licensed practicing Attorney for two years. *Ky.*, 218.
48

—The General Assembly may provide for the election or appointment, for a term not exceeding four years, of such other county or district ministerial and executive officers as shall, from time to time, be necessary and proper. *Ky.*, 219.

—A Sheriff shall be elected in each county, by the qualified voters thereof, whose term of office shall, after the first term, be two years, and until his successor be qualified; and he shall be re-eligible for a second term; but no Sheriff shall, after the expiration of the second term, be re-eligible, or act as deputy, for the succeeding term. The first election of Sheriff shall be on the second Monday in May, 1851; and the Sheriffs then elected shall hold their offices until the first Monday in January, 1853, and until their successors be qualified; and on the first Monday in August, 1852, and on the first Monday of August in every second year thereafter, elections for Sheriffs shall be held: *Provided*, That the Sheriffs first elected shall enter upon the duties of their respective offices on the first Monday in June, 1851, and after the first election on the first Monday in January next succeeding their election. *Ky.*, 218.

—Officers for towns and cities shall be elected for such terms, and in such manner, and with such qualifications as may be prescribed by law. *Ky.*, 219.

—Clerks, Sheriffs, Surveyors, Coroners, Constables, and Jailors, and such other officers as the General Assembly may from time to time require, shall, before they enter upon the duties of their respective offices, and as often thereafter as may be deemed proper, give such bond and security as shall be prescribed by law. *Ky.*, 219.

—A Sheriff and a Coroner shall be elected in each parish by the qualified voters thereof, who shall hold their offices for the term of two years. The Legislature shall have the power to increase the number of Sheriffs in any parish. Should a vacancy occur in either of these offices subsequent to an election, it shall be filled by the Governor, and the person so appointed shall continue in office until his successor shall be elected and qualified. *La.*, 232.

—[Sheriffs, Coroners, &c., appointed by the Governor and Council.] *Me.*, 241.

—There shall be elected in each county, and in the city of Baltimore, in every second year, one person, resident in said county or city, above the age of twenty-five years, and at least five years preceding his election, a citizen of this State, to the office of Sheriff. He shall hold his office for two years and until his successor is duly elected and qualified; shall be ineligible for two years thereafter; shall give such bond, exercise such powers and perform such duties as now are or may hereafter be fixed by law. In case of a vacancy by death, refusal to serve or neglect to qualify or give bond, by disqualification or removal from the county or city, the Governor shall appoint a person to be Sheriff for the remainder of the official term. *Md.*, 270.

—Coroners, Elisors, and Notaries Public may be appointed for each county and the city of Baltimore, in the manner, for the purposes, and with the powers now fixed or which may hereafter be prescribed by law. *Md.*, 270.

—The Legislature shall prescribe, by general law, for the election of Sheriffs, Registers of Probate, Commissioners of Insolvency, and Clerks of the Courts, by the people of the several counties, and that District Attorneys shall be chosen by the people of the several districts, for such term of office as the Legislature shall prescribe. *Mass.*, 298.

—No person shall be capable of holding or exercising at the same time, within this State, more than one of the following offices, viz.: Judge of Probate, Sheriff, Register of Probate, or Register of Deeds; and never more than any two offices, which are to be held by appointment of the Governor, or the Governor and Council, or the Senate, or the House of Representatives, or by the election of the people of the State at large, or of the people of any county, military offices and the offices of Justices of the Peace excepted, shall be held by one person. *Mass.*, 292.

—There shall be elected annually, on the first Monday of April, in each organized township, one Supervisor, one Township Clerk, who shall be *ex officio* School Inspector, one Commissioner of Highways, one Township Treasurer, one School Inspector, not exceeding four Constables, and one Overseer of Highways for each highway district, whose powers and duties shall be prescribed by law. *Mich.*, 309.

—In each organized county there shall be a Sheriff, a County Clerk, a County Treasurer, a Register of Deeds, and a Prosecuting Attorney, chosen by the electors thereof, once in two years, and as often as vacancies shall happen, whose duties and powers shall be prescribed by law. The Board of Supervisors in any county may unite the offices of County Clerk and Register of Deeds in one office, or disconnect the same. *Mich.*, 309.

—The Sheriff, County Clerk, County Treasurer, Judge of Probate, and Register of Deeds, shall hold their offices at the county seat. *Mich.*, 309.

—The Sheriff shall hold no other office and shall be incapable of holding the office of Sheriff longer than four in any period of six years. He may be required by law to renew his security from time to time, and in default of giving such security, his office shall be deemed vacant. The county shall never be responsible for his acts. *Mich.*, 309.

- Provision shall be made by law for the election of such county or township officers as may be necessary. *Min.*, 328.

—A Sheriff, and one or more Coroners, a Treasurer, Surveyor, and Ranger shall be elected in each county by the qualified electors thereof, who shall hold their offices for two years, unless sooner removed; except that the Coroner shall hold his office until his successor be duly qualified. *Miss.*, 342.

—There shall be elected by the qualified voters in each county, at the time and places of electing Representatives, a Sheriff and a Coroner. They shall serve for two years, and until a successor be duly elected and qualified, unless sooner removed for malfeasance in office, and shall be ineligible four years in any period of eight years. Before entering on the duties of their office they shall give security in such amount, and in such manner, as shall be prescribed by law. Whenever a county shall be hereafter established, the Governor shall appoint a Sheriff and a Coroner therein, who shall continue in office until the next succeeding general election, and until a successor shall be duly elected and qualified. *Mo.*, 356.

—Whenever a vacancy shall happen in the office of Sheriff or Coroner, the same shall be filled by the County Court. If such vacancy happen in the office of Sheriff more than nine months prior to the time of

holding a general election, such County Court shall immediately order a special election to fill the same; and the person by it appointed shall hold office until the person chosen at such election shall be duly qualified; otherwise the person appointed by such County Court shall hold office until the person chosen at such general election shall be duly qualified. If any vacancy happen in the office of Coroner, the same shall be filled, for the remainder of the term, by such County Court. No person elected or appointed to fill a vacancy in either of said offices shall thereby be rendered ineligible for the next succeeding term. *Mo.*, 357.

—In all elections for Sheriff and Coroner, when two or more persons have an equal number of votes, and a higher than any other person, the Presiding Judge of the County Court of the county shall give the casting vote; and all contested elections for the said offices shall be decided by the Circuit Court of the proper county, in such manner as the General Assembly may, by law, prescribe. *Mo.*, 357.

—In the absence of any contrary provision, all officers now or hereafter elected or appointed, shall hold office during their official term, and until their successors shall be duly elected or appointed, and qualified. *Mo.*, 362.

—The Legislature shall establish a system of county and township government, which shall be uniform throughout the State. *Nev.*, 383.

—The Legislature shall provide for the election by the people of a Clerk of the Supreme Court, County Clerk, County Recorder, who shall be *ex officio* County Auditor, District Attorneys, Sheriffs, County Surveyors, Public Administrators, and other necessary officers, and fix by law their duties and compensation. County Clerks shall be *ex officio* Clerks of the Courts of Record and of the Board of County Commissioners in and for their respective counties. *Nev.*, 383.

—The County Treasurers and Registers of Deeds shall be elected by the inhabitants of the several towns, in the several counties in the State, according to the method now practiced, and the laws of the State. *N. H.*, 408.

—*Provided, nevertheless*, The Legislature shall have authority to alter the manner of certifying the votes and the mode of electing those officers, but not so as to deprive the people of the right they now have of electing them. *N. H.*, 408.

—Clerks and Surrogates of Counties shall be elected by the people of their respective counties, at the annual elections for members of the General Assembly. They shall hold their offices for five years. *N. J.*, 419.

—Sheriffs and Coroners shall be elected annually, by the people of their respective counties, at the annual elections for members of the General Assembly. They may be re-elected until they have served three years, but no longer; after which, three years must elapse before they can be again capable of serving. *N. J.*, 419.

—That there shall be a Sheriff, Coroner or Coroners, and Constables, in each county within this State. *N. C.*, 426.

—There shall be elected in each county, by the qualified electors thereof, at the time of holding general elections, a County Clerk, Treasurer, Sheriff, Coroner and Surveyor, who shall severally hold their offices for the term of two years. *Or.*, 453.

—A Sheriff shall be elected in each county for the term of two years, who shall be the ministerial officer of the Circuit and County Courts, and shall perform such other duties as may be prescribed by law. *Or.*, 455.

—Such other county, township, precinct and city officers as may be necessary, shall be elected, or appointed in such manner as may be prescribed by law. *Or.*, 454.

—County officers shall be elected on the second Tuesday of October, until otherwise directed by law, by the qualified electors of each county, in such manner and for such term, not exceeding three years, as may be provided by law. *Ohio*, 440.

- Township officers shall be elected on the first Monday of April, annually, by the qualified electors of their respective townships, and shall hold their offices for one year, from the Monday next succeeding their election, and until their successors are qualified. *Ohio*, 440.

—No person shall be eligible to the office of Sheriff or County Treasurer for more than four years, in any period of six years. *Ohio*, 440.

—The General Assembly shall provide, by law, for the election of such county and township officers as may be necessary. *Ohio*, 440.

—Sheriffs and Coroners shall, at the times and places of election of Representatives, be chosen by the citizens of each county. One person shall be chosen for each office, who shall be commissioned by the Governor. They shall hold their offices for three years, if they shall so long behave themselves well, and until a successor be duly qualified; but no person shall be twice chosen or appointed Sheriff in any term of six years. Vacancies in either of the said offices shall be filled by an appointment, to be made by the Governor, to continue until the next general election, and until a successor shall be chosen and qualified as aforesaid. *Pa.*, 465.

—All other officers shall be appointed as they hitherto have been, until otherwise directed by law; but the same person shall not hold the office of Sheriff for two consecutive terms. *S. C.*, 487.

—There shall be elected in each county, by the qualified voters therein, one Sheriff, one Trustee, and one Register; the Sheriff and Trustee for two years, and the Register for four years: *Provided*, That no person shall be eligible to the office of Sheriff more than six years in any term of eight years. There shall be elected for each county, by the Justices of the Peace, one Coroner and one Ranger, who shall hold their offices for two years. Said officers shall be removed for malfeasance, or neglect of duty, in such manner as may be prescribed by law. *Tenn.*, 497.

—Should a vacancy occur, subsequent to an election, in the office of Sheriff, Trustee, or Register, it shall be filled by the Justices; if in that of the clerks to be elected by the people, it shall be filled by the courts; and the person so appointed shall continue in office until his successor shall be elected and qualified; and such office shall be filled by the qualified voters at the first election for any of the county officers. *Tenn.*, 497.

—The Legislature shall provide, that the election of the county and other officers by the people, shall not take place at the same time that the general elections are held for members of Congress, members of the Legislature, and Governor. The elections shall commence and terminate on the same day. *Tenn.*, 497.

—There shall be elected for each county, by the qualified voters, a County Clerk, who shall hold his office for four years years, who shall be the Clerk of the County and Police Courts, whose duties and perquisites, and fees of office shall be prescribed by the Legislature, and a vacancy in whose office shall be filled by the Judge of the County Court, until the next general election for county or State offices, who may be removed from office for such cause and in such manner as may be prescribed by law. *Tex.*, 512.

—Sheriffs and High Bailiffs shall be elected by the freemen of their respective counties. *Vt.*, 529.

—The voters of each county shall elect a Clerk of the County Court, a Surveyor, an Attorney for the Commonwealth, a Sheriff, and so many Commissioners of the Revenue as may be authorized by law, who shall hold their respective offices as follows: The Clerk, the Commissioner of the Revenue, and the Surveyor for the term of six years; the Attorney for the term of four years, and the Sheriff for the term of two years. Constables and Overseers of the Poor shall be elected by the voters as may be prescribed by law. *Va.*, 543.

—The officers mentioned in the preceding section, except the Attorneys, shall reside in the counties or districts for which they were respectively elected. No person elected for two successive terms to the office of Sheriff shall be re-eligible to the same office for the next succeeding term; nor shall he, during his term of service, or within one year thereafter, be eligible to any political office. *Va.*, 544.

—All officers appertaining to the cities and other municipal corporations, shall be elected by the qualified voters, or appointed by the constituted authorities of such cities, or corporations, as may be prescribed by law. *Va.*, 544.

—The voters of every county shall elect a Sheriff, Prosecuting Attorney, Surveyor of Lands, Recorder, one or more Assessors, and such other county officers as the Legislature may from time to time direct or authorize; the duties of all of whom shall be prescribed and defined, as far as practicable, by general laws. All the said county officers shall hold their offices for two years, except the Sheriff, whose term of office shall be four years. The same person shall not be elected Sheriff for two consecutive full terms, nor shall any person who has acted as deputy of any Sheriff be elected his successor, nor shall any Sheriff act as the deputy of his successor; but the retiring Sheriff shall finish all business remaining in his hands at the expiration of his term, for which purpose his commission and official bond shall continue in force. The duties of all the said officers shall be discharged by the incumbents thereof in person, or under their superintendence. The Board of Supervisors shall designate one or more Constables of their respective counties to serve process and levy executions, when the Sheriff thereof is a party defendant in a suit instituted therein, or is under any other disability. *W. Va.*, 554.

—Sheriffs, Coroners, Registers of Deeds, and District Attorneys shall be chosen by the electors of the respective counties, once in every two years, and as often as vacancies shall happen. Sheriffs shall hold no other office, and be ineligible for two years next succeeding the termination of their offices. They may be required by law to renew their security from time to time; and in default of giving such new security, their offices shall be deemed vacant. But the county shall never be made responsible for the acts of the Sheriff. The Governor may remove any officer in this section mentioned, giving to such officer a copy of the charges against him, and an opportunity of being heard in his defense. *Wis.*, 565.

—All county officers whose election or appointment is not provided for by this Constitution, shall be elected by the electors of the respective counties, or appointed by the Boards of Supervisors or other county authorities, as the Legislature shall direct. All city, town and village officers whose election or appointment is not provided for by this Constitution shall be elected by the electors of such cities, towns and villages, or of some division thereof, or appointed by such authorities thereof as the Legislature shall designate for that purpose. All other officers whose election or appointment is not provided for by this Constitution, and all officers whose offices may hereafter be created by law shall be elected by the people, or appointed as the Legislature may direct. *Wis.*, 571.

—Each town shall annually elect Selectmen, and such officers of local police as the laws may prescribe. *Ct.*, 113.

—Each county, town, city and incorporated village, shall make provision for the support of its own officers, subject to such regulations as may be prescribed by law. *Nev.*, 395.

—All deeds and conveyances of land shall be recorded in the Town Clerk's office, in their respective towns, and for want thereof, in the County Clerk's office of the same county. *Vt.*, 526.

—The Legislature shall, at their first session, by general laws, provide for carrying into effect the foregoing provisions of this article. They shall also provide for commissioning such of the officers therein mentioned as they may deem proper, and may require any class of them to give bond with security for the faithful discharge of the duties of their respective offices, and for accounting for and paying over, as required by law, all money which may come to their hands by virtue thereof. They shall further provide for the compensation of the said officers by fees, or from the county treasury; and for the appointment, when necessary, of deputies and assistants, whose duties and responsibilities shall be prescribed and defined by general laws. When the compensation of an officer is paid from the county treasury, the amounts shall be fixed by the Board of Supervisors, within limits to be ascertained by law, *W. Va.*, 555.

SUPERVISORS — COUNTY COMMISSIONERS.

—The General Assembly shall have power to establish in each county a Board of Commissioners, for the regulation of the county business therein. *Fl.*, 135.
—The Legislature shall have power to provide for the election of a Board of Supervisors in each county; and these Supervisors shall jointly and individually perform such duties as may be prescribed by law. *Cal.*, 104.
—The County Boards shall have power to provide farms as an asylum for those persons who, by reason of age, infirmity, or other misfortune, may have claims upon the sympathies and aid of society. *Ind.*, 178.
—The General Assembly may confer upon the Boards doing county business in the several counties, powers of a local administrative character. *Ind.*, 176.
— The Legislature may confer upon tribunals transacting the county business of the several counties such powers of local legislature and administration as it shall deem expedient. *Kan.*, 200.
—The General Assembly shall provide by law for the appointment of Road Supervisors in the several counties by the County Commissioners, and the number of said Supervisors, as well as their powers and duties in the several counties, shall be determined by the said County Commissioners. *Md.*, 274.
—The County Commissioner shall be elected, on a general ticket, by the qualified voters of the several counties in this State; an election for County Commissioners shall be held on the Tuesday next after the first Monday in the month of November, eighteen hundred and sixty-five, and as nearly one-half as may be of said Commissioners shall hold their office for two years, and the other half for four years. At the first meeting after their election and qualification, or as soon thereafter as practicable, the said commissioners shall determine by lot which of their number shall hold office for two and four years respectively; and thereafter there shall be elected as aforesaid, at each general election for county officers, County Commissioners for four years, to fill the places of those whose term has expired. The said commissioners shall exercise such powers and perform such duties (which shall be similar throughout the State) as are now or may hereafter be prescribed by law. Their number in each county, and their compensation, their powers and duties, may at any time hereafter be changed and regulated by the General Assembly. *Md.*, 274.
—A Board of Supervisors, consisting of one from each organized township, shall be established in each county, with such powers as shall be prescribed by law. *Mich.*, 309.
—Cities shall have such representation in the Board of Supervisors of the counties in which they are situated, as the Legislature may direct. *Mich.*, 309.
—The Board of Supervisors, or, in the county of Wayne, the Board of County Auditors, shall have the exclusive power to prescribe and fix the compensation for all services rendered for, and to adjust all claims against their respective counties, and the sum so fixed or defined shall be subject to no appeal. *Mich.*, 309.
—The Board of Supervisors of each organized county may provide for laying out highways, constructing bridges, and organizing townships, under such restrictions and limitations as shall be prescribed by law. *Mich.*, 309.
—The Legislature may confer upon organized townships, incorporated cities and villages, and upon the Board of Supervisors of the several counties, such powers of a local, legislative and administrative character as they may deem proper. *Mich.*, 304.
—The qualified electors of each county shall elect five persons by districts, for the term of two years, who shall constitute a Board of Police for each county, a majority of whom may transact business; which body shall have full jurisdiction over roads, highways, ferries, and bridges, and all other matters of county police, and shall order all county elections to fill vacancies that may occur in the offices of their respective counties; the Clerk of the Court of Probate shall be the Clerk of the Board of County Police. *Miss.*, 340.
—No person shall be eligible as a member of said Board, who shall not have resided one year in the county; but this qualification shall not extend to such new counties as may hereafter be established until one year after their organization; and all vacancies that may occur in said Board shall be supplied by election as aforesaid to fill the unexpired term. *Miss.*, 340.
—The Legislature shall provide by law for the election of a Board of County Commissioners in each county, and such County Commissioners shall jointly and individually perform such duties as may be prescribed by law. *Nev.*, 383.
—There shall be elected in each county in the State, by the persons qualified to vote for members of the Legislature, four County Commissioners, whose term of office shall be four years, who, with the Judge of the County Court, shall constitute, and be styled, the Police Court for the county, whose powers, duties and mode of action, in regulating, promoting and protecting the public interest relating to the county, shall be the same as that now prescribed by law for the Commissioners' Court of Roads and Revenue, until otherwise provided for and regulated by the Legislature. *Tex.*, 512.
—The voters of each township, assembled in stated or special township meeting, shall transact all such business relating exclusively to their township as is herein, or may be by law, required or authorized. They shall annually elect a Supervisor, Clerk of the Township, Surveyor of Roads for each precinct in their township, Overseer of the Poor, and such other officers as may be directed by law. They shall also, every four years, elect one Justice, and if the white population of their township exceeds twelve hundred in number, may elect an additional Justice; and every two years shall elect as many Constables as Justices. The Supervisor, or, in his absence, a voter chosen by those present, shall preside at all township meetings and elections, and the clerk shall act as clerk thereof. *W. Va.*, 554.
—The Supervisors chosen in the townships of each county shall constitute a board, to be known as "the Supervisors of the county of ———," by which name they may sue and be sued, and make and use a common seal, and enact ordinances and by-laws not inconsistent with the laws of the State. They shall meet statedly at least four times in each year at the court-house of their county, and may hold special and adjourned meetings. At their first meeting after the annual township election, and whenever a vacancy may occur, they shall elect one of their number president of the board, and appoint a clerk, who shall keep a journal of their proceedings, and transact such other business pertaining to his office as may be by them or by law required, and whose compensation they shall fix by ordinance and pay from the county treasury. *W. Va.*, 554.
—The Board of Supervisors of each county, a majority of whom shall be a quorum, shall, under such general regulations as may be prescribed by law, have the superintendence and administration of the internal affairs and fiscal concerns of their county, including the establishment and regulation of roads, public landings, ferries and mills; the granting of ordinary and other licenses; and the laying collecting and disbursement of the county levies; but all writs

1   § 3. When the duration of any office is not provided by this Constitution,
2 it may be declared by law, and if not so declared, such office shall be held
3 during the pleasure of the authority making the appointment.

1   § 4. The time of electing all officers named in this article shall be prescribed
2 by law.

1   § 5. The Legislature shall provide for filling vacancies in office, and in case
2 of elective officers, no person appointed to fill a vacancy shall hold his office
3 by virtue of such appointment longer than the commencement of the political
4 year next succeeding the first annual election after the happening of the
5 vacancy.

of *ad quod damnum* shall issue from the Circuit Courts. They shall from time to time appoint the places for holding elections in the several townships of their county; and shall be the judges of the election, qualifications and returns of their own members, and of all county and township officers. *W. Va.*, 554.
—The Legislature may confer upon the Boards of Supervisors of the several counties of the State, such powers of a local, legislative and administrative character as they shall from time to time prescribe. *Wis.*, 563.

TENURE OF OFFICES.

—All officers whose election or appointment is not provided for by this Constitution, and all officers whose offices may hereafter be created by law, shall be elected by the people, or appointed as the Legislature may direct. *Cal.*, 104; (nearly similar), *Ind.*, 180; *Kan.*, 206; *Mo.*, 357.
—All officers shall continue in office until their successors shall be chosen and qualified. *Ohio*, 445; *Or.*, 458.
—The tenure that all commission officers shall by law have in their offices, shall be expressed in their respective commissions. *Mass.*, 230.
—All other officers, whose appointments are not otherwise provided for by law, shall be nominated by the Governor, and appointed by him, with the advice and consent of the Senate; and shall hold their offices for the time prescribed by law. *N. J.*, 419.
—The Legislature shall provide in what cases officers shall continue to perform the duties of their offices until their successors shall be duly qualified. *Tex.*, 516.
—The tenure of all offices, which are not or shall not be otherwise provided for, shall be during the pleasure of the Governor and Council. *Me.*, 247.
—The tenure of any office not herein provided for, may be declared by law, or when not so declared, such office shall be held during the pleasure of the authority making the appointment; but the Legislature shall not create any office, the tenure of which shall be longer than four years, except as herein otherwise provided in this Constitution. *Nev.*, 392; (nearly similar), *Kan.*, 206; *Ind.*, 180.
—In all cases in which it is provided that an office shall not be filled by the same person more than a certain number of years continuously, an appointment *pro tempore* shall not be reckoned a part of that term. *Ind.*, 172; *Or.*, 449.
—All public officers in this State, legislative, executive and judicial, whose terms of office expire at the general election, to be held in the year one thousand eight hundred and fifty-seven, or at any subsequent general election, shall continue to hold their offices

until the first Monday of January next following the expiration of said terms, and until their successors shall be qualified: *Provided*, Such of said officers as are required to give bond for the discharge of their duties, shall give bond and security for said extended terms, as may be provided by the Legislature; and the terms of office of all officers chosen at the general election in the year eighteen hundred and fifty-seven, or at any subsequent general election, shall commence on the first Monday of January next succeeding the election, and shall continue for the time now fixed by the Constitution, and until their successors shall be qualified. *Mich.*, 344.
—The terms of office of all State and county officers, of the Circuit Judges, members of the Board of Education, the members of the Legislature, shall begin on the first day of January next succeeding their election. *Mich.*, 318.
—All officers holding their offices during good behavior may be removed by joint resolution, of the two Houses of the Legislature, if two-thirds of all the members elected to the Assembly, and a majority of all the members elected to the Senate, concur therein. *N. Y.* (1821), 36.
—When the duration of any office is not provided for by this Constitution, it may be declared by law, and if not so declared, such office shall be held during the pleasure of the authority making the appointment; nor shall the duration of any office not fixed by this Constitution ever exceed four years. *Cal.*, 104; *Or.*, 458.
—All officers for a term of years shall hold their offices for the terms respectively specified, only on the condition that they so long behave themselves well; and shall be removed on conviction of misbehavior in office or of any infamous crime. *La.*, 466.
—That no inconvenience may arise from a change of the Constitution, it is declared, that all officers, civil and military, shall continue to hold their offices; and all the functions appertaining to the same shall be exercised and performed according to the existing laws and Constitution, until the end of the first session of the General Assembly, which shall sit under this Constitution, and until the government can be reorganized and put into operation under this Constitution, in such manner as the first General Assembly aforesaid shall prescribe, and no longer. *Tenn.*, 560.
—The Senators first elected in the even numbered senate districts, the Governor, Lieutenant-Governor, and other State officers first elected under this Constitution, shall enter upon the duties of their respective offices on the first Monday of June next, and shall continue in office for one year from the first Monday of January next. The Senators first elected in the odd numbered senate districts, and the members of the Assembly first elected, shall enter upon their

duties respectively on the first Monday in June next, and shall continue in office until the first Monday in January next. *Wis.*, 575.

—All officers, civil and military, now holding office, whether by election or appointment under the State, shall continue to hold and exercise their offices, according to their present tenure, unless otherwise provided in this Constitution until they shall be superseded pursuant to its provisions, and until their successors be duly qualified; and the compensation of such officers which has been increased by this Constitution shall take effect from the first day of January, eighteen hundred and sixty-five. *Md.*, 277.

—All county and township officers and justices of the peace in office on the first day of September, one thousand eight hundred and fifty-one, shall continue in office until their terms expire, respectively. *Ohio*, 445.

—The election of all officers, and the filling of all vacancies that may happen by death, resignation, or removal, not otherwise directed or provided for by this Constitution, shall be made in such manner as the General Assembly shall direct; *Provided*, that no such officer shall be elected by the General Assembly. *Ill.*, 161.

—Township officers, except Justices of the Peace, shall hold their offices one year from the Monday next succeeding their election, and until their successors are qualified. *Kan.*, 203.

—The term of the office of all officers elected or appointed pursuant to the provisions of this Constitution, except when herein otherwise directed, shall commence on the day of the date of their respective commissions; but no commission for any office shall bear date prior to the expiration of the term of the incumbent of said office. *N. J.*, 419.

—The duration of all offices, not fixed by this Constitution, shall never exceed four years, except the office of Superintendent of the lunatic asylum, or other asylums that may be established by law, who shall continue in office during good behavior; *Provided*, That in all cases where the Governor has the authority under this Constitution, or laws made in pursuance thereof, to appoint to office, he shall also have power to remove from the same for malfeasance in office, neglect of duty, or other good cause; *Provided*, That a statement of the cause shall, at the time of removal, be furnished the party interested, and a copy thereof shall also be recorded in the office of the Secretary of State. *Tex.*, 515.

—*And be it further ordained*, That where, by this Convention, the duration of any office shall not be ascertained, such office shall be construed to be held during the pleasure of the Council of Appointment: *Provided* that new commissions shall be issued to judges of the county courts, other than to the first judge, and to justices of the peace, once at the least in every three years. *N. Y.* (1777), 30.

—The term of State officers, except judicial, elected at the first election under this Constitution, shall continue until the Tuesday after the first Monday of January, A. D. eighteen hundred and sixty-seven, and until the election and qualification of their successors. *Nev.*, 391.

—Where the duration of any office is not prescribed by this Constitution, it may be declared by law; and if not so declared, such office shall be held during the pleasure of the authority making the appointment. *N. Y.* (1821), 40; *Ind.*, 180.

—The term of each of the executive officers named in this article, shall commence on taking the oath of office, on or after the first day of May, 1858, and continue until the first Monday of January, 1860, except the Auditor, who shall continue in office until the first Monday of January, 1861, and until their successors shall have been duly elected and qualified; and the same above-mentioned time for qualification and entry upon the duties of their respective offices shall extend and apply to all other officers elected under the State Constitution who have not already taken the oath of office and commenced the performance of their official duties. *Minn.*, 324.

—The terms of such officers and members, not elected or appointed to fill a vacancy, shall, unless herein otherwise provided, begin on the first day of January next succeeding their election. *W. Va.*, 548.

—Whenever it is provided in this Constitution, or in any law which may be hereafter passed, that any officer, other than a member of the General Assembly, shall hold his office for any given term, the same shall be construed to mean that such officer shall hold his office for such term, and until his successor shall have been elected and qualified. *Ind.*, 180.

—The Governor, Lieutenant-Governor, Secretary of State, Treasurer and Attorney-General shall hold their offices for two years; and the Auditor for four years. Their terms of office shall commence on the second Monday of January next after their election and continue until their successors are elected and qualified. *Ohio*, 435.

—That the first General election of Governor, Secretary of State, Auditor, Treasurer, and members of the General Assembly, and of such other officers as are to be elected at the same time, shall be held on the first Monday of August, eighteen hundred and forty-eight, anything in this Constitution to the contrary notwithstanding. County officers then elected shall hold their respective offices, until their successors are elected or appointed, in conformity with laws hereafter enacted. *Ill.*, 168.

—To the end there may be no failure of justice, or danger arise to the Commonwealth, from a change of the form of Government, all officers, civil and military, holding commissions under the government and people of Massachusetts Bay, in New England, and all other officers of the said government and people, at the time this Constitution shall take effect, shall have, hold, use, exercise and enjoy all the powers and authority to them granted or committed, until other persons shall be appointed in their stead; and all courts of law shall proceed in the execution of the business of their respective departments; and all the Executive and Legislative officers, bodies and powers, shall continue in full force, in the enjoyment and exercise of all their trusts, employments and authority, until the General Court, and the Supreme and Executive officers under this Constitution, are designated and invested with their respective trusts, powers and authority. *Mass.*, 293.

—All the officers named in the preceding articles of amendment (Articles 14 to 18), shall be annually elected by ballot, and shall hold their offices for one year, said year commencing on the first day of December next after their election. *Vt.*, 530.

—The General Assembly may provide by law for the continuance in office of any officers of annual election or appointment until other persons are qualified to take their places. *R. I.*, 476.

—The Governor, Lieutenant-Governor, Senators, Representatives, Secretary of State, Attorney-General and General Treasurer, shall be elected at the town, city or ward meetings to be holden on the first Wednesday of April, annually; and shall severally hold their offices for one year, from the first Tuesday of May next succeeding, and until others are legally chosen and duly qualified to fill their places. If elected or qualified after the first Tuesday of May, they shall hold their offices for the remainder of the political year, and until their successors are qualified to act. *R. I.*, 478.

—The General Assembly shall, by law, prescribe the time when the several officers authorized or directed by this Constitution to be elected or appointed, shall enter upon the duties of their respective offices, except where the time is fixed by this Constitution. *Ky.*, 220.

—No person shall ever be appointed or elected to any office in this State for life or during good behavior; but the tenure of all offices shall be for some limited period of time, if the person appointed or elected thereto shall so long behave well. *Miss.*, 336.

—The Legislature may provide by law in what case officers shall continue to perform the duties of their offices until their successors shall have been inducted into office. *La.*, 235.

RESIDENCE OF CIVIL OFFICERS—SEAT OF GOVERNMENT.

—Sheriffs, Coroners, and County Surveyors must reside in their counties during their continuance in office. *Ark.*, 92.

—All county, township, and town officers shall reside within their respective counties, townships and towns, and shall keep their respective offices, at such places therein, and perform such duties as may be directed by law. *Ind.*, 176.

—All civil officers for the Commonwealth, at large, shall reside within the State, and all district, county, or town officers, within their respective districts, counties, or towns, trustees of towns excepted, and shall keep their offices at such places therein as may be required by law; and all militia officers shall reside in the bounds of the division, brigade, regiment, battalion, or company, to which they may severally belong. *Ky.*, 220.

—All county officers shall hold their respective offices at the county seat of their respective counties. *Nev.*, 392.

—No person shall be elected or appointed to a county office who shall not be an elector of the county; and all county, township, precinct and city officers shall keep their respective offices at such places therein, and perform such duties as may be prescribed by law. *Or.*, 454.

—Prothonotaries, Clerks of the Peace and Orphans' Courts, Recorders of Deeds, Registers of Wills, and Sheriffs, shall keep their offices in the county town of the county in which they, respectively, shall be officers, unless when the Governor shall, for special reasons, dispense therewith, for any term not exceeding five years after the county shall have been erected. *Pa.*, 466.

—All civil officers shall reside within the State; and all district or county officers within their districts or counties; and shall keep their offices at such places therein as may be required by law. *Tex.*, 515.

—The Governor shall reside at the seat of government. *Va.*, 539; *W. Va.*, 552; *Ark.*, 90.

—He [the Governor] shall always reside during the session of the General Assembly, at the place where their session may be held, and at other times wherever, in their opinion, the public good may require. *Ala.*, 78.

—It shall be the duty of the General Assembly to provide for the purchase or erection of a suitable building for the residence of the Governor, and the Governor shall reside at the seat of government; but whenever, by reason of danger from an enemy, or from disease, the Governor may deem the Capital unsafe, he may, by proclamation, fix the seat of government at some secure place within the State, until such danger shall cease. *Fl.*, 131.

—All civil officers of the State at large shall reside within the State, and all district or county officers within their respective districts or counties, and shall keep their respective offices at such places therein as may be required by law. *Fl.*, 136.

—The seat of government shall be and remain permanent at the City of Tallahassee, until otherwise provided for by the action of a Convention of the people of the State. *Fl.*, 139.

—The seat of government is hereby permanently established, as now fixed by law, at the city of Des Moines, in the county of Polk, and the State University at Iowa City, in the county of Johnson. *Iowa*, 194.

—The temporary seat of government is hereby located at the City of Topeka, county of Shawnee. The first Legislature under this Constitution shall provide by law for submitting the question of the permanent location of the Capital to a popular vote,

and a majority of all the votes cast at some general election shall be necessary for such location. *Kan.*, 206.

—The Governor, Secretary of State, Auditor of State, Treasurer of State, Attorney-General, and Superintendent of Public Instruction, shall keep their respective offices at the seat of government. *Kan.*, 207.

—The first and all future sessions of the Legislature shall be held in the town of Jackson, in the county of Hinds, until the year 1850. During the first session thereafter, the Legislature shall have power to designate by law the permanent seat of government; *Provided, however*, That unless such designation be then made by law, the seat of government shall continue permanently at the town of Jackson. The first session shall commence on the third Monday in November, in the year 1833, and in every two years thereafter, at such time as may be prescribed by law. *Miss.*, 338.

—The Governor, Secretary of State, Treasurer, Auditor of Public Accounts, and Attorney-General, shall reside at the seat of government. *Miss.*, 338.

—The seat of Government of this State shall remain at the City of Jefferson. *Mo.*, 362.

—The Governor, Secretary of State, State Treasurer, State Controller, and Clerk of the Supreme Court, shall keep their respective offices at the seat of government. *Nev.*, 392.

—Columbus shall be the seat of government, until otherwise directed by law. *Ohio*, 443.

—The Legislative Assembly shall not have power to establish a permanent seat of government for this State, but at the first regular session after the adoption of this Constitution the Legislative Assembly shall provide by law for the submission to the electors of this State, at the next general election thereafter, the matter of the selection of a place for a permanent seat of government; and no place shall ever be the seat of government under such law which shall not receive a majority of all the votes cast on the matter of such election. *Or.*, 458.

—The seat of government, when established as provided in section one, shall not be removed for the term of twenty years from the time of such establishment, nor in any other manner than as provided in the first section of this article; *Provided*, That all public institutions of the State hereafter provided for by the Legislative Assembly shall be located at the seat of Government. *Or.*, 458.

—The Governor and the Secretary and Treasurer of State shall severally keep the public records, books and papers in any manner relating to their respective offices, at the seat of government, at which place also the Secretary of State shall reside. *Or.*, 453.

—The Governor shall reside during the sitting of the General Assembly, at the place where its session may be held; and the General Assembly may, by law, require him to reside at the capital of the State. *S. C.*, 486.

—The General Assembly which shall sit after the first apportionment of representation under the new Constitution, to wit: in the year one thousand eight hundred and forty-three, shall, within the first week after the commencement of the session, designate and fix the seat of government; and when so fixed, it shall not be removed, except by the consent of two-thirds of the members of both Houses of the General Assembly. The first and second sessions of the General Assembly under this Constitution shall be held in Nashville. *Tenn.*, 500.

—The Governor shall reside, during the session of the Legislature, at the place where the session may be held, and at all other times wherever, in their opinion, the public good may require. *Tex.*, 514.

—The seat of government shall be at the city of Wheeling until a permanent seat of government be established by law. *W. Va.*, 551.

1   § 6. The political year and legislative term shall begin on the first day of

2 January ; and the Legislature shall, every year, assemble on the first Tuesday

3 in January, unless a different day shall be appointed by law.

1   § 7. Provision shall be made by law for the removal, for misconduct or

2 malversation in office, of all officers (except judicial) whose powers and duties

3 are not local or legislative, and who shall be elected at general elections, and

4 also for supplying vacancies created by such removal.

1   § 8. The Legislature may declare the cases in which any office shall be

2 deemed vacant, when no provision is made for that purpose in this Constitution.

FISCAL YEAR—POLITICAL YEAR.

—The fiscal year shall commence on the first day of July. *Cal.*, 104.

—The political year shall begin on the first Wednesday of January, instead of the last Wednesday of May ; and the General Court shall assemble every year on the said first Wednesday of January, and shall proceed, at that session, to make all the elections, and do all the other acts, which are by the Constitution required to be made and done at the session which has heretofore commenced on the last Wednesday of May. And the General Court shall be dissolved on the day next preceding the first Wednesday of January, without any proclamation or other act of the Governor. But nothing herein contained shall prevent the General Court from assembling at such other times as they shall judge necessary, or when called together by the Governor. The Governor, Lieutenant-Governor and Councillors, shall also hold their respective offices for one year next following the first Wednesday of January, and until others are chosen and qualified in their stead. *Mass.*, 295.

—Fiscal year shall commence on the first day of January in each year. *Nev.*, 389.

—The political year for the State of Wisconsin shall commence on the first Monday in January in each year, and the general election shall be holden on the Tuesday succeeding the first Monday in November in each year. *Wis.*, 570.

REMOVALS FROM OFFICE.

—Officers shall be removed from office for incapacity, misconduct or neglect of duty, in such manner as may be provided by law, when no mode of trial or removal is provided in this Constitution. *Fl.*, 133.

—The Legislature shall provide by law for the trial, punishment and removal from office of all other offices of the State by indictment or otherwise. *La.*, 232.

—The Legislature shall provide by law for the removal of any officer elected by a county, township or school district, in such manner and for such cause as to them shall seem just and proper. *Mich.*, 310.

—Provision shall be made by law for the removal from office of any civil officer, other than those in this article previously specified, for malfeasance or non-feasance in the performance of his duties. *Nev.*, 388.

—All judicial officers, duly appointed, commissioned and sworn shall hold their offices during good behavior, excepting such concerning whom there is different provision made in this Constitution: *Provided, nevertheless,* The Governor, with the consent of

the Council, may remove them upon the address of both Houses of the Legislature. *Mass.*, 290.

—The Legislature shall provide for the trial, punishment and removal from office of all other officers of the State, by indictment or otherwise. *Tex.*, 519.

ELECTIONS OR APPOINTMENTS TO OFFICE

—VACANCIES IN OFFICE.

—All officers, other than those who, by this Constitution, are directed to be otherwise appointed, shall be appointed in the manner following, to wit: The Assembly shall, once in every year, openly nominate and appoint one of the Senators from each great district, which Senators shall form a Council for the Appointment of the said officers, of which the Governor for the time being, or the Lieutenant-Governor, or the President of the Senate, when they shall respectively administer the government, shall be President and have a casting voice, *but no other vote ;* and with the advice and consent of the said Council, shall appoint all the said officers; and that a majority of the said Council be a quorum. *And further,* The said Senators shall not be eligible to the said Council for two years successively. *N. Y.* (1777), 30.

—All officers, whose election or appointment is not otherwise provided for, shall be chosen or appointed, as may be prescribed by law. *Nev.*, 392; *Pa.*, 466.

—The General Assembly shall, by law, provide for the appointment or election, and removal from office, of all officers, civil and military, in this State, not provided for in this Constitution. *Fl.*, 136.

—All vacancies that may occur in said court, from death, resignation or removal, shall be filled by election as aforesaid; *Provided, however,* That if the unexpired term do not exceed one year, the vacancy shall be filled by executive appointment. *Miss.*, 338.

—Vacancies that may occur in offices, the election of which is vested in the people, within less than one year before the expiration of their term, shall be filled by the Governor granting commissions, which shall expire at the end of the next term : but if one year or a longer period remains unexpired at the time of the vacancy, then, and in that case, the Governor shall order an election to be held to fill the vacancy. *Ark.*, 89.

—Vacancies in office occurring after the first day of September, one thousand eight hundred and fifty-one, shall be filled as is now prescribed by law, and until officers are elected or appointed, and qualified under this Constitution. *Ohio*, 445.

—Vacancies that may happen in offices, the election of which is vested in the General Assembly, shall be filled by the Governor during the recess of the General Assembly, by granting commissions, which shall expire at the end of the next session. *Ark.*, 89..

—The Legislature may declare the cases in which any office shall be deemed vacant, and also the manner of filling the vacancy, where no provision is made for that purpose in this Constitution. *Mich.*, 304.

—Vacancies that happen in offices, the appointment to which is vested in the General Assembly, or given to the Governor, with the advice and consent of the Senate, and shall be filled by the Governor during the recess of the General Assembly, by granting commissions which shall expire at the end of the next session. *Fl.*, 131.

—And during the recess of the General Assembly, fill, *pro tempore*, all vacancies in those offices for which the Constitution and laws make no provision; but his appointments to such vacancies shall be by commission to expire at the end of thirty days after the commencement of the next session of the General Assembly. *Va.*, 539.

—Vacancies in offices under this article shall be filled, until the next regular election, in such manner as the General Assembly may provide. *Ky.*, 219.

—All vacancies not provided for in this Constitution, shall be filled in such manner as the Legislature may prescribe. *Miss.*, 341.

—It shall have the power to provide for the election or appointment of all officers, and the filling of all vacancies not otherwise provided for in this Constitution. *Kan.*, 200.

—When any officer, the right of whose appointment is by this Constitution vested in the General Assembly, shall, during the recess, die, or the office, by the expiration of the term, or by other means become vacant, the Governor shall have the power to fill such vacancy, by granting a temporary commission, which shall expire at the end of the next session of the Legislature. *Tenn.*, 495.

—When, during a recess of the General Assembly, a vacancy shall happen in any office, the appointment to which is vested in the General Assembly; or when at any time a vacancy shall have occurred in any other State office, or in the office of judge of any court, the Governor shall fill such vacancy by appointment, which shall expire when a successor shall have been elected and qualified. *Ind.*, 175.

—When any office shall from any cause become vacant, and no mode is provided by the Constitution and laws for filling such vacancy, the Governor shall have power to fill such vacancy by granting a commission, which shall expire at the end of the next session of the Legislature, or at the next election by the people. *Cal.*, 100; (nearly similar), *Iowa*, 188; *Ky.*, 213; *Mo.*, 355; *Nev.*, 389; *Ohio*, 459; *R. I.*, 477; *La.*, 230.

—If a vacancy shall occur in said court from any cause, the Governor shall issue a writ of election to the proper district to fill such vacancy for the residue of the term: *Provided*, That if the unexpired term be less than one year, the Governor shall appoint a judge to fill such vacancy. *Ky.*, 215.

—Whenever a vacancy shall occur in any of the State offices, the Governor shall fill the same by appointment, by and with the advice and consent of the Senate, if in session. *Mich.*, 308.

—When vacancies happen in either House, the Governor for the time being shall issue writs of election to fill such vacancies *Tenn.*, 493.

—Vacancies that may happen in offices, the appointment of which is vested in the General Assembly, shall, during the recess of the General Assembly, be filled by the Governor, by granting commissions, which shall expire at the end of the next session. *Ala.*, 79.

—But no person who has been nominated for office and rejected by the Senate, shall be appointed to the same office during the recess of the Senate. *La.*, 230.

—It shall be the duty of the Governor to fill all vacancies in office happening between the adoption of this Constitution and the first session of the Senate, and not otherwise provided for; and the commissions shall expire at the end of the first session of the Senate, or when successors shall be elected or appointed and qualified. *N. J.*, 421.

—The Legislature may declare the cases in which any office shall be deemed vacant, and also the man-

ner of filling the vacancy where no provision is made for that purpose in this Constitution. *Neb.*, 373; *La.*, 235; *Wis.*, 571.

—That, in every case, where any officer, the right of whose appointment is, by this Constitution, vested in the General Assembly, shall, during their recess, die, or his office by other means become vacant, the Governor shall have power, with the advice of the Council of State, to fill up such vacancy, by granting a temporary commission, which shall expire at the end of the next session of the General Assembly. *N. C.*, 425.

—The General Assembly may provide by law for the election or appointment of such other officers as may be required, and are not herein provided for and prescribe their tenure of office, powers and duties. *Md.*, 274.

—In the election and appointment of all officers, and the filling of all vacancies, not otherwise provided for by this Constitution, or the Constitution of the United States, shall be made in such manner as may be directed by law; but no appointing power shall be exercised by the General Assembly, except as prescribed in this Constitution. *Ohio*, 435.

—All officers heretofore elective by the people, shall continue to be elected; and all other officers, whose appointment is not provided for, by this Constitution, and all officers, whose offices may be hereafter created by law, shall be elected by the people, or appointed, as may by law be directed. *N. Y.* (1821), 40.

—The appointment of all officers not otherwise directed by this Constitution, shall be made in such manner as may be proscribed by law; and all officers, both civil and military, acting under the authority of this State, shall before entering on the duties of their respective offices, take an oath or affirmation to support the Constitution of the United States and of this State, and to demean themselves faithfully in office. *Ark.*, 87.

—Elections to fill vacancies shall be for the unexpired term. Vacancies shall be filled in such manner as may be prescribed by law. *W. Va.*, 548.

—In order to prevent those who are vested with authority from becoming oppressors, the people have a right at such periods and in such manner as they shall establish by their frame of government, to cause their public officers to return to private life; and to fill up vacant places by certain and regular elections and appointments. *Mass.*, 281.

[The Governor shall nominate, and with the advice of the Council, appoint all other civil and military officers whose appointment is not by this Constitution, nor by law, otherwise provided for, and every such nomination shall be made at least seven days prior to such appointment.] *Me.*, 244.

—All the provisions of the Constitution, respecting the election and proceedings of the members of the General Court, or of any other officers or persons whatever, that have reference to the last Wednesday of May as the commencement of the political year, shall be so far altered as to have like reference to the first Wednesday of January. *Mass.*, 295.

—No person shall be elected or appointed to any office in this State, civil or military, who is not a citizen of the United States, and who shall not have resided in this State one year next before the election or appointment. *Ill.*, 162.

—When any office shall become vacant by death, resignation or otherwise, the Governor shall have power to fill such vacancy unless otherwise provided for by law; and persons so appointed shall continue in office until a successor is appointed agreeably to the mode pointed out by this Constitution, or by law in pursuance thereof. *Ga.*, 147.

—When a vacancy happens during the recess of the Legislature, in any office which is to be filled by the Governor and Senate, or by the Legislature, in joint meeting, the Governor shall fill such vacancy, and the commission shall expire at the end of the next session of the Legislature, unless a successor shall be sooner appointed. When a vacancy happens in the office of Clerk or Surrogate of any county, the Gov-

ARTICLE XI.

1   Section 1. The militia of this State shall, at all times hereafter, be armed
2 and disciplined, and in readiness for service; but all such inhabitants of this
3 State, of any religious denomination whatever, as from scruples of conscience
4 may be averse to bearing arms, shall be excused therefrom, upon such condi-
5 tions as shall be prescribed by law.

ernor shall fill such vacancy, and the commission shall expire when a successor is elected and qualified. *N. J.*, 417.

—No appointment or nomination to office shall be made by the Governor during the last week of his said term. *N. J.*, 415.

—The election of all officers, and the filling of all vacancies that may happen, by death, resignation, or removal, not otherwise directed or provided for by this Constitution, shall be made in such manner as the Legislature shall direct. *Tenn.*, 497.

—In all cases of elections to fill vacancies in office occurring before the expiration of a full term, the person so elected shall hold for the residue of the unexpired term; and all persons appointed to fill vacancies in office, shall hold until the next general election, and until their successors are elected and qualified. *Iowa*, 194.

—Vacancies in county, township, precinct, and city offices shall be filled in such manner as may be prescribed by law. *Or.*, 454.

—No person holding an office of profit under the United States, shall, during his continuance in such office, hold any office of profit under this State. *Mo.*, 362.

—If, at any election directed by this Constitution, any two or more candidates shall have the highest and an equal number of votes, a new election shall be ordered, except in cases specially provided for by this Constitution. *Md.*, 277.

—Every person holding any office created by or existing under the Constitution or laws of the State, the entire amount of whose pay or compensation received for the discharge of his official duties shall exceed the yearly sum of three thousand dollars, except wherein otherwise provided by this Constitution, shall keep a book in which shall be entered any sum or sums of money received by him or on his account as a payment or compensation for his performance of official duties, a copy of which entries in said book, verified by the oath of the officer by whom it is directed to be kept, shall be returned yearly to the Comptroller of the State for his inspection and that of the General Assembly of the State, and each of the said officers, when the amount received by him for the year shall exceed three thousand dollars, shall yearly pay over to the Treasurer of the State the amount of such excess by him received, subject to such disposition thereof as the General Assembly may direct; and such officer failing to comply with this requisition shall be deemed to have vacated his office and be subject to suit by the State for the amount that ought to be paid into the treasury. *Md.*, 276.

—If any civil officer shall become disabled from discharging the duties of his office, by reason of any permanent bodily or mental infirmity, his office may be declared to be vacant, by joint resolution, agreed to by two-thirds of the whole representation in each House of the General Assembly: *Provided*, That such resolution shall contain the grounds for the proposed removal, and before it shall pass either House, a copy of it shall be served on the officer, and a hearing be allowed him. *S. C.*, 487.

—All civil officers shall be removable by an address of a majority of the members elected to both Houses, except those the removal of whom has been otherwise provided by this Constitution. *La.*, 233.

ORGANIZATION OF THE MILITIA.

—*And whereas* it is of the utmost importance to the safety of every State, that it should always be in a condition of defense; and it is the duty of every man, who enjoys the protection of society, to be prepared and willing to defend it: this Convention, therefore, in the name and by the authority of the good people of this State, doth ORDAIN, DETERMINE AND DECLARE, that the militia of this State, at all times hereafter, as well in peace as in war, shall be armed, and disciplined, and in readiness for service. That all such of the inhabitants of this State (being of the people called Quakers) as, from scruples of conscience, may be averse to the bearing of arms, be therefrom excused by the Legislature; and do pay to the State, such sums of money, in lieu of their personal service, as the same may, in the judgment of the Legislature, be worth: And that a proper magazine of warlike stores, proportionate to the number of inhabitants, be, forever hereafter, at the expense of this State, and by acts of the Legislature, established, maintained, and continued, in every county in this State. *N. Y.* (1777), 33.

—The General Assembly shall provide by law for organizing and disciplining the militia of this State, in such manner as they may deem expedient, not incompatible with the Constitution and laws of the United States; shall fix the rank of all staff officers, and prescribe the manner in which all officers shall be appointed or elected. *Ala.*, 78.

—The militia of this State shall be divided into convenient divisions, brigades, regiments and companies, and other officers of corresponding titles and rank elected to command them, conforming, as nearly as practicable, to the general relations of the army of the United States; and all officers shall be elected by those subject to military duty in their several districts, except as hereinafter provided. *Ark.*, 90.

—The Legislature shall provide by law for organizing and disciplining the militia, in such manner as they shall deem expedient, not incompatible with the Constitution and laws of the United States. *Cal.*, 102; *Miss.*, 342.

—The Governor shall have power to call forth the militia to execute the laws of the State, to suppress insurrections, and repel invasions. *Cal.*, 102; *Tex.*, 514.

—All offenses against the Militia laws shall be tried by court-martial, or before a court and jury, as the General Assembly may direct. *Fl.*, 137.

—The militia of the State of —— shall consist of all free male able-bodied persons (negroes, mulattoes and Indians excepted), resident of the State, between the ages of eighteen and forty-five years, except such persons as now are or hereafter may be exempted by the laws of the United States or of this State, and shall be armed, equipped and trained, as the General Assembly may provide by law. *Ill.*, 163; (nearly similar), *Ky.*, 210.

—The militia shall consist of all able-bodied white male persons between the ages of eighteen and forty-five years, except such as may be exempted by the laws of the United States or of this State; and shall be organized, officered, armed, equipped and trained, in such manner as may be provided by law. *Ind.*, 170; (nearly similar), *Mich.*, 312; *Or.*, 456; *Tex.*, 514.

—The militia may be divided into classes of sedentary and active militia, in such manner as shall be prescribed by law. *Ind.,* 180.

—The General Assembly shall determine the method of dividing the militia into divisions, brigades, regiments, battalions and companies, and fix the rank of all staff officers. *Ind.,* 180.

—The militia of this State shall be composed of all able-bodied white male citizens between the ages of eighteen and forty-five years, except such as are or may hereafter be exempt by the laws of the United States or of this State, and shall be armed, equipped and trained as the General Assembly may provide by law. *Iowa,* 190; (nearly similar), *Kan.,* 203.

—The Legislature shall provide for organizing, equipping and disciplining the militia in such manner as it shall deem expedient, not incompatible with the laws of the United States. *Kan.,* 203; *Mich.,* 314.

—The militia of the State shall be organized in such manner as may be hereafter deemed most expedient by the Legislature. *La.,* 231.

—All able-bodied men in the State shall be armed and disciplined for its defense. *La.,* 231.

—The militia, as divided into divisions, brigades, regiments, battalions and companies, pursuant to the laws now in force, shall remain so organized, until the same shall be altered by the Legislature. *Me.,* 246; (nearly similar), *Mass.,* 288.

—The militia shall be composed of all able-bodied male citizens, residents of this State, being eighteen years of age, and under the age of forty-five years, who shall be enrolled in the militia, and perform military duty in such manner, not incompatible with the Constitution and laws of the United States, as may be prescribed by the General Assembly of Maryland. *Md.,* 275.

—The General Assembly shall provide at its first session after the adoption of this Constitution, and from time to time thereafter, as the exigency may require, for organizing, equipping and disciplining the militia in such a manner, not incompatible with the laws of the United States, as shall be most effective to repel invasion and suppress insurrection, and shall pass such laws as shall promote the formation of volunteer militia associations in the city of Baltimore and in every county, and to secure them such privileges or assistance as may afford them effectual encouragement. *Md.,* 275.

—The Governor may suspend or arrest any military officer of the State for disobedience of orders, or other military offense, may remove him in pursuance of the sentence of a court-martial; and may remove, for incompetency or misconduct, all civil officers who received appointments from the executive for a term not exceeding two years. *Md.,* 260.

—All public boards, the Commissary-General, all superintending officers of public magazines and stores, belonging to this Commonwealth, and all commanding officers of forts and garrisons within the same, shall, once in every three months, officially and without requisition, and at other times, when required by the Governor, deliver to him an account of all goods, stores, provisions, ammunition, cannon with their appendages, and small arms with their accoutrements, and of all other public property whatever under their care, respectively; distinguishing the quantity, number, quality and kind of each, as particularly as may be; together with the condition of such forts and garrisons; and the said commanding officer shall exhibit to the Governor, when required by him, true and exact plans of such forts, and of the land and sea, or harbor or harbors adjacent.

And the said Boards, and all public officers, shall communicate to the Governor, as soon as may be after receiving the same, all letters, dispatches, and intelligences of a public nature, which shall be directed to them respectively. *Mass.,* 288.

—All officers, civil and military, now holding any office or appointment, shall continue to hold their respective offices, unless removed by competent authority, until superseded under the laws now in force, or under this Constitution. *Mich.,* 316.

—It shall be the duty of the Legislature to pass such laws for the organization, discipline, and service of the militia of the State as may be deemed necessary. *Minn.,* 328.

—The Governor shall have power to call forth the militia to execute the laws of the State, to suppress insurrection, and repel invasion. *Miss.,* 342; *Nev.,* 391.

—All able-bodied male inhabitants of the State of Missouri shall be liable to military duty under this ordinance, except as is hereinafter provided, and, when organized, shall constitute and be known and designated as the "Missouri Militia." *Mo.,* 365.

—All able-bodied male inhabitants of this State, between the ages of eighteen and forty-five years, who are citizens of the United States, or have declared their intention to become citizens of the United States, shall be liable to military duty in the milita of this State; and there shall be no exemption from such duty, except of such persons as the General Assembly may, by law, exempt. *Mo.,* 361.

—The General Assembly shall, by law, provide for the organization of the militia, and for the paying of the same when called into actual service; but there shall be no officer above the grade of Brigadier-General, nor shall there be more than two officers of that grade. *Mo.,* 361.

—There shall be an enrolling officer for each county, with the rank of a lieutenant, appointed by the commanding officer of each sub-district, whose duty it shall be to enroll all persons in said county, liable to do military duty, once in each year; and all enrollments heretofore made under existing laws shall be taken and considered as made under this ordinance. *Mo.,* 366.

—The militia, as soon as enrolled, shall be organized into platoons, companies, regiments and brigades. A platoon shall be composed of not less than thirty-two nor more than forty-six privates, two sergeants, four corporals, and one lieutenant. A company shall consist of the number of men, commissioned and non-commission officers prescribed by the Revised Regulations of the Army of the United States. A regiment shall consist of eight companies or more, with the number of field and staff officers prescribed by "Army Regulations" for the particular branch of service to which it may be assigned. A brigade shall consist of three or more regiments. *Mo.,* 366.

- -Platoons or companies, as soon as organized, shall elect their commissioned officers, which officers, together with all brigade, regimental, and staff officers appointed by the Governor, and all non-commissioned company officers, shall, before commissions or warrants, as the case may be, [be] issue[d] to them, take and subscribe the following oath: "I, A. B., aged —— years, of the county of ——, in the State of Missouri, and a native of ——, do on oath (or affirmation) declare that I have not, during the present rebellion, taken up arms or levied war against the United States nor against the State of Missouri, nor have I willfully adhered to the enemies of either, whether domestic or foreign, by giving aid or comfort, by denouncing said governments, or either of them, by going into or favoring or encouraging others to go into, or favor secession, rebellion, or disunion, but have always in good faith opposed the same; and further, that I will support, protect, and defend the Constitution of the United States and of the State of Missouri against all enemies or opposers, whether domestic or foreign, any ordinance, law, resolution of any State Convention or Legislature, or of any orders, organization, secret or otherwise, to the contrary notwithstanding; and that I do this with an honest purpose, pledge and determination faithfully to perform the same, without any mental reservation or evasion whatever, so help me God. *Mo.,* 366.

—The staff of general officers shall be the same as for the time may be prescribed by the Regulations of the United States Army, or orders of the War Department, governing appointments of officers of the same grade in the United States service, all of whom shall be detailed from the line of the command of the officer to whose staff they are attached. *Mo.*, 366.

—It shall be lawful for the Commander-in-Chief to call into service such platoons, companies or regiments as the safety and peace of the State may require, and to issue such instructions as may be necessary to insure strict discipline and familiarity in drill. *Mo.*, 366.

—The publication of the proclamation of the Governor shall be deemed sufficient notice to all persons, subject to military duty, to report to their respective commanding officer for active service. *Mo.*, 366.

—The Articles of War and Army Regulations, as published by authority of the War Department of the United States, shall be observed by the Missouri Militia in every particular not otherwise provided by this Ordinance, and the manner of drill shall be such as is prescribed in the tactics adopted for the United States Army. *Mo.*, 367.

—Whenever the militia, or any part of it, is called into service, the Inspector-General or his assistants, shall muster such force into the service on the rolls of the platoon or company, one of which rolls shall be retained by the commanding officer of the platoon or company, one copy shall be returned to the Adjutant-General of the State, and one copy to the district head-quarters. He shall administer to each platoon or company separately on the following oath : " You and each of you do solemnly swear that you will support, protect and defend the United States and the State of Missouri, and the Constitution and laws thereof, against all their enemies; that you will assist in enforcing the laws, and will obey all lawful orders of the officers having authority to command you whilst in the service, so help your God." And any person subject to military duty who shall refuse to take said oath, shall be considered and treated as a prisoner of war. *Mo.*, 367.

—Every person who neglects or refuses to enroll himself shall pay the sum of twenty dollars, to be levied upon his goods and chattels, by order of the commanding officer of the district, and may be imprisoned or put at hard labor by said officer until said fine is paid, and shall then be enrolled and assigned to such platoon or company as the commanding officer of the district may di ect; and any person duly enrolled and liable to militia service who shall refuse or neglect to perform such service, shall pay a fine of five dollars per day for every day he fails to render such service, after having been thereto required by his officers, and in addition thereto such delinquent shall be subject to arrest, trial and punishment, within the discretion of a court-martial, and nothing in this section shall be construed to exempt any man from military service. *Mo.*, 367.

—The commanding officer of each platoon or company shall certify, to the commanding officer of the battalion or regiment to which he is attached, a list of all persons liable to fine under the provisions of this ordinance, with the number of days each person has neglected or refused to do duty, which list shall be, by the commanding officer of the battalion or regiment, certified to the clerk of the Circuit Court of the county ten days before the next term of the said court, who shall place a copy of said list in a conspicuous place in his office at lea-t five days before the first day of the term. *Mo.*, 367.

—It shall be the duty of the Circuit Court to render a judgment and award an execution against each person named in said lists for the sum due by him, and costs which shall be collected as other fines. The Sheriff of the County may collect all sums due in said lists before judgment, and shall pay over the same to the State treasury to the credit of the " Union Military Fund." He shall certify to the commanding officer of the district the names of all persons who fail to pay the amount stated against them in said lists, or who have no property whereof to levy such execution. An i the commanding officer of the district shall arrest and put at labor the persons mentioned in the last named list until the amounts due by them are paid. And it shall be the duty of the

Circuit Attorney of the proper circuit to prosecute all such matters as shall come before the said court by virtue of this section. *Mo.*, 367.

—The sum of fifty cents per day shall be reckoned to every person put at labor, under the provisions of this ordinance, until the fine or penalty due by him is fully paid. *Mo.*, 367.

—The uniform of the Missouri militia shall be the same as prescribed by the United States Army Regulations for the army of the United States, until otherwise ordered by the Commander-in-Chief. *Mo.*, 367.

—All officers when on duty, shall wear the uniform of their rank, and no person not in the military service of the State or the United States, shall wear any insignia of rank, or any part of uniform, under a penalty of twenty dollars for every offense, to be recovered by suit and summary trial before any Justice of the Peace. *Mo.*, 367.

—The pay of the militia shall be the same for officers and men as allowed for the time by the United States to officers and soldiers, and fifty cents for each day's service of his horse, when he is mounted ; and such pay shall be in the same funds in which the United States Volunteers are paid, or their equivalent. *Mo.* 368.

—All taxes levied and collected for military purposes, and all fines imposed upon militiamen by this ordinance, all proceeds of the sale of contraband or captured property, seized or captured by the militia, and all other appropriations and levies made for the benefit of the militia, shall likewise be paid into the treasury, to the credit of the said union military fund. Out of said fund shall be paid, first, all sums now due the enrolled Missouri militia for services rendered, and union military bonds now outstanding or hereafter issued, and second, all expenses incurred according to law, and audited by the proper officers, and appropriations for military purposes, as other claims against the State. *Mo.*, 368.

—The Governor of the State shall lay before the General Assembly, at each regular session thereof, a report of the moneys expended for militia purposes, and an estimate of the funds necessary for support of the militia for the next two years. *Mo.*, 368.

—The Commander-in-Chief may assign to duty as paymasters, such officers as may to him seem proper, not exceeding four (4) in number, with the rank and pay of majors of infantry, and require them, before entering upon the discharge of the duties of the office, to execute a bond in a sum and with such securities as he shall order, conditioned for the faithful performance of their duty. *Mo.*, 368.

—Any officer, civil or military, who may refuse to account for and pay over, according to law, any moneys or property coming to his hands belonging to the militia fund, shall, upon conviction thereof in the Circuit or Criminal Court, on indictment, be sentenced to imprisonment in the penitentiary for a term of not less than five nor more than ten years. *Mo.*, 368.

—Courts-Martial shall be constituted and shall proceed in all cases, and be governed by the laws and regulations prescribed for the United States Army. *Mo* , 368.

—The General Assembly of this State shall provide the ways and means for the payment of the Missouri militia, and may, at any time, amend or repeal this ordinance. *Mo.*, 368.

—The Legislature shall determine what persons shall constitute the militia of the State, and may provide for organizing and disciplining the same, in such manner as shall be prescribed by law. *Neb.*, 373.

—The Legislature shall provide by law for organizing and disciplining the militia of this State, for the effectual encouragement of volunteer corps, and the safe keeping of the public arms. *Nev.*, 391.

—The division of the militia into brigades, regiments and companies, made in pursuance of the militia laws now in force, shall be considered as the proper division of the militia of this State, until the same shall be altered by some future law. *N. H.*, 406.

—All public boards, the commissary-general, all superintending officers of public magazines, and

1 § 2. Militia officers shall be chosen or appointed as follows: Captains, sub-

2 alterns and non-commissioned officers shall be chosen by the written votes of

3 the members of their respective companies; field officers of regiments and

4 separate battalions, by the written votes of the commissioned officers of the

5 respective regiments and separate battalions; Brigadier-Generals and Brigade

6 Inspectors by the field officers of their respective brigades; Major-Generals,

7 Brigadier-Generals and commanding officers of regiments or separate battal-

8 ions, shall appoint the staff officers to their respective divisions, brigades,

9 regiments or separate battalions.

stores, belonging to this State, and all commanding officers of forts and garrisons within the same, shall, once in every three months, officially, and without requisition, and at other times when required by the Governor, deliver to him an account of all goods, stores, provisions, ammunition, cannon with their appendages, and all small arms with their accoutre-ments, and of all other public property under their care respectively; distinguishing the quantity and kind of each as particularly as may be, together with the condition of such forts and garrisons; and the commanding officer shall exhibit to the Governor, when required by him, true and exact plans of such forts, and of the land and sea, or harbor or harbors adjacent. *N. H.*, 407.

—The Legislature shall provide by law for enrolling, organizing, and arming the militia. *N. J.*, 418.

—All white male citizens, residents of this State, being eighteen years of age, and under the age of forty-five years, shall be enrolled in the militia, and perform military duty, in such manner, not incompatible with the Constitution and laws of the United States, as may be prescribed by law. *Ohio*, 440.

—The Governor shall commission all officers of the line and staff, ranking as such; and shall have power to call forth the militia, to execute the laws of the State, to suppress insurrection and repel invasion. *Ohio*, 440.

—The General Assembly shall provide, by law, for the protection and safe keeping of the public arms. *Ohio*, 440.

—The Legislative Assembly shall fix by law the method of dividing the militia into divisions, bri-gades, regiments, battalions and companies, and make all other needful rules and regulations in such man-ner as they may deem expedient, not incompatible with the Constitution or laws of the United States, or of the Constitution of this State, and shall fix the rank of all staff officers. *Or.*, 456.

—The freemen of this Commonwealth shall be armed, organized, and disciplined for its defense, when and in such manner as may be directed by law. Those who conscientiously scruple to bear arms, shall not be compelled to do so, but shall pay an equivalent for personal service. *Pa.*, 465.

—All militia officers shall be elected by persons sub-ject to military duty within the bounds of their several companies, battalions, regiments, brigades and divisions, under such rules and regulations as the legislature may, from time to time, direct and estab-lish. *Tenn.*, 497.

—The inhabitants of this State shall be trained and armed for its defense, under such regulations, restric-tions and exceptions, as Congress, agreeably to the Constitution of the United States, and the Legislature of this State shall direct. The several companies of militia shall, as often as vacancies happen, elect their captain and other officers, and the captains and sub-alterns shall nominate and recommend the field

officers of their respective regiments, who shall appoint their staff officers. *Vt.*, 525.

—The Legislature shall determine what persons shall constitute the militia of the State, and may provide for organizing and disciplining the same in such man-ner as shall be prescribed by law. *Wis.*, 563.

ELECTION OR APPOINTMENT OF MILITIA

OFFICERS.

—That all military officers be appointed during pleasure; that all commissioned officers, civil and military, be commissioned by the Governor; and that the Chancellor, the Judges of the Supreme Court, and the first Judge of the County Court in every county, hold their offices during good behavior, or until they shall have respectivley attained the age of fifty years. *N. Y.* (1777), 30.

[The provisions of Art. XI, §§ 2, 4, 5 and 6 are copied from the Constitution of 1821, except the words "Brigade Inspectors," which were introduced in 1846.] *P.* 38.

—The Governor shall nominate, and with the con-sent of the Senate appoint, all Major-Generals, brigade inspectors, and chiefs of the staff departments, except the Adjutant-General and Commissary-General. The Adjutant-General shall be appointed by the Governor. *N. Y.* (1821), 38.

—No other officers than Adjutant-Generals and Quartermaster-Generals shall be appointed by the General Assembly. *And provided further*, that Major-Generals shall appoint their aids and all division and staff officers, Brigadier-Generals shall appoint their aids and all other brigade staff officers, and Colonels shall appoint their regimental staff officers. *Ala.*, 78.

—The Governor shall appoint the Adjutant-General and other members of his staff; Major-Generals, Brigadier-Generals, and commanders of regiments, shall respectively appoint their own staff; and all commissioned officers may continue in office during good behavior, and staff officers during the same time, subject to be removed by the superior officer from whom they respectively derive their commissions. *Ark.*, 90.

—Officers of the militia shall be elected or appointed, in such a manner as the Legislature shall from time to time direct, and shall be commissioned by the Gov-ernor. *Cal.*, 102; (nearly similar), *Fl.*, 137; *Kan.*, 203.

—Officers of the militia shall be elected or appointed, and be commissioned in such manner as may be pro-vided by law. *Mich.*, 314.

—No commission shall be vacated except by sentence of a court-martial. *Fl.*, 137.

—All militia and county officers shall be elected by the people, under such regulations as have been or may be prescribed by law. *Va.*, 150.

51

—Company, battalion, and regimental officers, staff officers excepted, shall be elected by the persons composing their several companies, battalions, and regiments. *Ill.*, 163.

—Brigadier and Major-Generals shall be elected by the officers of their brigades and divisions, respectively. *Ill.*, 163.

—All militia officers shall be commissioned by the Governor, and may hold their commissions for such time as the Legislature may provide. *Ill.*, 163.

—The Governor shall appoint the Adjutant, Quartermaster, and Commissary-General. *Ind.*, 180.

—All militia officers shall be commissioned by the Governor, and shall hold their offices not longer than six years. *Ind.*, 180.

—All commissioned officers of the militia, (staff officers excepted), shall be elected by the persons liable to perform military duty, and shall be commissioned by the Governor. *Iowa*, 190.

—The Governor shall appoint the Adjutant-General and his other staff officers; the Major-Generals, Brigadier-Generals, and commandants of regiments, shall respectively appoint their staff officers; and commandants of companies shall appoint their non-commissioned officers. *Ky.*, 219; *Tenn.*, 498.

—All militia officers, whose appointment is not herein otherwise provided for, shall be elected by persons subject to military duty, within their respective companies, battalions, regiments, brigades, and divisions, under such rules and regulations, and for such terms, not exceeding six years, as the General Assembly may, from time to time, direct and establish. *Ky.*, 219.

—The Captains and subalterns of the militia shall be elected by the written votes of the members of their respective companies. The field officers of regiments by the written votes of the Captains and subalterns of their respective regiments. The Brigadier-Generals, in like manner, by the field officers of their respective brigades. *Me.*, 246.

—The Major-General shall be elected by the Senate and House of Representatives, each having a negative on the other. The Adjutant-General and Quartermaster-General shall be appointed by the Governor and Council; but the Adjutant-General shall perform the duties of Quartermaster-General, until otherwise directed by law. The Major-Generals and Brigadier-Generals, and the commanding officers of regiments and battalions shall appoint their respective staff officers; and all military officers shall be commissioned by the Governor. *Me.*, 246.

—And he shall also nominate, and with the advice and consent of the Council, appoint all other civil and military officers whose appointment is not, by this Constitution, or shall not by law, be otherwise provided for; and every such nomination shall be made seven days at least prior to such appointment. *Me.*, 244.

—There shall be an Adjutant-General, who shall be appointed by the Governor, by and with the advice and consent of the Senate. He shall hold his office at the pleasure of the Governor; shall perform such duties, and shall receive such compensation or emoluments as are now or may be hereafter fixed by law. *Md.*, 275.

—And no officer, duly commissioned to command in the militia, shall be removed from his office, but by the address of both Houses to the Governor, or by fair trial in court-martial, pursuant to the laws of the Commonwealth for the time being. *Mass.*, 288.

—The Major-Generals shall be appointed by the Senate and House of Representatives, each having a negative upon the other; and be commissioned by the Governor. *Mass.*, 288.

—And if the electors of brigadiers, field officers, captains or subalterns shall neglect or refuse to make such elections, after being duly notified, according to the laws for the time being, then the Governor, with the advice of Council, shall appoint suitable persons to fill such offices. *Mass.*, 288.

—The commanding officers of regiments shall appoint their adjutants and quartermasters; the brigadiers

their brigade-majors; and the major-generals their aids; and the Governor shall appoint the Adjutant-General. *Mass.*, 288.

—Whenever the exigencies of the Commonwealth shall require the appointment of a Commissary-General, he shall be nominated, appointed, and commissioned, in such manner as the Legislature may, by law, prescribe. *Mass.*, 294.

—All officers commissioned to command in the militia, may be removed from office in such manner as the Legislature may, by law, prescribe. *Mass.*, 294.

—In the elections of captains and subalterns of the militia, all the members of their respective companies, as well those under as those above the age of twenty-one years, shall have a right to vote. *Mass.*, 294.

—Commissioned officers of the militia (staff officers and the officers of volunteer companies excepted), shall be elected by the persons liable to perform military duty, and the qualified electors within their respective commands, and shall be commissioned by the Governor. *Miss.*, 342.

—Each company and regiment shall elect its own company and regimental officers; but if any company or regiment shall neglect to elect such officers within the time prescribed by law, or by the order of the Governor, they may be appointed by the Governor. *Mo.*, 361.

—The said election shall be conducted, and the returns thereof made to the clerks of the several County Courts, and by them immediately certified to the Secretary of State, as provided by law in the case of elections of State officers; and where an election shall be held in a regiment or company, the returns thereof, with the poll books, shall be certified to the Secretary of State, and may be transmitted by mail, or by any messenger to whom the judges of the election may intrust the same for that purpose. *Mo.*, 363.

—The Governor shall nominate, and by and with the advice and the consent of the Senate, appoint two Brigadier-Generals, and no more, and as many Colonels, Lieutenant-Colonels and Majors as may be necessary for properly disciplining and governing the force organized under this ordinance; *Provided, however,* That the officers and men thus commissioned and organized shall not be entitled to, nor receive any pay, rations or emoluments, when not in actual service. *Mo.*, 366.

—The staff of the Commander-in-Chief shall be an Adjutant-General, with the rank and pay of Colonel of cavalry; a Quartermaster-General, an Inspector-General and a Commissary-General, each with the rank and pay of a Colonel of cavalry; a Paymaster-General, with the rank and pay of Lieutenant-Colonel of infantry; a Surgeon-General, with the rank and pay of Colonel of infantry; a Judge-Advocate-General, with the rank and pay of Lieutenant-Colonel of infantry; three aids-de-camp, with the rank and pay of Major of infantry. He may detail from the line and field officers of any regiment such officers as he may deem proper, and assign them to duty on his staff. *Mo.*, 366.

—The captains and subalterns in the respective regiments shall be nominated and recommended by the field officers to the Governor, who is to issue their commissions immediately on receipt of such recommendations. *N. H.*, 406.

—No officer duly commissioned to command in the militia, shall be removed from his office but by the address of both Houses to the Governor, or by fair trial in court-martial, pursuant to the laws of the State for the time being. *N. H.*, 406.

—The commanding officers of the regiment shall appoint their adjutants and quartermasters; the brigadiers, their brigade majors; the major-generals, their aids; the captains and subalterns, their non-commissioned officers. *N. H.*, 406.

—The Governor shall classify and arrange the aforesaid returned list, and shall make therefrom separate lists of the electors belonging to each regiment, battalion, squadron and battery, from said Territory in the service of the United States, and shall, on or

1 § 3. The Governor shall nominate, and, with the consent of the Senate,

2 appoint all Major-Generals, and the Commissary-General. The Adjutant-

3 General and other chiefs of staff departments, and the Aides-de-Camp of the Com-

4 mander-in-Chief, shall be appointed by the Governor, and their commissions

5 shall expire with the time for which the Governor shall have been elected. The

6 Commissary-General shall hold his office for two years. He shall give security

7 for the faithful execution of the duties of his office, in such manner and

8 amount as shall be prescribed by law.

1 § 4. The Legislature shall, by law, direct the time and manner of electing

2 militia officers, and of certifying their elections to the Governor.

---

before the fifteenth day of August following, transmit, by mail or otherwise, to the commanding officer of each regiment, battalion, squadron and battery, a list of electors belonging thereto, which said list shall specify the name, residence and rank of each elector, and the company to which he belongs, if to any, and also the county and township to which he belongs, and in which he is entitled to vote. *Nev.*, 397.
—Between the hours of nine o'clock, A. M. and three o'clock, P. M., on each of the election days hereinbefore named, a ballot box, or suitable receptacle for votes, shall be opened, under the immediate charge and direction of three of the highest officers in command, for the reception of votes from the electors whose names are upon said list, at each place where a regiment, battalion, squadron, or battery of soldiers from the said Territory, may be on that day, at which time and place said electors shall be entitled to vote for all officers for which, by reason of their residence in the several counties in the said Territory, they are authorized to vote, as fully as they would be entitled to vote in the several counties or townships in which they reside, and the votes so given by such electors at such time and place, shall be considered, taken and held to have been given by them in the respective townships in which they are resident. *Nev.*, 397.
—Captains, subalterns, and non-commissioned officers shall be elected by the members of their respective companies. *N. J.*, 418.
—Field officers of regiments, independent battalions, and squadrons, shall be elected by the commissioned officers of their respective regiments, battalions, or squadrons. *N. J.*, 418.
—Brigadier-Generals shall be elected by the field officers of their respective brigades. *N. J.*, 418.
—Major-Generals shall be nominated by the Governor, and appointed by him, with the advice and consent of the Senate. *N. J.*, 418.
—The Legislature shall provide, by law, the time and manner of electing militia officers, and of certifying their elections to the Governor, who shall grant their commissions and determine their rank, when not determined by law; and no commissioned officer shall be removed from office but by the sentence of a court-martial pursuant to law. *N. J.*, 418.
—In case the electors of subalterns, captains, or field officers, shall refuse or neglect to make such elections, the Governor shall have power to appoint such officers, and to fill all vacancies caused by such refusal or neglect. *N. J.*, 418.
——Brigade inspectors shall be chosen by the field officers of their respective brigades. *N. J.*, 418.
—The Governor shall appoint the Adjutant-General, Quartermaster-General, and all other militia officers whose appointment is not otherwise provided for in this Constitution. *N. J.*, 418.

—Major-Generals, Brigadier-Generals, and commanding officers of regiments, independent battalions, and squadrons shall appoint the staff officers of their divisions, brigades, regiments, independent battalions and squadrons, respectively. *N. J.*, 419.
—The General Assembly shall have power to pass laws regulating the mode of appointing and removing militia officers. *N. C.*, 428.
—Majors-General, Brigadiers-General, Colonels, Lieutenant-Colonels, Majors, Captains, and subalterns, shall be elected by the persons subject to military duty, in their respective districts. *Ohio*, 440.
—The Governor shall appoint the Adjutant-General, Quartermaster-General, and such other staff officers as may be provided for by law. Majors-General, Brigadiers-General, Colonels or Commandants of regiments, battalions, or squadrons, shall, severally, appoint their staff, and Captains shall appoint their non-commissioned officers and musicians. *Ohio*, 440.
—The Major-Generals, Brigadier-Generals, Colonels, or commandants of regiments, battalions, or squadrons, shall severally appoint their staff officers, and the Governor shall commission all officers of the line and staff ranking as such. *Or.*, 456.
—The Governor shall appoint the Adjutant-General and the other chief officers of the general staff and his own staff, and all officers of the line shall be elected by the persons subject to military duty in their respective districts. *Or.*, 456.
—The manner of appointing militia officers shall be prescribed by law. *Va.*, 540.
- -The Governor shall nominate and by and with the advice and consent of the Senate appoint all military officers above the rank of Colonel. *W. Va.*, 552.

EXEMPTIONS FROM MILITIA SERVICE.

—That all such of the inhabitants of this State (being of the people called Quakers) as, from scruples of conscience, may be averse to the bearing of arms, be therefrom excused by the Legislature; and to pay to the State, such sums of money in lieu of their personal service, as the same may, in the judgment of the Legislature, be worth. *N. Y.* (1777), 33.
—The militia shall in all cases, except treason, felony, or breach of the peace, be privileged from arrest during their attendance at musters and elections of officers, and in going to and returning from the same. *Ill.*, 163.
—But all citizens of any religious denomination whatever, who, from scruples of conscience, may be averse to bearing arms, shall be exempted therefrom, upon such conditions as may be prescribed by law. *Kan.*, 203.
—But those who belong to religious societies, whose tenets forbid them to carry arms, shall not be com-

1   § 5. The commissioned officers of the militia shall be commissioned by the

2 Governor; and no commissioned officer shall be removed from office, unless by

3 the Senate on the recommendation of the Governor, stating the grounds on

4 which such removal is recommended, or by the decision of a court-martial,

5 pursuant to law. The present officers of the militia shall hold their commis-

6 sions subject to removal as before provided.

1   § 6. In case the mode of election and appointment of militia officers hereby

2 directed, shall not be found conducive to the improvement of the militia, the

3 Legislature may abolish the same and provide by law for their appointment

4 and removal, if two-thirds of the members present in each House shall concur

5 therein.

pelled to do so, but shall pay an equivalent for personal services. *Ky.*, 219.

— Persons of the denomination of Quakers and Shakers, Justices of the Supreme Judicial Court, and ministers of the gospel, may be exempted from military duty; but no other person, of the age of eighteen and under the age of forty-five years, excepting officers of the militia who have been honorably discharged, shall be so exempted, unless he shall pay an equivalent, to be fixed by law. *Me.*, 246.

—But persons whose religious opinions and conscientious scruples forbid them to bear arms shall be relieved from doing so on producing to the proper authorities satisfactory proof that they are thus conscientious. *Md.*, 275.

—But all such citizens of any religious denomination whatever, who, from scruples of conscience, may be averse to bearing arms, shall be excused therefrom, upon such conditions as shall be prescribed by law. *Mich.*, 313.

— Persons over the age of forty-five years, and under the age of eighteen years; United States mail carriers, when actually employed as such; United States and State officers; one miller to each public mill, and an engineer for the same, when actually employed in said capacity; teachers of public schools; ministers of the Gospel; regular practicing physicians, and railroad employees, shall be exempt from duty in the militia, and shall be entitled to, and receive from the "enrolling officer," a "certificate" to that effect, on producing to said "enrolling officer" satisfactory evidence of their respective avocations or employments. *Mo.*, 366.

—The Surgeon-General shall appoint a physician or surgeon for each county to examine persons claiming exemption, who shall give to every person exempted by him a certificate, and shall return to the office of the Adjutant of the district, within five days after the close of each of his sittings, a complete list of all persons so exempted. The physician or surgeon so employed shall receive the pay of a Major of infantry while actually engaged in such service. *Mo.*, 367.

—Any physician or surgeon authorized by the provisions of this ordinance to issue certificates of exemption, who shall fraudulently issue any such certificates, shall be liable to a fine of not less than five hundred dollars, to be recovered by indictment before the Circuit Court of the proper county, except St. Louis county, where the indictment shall be before the Criminal Court. *Mo.*, 367.

ARTICLE XII.

1   SECTION 1. Members of the Legislature, and all officers, executive and

2 judicial, except such inferior officers as may be by law exempted, shall, before

3 they enter on the duties of their respective offices, take and subscribe the

4 following oath or affirmation:

5   " I do solemnly swear (or affirm, as the case may be) that I will support the

6 Constitution of the United States, and the Constitution of the State of New

7 York; and that I will faithfully discharge the duties of the office of

8 according to the best of my ability."

9   And no other oath, declaration or test, shall be required as a qualification

10 for any office or public trust.

OATHS.

[Under the New York Constitution of 1777, an an oath or affirmation of allegiance to the State was required of electors, but no oath of office was prescribed; the oath of office now required was introduced in 1821.]

—All civil officers of this State, legislative, executive, and judicial, before they enter upon the execution of the duties of their respective offices, shall take the following oath: "I solemnly swear" (or affirm, as the case may be), " that I will support the Constitution of the United States, and the Constitution of the State of —— so long as I continue a citizen thereof; and that I will faithfully discharge, to the best of my abilities, the duties of the office of —— so help me God." *Ala.*, 86; (nearly similar), *Ct.*, 113.

—Members of the Legislature, and all officers, executive and judicial, except such inferior officers as may be by law exempted, shall, before they enter on the duties of their respective offices, take and subscribe the following oath or affirmation: "I do solemnly swear" (or affirm, as the case may be) "that I will support the Constitution of the United States, and the Constitution of the State of ——, and that I will faithfully discharge the duties of the office of ——, according to the best of my ability." And no other oath, declaration or test, shall be required as a qualification for any office or public trust. *Cal.*, 104; *Iowa*, 187; *Mich.*, 314; *Miss.*, 342; *N. J.*, 415; *Or.*, 452.

—All persons thus declared to be State officers, shall enter upon the discharge of their respective offices as soon thereafter as they take and subscribe an oath before any Justice of the Peace, or other officer authorized to administer oaths, as follows: That they will faithfully perform the duties of their respective offices; that they will support the Constitution and laws of the State and of the United States; and said oath, in case of State officers, shall be filed in the office of the Secretary of State; and in case of county officers, they shall enter upon the duties of their respective offices immediately after the election upon filing said oath with the county commissioners. *Ark.*, 94.

—Members of the General Assembly and all officers, executive and judicial, shall be bound by oath or affirmation, to support the Constitution of this State, and to perform the duties of their respective offices with fidelity. *Del.*, 126.

—Members of the General Assembly, and all officers, civil or military, before they enter upon the execution of their respective offices, shall take the following oath or affirmation: "I do swear (or affirm) that I am duly qualified according to the Constitution of

this State, to exercise the office to which I have been elected (or appointed), and will to the best of my abilities, discharge the duties thereof, and preserve, protect and defend the Constitution of this State, and of the United States of America." *Fl.*, 136.

—The oaths of officers directed to be taken under this Constitution, may be administered by any judge, or justice of the peace, in the State of Florida, until until otherwise provided by law. *Fl.*, 140.

—The Governor shall, before he enters on the duties of his office, take the following oath or affirmation : " I do solemnly swear or affirm (as the case may be), that I will faithfully execute the office of Governor of the State of ——; and will, to the best of my abilities, preserve, protect and defend the Constitution thereof, and of the Constitution of the United States of America." *Ga.*, 147; (nearly similar), *Ill.*, 158.

—Every Senator and Representative, before taking his seat, shall take an oath or affirmation to support the Constitution of the United States and of this State; and also that he hath not practiced any unlawful means, either directly or indirectly, to procure his election. And every person convicted of having given or offered a bribe, shall be disqualified from serving as a member of either House for the term for which he was elected. *Ga.*, 145.

—Every person elected or appointed to any office under this Constitution shall, before entering on the duties thereof, take an oath or affirmation to support the Constitution of this State and of the United States, and also an oath of office. *Ill.*, 154; *Iowa*, 194; *Ohio*, 443; *Or.*, 458; *Tenn.*, 498.

—Members of the General Assembly are hereby empowered to administer to each other the oath or affirmation. *Iowa*, 187.

—All State officers, before entering upon their respective duties, shall take and subscribe an oath or affirmation to support the Constitution of the United States and the Constitution of this State, and faithfully to discharge the duties of their respective offices. *Kan.*, 199.

—Members of the General Assembly and all officers, before they enter upon the duties of their offices shall take the following oath or affirmation: " I, A. B., do solemnly swear (or affirm) that I will support the Constitution and laws of the United States, and of this State, and that I will faithfully and impartially discharge and perform all the duties incumbent on me as ——, according to the best of my abilities and understanding, so help me God !" *La.*, 232.

—Members of the General Assembly, and all officers, before they enter upon the execution of the duties of their respective offices, and all members of the bar, before they enter upon the practice of their

52

profession, shall take the following oath or affirmation :
" I do solemnly swear (or affirm, as the case may be),
that I will support the Constitution of the United
States, and the Constitution of this State, and be
faithful and true to the Commonwealth of ——, so
long as I continue a citizen thereof, and that I will
faithfully execute, to the best of my abilities, the
office of ——, according to law ; and I do further
solemnly swear (or affirm), that since the adoption of
the present Constitution, I, being a citizen of this
State, have not fought a duel, with deadly weapons,
within this State or out of it, with a citizen of this
State, nor have I sent or accepted a challenge to
fight a duel with deadly weapons, with a citizen of
this State ; nor have I acted as second in carrying a
challenge, or aided, or assisted any person thus
offending—so help me God." *Ky.* 219; (nearly similar), *Tex.* 514.
- The oaths of office herein directed to be taken
may be administered by any Judge or Justice of the
Peace, until the General Assembly shall otherwise
direct. *Ky.*, 224.
—The General Assembly shall pass laws requiring the president, directors, trustees or agents of corporations, created or authorized by the laws of this
State, teachers, or superintendents of public schools,
colleges or other institutions of learning ; attorneys-
at-law, jurors and such other persons as the General
Assembly shall from time to time prescribe, to take
the oath of allegiance to the United States set forth
in the first article of this Constitution. *Md.*, 264.
—And every person chosen to either of the places or
offices aforesaid, as also any person appointed or commissioned to any judicial, executive, military or other
office under the government, shall, before he enters
on the discharge of the business of his place or office,
take and subscribe the following declaration and oaths
or affirmations, viz. : *Mass.*, 291.
—" I, A. B., do solemnly swear, that I will bear true
faith and allegiance to the Commonwealth of Massachusetts, and will support the Constitution thereof.
So help me God." *Mass.*, 294.
—*Provided*, That when any person shall be of the
denomination called Quakers, and shall decline taking
said oath, he shall make his affirmation in the foregoing form, omitting the word "swear," and inserting,
instead thereof, the word " affirm," and omitting the
words, " so help me, God," and subjoining, instead
thereof, the words "This I do under the pains and
penalties of perjury." *Mass.*, 294.
—No oath, declaration, or subscription, excepting the
oath prescribed in the preceding article, and the oath
of office, shall be required of the Governor, Lieutenant-Governor, Councillors, Senators, or Representatives, to qualify them to perform the duties of their
respective offices. *Mass.*, 291.
—" I, A. B., do solemnly swear and affirm that I will
faithfully and impartially discharge and perform all
the duties incumbent on me as ——, according to the
best of my abilities and understanding, agreeably to
the rules and regulations of the Constitution and
the laws of the Commonwealth, so help me God."
Mass., 291.
—And the said oaths or affirmations shall be taken
and subscribed by the Governor, Lieutenant-Governor and Councillors, before the President of the
Senate, in the presence of the two Houses of Assembly ; and by the Senators and Representatives first
elected under this Constitution, before the President
and five of the Council of the former Constitution ;
and forever afterwards before the Governor and
Council for the time being ; and by the residue of the
officers aforesaid, before such persons, and in such
manner as from time to time shall be prescribed by
the Legislature. *Mass.*, 291.
—Every person elected or appointed to either of the
places or offices provided in this Constitution, and
every person, elected, appointed, or commissioned to
any judicial, executive, military, or other office under
this State, shall, before he enters on the discharge of
the duties of his place or office, take and subscribe
the following oath or affirmation : "I, ——, do swear,

that I will support the Constitution of the United
States and of this State, so long as I shall continue a
citizen thereof. So help me God."
"I, ——, do swear, that I will faithfully discharge,
to the best of my abilities, the duties incumbent on
me as ——, according to the Constitution and the
laws of the State. So help me God." *Provided*,
That an affirmation in the above forms may be sub-
stituted, when the persons shall be conscientiously
scrupulous of taking and subscribing an oath.
The oaths or affirmations shall be taken and subscribed by the Governor and Counsellors before the
presiding officer of the Senate, in the presence of
both Houses of the Legislature, and by the Senators
and Representatives before the Governor and Council, and by the residue of said officers before such person as shall be prescribed by the Legislature ; and,
whenever the Governor or any Counsellor shall not
be able to attend, during the session of the Legislature, to take and subscribe said oaths or affirmations,
such oaths or affirmations may be taken and subscribed, in the recess of the Legislature, before any
Justice of the Supreme Judicial Court ; *Provided*,
That the Senators and Representatives first elected
under this Constitution shall take and subscribe such
oaths or affirmations before the President of the Convention. *Me.*, 247.
—All members and officers of both branches of the
Legislature shall, before entering upon the duties of
their respective trusts, take and subscribe an oath or
affirmation to support the Constitution of the United
States, the Constitution of the State of ——, and
faithfully and impartially to discharge the duties de-
volving upon him as such member or officer. *Minn.*,
323.
—Each officer created by this article shall, before
entering upon his duties, take an oath or affirmation
to support the Constitution of the United States, and
of this State, and faithfully discharge the duties of his
office to the best of his judgment and ability. *Minn.*,
324.
—The Legislature shall provide for a uniform oath or
affirmation to be administered at elections ; and no
person shall be compelled to take any other or different form of oath to entitle him to vote. *Minn.*, 329.
—Within sixty days after this Constitution takes
effect, every person in this State holding any office
of honor, trust, or profit under the Constitution or
laws thereof, or under any municipal corporation, or
any of the other offices, positions, or trusts mentioned
in the third section of this article, shall take and subscribe the said oath. If any officer or person referred
to in this section shall fail to comply with the requirements thereof, his office, position, or trust shall, *ipso
facto*, become vacant, and the vacancy shall be filled
according to the law governing the case. *Mo.*, 350.
—The oath to be taken as aforesaid shall be known
as the Oath of Loyalty, and shall be in the following
terms : *Mo.*, 349.
"I, A. B., do solemnly swear, that I am well ac-
quainted with the terms of the third section of the
second article of the Constitution of the State of ——,
adopted in the year 1865, and have carefully considered the same ; that I have never, directly or indirectly, done any of the acts in said section specified ;
that I have always been truly and loyally on the
side of the United States against all enemies thereof,
foreign and domestic : that I will bear true faith
and allegiance to the United States, and will support
the Constitution and laws thereof, as the supreme
law of the land, any law or ordinance of any State
to the contrary notwithstanding ; that I will, to the
best of my ability, protect and defend the Union of
the United States, and not allow the same to be
broken up and dissolved, or the Government thereof
to be destroyed or overthrown, under any circumstances, if in my power to prevent it; that I will
support the Constitution of the State of ——, and
that I make this oath without mental reservation or
evasion, and hold it to be binding on me."
—Members of the Legislature, and all officers, executive and judicial, except such inferior officers as may

be by law exempted, shall, before they enter upon the duties of their respective offices, take and subscribe an oath or affirmation to support the Constitution of the United States, and the Constitution of the State of——, and faithfully to discharge the duties of their respective offices to the best of their ability. *Neb.*, 373.

—Members of the Legislature, and all officers, executive, judicial and ministerial, shall, before they enter upon the duties of their respective offices, take and subscribe to the following oath or affirmation: I, ——, do solemnly swear (or affirm), that I will support, protect and defend the Constitution and government of the United States, and the Constitution and government of the State of ——, against all enemies, whether domestic or foreign; and that I will bear true faith, allegiance and loyalty to the same, any ordinance, resolution, or law of any State, Convention or Legislature, to the contrary notwithstanding; and further, that I do this with a full determination, pledge and promise, without any mental reservation or evasion whatsoever. And I do further solemnly swear (or affirm), that I have not fought a duel, nor sent or accepted a challenge to fight a duel, nor been a second to either party, nor in any manner aided or assisted in such duel, nor been knowingly the bearer of such challenge or acceptance, since the Constitution of the State of ——, and that I will not be so engaged or concerned, directly or indirectly, in or about such duel, during my continuance in office. And further, that I will well and faithfully perform all the duties of the office of ——, on which I am about to enter; (if on oath), so help me God; (if on affirmation), under the pains and penalties of perjury." *Nev.*, 391.

—Any person chosen Governor, Councillor, Senator or Representative, military or civil officer, (town officers excepted) accepting the trust, shall, before he proceeds to execute the duties of his office, make and subscribe to the following declaration, viz. :

I, A. B., do solemnly swear that I will bear true faith and true allegiance to the State of——, and will support the Constitution thereof. So help me God.

I, A. B., do solemnly and sincerely swear and affirm that I will faithfully and impartially discharge and perform all the duties incumbent on me as , according to the best of my abilities; agreeable to the rules and regulations of this Constitution, and the laws of the State of —— So help me God.

Any person having taken and subscribed the oath of allegiance, and the same being filed in the Secretary's office, he shall not be obliged to take said oath again :

Provided, always, When any person, chosen or appointed as aforesaid, shall be of the denomination called Quakers, or shall be scrupulous of swearing, and shall decline taking the said oaths, such person shall take and subscribe them, omitting the word "swear," and likewise the words, "So help me God," subjoining instead thereof, "This I do under the pains and penalties of perjury." *N. H.*, 409.

—And the oaths or affirmation shall be taken and subscribed by the Governor, before the President of the Senate, in presence of both Houses of the Legislature, and by the Senators and Representatives first elected under this Constitution, as altered and amended, before the President of the State and a majority of the Council then in office, and forever afterward before the Governor and Council for the time being; and by all other officers, before such persons and in such manner as the Legislature shall from time to time appoint. *N. H.*, 409.

—And members elect of the Senate or General Assembly are hereby empowered to administer to each other the said oath or affirmation. *N. J.*, 415.

—The Governor elect shall enter on the duties of the office on the first day of January next after his election, having previously taken the oaths of office in presence of the members of both branches of the General Assembly, or before the Chief Justice of the Supreme Court, who, in case the Governor elect

should be prevented from attendance before the General Assembly, by sickness or other unavoidable cause, is authorized to administer the same. *N. C.*, 429.

—That every person who shall be chosen a member of the Senate or House of Commons, or appointed to any office or place of trust, before taking his seat, or entering upon the execution of his office, shall take an oath to the State; and all officers shall take an oath of office. *N. C.*, 424.

—And such oath may be administered by the Governor, Secretary of State, or a Judge of the Supreme Court. *Or.*, 452.

—Every Judge of the Supreme Court, before entering upon the duties of his office, shall take and subscribe, and transmit to the Secretary of State the following oath :

"I —— ——, do solemnly swear (or affirm) that I will support the Constitution of the United States and the Constitution of the State of Oregon, and that I will faithfully and impartially discharge the duties of a Judge of the Supreme and Circuit Courts of said State according to the best of my ability, and that I will not accept any other office except judicial offices during the term for which I have been elected. *Or.*, 455.

—Members of the General Assembly, and officers executive and judicial, shall be bound by oath or affirmation to support the Constitution of this Commonwealth, and to perform the duties of their respective offices with fidelity. *Pa.*, 467.

– All general officers shall take the following engagement before they act in their respective offices, to wit: *R. I.*, 479.

You, —— ——, being by the free vote of the electors of this State of Rhode Island and Providence Plantations, elected unto the place of do solemnly swear (or affirm) to be true and faithful unto this State, and to support the Constitutions of this State and of the United States; that you will faithfully and impartially discharge all the duties of your aforesaid office to the best of your abilities, according to law ; so help your God. *R. I.*, 479.

Or, this affirmation you make and give upon the perils of the penalty of perjury. *R. I.*, 479.

—The oath or affirmation shall be administered to the Governor, Lieutenant-Governor, Senators and Representatives, by the Secretary of State, or, in his absence, by the Attorney-General. The Secretary of State, Attorney-General and General Treasurer, shall be engaged by the Governor, or by a Justice of the Supreme Court. *R. I.*, 479.

—The members of the General Assembly, the Judges of all the Courts, and all other officers, both civil and military, shall be bound by oath or affirmation to support this Constitution, and the Constitution of the United States. *R. I.*, 479.

—The Governor and the Lieutenant-Governor, before entering upon the duties of their respective offices, shall, in the presence of the General Assembly, take the oath of office prescribed in this Constitution. *S. C.*, 486.

—All persons who shall be elected or appointed to any office of profit or trust, before entering on the execution thereof, shall take, beside special oaths, not repugnant to this Constitution, prescribed by the General Assembly, the following oath : "I do swear (or affirm) that I am duly qualified, according to the Constitution of this State, to exercise the office to which I have been appointed, and that I will, to the best of my ability, discharge the duties thereof, and preserve, protect and defend the Constitution of this State, and that of the United States. So help me God." *S. C.*, 487.

—I solemnly swear that I will henceforth support the Constitution of the United States and defend it against the assaults of all its enemies; that I am an active friend of the government of the United States; and the enemy of the so-called Confederate States; that I ardently desire the suppression of the present rebellion against the government of the United States; that I sincerely rejoice in the triumph of the armies and navies of the United States, and in the defeat and overthrow of the armies, navies, and of all armed combinations in the so-called Confederate States; that I will cordially oppose all armistices or negotiations for peace with rebels in arms, until the Constitution of the United States, and all laws and proclamations made in pursuance thereof, shall be established over all the people of every State and Territory embraced within the National Union; and that I will heartily aid and assist the loyal people in whatever measures may be adopted for the attainment of those ends; and further, that I take this oath freely and voluntarily and without mental reservation. So help me God. *Tenn.*, 504.

—Each member of the Senate and House of Representatives shall, before they proceed to business, take an oath or affirmation to support the Constitution of this State, and of the United States, and also the following oath: "I, ——, do solemnly swear (or affirm), that, as a member of this General Assembly, I will, in all appointments, vote without favor, affection, partiality or prejudice ; and that I will not propose or assent to any bill, vote or resolution which shall appear to me injurious to the people, or consent to any act or thing whatever that shall have a tendency to lessen or abridge their rights and privileges, as declared by the Constitution of this State. *Tenn.*, 498.

—The Representatives having met and chosen their Speaker and Clerk, shall, each of them, before they proceed to business, take and subscribe, as well the oath or affirmation of allegiance hereinafter directed (except where they shall produce certificates of their having heretofore taken and subscribed the same), as the following oath or affirmation, viz.:

"You, do solemnly swear (or affirm) that as a member of this Assembly you will not propose or assent to any bill, vote, or resolution, which shall appear to you injurious to the people, nor do or consent to any act or thing whatever, that shall have a tendency to lessen or abridge their rights and privileges, as declared by the Constitution of this State ; but will in all things conduct yourselves as a faithful, honest Representative and guardian of the people, according to the best of your judgment and abilities. (In case of an oath)—So help you God, (and in case of an affirmation) under the pains and penalties of perjury." *Vt.*, 524.

"You do solemnly swear (or affirm) that you will be true and faithful to the State of Vermont, and that you will not, directly or indirectly, do any act or thing injurious to the Constitution or government thereof, as established by Convention. (If an oath), So help you God, (if an affirmation) under the pains and penalties of perjury." *Vt.*, 526.

"You do solemnly swear (or affirm) that you will faithfully execute the office of for the of and will therein do equal right and justice to all men, to the best of your judgment and abilities according to law. (If an oath), So help you God, (if an affirmation) under the pains and penalties of perjury." *Vt.*, 526.

—Every person elected or appointed to any office or trust, civil or military, shall, before proceeding to exercise the authority or discharge the duties of the same, make oath or affirmation that he will support the Constitution of the United States, and the Constitution of this State; and every citizen of this State may, in time of war, insurrection, or public danger, be required by law to make like oath or affirmation, upon pain of suspension of his right of voting and holding office under this Constitution. *W. Va.*, 548.

—Members of the Legislature and all officers, executive and judicial, except such inferior officers as may be by law exempted, shall, before they enter upon the duties of their respective offices, take and subscribe an oath or affirmation to support the Constitution of the United States, and the Constitution of the State of Wisconsin, and faithfully to discharge the duties of their respective offices to the best of their ability. *Wis.*, 563.

—The oath of office may be administered by any Judge or Justice of the Peace, until the Legislature shall otherwise direct. *Wis.*, 575.

—That the oaths of office herein required to be taken may be administered by a Justice of the Peace until otherwise provided for by law. *Ill.*, 167.

—No person shall assume the duties of any State, county, city, town or other office, to which he may be appointed, otherwise than by a vote of the people ; nor shall any person, after the expiration of sixty days after this Constitution takes effect, be permitted to practice as an attorney or counselor-at-law ; nor, after that time, shall any person be competent as a bishop, priest, deacon, minister, elder or other clergyman of any religious persuasion, sect or denomination, to teach or preach, or solemnize marriages, unless such person shall have first taken, subscribed and filed said oath [of allegiance to the United States and State.] *Mo.*, 350.

—In addition to the oath of loyalty aforesaid, every person who may be elected or appointed to any office shall, before entering upon its duties, take and subscribe an oath or affirmation that he will, to the best of his skill and ability, diligently and faithfully, without partiality or prejudice, discharge the duties of such office according to the Constitution and laws of this State. *Mo.*, 350.

—Whoever shall, after the times limited in the seventh and ninth sections of this article, hold or exercise any of the offices, positions, trusts, professions, or functions therein specified, without having taken, subscribed, and filed said oath of loyalty, shall, on conviction thereof, be punished by fine, not less than five hundred dollars, or by imprisonment in the county jail not less than six months, or by both such fine and imprisonment; and whoever shall take said oath falsely, by swearing or by affirmation, shall, on conviction thereof, be adjudged guilty of perjury, and be punished by imprisonment in the penitentiary not less than two years. *Mo.*, 350.

—Every person holding any office of trust or profit under the late Constitution, or under any law of this State, and who shall be continued in office under this Constitution, or under any law of this State, shall within thirty days after this Constitution shall have gone into effect take and subscribe the oath or affirmation set forth in the seventh section of this article, and if any such person shall fail to take said oath his office shall be *ipso facto* vacant. And every person hereafter elected or appointed to office in this State, who shall refuse or neglect to take the oath or affirmation of office provided for in the said seventh section of this article shall be considered as having refused to accept the said office, and a new election or appointment shall be made as in case of refusal to accept or resignation of an office. And any person swearing or affirming falsely in the premises shall, on conviction thereof in a court of law, incur the penalties for willful and corrupt perjury, and thereafter shall be incapable of holding any office of profit or trust in this State. *Md.*, 258.

—Every person elected or appointed to any office of trust or profit under this Constitution, or under the laws made pursuant thereto, before he shall enter upon the duties of such office, shall take and subscribe the following oath or affirmation: I, ——, do swear, (or affirm, as the case may be) that I will, to the best of my skill and judgment, diligently and faithfully, without partiality or prejudice, execute the office of ——; according to the Constitution and laws of this State, and that since the fourth day of July, in the year eighteen hundred and fifty-one, I have not in any manner violated the provisions of the present, or of the late Constitution, in relation to the bribery of voters, or preventing legal votes or procuring illegal votes to be given (and if a Governor, Senator, member of the House of Delegates, or Judge), that I will not, directly or indirectly, receive the profits or any part of the profits of any other office during the term of my acting as ——. I do further swear or affirm that I will bear true allegiance to the State of Maryland and support the Constitution and laws thereof, and that I will bear true allegiance to the United States, and support, protect and defend the Constitution, laws and government thereof, as the supreme

ARTICLE XIII.

1 Section 1. Any amendment or amendments to this Constitution may be
2 proposed in the Senate and Assembly; and if the same shall be agreed to by
3 a majority of the members elected to each of the two Houses, such proposed
4 amendment or amendments shall be entered on their journals with the yeas
5 and nays taken thereon, and referred to the Legislature to be chosen at the
6 next general election of Senators, and shall be published for three months
7 previous to the time of making such choice, and if in the Legislature so next
8 chosen as aforesaid, such proposed amendment or amendments shall be agreed
9 to by a majority of all the members elected to each House, then it shall be the
10 duty of the Legislature to submit such proposed amendment or amendments
11 to the people, in such manner and at such time as the Legislature shall pre-
12 scribe ; and if the people shall approve and ratify such amendment or amend-
13 ments, by a majority of the electors qualified to vote for members of the
14 Legislature voting thereon, such amendment or amendments shall become part
15 of the Constitution.

law of the land, any law or ordinance of this or any State to the contrary notwithstanding; that I have never directly or indirectly, by word, act or deed, given any aid, comfort or encouragement to those in rebellion against the United States or the lawful authorities thereof, but that I have been truly and loyally on the side of the United States against those in armed rebellion against the United States; and I do further swear (or affirm) that I will to the best of my abilities protect and defend the Union of the United States, and not allow the same to be broken up and dissolved, or the government thereof to be destroyed, under any circumstances, if in my power to prevent it, and that I will at all times discountenance and oppose all political combinations having for their object such dissolution or destruction. *Md.*, 258.

VOTE ON ADOPTION OF THE CONSTITUTION.

[Extended and minute provisions made for holding the election on the adoption of the Constitution.] *Ark.*, 94; *Cal.*, 105; *Iowa*, 195; *Mich.*, 317; *Mo.*, 363; *Neb.*, 378; *Nev.*, 397; *Tenn.*, 500; *Wis.*, 572.
—Every citizen of ——— declared a legal voter by this Constitution, and every citizen of the United States, a resident of this State on the day of election, shall be entitled to vote at the first general election under this Constitution, and on the question of the adoption thereof. *Cal.*, 105.
—If this Constitution shall be ratified by the people of ———, the Executive of the existing government is hereby requested immediately after the same shall be ascertained, in the manner herein directed, to cause a fair copy thereof to be forwarded to the President of the United States, in order that he may lay it before the Congress of the United States. *Cal.*, 106.
—On the organization of the Legislature it shall be the duty of the Secretary of State to lay before each

House a copy of the abstract made by the Board of Canvassers, and if called for, the original returns of election, in order that each House may judge of the correctness of the report of said Board of Canvassers. *Cal.*, 106.
—That this Constitution shall be submitted to the people for their adoption or rejection at an election to be held on the   , and there shall also be submitted for adoption or rejection at the same time, the separate articles in relation to the emigration of colored persons and the public debt. *Ill.*, 167.
—That every person entitled to vote for members of the General Assembly, by the Constitution and laws now in force, shall on the   , be entitled to vote for the adoption or rejection of this Constitution, and for and against the aforesaid articles separately submitted, and the said qualified electors shall vote in the counties in which they respectively reside, at the usual places of voting, and not elsewhere; and the said election shall be conducted according to the laws now in force in relation to the election of Governor, so far as applicable, except as herein otherwise provided. *Ill.*, 168.
—That the returns of the votes for the adoption or rejection of this Constitution, and for and against the separate articles submitted shall be made to the Secretary of the State within fifty days after the election, and the returns of the votes shall, within five days thereafter, be examined and canvassed by the Auditor, Treasurer, and Secretary of State, or any two of them, in the presence of the Governor, and proclamation shall be made by the Governor forthwith of the result of the polls. If it shall appear that a majority of all the votes polled are for the adoption of this Constitution, it shall be the supreme law of the land, from and after the first day of April, A. D. 1848, but if it shall appear that a majority of the votes polled, were given against the Constitution, it shall be null and void. If it shall further appear that a majority of the votes polled shall have been given for the separate article in relation to colored persons, or the

article for the two mill tax, then said article or articles shall be and form a part of this Constitution, otherwise said article or articles shall be null and void. *Ill.*, 168.

—No article or section of this Constitution shall be submitted as a distinct proposition to a vote of the electors, otherwise than is herein provided. *Ind.*, 182.

—Each elector shall express his assent or dissent by voting a written or printed ballot labelled "For the Constitution," or "Against the Constitution." *Kan.*, 207.

—If a majority of all the votes cast at such election shall be in favor of the Constitution, then there shall be an election held in the several voting precincts on the first Tuesday in December, A. D. 1859, for the election of members of the first Legislature, of all State, district, and county officers provided for in this Constitution, and for a Representative in Congress. *Kan.*, 207.

—All persons having the qualifications of electors, according to the provisions of this Constitution, at the date of each of said elections, and who shall have been duly registered according to the provisions of the registry law of this Territory, and none others, shall be entitled to vote at each of said elections. *Kan.*, 207.

—The persons who may be judges of the several voting precincts of this Territory at the date of the respective elections in this schedule provided for, shall be the judges of the respective elections herein provided for. *Kan.*, 207.

—That "article XI," entitled "Commons," is hereby adopted as a part of the Constitution of this State, without being submitted to be voted upon by the people. *Ill.*, 167.

—Immediately after the adjournment of the Convention, the Governor shall issue his proclamation directing the several officers of this State, authorized by law to hold elections, or in default thereof such officers as he shall designate, to open and hold polls in the several parishes of the State, at the places designated by law, on the first Monday of September, 1864, for the purpose of taking the sense of the good people of this State in regard to the adoption or rejection of this Constitution; and it shall be the duty of said officers to receive the suffrages of all qualified voters. Each voter shall express his opinion by depositing in the ballot-box a ticket whereon shall be written "The Constitution accepted," or, "The Constitution rejected." At the conclusion of the said election, the officers and commissioners appointed to preside over the same shall carefully examine and count each ballot as deposited, and shall forthwith make due return thereof to the Secretary of State, in conformity to the provisions of law and usages in regard to elections. *La.*, 237.

—Upon the receipt of said returns, or on the third Monday of September, if the returns be not sooner received, it shall be the duty of the Governor, the Secretary of State, the Attorney-General and the State Treasurer, in the presence of all such persons as may choose to attend, to compare the votes at the said election for the ratification or rejection of this Constitution, and if it shall appear at the close, that a majority of all the votes given is for ratifying this Constitution, then it shall be the duty of the Governor to make proclamation of the fact, and thenceforth this Constitution shall be ordained and established as the Constitution of the State of Louisiana. But whether this Constitution be accepted or rejected, it shall be the duty of the Governor to cause to be published the result of the polls, showing the number of votes cast in each parish for and against this Constitution. *La.*, 237.

—The canvass of the votes cast for the adoption or rejection of this Constitution, and the provision in relation to the elective franchise separately submitted, and the returns thereof shall be made by the proper canvassing officers, in the same manner as now provided by law for the canvass and return of the votes cast at an election for Governor, as near as may

be, and the return thereof shall be directed to the Secretary of State. On the _____, or within five days thereafter, the Auditor-General, State Treasurer, and Secretary of State, shall meet at the Capitol, and proceed, in the presence of the Governor, to examine and canvass the returns of the said votes, and proclamation shall forthwith be made by the Governor of the result thereof. If it shall appear that a majority of the votes cast upon the question have thereon " Adoption of the Constitution —yes," this Constitution shall be the supreme law of the State from and after the first day of January, one thousand eight hundred and fifty-one, except as is herein otherwise provided; but if a majority of the votes cast upon the question have thereon " Adoption of the Constitution—no," the same shall be null and void. *Mich.*, 317.

—At the next general election, and at the same time when the votes of the electors shall be taken for the adoption or rejection of this Constitution, an additional amendment to section one of article seven, in the words following :

" Every colored male inhabitant possessing the qualifications required by the first section of the second article of the Constitution, shall have the rights and privileges of an elector." *Mich.*, 318.

—This Constitution shall be submitted to the people for their adoption or rejection, at the general election to be held on the _____, and there shall also be submitted for adoption or rejection, at the same time, the separate resolution in relation to the elective franchise; and it shall be the duty of the Secretary of State, and all other officers required to give or publish any notice in regard to the said general election, to give notice, as provided by law in case of an election of Governor, that this Constitution has been duly submitted to the electors at said election. Every newspaper within this State publishing, in the month of September next, this Constitution as submitted, shall receive, as compensation therefor, the sum of twenty-five dollars, to be paid as the Legislature shall direct. *Mich.*, 317.

—Shall be separately submitted to the electors of this State for their adoption or rejection, in form following, to wit: A separate ballot may be given by every person having the right to vote for the revised Constitution, to be deposited in a separate box. Upon the ballots given for the adoption of the said separate amendment shall be written or printed, or partly written and partly printed, the words "Equal suffrage to colored persons? Yes;" and upon all ballots given against the adoption of the said separate amendment, in like manner, the words "Equal suffrage to colored persons? No." And on such ballots shall be written or printed, or partly written and partly printed, the words "Constitution: Suffrage," in such manner that such words shall appear on the outer side of each ballot when folded. If, at said election, a majority of all the votes given for and against the said separate amendment shall contain the words "Equal suffrage to colored persons? Yes," then there shall be inserted in the first section of the article, between the words " tribe and shall," these words, "and every colored male inhabitant," anything in the Constitution to the contrary notwithstanding. *Mich.*, 318.

—Any person entitled to vote for members of the Legislature, by the Constitution and laws now in force, shall, at the said election, be entitled to vote for the adoption or rejection of this Constitution, and for or against the resolution separately submitted, at the places and in the manner provided by law for the election of members of the Legislature. *Mich.*, 317.

—At the said general election a ballot box shall be kept by the several boards of inspectors thereof, for receiving the votes cast for or against the adoption of this Constitution; and on the ballots shall be written or printed, or partly written and partly printed, the words, "Adoption of the Constitution—yes," or "Adoption of the Constitution—no." *Mich.*, 317.

—Upon the _____, an election shall be held for members of the House of Representatives of the United States, Governor, Lieutenant-Governor, Supreme and District Judges, members of the Legislature, and all other officers designated in this Constitution, and also for the submission of this Constitution to the people, for their adoption or rejection. *Min.*, 331.

—Upon the day so designated as aforesaid, every free white male inhabitant over the age of twenty-one years, who shall have resided within the limits of the State for ten days previous to the day of said election, may vote for all officers to be elected under this Constitution at such election, and also for or against the adoption of this Constitution. *Minn.*, 332.

—The returns of said election for and against this Constitution, and for all State officers and members of the House of Representatives of the United States, shall be made, and certificates issued, in the manner now prescribed by law for returning votes given for delegate to Congress, and the returns for all district officers, judicial, legislative or otherwise, shall be made to the Register of Deeds of the senior county in each district, in the manner prescribed by law, except as otherwise provided. The returns for all officers elected at large shall be canvassed by the Governor of the Territory, assisted by Joseph R. Brown and Thomas J. Galbraith, at the time designated by law for canvassing the vote for delegate to Congress. *Minn.* 332.

—If, upon canvassing the votes for and against the adoption of this Constitution, it shall appear that there has been polled a greater number of votes against than for it, then no certificates of election shall be issued for any State or district officer provided for in this Constitution, and no State organization shall have validity within the limits of the territory until otherwise provided for, and until a Constitution for a State government shall have been adopted by the people. *Minn.*, 332.

—In voting for or against the adoption of this Constitution, the words "for Constitution," or "against Constitution," may be written or printed on the ticket of each voter; but no voter shall vote for or against this Constitution on a separate ballot from that cast by him for officers to be elected at said election under this Constitution; and if, upon the canvass of the vote so polled, it shall appear that there was a greater number of votes polled for than against said Constitution, then this Constitution shall be deemed to be adopted as the Constitution of the State of Minnesota; and all the provisions and obligations of this Constitution, and of the schedule hereunto attached, shall thereafter be valid, to all intents and purposes, as the Constitution of this State. *Min.*, 332.

—The preceding parts of this instrument shall not take effect unless this Constitution be adopted by the people at the election to be held as hereinafter directed; but the provisions of this article shall be in force from the day of the adoption of this Constitution by the Representatives of the people in this Convention assembled. *Mo.*, 363.

—The election provided for in the next preceding section shall be by ballot. Those ballots in favor of the Constitution shall have written or printed thereon the words "New Constitution—yes," those against the Constitution shall have written or printed thereon the words "New Constitution—no." *Mo.*, 363.

—Each ballot deposited for the adoption or rejection of this Constitution, in the army of the United States, shall have distinctly written or printed thereon, "Constitution, Yes," or "Constitution, No," or words of a similar import. *Nev.* 397.

—*Be it ordained*, That the amendments to the Constitution of the State, adopted by this Convention, be submitted by the Governor to the people on the second Monday in November next, thirty days' notice having been given, and that the polls be opened by the respective Sheriffs, and kept open for three successive days, at the several election precincts in each and every county in the State, under the same rules and regulations as now exist for the election of members to the General Assembly. That the said Sheriffs

be required to compare and certify the results of the elections, on or before the Monday following, and transmit the same in twenty days thereafter to the Governor of the State. That all persons qualified to vote for members of the House of Commons, may vote for or against a ratification of the amendments. Those who wish a ratification of the amendments, voting with a printed or written ticket, "Ratification," —those of a contrary opinion, "Rejection." *N. C.*, 430.

—The foregoing Constitution shall be submitted to the electors of the State, at an election to be held on the third Tuesday of June, one thousand eight hundred and fifty-one, in the several election districts of this State. The ballots at such election shall be written or printed as follows: Those in favor of the Constitution, "New Constitution, Yes;" those against the Constitution, "New Constitution, No." The polls at the said election shall be opened between the hours of eight and ten o'clock A. M., and closed at six o'clock P. M.; and the said election shall be conducted, and the returns thereof made and certified to the Secretary of State, as provided by law for annual elections of State and county officers. Within twenty days after such election the Secretary of State shall open the returns thereof in the presence of the Governor; and if it shall appear that a majority of all the votes cast at such election are in favor of the Constitution, the Governor shall issue his proclamation, stating that fact, and said Constitution shall be the Constitution of the State of Ohio, and not otherwise. *Ohio*, 445.

—At the time when the votes of the electors shall be taken for the adoption or rejection of this Constitution, the additional section, in the words following, to wit: "No license to traffic in intoxicating liquors shall hereafter be granted in this State; but the General Assembly may, by law, provide against evils resulting therefrom," shall be separately submitted to the electors for adoption or rejection, in form following, to wit: A separate ballot may be given by every elector and deposited in a separate box. Upon the ballots given for said separate amendment shall be written or printed, or partly written and partly printed, the words: "License to sell intoxicating liquors—Yes;" and upon the ballots given against said amendment, in the like manner, the words: "License to sell intoxicating liquors—No." If, at the said election, a majority of all the votes given for and against said amendment shall contain the words: "License to sell intoxicating liquors—No," then the said amendment shall be a separate section of article fifteen of the Constitution. *Ohio*, 445.

—For the purpose of taking the vote of the electors of the State for the acceptance or rejection of this Constitution, an election shall be held on the ——, to be conducted according to existing laws regulating the election of Delegate in Congress, so far as applicable, except as herein otherwise provided. *Or.*, 459.

—If a majority of all the votes given for and against the Constitution shall be given for the Constitution, then this Constitution shall be deemed to be approved and accepted by the electors of the State, and shall take effect accordingly; and if a majority of such votes shall be given against the Constitution, then this Constitution shall be deemed to be rejected by the electors of the State, and shall be void. *Or.*, 459.

—If this Constitution shall be ratified, an election shall be held on the first Monday in June, 1858, for the election of members of the Legislative Assembly, a Representative in Congress, and State and county officers; and the Legislative Assembly shall convene at the capital the first Monday of July, 1858, and proceed to elect two Senators in Congress, and make such further provisions as may be necessary to the complete organization of a State government. *Or.*, 460.

—Each elector who offers to vote upon this Constitution shall be asked by the judges of election this question:

Do you vote for the Constitution—yes or no?

And also this question:

1 § 2. At the general election to be held in the year eighteen hundred and
2 sixty-six, and in each twentieth year thereafter, and also at such time as the
3 Legislature may by law provide, the question, "Shall there be a Convention
4 to revise the Constitution and amend the same?" shall be decided by the
5 electors qualified to vote for members of the Legislature; and in case a
6 majority of the electors so qualified, voting at such elections, shall decide in
7 favor of a Convention for such purpose, the Legislature at its next session,
8 shall provide by law for the election of delegates to such Convention.

Do you vote for slavery in Oregon—yes or no?
And also this question:

Do you vote for free negroes in Oregon—yes or no?
And in the poll-books shall be columns headed,
respectively, "Constitution, yes;" Constitution, no;"
"Slavery, yes;" "Slavery, no:" "Free negroes, yes;"
"Free negroes, no." And the names of electors
shall be entered in the poll-books, together with their
answers to the said questions under their appropriate
heads. The abstracts of the votes transmitted to the
Secretary of the Territory shall be publicly opened,
and canvassed by the Governor and Secretary, or by
either of them, in the absence of the other; and the
Governor, or, in his absence, the Secretary, shall
forthwith issue his proclamation, and publish the
same in the several newspapers printed in this State,
declaring the result of the said election upon each of
said questions. *Or.*, 459.

—It shall be the duty of said returning officers in
each county in this State, to prepare poll books, which
shall be opened on said days of election, and in which
shall be enrolled the name of each voter by the assistance of clerks, who shall be appointed and sworn as
clerks in other elections. Said officers shall prepare
a ballot box, in which shall be placed the ticket of
each voter. Each ticket shall have written thereon
the words, "I ratify the amended Constitution;" or
if the voter is opposed to it, "I reject the amended
Constitution;" or the words "Ratification" or "Rejection," or some such words as will distinctly convey
the intention of the voter. The justices of the several
County Courts in this State, at some time previous
to the day of said election, shall appoint three inspectors for each precinct; and in case of failure of the
courts to appoint inspectors, then said returning officers shall appoint them. It shall be the duty of said
returning officers, in presence of the said inspectors,
to count the votes given for the ratification and rejection of the Constitution, of which they shall keep a
true and correct estimate in said poll book. Said
returning officer shall deposit the original poll books
of said election with the Clerk of the County Court
in their respective counties, and shall, within five days
after said election, make out duplicate statements of
the number of votes in their respective counties for
ratifying and rejecting the Constitution; and shall
forward by mail one of said certificates to the Governor, one to the Secretary of State, and shall likewise
deposit one with the Clerk of the County Court. It
shall be the duty of said several clerks carefully to
examine the said poll books, and forthwith to certify
to the Secretary of State, a full, true, and perfect
statement of the number of votes taken for and against
the Constitution, as appears from the poll books, filed
in their office. Should said returning officers, or any
of them, fail to make returns in due time, as above
directed, the Secretary of State shall then be authorized to dispatch a special messenger for the purpose
of obtaining a certified copy of the result of said election. *Minn.*, 500.

—*Be it further ordered,* That if any Sheriff or other
acting officer shall fail, within the time prescribed by

this ordinance, to discharge any of the duties hereby
required, such Sheriff or other returning officer so
failing as aforesaid, shall forfeit and pay the sum of
five thousand dollars, to be recovered by action of
debt in any of the Courts of Record in this State; to
be sued for in the name of the Governor, for the use
and benefit of common schools. *Tenn.*, 501.

[Soldier's vote taken in camps.] *Ark.*, 94; *Mo.*,
363; *Nev.*, 397; *Md.*, 277.

[In the Constitutions of *N. Y.* (1777), *Ala.*, *Ct.*,
Del., *Fl.*, *Ga.*, *Ky.*, *Miss.*, *S. C.*, *Tex.* and *Va.*, there
are no forms prescribed for submitting the Constitu-
tion to a vote, although in some, the question of a
Convention is thus decided.]

AMENDMENTS TO THE CONSTITUTION.

[The mode of amendment specified in § 1, of Art.
XIII, was adopted in 1821]. *P.* 43; (nearly similar),
Cal., 103; *La.*, 237; *N. J.*, 420; *Or.*, 459; *W. Va.*,
558; *Wis.*, 570.

—The General Assembly may, whenever two-thirds
of each House shall deem it necessary, propose
amendments to this Constitution; which proposed
amendments shall be duly published in print (in such
manner as the General Assembly may direct), at least
three months before the next general election for
Representatives, for the consideration of the people;
and it shall be the duty of the several returning
officers, at the next ensuing general election for Representatives, to open a poll for the vote of the qualified
electors on the proposed amendments, and to make a
return of said vote to the Secretary of State; and if
it shall thereupon appear that a majority of all the
qualified electors of the State, who voted for Representatives, voted in favor of the proposed amendments, and two-thirds of each house of the next
General Assembly, before another election, shall
ratify said amendments, each house voting by yeas
and nays, said amendments shall be valid, to all
intents and purposes, as parts of this Constitution.
Provided, that said proposed amendments shall, at
each of said sessions of the General Assembly, have
been read three times, on three several days, in each
house. *Ala.*, 82.

—After the expiration of twelve months from the adoption of this Constitution, no Convention shall be held
for the purpose of altering or amending the Constitution of this State, unless the question of Convention
or no Convention, shall be first submitted to a vote
of the qualified electors of the State, and approved by
a majority of the electors voting at said election.
Ala., 82.

—The General Assembly may, at any time, propose
such amendments to this Constitution as two-thirds
of each House shall deem expedient, which shall be
published in all the newspapers published in this
State, three several times, at least twelve months
before the next general election; and if, at the first
session of the General Assembly after such general
election, two-thirds of each House shall, by yeas and

nays, ratify such proposed amendments, they shall be valid to all intents and purposes as parts of this Constitution: *Provided*, That such proposed amendments shall be read on three several days in each House, as well when the same are proposed as when they are finally ratified. *Ark.*, 88.

—The General Assembly, whenever two-thirds of each House shall deem it necessary, may. with the approbation 'of the Governor, propose amendments to this Constitution, and at least three, and not more than six, months before the next general election of Representatives, duly publish them in print for the consideration of the people; and if three-fourths of each branch of the Legislature shall. after such an election and before another, ratify the said amendments, they shall be valid to all intents and purposes as parts of this Constitution. No Convention shall be called but by the authority of the people; and an unexceptionable mode of making their sense known will be for them at a special election on the third Tuesday of May in any year, to vote by ballot for or against a Convention, as they shall severally choose to do; and if thereupon it shall appear that a majority of all the citizens in the State, having right to vote for Representatives, have voted for a Convention, the General Assembly shall accordingly at their next session call a Convention, to consist of at least as many members as there are in both Houses of the Legislature, to be chosen in the same manner, at the same places and at the same time that Representatives, are by the citizens entitled to vote for Representatives, on due notice given for one month, and to meet within three months after they shall be elected. The majority of all the citizens in the State having right to vote for Representatives shall be ascertained by reference to the highest number of votes cast in the State at any one of the three general elections, next preceding the day of voting for a Convention, except when they may be less than the whole number of votes voted both for and against a Convention, in which case the said majority shall be ascertained by reference to the number of votes given on the day of voting for or against a Convention; and whenever the General Assembly shall deem a Convention necessary, they shall provide by law for the holding of a special election for the purpose of ascertaining the sense of the majority of the citizens of the State entitled to vote for Representatives. *Del.*, 126.

—And if at any time two-thirds of the Senate and Assembly shall think it necessary to revise and change this entire Constitution, they shall recommend to the electors, at the next election for members of the Legislature, to vote for or against the Convention; and if it shall appear that a majority of the electors voting at such election have voted in favor of calling a Convention, the Legislature shall at its next session provide by law for calling a Convention, to be holden within six months after the passage of such law; and such Convention shall consist of a number of members not less than that of both branches of the Legislature. *Cal.*, 103.

—Whenever a majority of the House of Representatives shall deem it necessary to alter or amend this Constitution, they may propose such alterations and amendments; which proposed amendments shall be continued to the next General Assembly, and be published with the laws which may have been passed at the same session; and if two-thirds of each House, at the next session of said Assembly, shall approve the amendment proposed, by yeas and nays, said amendment shall by the Secretary be transmitted to the Town Clerk in each town in the State, whose duty it shall be to present the same to the inhabitants thereof for their consideration, at a town meeting legally warned and held for that purpose; and if it shall appear, in manner to be provided by law, that a majority of the electors present at such meetings shall have approved such amendments, the same shall be valid, to all intents and purposes, as a part of this Constitution. *Ct.*, 113.

—No part of this Constitution shall be altered except by a Convention duly elected. *Fl.*, 139.

54

—Whenever a Convention shall be called, proclamation of an election for Delegates shall be made by the Governor at least thirty days before the day of election. Every county and Senatorial District shall be entitled to as many Delegates as it has Representatives in the General Assembly. The same qualifications shall be required in Delegates, and in Electors, that are required in members of the General Assembly, and voters for the same respectively, and the elections for Delegates to a Convention, and the returns of such election, shall be held and made in the manner prescribed by law for regulating elections for members of the General Assembly, but the Convention shall judge of the qualifications of its members. *Fl.*, 139.

—No Convention of the people shall be called unless by the concurrence of two-thirds of all the members of each House of the General Assembly, made known by the passing of a bill, which shall be read three times on three several days in each House. *Fl.*, 139.

—This Constitution shall be altered or amended only by a Convention of the people, called for that purpose by act of the General Assembly. *Ga.*, 150.

—. Whenever two-thirds of all the members elected to each branch of the General Assembly shall think it necessary to alter or amend this Constitution, they shall recommend to the electors at the next election of members of the General Assembly, to vote for or against a Convention; and if it shall appear that a majority of all the electors of the State voting for Representatives have voted for a Convention, the General Assembly shall, at their next session, call a Convention to consist of as many members as the House of Representatives at the time of making said call, to be chosen in the same manner, at the same place, and by the same electors, in the same districts that chose the members of the House of Representatives; and which Convention shall meet within three months after the said election, for the purpose of revising, altering, or amending this Constitution. *Ill.*, 165; (nearly similar), *Min.*, 329; *Ohio*, 444.

—Any amendment or amendments to this Constitution may be proposed in either branch of the General Assembly; and if the same shall be agreed to by two-thirds of all the members elect in each of the two Houses, such proposed amendment or amendments shall be referred to the next regular session of the General Assembly, and shall be published at least three months previous to the time of holding the next election for members of the House of Representatives; and if, at the next regular session of the General Assembly after said election, a majority of all the members elect in each branch of the General Assembly shall agree to said amendment or amendments, then it shall be their duty to submit the same to the people at the next general election for their adoption or rejection, in such manner as may be prescribed by law; and if a majority of all the electors voting at such election for members of the House of Representatives shall vote for such amendment or amendments, the same shall become a part of the Constitution. But the General Assembly shall not have power to propose an amendment or amendments to more than one article of the Constitution at the same session.' *Ill.*, 165.

—Any amendment or amendments to this Constitution may be proposed in either branch of the General Assembly, and if the same shall be agreed to by a majority of the members elected to each of the two Houses, such proposed amendment or amendments shall, with the yeas and nays thereon, be entered on their journals, and referred to the General Assembly to be chosen at the next general election; and if, in the General Assembly so next chosen, such proposed amendment or amendments shall be agreed to by a majority of all the members elected to each House, then it shall be the duty of the General Assembly to submit such amendment or amendments to the electors of the State; and if a majority of said electors shall ratify the same, such amendment or amendments shall become a part of this Constitution. *Ind.*, 181; (nearly similar), *Iowa*, 193; *Nev.*, 392; *Pa.*, 468.

—If two or more amendments shall be submitted at the same time, they shall be submitted in such manner that the electors shall vote for or against each of such amendments separately; and while an amendment or amendments which shall have been agreed upon by one General Assembly shall be awaiting the action of a succeeding General Assembly, or of the electors, no additional amendment or amendments shall be proposed. *Ind.*, 181; *Or.*, 459.

—At the general election to be held in the year one thousand eight hundred and seventy, and in each tenth year thereafter, and also at such time as the General Assembly may, by law, provide, the question, " Shall there be a Convention to revise the Constitution, and amend the same ?" shall be decided by the electors qualified to vote for members of the General Assembly; and in case a majority of the electors so qualified, voting at such election for and against such proposition, shall decide in favor of a Convention for such purpose, the General Assembly, at its next session shall provide by law for the election of delegates to such convention. *Iowa*, 193.

—If two or more amendments shall be submitted at the same time, they shall be submitted in such manner that the electors shall vote for or against each of such amendments separately. *Iowa*, 193.

—Propositions for the amendment of this Constitution may be made by either branch of the Legislature; and if two-thirds of all the members elected to each House shall concur therein, such proposed amendments, together with the yeas and nays, shall be entered on the journal; and the Secretary of State shall cause the same to be published, in at least one newspaper in each county of the State where a newspaper is published, for three months preceding the next election for Representatives, at which time the same shall be submitted to the electors for their approval or rejection; and if a majority of the electors voting on said amendments, at said election, shall adopt the amendments, the same shall become a part of the Constitution. When more than one amendment shall be submitted at the same time, they shall be so submitted as to enable the electors to vote on each amendment separately; and not more than three propositions to amend shall be submitted at the same election. *Kan.*, 205.

—Whenever two-thirds of the members elected to each branch of the Legislature shall think it necessary to call a Convention to revise, amend or change this Constitution, they shall recommend to the electors to vote at the next election of members to the Legislature, for or against a Convention; and if a majority of all the electors voting at such election shall have voted for a Convention, the Legislature shall, at the next session, provide for calling the same. *Kan.*, 206.

—When experience shall point out the necessity of amending this Constitution, and when a majority of all the members elected to each House of the General Assembly shall, within the first twenty days of any regular session, concur in passing a law for taking the sense of the good people of this Commonwealth, as to the necessity and expediency of calling a convention, it shall be the duty of the several Sheriffs, and other officers of elections, at the next general election which shall be held for Representatives in the General Assembly, after the passage of such law, to open a poll for, and make return to the Secretary of State, for the time being, of the names of all those entitled to vote for Representatives, who have voted for calling a Convention; and if, thereupon, it shall appear that a majority of all the citizens of this State, entitled to vote for Representatives, have voted for calling a Convention, the General Assembly shall, at their next regular session, direct that a similar poll shall be opened, and return made for the next election for Representatives; and if, thereupon, it shall appear that a majority of all the citizens of this State, entitled to vote for Representatives, have voted for calling a Convention, the General Assembly shall, at their next session, pass a law calling a Convention, to consist of as many members

as there shall be in the House of Representatives, and no more; to be chosen on the first Monday in August thereafter, in the same manner and proportion, and at the same places, and possessed of the same qualifications of a qualified elector, by citizens entitled to vote for Representatives; and to meet within three months after their election, for the purpose of re-adopting, amending, or changing this Constitution; but if it shall appear by the vote of either year, as aforesaid, that a majority of all the citizens entitled to vote for Representatives did not vote for calling a Convention, a Convention shall not then be called. And for the purpose of ascertaining whether a majority of the citizens, entitled to vote for Representatives, did or did not vote for calling a Convention, as above, the General Assembly passing the law authorizing such vote, shall provide for ascertaining the number of citizens entitled to vote for Representatives within the State. *Ky.*, 222.

—The Convention, when assembled, shall judge of the election of its members and decide contested elections, but the General Assembly shall, in calling a Convention, provide for taking testimony in such cases and for issuing a writ of election in case of a tie. *Ky.*, 222.

—The Legislature, whenever two-thirds of both Houses shall deem it necessary, may propose amendments to this Constitution; and when any amendment shall be so agreed upon, a resolution shall be passed and sent to the selectmen of the several towns and the assessors of the several plantations, empowering and directing them to notify the inhabitants of their respective towns and plantations, in the manner prescribed by law, at their next annual meeting in the month of September, to give in their votes on the question whether such amendment shall be made; and if it shall appear that a majority of the inhabitants voting on the question are in favor of such amendment, it shall become a part of this Constitution. *Me.*, 249.

—The General Assembly may propose any amendment or amendments to this Constitution, which shall be agreed to by three-fifths of all the members elected to both Houses. Such proposed amendment or amendments, with the yeas and nays thereon, shall be entered on the journal of each House; shall be printed with the laws passed at the same session, and shall be published, by order of the Governor, in all the newspapers printed in the different counties of this State, and in three newspapers printed in the city of Baltimore (one of which shall be printed in the German language) for at least three months preceding the next election for members of the General Assembly, at which election the said proposed amendment or amendments shall be submitted to the qualified electors of the State for their confirmation or rejection; and if it shall appear to the satisfaction of the Governor, from the returns of said election made to him by the proper authorities, that a majority of the qualified votes cast at said election on the proposed amendment or amendments were in favor of the said proposed amendment or amendments, he shall, by proclamation, declare said amendment or amendments to be part of the Constitution of this State. When two or more amendments shall be submitted by the General Assembly to the qualified electors of the State at the same election, they shall be so submitted that the electors may vote for or against each amendment separately. *Md.*, 276.

—Whenever two-thirds of the members elected to each branch of the General Assembly shall think it necessary to call a Convention to revise, amend or change this Constitution, they shall recommend to the electors to vote at the next election for members of the General Assembly for or against a Convention; and if a majority of all the electors voting at said election shall have voted for a Convention, the General Assembly shall, at their next session, provide by law for calling the same. *Md.*, 276.

—The Convention shall consist of as many members as both Houses of the General Assembly, who shall be chosen in the same manner, and shall meet within three months after their election for the purpose aforesaid. *Md.* 276.

[A vote for or against a Convention, to be taken in 1882, and every twenty years after. *Md.,* 276.]

[A vote to be taken in 1866, and every sixteenth year after. *Mich.,* 315.]

—All the amendments shall take effect at the commencement of the political year after their adoption. *Mich.,* 315.

—Any amendment or amendments to this Constitution may be proposed in the Senate or House of Representatives. If the same shall be agreed to by two-thirds of the members elected to each House, such amendment or amendments shall be entered on their journals respectively, with the yeas and nays taken thereon; and the same shall be submitted to the electors at the next general election thereafter, and if a majority of the electors qualified to vote for members of the Legislature voting thereon shall ratify and approve such amendment or amendments, the same shall become part of the Constitution. *Mich.,* 315.

—If, at any time hereafter, any specific and particular amendment or amendments to the Constitution be proposed in the General Court and agreed to by a majority of the Senators and two-thirds of the members of the House of Representatives present and voting thereon, such proposed amendment or amendments shall be entered on the journals of the two houses, with the yeas and nays taken thereon, and referred to the General Court then next to be chosen, and shall be published; and if, in the General Court next chosen as aforesaid, such proposed amendment or amendments shall be agreed to by a majority of the Senators and two-thirds of the members of the House of Representatives present and voting thereon, then it shall be the duty of the General Court to submit such proposed amendment or amendments to the people; and if they shall be approved and ratified by a majority of the qualified voters, voting thereon, at meetings legally warned and holden for that purpose, they shall become part of the Constitution of this Commonwealth. *Mass.,* 295.

—Whenever a majority of both Houses of the Legislature shall deem it necessary to alter or amend this Constitution, they may propose such alterations or amendments, which proposed amendments shall be published with the laws which have been passed at the same session, and said amendments shall be submitted to the people for their approval or rejection; and if it shall appear, in a manner to be provided by law, that a majority of voters present and voting shall have ratified such alterations or amendments, the same shall be valid to all intents and purposes, as a part of this Constitution. If two or more alterations or amendments shall be submitted at the same time, it shall be so regulated that the voters shall vote for or against each separately. *Minn.,* 329.

—Whenever two-thirds of each branch of the Legislature shall deem any change, alteration, or amendment necessary to this Constitution, such proposed change, alteration, or amendment shall be read and passed by a majority of two-thirds of each House respectively on each day, for three several days. Public notice thereof shall then be given by the Secretary of State, at least six months preceding the next general election, at which the qualified electors shall vote directly for or against such change, alteration, or amendment; and if it shall appear that a majority of the qualified electors voting for members of the Legislature, shall have voted for the proposed change, alteration, or amendment, then it shall be inserted by the next succeeding Legislature, as a part of this Constitution, and not otherwise. *Miss.,* 344.

—This Constitution may be amended and revised in pursuance of the provisions of this article. *Mo.,* 362.

—The General Assembly, at any time, may propose such amendments to this Constitution as a majority of the members elected to each House shall deem expedient; and the vote thereon shall be taken by yeas and nays, and entered in full on the journals.

And the proposed amendments shall be published with the laws of that session, and also shall be published weekly in two newspapers, if such there be, within each congressional district in the State, for four months next preceding the general election then next ensuing. The proposed amendments shall be submitted to a vote of the people, each amendment separately, at the next general election thereafter, in such manner as the general Assembly may provide. And if a majority of the qualified voters of the State, voting for and against any one of said amendments shall vote for such amendment, the same shall be deemed and taken to have been ratified by the people, and shall be valid and binding, to all intents and purposes as a part of this Constitution. *Mo.,* 362.

—The General Assembly shall have power to repeal or modify all ordinances adopted by any previous Convention. *Mo.,* 362.

—The General Assembly may, at any time, authorize by law, a vote of the people to be taken upon the question whether a Convention shall be held for the purpose of revising and amending the Constitution of this State; and if, at such election, a majority of the votes on the question be in favor of a Convention, the Governor shall issue writs to the Sheriffs of the different counties, ordering the election of delegates to such a Convention, on a day within three months after that on which the said question shall have been voted on. At such election, each senatorial district shall elect two Delegates for each Senator to which it may be then entitled in the General Assembly, and every such Delegate shall have the qualifications of a Senator. The election shall be conducted in conformity with the laws regulating the election of Senators. The Delegates so elected shall meet at such time and place as may be provided by law, and organize themselves into a Convention, and proceed to revise and amend the Constitution; and the Constitution, when so revised and amended, shall, on a day to be therein fixed, not less than sixty nor more than ninety days after that on which it shall have been adopted by the Convention, be submitted to a vote of the people for and against it, at an election to be held for that purpose only; and if a majority of all the votes given be in favor of such Constitution, it shall, at the end of thirty days after such election, become the Constitution of this State. The result of such election shall be made known by proclamation by the Governor. The General Assembly shall have no power, otherwise than as in this section specified, to authorize a Convention for revising and amending the Constitution. *Mo.,* 369.

—If at any time a majority of the Senate and House of Representatives shall deem it necessary to call a Convention to revise or change this Constitution, they shall recommend to the electors to vote for or against a Convention at the next election for members of the Legislature; and if it shall appear that a majority of the electors voting thereon have voted for a Convention, the Legislature shall at its next session provide for calling such convention. *Neb.,* 377; *Nev.,* 392.

—To be holden within six months after the passage of such law; and such convention shall consist of a number of members not less than both branches of the Legislature. In determining what is a majority of the electors voting at such election, reference shall be had to the highest number of votes cast at such election for the candidates for any office or on any question. *Nev.,* 392.

—To the end that there may be no failure of justice or danger to the State, by the alterations and amendments made in the Constitution, the General Court is hereby fully authorized and directed to fix the time when the alterations and amendments shall take effect, and make the necessary arrangements accordingly. *N. H.,* 410.

—It shall be the duty of the Selectmen and Assessors of the several towns and places in this State, in warning the first annual meetings for the choice of Senators, after the expiration of seven years from the adoption of this Constitution as amended, to insert expressly in the warrant this purpose among others

216

for the meeting, to wit: to take the sense of the qualified voters on the subject of a revision of the Constitution; and the meeting being warned accordingly, and not otherwise, the moderator shall take the sense of the qualified voters present as to the necessity of a revision; and a return of the number of votes for and against such necessity shall be made by the clerk, sealed up and directed to the General Court at their then next session; and if it shall appear to the General Court by such return, that the sense of the people of the State has been taken, and that in the opinion of the majority of the qualified voters in the State, present and voting at the said meetings, there is a necessity for a revision of the Constitution, it shall be the duty of the General Court to call a Convention for that purpose; otherwise the General Court shall direct the sense of the people to be taken, and then proceed in the manner before mentioned; the delegates to be chosen in the same manner, and proportioned as the Representatives to the General Court: *Provided*, That no alterations shall be made in this Constitution before the same shall be laid before the towns and unincorporated places, and approved by two-thirds of the qualified voters present and voting on the subject. *N. H.*, 410.

—And the same method of taking the sense of the people as to the revision of the Constitution, and calling a Convention for that purpose, shall be observed afterward, at the expiration of every seven years. *N. H.*, 411.

—No convention of the people shall be called by the General Assembly, unless by the concurrence of two-thirds of all the members of each House of the General Assembly. *N. C.*, 430; *S. C.*, 488.

—No part of the Constitution of this State shall be altered, unless a bill to alter the same shall have been read three times in each House of the General Assembly, and agreed to by three-fifths of the whole number of members of each House respectively; nor shall any alteration take place until the bill so agreed to shall have been published six months previous to a new election of members to the General Assembly. If, after such publication, the alteration proposed by the preceding General Assembly shall be agreed to in the first session thereafter, by two-thirds of the whole representation in each House of the General Assembly, after the same shall have been read three times on three several days, in each House, then the said General Assembly shall prescribe a mode by which the amendment or amendments may be submitted to the qualified voters of the House of Commons throughout the State; and if, upon comparing the votes given in the whole State, it shall appear that a majority of the voters have approved thereof, then and not otherwise, the same shall become a part of the Constitution. *N. C.*, 430.

—It shall be the duty of the Legislature to submit such proposed amendment or amendments, or such of them as may have been agreed to as aforesaid by the two Legislatures, to the people in such manner and at such time, at least four months after the adjournment of the Legislature, as the Legislature shall prescribe: and if the people, at a special election to be ·held for that purpose only, shall approve and ratify such amendment or amendments, or any of them, by a majority of the electors qualified to vote for members of the Legislature voting thereon, such amendment or amendments, so approved and ratified, shall become part of the Constitution; *Provided*, That if more than one amendment be submitted, they shall be submitted in such manner and form that the people may vote for or against each amendment separately and distinctly; but no amendment or amendments shall be submitted to the people by the Legislature oftener than once in five years. *N. J.*, 420.

—No part of this Constitution shall be altered, unless a bill to alter the same shall have been read on three several days in the House of Representatives, and on three several days in the Senate, and agreed to, at the second and third reading, by two-thirds of the

whole representation in each House of the General Assembly; neither shall any alteration take effect, until the bill, so agreed to, shall be published for three months previous to a new election for members of the House of Representatives; and the alteration proposed by the preceding General Assembly shall be agreed to by the new General Assembly, in their first session, by the concurrence of two-thirds of the whole representation in each House, after the same shall have been read on three several days in each; then and not otherwise the same shall become a part of the Constitution. *S. C.*, 488.

—Either branch of the General Assembly may propose amendments to this Constitution; and, if the same shall be agreed to by three-fifths of the members elected to each House, such proposed amendments shall be entered on the journals, with the yeas and nays, and shall be published in at least one newspaper in each county of the State, where a newspaper is published, for six months preceding the next election for Senators and Representatives, at which time the same shall be submitted to the electors, for their approval or rejection; and if a majority of the electors voting at such election, shall adopt such amendments, the same shall become a part of the Constitution. When more than one amendment shall be submitted at the same time, they shall be so submitted, as to enable the electors to vote on each amendment separately. *Ohio*, 444.

[An election for or against a Constitution to be held in 1871 and each twentieth year after] *Ohio*, 444.

—But no amendment or amendments shall be submitted to the people oftener than once in five years; *Provided*, That if more than one amendment be submitted, they shall be submitted in such manner and form, that the people may vote for or against each amendment separately and distinctly. *Pa.*, 468.

—In the words of the Father of his Country, we declare: "That the basis of our political systems is the right of the people to make and alter their constitutions of government; but that the Constitution which at any time exists, till changed by an explicit and authentic act of the whole people, is sacredly obligatory upon all." *R. I.*, 473.

—The General Assembly may propose amendments to this Constitution, by the votes of a majority of all the members elected to each House. Such propositions for amendments shall be published in the newspapers, and printed copies of them shall be sent by the Secretary of State, with the names of all the members who shall have voted thereon, with the yeas and nays, to all the Town and City Clerks in the State. The said propositions shall be, by said clerks, inserted in the warrants or notices by them issued, for warning the next annual town and ward meetings in April; and the clerks shall read said propositions to the electors, when thus assembled, with the names of all the Representatives and Senators who shall have voted thereon, with the yeas and nays, before the election of Senators and Representatives shall be had. If a majority of all the members elected to each House, at said annual meeting, shall approve any proposition thus made, the same shall be published and submitted to the electors in the mode provided in the act of approval; and if then approved by three-fifths of the electors of the State present and voting thereon, in town and ward meetings, it shall become a part of the Constitution of the State. *R. I.*, 480.

—Any amendment or amendments to this Constitution may be proposed in the Senate or House of Representatives; and if the same shall be agreed to by a majority of all the members elected to each of the two Houses, such proposed amendment or amendments shall be entered on their journals, with the yeas and nays thereon, and referred to the General Assembly then next to be chosen; and shall be published for six months previous to the time of making such choice. And if, in the General Assembly next chosen as aforesaid, such proposed amendment or amendments shall be agreed to by two-thirds of all the members elected to each House, then it shall be the

217

ARTICLE XIV.

1   SECTION 1. The first election of Senators and Members of Assembly,

2 pursuant to the provisions of this Constitution, shall be held on the Tuesday

3 succeeding the first Monday of November, one thousand eight hundred and

4 forty-seven. The Senators and Members of Assembly who may be in office

5 on the first day of January, one thousand eight hundred and forty-seven, shall

6 hold their offices until and including the thirty-first day of December follow-

7 ing and no longer.

duty of the General Assembly to submit such proposed amendment or amendments to the people, in such manner and at such time as the General Assembly shall prescribe. And if the people shall approve and ratify such amendment or amendments, by a majority of all the citizens of the State voting for Representatives, voting in their favor, such amendment or amendments shall become part of this Constitution. When any amendment or amendments to the Constitution shall be proposed in pursuance of the foregoing provisions, the same shall at each of the said sessions be read three times on three several days in each House. The Legislature shall not propose amendments to the Constitution oftener than once in six years. *Tenn.*, 499.

—The Legislature, by a vote of three-fourths of all the members of each House, with the approval of the Governor, shall have the power to call a Convention of the people, for the purpose of altering, amending or reforming the Constitution of this State; the manner of electing delegates to the Convention, the time and place of assembling them, to be regulated by law. *Tex.*, 517.

—The Legislature, at any biennial session, by a vote of two-thirds of all the members of each House, may propose amendments to the Constitution, to be voted upon by persons legally qualified to vote for members of the House of Representatives of the State; which proposed amendments shall be duly published in the public prints of this State, at least three months before the next general election for the Representatives to the Legislature for the consideration of the people; and it shall be the duty of the several returning officers, at said general election, to open a poll for, and make returns to the Secretary of State, of the number of legal votes cast at said election, for and against said amendment, and if more than one be proposed, then the number of legal votes cast for and against each of them; and if it shall appear, from said return, that a majority of the votes cast upon said proposed amendment or amendments have been cast in favor of the same, and two-thirds of each House of the Legislature, at the next regular session thereafter shall ratify said proposed amendment, or amendments so voted upon by the people, the same shall be valid to all intents and purposes, as parts of the Constitution of the State of Texas; provided that the said proposed amendments shall, at each of said sessions, have been read on three several days, in each House of the Legislature, and the vote thereon shall have been taken by yeas and nays; and provided further, that the rule in the above proviso shall never be suspended by either of said Houses. *Tex.*, 517.

[A *Council of Censors*, elected at intervals of seven years, to inquire whether the Constitution has been preserved inviolate in every part during the last septennary, and whether the Legislative or Executive branches have performed their duty. They have power to call a Convention, and to perform other acts tending to preserve the integrity of the government] *Vt.* 527

—No Convention shall be called, having authority to alter the Constitution of the State, unless it be in pursuance of a law passed by the affirmative vote of a majority of the members elected to each branch of the Legislature, and providing that polls shall be held throughout the State, on some day therein specified, which shall not be less than three months after the passage of such law, for the purpose of taking the sense of the voters on the question of calling a Convention. And such Convention shall not be held unless a majority of the votes cast at such polls be in favor of calling the same; nor shall members be elected to such Convention, until at least one month after the result of the polls shall be duly ascertained, declared and published. And all acts and ordinances of said Convention shall be submitted to the voters of the State for ratification, or rejection, and shall have no validity whatever until they are ratified, and in no event shall they, by any shift or device, be made to have any retrospective operation or effect. *W. Va.*, 558.

FIRST ELECTIONS UNDER THE CONSTITUTION.

—All Officers of State and District Judges first elected under this Constitution, shall be commissioned by the Governor of this Territory, which commission shall be countersigned by the Secretary of the same, and shall qualify before entering upon the discharge of their duties, before any officer authorized to administer oaths under the laws of this territory; and also the State Comptroller and State Treasurer shall each respectively, before they shall qualify and enter upon the discharge of their duties, execute and deliver to the Secretary of the Territory of Nevada an official bond, made payable to the people of the State of Nevada, in the sum of thirty thousand dollars, to be approved by the Governor of the Territory of Nevada, and shall also execute and deliver to the Secretary of State such other or further official bond or bonds as may be required by law. *Nev.*, 395.

—That the Sheriffs, State Attorneys, and all other officers elected under this Constitution, shall perform such duties as shall be prescribed by law. *Ill.*, 167.

—The first election for Governor, Secretary of State, Auditor of State, one Representative to Congress, the Justices to the Supreme Court, the members of the Senate and House of Representatives, shall be held on the second day of June, one thousand eight hundred and sixty-six, at the places, and in the manner now prescribed by law for general elections. The members of the Senate shall be elected in and from the same districts that are now prescribed by law for councilmen districts. The members of the House of Representatives shall be elected in and from the same districts that are now prescribed by law for members to the House of Representatives of the Territory of Nebraska, and all the officers mentioned, to wit: Senators and Representatives, shall hold their offices until

55

the first Monday in January, A. D. 1867: Governor, Secretary of State, State Auditor and Treasurer, until the second Monday in January, A. D. 1869, and until their successors are elected and qualified; the Supreme Judges until the first day of January, A. D. 1873. *Neb.*, 377.

—The Legislature at its first session shall elect such officers as may be ordered by this Constitution to be elected by that body, and within four days after its organization proceed to elect two Senators to the Congress of the United States. But no law passed by this Legislature shall take effect until signed by the Governor after his installation into office. *Cal.*, 106.

—The limitation of the powers of the Legislature, contained in article eighth of this Constitution, shall not extend to the first Legislature elected under the same, which is hereby authorized to negotiate for such amount as may be necessary to pay the expenses of the State government. *Cal.*, 106.

—The provisions of this Constitution concerning the term of residence necessary to enable persons to hold certain offices therein mentioned, shall not be held to apply to officers chosen by the people at the first election, or by the Legislature at its first session. *Cal.*, 105.

—The first election for Secretary, Auditor, and Treasurer of State, Attorney-General, District Judges, members of the Board of Education, District Attorneys, members of Congress, and such State officers as shall be elected at the April election, in the year one thousand eight hundred and fifty-seven, except the Superintendent of Public Instruction, and such county officers as were elected at the August election, in the year one thousand eight hundred and fifty-six, except prosecuting Attorneys, shall be held on the Second Tuesday of October, one thousand eight hundred and fifty-eight, provided that the time for which any District Judge or any other State or county officer elected at the April election in 1858, shall not extend beyond the time fixed for filling like offices at the October election. *Iowa*, 194.

—The first election under this Constitution shall be held on the second Tuesday in October, in the year one thousand eight hundred and fifty-seven, at which time the electors of the State shall elect the Governor and Lieutenant-Governor. There shall also be elected at such election, the successors of such State Senators as were elected at the August election, in the year one thousand eight hundred and fifty-four, and members of the House of Representatives, who shall be elected in accordance with the act of apportionment, enacted by the seventh General Assembly of the State. *Iowa*, 194.

—The first general election under this Constitution shall be held in the year one thousand eight hundred and fifty-two. *Ind.*, 181 (date specified); *Ohio*, 444.

—The first regular session of the Legislature shall commence on the first Monday of December, A. D. eighteen hundred and sixty-four; and the second regular session of the same shall commence on the first Monday of January, eighteen hundred and sixty-six; and the third regular session of the Legislature shall be the first of the biennial sessions, and shall commence on the first Monday of January, A. D. eighteen hundred and sixty-seven; and the regular sessions of the Legislature shall be held thereafter biennially, commencing on the first Monday of January. *Nev.*, 394.

—The Governor, Lieutenant-Governor, Secretary of State, State Treasurer, State Controller, Attorney-General, Surveyor-General, Clerk of the Supreme Court, and Superintendent of Public Instruction, to be elected at the first election under this Constitution, shall each qualify and enter upon the duties of their respective offices on the first Monday of December succeeding their election, and shall continue in office until the first Tuesday after the Monday of January, eighteen hundred and sixty-seven, and until the election and qualification of their successors respectively. *Nev.*, 395.

—The first election for Aldermen and Justices of the Peace shall be held in the year eighteen hundred and forty, at the time fixed for the election of Constables. The Legislature at its first session under the amended Constitution, shall provide for the said election, and for subsequent similar elections. The Aldermen and Justices of the Peace now in commission, or who may in the interim be appointed, shall continue to discharge the duties of their respective offices until fifteen days after the day which shall be fixed by law for the issuing of new commissions, at the expiration of which time their commissions shall expire. *Pa.*, 470.

—The first election under this Constitution for Governor, Lieutenant-Governor, Treasurer, Auditor of Public Accounts, Register of the Land Office, and Attorney-General, shall be held on the first Monday in August, in the year 1851. *Ky.*, 214.

—As soon as the general election can be held under this Constitution in every parish of the State, the the Governor shall, by proclamation, or in case of his failure to act, the Legislature shall, by resolution, declare the fact, and order an election to be held on a day fixed in said proclamation or resolution, and within sixty days from the date thereof, for Governor, Lieutenant-Governor, Secretary of State, Auditor, Treasurer, Attorney-General and Superintendent of Education. The officers so chosen shall, on the fourth day after their election, be installed into office; and shall hold their offices for the terms prescribed in this Constitution, counting from the second Monday in January next preceding their entering into office in case they do not enter into office on that date. The terms of office of the State officers elected on the 22d day of February, 1864, shall expire on the installation of their successors as herein provided for; but under no state of circumstances shall their term of office be construed as extending beyond the length of the terms fixed for said offices in this Constitution; and, if not sooner held, the election of their successors shall take place on the first Monday of November, 1867, in all parishes where the same can be held, the officers elected on that date to enter into office on the second Monday in January, 1868. *La.*, 238.

—The first election for Governor, Lieutenant-Governor, Auditor, Treasurer, and Secretary of State, and Attorney-General, shall be held on the second Tuesday of October, one thousand eight hundred and fifty-one. The persons holding said offices on the first day of September, one thousand eight hundred and fifty-one, shall continue therein, until the second Monday of January, one thousand eiget hundred and fifty-two. *Ohio*, 444.

—The first election for Governor, Lieutenant-Governor, Judges of the Supreme Court and Circuit Courts, Clerk of the Supreme Court, Prosecuting Attorney, Secretary, Auditor, and Treasurer of State, and State Superintendent of Public Instruction, under this Constitution, shall be held at the general election in the year one thousand eight hundred and fifty-two; and such of said officers as may be in office when this Constitution shall go into effect, shall continue in their respective offices until their successors shall have been elected and qualified. *Ind.*, 181.

—That if this Constitution shall be ratified by the people, the Governor shall forthwith, after having ascertained the fact, issue writs of election to the Sheriffs of the several counties in this State; or, in case of vacancy, to the Coroners, for the election of all the officers, the time of whose election is fixed by this Constitution, or schedule; and it shall be the duty of said Sheriffs or Coroners, to give at least twenty days' notice of the time and place of said election, in the manner now prescribed by law. *Ill.*, 168.

—General elections shall be held throughout the State, on the Tuesday next after the first Monday in the month of November of each and every year; at the election held in the year eighteen hundred and sixty-four, all State officers required to be elected under this Constitution during that year shall be elected, and in like manner in every second year thereafter,

219

1 § 2. The first election of Governor and Lieutenant-Governor under this
2 Constitution, shall be held on the Tuesday succeeding the first Monday of
3 November, one thousand eight hundred and forty-eight; and the Governor
4 and Lieutenant-Governor in office when this Constitution shall take effect,
5 shall hold their respective offices until and including the thirty-first day of
6 December of that year.

1 § 3. The Secretary of State, Comptroller, Treasurer, Attorney-General,
2 District Attorney, Surveyor-General, Canal Commissioners and Inspectors of
3 State Prisons, in office when this Constitution shall take effect, shall hold their
4 respective offices until and including the thirty-first day of December one
5 thousand eight hundred and forty-seven, and no longer.

an election shall be held for those State officers whose terms are about to expire; at the election held in the year eighteen hundred and sixty-five, all county officers required to be elected under this Constitution in that year shall be elected, and in like manner in every second year thereafter, an election shall be held for those county officers whose terms are about to expire. *Md.*, 277.

CONTINUANCE OF OFFICERS AND OF OFFICES.

—That no inconveniences may arise from the amendments of the Constitution of this State, and in order to carry the same into complete operation, it is hereby declared and ordained as follows:
—The offices of the present Senate and Representatives shall not be vacated by any amendment of the Constitution made in this Convention, nor otherwise affected, except that the terms of the Representatives and the terms of the Senators which will expire on the first Tuesday of October, in the year of our Lord one thousand eight hundred and thirty-two, are hereby extended to the second Tuesday of November in that year; and the terms of the Senators which will expire on the first Tuesday of October in the year of our Lord one thousand eight hundred and thirty-three, are hereby extended to the second Tuesday of November in that year; and the terms of the Senators which will expire on the first Tuesday of October in the year of our Lord one thousand eight hundred and thirty-four, are hereby extended to the second Tuesday of November in that year. *Del.*, 126.
—The Registers' Courts and Justices of the Peace shall not be affected by any amendments of the Constitution made in this Convention; but the said courts and the terms of office of Registers and Justices of the Peace shall remain the same as if said amendments had not been made. *Del.*, 128.
·· The provision in the twentieth section of the sixth article of this amended Constitution (being the thirtieth section of the sixth article of the original Constitution) of limitation of writs of error, shall have relation to, and take date from, the twelfth day of June, in the year of our Lord one thousand seven hundred and ninety-two, the date of said original Constitution. *Del.*, 128.
—It is declared that nothing in this amended Constitution gives a writ of error from the Court of Errors and Appeals to the Court of Oyer and Terminer or Court of General Sessions of the Peace and Jail Delivery, nor an Appeal from the Court of General Sessions of the Peace and Jail Delivery. *Del.*, 128.

—All civil officers heretofore commissioned by the Governor, or who have been duly appointed, or elected, since the first day of January last, but who have not received their commission and who have not resigned, nor been removed from office, and whose terms of office shall not have expired, shall continue in the exercise of the duties of their respective offices during the periods for which they were duly appointed or duly elected as aforesaid, and commissioned, and until their successors shall be appointed under the provisions of this Constitution; unless removed from office as herein provided. *Ga.*, 150.
—The County Commissioners' Courts and the Probate Justices of the several counties, shall continue in existence and exercise their present jurisdiction, until the County Court provided in this Constitution, is organized in pursuance of an act of the General Assembly to be passed at its first session. *Ill.*, 157.
—Every person elected by popular vote, and now in any office which is continued by this Constitution, and every person who shall be so elected to any such office before the taking effect of this Constitution (except as in this Constitution otherwise provided), shall continue in office until the term for which such person has been, or may be elected, shall expire: *Provided*, That no such person shall continue in office after the taking effect of this Constitution for a longer period than the term of such office in this Constitution prescribed. *Ind.*, 182; (nearly similar), *Iowa*, 195.
—On the taking effect of this Constitution, all officers thereby continued in office shall, before proceeding in the further discharge of their duties, take an oath or affirmation to support this Constitution. *Ind.*, 182.
—All vacancies that may occur in existing offices prior to the first general election under this Constitution, shall be filled in the manner now prescribed by law. *Ind.*, 182.
—Senators elected at the August election, in the year one thousand eight hundred and fifty-six, shall continue in office until the second Tuesday of October, in the year one thousand eight hundred and fifty-nine, at which time their successors shall be elected as may be prescribed by law. *Iowa*, 195.
—The Governor, Secretary, and Judges, and all other officers both civil and military, under the territorial government, shall continue in the exercise of the duties of their respective departments until the said officers are superseded under the authority of this Constitution. *Kan.*, 207.
—No office shall be superseded by the adoption of this Constitution, but the laws of the State relative to the duties of the several officers, Legislative, Executive, Judicial and Military, shall remain in full

1 § 4. The first election of Judges and Clerk of the Court of Appeals, Justices
2 of the Supreme Court, and County Judges, shall take place at such time be-
3 tween the first Tuesday of April and the second Tuesday of June, one thousand
4 eight hundred and forty-seven, as may be prescribed by law. The said courts
5 shall respectively enter upon their duties on the first Monday of July next
6 thereafter; but the term of office of said Judges, Clerk and Justices, as
7 declared by this Constitution, shall be deemed to commence on the first day
8 of January, one thousand eight hundred and forty-eight.

force, though the same be contrary to this Constitution, and the several duties shall be performed by the respective officers of the State, according to the existing laws, under the organization of the Government, as provided for under this Constitution, and the entering into office of the officers to be elected or appointed under said Government and no longer. *Ky.*, 224.

—In order that no inconvenience may result to the public service from the taking effect of this Constitution, no officer shall be superseded thereby; but the laws of this State relative to the duties of the several officers, Executive, Judicial and Military, except those made void by military authority, and by the ordinance of emancipation, shall remain in full force, though the same be contrary to this Constitution, and the several duties shall be performed by the respective officers of the State, according to the existing laws, until the organization of the government under this Constitution, and the entering into office of the new officers to be appointed under said government, and no longer. *Ia.*, 237.

—The members of the House of Representatives of the Legislature of one thousand eight hundred and fifty-one, shall continue in office under the provisions of law until superseded by their successors elected and qualified under this Constitution. *Mich.*, 316.

—All county officers, unless removed by competent authority, shall continue to hold their respective offices until the first day of January, in the year one thousand eight hundred and fifty-three. The laws now in force as to the election, qualification, and duties of township officers, shall continue in force until the Legislature shall, in conformity to the provisions of this Constitution, provide for the holding of elections to fill such offices and prescribe the duties of such officers respectively. *Mich.*, 316.

—All territorial officers, civil and military, now holding their offices under the authority of the United States or of the Territory of Minnesota, shall continue to hold and exercise their respective offices until they shall be superseded by the authority of the State. *Min.*, 330.

—The Governor and all officers, civil and military, now holding commissions under the authority of this State, shall continue to hold and exercise their respective offices until they shall be superseded, pursuant to the provisions of this Constitution, and until their successors be duly qualified. *Miss.*, 344.

—The Governor and all other officers of the Territorial Government, shall continue to discharge and exercise the duties of their respective offices, until superseded by the provisions of this Constitution or the officers appointed or elected by authority of its provisions. *Neb.* 377.

—The Governor, Secretary, Treasurer, and Superintendent of Public Instruction of the Territory of Nevada, shall each continue to discharge the duties of their respective offices after the admission of this State into the Union, and until the time designated for the qualification of the above-named officers to be

elected under the State government; and the Territorial Auditor shall continue to discharge the duties of his said office until the time appointed for the qualification of the State Comptroller; *Provided*, That the said officers shall each receive the salaries and be subject to the restrictions and conditions provided in this Constitution; *And, provided further*, That none of them shall receive to his own use any fees or perquisites for the performance of any duty connected with his office. *Nev.*, 394.

—All officers now filling any office or appointment, shall continue in the exercise of the duties thereof, according to their respective commissions or appointments, unless by this Constitution it is otherwise directed. *N. J.*, 420.

—The present Governor, Chancellor and Ordinary or Surrogate-General, and Treasurer, shall continue in office until successors elected or appointed under this Constitution shall be sworn or affirmed into office. *N. J.*, 420.

—In case of the death, resignation, or disability of the present Governor, the person who may be Vice-President of Council at the time of the adoption of this Constitution, shall continue in office, and administer the government until a Governor shall have been elected and sworn, or affirmed into office under this Constitution. *N. J.*, 420.

—The Register and Receiver of the Land Office, Directors of the Penitentiary, Directors of the benevolent institutions of the State, the State Librarian, and all other officers, not otherwise provided for in this Constitution, in office on the first day of September, one thousand eight hundred and fifty-one, shall continue in office until their terms expire, respectively, unless the General Assembly shall otherwise provide. *Ohio*, 444.

—All officers of the Territory, or under its laws, when this Constitution takes effect, shall continue in office until superseded by the State authorities. *Or.*, 460.

—All civil and military officers which have been or may hereafter be appointed by the acting Governor of the State, are hereby ratified and affirmed, and they shall continue to hold and exercise the functions of their respective offices until their successors shall be elected or appointed, and qualified as prescribed by the laws and Constitution of the State and United States. *Tenn.*, 504.

—All officers, civil and military, now holding their offices under the authority of the United States, or of the Territory of Wisconsin, shall continue to hold and exercise their respective offices until they shall be superseded by the authority of the State. *Wis.*, 572.

—All county, precinct, and township officers, shall continue to hold their respective offices, unless removed by the competent authority, until the Legislature shall, in conformity with the provisions of this Constitution, provide for the holding of elections to fill such offices respectively. *Wis.*, 572.

—The acts of the General Assembly, increasing the number of Justices of the Peace, shall remain in force

1 § 5. On the first Monday of July, one thousand eight hundred and forty-seven

2 jurisdiction of all suits and proceedings then pending in the present Supreme

3 Court and Court of Chancery, and all suits and proceedings originally com-

4 menced and then pending in any Court of Common Pleas (except in the city

5 and county of New York), shall become vested in the Supreme Court hereby

6 established. Proceedings pending in Courts of Common Pleas, and in suits

7 originally commenced in Justices' Courts, shall be transferred to the County

8 Courts provided for in this Constitution, in such manner and form and under

9 such regulations as shall be provided for by law. The Courts of Oyer and

until repealed by the General Assembly; and no office shall be vacated by the amendment to this Constitution, unless the same be expressly vacated thereby, or the vacating the same is necessary to give effect to the amendments. *Del.*, 128.

—The salaries or compensation of all persons holding office under the present Constitution, shall continue to be the same as now provided by law, until superseded by their successors elected or appointed under this Constitution; and it shall not be lawful hereafter for the Legislature to increase or diminish the compensation of any officer during the term for which he is elected or appointed. *Mich.*, 317.

—All executive, judicial and other officers and members of the General Assembly now elected shall continue in office until their present terms expire, in the same manner as if this Constitution had not been adopted. The Senate may so fix the term of members first elected thereto from districts not now represented, that one-half the number of Senators (or as near that number as may be) shall be elected every two years. *Va.*, 544.

—In order that no inconvenience may result to the public service from the taking effect of this Constitution, no office shall be superseded thereby, nor the laws relative to the duties of the several officers be changed, until the entering into office of the new officers to be appointed under this Constitution. *Cal.*, 105.

—The Governor, at the expiration of the present official term, shall continue to act until his successor shall have been sworn into office. *Ind.*, 181.

—Senators now in office and holding over under the existing Constitution, and such as may be elected at the next general election, and the Representatives then elected, shall continue in office until the first general election under this Constitution. *Ind.*, 181.

—The members of the present Legislature shall, on the first Monday of March next, take and subscribe an oath or affirmation, to support this Constitution, so far as the same shall then be in force. Sheriffs, clerks of counties, and coroners, shall be elected at the election hereby directed to commence on the first Monday of November, in the year one thousand eight hundred and twenty-two; but they shall not enter on the duties of their offices before the first day of January then next following. The commissions of all persons holding civil offices on the last day of December, one thousand eight hundred and twenty-two, shall expire on that day; but the officers then in commission, may respectively continue to hold their said offices until new appointments, or elections, shall take place under this Constitution. *N.Y.* (1821), 43.

—All civil and military officers now elected, or who shall be hereafter elected by the General Assembly, or other competent authority, before the said first Wednesday of April, shall hold their offices and may exercise their powers until the said first Tuesday of May, or until their successors shall be qualified to act. *R.I.*, 481.

CONTINUANCE OF LAWS, RIGHTS AND LEGAL PROCEEDINGS.

—That no inconvenience may arise from the alterations and amendments made in the Constitution of this State, and to carry the same into complete effect, it is hereby ordained and declared : *Ill.*, 167., &c.,

That all laws in force at the adoption of this Constitution, not inconsistent therewith, and all rights, actions, prosecutions, claims and contracts of the State, individuals or bodies corporate, shall continue and be as valid as if this Constitution had not been adopted. *Ill.*, 167; (nearly similar), *Cal.*, 105; *Ind.*, 181; *Iowa*, 199; *Kan.*, 200; *Ky.*, 229; *La.*, 237; *Mich.*, 316; *Min.*, 330; *Miss.*, 344; *Neb.*, 377; *Nev.*, 393; *Pa.*, 469; *Wis.*, 571.

—All laws of the State passed during and since the tenth session of the Legislature thereof, in 1860, not repugnant to the Constitution of this State, or of the United States, shall be valid; all writs, actions, prosecutions, judgments and decrees, of the courts of the State, all executions and sales made thereunder, and all acts, orders and proceedings of the Judges of Probate; and of executors, administrators, guardians and trustees, provided they were in conformity to the laws then in force, and not fraudulent, shall be as valid as if made under the usual and ordinary legislation of the country, provided that the same be not repugnant to the Constitution of the State and of the United States. *Fl.*, 140.

—The clauses, sections, and articles of the said Constitution which remain unaltered, shall continue to be construed and have the effect as if the said Constitution had not been amended. *Pa.*, 469.

—All fines, penalties, and forfeitures, owing to the Territory of ——, or any county, shall inure to the use of the State or county. All bonds executed to the Territory, or any officer thereof, in his official capacity, shall pass over to the Governor, or other officers of the State or county, and their successors in office, for the use of the State or county, or by him or them to be repectively assigned over to the use of those concerned, as the case may be. *Kan.*, 206; (nearly similar), *Nev.*, 393.

—The rights and duties of all corporations shall remain as if this Constitution had not been adopted, with the exception of such regulations and restrictions as are contained in this Constitution. All judicial and civil officers now in office, who have been appointed by the General Assembly and commissioned according to law, and all such officers as shall be appointed by the said Assembly, and commissioned as aforesaid, before the first Wednesday of May next, shall continue to hold their offices until the first day of June next, unless they shall, before that time, resign, or be removed from office according to law. The Treasurer and Secretary shall continue in office until a Treasurer and Secretary shall be appointed under this Constitution. All military officers shall continue to hold and exercise their respec-

56

222

10 Terminer hereby established shall, in their respective counties, have jurisdic-

11 tion, on and after the day last mentioned, of all indictments and proceedings

12 then pending in the present Courts of Oyer and Terminer, and also of all

13 indictments and proceedings then pending in the present Courts of General

14 Sessions of the Peace, except in the city of New York, and except in cases of

15 which the Courts of Sessions hereby, established may lawfully take cognizance;

16 and of such indictments and proceedings as the Courts of Sessions hereby

17 established shall have jurisdiction on and after the day last mentioned.

tive offices until they shall resign, or be removed according to law. All laws not contrary to or inconsistent with the provisions of this Constitution shall remain in force until they shall expire by their own limitation, or shall be altered or repealed by the General Assembly, in pursuance of this Constitution. The validity of all bonds, debts, contracts, as well of individuals as of bodies corporate, or the State, of all suits, actions, or rights of action, both in law and equity, shall continue as if no change had taken place. The Governor, Lieutenant-Governor, and General Assembly which is to be formed in October next, shall have and possess all the powers and authorities not repugnant to or inconsistent with this Constitution, which they now have and possess, until the first Wednesday of May next. *Ct.*, 113.

—All suits, proceedings, and matters which, on the third Tuesday of January, in the year of our Lord one thousand eight hundred and thirty-two, shall be depending in the Supreme Court, or Court of Common Pleas, and all books, records, and papers of the said courts shall be transferred to the Superior Court established by this amended Constitution, and the said suits, proceedings, and matters shall be proceeded in to final judgment or determination in the said Superior Court. All indictments, proceedings, and matters which, on the third Tuesday of January, in the year of our Lord one thousand eight hundred and thirty-two, shall be depending in the Court of General Quarter Sessions of the Peace and Jail Delivery, shall be transferred to and proceeded in to final judgment and determination in the Court of General Sessions of the Peace and Jail Delivery established by this amended Constitution, and all books, records, and papers of said Court of General Quarter Sessions of the Peace and Jail Delivery shall be transferred to the said Court of General Sessions of the Peace and Jail Delivery. All suits, proceedings, and matters which, on the third Tuesday of January, in the year of our Lord one thousand eight hundred and thirty-two, shall be depending in the Court of Chancery or in the Orphans' Court and all records, books and papers of said courts respectively, shall be transferred to the Court of Chancery or Orphans' Court established by this amended Constitution, and the said suits, proceedings, and matters shall proceed into final decree, order, or other determination. *Del.*, 127.

—All recognizances heretofore taken shall remain valid, and all bonds executed to the Governor of the State of Florida, either before or since the first day of January, 1861, or to any other officer of the State in his official capacity, shall be of full force and virtue for the uses therein respectively expressed, and may be sued for and recovered accordingly; and all criminal prosecutions, and penal actions which have arisen may be prosecuted to judgment and execution in the name of the State. *Fl.*, 140.

—Local and private statutes heretofore passed intended for the benefit of counties, cities, towns, corporations, and private persons not inconsistent with the supreme law, nor with this Constitution, and which have neither expired by their own limita-

tions nor been repealed, shall have the force of statute law subject to judicial decision, as to their validity when enacted, and to any limitations imposed by their own terms. *Ga.*, 150.

—All acts of incorporation for municipal purposes shall continue in force under this Constitution, until such time as the General Assembly shall, in its discretion, modify or repeal the same. *Ind.*, 181.

—All bonds executed to the State, or to any officer in his official capacity, shall remain in force and inure to the use of those concerned. *Iowa*, 194.

—All recognizances heretofore taken, or which may be taken before the organization of the Judicial Department under this Constitution, shall remain as valid as though this Constitution had not been adopted, and may be prosecuted in the name of the Commonwealth. All criminal prosecutions and penal actions which have arisen, or may arise before the reorganization of the Judicial Department under this Constitution, may be prosecuted to judgment and execution, in the name of the Commonwealth. *Ky.*, 224.

—All writs, actions, causes of action, prosecutions, and rights of individuals and of bodies corporate, and of the State, and all charters of incorporation, shall continue; and all indictments which shall have been found, or which may hereafter be found, for any crime or offense committed before the adoption of this Constitution, may be proceeded upon as if no change had taken place. The several courts, except as herein otherwise provided, shall continue with the like powers and jurisdiction, both at law and in equity, as if this Constitution had not been adopted, and until the organization of the judicial department under this Constitution. *Mich.*, 316.

—That all fines, penalties, forfeitures, and escheats accruing to the State of Michigan under the present Constitution and laws, shall accrue to the use of the State under this Constitution. *Mich.*, 316.

—That all recognizances, bonds, obligations, and all other instruments entered into or executed before the adoption of this Constitution, to the people of the State of Michigan, to any State, county, or township, or any public officer or public body, or which may be entered into or executed, under existing laws, "to the people of the State of Michigan," to any such officer or public body, before the complete organization of the departments of government under this Constitution, shall remain binding and valid; and rights and liabilities upon the same shall continue, and may be prosecuted as provided by law. And all crimes and misdemeanors, and penal actions, shall be tried, punished, and prosecuted, as though no change had taken place, until otherwise provided by law. *Mich.*, 316.

—The cases pending and undisposed of in the late Court of Chancery at the time of the adoption of this Constitution, shall continue to be heard and determined by the Judges of the Supreme Court. But the Legislature shall, at its session in one thousand eight hundred and fifty-one, provide by law for the transfer of said causes that may remain undisposed of on the first day of January, one thousand eight hundred and fifty-two, to the Supreme or Circuit Court established by this Constitution, or require that the same may be heard and determined by the Circuit Judges. *Mich.*, 318.

—All rights vested, and all liabilities incurred, shall remain the same as if this Constitution had not been adopted. *Miss.*, 344.

—All debts and liabilities of the Territory of ——, lawfully incurred, and which remain unpaid at the time of the admission of this State into the Union, shall be assumed by and become the debt of the State of ——: *Provided,* That the assumption of such indebtedness shall not prevent the State from contracting the additional indebtedness, provided in section three of article nine of this Constitution. *Nev.*, 394.

—All property and rights of the Territory, and of the several counties, subdivisions and political bodies corporate of or in the Territory, including fines, penalties, forfeitures, debts, and claims of whatsoever nature, and recognizances, obligations and undertakings to or for the use of the Territory, or any county, political corporation, officer, or otherwise, to or for the public, shall inure to the State, or remain to the county, local division, corporation, officer, or public, as if the change of government had not been made. And private rights shall not be affected by such change. *Or.*, 400.

—All debts contracted and engagements entered into before the adoption of this Constitution, shall be as valid against this State, as if this Constitution had not been adopted. *R. I.*, 481.

—All fines, penalties, or forfeitures accruing to the Territory of —— shall inure to the State. *Min.*, 330; *Wis.*, 571.

—That all fines, penalties, and forfeitures due and owing to the State of Illinois under the present Constitution and laws, shall inure to the use of the people of the State of Illinois under this Constitution. *Ill.*, 167.

—All fines, penalties, or forfeitures due, or to become due or accruing to the State, or to any county therein, or to the school fund, shall inure to the State, county or school fund in the manner prescribed by law. *Iowa*, 194.

—All suits at law or in equity, now pending in the several courts of this State, shall be transferred to such court as may have proper jurisdiction thereof. *Miss.*, 344.

—The territorial prison, as located under existing laws, shall, after the adoption of this Constitution, be and remain one of the State prisons of the State of ——. *Min.*, 329.

—All indictments, prosecutions, suits, pleas, plaints, and other proceedings pending in any of the courts, shall be prosecuted to final judgment and execution; and all appeals, writs of error, certiorari, and injunctions, shall be carried on in the several courts in the same manner as is now provided by law. *Ind.*, 181.

—All judgments, decrees, orders, and other proceedings of the several courts of this State heretofore made within the limits of their several jurisdictions, are hereby ratified and affirmed, subject only to past and future reversal, by motion for new trial, appeal, bill of review, or other proceedings, in conformity with the law of force when they were made. *Ga.*, 150; (nearly similar), *Iowa*, 194.

—Crimes and misdemeanors committed against the Territory of Oregon shall be punished by the State as they might have been punished by the Territory if the change of government had not been made. *Or.*, 400.

—Recognizances, bonds, obligations, and all other instruments entered into or executed, before the adoption of this Constitution to the people of the State of Illinois, to any State or county officer or public body, shall remain binding and valid, and rights and liabilities upon the same shall continue, and all crimes and misdemeanors shall be tried and punished as though no change had been made in the Constitution of the State. *Ill.*, 167.

—All fines, penalties, and forfeitures sued or accruing to the State, or to any county therein, shall inure to the State, or to such county, in the manner prescribed by law. All bonds executed to the State, or to any officer in his official capacity, shall remain in force, and inure to the use of those concerned. *Ind.*, 181.

—All recognizances heretofore taken, or which may be taken before the change from a territorial to a permanent State government, shall remain valid, and shall pass to, and may be prosecuted in the name of the State, and all bonds executed to the Governor of the Territory, or to any other officer or court, in his or their official capacity, shall pass to the Governor or the State authority, and their successors in office, for the uses therein respectively expressed, and may be sued for and recovered accordingly; and all the estate or property, real, personal, or mixed, and all judgments, bonds, specialties, choses in action, and claims, or debts of whatsoever description, of the Territory of ——, shall inure to and vest in the State of ——, and may be sued for and recovered in the same manner, and to the same extent, by the State of ——, as the same could have been by the Territory of ——. All criminal prosecutions and penal actions, which may have arisen, or which may arise before the change from a territorial to a State Government, and which shall then be pending, shall be prosecuted to judgment and execution in the name of the State. All offenses committed against the laws of the Territory of ——, before the change from a territorial to a State government, and which shall not be prosecuted before such change, may be prosecuted in the name and by the authority of the State of ——, with like effect as though such change had not taken place; and all penalties incurred shall remain the same as if this Constitution had not been adopted. All actions at law, and suits in equity, which may be pending in any of the courts of the Territory of ——, at the time of the change from a territorial to a State government, may be continued and transferred to any court of the State which shall have jurisdiction of the subject matter thereof. *Wis.*, 571.

—This Constitution as amended, so far as shall concern the Judicial Department, shall commence and be in operation from and after the third Tuesday of January, in the year of our Lord one thousand eight hundred and thirty-two. All the courts of justice now existing shall continue with their present jurisdiction, and the Chancellor and Judges and the Clerks of the said courts shall continue in office until the said third Tuesday of January, in the year of our Lord one thousand eight hundred and thirty-two; upon which day the said courts shall be abolished, and the offices of the said Chancellor, Judges and Clerks shall expire. All writs of error, and appeals and proceedings which, on the third Tuesday of January, in the year of our Lord one thousand eight hundred and thirty-two, shall be depending in the High Court of Errors and Appeals, and all the books, records and papers of said court shall be transferred to the Court of Errors and Appeals established by this amended Constitution; and the said writs of errors, appeals, and proceedings shall be proceeded in, in the said Court of Errors and Appeals, to final judgment, decree, or other determination. *Del.*, 127.

—That the Clerk of the Circuit Court, in each county fixed by this Constitution as the place for holding the Supreme Court, except in the county of Sangamon, shall be *ex officio* Clerk of the Supreme Court, until the clerks of said Court shall be elected and qualified, as provided in this Constitution, and all laws now in force, in relation to the Clerk of the Supreme Court, shall be applicable to said clerks and their duties. *Ill.*, 167.

—All ordinances and laws in force when this Constitution is adopted, and not inconsistent therewith, shall continue and remain in force, and so of all rights, prosecutions, actions, claims and contracts. *Va.*, 544.

—The Legislature shall provide for the removal of all causes which may be pending when this Constitution

1   § 6. The Chancellor and the present Supreme Court shall respectively,

2 have power to hear and determine any of such suits and proceedings ready on

3 the first Monday of July, one thousand eight hundred and forty-seven, for hear-

4 ing or decision, and shall, for their services therein, be entitled to their present

5 rates of compenation, until the first day of July, one thousand eight hundred

6 and forty-eight, or until all such suits and proceedings shall be sooner heard

7 and determined. Masters in Chancery may continue to exercise the functions

8 of their offices in the Court of Chancery, so long as the Chancellor shall con-

9 tinue to exercise the functions of his office under the provisions of this Con-

10 stitution. And the Supreme Court hereby established shall also have power

11 to hear and determine such of said suits and proceedings as may be prescribed

12 by law.

1   § 7. In case any vacancy shall occur in the office of Chancellor or Justice

2 of the present Supreme Court, previous to the first day of July, one thousand

goes into effect, to courts created by the same. *Cal.*, 105.

—All statutes, public and private, not repugnant to this Constitution, shall continue in force until they expire by their own limitations, or are repealed by the General Assembly. All charters, contracts, judgments, actions and rights of action, shall be as valid as if this Constitution had not been made. The present government shall exercise all the powers with which it is now clothed, until the said first Tuesday of May, one thousand eight hundred and forty-three, and until the government under this Constitution is duly organized. *R. I.*, 181.

PUBLICATION OF THE CONSTITUTION.

—This Constitution shall be published in three papers to be selected by the President of the Convention, whereof two shall publish the same in English and French, and one in German, from the period of the adjournment of the Convention until the election for ratification or rejection on the first Monday of September, 1864. *La.*, 238.

—This form of government shall be enrolled on parchment, and deposited in the Secretary's office, and be a part of the laws of the land; and printed copies thereof shall be prefixed to the book containing the laws of this Commonwealth, in all future editions of the said laws. *Mass.*, 294; (similar provision), *Me.*, 252.

—The Legislature, at their first session, shall provide for the payment of all expenditures of the Convention to revise this Constitution, and of the publication of the same as is provided in this article. *Mich.*, 317.

—At the first regular session of the Legislature, to convene under the requirements of this Constitution, provision shall be made by law for paying for the publication of six hundred copies of the debates and proceedings of this Convention, in book form, to be disposed of as the Legislature may direct; and the Hon. J. Neely Johnson, President of this Convention, shall contract for, and A. J. Marsh, official reporter of this Convention, under the direction of the President, shall supervise the publication of such debates and proceedings. Provision shall be made by law at such first session of the Legislature for the compensation of the official reporter of this Convention, and he

shall be paid in coin or its equivalent. He shall receive for his services in reporting the debates and proceedings, fifteen dollars per day during the session of the Convention, and seven and one-half dollars additional for each evening session, and thirty cents per folio for one hundred words for preparing the same for publication, and for supervising and indexing such publication, the sum of fifteen dollars per day during the time actually engaged in such service. *Nev.* 395.

—The President of the Convention shall, immediately after the adjournment thereof, cause this Constitution to be deposited in the office of the Governor of the Territory; and if after the submission of the same to a vote of the people, as hereinafter provided, it shall appear that it has been adopted by a vote of the people of the State, then the Governor shall forward a certified copy of the same, together with an abstract of the votes polled for and against the said Constitution, to the President of the United States, to be by him laid before the Congress of the United States. *Minn.* 330.

—This form of government shall be enrolled on parchment, and deposited in the Secretary's office, and be a part of the laws of the land, and printed copies thereof shall be prefixed to the books containing the laws of this State in all future editions thereof. *N. H.*, 411.

1. It shall be the duty of the President of this Convention, immediately on its adjournment, to certify to the Governor a copy of the Bill of Rights and Constitution adopted, together with this schedule.

2. Upon the receipt of such certified copy, the Governor shall forthwith announce the fact by proclamation, to be published in such manner as he may deem requisite for general information, and shall annex to his proclamation a copy of the Bill of Rights and Constitution, together with this schedule, all of which shall be published in the manner indicated. Ten printed copies thereof shall, by the Secretary of the Commonwealth, be immediately transmitted by mail to the clerk of each County and Corporation Court in this Commonwealth, to be by such clerk submitted to the examination of any person desiring the same. *Va.*, 514.

—This Constitution shall be prefixed to every edition of the laws made by direction of the Legislature. *Del.*, 125.

3 eight hundred and forty-eight, the Governor may nominate, and by and with
4 the advice and consent of the Senate, appoint a proper person to fill such
5 vacancy. Any Judge of the Court of Appeals or Justice of the Supreme
6 Court, elected under this Constitution, may receive and hold such appoint-
7 ment.

1   § 8.   The offices of Chancellor, Justice of the existing Supreme Court,
2 Circuit Judge, Vice-Chancellor, Assistant Vice-Chancellor, Judge of the exist-
3 ing County Courts of each county, Supreme Court Commissioner, Master in
4 Chancery, Examiner in Chancery, and Surrogate (except as herein otherwise
5 provided), are abolished from and after the first Monday of July, one thousand
6 eight hundred and forty-seven (1847).

1   § 9.   The Chancellor, the Justices of the present Supreme Court, and the
2 Circuit Judges, are hereby declared to be severally eligible to any office at the
3 first election under this Constitution.

1   § 10.   Sheriffs, Clerks of Counties (including the Register and Clerk of the
2 city and county of New York), and Justices of the Peace and Coroners, in
3 office when this Constitution shall take effect, shall hold their respective offices
4 until the expiration of the term for which they were respectively elected.

1   § 11.   Judicial officers in office when this Constitution shall take effect,
2 may continue to receive such fees and perquisites of office as are now author-
3 ized by law, until the first day of July, one thousand eight hundred and forty-
4 seven, notwithstanding the provisions of the twentieth section of the sixth
5 article of this Constitution.

1   § 12.   All local courts established in any city or village, including the
2 Superior Court, Common Pleas, Sessions and Surrogates' Courts of the city
3 and county of New York, shall remain, until otherwise directed by the Legis-
4 lature, with their present powers and jurisdictions; and the Judges of such
5 courts, and any Clerks thereof, in office on the first day of January, one
6 thousand eight hundred and forty-seven, shall continue in office until the ex-
7 piration of their terms of office, or until the Legislature shall otherwise direct

1   § 13. This Constitution shall be in force from and including the first day

2 of January, one thousand eight hundred and forty-seven, except as herein

3 otherwise provided.

Done in Convention, at the capitol in the city of Albany, the ninth day of

October, in the year one thousand eight hundred and forty-six, and of the Inde-

pendence of the United States of America the seventy-first. In witness

whereof, we have hereunto subscribed our names.

JOHN TRACY,

President, and Delegate from the County of Chenango.

JAMES F. STARBUCK, }
H. W. STRONG,   } *Secretaries.*
FR. SEGER,   }

SUPREMACY OF THE CONSTITUTION — LAWS FOR CARRYING IT INTO EFFECT.

—This Constitution shall be the supreme law of the State, and any law inconsistent therewith shall be void. The General Assembly shall pass all laws necessary to carry this Constitution into effect. *Iowa*, 194; *R. I.*, 475.

—That the declaration of rights is hereby declared to be a part of the Constitution of this State, and ought never to be violated on any pretense whatsoever. *N. C.*, 426.

—The Legislature shall pass all laws necessary to carry into effect the provisions of this Constitution. *N. J.*, 421; (nearly similar), *Del.*, 128; *Ill.*, 169; *Va.*, 514.

—It shall be the duty of the Legislature, at their first session, to adapt the present laws to the provisions of this Constitution, as far as may be. *Mich.*, 316.

—The General Assembly shall have power to make all laws and ordinances consistent with this Constitution, and not repugnant to the Constitution of the United States, which they shall deem necessary and proper for the welfare of the State. *Ga.*, 146.

—The General Assembly shall have power to pass all such laws as may be necessary and proper for carrying into execution the powers vested by this Constitution, in any department or office of the Government, and the duties imposed upon them thereby. *Md.*, 265.

—The General Assembly shall declare by law what parts of the common law, and what parts of the civil law, not inconsistent with this Constitution, shall be in force in this State. *Fl.*, 140.

—All the provisions of the existing Constitution inconsistent with the provisions herein contained, are hereby wholly annulled. *Mass.*, 295, 296.

DATES OF GOING INTO EFFECT.

—New York (1777), April 20, 1777.
— "   "   (1821), January 1, 1822, with such exceptions as are made in Art. IX, § 1. P. 102.
—Ohio, September 1, 1851. P. 445.
—Indiana, November 1, 1851. P. 181.
—New Jersey, September 2, 1844. P. 420.
—All officers of this State, other than members of the Legislature, shall be installed into office on the fifteenth day of December next, or as soon thereafter as practicable. *Cal.*, 106.
—The first session of the Legislature of the State of Wisconsin shall commence on the first Monday in June next, and shall be held at the village of Madison, which shall be and remain the seat of government until otherwise provided by law. *Wis.*, 572.
—This Constitution, if adopted, shall go into operation on the first Tuesday of May, in the year one thousand eight hundred and forty-three. The first election of Governor, Lieutenant-Governor, Secretary of State, Attorney-General and General Treasurer, and of Senators and Representatives under said Constitution, shall be had on the first Wednesday of April next preceding, by the electors qualified under said Constitution. And the town and ward meetings therefor shall be warned and conducted as is now provided by law. *R. I.*, 481.

ARRANGEMENT OF SUBJECTS.

58

232

INDEX.